modernism and M

AN ANTHOLOGY OF SOURCES

Edited and with Commentary by Daniel Albright

The University of Chicago Press CHICAGO AND LONDON

Daniel Albright is professor

of English and American

Literature at Harvard

University. He is the author

of *Untwisting the Serpent:*

Modernism in Music,

Literature, and Other Arts,

also published by the

University of Chicago Press.

The University of Chicago Press, Chicago 60637

The University of Chicago Press, Ltd., London

© 2004 by The University of Chicago

All rights reserved. Published 2004

Printed in the United States of America

13 12 11 10 09 08   5 4 3 2

ISBN (cloth): 0-226-01266-2

ISBN (paper): 0-226-01267-0

Library of Congress Cataloging-in-Publication Data

Modernism and music : an anthology of sources / edited and with
     commentary by Daniel Albright.
          p.   cm.
     Includes bibliographical references (p.   ) and index.
     ISBN 0-226-01266-2 (cloth : alk. paper)—
     ISBN 0-226-01267-0 (pbk. : alk. paper)
     1. Music—20th century—History and criticism.
     2. Modernism (Aesthetics)   I. Albright, Daniel, 1945–
ML197 .M58   2004
780′.9′04—dc22

                                        2003017899

Contents

List of Illustrations *ix*
Acknowledgments *xi*

1 Introduction *1*

→Arnold Schoenberg, from "The Future of the Opera" (1927) *15*
Sergei Prokofiev, from *From My Life* (1944) *20*

2 Testing the Boundaries between Speech and Music *23*

→Harry Partch, from *Genesis of a Music* (1949) *30*
→Arnold Schoenberg, Foreword to *Pierrot Lunaire* (1912) *38*
→Arnold Schoenberg, "The Relationship to the Text" (1912) *39*
→Alban Berg, "Voice in Opera" (1929) *43*
James Joyce, from "Sirens" (1922) *45*
Virginia Woolf, from *The Waves* (1931) *49*
T. S. Eliot, from "The Music of Poetry" (1942) *52*
Carl Nielsen, from "Words, Music, and Program Music" (1925) *55*
Paul Hindemith, from *A Composer's World* (1949–50) *60*

3 Testing the Boundaries between the Visual Arts and Music *64*

PAINTING AND ARCHITECTURE *64*
Arnold Schoenberg, from *Harmonielehre* (1911) *66*
George Antheil, Letter to Nicolas Slonimsky (1936) *71*
George Antheil, "Composer's Notes on 1952–53 Re-Editing" [of *Ballet Mécanique*]
   (1953) *71*
→Theodor Adorno, from *Philosophy of Modern Music* (1948) *72*
Morton Feldman, [Time-canvas] (1983) *80*
Iannis Xenakis, from *Formalized Music* (1971) *82*

EMBODYING PHYSICAL MOVEMENT: BALLET AND FILM *84*
Émile Jaques-Dalcroze, "The Technique of Moving Plastic" (1922) *86*
Hanns Eisler, from *Composing for the Films* (1947) *93*

4 **The New Music Theater** *103*

Friedrich Nietzsche, from *The Birth of Tragedy* (1872) *108*
Hugo von Hofmannsthal, Letter to Richard Strauss (1911) *114*
Kurt Weill, "Shifts in Musical Composition" (1927) *117*
Kurt Weill, "Opera—Where To?" (1929) *120*
Alban Berg, "The 'Problem of Opera'" (1928) *124*
Ernst Krenek, from "Is Opera Still Possible Today?" (1936) *127*
W. H. Auden, from "The World of Opera" (1967) *134*

5 **Fuller Universes of Music** *137*

ABOLISHING THE OLD RULES *137*
Claude Debussy, from *Monsieur Croche antidilettante* (1901) *139*
Ferruccio Busoni, from *Sketch of a New Esthetic of Music* (1907) *141*
Max Reger, "Degeneration and Regeneration in Music" (1907) *148*
Charles Ives, from *Essays before a Sonata* (1920) *157*
Charles Ives, from "Postface to 114 Songs" (1922) *159*
Charles Ives, "Music and Its Future" (1929) *159*
Percy Grainger, "Free Music" (1938) *165*

PANTONALITY *167*
Arnold Schoenberg and Vassily Kandinsky, Correspondence (1911) *169*

NOISE *172*
Luigi Russolo, "The Art of Noises: Futurist Manifesto" (1913) *177*
Edgard Varèse, "Music and the Times" (1936) *185*
John Cage, Fragments from *Silence* (1961) *190*

6 **New Discipline: The Twelve-Tone Method** *193*

Arnold Schoenberg, from "Composition with Twelve Tones": [*fiat lux*] (1941) *194*
Anton Webern, from "The Path to Twelve-Note Composition" (1932) *202*
Thomas Mann, from *Dr. Faustus* (1947) *216*
Arthur Honegger, [The Twelve-Tone Method] (1951) *222*
Leonard Bernstein, [The Twelve-Tone Method] (1976) *222*
Benjamin Britten, [The Twelve-Tone Method] (1963) *223*

7 Isms 224

SYMBOLISM 226
Charles Baudelaire, from *Richard Wagner and Tannhäuser in Paris* (1861) 229
→ Marcel Proust, from *Swann's Way* (1913) 231

PRIMITIVISM AND EXOTICISM 234
Igor Stravinsky, "What I Wished to Express in *The Consecration of Spring*" (1913) 237
Igor Stravinsky, from *An Autobiography* (1934) 239
→ Béla Bartók, "The Influence of Peasant Music on Modern Music" (1931) 244

EXPRESSIONISM 251
Richard Wagner, "Beethoven" (1870) 255
Oskar Kokoschka, *Murderer, Hope of Women* (1907, 1917) 265
Arnold Schoenberg, from *Die glückliche Hand* (1910–13): [brain-storm] 271
Theodor Adorno, from *Philosophy of Modern Music* (1948) 272

NEOCLASSICISM AND THE NEW OBJECTIVITY 276
Rainer Maria Rilke, *Sonnets to Orpheus* 1.3 (1922) 280
Igor Stravinsky, from *An Autobiography* (1936) 282
Igor Stravinsky and Robert Craft, from *Expositions and Developments* [Expressivity] (1962) 283
Igor Stravinsky and Robert Craft, from *Expositions and Developments* [Pulcinella] (1962) 284
Igor Stravinsky and Robert Craft, from *Dialogues* (1968) 286
Igor Stravinsky and Robert Craft, from *Themes and Conclusions* (1969) 288
Arnold Schoenberg, from *Three Satires* (1925) 289
Ernst Krenek, from "New Humanity and Old Objectivity" (1931) 291
Ernst Krenek, "Music and Mathematics" (1937) 295
→ Constant Lambert, "The Age of Pastiche" (1934) 297
Constant Lambert, [Stravinsky as Pasticheur] (1934) 300
→ Gertrude Stein, from *Lectures in America* (1935) 305
→ Maurice Ravel, Interview: [Ravel's Toys] (1933) 307
→ Maurice Ravel, Interview: "Finding Tunes in Factories" (1933) 308

DADAISM AND SURREALISM 309
Kurt Schwitters: *Ursonate:* Rondo (1921–32) 318
→ Guillaume Apollinaire, Program Note for *Parade* (1917) 320
→ Erik Satie, from *Memoirs of an Amnesiac* (1912) 322

Jean Cocteau, from *Cock and Harlequin* (1918) *324*

Erwin Schulhoff, "For General Intelligibility as a Confession" (1919) *327*

Edith Sitwell, "Hornpipe" (1922) *329*

Ernst Krenek, from "What Is Called the New Music, and Why?" (1937) *330*

8 Music, Social Responsibility, and Politics *337*

Hanns Eisler, "On Old and New Music" (1925) *339*

Bertolt Brecht and Peter Suhrkamp, "The Modern Theatre Is the Epic Theatre" (1930) *343*

Friedrich Hollaender, *Münchhausen* (1931) *349*

Friedrich Hollaender, "Cabaret" (1932) *351*

Paul Hindemith, from *A Composer's World* (1949–50) *355*

Peter Kien, *Der Kaiser von Atlantis:* Final Scene (1943–44) *360*

Arnold Schoenberg, *A Survivor from Warsaw* (1947) *361*

L. N. Lebedinski, *Rayok:* The Music Lesson (1957) *364*

9 Testing the Boundaries between Popular and High Art *367*

Ernest Ansermet, "On a Negro Orchestra" (1919) *368*

Langston Hughes, from *The Big Sea* (1940) *375*

Langston Hughes, "Moon-Faced, Starry-Eyed" (1946–47) *377*

Ivan Goll, "The Negroes Are Conquering Europe" (1926) *378*

Daniel Gregory Mason, from *Tune In, America* (1931) *381*

George Gershwin, "The Composer and the Machine Age" (1933) *386*

George Antheil, "The Negro on the Spiral, or A Method of Negro Music" (1934) *390*

Gene Krupa and Leonard Bernstein, "Has Jazz Influenced the Symphony?" (1947) *398*

Elliott Carter, "Once Again Swing" (1939) *404*

Elliott Carter, from "The Rhythmic Basis of American Music" (1955) *405*

Bibliographical Note *409*

Credits *411*

Index *415*

Illustrations

Harry Partch's setting of Li Po 29

Morton Feldman, Projection 4 for violin and piano (1951) 81

Marcel Duchamp, *Nude Descending a Staircase, no. 2* (1912) 175

Luigi Russolo, *Music* (1911–12) 176

Giacomo Balla, *Rhythms of a Bow* (1912) 177

Giacomo Balla, set design for Stravinsky's *Fireworks* (reconstruction) 184

Pierre Boulez, symmetry diagram of a Webern series 203

Piet Mondrian, *Composition with Grid 5 (Lozenge)* (1919) 204

Edvard Munch, *The Scream* (1895) 254

Ernest Ludwig Kirchner, *The Women at Potsdamer Platz* (1914) 261

Erich Heckel, *Glassy Day* (1913) 262

Georg Grosz, *Jack the Ripper* (1918) 263

Oskar Kokoschka, drawing for *Mörder, Hoffnung der Frauen* (1908) 266

Fernand Léger, *The Mechanic* (1920) 279

René Magritte, *The Discovery of Fire* (ca. 1934–35) 311

Hugo Ball in costume 314

Kurt Schwitters, *The Hitler Gang* (1944) 316

Pablo Picasso, costumes for the Managers in *Parade* (1917) 326

Acknowledgments

Most of all I'm grateful to Kathleen Hansell, the music editor at the University of Chicago Press and the onlie begetter of this volume. She wanted it to exist, and bringing it into being has been one of the most enjoyable tasks of my professional life.

I also owe an enormous debt to a number of people at the Eastman School of Music, most conspicuously Kim Kowalke, Ralph Locke, Olivia Mattis, and David Headlam. If I asked one of them a question, he or she did not tell me where to go to find the answer, but simply answered it, in a shocking display of erudition. Furthermore, they told me things I needed to know but didn't know I needed to know. A special expression of gratitude goes to Antonius Bittmann, who went to endless trouble to check some of my translations from the German. He has that greatest of scholarly gifts, the gift to attend intensely and minutely to small things, without losing control of the largest themes. I also thank Peter J. Rabinowitz of Hamilton College, who made a number of shrewd and brilliantly well-informed suggestions. Beyond those I name here there lie many others, whose names grow indistinct in the radiance of their wit.

[ON THE ANTIQUITY OF THE MODERN]

As I was due to take part in these festivities with you, dear guests, I was in the vestibule, on the point of coming upstairs, when—just listen to this peculiar tale—I was approached by an old man in a hat so wide you could have cooked cabbage in it, with a decrepit old beard and scholar's robes. He was carrying a huge bundle of yellowing old paper strung across his body from his rump to his left shoulder, and addressed me in these words: "Go no further, o PLEASURE! You are not expected here, for the Author did not wish to have me as Master of the Music—I whom the theoreticians call RIGOR—, thus openly flouting the chromatic and harmonic rules which give all true music its harmony and reason; he has replaced them with harsh, uncouth proportions, composed diatonically, with no regard for reason. So if indeed you are PLEASURE, turn back, for in this place there can be no place for you."

After listening to this impudent chatter, I looked at him darkly and gave him an answer he certainly wasn't expecting: "I am PLEASURE, but the MODERN kind. I'll have you know that the Author—none other than myself, if the truth be told—may not have obeyed the rules on your bits of paper; but he claims to have done well nevertheless, and you, with all your hair-splitting and caviling, you insinuate that modern composers should go along with your antiquated nonsense. Oh, how amazed you would be if you realized that out of a hundred intelligent people, ninety are quite happy to accept the great precept: *Everything new gives pleasure.*

So my advice to you, o ANTIQUE RIGOR, is to sell your old papers to a grocer—they will make a most excellent brine for his sardines, tuna, herrings and caviar in no time."

His impudent nonsense started up all over again, whereupon I was inspired by a brilliant idea and returned his fire with a shower of black notes: *Oh, what a big nose.*

Prologue, Adriano Banchieri, *Festino nella sera del Giovedì Grasso avanti Cena* [*Fête for the Evening of Carnival Thursday, before Supper*], 1608, trans. John Sidgwick.

1 Introduction

Terms such as "modern" and "Modernism" seem to possess a certain security, even prestige, but they were long regarded with suspicion. Shakespeare used "modern" to mean commonplace—in his day, the word was uncomfortably close in meaning to "trivial." The culture of the Renaissance, like that of the eighteenth century, tended to revere the classical, the ancient; something that was modern (a word derived from *modus,* that is, fashion) was merely fashionable, transitory, perhaps gaudy, like an ostrich plume on a hat. To praise an excellent book, one compared it to the work of Horace or Cicero; to praise an excellent sculpture, one compared it to the work of Greek antiquity, which survived (in Roman copies) throughout Europe.

But the situation in music was a little different. Musical compositions could not be judged against models from remote antiquity. Certainly composers could evoke standards of comparison from classical Greece, as when Antoine Busnoys, in his motet *In hydraulis* (written before 1467), looked to Pythagoras for sanction for the polyphonic art that he, Busnoys, had inherited from Johannes Ockeghem. But no one knew what Greek music sounded like; and Busnoys could scarcely have imagined that Pythagoras, long before the birth of Christ, devised on his one-stringed lyre a music as intricate as that of the fifteenth century. From before the Renaissance until the later eighteenth century, music was usually modern. Plainchant persisted in church services; Gregorio Allegri's *Miserere* continued to be sung in the Vatican; the operas of Jean-Baptiste Lully held the stage long after the composer's death; but, for the most part, music meant new music. The art of music evolved so rapidly, and with such a strong general presupposition that the newer was *better* than the older, that the reverence for the classical, so common in other artistic media, was as much a matter of lip service as a matter of actual practice.

When, in the late nineteenth century, the artistic movement we call Modernism began, music was the artistic medium best equipped to participate, since it had always tended to assign privilege to the up to date and the novel. Music has always been the most temporally immediate of the arts, the medium most sensitive to the Now. And it is not surprising that, at the dawn of the twentieth century, music became the vanguard medium of the Modernist aesthetic.

The sudden importance of music was itself something new. For most of the history of Western art, music seemed somewhat slow to respond to advances in the other artistic media: in the words of Pierre Boulez, "we are always being told that musicians lag behind their literary rivals and colleagues."[1] For example, scholars of literature might date the beginning of the Renaissance from the time of Dante and Petrarch, in the fourteenth century, whereas scholars of music might date the beginning of the Renaissance from the time of Guillaume Dufay, a whole century later; similarly, the Romantic movement in literature was losing impetus by the time of the deaths of E. T. A. Hoffmann (1822), Lord Byron (1824), and Jean Paul (1825), that is, approximately the moment when musical Romanticism was catching fire, in the impassioned works of Schubert, Bellini, Berlioz, and others. But in the universe of Modernism, music shook off its belatedness, and took charge.

There are many signs that music is now the instigator, not the sluggish follower. For example, in 1925 T. S. Eliot wrote *The Hollow Men* ("We are the stuffed men . . . Headpiece filled with straw") partly in response to the eerie energy of the marionette in Stravinsky's 1911 ballet *Petrushka;*[2] and in 1947, W. H. Auden—arguably the most distinguished English poet of the generation following Eliot—wrote a letter concerning the proposed opera *The Rake's Progress* in which he told Stravinsky, "I need hardly say that the chance of working with you is the greatest honor of my life."[3] But well before Eliot's or Auden's time, literary folk were starting to bow to composers. When the poet Charles Baudelaire attended, in 1861, the new version of Richard Wagner's *Tannhäuser,* he felt that he was hearing something that should change the evolution of literature. When the philosopher Friedrich Nietzsche published his first book, in 1872, *The Birth of Tragedy out of the Spirit of Music,* he prophesied that Wagner's *Tristan und Isolde* (1865) would inaugurate a rebirth of the Dionysiac energy that informs all artistic and intellectual achievement. In the next year, 1873, Walter Pater published *The Renaissance,* in which he argued that *"All art constantly aspires toward the condition of music."*[4] The italics are Pater's own, and the prose style of his book, sinuously gorgeous, suggests that Pater was himself trying to write a text that sounds like music.

Already by the 1870s the prestige of the composer was so great that some poets, particularly in France, were starting to conceive themselves as surrogate composers, composers *manqués:* Paul Verlaine begins his "Art poétique" (1874) with the line "Before everything else, music"; and Stéphane Mallarmé writes, in "L'après-midi d'un faune" (1876),

---

1. Pierre Boulez, *Orientations: Collected Writings,* ed. Jean-Jacques Nattiez, trans. Martin Cooper (London: Faber and Faber, 1986), 208.

2. B. C. Southam, *A Guide to the Selected Poems of T. S. Eliot* (San Diego: Harvest, 1994), 210.

3. Igor Stravinsky and Robert Craft, *Memories and Commentaries* (Berkeley: University of California Press, 1981), 155.

4. Walter Pater, *The Renaissance,* ed. Donald L. Hill (Berkeley: University of California Press, 1980), 106.

Inerte, tout brûle dans l'heure fauve

Sans marquer par quel art ensemble détala

Trop d'hymen souhaité de qui cherche le *la*

Torpid, all things burn in that wild hour

Not noting how the too-much-marriage slipped away

Desired by the one who seeks the A

These lines are so shadowy, so evacuated of solid objects and determinate meaning, that they become correspondingly rich in musical suggestiveness; the only conspicuous feature in the poem is the faun's piercing A♮. Debussy's famous *Prélude* (1894) seems designed to tease out of Mallarmé's poem the music already latent within it.

The essays gathered in this anthology reflect a sense, not always present in the pre-Modernist world, that the composer is an important person whose words should be pondered carefully—and not just by other artists, but also by the general public. The Modernist composer is typically an intellectual—a pontificator at large, orating on the largest stages. Some of these composers took a strong interest in politics: Arnold Schoenberg, for example, wrote to a newspaper on the difficulties of writing an international hymn for peace (1928) and even wrote a play, *The Biblical Way* (1926–27), concerning the establishment of a Zionist homeland in Africa. Charles Ives corresponded with William Howard Taft in 1920 to gain his support for a constitutional amendment to combine presidential elections with a national referendum.

But the twentieth-century composer is rarely a crusader, and still more rarely a successful crusader: Schoenberg's play ends with the failure of the Moses figure to achieve what he worked for; and Taft brusquely dismissed Ives's plan for majoritarian rule. Typically, the composer tries to effect change in the larger culture not by direct action but by illustrating technical possibilities for advancement in the arts and letters—by exploring regions of liberation undreamed of in previous ages. The Modernist composer devises theories, theories that themselves become forms of action, forms of art. As music starts to become self-consciously smart—intricate, cerebral, generated from pre-compositional ideas—the composer starts to become engaged with every sort of intellectual activity, from philosophy to sociology; musical compositions become models for problem-solving, as if music were a species of thinking carried out by other means.

The clearest nineteenth-century prefiguration of the Modernist composer-intellectual can be found in the example of Richard Wagner: not only a political rebel who fled Germany after a warrant was issued for his arrest during the upheavals of 1848–49, but also a man who felt free to opine in print on every subject under the sun, such as the origins of classical Greek drama in folk art; the corruption of European culture by Jews; the relation between early Christian asceticism and Buddhist rejection of desire; the psychoacoustics of alliteration in German verse; and the role of dreaming in the philosophy of Arthur Schopenhauer. Before Wagner's time, when composers felt impelled to write, they usually wrote treatises on harmony (Johannes Tinctoris, Jean-Philippe Rameau) or practical advice for instrumentalists (Leopold Mozart, Johann Joachim Quantz). But Wagner was an intellectual-at-large, confrontational and sometimes erudite, whose public presence was more like that of Jean-Paul Sartre than like that of a musician trying to improve performance standards.

Wagner, of course, wrote a great deal about music, but much of his speculation concerns the music of the past and the music of the future; earlier composers, by contrast, tended to be interested in questions pertinent to the immediate present—questions of writing a fugue that offends no one's ears, or of properly differentiating legato, spiccato, and staccato when playing a violin. For Wagner, music is not an art of evanescent compositions, sounds that reverberate a moment and then die away, but an art of timeless masterpieces: Wagner (and in this respect he resembles Felix Mendelssohn and Johannes Brahms) devoted much energy to rehabilitating the music of the past, by editing Giovanni Pierluigi da Palestrina's Stabat Mater, or by preparing a new German performing edition of Christoph Willibald Gluck's *Iphigenia in Aulis.* Even in the eighteenth century there were tentative signs that a canon of classic music was taking shape, immune from time's ravages: Wolfgang Amadeus Mozart, for example, evidently added his own adagios (K. 404a) to some fugues from J. S. Bach's *Well-Tempered Clavier,* and certainly rewrote George Frideric Handel's *Acis and Galatea* and *Messiah* for the orchestra of his own time; but the nineteenth and twentieth centuries bear most of the responsibility for giving music a history, for making music more than thirty years old part of the normal experience of listening. Sometimes nineteenth- and twentieth-century composers even wrote music *about* music history: an early example is Louis Spohr's Sixth Symphony (1840), the *Historical* Symphony, which recapitulates the evolution of the art. The first movement is called the "Bach-Handel Period," the second the "Haydn-Mozart Period," the scherzo the "Beethoven Period," and the finale "The Newest of the New," a movement that sounds perhaps like the operas of Daniel François Auber; it is hard to be certain whether Spohr treats this ultra-modern stuff respectfully or sneers at it for being laboriously trivial. Nowadays we often deplore the fact that the life of the concert hall and opera house is a museum culture, in which recently written works are rarely heard; but the older sort of culture, in which concertgoers sometimes heard *only* recently written works, was (as Spohr tried to show) a still unhealthier situation.

■ If the caricature of the Romantic composer is the eccentric genius or mesmerizing satyr—Paganini or Liszt playing with fingers inhumanly long—the caricature of the Modernist composer is a sort of scientist, conducting, with scalpels of sound, research into the darkest regions of the human psyche. Schoenberg seems to join Sigmund Freud

Milhaud was in this sense a Wagner epigone

(and the painter Edvard Munch and the novelist Joseph Conrad) in a common project to map areas of feeling little explored in previous ages. The Modernist composer is considered the master of an arcane and forbidding art, like tensor calculus; as the elderly Schoenberg wrote, reviewing his career, there was a time "when everybody made believe he understood Einstein's theories and Schoenberg's music."[5] Modernist music (according to the cartoon version) may provide exquisite pleasure to those of refined taste, who enjoy tone clusters, irregular rhythms, and bizarre timbres, but sounds intolerably shrill, aggressive, aimless, banging, to normal people who like good tunes with dominant seventh chords and clear cadences. The nineteenth-century composer always has a full head of hair, or at least a long beard; but the twentieth-century composer has the bald pate of Schoenberg or Igor Stravinsky or Sergei Prokofiev or Paul Hindemith, as well as the severe scowl of Anton Webern, appropriate for a music that seems to reject all ornament and charm in favor of research into the essence of things, the phonic equivalent of the physics of subatomic particles. The purpose of the earlier composers (speaking very roughly) was to *praise:* to praise God, to congratulate the Hamburg city council, to sing happy birthday to the king's eleven-year-old son, to provide cheer at the local university's commencement ceremony; the purpose of the nineteenth-century composer was to *move,* to make the audience shudder, weep, break out in laughter; but the purpose of the twentieth-century composer seems to be to *think,* to provide transcendental philosophy with fretful and opaque analogues in sound.

How much truth is there in these caricatures of Modernism? In order to answer this question, it is necessary to study its central assumption: that Modernist art is *difficult.*

Perhaps the classic statement of this assumption occurs in T. S. Eliot's essay "The Metaphysical Poets" (1921): "it appears likely that poets in our civilization, as it exists at present, must be *difficult.* Our civilization comprehends great variety and complexity, and this variety and complexity, playing upon a refined sensibility, must produce various and complex results."[6] Those who discuss Modernism in music have tended to agree. The well-informed and taxonomically passionate musicologist Carl Dahlhaus, for example, argues that composers are Modernist if they are progressive:

> The year 1890 . . . lends itself as an obvious point of historical discontinuity. . . . The "breakthrough" of Mahler, Strauss, and Debussy implies a profound historical transformation. . . . If we were to search for a name to convey the breakaway mood of the 1890s (a mood symbolized musically by the opening bars of Strauss's *Don Juan* [1888]) but without imposing a fictitious unity of style on the age, we could do worse

5. Arnold Schoenberg, *Style and Idea: Selected Writings of Arnold Schoenberg,* ed. Leonard Stein, trans. Leo Black (Berkeley: University of California Press, 1984), 51–52.

6. T. S. Eliot, *Selected Essays* (New York: Harcourt, Brace and World, 1960), 248.

than revert to [the] term "modernism" extending (with some latitude) from 1890 to the beginnings of our own twentieth-century modern music in 1910. . . . The label "late romanticism" . . . is a terminological blunder of the first order and ought to be abandoned forthwith. It is absurd to yoke Strauss, Mahler, and the young Schönberg, composers who represented modernism in the minds of their turn-of-the-century contemporaries, with the self-proclaimed anti-modernist Pfitzner, calling them all "late romantics" in order to supply a veneer of internal unity to an age fraught with stylistic contradictions and conflicts.[7]

Dahlhaus presents a strong case for restricting the term Modernism to a somewhat narrow spectrum of musical activity, and to a short chronological span, only twenty years. I believe that Modernism embraces a broader bandwidth, but Dahlhaus's nice strictures deserve serious attention. If Modernism is a movement confined to the progressive music of 1890–1910, then its main features are:

1. *Comprehensiveness and depth.* Gustav Mahler's symphonies, for example, aspire to become vehicles for the transmission of universal vibrations into the domain of human perception: as he wrote concerning his Third Symphony of 1895–96, "Now think of a work so *great* that it actually mirrors the *whole world*—one is, so to speak, oneself only an instrument on which the universe plays. . . . My symphony will be something that *the world has never heard!* All nature finds in it a voice, and tells a deep secret, like the tinglings of a dream! I tell you, I get uncanny feelings when I look at certain passages, as if I hadn't written them."[8] To write a symphony that comprised the whole world's music, Mahler agglomerated military fanfares, vulgar dance tunes, whirling gestures of rapture—in Terence's phrase, nothing human was alien to him. He strove for depth as well as for range. Just as Nietzsche located ultimate reality in Dionysiac rending, in which the ego is torn to pieces in order that we may glimpse the terror at the center of things, so Mahler felt possessed. In the words of his wife, "One day in the summer he came running down from his hut in a perspiration and scarcely able to breathe. At last he came out with it: it was the heat, the stillness, the Panic horror. He was often overcome by this feeling of the goat-god's frightful and ebullient eye upon him."[9] The fourth movement of the Third Symphony is a setting of the Midnight Song from Nietzsche's *Also sprach Zarathustra,* as if to honor Nietzsche as the chief modern prophet of Dionysus. At the very time when Mahler was seized by Pan, Richard Strauss was composing *Also sprach*

7. Carl Dahlhaus, *Nineteenth-Century Music,* trans. J. Bradford Robinson (Berkeley: University of California Press), 334.

8. *Gustav Mahler Briefe,* ed. Herta Blaukopf (Vienna: Paul Zsolnay Verlag, 1982), 164–65.

9. Alma Mahler, *Gustav Mahler: Memories and Letters,* ed. Donald Mitchell, trans. Basil Creighton (Seattle: University of Washington Press, 1975), 116.

Zarathustra (1896), which also climaxes on Nietzsche's vision of the soul's ultimate midnight; soon thereafter Frederick Delius began setting texts from Nietzsche's *Also sprach Zarathustra* in *A Mass of Life* (1899–1909).

2. *Semantic specificity and density.* Not only did the new music of the 1890s appeal to an astonishing range of experience, but it also arrested its listeners through vividness of detail. The bleating sheep (flutter-tonguing winds) and the pair of strolling Benedictines (bassoons exchanging lines) in *Don Quixote* (1898) are among the most conspicuous examples of the remarkable extension of musical onomatopoeia and metaphor that Strauss achieved in this decade. It seemed possible that music could go beyond imitation to an actual embodiment of the outer world; perhaps a powerfully reified music could compete with literature and painting as a direct seizure of reality. Another form of detailed acoustic realism could be found in certain violently heterogeneous works of Charles Ives: for example, Ives created an interweaving of popular tunes in *Central Park in the Dark* (1906). As Ives explained, "The piece purports to be a picture-in-sounds of the sounds of nature and of happening that men would hear . . . when sitting on a bench in Central Park on a hot summer night. The strings represent the night sounds and silent darkness—interrupted by sounds (the rest of the orchestra) from the Casino over the pond—of street singers coming up from the Circle singing, in spots, the tunes of those days. . . . A street car and a street band join in the chorus." [10]

3. *Extensions and destructions of tonality.* When a hostile critic said of the young Schoenberg's sextet *Verklärte Nacht* (1899) that "it sounds as if someone had smeared the score of *Tristan* while it was still wet," [11] he provided a clever description for the Jugendstil (or art nouveau) way in which Schoenberg's melodies seem to curl themselves in continuous tendrils, instead of pausing on harmonically significant notes. In his next work, the tone poem *Pelleas und Melisande,* Schoenberg invented (or so he claimed) the trombone glissando; and the texture of much of his early work can sometimes sound like a general gliss, as if themes were generated by something more like finger painting than like the normal method of arranging finite notes on staves. Schoenberg's verticals are just as chromatically charged as his horizontals: soon after Debussy began to write with sonorous puddles of ninth chords, Schoenberg was experimenting with all sorts of non-triadic formations, sometimes full of such exotic intervals as major sevenths, major and minor seconds, and augmented fourths. This exploration of the gaps between the notes of the diatonic scale is strongly related to the Expressionist desire to investigate subtler,

10. Charles Ives, "Note," in *Central Park in the Dark,* ed. Jacques-Louis Monod (Hillsdale, N.Y.: Boelke-Bomart, 1973), 31.

11. See Arnold Whittall, *Schoenberg Chamber Music* (Seattle: University of Washington Press, 1979), 11.

more intimate, more powerful emotions that those expressible by diatonic means—musical dissonance is an attractive metaphor for emotional dissonance. Just as there are notes that dwell in the forbidden gaps of the scale, so there are feelings that hide in the cracks between such familiar and acceptable feelings as love, anger, rage, sadness, and so forth. Mahler's marital troubles led him to consult Sigmund Freud in 1910, and Freud was struck by Mahler's quick comprehension of the principles of psychoanalysis; the author of the libretto for Schoenberg's *Erwartung* (1909)—which sounds like the monologue of a psychoanalyzed patient—was an Austrian medical student, Marie Pappenheim. Pappenheim was a relative of Bertha Pappenheim, one of psychoanalysis's most closely investigated patients, called in Freud's case history "Anna O."; and a certain strain of Modernist music can be best understood as an investigation of music's unconscious. What onomatopoeia is to outer realism, chromaticism is to inner realism.

So it seems that the motto of Modernism is the poet Ezra Pound's favorite slogan, "Make it new." On the other hand, "Make it new" is an extremely old slogan: Pound discovered it in the Great Digest of Confucius, who noted that it was written in letters of gold on the Emperor T'ang's bathtub.[12] Against this ancient call for novelty, we should remember King Solomon's warning: "there is no new thing under the sun."[13]

Each of the three sorts of originalities listed above can be shown to be nothing new. The world-comprehending symphonies of Mahler have a number of old precedents, especially in the domain of world theater—a name for the sort of theater developed in the medieval mystery and morality plays in order to embrace the whole range of human experience, from the temptations of the flesh to the soul's departure for heaven or hell; from the creation of the world to the Last Judgment. The Elizabethan stage was a world theater, in that the ceiling of the stage's overhang was painted with stars and called heaven; and the part of the stage beneath the trap door was called hell. World theater has often been associated with music: a very early example is Hildegard's *Ordo Virtutum* (ca. 1152), a morality play in which every speech, except the devil's, is set to plainchant. It is perhaps odd to think of Hildegard as a precursor of Mahler, but they had similarly vast ambitions for their music. Other examples of composers with strong aspirations toward comprehensiveness include Orlando Gibbons in his madrigal *The Cries of London* (the closest approach in the world of Elizabethan music to rich Shakespearean disorder), Heinrich Schütz in the *Psalmen Davids,* Joseph Haydn in *The Creation,* and Beethoven in his Ninth Symphony—a work that comprises gestures of immediate rage, a toy march for Turkish soldiers, a plunge into the abyss, and swells of interplanetary harmony.

---

12. Ezra Pound, *Confucius* (New York: New Directions, 1951), 36.
13. Ecclesiastes 1:9.

As for examples of semantic specificity, the history of music overflows with them: the whole aviary in Clément Janequin's *Le chant des oyseaulx,* the nightingale in Alessandro Poglietti's large harpsichord suite *Rossignolo,* the barking dog in Antonio Vivaldi's *Four Seasons,* the nightingale, quail, and cuckoo in Beethoven's Sixth Symphony, the notorious frog croaks in Haydn's *The Seasons.* This last composition so angered Schopenhauer that he rejected it entirely, called it a wretched instance of what happens when composers take their inspirations secondhand from exterior ideas instead of firsthand from the depths of experience.[14] Examples of semantic density are perhaps a little harder to find, but Heinrich Biber in the seventeenth century and Georg Philipp Telemann in the eighteenth both provide clear foreshadowings of Ives's overlay technique: Biber in his *Battalia a 10,* where a gang of rowdy drunken soldiers is illustrated by a string consort in which each instrument bawls its own tune; Telemann in his *Gulliver Suite* for two violins, in which (in the movement called "Loure of the well-mannered Houyhnhnms and furie of the ill-mannered Yahoos") one violin plays a slow, stately tune and the other a wild dance, at the same time. These two pieces are jokes, but the older music sometimes uses overlay for serious purposes as well: in a Salve Regina (1541) subtitled *Diversi diversa orant* (different people pray different things), Nicholas Gombert has four singers singing four different antiphons in praise of the Virgin Mary simultaneously, as if in imitation of a heavenly perspective in which Mary's ear catches all prayers directed toward her, distinct yet intermingled.

The chromaticism so characteristic of the progressive music of 1890–1910 also generated a series of important precursors: Carlo Gesualdo, born in 1566, almost became an honorary Modernist on the strength of the chromatic contortion of such works as the responsory *Tristis est anima mea;* Stravinsky was sufficiently impressed that he reworked three of Gesualdo's motets (*Tres Sacrae Cantiones di Gesualdo*) and wrote a *Monumentum pro Gesualdo.* Even before Gesualdo's time, Nicola Vicentino, born in 1511, experimented with microtones by devising an *archicembalo,* a harpsichord with split black keys, capable of making fine differentiations between, say, F♯ and G♭. In the twentieth century Ives wrote music for quarter-tone piano, and Alois Hába and Harry Partch built whole orchestras to play music written in intervals much smaller than the semitones that represent the limit of subtlety in the well-tempered scale; but these exotic instruments were, in a sense, only refinements and extensions of the old *archicembalo.*

■ If there is nothing new under the sun, however, there are new shifts of emphasis. The overlay of incomprehensible counterpoints, the juxtaposition of bizarrely mismatched material, the flaunting of forbidden notes, the creating of undreamed-of notes in the

14. Arthur Schopenhauer, *The World as Will and Idea,* trans. R. B. Haldane and J. Kemp, 2 vols. (New York: Scribner's, 1950), 1:341.

interstices of the scale—these were once fringe phenomena of the art of music; but from 1890 on, they became a central line of development. Perhaps the true breakthrough of Modernism is the assumption that technical liberation can lead to artistic liberation—in other words, that tinkering with the basic material of compositional technique (the scale, the rules of voice leading, all the proprieties that govern construction) is a delight in itself, an end in itself, and requires no justification. T. S. Eliot and Ezra Pound were much struck by the comment of a French critic named Davray, who, reviewing an early collection of Modernist English poetry, wrote, "They seek sentiments in order to accommodate them to their vocabulary, instead of seeking words to express their passions and ideas." [15] If Davray is right, odd words are more important to a Modernist poet for the sake of their sonority and flavor than for the sake of their appropriate meaning. A Romantic composer, when breaking a rule, might justify his or her transgression on the grounds that the emotion was too intense to be confined to the old formality of the sonata-allegro form; a Modernist composer seems to transgress for transgression's sake, and then to seek some landscape of affect to which the bold music might pertain. Debussy asked his friends for help in inventing the titles of his piano pieces, as in the case of *Et la lune descend sur le temple qui fut (And the Moon Descends above the Ruins of the Temple),* from *Images 2,* no. 2 (1907)—a poised Alexandrine line supposedly suggested by Louis Laloy—as if the meaning of the music, even the intention of the music, came into being at some point after the music was written. Yet even this emphasis on generating music through technical experiment isn't quite unprecedented in the history of music: the composers of the *ars subtilior* movement in the late fourteenth century, such as Solage, Grimace, and Baude Cordier, wrote a sort of mannerist music characterized by exuberance in notational games—Baude Cordier's canon *Tout par compas* is written on a circular staff, as if it were to be sung until the end of time. In this fourteenth-century Modernism, as in the twentieth-century kind, the listener sometimes feels that the music arises not from expressive urgency or from obedience to the rules of good craft, but from an autonomous delight in extending the kingdom of sound.

Dahlhaus's triumphalist definition of Modernism (cited earlier) is far from negligible, since the expansion of phonic resources has been one of the predominant themes of twentieth-century music: composers have explored not only the more anxious intervals of the chromatic scale, but also quarter-tones, the forty-three-part division of the octave, tape-recorded noise, and other sounds that might have caused Mozart to wince. But this definition of Modernism tends to create an artificial distinction between his-

---

15. T. S. Eliot, *The Waste Land: A Facsimile and Transcript of the Original Drafts Including the Annotations of Ezra Pound,* ed. Valerie Eliot (New York: Harcourt Brace Jovanovich, 1971), 126.

tory's winners (Richard Strauss until about 1909, Debussy, Schoenberg, Stravinsky from about 1911 to 1917, Alban Berg, Webern, Edgard Varèse, Partch, Elliott Carter) and history's losers (Giacomo Puccini, Jean Sibelius, Sergei Rachmaninov, Francis Poulenc, the later Richard Strauss, Stravinsky from about 1919 to 1951)—between brave progressives willing to endure humiliation as they blazed trails through the jungles of unheard acoustic phenomena and slothful retrogressives eager to flatter the tastes of a complacent bourgeois public. A great many points could be made to refute this (basically political) narrative of Modernism, including the fact that Strauss built his villa at Garmisch-Partenkirchen on the royalties of his challenging but wildly successful "Modernist" opera *Salome.* But the fundamental problem is this: to define musical Modernism in terms of dissonance is to ignore the fact that a composer can be original in dimensions other than harmonic novelty. Extremely simple music (as Erik Satie demonstrated) can be as radical as a continuous succession of discords. Dahlhaus was eager to choose Hans Pfitzner as his specimen anti-Modernist—too reactionary even for the Nazis, who brushed off his attempts to ingratiate himself with them; but Pfitzner's gnarled, anxious, willful diatonicism, his self-conscious and confrontational rejection of every newfangle of the twentieth century, his sense of working in the limbo between two musical worlds, one dead and the other unable to be born, are original, striking, even visionary. He might be called a Modernist in spite of himself, for Modernism is a movement that embraces even its enemies. Where there is technical aggressiveness, there is Modernism.

■ A theory of the Modernist movement that might embrace both Pfitzner and Schoenberg, or Balthus and Picasso, could be constructed along the following lines: Modernism is *a testing of the limits of aesthetic construction.* According to this perspective, the Modernists tried to find the ultimate bounds of certain artistic possibilities: volatility of emotion (Expressionism); stability and inexpressiveness (the New Objectivity); accuracy of representation (Hyperrealism); absence of representation (Abstractionism); purity of form (Neoclassicism); formless energy (Neobarbarism); cultivation of the technological present (Futurism); cultivation of the prehistoric past (the Mythic Method). I have, of course, arranged these extremes in pairs, because aesthetic heresies, like theological ones, often come in binary sets: each limit point presupposes an opposite limit point, a counterextreme toward which the artist can push. Much of the strangeness, the stridency, the exhilaration of Modernist art can be explained by this strong thrust toward the verges of the aesthetic experience: after the nineteenth century had established a remarkably safe, intimate center where the artist and the audience could dwell, the twentieth century reached out to the freakish circumferences of art. Perhaps this sense of the comfortableness of nineteenth-century music is merely an artifact of the twentieth-century spectator, a deceptive nostalgia; on the other hand, Schubert, Brahms, and

Dvořák were companionable and convivial composers, more easily envisaged playing their songs in the evening with an agreeable chorus of friends than is, say, Pierre
Boulez.

The extremes of the aesthetic experience tend to converge: in the Modernist movement, the most barbaric art tends to be the most up-to-date and sophisticated. For example, when T. S. Eliot first heard *The Rite of Spring,* he wrote that the music seemed to
"transform the rhythm of the steppes into the scream of the motor-horn, the rattle of
machinery, the grind of wheels, the beating of iron and steel, the roar of the underground railway, and the other barbaric noises of modern life." [16] *The Waste Land* is itself
written to the same recipe: the world of London, with its grime, boredom, and abortifa-
cient drugs, overlays the antique world of primal rites for the rejuvenation of the land
through the dismemberment of a god. In the Modernist movement, things tend to coexist uncomfortably with their exact opposites. But it would wrong to overstress the aesthetic, formal qualities of Modernism: as the quotation from Eliot suggests, Modernism
also challenges the boundaries between art and the rest of human experience: industry,
domestic life, politics, and all that we mean by the word "culture."

■ When did the Modernist movement end? This is not easy to answer. For Dahlhaus,
the purest strain was over by 1910; but for other critics, Modernism terminated around
the end of one or the other of the world wars. Such claims tend to make Modernism
a phenomenon of the first half of the twentieth century; after it is over comes Postmodernism. The main tendencies of Postmodernism can be summarized roughly as
follows:

1. *Bricolage:* the jury-rigging of art, the assembling of the art object from the odds and
ends of older art, in a denatured and desecrated fashion, in order to expose the purely
arbitrary character of the signs that all artists, past and present, employ. In this sense the
modality of Postmodernist art is a collage of ironic quotations. Art history is wholly flattened, denarratized: the passage of centuries shows no progress, development, or flowering of art, only a steady accumulation of shiny familiar junk, such as the plagal cadence, the first four notes of Beethoven's Fifth Symphony, or the *Tristan* chord. As the
philosopher Jacques Derrida has written, "Every sign, linguistic or non-linguistic, spoken or written . . . , in a small or large unit, can be *cited,* put between quotation marks;
in so doing it can break with every context, engendering an infinity of new contexts in a
manner which is absolutely illimitable." [17]

2. *Polystylism:* this is *bricolage* on the level of technique instead of content. The poly-

16. T. S. Eliot, "London Letter," *Dial,* September 1921.
17. Jacques Derrida, "Signature Event Context," in *Glyph* 1 (1977): 185.

stylist may combine Gregorian chant, tuneful tonalism, and obnoxious dissonances into a single composition, in order to create incongruities that deny the propriety or the tenability of any single style.

3. *Randomness:* a technique for depersonalizing the artist, for demonstrating the transcendental anonymity of the work of art. If artistic decisions are governed by the rolling of dice, then the artwork is liberated from human responsibility. Roland Barthes's influential essay "The Death of the Author" (1968) has helped bring into being a sort of art in which the maker dramatizes the absence of authority within the made object.

The student of Postmodernism can point to any number of late-twentieth-century works that display these characteristics: for example, the third movement of Luciano Berio's *Sinfonia* (1969) paraphrases the sermon to the fishes in Mahler's Second Symphony (1895), treats it as a music stream in which swim strips of text by Samuel Beckett, as well as audible quotation wriggles from Bach, Beethoven, Ravel, Boulez, and many other composers; or Alfred Schnittke's *Peer Gynt* (1987), in which huge, loud, athematic arrhythmias are interrupted by pseudo-Grieg sections, and by a tune stolen from Rachmaninov's Fourth Piano Concerto. One attractive date for the beginning of Postmodernism is 1951, when John Cage composed the first extended composition determined by purely chance procedures, *Music of Changes.*

■

As a rough guide for assembling this anthology, I have taken 1951, when Cage wrote *Music of Changes,* as an ending point for Modernism, just as I have taken 1894–95 as a starting point, when Debussy wrote his *Prélude à l'après-midi d'un faune* and Strauss wrote his *Till Eulenspiegels lustige Streiche*—works charged with semantic intensities almost unprecedented in the history of music. But the narrative threads of story of Modernism begin well before 1894 and extend well after 1951, and so I have not hesitated to print a few texts, both early and late, that seem necessary to give a fuller sense of the movement.

The student of Modernism should be suspicious of any terminal date whatsoever. There is scarcely any characteristic attributed to Postmodernism that cannot be found within the earlier Modernism. Stravinsky's *Pulcinella* (1920), with its relentless appropriation of the works of Giovanni Battista Pergolesi, and of various compositions misattributed to Pergolesi, has that quality of theft-verging-on-hoax so typical of the later twentieth century; and Stravinsky's *Oedipus Rex* (1927), with its flagrant Handelisms, Verdi-isms, and Musorgskyisms, is as blatant a piece of polystylism as anything by Alfred Schnittke. Erik Satie was a master of *bricolage* by the time of the First World War: for example, his ballet *Parade* (1917) quotes a rag by Irving Berlin in a conspicuously dry, sterilized context, as if Satie were picking up the pop tune with tweezers and holding it up to the light. Marcel Duchamp, as early as 1913, was composing his *Musical Erratum* by means of blind chance: he wrote the names of notes on slips of paper and mixed them in a hat. (Again, in the domain of *bricolage,* polystylism, and randomness, the art of music, far from being belated, was more the leader than the follower.) A skeptical critic might claim that what is called Postmodernism is such an obvious realization of certain potentialities within earlier Modernism that it shouldn't be labeled a separate artistic movement; he or she might also claim that the ego assertion of Modernism and the egolessness of Postmodernism are coextensive, not successive. If the skeptical critic is right, there isn't any Postmodernism; we're still living in the Modernist world.

As an artistic movement, Postmodernism is pluralistic and hard to define. But as a movement in criticism, Postmodernism has a certain coherence—and tremendous influence.

Postmodernist criticism starts with the premise that art, science, and human thought of any sort are governed by a search for validation. If I write a poem, or compose a piece of music, or develop a scientific theory, what guarantees that it will be of value? For Jacques Derrida, the authority of an utterance lies in the presumed speaking voice of the person who utters it; once we learn to regard our libraries as assemblages of *written* texts, texts that have behind them no king or priest or father figure whose deep, commanding voice upholds their meaning, then we are on the path to enlightenment. Similarly (perhaps), if we can learn to hear a composition by Beethoven or Schoenberg as if no one in particular had written it—that is, without feeling behind the notes the myth of the man, the thunder of his presence—we can hear it more freely, more critically. Shorn of the fiction of the composer's ego, deprived of the normal context that music historians have contrived, a piece of music loses its sacred aura and recedes into a tame, culturally plastic, cooperative state. Romanticism and Modernism tend to enforce the awe of genius; but Postmodernism tends to assume that the author is dead, and that pages of text circulate endlessly in the slow whirlwind of culture.

Other Postmodernist critics treat the issue of validation differently. Jean-François Lyotard claims that we warrant the worth of our theories, our artifacts, by telling ourselves stories about them. The technical term for such a validating story is metanarrative. If I am a Modernist composer, how do I assert the value of tone clusters, nonfunctional harmony, and dissonant counterpoint—anything that might make the audience run, hands over ears, from the concert hall? Well, I might construct a metanarrative, roughly along the following lines: "The history of music is a continual extension of the concept of the beautiful, a continual emancipation of the dissonance; in the Middle Ages, the third was considered a dissonance, and the tritone was considered diabolical; but in recent centuries, the third has been treated as a consonance, and the tritone probingly explored in diminished seventh chords; now I have come to show you the path toward a full liberation of the resources of the chromatic scale; if you dislike what you hear, it is because you are either a complacent bourgeois or a fool." Note that the composer who makes this claim is locating the value of the composition not inside the composition itself, but inside the metanarrative: a story about aesthetic progressivity. But Lyotard says: "I define *postmodern* as incredulity toward metanarratives";[18] and in the devalued and equable spaces of Postmodernism, works of art are no longer sheathed in the stories that formerly puffed them up and guaranteed their importance. If we today enjoy Henry Cowell's tone clusters, or Schoenberg's successions of chords made up of major sevenths, it is for some reason other than the metanarrative of resource extension that once justified them.

Postmodernist criticism, then, is sensitive to the fictions of valuation that cling to works of art—perhaps partly because Modernist art was so furiously defended that the artwork itself sometimes seems buried amid the enormous body of vindications that grew around it. And Postmodernist criticism is especially sensitive to the political values that occlude themselves in works of art. The teasing out of metanarratives from the work of art usually exposes struggles for power. Chapter 8 of this anthology is devoted to music and politics, concerning mostly the extreme situations of Hitler's Germany and Stalin's Russia; but it is important to remember that *all* the essays in this volume can be studied from a political point of view. Consider for a moment some remarks by Schoenberg.

ARNOLD SCHOENBERG
from "The Future of the Opera" (1927)

It is self-evident that art which treats deeper ideas can not address itself to the many. "Art for everyone": anyone regarding that as possible is unaware how "everyone" is constituted and how art is constituted. So here, in the end, art and success will yet again part company.

The erosion of the theatre began as the emotions of the people acting on the stage came to absorb more and more of the audience's interest. The result of this, and of the attempt to interest as many people as possible in the emotion concerned, was that the characters represented necessarily became even more ordinary, their emotions even more comprehensible to all. The result is that nowadays one sees on the stage almost exclusively the kind of philistines one also meets in life, whether they are supposed to represent heroes, artists, or men-in-the-street.

The opera is in a comparable situation. It has less to offer the eye than the film has—

18. Jean-François Lyotard, *The Postmodern Condition: A Report on Knowledge*, trans. Geoff Bennington and Brian Massumi (Minneapolis: University of Minnesota Press, 1997), xxiv.

and color-film will soon be here, too. Add music, and the general public will hardly need to hear an opera sung and acted any more, unless a new path is found.

Fortunately it so expensive to make a film that producers will not be able to renounce widespread popular appeal. This again makes clear the need to seek some individual form for the newest art.

From *Style and Idea: Selected Writings of Arnold Schoenberg*, ed. Leonard Stein, trans. Leo Black (Berkeley: University of California Press, 1984), 336–37. First published as "Die Zukunft der Oper," *Neues Wiener Tageblatt*, 1927.

This passage seems fairly innocuous, and yet it presupposes a political critique along the following lines: art music is a domain of rarefied spiritual sensations, much threatened by popular culture; art music can never hope for financial success; democratic culture naturally tends to decay into the coarse, the universally accessible; the cinema, with its powers of sensory glamour, might overwhelm and drive out new developments in opera, except that the economics of filmmaking require a certain obvious pandering to the masses; and so the ambitious projects of art music should be financed by educated benefactors who can appreciate the narrow and intense bandwidths of genius. Schoenberg's monarchist politics,[19] his belief that music is ideally supported by princes, lies only a little way beneath the conventional elitism of this essay.

And yet, we can hear in this passage odd resonances of contradictory political opinions, a sense that the future lies not with staged operas addressed to the six most cultivated ears in Europe, but with the vulgar, prepotent art of the movies. Opera seems weak, pale, static, nearly helpless, compared with the films that Schoenberg anticipates—films in *color!* As early as 1913 Schoenberg had written detailed instructions for a possible film version of his short opera *Die glückliche Hand;*[20] and in 1930 Schoenberg wrote *Music to Accompany a Film Scene,* a piece of such extreme ambivalence that it managed simultaneously to be and not to be film music: the score provides mood cues (Threatening Danger; Anxiety; Catastrophe) in the normal film-music manner, but the music is a concert piece, intended for no specific film. The argument of "The Future of the Opera" contains a built-in counterargument encouraging the very accommodations that the main line strenuously denies. Postmodernist criticism is suspicious of univocal assertions: every text, even the most polemical, tends to deconstruct itself into a welter of competing opinions.

Another important aspect of Postmodernist criticism is the refusal to countenance the organizing force of binary poles—such basic antitheses as nature-culture, body-

19. Schoenberg, *Style and Idea*, 505.

20. *Arnold Schoenberg: Letters*, ed. Erwin Stein, trans. Eithne Wilkins and Ernst Kaiser (Berkeley: University of California Press, 1987), 43.

mind, essence-construct, instinct-reason, and the like. This is the Poststructuralist area of Postmodernist thought. For a Structuralist like the anthropologist Claude Lévi-Strauss, life tends to be governed by simple binary categories: if I am a hunter, I need to know whether my quarry is inedible or edible; if edible, then whether it should be eaten raw or cooked; if cooked, then whether boiled or roasted . . . and so on, and so on. (This is all explained in such books as *The Raw and the Cooked.*) Though Lévi-Strauss was reluctant to go too far, the possibility remains open that all human thought can be broken down into an infinitely complex network of elementary yes-no decisions, like the on-off bits that a computer uses for thinking.

But Poststructuralism assumes that these neat binaries are subject to all manner of lurching destabilizations. For Derrida, culture is at once the antithesis of nature and a sort of surrogate or usurpation of nature: "one could reconsider all the pairs of opposites on which philosophy is constructed and on which our discourse lives, not in order to see opposition erase itself but to see what indicates that each of the terms must appear as . . . the other different and deferred . . . nature as culture different and deferred."[21] So, when we talk about nature, we are, perhaps without realizing it, talking cryptically about culture. Nature is, from one point of view, something constructed, a cultural artifact, carefully doled out to us in the form of signposted landscapes, understood through the mediation of handbooks of botany; the more closely we try to isolate nature from culture, the more strongly the impossibility of the task grows clear. The same is true for mind and body:

Cut off a "mental" and a "physical" world, dissect and classify the phenomena of each: the mental resolves into a curious and intricate mechanism, and the physical reveals itself as a mental construct. If you will find the mechanical anywhere, you will find it in the workings of mind; and to inspect the living mind, you must look to the world outside.[22]

This passage, if written by a French Poststructuralist in the 1980s, would seem unexceptional; but in fact it was written by T. S. Eliot in 1916.

This wobbliness, this loss of precision in binary categories, has important consequences for the study of Modernism. Much of Modernism in music consists of the search for authenticity—a search that sometimes finds authenticity in strange places, such as the microtonal intervals of peasant fiddlers, or the noise of an airplane propeller,

21. Jacques Derrida, *Margins of Philosophy,* trans. Alan Bass (Chicago: University of Chicago Press, 1982), 17.

22. T. S. Eliot, *Knowledge and Experience in the Philosophy of F. H. Bradley* (New York: Farrar, Straus, 1964), 154.

or the principle of equal value to each note in the chromatic scale. Indeed each of the subordinate isms of Modernism, such as Primitivism, Exoticism, Futurism, and Serialism, can be understood as an investigation of a certain locus of authenticity, a refuge from the exhaustion of the tonal system, a revivification of the art. Modernist isms can be easily analyzed through Structuralist models, in that value inheres on one side of a binary dialectic. Up with the primitive, down with the slick; up with the future, down with the worn-out past.

On the other hand, though the theory that justifies Primitivism, or Futurism, sounds Structuralist, the actual artistic practice can be better understood with a Poststructuralist model. The definition of Modernism I have offered above—a definition that stresses the convergence of such extremes as the barbaric and the sophisticated—is Poststructuralist. If Béla Bartók had been a strict Primitivist, he might have simply composed new tunes using Hungarian, Turkish, or Arabic principles of mode and rhythm, suitable for singing by actual peasants. But of course Bartók integrated what he learned from field research into the evolved large-scale forms of Western art music—he wrote concertos and sonatas and favored that expensive instrument the piano. His theory exalted the primitive, but his practice exalted folk practices and the practices of European conservatories in roughly equal measure. In, say, the First Piano Concerto (1926), folksong defers to Franz Liszt, and vice versa. It is not simply that "natural" folk modes are embedded in the "artificial" form of the concerto; in practice, the boundaries of the natural and the artificial, the authentic and the secondhand, are elusive, indeterminate.

An especially sensitive area of Poststructuralist theory concerns gender. The binary pair male/female has received close critical scrutiny, and it too has been found unstable, liable to crossovers of every sort. In the domain of Modernist music, we sometimes find composers who insist on dividing male from female in the strongest manner possible—most conspicuously in the aggressively masculinist Ives, as we shall see later. But just as Modernism at once establishes and subverts many sorts of claims of authenticity, so it establishes and subverts many sorts of claims of male privilege. This can be seen in different areas.

First, Modernism was a little more open to participation by women than Romanticism was. Her brother's sense of feminine decorum tended to subdue the presence of Fanny Mendelssohn Hensel; Clara Wieck Schumann, who wrote an ambitious piano concerto at the age of sixteen, found it difficult to continue her own career as a composer as she gave birth to child after child; but such later composers as Germaine Tailleferre, Lili Boulanger, Rebecca Clarke, and, perhaps most impressive of all, Ruth Crawford Seeger had productive and quite public careers as composers. (Alma Schindler Mahler, however, found her gift for composition stunted by her husband's disapproval.) Women also participated in Modernist music in other ways: Colette, Gertrude Stein, and Marie

Pappenheim as librettists (for Maurice Ravel, Virgil Thomson, and Schoenberg, respectively; Schoenberg's second wife also wrote a libretto for him); and Nadia Boulanger as the most versatile composition teacher of the century—her pupils included such diverse figures as Aaron Copland and Philip Glass.

Second, the Modernists created works in which issues of gender were called into question; in certain theatrical pieces sexual divisions waver, grow untenable. Homosexuality and transvestism became explicit themes. Of course, homosexuality has always been present in art music: Louis XIV censured Lully for homosexual escapades, and Baroque opera, with its flamboyant castrati and its travesty roles, continued for centuries to destabilize gender. But the notion of a music theater designed by "inverts" and partially addressing itself to an audience of "inverts" is chiefly a twentieth-century phenomenon. Serge Diaghilev's Ballets Russes, to take the most famous example, managed to homoeroticize the whole genre of ballet, formerly regarded as a site in which rich men could contemplate the charms of more-or-less available ballerinas. Diaghilev himself was a passive homosexual who sometimes seduced his stars, such as the dancer Vaslav Nijinsky. Nijinsky's stage presence struck critics as at once epicene and sexually confrontational: he could dance *en pointe,* an unheard-of skill in a male dancer; but, in choreographing his own role as the faun in *L'après-midi d'un faune,* Nijinsky did not hesitate, as the music came to its delicate, languid conclusion, to masturbate with the nymph's scarf.

One of Diaghilev's notable collaborators was the homosexual poet Jean Cocteau, the scenarist of Satie's *Parade* and Stravinsky's *Oedipus Rex.* Cocteau devised some extraordinarily imaginative ways of relating the instabilities of Modernist music to the uncertainty of gender. When he heard Darius Milhaud's *Le boeuf sur le toit* (1919), based on South American tunes, he devised a ballet set in an American speakeasy whose customers include a dwarf and a transvestite; a policeman arrives to enforce the national prohibition against alcoholic drinks, and the bar transforms itself into a milk bar; soon the policeman is decapitated by a ceiling fan, but at the end of the ballet he revives, and the effeminate bartender asks him to pay the bill. Milhaud himself imagined the music as an accompaniment to a Charlie Chaplin silent film, but Cocteau may have noticed that the bitonality of the music could provide an effective metaphor for bisexuality. If there is a composition in which two musical keys can be present at once, then it might properly accompany a spectacle in which male and female coexist in the same person; in which an alcohol bar and a milk bar coexist on the same premises; and in which a policeman can be simultaneously living and dead. Cocteau impudently deranged the basic categories through which we organize our lives, and Milhaud's music assisted him in this project. This gender torsion was no isolated incident: in Poulenc's opera *Les mamelles de Tirésias* (1944), to a text by Guillaume Apollinaire, the heroine takes her breasts out of her blouse—they turn out to be rubber balloons—pops them with her cigarette lighter, and announces that she's henceforth a man. Gender is an artificial construct, a reversible jacket. Here and elsewhere, Modernist music provides a rich quarry for Postmodernist speculation.

■ What would be the conditions that would truly terminate the Modernist/Postmodernist movement? Perhaps the answer lies in the development of a musical language that feels *natural*, both to the composer and to the audience. Such natural styles seem to exist in the domain of popular music—if Harold Arlen or Willie Nelson or the artist once again known as Prince was ever consumed by stylistic anguish, by fear of the propriety of the triad, such anxieties aren't manifest in the music. But in the highbrow areas of the twentieth century, the spectrum of styles has been so wide, and the styles themselves so mutually hostile—how do the Darmstadt serialist and the Glassy minimalist talk to one another, or even feel engaged in the same sort of enterprise?—that all style has felt like artifice. This is true not only for obviously avant-garde composers, but also for the comparatively conservative. Here is Prokofiev, talking like a man with multiple personality disorder.

SERGEI PROKOFIEV
from *From My Life* (1944)

I would like to . . . characterize the fundamental lines of my creative development up to this point. Above all there was the line of the classics, which could be followed back to my earliest childhood, to the Beethoven sonatas that my mother used to play. This line conditions many neoclassical forms (sonatas, concertos), many imitations of eighteenth-century forms (gavottes, my *Classical Symphony,* and especially my sinfonietta). The second—the "modern"—line began with my encounter with Taneyev, when he reproached me for the "harshness" of my harmony. . . . Chiefly this led me to strive for a harmonic language of my own, and later to the expression of powerful feelings (. . . *Suggestion diabolique, Sarcasms,* the *Scythian Suite,* . . . my Second Symphony). . . . The third line is the "motoric," perhaps derived from Schumann's toccata, which, when I first heard it, made a violent impression on me (*Études* op. 2, *Toccata* op. 11, *Scherzo* op. 12, the scherzo in my Second Piano Concerto, the toccata in my Fifth Piano Concerto, the steadily intensifying repetition of certain melodic figures in the *Scythian Suite,* the *Pas d'acier,* and some passages in the Third Piano Concerto). This line is perhaps the least important. The fourth line is the "lyrical." It appears above all in reflective, meditative moods and not always in connection with melody. . . . This line became recognized much later than the others. For a long time it was thought that I had no lyrical gift, and because of this lack of encouragement it developed slowly. But in the course of time I cultivated this side of my creativity more and more.

I would prefer to limit myself to these four lines and to conceive the fifth one, which many people ascribe to me—the "grotesque"—simply as a deviation from the other lines. . . . My music should rather be called "scherzo-like," or described with the three words that express the different gradations of the scherzo character: capricious, cheerful, and mocking.

From *Aus meinem Leben* (Zürich: Peter Schifferli, 1962), 44–46.

A nineteenth-century composer, such as Liszt, could write music in each of these five lines without seeming to be torn in pieces because he could employ the varying dialects of a single musical language. Prokofiev, on the other hand, needs to reconcile nearly incompatible languages within the compass of his own creative effort.

Multilingualism remains either the chief curse or blessing of Modernist music. Poets have always lamented the confounding of human languages after God destroyed the Tower of Babel; but the twentieth century has seen, for the first time in history, a confounding of the languages of music. Composers have tried to make the best of this, often by becoming polyglots. Schoenberg continued to write tonal music even in his old age (such as the agreeable Theme and Variations for Band, op. 43a), side by side with his difficult twelve-tone music, and he evidently believed (though the source of this remark is difficult to trace) that there was a great deal of music left to be written in C major. The older Stravinsky taught himself to "speak" Schoenbergian by becoming a serialist of sorts—but only after Schoenberg's death in 1951, as if he feared losing face to his great competitor. Outside the domain of popular music, every composer born in the twentieth century has had to adopt or invent a tongue before he or she could think of finding anything to say. Highbrow Modernism will be over—if it ever is—when syntax and technique stop being charged issues; when a single compositional style becomes so attractive that the composer can use it spontaneously, without having to think about it; when music abandons every desire to be difficult, or even to be easy, but simply goes its way without strenuous intention, without precondition by theory.

But perhaps one of the benefits of all this Modernist strain and self-consciousness, this anxiety about musical language, has been the cultivation of written language as a secondary medium. The urgency that inspired musical innovation also inspired polemic texts of every sort. Not every important composer was a gifted writer—neither Strauss, nor Bartók, nor Britten, for example, was particularly comfortable with the medium of words—but a number of them, including Stravinsky and Schoenberg, had real flair in this domain; Hindemith and Eisler could have been distinguished men of letters if they had applied themselves in that direction; and Virgil Thomson *was* a distinguished man of letters. The point of the present anthology is to allow the voices of composers to be heard, in the astonishingly rich context of twentieth-century art and ideas. Their essays not only improve the experience of hearing their music, but even constitute in themselves a sort of music.

2 Testing the Boundaries between Speech and Music

One important characteristic of Modernism is the uneasy relationship between a given artistic medium and all others. For certain twentieth-century composers, the borders between music and the other arts were strict and impermeable; but for others, these borders were fluid, perhaps even wholly unreal. This point of contention was especially noticeable with respect to music and spoken language, since it has always been difficult to tell exactly where one ends and the other begins: both of these artistic media consist of sound that varies over time, though in one case those sounds are called notes and in the other case phonemes.

The word "music"—roughly the same in all European languages—is derived from the Greek *mousikē,* which refers to anything governed by the Muses, that is, to any fine art whatsoever. Therefore, in Western culture there has been a certain primary feeling that the arts are fundamentally one, and that any attempt to divide music from poetry, painting, and other arts is bound to be somewhat arbitrary and infirm.

Since the eighteenth century, speculation about the origin of language has often supposed that, in prehistoric times, all speech was song. Jean-Jacques Rousseau—both a philosopher and a composer—attempted to describe (in his *Essay on the Origin of Languages,* written around 1749–55) the nature of the First Language, the language from which all modern languages were distantly derived: because the First Language was formed directly out of nature, it consisted almost exclusively of vowels, crooning and yowling:

> Since natural sounds are inarticulate, words have few articulations. Interposing some consonants to fill the gaps between vowels would suffice to make them fluid and easy to pronounce. . . . Since sounds, accent, and number, which are natural, would leave little to articulation, which is conventional, *it would be sung rather than spoken.*[1]

Thousands of years ago, the first men, solitary hunters and gatherers, dwelt within a perpetual opera. Rousseau thought that the Oriental languages of the present day, with their pitch-differentiated phonic systems, carried strong traces of the First Language, and were, therefore, irresistible and overwhelming media of expression: Rousseau even

---

1. Jean-Jacques Rousseau, *On the Origin of Language,* trans. John Moran (New York: Frederick Ungar, 1966), 15–16; my emphasis.

imagined that a modern European, only faintly acquainted with Arabic, would prostrate himself, abandon his Christian beliefs, and march in the armies of Islam, if he had heard Mohammed preach, burning with the enthusiasm of his prophecy.[2] Modern Western languages, Rousseau taught, are exact, but cold, dull, prolix, impoverished by abstraction; but the Eastern languages still vibrate with passionate intensity. In order to hear the First Language, we need not take a ride in a time machine back to the prehistoric, nor even a sea voyage to Arabia—a short walk to a concert hall, it seems, will suffice:

> By imitating the inflections of the voice, melody expresses pity, cries of sorrow and joy, threats and groans. All the vocal signs of passion are within its domain. It imitates the tones of languages, and the twists produced in every idiom by certain psychic acts [*mouvemens de l'âme*].[3]

According to Rousseau, language may have lost its music, but music has in no way lost its linguistic power.

It is a short step from Rousseau's praise of vocal music to Richard Wagner's attempt, a century later, to recover this archaic purity and intensity of music-speech through the *Gesamtkunstwerk*—the total artwork, which unites speech and music and the visual arts in a fused, indissoluble whole:

> If we look closer at the evolutionary history of the modern European languages, even today we meet in their so-called word roots a rudiment that plainly shows us how at the first beginning the formation of the mental concept of an object ran almost completely parallel with the subjective feeling of it; and the supposition that the earliest speech of man must have borne a great analogy with song, might not perhaps seem quite ridiculous.[4]

Wagner's career as a composer can be seen as a continual attempt to enrich the semantic content of music, to make the structure of music more profoundly analogous to the grammar of that primitive Germanic that he caricatured in the libretto to *Der Ring des Nibelungen*. Wagner's contemporaries responded deeply to the linguistic stress of his music: the philosopher Friedrich Nietzsche wrote that Wagner "*has increased music's language-capacity into the immeasurable.*"[5]

The twentieth century has been, in some ways, particularly friendly to composers who want to increase music's capacity for language. The linguistics of Ferdinand de

2. Ibid., 49.

3. Ibid., 57.

4. *Wagner on Music and Drama,* trans. H. Ashton Ellis, ed. Albert Goldman and Evert Sprinchorn (New York: Da Capo Press, 1964), 153.

5. Friedrich Nietzsche, *Werke in drei Bänden,* ed. Karl Schlechta (München: Carl Hanser Verlag, 1966), 2:919.

Saussure and the philosophy of Ludwig Wittgenstein, both extremely influential, tend to cut the word free from any reference in the physical world; and as language becomes a dereferentialized, self-enclosed system of signs—signs that point at other signs, never at actual concrete objects—speech becomes more and more like music. As Wittgenstein claimed, "To say that a word has meaning does not imply that it *stands for* or *represents* a thing. . . . The sign plus the rules of grammar applying to it is all we need [to make a language]. We need nothing further to make the connection with reality. If we did we should need something to connect that with reality, which would lead to an infinite regress."[6] And, for Wittgenstein, the consequence of this disconnection was clear: "Understanding a sentence is much more akin to understanding a theme in music than one may think."[7] Perhaps the intellectual world that Wittgenstein helped to build has made composers feel comfortable with the notion that musical themes are simply speech pursued by means other than consonants and vowels.

While composers were trying to do the work of poets, poets were also trying to usurp the role of composers. In 1873 the Victorian literary critic Walter Pater grandly announced that "*all art constantly aspires towards the condition of music*";[8] and the notion that literature, as it evolves, becomes less denotative and more shadowy, elusive, and teasing—more musical—marked the poetry of Paul Verlaine and Stephane Mallarmé in France, and much of British Modernist literature as well. Not only does speech equal song at the beginning of time; at the end of time, the same condition will apply.

Ezra Pound considered that the ideal poet was the troubadour, simultaneously writer and composer: "both in Greece and in Provence the poetry attained its highest rhythmic and metrical brilliance at times when the arts of verse and music were closely knit together, when each thing done by the poet had some definite musical urge or necessity behind it."[9] Pound further argued that "the divorce [of music and poetry] had been to the advantage of neither, and that melodic invention had declined simultaneously and progressively with their divergence. The rhythms of poetry grew stupider."[10] He took the necessity of music so seriously that in 1921 he composed his own neo-medieval music for an opera, *Le testament,* to texts by François Villon. Pound regarded this opera as a sort of stylistic refutation of Debussy's *Pelléas et Mélisande,* which Pound detested for its thick soft harmonies and reticent drama—Pound, by contrast, wanted energetic

6. *Wittgenstein's Lectures: Cambridge 1930–32,* ed. Desmond Lee (Chicago: University of Chicago Press, 1980), 45, 59.

7. Ludwig Wittgenstein, *Philosophical Investigations,* trans. G. E. M. Anscombe (New York: Macmillan, 1958), no. 527.

8. Walter Pater, *The Renaissance,* ed. Donald L. Hill (Berkeley: University of California Press, 1980), 106.

9. Ezra Pound, *Literary Essays* (New York: New Directions, 1935), 91.

10. Ezra Pound, *Criterion,* March 1924, 321.

monody. But Debussy and Pound, in their different ways, both exemplify a Modernist hope for an art that takes place in the limbo between speech and music.

The Anglo-Irish poet and playwright William Butler Yeats (1865–1939) was a member of the same generation as Strauss and Mahler—a transitional generation between Romanticism and Modernism. "We were the last romantics," Yeats wrote in "Coole and Ballylee, 1931," and yet the spare diction and the lashing rhythmic energy of his later poems exhibit strong Modernist tendencies; indeed he spent the winters of 1913–16 in the company of Ezra Pound partly in order to modernize his literary style, rid it of all languor and self-conscious intricacy. Yeats's evolution was remarkable. By the time he was thirty-five, in 1900, Yeats had written such anthology pieces as "The Lake Isle of Innisfree," but still seemed an ill-educated, fey, and superstitious provincial, whose chief theme was Irish fairy lore; by the age of seventy, after having written "Sailing to Byzantium" and *A Vision,* Yeats seemed the closest twentieth-century equivalent of Dante. Like Picasso and Stravinsky, Yeats lived long and kept himself open to all recent currents of art and thought: his pagan philosophy, his rejection of Christianity as a slave religion, was partly derived from reading Nietzsche; and Yeats's habit of seeking poetic inspiration through his wife's spiritualistic trances may be related to the automatism cultivated by such Surrealists as André Breton.

Yeats was all but tone-deaf: as Pound wrote, "Mr. Yeats probably would distinguish between a *g* and a *b flat,* but he is happy to think that he doesn't, and would certainly be incapable of whistling a simple melody or tune. Nevertheless before writing a lyric he is apt to 'get a chune in his head.'"[11] Despite his incompetence at formal music, Yeats's poetry always verges on chant, fiercely marked both in pitch and in rhythm. Stravinsky, listening to the records of Yeats's BBC broadcasts, recognized a fellow rhythmician. "Yeats pauses at the end of each line, he dwells a precise time on and in between each word— one could as easily notate his verses in musical rhythm as scan them in poetic meters."[12] Yeats indeed hoped to recreate the aboriginal union of music and poetry; and in the first decade of the twentieth century he toured with his close friend, the actress and theosophist Florence Farr, who devised musical settings for Yeats's poems and chanted them to the accompaniment of a psaltery:

> Since I was a boy I have always longed to hear poems spoken to a harp, as I imagined Homer to have spoken his. . . . Images used to rise up before me, as I am sure they have arisen before nearly everybody else who cares for poetry, of wild-eyed men speaking harmoniously to murmuring wires while audiences in many-colored robes

11. Ezra Pound, *ABC of Reading* (New York: New Directions, 1960), 197–98.

12. Igor Stravinsky and Robert Craft, *Conversations with Igor Stravinsky* (Berkeley: University of California Press, 1980), 120.

listened, hushed and excited. Whenever I spoke of my desire to anybody they said I should write for music, but when I heard anything sung I did not hear the words, or if I did their natural pronunciation was altered and their natural music was altered, or it was drowned in another music which I did not understand. What was the good of writing a love-song if the singer pronounced love "lo-o-o-o-o-ve" . . . ? Like every other poet, I spoke verses in a kind of chant when I was making them; and sometimes, when I was alone on a country road, I would speak them in a loud chanting voice. . . .

Even when one is speaking to a single note sounded faintly on the psaltery, if one is sufficiently practiced to speak on it without thinking about it one can get an endless variety of expression. All art is, indeed, a monotony in external things for the sake of an interior variety, a sacrifice of gross effects to subtle effects, an asceticism of the imagination.[13]

The psaltery had been built by Arnold Dolmetsch (1858–1940), the pioneer in the revival of early instruments and historical performance practice and one of Ezra Pound's heroes—Pound claimed that Dolmetsch's writings helped poets to learn how to write free verse, since "vers libre exists in old music."[14] The old and the new seemed conjoined, just as word and music were conjoined. Florence Farr herself attempted to link her method of psaltery chanting to the restoration of Greek music-poetry devised by the Renaissance inventors of opera:

I made an interesting discovery after I had been elaborating the art of speaking to the psaltery for some time. I had tried to make it more beautiful than the speaking by priests at High Mass, the singing of recitative in opera and the speaking through music of actors in melodrama. My discovery was that those who had invented these arts had all said about them exactly what Arnold Dolmetsch and Mr. W. B. Yeats said about my art. Any one can prove this for himself who will go to a library and read the authorities that describe how early liturgical chant, plain-song and jubilations or melismata were adapted from the ancient traditional music; or if they read the history of the beginning of opera and the "nuove musiche" by Caccini, or study the music of Monteverdi and Carissimi[15] who flourished at the beginning of the seventeenth century, they will find these masters speak of doing all they can to give an added

13. "Speaking to the Psaltery" (1902), from W. B. Yeats, *Essays and Introductions* (New York: Macmillan, 1961), 14, 18.

14. Ezra Pound, *Literary Essays* (New York: New Directions, 1935), 440.

15. Giulio Caccini (c. 1550–1618) published *Le nuove musiche* in 1601, one of the most important texts in the reform movement called the *seconda prattica,* which valued the expressive refinements of solo singing over the sort of polyphony that seemed to promote complexity for complexity's sake;

beauty to the words of the poet. . . . There is no more beautiful sound than the alter-
nation of caroling or keening and a voice speaking in regulated declamation.[16]

This is another specimen of how strongly the supposed primal oneness of music and
speech has influenced the development of Modernist art.

In addition to the special recitations with Florence Farr, Yeats worked with a number
of more traditional composers, including Edward Elgar, who wrote some incidental
music for *Diarmuid and Grania* (1901), and George Antheil, who wrote music for Yeats's
adaptation of Japanese Noh dramaturgy, *Fighting the Waves* (1929)—music in which a
lilting, Irish-sounding melody is mixed into implacabilities out of Stravinsky's *Oedipus
Rex* (1927). A number of song composers also took an interest in Yeats's poetry, notably
Peter Warlock (the pseudonym of Philip Heseltine), whose cycle *The Curlew* (1920–22)
subtly evokes the haunted twilight of Yeats's early poetry—though Heseltine, like most
composers, had great trouble in getting Yeats's permission to use his lyrics.

But Yeats's most fruitful collaboration with a composer came from an unexpected
source: a California hobo. In 1930 Harry Partch (1901–74), a largely self-taught composer who had survived the depression as a migrant laborer, picking grapes and plums,
looked at the whole history of Western music and thought he could do better. He decided to discard it and marked this revolution by burning all his previous compositions.
Farr understood her music for Yeats's poems as a sort of sequel to the work of the Florentine camerata, in which Giulio Caccini and others labored to recreate the art of Greek
tragedy; Partch understood his mission in similar but more radical terms. He thought
that the human body, especially as expressed in the speaking voice, was the ultimate
source of authority and virtue in music: all music that abstracted itself from the body, by
engrossing itself in artificial procedures of counterpoint, development, and other formalities, was insipid and useless.

Partch's first mature compositions struggle to recenter the art of music on the speaking voice. But he felt that neither the twelve-note scale of Western music nor the instruments of the Western orchestra were viable tools for achieving a genuinely concrete music, a music attentive to the nuances of speech. A speaking sort of music needs to imitate
intervals far smaller than the semitones to which most woodwind, brass, and keyboard
instruments are confined. So Partch devised his own forty-three-tone scale, which begins by achieving the major second (defined by a pitch ratio of 9/8) as the termination
of a widening series of near-unison pitch ratios (1/1, 81/80, 33/32, 21/20, 16/15, 12/11, 11/10,
10/9, and at last 9/8); and he devised his own instrumentarium in order to be able to play

Claudio Monteverdi (1567–1643) secured the status of opera with his *Orfeo* (1607); Giacomo Carissimi
(1605–74) was a pioneer in the field of oratorio.

16. "Note by Florence Farr upon Her Settings" (1907), from W. B. Yeats, *Essays and Introductions*
(New York: Macmillan, 1961), 21–22.

Harry Partch's setting of Li Po. From Partch, *Genesis of a Music* (Madison: University of Wisconsin Press, 1949), 221. Courtesy of the Harry Partch Foundation.

these pitches. The earliest novelties were stringed instruments such as the adapted viola (a viola with a huge neck grafted on), used to accompany the precisely notated intoning voice in *Seventeen Lyrics by Li Po* (1931). Later, Partch used all sorts of technological junk, including artillery casings, light-bulb tops, airplane fuel tanks, and hubcaps, to create an enormous variety of instruments, to which he gave whimsical names, such as diamond marimba, spoils of war, zymo-xyl, boo, harmonic canon, gourd tree, and cloud chamber bowls.

Partch's first major ambition was to recreate Yeats's translation of Sophocles' *King Oedipus* as a opera of speech: "It is in no sense opera. The drama is paramount always—there is no attempt to reconcile it with musical form. It is drama heightened throughout, and finally purged, by music."[17] In 1934 a Carnegie grant enabled Partch to visit Dublin, meet Yeats, hear a performance of the play at Yeats's Abbey Theatre, and notate the pitches and rhythms of the actors' voices. Yeats was excited by Partch's method of speaking, often without melody, to musical instruments that employ "very minute intervals"; he wrote to Partch that "so far as I can understand your method [it has] my complete sympathy."[18] It was not until 1952, after Yeats's death, that the finished opera was performed at Mills College; but Partch's *King Oedipus* remains one of the twentieth century's most compelling resurrections of the speech-oriented aesthetic of the earliest operas, those by Jacopo Peri and Claudio Monteverdi. Other Modernist operas in this line include Pound's *Le testament* and Carl Orff's *Antigone* (1949)—Partch admired Orff's neo-archaic musical style, melismatic and percussive. Orff, like Partch, understood himself as a kind of successor to the early opera composers, as can be seen from such adaptations of Monteverdi as *Klage der Ariadne* and *Orpheus* (both 1925).

17. From Partch's project report to the Carnegie Foundation, from Philip Blackburn, *Enclosure 3: Harry Partch* (St. Paul, Minn.: American Composer's Forum, 1997).

18. Ibid., 28.

Partch's later works continue his exploration of reviving Greek drama—what might be call the Partchian Renaissance—most notably in *Revelation in the Courthouse Square* (1962), loosely based on Euripides' *Bacchae;* here Dionysus is reimagined as a rock singer. But in other works Partch investigated ways of writing a corporeal music less dependent on the human voice: in *Water! Water!* (1962), a satire about dam-building in California, the text is gibberish; and in such long instrumental compositions as *And on the Seventh Day Petals Fell in Petaluma* (1963–66), he allowed the "sound-magic," the timbre collage of his strange instruments, to evoke the image of the dryness of wood, the heft of rock, the physical presence of the earth as it impinges on the human body. As the following excerpts from Partch's private history of music show, few composers have achieved such an intense witness of the reifying power of music, its textures of scrape and hit and pluck, its mouth-feel. Roland Barthes wrote an essay, "Rasch," in which he described what he called somathemes:

> In Schumann's *Kreisleriana* (Opus 16; 1838), I actually hear no note, no theme, no contour, no grammar, no meaning, nothing which would permit me to reconstruct an intelligible structure of the work. No, what I hear are blows: I hear what beats in the body, what beats the body, or better: I hear this body that beats.[19]

But it could be argued that *Kreisleriana* is full of themes, grammar, meaning. Barthes's words better apply to the extremely somathematic music of Partch.

HARRY PARTCH
from *Genesis of a Music* (1949)
"FROM EMPEROR CHUN TO THE VACANT LOT"

The origin of music in speech intonation among the early peoples to whom we ascribe civilizations—the Greeks and the Chinese particularly—seems pretty well established. . . .

From Terpander,[20] about 700 B.C., to the nineteenth-century Beethoven, the more approved and more serious types of European music may be indexed according to the extent to which they preserved the vitality of words or, conversely, the extent to which they were "independent" of words.

For the essentially vocal and verbal music of the individual—a Monophonic concept—the word Corporeal may be used, since it is a music that is vital to a time and place, a here and now. The epic chant is an example, but the term could be applied with

---

19. See Roland Barthes, *The Responsibility of Forms: Critical Essays on Music, Arts, and Representation,* trans. Richard Howard (New York: Hill and Wang, 1985), 299.

20. Terpander, early Greek musician who expanded the compass of the lyre from four strings to seven, and founded the first Greek music school.

equal propriety to almost any of the important ancient and near-ancient cultures—the Chinese, Greek, Arabian, Indian, in all of which music was physically allied with poetry or the dance. Corporeal music is emotionally "tactile." It does not grow from the root of "pure form." It cannot be characterized as either mental or spiritual.

The word Abstract, on the other hand, may be used to denote a mass expression, in its highest application, the spirits of all united into one and transported into a realm of unreality, neither here nor now, but transcending both. The symphony is an example. Abstract music grows from the root of non-verbal "form," how "pure" being a matter of individual opinion. It may be characterized as either mental or spiritual. It is always "instrumental," even when it involves the singing of words, because the emotion of an individual conveyed through vitally rendered words would instantly end the characteristic domination of nonverbal "form."

Thus the mere presence of words in music is not in itself the criterion of its classification. The chants of the Roman church, early in its history, were actually in a language that none but the learned clergy understood, though some of them were sung with the natural rhythm and inflections of the Latin words. An important distinction, then, as regards the Corporeal and the Abstract, is between an individual's vocalized words, intended to convey meaning, and musicalized words that convey no meaning, whether rendered by an individual or a group, because they are beyond the hearers' understanding, because they have been ritualized, or because of other evolvements of rendition.

The peoples of history have radicated their instinctive Corporeal attitudes in many variations of musical utterance, in:

Stories sung or chanted, including much folk music.
Poems recited or intoned, including some folk music and some, but not all, popular music.
Dramas, such as the early seventeenth-century Florentine music-dramas, for example.
Music intended specifically for dances which tell a story or describe a situation; both ancient and modern.

The tendency toward an Abstract character, on the other hand, is evident in such musical forms as:

Songs with words that are intended not to convey meaning but simply to set the mood of the music.
Songs or dramas with words that do not convey meaning because of the style of composition or manner of rendition; most modern operas come under this head.
All purely instrumental music, whether programmed or not, though programmed music often tends toward the Corporeal. . . .

By a canon of the decade 360–70 "the people" were forbidden to "sing out of the parchment" because their uncultivated voices "destroyed the harmony," and since the service from which they were barred as participants was in Greek or Latin it became quite beyond their comprehension as time went on. The listener perforce came to think of music itself as conveying meaning. Plato's [21] complaint that "harmony" had no "meaning" without words implied understood words, and the evolution from sung words that conveyed no meaning—except in a general moodlike way—to an Abstract music entirely without words was easy and inevitable.

Whether one interprets history in such a way as to ascribe the "independence" of music to the beginning of the Christian era or to a later time, there is no question but that, very close to the beginning, it became a new art. It became a language in itself. The insistence with which this simulation was carried on is manifest in the "motives," "subjects," "phrases," "questions," "responses," and "periods" of our musical forms, all entirely apart from the circumstance that sung words might be involved.

The fact is that the ancient spirit was gone. And it was gone because the ancient, lovely, and fearless attitude toward the human body was gone. Musical "morals" denied the human body—through the one agent of the body that they could control: words from the vocal organ—because the "mother morals" denied it and have succeeded in nursing this denial, yea these many centuries. D. H. Lawrence advises us never to forget that "modern morality has its roots in hatred a deep, evil hate of the instinctive, intuitional, procreative body." [22] How could the "morality" of music conceive anything different, anything different at all, than occasionally a bastard exception? . . .

Those who have wondered how pregnant or sterile for the creation of significant art the house of the dilettante actually is . . . must be reminded of the house of Count Bardi [23] in Florence, in the last decades of the sixteenth century. Among the circle of accomplished men—composers, poets, actors—who met in this house of dilettantism

21. Plato (ca. 427–348 B.C.), seminal Greek philosopher, discipline of Socrates, teacher of Aristotle. His attitude toward music was ambiguous: in *The Republic* he rhapsodizes over the music of the spheres, generated by sirens singing on the whirling planets; but elsewhere in the same dialogue he suggests that musicians should be expelled from the ideal city, since some of the musical modes are conducive to idleness.

22. David Herbert Lawrence (1885–1930), English novelist, poet, and painter, who taught that the physical body was the source of all health, and that mental constructs tended to limit and deprave the human subject. His novel *Lady Chatterley's Lover* (1927), concerning the sexual relationship between an upper-class woman and a gamekeeper, and some of his paintings, were banned because of indecency. Partch's quotation is from *Phoenix: The Posthumous Papers of D. H. Lawrence* (New York: Viking, 1936), 558.

23. Giovanni de' Bardi (1534–1612), patron of the Florentine camerata.

was Galilei.[24] Blazing the way toward a reproduction of the tonal effect of ancient drama, Galilei wrote and sang—or intoned—a dramatic *scena* from Dante's *Purgatorio*,[25] playing the viola as he intoned. . . .

Similar efforts followed Galilei's success in fairly quick succession. Giulio Caccini (*c.* 1558–1615) declared that the "wise and noble personages" with whom he associates in Florence "determined me to place no value upon that music which makes it impossible to understand the words." . . .

Here, at long last, was a highly conceived attempt to transfer the spirit of the Corporeal music of ancient Greece to a time and place characteristic of Western Europe. . . .

In his expressed ideals, Modest Petrovich Moussorgsky (1839–81) is part of the taproot of the Corporeal spirit, whatever the current mode of rendition makes of his music. The harrying opposition of those to whom Abstract beauty is or should be *de rigueur* provoked in Moussorgsky a rather indefensible deprecation of the idea of sheer beauty, but one also in which his Corporeal banner is clearly displayed: "The artistic presentment of beauty alone, to use the word in its material sense, is sheer childishness, only fit for the babes and sucklings of art. To trace the finer characteristics of human nature and of the mass of mankind, resolutely to penetrate into these unexplored regions and to conquer them—that is the mission of the genuine artist."[26]

. . . The first tentative antecedent in Russia of Moussorgsky's "mad idea" was Alexander Dargomizhky (1813–69), on the fringe of the "Coterie." Dargomizhky wrote an opera, *The Stone Guest,* for which his generating Corporeal declaration was simply: "I insist that the note shall be the direct expression of the word." Moussorgsky also stressed this theme: "Whenever I hear people speaking, no matter who it is or what they say, my brain immediately sets to work to translate what I have heard into music"; and again, "In my 'opera dialogue' I endeavor, as far as possible, to show up very clearly the slight changes in intonation that occur in the course of conversation apparently for the most trivial reasons and in the least important words."[27] (The phrase "slight changes in intonation" causes one to speculate on what Moussorgsky might have done in a more sensitive system of music, that is, one which offered smaller intervals than are available in the twelve-tone "octave.")

While working on his second completed opera, *Khovanshchina,* Moussorgsky wrote:

24. Vicenzo Galilei (d. 1591), central figure in the development of monody as the basis of a revived art of Greek tragedy, and father of the astronomer Galileo.

25. Dante Alighieri (1265–1321) wrote the *Divine Comedy,* a comprehensive tour of the afterlife, of which the *Purgatorio* is the second part.

26. Oskar v. Riesemann, *Mussorgsky* (Tudor), 104. [Partch's note.]

27. Ibid., 162, 171, 172, 176. [Partch's note.]

"I am now deep in the study of human speech; I have come to recognize the melodic element in ordinary speech and have succeeded in turning recitative into melody. I might call it 'melody justified by the meaning.'" In a "confession of faith" he asserts that only the great reformers have given laws to music, that these laws are continually subject to alteration, that it is his task "to reproduce not only the voice of emotion, but, more especially, the varying modulations of human speech." [28] Virtually single-handed, Moussorgsky was trying to fill a vacuum which he alone could discern.

. . . To find true Corporeality in manner of presentation it is necessary to go to the folk and popular singers, for it is present-day fact that few if any of the singers and masters of the concert ever escape their bondage to pure tone and vocal amplitude in the rendition of the word-loving, sensitive, subtle, and natural Moussorgsky.

Russia seems quite content to have only one really bad Corporeal boy to remember, but the spirit was infectious elsewhere . . . and quickly touched another Slav, the Bohemian Leoš Janáček (1854–1928). Janáček's chief work, called at various times *Her Stepmother* and *Jenůfa,* and widely performed in Europe after World War 1, brought this comment from one reviewer: "It is perhaps the most intensely national of all operas. Its vocal music gives living expression to the intrinsic nature of peasant song and speech. As in Moussorgsky's operas, the music that carries the dialogue is entirely in speech-rhythm and includes no songs or other formal pieces."

"AMERICA'S MUSICAL TENDENCIES"

. . . From one standpoint the twentieth century is a fair historic duplicate of the eleventh. At that time the standard and approved ecclesiastical expression failed to satisfy an earthly this-time-and-this-place musical hunger; result: the troubadours. Today, and especially in America, the approved Abstraction is a full musical fare for only a small percentage of our people, and the resulting hunger is satisfied by anything that breaks the formal barriers in the direction of Corporeality—hillbilly, cowboy, and popular music, which, whatever its deficiencies, owes nothing to sciolist and academic Europeanisms.

The devitalized tricks of "serious" singing, if they belong anywhere, certainly do not belong here, and they are nationally resented, consciously or otherwise. Examples are (1) the ubiquitous rolled *r*'s, an articulation common in European tongues but alien to America; (2) precise attack and precise release (like the tones of an organ), as opposed to the gliding tones so characteristic of American speech, the *portamento* of "faulty attack" and "faulty release"; and (3) the affected stylization of "refined" English. Many of our folk and popular singers unconsciously tend to preserve word form and drama. Frequently their manner is simple. Frequently they "explode" consonants, and sustain

28. Ibid., 108, 142 . . . [Partch's note.]

such consonants as *l, m, n,* and *z* rather than the vowels preceding them.[29] Frequently they break a word off short of its notated time and let it fall or rise in a gliding inflection regardless of the notation. Frequently they personify a directness of word appeal, characteristic of this age and this land, and characterized by suggestions of actual times, actual localities, actual identities, and actual human situations, all of which is the very antithesis of the Abstract concept.

By mere control of the lips, mouth, tongue, palate, glottis, and diaphragm under emotional stimulus, the human voice is ready to express all the feelings and attitudes which the cumulative centuries have symbolized in words and poured into the dictionary—from joyful spite to tragic ecstasy, from ecstatic melancholy to hedonic fatuity, from furtive beatitude to boisterous grotesquerie, from portentous lechery to obdurate athanasia—prescience, felicity, urbanity, hauteur, surfeit, magniloquence, enravishment, execration, abnegation, anguish, riot, debauch, hope, joy, death, grief, effluent life, and a lot more.

This bottle of cosmic vintage is the endowment of all of us. Do the freedom-fearing music schools of Europe and America train singers to give us even a little draught of these vocal potentialities? They concoct one special brand of their own, put it in an atomizer in the singers' throats, and send it in a sweet sickening stream over the proscenium and the kilocycles; it anoints the hair, it titillates the brows, it mizzles on the temples, and this wretchedest of intellectual infamies in the name of music—mark the term!—is called "musical tone."

Couple these shortcomings of "serious" music with the austerity of the concert hall—rampant formality, huge impersonal assemblies with closely placed, hard, stiff-backed seats, black and white "tails," brisk robots on stage. . . .

Can we take no pride in a human gathering of smaller proportions than would fill a stadium? And will someone tell us the name of the presumptuous god who ordained that the respective appetites of spirit and flesh must remain forever strangers? And if there is none such, will the Arbiters of Pure Beauty please close their eyes on this sordid world and then inform us what is wrong with having tables strewn with glasses of beer and chocolate malteds along with music, at least in some situation more intimate than the concert hall?

Except for the brief release of a ten-minute intermission, to allow Abstractionism's communicants the "smoke" of self-fortification for the remainder of something that frequently takes on the character of an "ordeal by Abstract beauty," the Masters of the Concert arrest all the simple, uncomplicated, uncontroversial appetites of the flesh,

---

29. Ogden asserts that the vowel sounds in speech are normally ten times the duration of consonants (*Hearing,* 221). Most composers and singers seem to feel that 10,000 to 1 is also a good ratio! [Partch's note.]

slap them into jail, and hold them incommunicado for the duration of the concert.[30] See, in the obscure background, the ancient ghost in its ecclesiastical habit? For they shall not "sing out of the parchment," nor shall they contribute anything except their stiff and reverent presence!

Considering the widespread vegetation of such and similar traditions, perhaps it becomes apparent why our bars are filled with rebelling youngsters, groping among bar entertainers for a better value. And the guess might be hazarded that the crux of rebellion isn't the Abstract fare quite so much as the cold punctilio of its dishing. Again — a vacuum, which is filled by the first thing that comes along, in this case the bar.

Contemporary visual art, and attitudes toward it, which arouse explosive resentment in D. H. Lawrence, in many ways parallel this situation in "serious" music. In viewing paintings, he maintains, we "are only undergoing cerebral excitation. . . . The deeper responses, down in the intuitive and instinctive body, are not touched. They cannot be, because they are dead. A dead intuitive body stands there and gazes at the corpse of beauty: and usually it is completely and honestly bored."

And intuition died, declares Lawrence, because "Man came to have his own body in horror." We are afraid of the "procreative body" and its "warm flow of intuitional awareness," and fear is "poison to the human psyche." "We don't live in the flesh. Our instincts and intuitions are dead, we live wound round with the winding sheet of abstraction." Our youngsters who look forward to creative careers are "totally enclosed in pale-blue glass bottles of insulated inexperience"; in speaking to one of them Lawrence felt that he was "like my grandfather."

Finally: "The history of our era is the nauseating and repulsive history of the crucifixion of the procreative body for the glorification of the spirit, the mental consciousness. Plato was an arch-priest of this crucifixion. . . . in the eighteenth century it became a corpse, a corpse with an abnormally active mind: and today it stinketh."[31] . . .

I am trying to hope that we are not entering an era where the only men of significance in music will be those facile at quoting Bach and Beethoven, Brahms and Tschaikowsky. . . . If we are entering such an age it is already dead, and I can think of no epitaph more fitting than this: "They did not like modern music."

From *Genesis of a Music* (Madison: University of Wisconsin Press, 1949), 8–9, 15–16, 21–22, 31–33, 52–54.

30. Contrast the deportment of an audience of Greeks at their ancient music-dramas: "it is a lively audience, not less or more mannerly than such assemblages in other lands. It eats nuts and fruit and drinks wine as it listens; Aristotle proposes to measure the failure of a play by the amount of food eaten during the presentations." Durant, *Life of Greece*, 381. Presumably, much food consumed would indicate failure. [Partch's note.]

31. *Phoenix* [D. H. Lawrence, *Phoenix*, ed. Edward D. McDonald (New York: Viking, 1936)] 552, 554, 556, 569, 570, 584. [Partch's note.]

■

While Yeats was approaching the common ground of speech and music from the direction of speech, certain advanced composers, including Partch, were approaching it from the direction of music. Caccini himself, at the beginning of the seventeenth century, wrote that singing should be like "speaking musically," and composers have often written recitatives in which singers were encouraged to provide the inflections of speech; but the task of writing vocal lines that did not simply provide opportunities for speaking, but actually embodied spoken nuances, small fluctuations in pitch, fell in part on the Modernists.

Central European Modernists also investigated the intersections of speech and music. For some composers in the 1920s and 1930s, such as Alois Hába, this meant actual notation in quarter-tones and even smaller intervals; but in the earlier part of the century other strategies for intensifying the speechlikeness of music were found. One of the pioneers in this movement was Leoš Janáček (1854–1928), the late-blooming Moravian composer who had an almost sacred regard for the importance of speech—as if all authenticity in music sprang from a sort of heightened talkiness. The vocal lines in his operas, especially from *Jenůfa* (1903) on, were derived from a close study of the inflections of the Czech language. As he wrote in an article in *Hlídka* (Brno, 1905) on speech melody,

> the melodic curves of speech are an expression of the complete organism and of all phases of its spiritual activities. They demonstrate whether a man is stupid or intelligent, sleepy or awake, tired or alert. They tell us whether he is a child or an old man, whether it is morning or evening, light or darkness, heat or frost, and disclose whether a person is alone or in company. The art of dramatic writing is to compose a melodic curve that will, as if by magic, reveal immediately a human being in one definite phase of his existence.[32]

This reliance on the revelatory power of the speaking voice follows from the practice of the Russian composer Modest Musorgsky (1839–1881).

Not long after *Jenůfa*, Arnold Schoenberg (1874–1951) found ways of increasing the speech tension of music, but with rather different aesthetic goals. Schoenberg devised a notational scheme in which extremely chromatic lines (but without intervals smaller than a semitone), combined with careful inflectional instructions to the performer, managed to simulate speech—not for the sake of simplicity or any naturalistic effect, but in order to heighten the artificiality, the eeriness of the music. Schoenberg states

32. Bohumír Štědroň, *Leoš Janáček: Letters and Reminiscences,* trans. Geraldine Thomsen (Prague: Artia, 1955), 90. Cited in *Composers on Music,* ed. Josiah Fisk (Boston: Northeastern University Press, 1997), 175–76.

these instructions in the foreword to *Pierrot Lunaire,* a setting of twenty-one poems by the Symbolist poet Albert Giraud concerning a clown who tries in vain to wipe a spot of moonbeam off his coat; finds himself eating a bleeding heart in a mock eucharist; and drills a hole into another clown's skull and stuffs tobacco into it, in order to convert him into a living pipe. To imagine a music for this studied insincerity, this fun depravity, this blasphemy against expression, Schoenberg devised a style of vocal recitation designed to be neither speech nor song, but some hybrid of the two, a translunar synthesis. Monteverdi wrote that musical expression should be concentrated "on the word and not on the meaning of the sentence";[33] and Schoenberg takes the minute examination of particular words to astonishing lengths, building (to take an example from the seventh song) a complicated apparatus of speech trills into the phrase-droop of "todeskranker Mond" ("sick-to-death moon"). Melodrama, in the technical sense, refers to the practice of speaking over a musical accompaniment (as in passages in Mozart's *Zaide,* and in Beethoven's *Egmont* and *Fidelio*); and in *Pierrot Lunaire* Schoenberg takes the concept of melodrama about as far as it will go.

ARNOLD SCHOENBERG
Foreword to *Pierrot Lunaire* (1912)

The melody given in the *Sprechstimme* [speaking voice] by means of notes is not intended for singing (except for specially marked isolated exceptions). The task of the performer is to transform it into a speech-melody, taking into account the given pitch. This is achieved by:

I. Maintaining the rhythm as accurately as if one were singing, i.e., with no more freedom than would be allowed with a singing melody;
II. Becoming acutely aware of the difference between *singing tone* and *speaking tone:* singing tone unalterably stays on the pitch, whereas speaking tone gives the pitch but immediately leaves it again by falling or rising. However, the performer must be very careful not to adopt a *singsong* speech pattern. That is not intended at all. Nor should one strive for realistic, natural speech. On the contrary, the difference between ordinary speaking and speaking that contributes to a musical form should become quite obvious. But it must never be reminiscent of singing.

Moreover, stress the following concerning performances:

It is never the task of performers to recreate the mood and character of the individual pieces on the basis of the meaning of the words, but rather solely on the basis of

---

33. *sopra alla parola et non sopra al senso de la clausula*—from a letter to Alessandro Striggio, 7 May 1627.

the music. The extent to which the tone-painting-like rendering of the events and emotions of the text was important to the author is already found in the music. Where the performer finds it lacking, he should abstain from presenting something that was not intended by the author. He would not be adding, but rather detracting.

From *Dreimal sieben Gedichte aus Albert Girauds Pierrot Lunaire, op. 21* (Vienna: Universal Edition, 1914); authorized translation.

But most of Schoenberg's vocal music is not parodic in character, nor is it written in the *Sprechstimme* mode of *Pierrot Lunaire.* In an essay written in the same year as *Pierrot Lunaire,* Schoenberg tried to indicate how he responded most intimately to literature: not on the level of word-by-word illustration (though this is exactly what he did in *Pierrot Lunaire*), nor on the level of conscious analysis, but on the level of phonic intuition. Schoenberg considered himself an essentialist, who felt the deep seizure of reality that inspired the poet and recreated that seizure in the domain of music. In this way Schoenberg thought that he met the text at its most fundamental level, even when his vocal music had nothing particularly speechlike in its surface sound.

ARNOLD SCHOENBERG
"The Relationship to the Text" (1912)

There are relatively few people who are capable of understanding, purely in terms of music, what music has to say. The assumption that a piece of music must summon up images of one sort or another, and that if these are absent the piece of music has not been understood or is worthless, is as widespread as only the false and banal can be. Nobody expects such a thing from any other art, but rather contents himself with the effects of its material, although in the other arts the material-subject, the represented object, automatically presents itself to the limited power of comprehension of the intellectually mediocre. Since music as such lacks a material-subject, some look beyond its effects for purely formal beauty, others for poetic procedures. Even Schopenhauer,[34] who at first says something really exhaustive about the essence of music in his wonderful thought, "The composer reveals the inmost essence of the world and utters the most profound wisdom in a language which his reason does not understand, just as a

---

34. Arthur Schopenhauer (1778–1860), pessimistic German philosopher, author of *The World as Will and Representation* (1819), which understands the universe as the blind, spastic groping of the will (all human or subhuman desire) toward further entanglements of itself; only through chaste intellection, through choosing a dispassionate life of ideas, can we hope to save ourselves from will. Schopenhauer thought that music was the only art that did not merely copy ideas, but actually embodied the will itself.

magnetic somnambulist gives disclosures about things which she has no idea of when awake" — even he loses himself later when he tries to translate details of this language *which the reason does not understand* into our terms. It must, however, be clear to him that in this translation into the terms of human language, which is abstraction, reduction to the recognizable, the essential, the language of the world, which ought perhaps to remain incomprehensible and only perceptible, is lost. But even so he is justified in this procedure, since after all it is his aim as a philosopher to represent the essence of the world, its unsurveyable wealth, in terms of concepts whose poverty is all too easily seen through. And Wagner too, when he wanted to give the average man an indirect notion of what he as a musician had looked upon directly, did right to attach programs to Beethoven's symphonies.[35]

Such a procedure becomes disastrous when it becomes general usage. Then its meaning becomes perverted to the opposite; one tries to recognize events and feelings in music as if they *must* be there. On the contrary, in the case of Wagner it is as follows: the impression of the "essence of the world" received through music becomes productive in him and stimulates him to a poetic transformation in the material of another art. But the events and feelings which appear in this transformation were not contained in the music, but are merely the material which the poet uses only because so direct, unpolluted and pure a mode of expression is denied to poetry, an art still bound to subject-matter. . . .

A few years ago I was deeply ashamed when I discovered in several Schubert[36] songs, well-known to me, that I had absolutely no idea what was going on in the poems on which they were based. But when I had read the poems it became clear to me that I had gained absolutely nothing for the understanding of the songs thereby, since the poems did not make it necessary for me to change my conception of the musical interpretation in the slightest degree. On the contrary, it appeared that, without knowing the poem, I had grasped the content, the real content, perhaps even more profoundly than if I had clung to the surface of the mere thoughts expressed in words. For me, even more decisive than this experience was the fact that, inspired by the sound of the first words of the text, I had composed many of my songs straight through to the end without troubling myself in the slightest about the continuation of the poetic events, without even grasping them in the ecstasy of composing, and that only days later I thought of looking back to see just what was the real poetic content of my song. It then turned

---

35. Ludwig von Beethoven (1770–1827). Some examples of these programs for Beethoven by Richard Wagner (1813–83) can be found in *Wagner on Music and Drama*, trans. H. Ashton Ellis, ed. Albert Goldman and Evert Sprinchorn (New York: Da Capo Press, 1964), 160–76.

36. Franz Schubert (1797–1828).

out, to my greatest astonishment, that I had never done greater justice to the poet than when, guided by my first direct contact with the sound of the beginning, I divined everything that obviously had to follow this first sound with inevitability.

Thence it became clear to me that the work of art is like every other complete organism. It is so homogeneous in its composition that in every little detail it reveals its truest, inmost essence. When one cuts into any part of the human body, the same thing always comes out—blood. When one hears a verse of a poem, a measure of a composition, one is in a position to comprehend the whole. Even so, a word, a glance, a gesture, the gait, even the color of the hair, are sufficient to reveal the personality of a human being. So I had completely understood the Schubert songs, together with their poems, from the music alone, and the poems of Stefan George [37] from their sound alone, with a perfection that by analysis and synthesis could hardly have been attained, but certainly not surpassed. However, such impressions usually address themselves to the intellect later on, and demand that it prepare them for general applicability, that it dissect and sort them, that it measure and test them, and resolve into details what we possess as a whole. And even artistic creation often goes this roundabout way before it arrives at the real conception. When Karl Kraus [38] calls language the mother of thought, and Wassily Kandinsky [39] and Oskar Kokoschka [40] paint pictures the objective theme of which is hardly more than an excuse to improvise in colors and forms and to express themselves as only the musician expressed himself until now, these are symptoms of a gradually expanding knowledge of the true nature of art. And with great joy I read Kandinsky's book *On the Spiritual in Art,* in which the road for painting is pointed out and the hope is aroused that those who ask about the text, about the subject-matter, will soon ask no more.

37. Stefan George (1868–1933), Symbolist poet with classicizing tendencies. Schoenberg set George's lyrics in *Zwei Lieder,* op. 14 (1907), and *Das Buch der hängenden Gärten,* op. 15 (1908–9), his most ambitious song sequence; two George poems appear, set for soprano, in the final movements of Schoenberg's Second String Quartet, op. 10 (1907–8), one of Schoenberg's first experiments with abandoning tonality—indeed, at the beginning of the finale, George's line "I feel air from other planets" seems redolent of the new atonal or pantonal universe that Schoenberg was exploring.

38. Karl Kraus (1874–1936), prolific writer and editor of the journal *Die Fackel,* was much concerned with precision in language.

39. Vassily Kandinsky (1866–1944), a Russian painter based in Germany and a friend of Schoenberg's, was a founder of the anti-naturalistic artistic movement called *Der blaue Reiter;* in his book *Concerning the Spiritual in Art* (1911), he argued for the spiritual superiority of nonrepresentational art—if art imitated nothing it would not be contaminated by the material world. Schoenberg here claims that music deserves the same privilege as painting.

40. Oskar Kokoschka (1886–1980), Expressionist painter and playwright.

Then there will become clear what was already made clear in another instance. No one doubts that a poet who works with historical material may move with the greatest freedom, and that a painter, if he still wanted to paint historical pictures today, would not have to compete with a history professor. One has to hold to what a work of art intends to offer, and not to what is merely its intrinsic cause. Furthermore, in all music composed to poetry, the exactitude of the reproduction of the events is as irrelevant to the artistic value as is the resemblance of a portrait to its model; after all, no one can check on this resemblance any longer after a hundred years, while the artistic effect still remains. And it does not remain because, as the Impressionists perhaps believe, a real man (that is, the one who is apparently represented) speaks to us, but because the artist does so—he who has expressed himself here, he whom the portrait must resemble in a higher reality. When one has perceived this, it is also easy to understand that the outward correspondence between music and text, as exhibited in declamation, tempo and dynamics, has but little to do with the inward correspondence, and belongs to the same stage of primitive imitation of nature as the copying of a model. Apparent superficial divergences can be necessary because of parallelism on a higher level. Therefore, the judgment on the basis of the text is just as reliable as the judgment of albumen according to the characteristics of carbon.

From "The Relationship to the Text," in *Style and Idea,* ed. Leonard Stein, trans. Leo Black (Berkeley: University of California Press, 1984), 141–45. First published as "Das Verhältnis zum Text," in *Der blaue Reiter,* ed. Wassily Kandinsky and Franz Marc (Munich: R. Piper Verlag, 1912).

The relationship of speech to music was not only a technical preoccupation of Schoenberg's, but a theme in his work: his unfinished opera *Moses und Aron* (1930–32) contrasts speech and song in the most direct way possible, by opposing Aron, a florid tenor, to Moses, who does not sing (with one brief exception) but only declaims in *Sprechstimme* (notated in the manner of *Pierrot Lunaire*). Moses's authenticity, his nearness to God, seems a reflex of the mouth impediment that forbids him to sing; while Aron's slipperiness, his compromising and devious character, seems a reflex of his coloratura agility. The voice of the Burning Bush, however, is depicted as a small chorus that simultaneously speaks and sings, as if God were divine because He comprised speech and song as a single field of sound.

The operas of Schoenberg's pupil Alban Berg (1885–1935) also used vocal styles as something like characters themselves, in counterpoint to the dramatis personae of the text. His scores show the subtlest gradations between pure spoken dialogue and unintelligibly virtuosic singing; Berg continually readjusts voice production according to the particular need of the dramatic moment.

ALBAN BERG
"Voice in Opera" (1929)

It goes without saying that an art form that makes use of the human voice must de-prive itself of none of the voice's many possibilities, so that even in opera the spoken word (either with or without musical accompaniment) has its place, just as much as the sung word: from recitative to *parlando,* from cantilena to coloratura. Therefore, even in today's operatic music, the possibility of using *bel canto* is given, and such a claim is justified. For it is not well understood that modern melodies made up of *cantabile* phrases (I might take one of hundreds of examples from Schoenberg's *Erwartung*)[41] not only *can* be "beautifully sung," but—if they are to have their proper value—*must* be "beautifully sung," just like the famous "La donna è mobile."[42]

The fact that here, as almost always in the arioso forms of Italian music, [the elabo-ration of] a single motive—which (as opposed to women) is not even changeable—is found sufficient and certainly provides a guarantee that everyone can immediately sing such a melodic idea. But it doesn't warrant the supposition that only with a so-called declamatory art of singing can one do justice to such a style that, germane specifically to German music, is characterized, whether tonal or atonal, by melodic, harmonic, and rhythmic richness and far-reaching variation. On the contrary: a composer who had such a concept of melody wants to know that the singer feels it and renders it (which makes the singer a really important part of the concept!). And I can speak from my own experience, how astonished I was when, in a review of *Wozzeck,*[43] only recently again a singer was reproached for having "too much ambition to show off her voice, to assert herself as a singer." Perhaps in my opera I've unequally exploited the possibilities of the voice (only a dozen measures of true recitative can be found there), but I have cer-tainly never sacrificed the possibility of using *bel canto.* I believe I've amply made up for the absence of recitative by using, for the first time in opera and at great length, what is called "rhythmical declamation" (which Schoenberg introduced twenty years ago in the spoken choruses of *Die glückliche Hand* and in the melodrama of *Pierrot*

41. Schoenberg's *Erwartung* (1909) is a monodrama sung by woman who has evidently killed (or has hallucinated that she has killed) her lover. Its dissonant, psychoanalytically intense style is a high point of the Expressionist movement. Berg quotes as his example of Schoenbergian *bel canto* the melody that accompanies "und alle Farben der Welt brachen aus deinen Augen."

42. "La donne è mobile": aria in Giuseppe Verdi's *Rigoletto* (1851), sung by the Duke, a cheerful lib-ertine who laughs at the fickleness of women.

43. *Wozzeck* (1925), Berg's first opera, concerns a sullen and visionary soldier, the victim of outra-geous medical experiments, who murders his unfaithful mistress. The opera is constructed out of strict musical forms, such as the passacaglia, the sonata-allegro, and the invention, in a manner that seems to offer a startling contrast to the Expressionistic freedom of the singing. (A fuller treatment of *Wozzeck* can be found in the Berg essay printed in chapter 4.)

Lunaire).[44] Note well: this manner of treating the voice safeguards, unlike recitative, all the prerogatives of absolute musical construction. It is proved that it represents one of the best means for assuring comprehensibility (as speech in opera must, now and then, be comprehensible); and also that it has enriched opera—from the tonelessly whispered word to the veritable *bel parlare*[45] of its wide-ranging speech-melodies—with a most valuable artistic means, drawn from the purest sources of music. United with song—and it makes a welcome complement to song, an attractive contrast in sound—this sort of melodically, rhythmically, dynamically fixed spoken word can naturally participate in every other form of dramatic music: I mean in the solo as well as in the duet, in the trio, in ensembles great and small, in choruses male, female, and mixed, in singing a capella and accompanied. These possibilities also show to what degree the opera, like no other musical form, is predestined to place itself in service to the human voice, to help it to safeguard its rights, those rights that have almost been lost in the music drama of recent decades, when opera music has often represented—to cite a remark of Schoenberg's—nothing more than a "symphony for large orchestra with vocal accompaniment."

From "Die Stimme in der Oper," in *Gesang*, the 1929 yearbook of Universal Edition, Vienna; cited in Willi Reich, *Alban Berg: Mit Bergs eigenen Schriften* (Vienna: Herbert Reichner Verlag, 1937), 164–65; translated by the editor.

The dream of a corporeal music, with a high specific gravity of meaning, can be related to certain literary experiments in trying to heighten the corporeality of words. The Irish novelist and poet James Joyce (1882–1941) offers several conspicuous examples. In the "Sirens" chapter of *Ulysses* (1922), Joyce opens with a sort of thematic catalog of sound-intensive phrases, phrases that will appear later in the chapter in a more intelligible narrative context. Here, then, we have language shorn of every aspect except its musicality, as if the sirens' song drifted in strange melodic snatches across the waves, before the reader gets close enough to the chapter to make out its events. It is possible to imagine this passage as a bundle of *Leitmotive;* Joyce himself referred to the chapter as a *fuga per canonem,* but it is not easy to analyze the chapter as a fugue.

The "sirens" are two flirtatious barmaids, Lydia Douce and Mina Kennedy, one brunette, one blonde ("Bronze by gold"), both listening to the viceroy's procession ("hoof-

44. *Die glückliche Hand* (*The Lucky Touch*, 1910–13), is Schoenberg's short opera concerning an artist beleaguered by hyena-bats and a seductive woman—an allegory of the artist's desperate need to retain his solitary integrity. The "Foreword to *Pierrot Lunaire*," is reprinted in this chapter.

45. *bel parlare:* Italian for "beautiful speaking," by analogy with *bel canto,* "beautiful song," a term used to describe the refined singing method of early-nineteenth-century opera.

irons") passing on the street. Some of the customers sing the popular songs of the day. But the most important customer, from Joyce's perspective, is Leopold Bloom, the middle-class advertising man who plays the role of Odysseus in Joyce's carefully wrought parallels between Homeric legend and the Dublin of 1904; he is bemused by the sentimental songs and by the percussion of bartending (ringing coins, snapping garters), but the sound that most preoccupies him is a constant imaginary jingling, the jaunty noise of Blazes Boylan, his wife's lover, on the way (as Bloom knows) to a tryst with her.

JAMES JOYCE
from "Sirens" (1922)
Bronze by gold heard the hoofirons, steelyringing.
Imperthnthn[46] thnthnthn.
Chips, picking chips off rocky thumbnail, chips.
Horrid! And gold flushed more.
A husky fifenote blew.
Blew. Blue bloom is on the.[47]
Goldpinnacled hair.
A jumping rose on satiny breast of satin, rose of Castile.[48]
Trilling, trilling: Idolores.[49]
Peep! Who's in the . . . peepofgold?
Tink cried to bronze in pity.
And a call, pure, long and throbbing. Longindying call.
Decoy. Soft word. But look: the bright stars fade.[50] Notes chirruping answer.
O rose! Castile. The morn is breaking.
Jingle jingle jaunted jingling.
Coin rang. Clock cracked.
Avowal. *Sonnez.* I could. Rebound of garter. Not leave thee. Smack.
   La cloche! Thigh smack. Avowal. Warm. Sweetheart, goodbye!
Jingle. Bloo.
Boomed crashing chords. When love absorbs. War! War! The tympanum.

46. "Impertinent" lisped.
47. A popular song, "When the Bloom Is on the Rye," by Edward Fitzball and Henry Bishop.
48. *The Rose of Castille* (1857), opera by Michael Balfe.
49. A song from Leslie Stuart's operetta *Florodora* (1899), "The Shade of the Palm," with a refrain "Oh, my Delores Queen of the Eastern Sea!"
50. "The bright stars fade" is the first line of the song "Goodbye, Sweetheart, Goodbye," by Jane Williams and John L. Hatton.

A sail! A veil awave upon the waves.
Lost. Throstle fluted. All is lost now.[51]
Horn. Hawhorn.
When first he saw. Alas!
Full tup. Full throb.
Warbling. Ah, lure! Alluring.
Martha! Come!
Clapclap. Clipclap. Clappyclap.
Goodgod henev erheard inall.
Deaf bald Pat brought pad knife took up.
A moonlit nightcall: far, far.
I feel so sad. P.S. So lonely blooming.[52]
Listen!
The spiked and winding cold seahorn. Have you the? Each, and for other,
    plash and silent roar.
Pearls: when she. Liszt's rhapsodies.[53] Hissss.
You don't? Did not: no, no: believe: Lidlyd.
With a cock with a carra.
Black. Deepsounding. Do, Ben, do.
Wait while you wait. Hee hee. Wait while you hee.
But wait!
Low in dark middle earth. Embedded ore.
Naminedamine. Preacher is he.
All gone. All fallen.
Tiny, her tremulous fernfoils of maidenhair.
Amen! He gnashed in fury.
Fro. To, fro. A baton cool protruding.
Bronzelydia by Minagold.
By bronze, by gold, in oceangreen of shadow. Bloom. Old Bloom.
One rapped, one tapped, with a carra, with a cock.
Pray for him! Pray, good people!
His gouty fingers nakkering.

51. "All is lost" is a translation of "Tutto è sciolto," a tenor aria from Vincenzo Bellini's *La sonnambula* (1831), which concerns a man's despair over his seemingly unfaithful girlfriend.
52. "Left blooming alone" is a line from Thomas Moore's "Last Rose of Summer," a song prominent in Friedrich von Flotow's *Martha.*
53. Probably the popular Hungarian rhapsodies by Franz Liszt (1811–86).

Big Benaben. Big Benben.[54]

Last rose Castile of summer left bloom I feel so sad alone.

Pwee! Little wind piped wee.

True men. Lid Ker Cow De and Doll. Ay, ay. Like you men. Will lift your tschink
   with tschunk.

Fff! OO!

Where bronze from anear? Where gold from afar? Where hoofs?

Rrrpr. Kraa. Kraandl.

Then not till then. My eppripfftaph. Be pfrwritt.[55]

Done.

Begin!

From "Sirens," in *Ulysses: A Critical and Synoptic Edition,* 3 vols., ed. Hans Walter Gabler et al. (New York: Garland, 1986), 1:549–553. I have consulted Weldon Thornton's *Allusions in Ulysses: An Annotated List* (Chapel Hill: University of North Carolina Press, 1968) in the textual notes.

Joyce's disciple and friend Samuel Beckett once wrote that in Joyce's later work, "form *is* content, content *is* form. . . . His writing is not *about* something; *it is that something itself.*" . . . When the sense is sleep, the words go to sleep. . . . When the sense is dancing, the words dance."[56] Similarly, when the sense is music, the words sing out, emphasize their phonic character. Joyce had training in music, and even contemplated a career as a tenor; and his prose is always sensitive to the acoustics of language.

Composers have often taken note of the musicality of Joyce's work. In 1909 Geoffrey Molyneux Palmer asked Joyce for permission to write music for Joyce's first book of poems, *Chamber Music;* Joyce liked Palmer's sensitively muted settings. Among better-known composers, Samuel Barber turned to Joyce on a number of occasions, including a striking setting of a passage from *Finnegans Wake, Nuvoletta* (1947), a spoof of (among other things) Wagner's *Tristan.* Luciano Berio set three poems from *Chamber Music* in 1953, and in 1958 wrote a remarkable *Thema (Omaggio a Joyce),* consisting entirely of tape manipulations of the voice of his wife (Cathy Berberian) reading the thematic catalog at the beginning of the "Sirens" chapter. Her voice is so contorted, so overfolded, that it

54. Joyce's friend Stuart Gilbert wrote that the booming noise of "Big Benben" was a dominant-tonic cadence (*James Joyce's Ulysses* [New York: Vintage, 1952], 256). Joyce may or may not have approved of such speculations.

55. A mangled version of the speech of the Irish revolutionary Robert Emmet (1778–1803), when he heard he was condemned to death: "When my country takes her place among the nations of the earth, then, and not till then, let my epitaph be written. I have done." This speech is quoted at the end of the "Sirens" chapter, as the customers toast by clinking their glasses ("Tschink. Tschunk").

56. Samuel Beckett, *Disjecta* (New York: Grove, 1984), 27.

generates the percussive noises, the melos, even the harmony, that Joyce could only suggest in his prose. Later composers, such as Steve Reich, would experiment with extracting music from tapes of the human voice, but in less highfalutin realms of expression—in *Come Out* (1966), for example, Reich phase-shifts the last five words of the phrase "I had to like open the bruise up and let some of the bruise blood come out to show them" (spoken by a boy arrested for murder after a riot in Harlem), until all sense of language reels, echoes out into a hallucinatory blur of rhythm.

The notion that prose can find ways of becoming music, can find strategies to compensate for the absence of notated pitch and simultaneous voicing of sounds, has been attractive throughout the twentieth century. Gertrude Stein's *A Sonatina Followed by Another* (1921) is another example, in which it is perhaps possible to distinguish a first thematic group (declamatory and formal) from a second thematic group (intimate and lyrical)—though Stein knew so little about music that it is venturesome to make such experiments.

One of the great artistic communes of the twentieth century was Bloomsbury, named after the London neighborhood near the British Museum, where, in 1904, the Stephen children set up house after the death of their father, the Victorian intellectual historian Sir Leslie Stephen. Vanessa Stephen Bell painted; Clive Bell and Roger Fry practiced art history (Fry named the school of Postimpressionism and in 1912 organized the first British exhibit of avant-garde French painting); Lydia Lopokova, the wife of the economist John Maynard Keynes, had been a dancer with Diaghilev's Ballets Russes; and, of course, there was Virginia Stephen Woolf (1882–1941), who wrote. In Bloomsbury music was the least represented of the major arts, though Woolf struck up a friendship with the elderly and formidable composer Ethel Smyth, whose spirited feminism Woolf found congenial. But Woolf's writings show a close acquaintance with and sensitivity to music; indeed when she summed up her life in "A Sketch of the Past" (1939–40), finished only four months before her suicide, Woolf described her philosophy

> that behind the cotton wool [of commonplace experience] is hidden a pattern; that we—I mean all human beings—are connected with this; that the whole world is a work of art; that we are parts of the work of art. *Hamlet* or a Beethoven quartet is the truth about this vast mass that we call the world. But there is no Shakespeare; there is no Beethoven; certainly and emphatically there is no God; we are the words; we are the music.[57]

57. Virginia Woolf, *Moments of Being: Unpublished Autobiographical Writings,* ed. Jeanne Schulkind (New York: Harcourt Brace Jovanovich, 1976), 72.

Music, for Woolf, offered a shuddery intuition into the deepest nature of reality; and often the most musical characters in Woolf's novels are the fevered and the insane, those who have closest access to the unbearable truths that most of us ignore. (Woolf herself was sometimes hospitalized for psychotic episodes.) In the excerpt that follows, from *The Waves* (1931), Rhoda—an unstable woman, ultimately a suicide, much disgusted with human life after an absurd accident kills her friend Percival—attends a concert in which a song recital is followed by the performance of a string quartet; she attains a certain relief through the strict formality of the music. Whereas Joyce evoked music by allowing phonetic residues in the reader's mind to reverberate against new strings of phonemes (and by the simpler means of quoting snippets of songs), Woolf evokes music by finding geometric metaphors to convey a sense of deep patternedness. When Rhoda hears the concert soprano, she hears expression of emotion; but when she hears the violinists, she experiences something poised and classical, an intuition of a music not written by Beethoven or any other human being—the music we are, instead of the music we write. Perhaps this is the Modernist equivalent of the music of the spheres, no longer something transcendent, but immanent in our lives.

VIRGINIA WOOLF
from *The Waves* (1931)

"Here is a hall where one pays money and goes in, where one hears music among somnolent people who have come here after lunch on a hot afternoon. We have eaten beef and pudding enough to live for a week without tasting food. Therefore we cluster like maggots on the back of something that will carry us on. Decorous, portly—we have white hair waved under our hats; slim shoes; little bags; clean-shaven cheeks; here and there a military moustache, not a speck of dust has been allowed to settle anywhere on our broadcloth. Swaying and opening programs, with a few words of greeting to friends, we settle down, like walruses stranded on rocks, like heavy bodies incapable of waddling to the sea, hoping for a wave to lift us, but we are too heavy, and too much dry shingle lies between us and the sea. We lie gorged with food, torpid in the heat. Then, swollen but contained in slippery satin, the sea-green woman comes to our rescue. She sucks in her lips, assumes an air of intensity, inflates herself and hurls herself precisely at the right moment as if she saw an apple and her voice was the arrow into the note, 'Ah!'

"An axe has split a tree to the core; the core is warm; sound quivers within the bark. 'Ah,' cried a woman to her lover, leaning from her window in Venice, 'Ah, Ah!' she cried, and again she cries 'Ah!' She has provided us with a cry. But only a cry. And what is a cry? Then the beetle-shaped men come with their violins; wait; count; nod; down come their bows. And there is ripple and laughter like the dance of olive trees and their myriad-tongued grey leaves when a seafarer, biting a twig between his lips where the many-backed steep hills come down, leaps on shore.

"'Like' and 'like' and 'like'—but what is the thing that lies beneath the semblance of the thing? Now that lightning has gashed the tree and the flowering branch has fallen and Percival, by his death, has made me this gift, let me see the thing. There is a square; there is an oblong. The players take the square and place it upon the oblong. They place it very accurately; they make a perfect dwelling-place. Very little is left outside. The structure is now visible; what is inchoate is here stated; we are not so various or so mean; we have made oblongs and stood them upon squares. This is our triumph; this is our consolation.

"The sweetness of this content overflowing runs down the walls of my mind, and liberates understanding. Wander no more, I say; this is the end. The oblong has been set upon the square; the spiral is on top. We have been hauled over the shingle, down to the sea. The players come again. But they are mopping their faces. They are no longer so spruce or so debonair. I will go. I will set aside this afternoon. I will make a pilgrimage. I will go to Greenwich. I will fling myself fearlessly into trams, into omnibuses. As we lurch down Regent Street, and I am flung upon this woman, upon this man, I am not injured, I am not outraged by the collision. A square stands upon an oblong. Here are mean streets where chaffering goes on in street markets, and every sort of iron rod, bolt and screw is laid out, and people swarm off the pavement, pinching raw meat with thick fingers. The structure is visible. We have made a dwelling-place. . . ."

"The still mood, the disembodied mood is on us," said Rhoda, "and we enjoy this momentary alleviation (it is not often that one has no anxiety) when the walls of the mind become transparent. Wren's palace,[58] like the quartet played to the dry and stranded people in the stalls, makes an oblong. A square is stood upon the oblong and we say, 'This is our dwelling-place. The structure is now visible. Very little is left outside.'"

From *The Waves* (New York: Harcourt, Brace, 1959), 161–63, 228.

For Woolf's Rhoda, a musical composition is a piece of architecture—square set on top of oblong—in which the inflamed mind can take refuge from expression. It is possible to understand the history of twentieth-century music in similar terms: after the brain fever, the gastroenteritis, of the Expressionism of the 1910s, music in the 1920s sought relief in Neoclassical severities. This is far from the whole story—Neoclassicism had its aggressive and vexing aspects, and Expressionism its intellectual artifices—but

58. An extension to Hampton Court, built by the architect Sir Christopher Wren (1631–1723).

in the 1920s the world sometimes felt so exhausted by the Great War that it thirsted for simplicity.

One of the major figures in the classicizing of Modernism was that most music-haunted of poets, Thomas Stearns Eliot (1888–1965)—born in St. Louis, but a British subject after 1927. Eliot's contemporaries sometimes found his poetry self-consciously erudite and allusive, dry, cerebral, and this impression was heightened by his critical essays: for example, Eliot argued in his famous essay "Tradition and the Individual Talent" (1919) that a poem is impersonal and inexpressive, for the poet's mind is only a shred of platinum that catalyzes a chemical reaction in which feelings precipitate into words— "the poet has, not a 'personality' to express, but a particular medium. . . . Poetry is not a turning loose of emotion, but an escape from emotion; it is not the expression of personality, but an escape from personality."[59] In its domain, this essay is as important a statement of Neoclassicism as Stravinsky's *Pulcinella,* written in the same year; and Eliot's artistic practice, like Stravinsky's, often entailed the resuscitation of extinct forms and themes from the history of his art.

But only a few of Eliot's poems actually show the sort of marmoreal formality that he seems here to advocate. *The Waste Land* (1922) can be seen as a scholarly attempt to embrace "the mind of Europe"[60] within the confines of a dehydrated epic; it can also be seen as the score to a Dada performance piece, since the poem is shot through with quotations from Wagner's *Tristan und Isolde* and *Götterdämmerung,* as well as less formal music—"O O O O that Shakespeherian Rag" (l. 128); "The pleasant whining of a mandoline" (l. 261); "A woman drew her long black hair out tight / And fiddled whisper music on those strings" (ll. 378–79). From 1935 to 1942, Eliot worked on his most ambitious project, the poem *Four Quartets,* which seems to look to such string quartets as Beethoven's Fifteenth (op. 132) and Bartók's Fifth for inspiration for its five-part structural model; but Eliot is never quite as highbrow as he seems, and the music of his poetry also comprises the music hall of the British comedian Marie Lloyd, and the jungle—"Poetry begins, I dare say, with a savage beating a drum in the jungle, and it retains that essential of percussion and rhythm; hyperbolically one might say that the poet is *older* than other human beings."[61]

Eliot's most searching investigation of literary musicality occurs in "The Music of Poetry," written just as he was completing *Four Quartets.* Here he argues that poetry is governed by a dialectic of music and speech: the history of literature shows a continual oscillation between one pole and the other—and a single poem also may show such

59. T. S. Eliot, *Selected Essays* (New York: Harcourt, Brace and World, 1950), 9–10.
60. Eliot, *Selected Essays,* 6.
61. T. S. Eliot, *The Use of Poetry and the Use of Criticism* (London: Faber and Faber, 1964), 155.

an oscillation. How can a text manage to *be* music? For Joyce, through self-assertion of phonemes; for Woolf, through metaphors responding to musical structure; for Eliot, through adoption of the patterns of recurrence found in music—sonata, rondo, fugue —as constitutive templates for a poem.

T. S. ELIOT
from "The Music of Poetry" (1942)

The music of verse is not a line by line matter, but a question of the whole poem. Only with this in mind can we approach the vexed question of formal pattern and free verse. In the plays of Shakespeare a musical design can be discovered in particular scenes, and in his more perfect plays as wholes. It is a music of imagery as well as sound: Mr. Wilson Knight[62] has shown in his examination of several of the plays, how much the use of recurrent imagery and dominant imagery, throughout one play, has to do with the total effect. A play of Shakespeare is a very complex musical structure; the more easily grasped structure is that of forms such as the sonnet, the formal ode, the ballade, the villanelle, rondeau or sestina. It is sometimes assumed that modern poetry has done away with forms like these. I have seen signs of a return to them; and indeed I believe that the tendency to return to set, and even elaborate patterns is permanent, as permanent as the need for a refrain or a chorus to a popular song. Some forms are more appropriate to some languages than to others, and any form may be more appropriate to some periods than to others. At one stage the stanza is a right and natural formalization of speech into pattern. But the stanza—and the more elaborate it is, the more rules to be observed in its proper execution, the more surely this happens—tends to become fixed to the idiom of the moment of its perfection. It quickly loses contact with the changing colloquial speech, being possessed by the mental outlook of a past generation; it becomes discredited when employed solely by those writers who, having no impulse to form within them, have recourse to pouring their liquid sentiment into a ready-made mould in which they vainly hope that it will set. In a perfect sonnet, what you admire is not so much the author's skill in adapting himself to the pattern as the skill and power with which he makes the pattern comply with what he has to say. Without this fitness, which is contingent upon period as well as individual genius, the rest is at best virtuosity: and where the musical element is the only element, that also vanishes. Elaborate forms return: but there have to be periods during which they are laid aside.

As for "free verse," I expressed my view twenty-five years ago[63] by saying that no verse is free for the man who wants to do a good job. No one has better cause to know

---

62. G. Wilson Knight (1897–1985), Shakespearean critic in the grand style.

63. T. S. Eliot, "Reflections on *Vers libre*," *New Statesman,* 3 March 1917.

than I, that a great deal of bad prose has been written under the name of free verse; though whether its authors wrote bad prose or bad verse, or bad verse in one style or in another, seems to me a matter of indifference. But only a bad poet could welcome free verse as a liberation from form. It was a revolt against dead form, and a preparation for new form or for the renewal of the old; it was an insistence upon the inner unity which is unique to every poem, against the outer unity which is typical. The poem comes before the form, in the sense that a form grows out of the attempt of somebody to say something; just as a system of prosody is only a formulation of the identities in the rhythms of a succession of poets influenced by each other.

Forms have to be broken and remade: but I believe that any language, so long as it remains the same language, imposes its laws and restrictions and permits its own licence, dictates its own speech rhythms and sound patterns. And a language is always changing; its developments in vocabulary, in syntax, pronunciation and intonation— even, in the long run, its deterioration—must be accepted by the poet and made the best of. He in turn has the privilege of contributing to the development and maintaining the quality, the capacity of the language to express a wide range, and subtle gradation, of feeling and emotion; his task is both to respond to change and make it conscious, and to battle against degradation below the standards which he has learnt from the past. The liberties that he may take are for the sake of order.

At what stage contemporary verse now finds itself, I must leave you to judge for yourselves. I suppose that it will be agreed that if the work of the last twenty years is worthy of being classified at all, it is as belonging to a period of search for a proper modern colloquial idiom. We have still a good way to go in the invention of a verse medium for the theatre, a medium in which we shall be able to hear the speech of contemporary human beings, in which dramatic characters can express the purest poetry without high-falutin and in which they can convey the most commonplace message without absurdity. But when we reach a point at which the poetic idiom can be stabilized, then a period of musical elaboration can follow. I think that a poet may gain much from the study of music: how much technical knowledge of musical form is desirable I do not know, for I have not that technical knowledge myself. But I believe that the properties in which music concerns the poet most nearly, are the sense of rhythm and the sense of structure. I think that it might be possible for a poet to work too closely to musical analogies: the result might be an effect of artificiality; but I know that a poem, or a passage of a poem, may tend to realize itself first as a particular rhythm before it reaches expression in words, and that this rhythm may bring to birth the idea and the image; and I do not believe that this is an experience peculiar to myself. The use of recurrent themes is as natural to poetry as to music. There are possibilities for verse which bear some analogy to the development of a theme by different groups of instruments; there are possibilities of transitions in a poem comparable to the different

movements of a symphony or a quartet; there are possibilities of contrapuntal arrangement of subject-matter. It is in the concert room, rather than in the opera house, that
the germ of a poem may be quickened. More than this I cannot say, but must leave the
matter here to those who have had a musical education. But I would remind you again
of the two tasks of poetry, the two directions in which language must at different times
be worked: so that however far it may go in musical elaboration, we must expect a time
to come when poetry will have again to be recalled to speech. The same problems arise,
and always in new forms.

From *On Poetry and Poets* (New York: Noonday, 1961), 30–33.

We have now seen a number of composers and writers experimenting with rap-
prochements between music and speech. But in the world of Modernism every position
is the object of contention—and certainly there were Modernists who strenuously re-
sisted any attempt to make music speak, or to understand music as a language. Carl
Nielsen (1865–1931) was a Danish composer who, beginning at the cultural margin of
Europe, grew into one of the twentieth century's major symphonists; he remained sensitive to the latest musical developments, and in the Humoreske in his Sixth Symphony
(1924–25) wrote what might be taken as a hilarious parody of "atonal" music. In the following essay Nielsen states the antilinguistic case with unusual vigor and flair. An earlier writer, such as the Viennese critic Eduard Hanslick, might have argued this case by
pointing to the formality and abstraction of music, superior to those of other arts; but
Nielsen approaches his theme from a distrust of simile. Woolf's Rhoda cried out, " 'Like'
and 'like' and 'like'—but what is the thing that lies beneath the semblance of the thing?";
and Nielsen too craves authenticity, refuses to admit the validity of figures of speech: to
say that a musical work is *like* a painting or a poem diminishes it, estranges it, pushes it
out into a domain where it doesn't belong. From this premise Nielsen develops a meditation about the trashiness of much modern art, contaminated by appeals to alien artistic media; and, more specifically, a meditation about music's nonrepresentationality,
music's resistance to having any plaster of words applied to it.

Nielsen begins his essay by writing about uncut stones, stones that bemuse us but resemble nothing at all, in order to stress that the fascination with phenomena has nothing to do with their power to represent or copy—he wants a sort of music that capti-
vates for its own sake, not for the sake of its resemblance to something outside itself. His
"Oriental" parable also concerns the futility of simile-making.

CARL NIELSEN
from "Words, Music, and Program Music" (1925)

The farmer is walking one morning across his freshly harrowed field. He stops, picks up an oddly shaped stone, turns it over in his hand, feels it, and examines it closely from all sides. Then he goes off with his find, meaning to put it with the other "funny" stones in his garden. Provided the man is not over-imaginative, seeing in the stone a dog, a cat, a bird, or some other creature, we have here that original sense of form which is so promising and on which indeed all appreciation of plastic art depends. This simple fact, that an object meaning or representing nothing at all is able to arouse our interest and sense of wonder solely by the true organic play of forms and lines, this is the primeval basis of what we call our mental life, as chalk, clay, and soil are of geology. It is from these strata that art must grow and become personal and individual. Without these basic substances—wonder, delight, and possessive desire—many sorts of plant will no doubt grow; but they will die again and will scarcely ever have delighted us, certainly never nourished us. . . .

We are experiencing a strange, impotent, abnormal tendency to mix the arts one with another: a singularly perverse craving to see what will come out of the most absurd conglomeration. It is not a sane breeder's attempt to improve his strains, but a queer, emasculate desire to see monsters. The general confusion of ideas which prevails on this point is best seen from the fact that terms like *music* in painting, *color* in music, *pictorial effect* in sculpture, and *architecture* in poetry are no longer just figures of speech but are taken quite literally by artists striving, in the sweat of their desperate brows, to express the essence of one art in the medium of another. All this is very individualistic and very lyrical, and no doubt these artists *feel* very intensely over their work. But it is an unmistakable sign that we are at the bottom in a period of decline. It's time to go up!

It is incredible that an artist should feel flattered at being viewed from the standpoint of an art not his own, and it is all the more absurd when he himself strives to that end. A composer should feel it the height of mockery to have his work praised for pictorial beauty. So also the sculptor. Conversely, the painter should object to the application of musical ideas to his art. It would be all to the good if every man stuck to his job, and he can have only one. Artists have quite enough to do trying to attain excellence in their own art, and should not waste their time. This is not a plea for partiality and exclusiveness. One art will not thrive without another, and it is a well-known fact that barley and oats sown together in the same field will be robuster than if kept separate. But the barley remains barley; the oats, oats. Where one art thrives, the other will be wanted; but attempts to run them together will never succeed and will only mislead those who might otherwise be "pure in heart."

There is an Oriental tale about a man who invited a friend to eat at his table. A slave brought in butter for their bread. The guest exclaimed when he saw it: "What delicious butter; as smooth and fragrant as oil!" The host instantly commanded the slave to take away the butter and bring oil instead. The guest enthusiastically declared that the oil was as pure and clear as water from a spring. "Ah, I see you prefer water," said the host; and the servant was given fresh orders and told to remove the oil and serve water.

To take words and music first.

Something could be done about this. A real word of advice could be given to composers who think that words and music can combine as intimately as silver and gold, and who therefore turn and twist them, compose and decompose them, until there is hardly anything left, what may have been an original talent being reduced to matchwood and perishing in the process.

Herbert Spencer,[64] who asserts that music has its origin in language, and in a sense is exalted, intensified, or enlarged and idealized speech, may have taken an interest in music, but he can never have been musical, in fact cannot have had the slightest real feeling for music. His example of a mistress calling her maid, first with an even voice in the middle register and then, as the maid fails to respond, ever louder and sharper, is so far from proving his theory as to be the very reverse. The louder and more insistently the lady calls the maid, the further she in fact gets from the essential character of music. Even though she were to work herself into a state of ecstasy, her stream of speech swaying and rocking through the whole scale of notes, the result would but correspond to a man sitting in a boat and being dragged across the land. Only when the boat glides into the water, moving freely in its own element, can it be called sailing. . . .

In another respect, in regard to concrete or positive ideas, music is completely silent. It can tell us nothing about the meaning of this or that, and cannot be translated into words or pictures. If one were to ask a composer what he meant by a particular chord or succession of tones, the only answer he could really give would be to play or sing the passage. All other explanation is nonsense.

But music in association with words, surely, can express something concrete? No; it is a confusion of ideas to think so. Take passages like the cry of "Barabbas" in Bach's *Matthew Passion*,[65] the "No" of the spirits in Act Two of *Orpheus*,[66] or Don Giovanni's

---

64. Herbert Spencer (1820–1903), British philosopher, who tried to adapt Charles Darwin's theory of evolution to the mental life of man, including the study of ethics.

65. Johann Sebastian Bach (1685–1750) wrote a *Passion According to St. Matthew* (1727) in which, at a climactic moment, the crowd of Jews shouts that Barrabas should live, and Christ should be crucified.

66. In *Orfeo ed Euridice* (1762), by C. W. Gluck (1714–87), Orpheus tries to enter Hades to rescue his dead wife, but the Furies repel him with a great "No!"

wild defiance in the final scene of the opera.[67] It is a mistake to think that music expresses anything very definite, even in strongly marked passages like these. The tones can just as well signify loud shouts for help or cries of warning, and the "No" in Orpheus might be just as effective a "Yes." The passages referred to are none the less brilliant for that; but I hope I shall make myself clear in what follows.

Not even when it musters all its effects, then, can music express the crudest ideas of Yes and No; even in association with words, it expresses one as much or as little as the other.

Then what is the relation of music to words?

We have to admit that it is a purely decorative relation; not, it is true, in the generally accepted sense of the word decorative, but in the sense of the sun's relation to things, illumining and coloring them, radiating and imparting luster to them, besides warming and vitalizing them, so every potentiality can develop. If we associate the word "decorative" in our minds with something which requires the sun to make it unfold and open itself and to beautify it, we will understand that it implies nothing derogatory. But many a good musician may feel it a derogation of the art into which he often thinks he has put so many ideas and *images*. One will come and tell us about all the palms, rivers, and canals he saw while working on an "Oriental suite"; another about all he *thought,* felt, and re-thought when composing this or that "symphonic poem." Few, however, will tell us what they heard. . . .

Meanwhile, music neither can nor will bind itself to concrete ideas; that would be completely contrary to its nature. It will be free; and although it serves and obeys, it does so only because in this way, too, it delights in itself, reveling in the flexibility of its nature like the sea-lion in the water or the swallow in flight. And the less we try to bind it, the more we allow it to follow its own strange laws, the better it serves and the richer it is. If, in common with architecture, it can proclaim nothing definite and cannot, like poetry, painting, and sculpture, convey information about what we call nature and reality, it can, more than any of these, illumine, emphasize, suggest, and clarify with swift assurance the most elementary feelings and most heavily charged emotions. These are the properties that are continually confused with concrete ideas. Understandably; for at such moments music can encircle and assail words with power so expansive that we think it speaks. And so, of course, it does, but in its own language, which is no language but a continual gliding in and out, up and down, between the words; now away from them, now very close, yet never touching; now urging on and now lingering, yet ever in vital motion. Thus music can come with a rush, inflaming and vitalizing the

67. Near the end of *Don Giovanni* (1787), by W. A. Mozart (1756–91), the title character is carried off to hell, shouting defiance.

words, vibrating them, encircling them in long, steady orbits so they slumber, inciting
and exciting them till it hurts, or warming and irradiating them so they swell and burst
in infinite delight. But to think thoughts, glow in colors, or speak in allusive metaphors
is beyond its powers. In this it resembles architecture, another art which tells us nothing about realities and which rests on the same distinguished foundation of mathematical certitude. Strange that music—even the most banal and the most hysterical—
should have so law-bound and immutable a foundation! . . .

Of the relationship between words and music there is little more to be said, unless
we embark on a school-masterly discussion of declamation and so forth. But it might
be interesting—also psychologically—to study the relationship of musicians to words
and absolute music. They can be divided into two groups. One group cannot manage
without words and stage; they must have something to hold on to, as it were. Their music clings to words as the hop to its pole or the vine to its trellis. We realize how dependent they are on a text or story when they compose absolute music.

The masters of the second group are quite capable of composing to a text, but seem
to be really free only when they apply themselves to tones alone. The first group includes Gluck, Weber, Marschner, Meyerbeer, Wagner, Verdi, Robert Franz, Grieg, and, in
Denmark, Hartmann;[68] the second, Bach, Haydn, Mozart, Beethoven, Brahms, and,
among Danish composers, Niels W. Gade.[69] It may be objected that Mozart wrote his
most celebrated works for the stage, *i.e.* to a text. But the best symphonies, sonatas,
and quartets are in no wise inferior to his operas; and in these, for all their brilliant dramatic qualities, the claims of absolute music are so fully met that he may be said to belong to this group. . . .

If music cannot express concrete ideas or action, nor its relation to words ever be
anything but decorative and illuminating, still less is it capable of expressing an entire,
long, coherent program. Yet just now—especially in Germany, the breeding-ground of
metaphysicians—there are many composers who hold to that view. It would be most
interesting to see what different listeners got out of a piece of program music the key
to which had been withheld. One thing is certain: not one would guess correctly. And
it would be found that most listeners—once the floodgates of imagination were
opened—would imagine all sorts of nonsense, going much further than the most poetical musician. The following occurrence is proof of this. A Danish composer had written a symphony [Nielsen's own First Symphony] of which the *allegro* movement was

68. Carl Maria von Weber (1786–1826), Romantic composer celebrated for such operas as *Der
Freischütz;* Heinrich Marschner (1795–1861), composer of supernatural operas such as *Der Vampyr;*
Giacomo Meyerbeer (1791–1864), grand opera composer, noted for lavish stage spectacles; Robert
Franz (1815–92); Edvard Grieg (1843–1907); J. P. E. Hartmann (1805–1900), Danish theater composer.
69. Niels W. Gade (1817–90), Mendelssohn-influenced Danish composer.

styled *allegro orgoglioso* (*orgoglioso* = proud). After the first performance the composer was congratulated by an elderly, cultured, and really intelligent lady who confessed that the first movement had given her most delight, because throughout it she
had clearly heard the organ-like character the composer had wished to express. The
movement, it should be said, contained nothing resembling organ music, but the mis-
understanding of the Italian word had given the old lady a rare treat—those who saw
the composer's face no doubt a still rarer one. A converse example of an artist who was
confused is given in the little story about a painter. He meets a friend in front of one of
his pictures at an exhibition, and asks his opinion of it. The friend gives another look at
the painting, which represents a garden with a white garden-seat and on it a woman's
shawl. He makes a few critical observations on the manner of painting the trees. The
artist acknowledges that the criticism may be justified, but hastens to add that it is a
minor point since what matters is the picture's *content*. The friend looks inquiring at
him, and suddenly the young artist bursts out: "Can't you see it's a vicarage and that
the parson's daughter has just got up from the seat, leaving her shawl behind, and that
the curate has been sitting on the same seat and has gone off behind those trees on the
right after a little scene?"

Is there nothing in the program idea, then? Many artists—including many gifted
ones—have practiced it. Yes; but very few know where to draw the line between the
fanciful and the possible. Now take music. If we confine ourselves to a brief suggestion
of a title, the music can from various angles and in many ways elucidate and emphasize
it, as we saw in its relation to words. Of course. But then the program or title must imply a mood or emotional theme, never a thought or concrete action theme.

Wagner keeps within bounds in *The Ride of the Valkyries*,[70] as does the Dane Hartmann in his little piano piece *The Butterfly*. But strictly speaking, nothing, as I have
said, is fixed, and *The Ride of the Valkyries* could be just as suggestive of the incessant
breaking of spray and Hartmann's piece of the rustle of leaves or the trickle of a spring.

The length to which we may go in this respect is obviously a matter of taste and tact.

Still, it would be all to the good if our general view of art were to tend in the direction of cleaner lines, that we might be rid of verse or prose captions to paintings, short
stories and novelettes as prefaces to music, and the carving or engraving of subtle
aphorisms on bronze and marble statues. . . .

If music were to assume human form and explain its essence, it might say something
like this: "I am everywhere and nowhere; I skim the wave and the tops of forests; I sit
in the throat of the savage and the foot of the negro, and sleep in the stone and the
sounding metal. None can grasp me, all can apprehend me; I live tenfold more intensely

---

70. Concert excerpt from *Die Walküre* (1856; 1870), based on the frenzied gathering of the warrior
maidens at the beginning of the third act.

than any living thing, and die a thousandfold deeper. I love the vast surface of silence; and it is my chief delight to break it. I know no sorrow or joy, no pleasure or pain; but I can rejoice, weep, laugh, and lament all at once and everlastingly."

From "Words, Music, and Program Music," in *Living Music,* trans. Reginald Spink (Copenhagen: Wilhelm Hansen, n.d.), 24, 26–37.

A more orthodox and philosophical case against the language function of music can be found in the Norton lectures of the German composer Paul Hindemith (1895–1963). Hindemith begins with the corporealist argument that music arises from our primary experience of our own bodies—our throats naturally express our experience in sound, by sobbing, laughing, and so forth. But Hindemith is acutely conscious that the interpretation of *musical* sounds (greatly refined from these naked cries) as expressions is quirky, private, and unpredictable; he believes that a dictionary of music words is an impossibility, for pieces of music mean different things to different people. For Hindemith, music is less expression than a halting *image* of expression—a picture-puzzle in sound, construable in a thousand different ways. If music is a language, it is a language that everyone can hear and no one can speak, since every meaning-intention of the composer is likely to be lost. Music is the domain of fleeting but intense "pseudo-feelings"— more like dreams than like words or direct sensation.

PAUL HINDEMITH
from *A Composer's World* (1949–50)

Some philosophers, psychologists, and musicologists . . . see in onomatopoetic imitation the source of all composition—in fact, of all organized music. . . . Melody, even in its most developed form, could, according to those theories, always be traced back to some primitive melodic model in free nature, such as the song of birds, the murmuring of water, the melodious dripping of falling drops, and it would be up to the composer to decide how far away from these natural sources he wanted to remove his melody. Harmony would be derived from natural harmonies, such as the chordal howling of the storm, the simultaneous chirping of many birds or crickets. And for rhythmical forms in music there would be many models in nature: anything pounding, beating, and ringing with a certain steadiness, such as the noises of primitive craftsmen at work, the beat of tribal dance rhythms, or the pecking of woodpeckers.

For a musician this theory of the origin of organized music is not too satisfactory. Although it is possible that even in a very early state of musical experience many stimulations came from such natural sources and prompted simple-minded musicians to imitate them, it is more likely that music stems from the bodily experiences of each individual human being. The baby's own crying, whining, and playful crowing is probably the primordial material which according to our former statements assumes a very primitive musical meaning after comparison with the already experienced feeling of general motion. Thus he bursts out spontaneously, without models, into the simplest songlike utterances, and with his growing experiences and a desire to self-expression develops them into audible forms of a slightly higher degree of musical significance. From here on it is a question of further experience and education, how—and how soon—these basic phenomena can be developed into organized music. . . .

Other analysts, in explaining the effects of music on the listener, see in music a kind of language which by its peculiar means of expression conveys some meaning, whatever this meaning may be. But the difference is, that in a spoken or written language each verbal expression used has unchangeable connotations, while in music each component of an audible form can be understood and interpreted emotionally in many different ways. The word "river" always means a stream of flowing water, but a certain phrase in C minor may cause one listener to experience some feeling of sadness, while to another listener the same phrase means something entirely different. This discrepancy in interpretation will be particularly obvious in the case of music that is unfamiliar to the recipient. Those who have had some experience with oriental people and their music will confirm this observation. In hearing oriental music for the first time, the Western listener usually cannot detect any musical significance in it—which it would have, if music was an internationally recognized and understandable language. The strangeness of its sounds will strike him as funny, even ridiculous, and the only emotional urge he will feel will be a desire to laugh heartily. But this same piece may induce the initiated to feel sad, pathetic, heroic, or whatnot. We do not even need to go so far away into foreign regions; sometimes in southern countries church music can be heard which for the visitor from the North has the most exhilarating effect, although it may be intended as funeral music and will have the proper effect of such on the native listener. On the other hand, there are people in whom Gilbert and Sullivan operettas[71] arouse only feelings of boundless desolation and despair.

A composer who wanted to use music in the same sense a language is used could do so only by preparing a voluminous dictionary, in which each particle of a musical form corresponded with a verbal equivalent. But apart from the fact that he never would find a strict definition of the term "particle of a musical form," he would have to come to an agreement with other composers as to the exact meaning of the entries in the musical-verbal vocabulary. Knowing what musicians are like, we can be sure that there will be as many different versions of the dictionary as there are musicians interested in the project; and even if through some supernatural influence the ideas of

---

71. The operettas of W. S. Gilbert (1836–1911), with music by Arthur Sullivan (1842–1900), are calculated to produce mirth, not despondency.

two or more musicians could be unified, the listeners would never want to get acquainted with the fixed symbolism of a musical language. This means that music, due to the absence of any stable connotations in its messages of sound, does not have the properties of a language and cannot be used in the same sense verbal communications are used.

. . . The reactions music evokes are not feelings, but the images, memories of feelings. . . .

Dreams, memories, musical reactions—all three are made of the same stuff. We cannot have musical reactions of any considerable intensity if we do not have dreams of some intensity, for musical reactions build up, like dreams, a phantasmagoric structure of feelings that hits us with the full impact of real feeling. Furthermore we cannot have any musical reactions of emotional significance, unless we have once had real feelings the memory of which is revived by the musical impression. . . . Reactions of a grievous nature can be aroused by music only if a former experience of real grief was stored up in our memory and is now again portrayed in a dreamlike fashion. "Musical" gaiety can be felt only if a feeling of real gaiety is already known to us; "musical" complacency arises in our memory only if complacency felt before without musical prompting was already part of our experience. It is only with the memory of feelings in our mind that we can have any feelinglike reaction caused by music. This can be proved. If, for example, we assume that music is able to arouse a reaction, which in the mind of a mass murderer uncovers the memory of the satisfaction he felt after having slaughtered a row of twenty victims, that feeling cannot be reproduced in our own minds unless we do as he did—murder twenty people and then listen to the adequate music. Certainly we can imagine what this fellow felt and we can direct our reactions to music so that in their dreamlike way they make us feel as if we had the mass murderer's experience and the memories thereof, released by music. But these reactions can never be like the genuine ones of the mass murderer, as we do not have the actual experience that left its imprints in his mind; they can be nothing but reactions of a similar—never identical—nature; reactions based on the feeling of satisfaction we had after other cruelties we committed. These are now substituted by us for the lacking experience of greater cruelty, and are rather artificially brought into contact with a musical impression.

If music did not instigate us to supply memories out of our mental storage rooms, it would remain meaningless, it would merely have a certain tickling effect on our ears. We cannot keep music from uncovering the memory of former feelings and it is not in our power to avoid them, because the only way to "have"—to possess—music, is to connect it with those images, shadows, dreamy reproductions of actual feelings, no matter how realistic and crude or, on the contrary, how denatured, stylized, and sublimated they may be. If music we hear is of a kind that does not easily lend itself or does not lend itself at all to this connection, we still do our best to find in our memory some feeling that would correspond with the audible impression we have. If we find nothing that serves this purpose, we resort to hilarity—as in the case of oriental music, mentioned above—and have a "funny feeling," but even this funny feeling is merely the image of some real funny feeling we had with some former nonmusical experience, and which is now drawn out of its storage place, to substitute for the memory of a more suitable feeling.

This theory gives us a reasonable explanation for the fact that one given piece of music may cause remarkably diversified reactions with different listeners. As an illustration of this statement I like to mention the second movement of Beethoven's Seventh Symphony, which I have found leads some people into a pseudo feeling of profound melancholy, while another group takes it for a kind of scurrilous scherzo, and a third for a subdued pastorale. Each group is justified in judging as it does. The difference in interpretation stems from the difference in memory-images the listeners provide, and the unconscious selection is made on the basis of the sentimental value or the degree of importance each image has: the listener chooses the one which is dearest and closest to his mental disposition, or which represents a most common, most easily accessible feeling.

From *A Composer's World: Horizons and Limitations* (Gloucester: Peter Smith, 1969), 38–41, 45–57.

3 Testing the Boundaries between the Visual Arts and Music

PAINTING AND ARCHITECTURE

Throughout history, the boundary between language and music has often seemed permeable; both speech and music can be produced with the vocal organs, and speech and music share such features as rhythm, phrase shape, and even pitch—as Professor Henry Higgins demonstrates with his little xylophone, plinking out the speech-melody of "The Rain in Spain Stays Mainly in the Plain" in the Lerner and Loewe musical *My Fair Lady* (1956). Indeed the history of music is full of suggestions that any attempt to oppose speech and music is somewhat futile: in one of the wisest explorations of this problem ever written, Marc-Antoine Charpentier's operatic divertissement *Les plaisirs de Versailles* (early 1680s), the two principal characters, La Musique and La Conversation (the first accompanied by sensuous flutes, the second by talky bass viols) quarrel violently; eventually Comus, the god of mirth, tries to appease them by offering hot chocolate and other indulgences; at last they make up and reveal that their dispute was only a sham, performed in order to provide a little entertainment for Louis XIV. Perhaps most of the antagonism between speech and music, in the twentieth as well as the seventeenth century, is only a sort of pretense.

But transgressions of the boundary between music and the visual arts, on the other hand, have always seemed venturesome. Many aesthetic thinkers have frowned severely at all attempts to confuse arts constituted in time (such as poetry and music) with arts constituted in space (such as painting and sculpture). As Gotthold Ephraim Lessing wrote in *Laokoon* (1766),

> this essential difference between [poetry and the visual arts] is found in that the former is a visible progressive act, the various parts of which take place little by little [*nach und nach*] in the sequence of time; whereas the latter is a visible static act, the various parts of which develop next to one another [*neben einander*] in space. But if painting, by virtue of its signs or its means of imitation, which it can combine in space alone, must completely renounce time, then progressive acts, because progressive, do not belong among its subjects—painting must content itself with acts next to one another, or with mere bodies. . . .[1]

1. Gotthold Ephraim Lessing, *Lessing's Laokoon,* ed. A. Hamann (Oxford: Oxford at the Clarendon Press, 1901); translated by the editor.

This is the source of Lessing's famous distinction between the arts of *nacheinander* (sequential, existing in time) and of *nebeneinander* (juxtapositive, existing in space). Lessing despised poetry that tries to do the work of the visual arts (by static description with strings of adjectives) and painting that tries to do the work of poetry (by trying to depict moving bodies, or a single thing in two different temporal states). For a critic of Lessing's temperament, any music that strives to enforce an unchanging mood, or to describe a physical object, or to name something by means of a *Leitmotiv*, has fallen into hopeless confusion. When Carl Nielsen (earlier in this anthology) wrote that a composer's butterfly might just as well be the rustling of leaves, or that Wagner's *Ride of the Valkyries* might just as well be the breaking of waves against rocks, he shows himself a true disciple of Lessing: music can depict action, but has no power to depict the thing that acts. Music is all verb, no noun.

Nevertheless, some Modernists felt that the arts were all one—that genius was an indiscriminate electrical charge that might channel itself into music, or might channel itself into painting. The painter Vassily Kandinsky wrote a play that is a sort of talking picture, *Der gelbe Klang* (discussed in chapter 5); and Arnold Schoenberg (1874–1951) was trained as a painter (unhappily, his first wife eloped with his art teacher). In Schoenberg's mid-thirties it seemed possible that he might become as successful an artist as he was a composer. His portraits and self-portraits, such as his stark and arresting image of a face with burning eyes, *Der rote Blick* (*The Red Gaze*, 1910), attracted the praise of Kandinsky. This was the period when Schoenberg was evolving the free "atonal" style, and he sometimes conceived the new emancipated music as a sort of painting in sound. For example, he called the third of the Five Orchestral Pieces (1909) "Farben" ("Colors"—the original title was "Morning at the Lake"), and it is indeed a quasi-pictorial study in static harmonies that acquire motion through delicate shifts of timbre. Schoenberg considered that he was exploring a new plane of musical activity, a plane of color. In his famous treatise *Harmonielehre* (*Theory of Harmony*, 1911), he explained that sound has other dimensions beyond the linear, forward-pushing dimension of pitch change. It should be noted that neither in 1911 nor later did Schoenberg show any interest in collage technique; his method of tone painting pertained, not to musical analogs of flat canvases, but to careful placement of sounds according to an intuitive spectrum of timbre (as opposed to placement according to position in a hierarchy of consonances and dissonances).

ARNOLD SCHOENBERG
from *Harmonielehre* (1911)

The chord, *c–e–g–d,* is then surely more immediate than *c–e–g–b* (or *b♭*). But what then can we do with the *g♯*? How is that to find a place in the system? As if the system had to be built up by thirds alone! Why not by fifths, which are indeed more immediate than thirds? Why built "up" in the first place? Perhaps sounds, too, have three dimensions, perhaps even more! All right! Build it up, but don't expect me to take your system for more than it is: a system for presenting events, not one that explains them. A junk dealer, having bought up a lot of old odds and ends, brings about some order as a by-product of picking out and sorting the better items. But the trash, which he can no longer sort, he leaves in a pile and says to a customer: "I have a number of things here that are better; over there are some more that I really don't know what to do with. Pick out what you can use." Now, this junk man is going about his business just the same way these "building-up" theorists go about theirs. For in that trash that the junk man really did not know what to do with, over which he gave preference to his old trousers and patched jackets, it was generally in just such trash that old works of art, valuable paintings, rare violins, and the like, were found. "I don't know what to do with it"—that doesn't bother me. You simply have to admit it! I shall be satisfied with that, and you may go right on building up. But that the system is false, or at least inadequate, because it cannot accommodate phenomena that do exist, or labels them trash, exceptions, accidental harmonic structures, piles of rejects—that had to be said. And yet the system would arrogate to itself the status of a natural system, whereas it will scarcely do as a system of presentation. Confess: "because I don't know what to do with it!" Then we shall be good friends. But the pretense must stop.

There are, then, no non-harmonic tones, no tones foreign to harmony, but merely tones foreign to the harmonic system. . . .

In a musical sound (*Klang*) three characteristics are recognized: its pitch, color [timbre], and volume. Up to now it has been measured in only one of the three dimensions in which it operates, in the one we call "pitch." Attempts at measurement in the other dimensions have scarcely been undertaken to date; organization of their results into a system has not been attempted at all. The evaluation of tone color (*Klangfarbe*), the second dimension of tone, is thus in a still much less cultivated, much less organized state than is the aesthetic evaluation of these last-named harmonies. Nevertheless, we go right on boldly connecting the sounds with one another, contrasting them with one another, simply by feeling. . . . How all that relates to the essence of natural sound we do not know, perhaps we can hardly guess at it yet; but we do write progressions of tone colors without a worry, and they do somehow satisfy the sense of beauty. What system underlies these progressions?

The distinction between tone color and pitch, as it is usually expressed, I cannot accept without reservations. I think the tone becomes perceptible by virtue of tone color, of which one dimension is pitch. Tone color is, thus, the main topic, pitch a subdivision. Pitch is nothing else but tone color measured in one direction. Now, if it is possible to create patterns out of tone colors that are differentiatied according to pitch, patterns we call "melodies," progressions, whose coherence (*Zusammenhang*) evokes an effect analogous to thought processes, then it must also be possible to make such progressions out of the tone colors of the other dimension, out of that which we call simply "tone color," progressions whose relations with one another work with a kind of logic which satisfies us in the melody of pitches. That has the appearance of a futuristic fantasy and is probably just that. But it is one which, I firmly believe, will be realized. I firmly believe it is capable of heightening in an unprecedented manner the sensory, intellectual, and spiritual pleasures offered by art. I firmly believe that it will bring us closer to the illusory stuff of our dreams; that it will expand our relationships to that which seems to us today inanimate as we give life from our life to that which is temporarily dead for us, but dead only by virtue of the slight connection we have with it.

Tone-color melodies! How acute the sense that would be able to perceive them! How high the development of spirit that could find pleasure in such subtle things?

In such a domain, who dares ask for theory!

From *Theory of Harmony*, trans. Roy E. Carter (Berkeley: University of California Press, 1983), 321, 421–22.

Some of the Modernists went far toward investigating music's potentiality for visuality—for constituting itself as a noun. One was Claude Debussy—though some observers felt that there was something meretricious, self-defeating, about all this eye-music:

> When Debussy was new to us, those of us who "heard" him at all found in the "Sunken Cathedral" [*Préludes 1,* no. 10], in "Sails" [*Préludes 1,* no. 2], in "Gold Fish" [*Images 2,* no. 3], in the "Granada" [*Estampes* no. 2 . . .] suggestion of colors, suggestion of visions . . . And this visionary world was a delight. By his very titles it was hinted to us that the composer wished to suggest scenes and visions and objects, and, to a great extent, he succeeded. He succeeded, I do not wish to be paradoxical, in writing music for the eye, with the result [that . . .] the effect of his music diminishes on repeated hearing.[2]

2. Ezra Pound, *Ezra Pound and Music,* ed. R. Murray Schafer (New York: New Directions, 1977), 71. Originally published in *New Age,* 24 January 1918, 248–49.

This is Ezra Pound, active as a London music critic in 1918, making a milder version of the same sort of complaint that Lessing raised in the mid-eighteenth century: by trying to contort itself into the wrong field of operation, music has crippled itself.

But others found eye music a viable and attractive goal. One strategy for increasing the opticality of music was to turn the musical score into a sort of canvas painted in time, by frustrating any sense of musical progression, development, or forward motion. In this sense, the sonata-allegro is a particularly unvisual sort of musical form, for it is felt as a drama of sound, in which tonic and dominant, or minor and major, are first vigorously opposed (in the exposition), then jiggled about (in the development), and finally reconciled (in the recapitulation). Similarly a fugue is understood as a forward pressure in time, in that a theme keeps jostling with itself, keeps making its intervallic structure felt in new ways from the continual exfoliation of its self-displacements. But in some of the older forms, such as the rondo (a sectionalized pattern of symmetrical digressions from a recurrent paragraph, such as ABACABA), a certain stasis, a sense of going nowhere, may result from the fact that sections A, B, and C don't seem to alter or impinge on one another; they simply happen.

This sense of motionlessness-within-movement—what T. S. Eliot called "the still point of the turning world"[3]—occasionally present in the work of older composers, becomes quite prominent in the work of such Modernists as Erik Satie (1866–1925), Igor Stravinsky (1882–1971), and, in a later generation, Olivier Messiaen (1908–92): composers who try to undo the concept of *development* in music in order to make hard-edged collages of sound, or to allude to the eternity that exists on time's far side, or simply to thumb their noses at bourgeois notions of musical satisfaction—or bourgeois notions of progress. In his *Furniture Music* (1920), Satie wrote music designed not to be listened to, music that simply decorated the background surface of the mind, like wallpaper:

> You know, there's a need to create furniture music, that is to say, music that would be a part of the surrounding noises and that would take them into account. I see it as melodious, as masking the clatter of knives and forks without drowning it out completely, without imposing itself. It would fill up the awkward silences that occasionally descend upon guests. It would spare them the usual banalities. Moreover, it would neutralize the street noises that indiscreetly force themselves into the picture.[4]

One piece of *Furniture Music* is entitled "Tapisserie en fer forgé" (which might be translated "Wallpaper in Wrought Iron"), and is to some extent the ancestor of the Minimalist music of the later twentieth century—though Philip Glass, unlike Satie, super-

---

3. See "Coriolan" I (1931) and "Burnt Norton" II (1936).
4. Cited in Alan M. Gillmor, *Erik Satie* (New York: Norton, 1988), 232.

imposes several layers of figured grids, creating moiré effects in sound. Satie's only public performance of *Furniture Music*—endlessly repeated commonplace figures from Saint-Saëns's *Danse macabre* and Ambroise Thomas's *Mignon,* played by a small band at the intermission of a play—turned out to be a fiasco when those within earshot insisted on listening to it instead of proceeding about their normal business, even though Satie kept shouting, "Don't listen!" It is hard to train spectators to make idle glances at music with their eyes, instead of listening with their ears, even for a composer who intends to be boring.

Stravinsky made far more ambitious attempts at translating the methods of visual arts into music. In a piece such as the burlesque *Renard* (1915–16), Stravinsky abuts one abrupt section against the next, as if he were stringing beads on a necklace instead of composing music with the usual fluency, the usual sensitivity to transition; the music seems to dwell in a continual present tense, because one music-bit seems to take no notice of previous musical events—there is neither retrospection nor anticipation. Just as Vladimir Nabokov wrote novels by writing a series of disconnected texts on small note cards, then writing on other note cards to fill in the gaps, so Stravinsky wrote music by assembling short chunks; in *Renard* the listener can, so to speak, hear the scissors and the glue pot at work. Many of Stravinsky's contemporaries were intrigued by this disintegrated approach to composition, this flattened musical surface, this bittiness of texture:

> Strawinsky's merit lies very largely in taking hard bits of rhythm, and noting them with great care. Antheil continues this; and these two composers mark a definite break with the "atmospheric" school; they both write horizontal music.[5]

This is Ezra Pound again. The comparison with Antheil is apt, because Antheil was strongly influenced by Stravinsky's methods; together Antheil and Pound worked out one of the first theories about the successful transposition of music into the visual arts—painting with sound instead of painting with pigment.

George Antheil (1900–1959), born in New Jersey, called his autobiography *Bad Boy of Music,* but he was a bad boy in a great many other venues as well: a virtuoso pianist who kept a revolver on the piano during his concerts; a writer of a manual on forensic endocrinology; an advice-to-the-lovelorn columnist; and the co-holder, with the actress Hedy Lamarr, of U.S. patent 2,292,387 for a device to aim torpedoes by radio waves. Most of his notoriety, though, came from his musical compositions, especially *Ballet Mécanique* (1926), scored for (among other strident or percussive things) airplane propellers, sirens, and a battery of pianos and player pianos; its première led to one of those

---

5. Pound, *Ezra Pound and Music,* 258.

Parisian concert riots that have been, since Stravinsky's *Rite of Spring* (1913), de rigueur for avant-garde success.

Earlier in the 1920s Antheil's cause had been taken up by his fellow American expatriate, the poet and propagandist Ezra Pound (1885–1972). Pound praised Antheil so extravagantly that even Antheil was embarrassed—and Antheil was not an easy man to embarrass: over a span of several decades, Pound compared Antheil with everyone from Stravinsky to Jimmy Cagney.[6] Pound considered Antheil a sort of subatomic physicist of music, breaking down the musical phenomenon into its barest constituents:

> This Sonata [Antheil's third violin sonata] thinks in time's razor edge. . . . It means that, via Stravinsky and Antheil . . . we are brought to a closer conception of time, to a faster beat, to a closer realization or, shall we say, "decomposition" of the musical atom.
>
> The mind, even the musician's mind, is conditioned by contemporary things, our minimum, in a time when the old atom is "bombarded" by electricity, when chemical atoms and elements are more strictly considered, is no longer the minimum of the sixteenth century pre-chemists. Both this composer and this executant [the violinist Olga Rudge, Pound's companion . . .] have acquired—perhaps only half-consciously—a new precision. . . .[7]

> Musical moralists have damned in my presence that very tough baby George Antheil. . . . He was imperfectly schooled, in music, in letters, in all things, but he nevertheless did once demand bits of SOLIDITY, he demanded short hard bits of rhythm hammered down, worn down so that they were indestructible and unbendable. He wanted these gristly and undeformable "monads."[8]

Antheil, therefore, became the musical equivalent of a mosaic-maker, taking harsh, simple fragments and carefully arranging them onto what he called a time-canvas. One of the most remarkable features of the *Ballet Mécanique* was its conscious play with the concept of figure and background—a concept derived, of course, from the visual arts: in the first third of the piece, Antheil poses his music bits against the background of a steady roar (the propellers' whap-whap); in the last third, against the background of long periods of silence. (Note that these remarks apply only to Antheil's original score, not to the bowdlerized version of 1952–53.)

6. Ibid., 344.
7. Ibid., 316.
8. Pound, *Guide to Kulchur* (New York: New Directions, 1970), 94–95.

GEORGE ANTHEIL
Letter to Nicolas Slonimsky (1936)

I personally consider that the *Ballet Mécanique* was important in one particular and this is that it was conceived in a new form, that form specifically being the filling out of a certain time canvas with musical abstractions and sound material composed and contrasted against one another with the thought of time values rather than tonal values. . . . Now in order to paint musical pictures one must admit right at the outset that the only canvas of music can be time. Music does not exist all at once like a painting but it unrolls itself. Nevertheless, we must consider it in the terms of painting as something that exists all at once. In other words, time is our musical canvas, not the notes and timbres of the orchestra or the melodies and tunes or the tonal forms handed down to us by the great masters. In the *Ballet Mécanique* I used time as Picasso might have used the blank spaces of his canvas. I did not hesitate, for instance, to repeat one measure one hundred times; I did not hesitate to have absolutely nothing on my pianola rolls for sixty-two bars; I did not hesitate to ring a bell against a certain given section of time or indeed to do whatever I pleased to do with the time canvas as long as each part of it stood up against the other. My ideas were the most abstract of the abstract.

From Linda Whitesitt, *Life and Music of George Antheil, 1900–1959* (Ann Arbor: University of Michigan Research Press, 1983), 105–6.

GEORGE ANTHEIL
"Composer's Notes on 1952–53 Re-Editing" [of *Ballet Mécanique*] (1953)

BALLET MECANIQUE, while utilizing (subconsciously, for at the time this work was written, 12 tone-ism was unknown as such) both systems [tonality and "12 tone-ism"], concentrated on what I then called "the time canvas." Rather than to consider musical form as a series of tonalities, atonalities with a tonal center, or a tonal center at all, it supposed that music actually takes place in time; and that, therefore, time is the real construction principle, "stuff of music," as it unreels. It is the musician's "canvas." The tones which he uses, therefore, are merely his crayons, his colors. The "Time-Space" principle, therefore, is an aesthetic of "looking," so to speak, at a piece of music "all at once." One might propose, therefore, that it is a sort of "Fourth Dimension"-al way of looking at music; its constructive principles may, or may not have been touched in this work, but they have been attempted.

From George Antheil, *Ballet Mécanique* (Water Gap, Del.: Shawnee Press, 1961).

■

Other sensitive listeners understood the collage-quality of certain Modernist musical compositions, but did not delight in it—especially Theodor Wiesengrund Adorno

(1903–69). A student of Alban Berg's, Adorno wrote a number of rather well-behaved atonal compositions, including some songs for a stage work, *The Treasure of Indian Joe,* based on (of all writers) Mark Twain. But Adorno left his mark less as a composer than as a brilliant philosopher-musician whose aesthetic and political theories were energized by powerful antagonisms—to capitalism, to nostalgia, and, perhaps most remarkably, to Stravinsky. Adorno understood Stravinsky as the source of most of the twentieth century's musical vices: in the course of *Philosophy of Modern Music* (1948), Adorno called Stravinsky an acrobat, a civil servant, a tailor's dummy, hebephrenic, psychotic, infantile, fascistic, and devoted to making money. What was Stravinsky's crime? Partly that the Neoclassicism Stravinsky had pioneered in *Pulcinella* (1919) seemed to Adorno a regression to a stupider world, a refusal to explore the paths of human advancement, namely the path taken, in music, by Schoenberg. But Adorno considered that much of Stravinsky's depravity comes from his essentially pictorial method of writing music: Adorno, like Lessing, thought that any composer who used models from the visual arts was perverse and destructive. Adorno insisted on musical progress, just as he insisted on historical progress; and a composer who denied progressivity, either on the level of the static individual composition or on the level of the centuries-long development of musical art, was to Adorno anathema.

Adorno leads into the theme of Stravinsky's pseudomorphism—that is, Stravinsky's adoption of visual models for music—through a meditation on Stravinsky's habit of writing music about music, music stitched together from the scattered limbs of old compositions. Adorno, then, begins with a consideration of Stravinsky as a willful child playing with the toys of long-established musical turns of phrase—and as the Frankenstein of music.

THEODOR ADORNO
from *Philosophy of Modern Music* (1948)

An artful *"mal fait"* [ill-made] replaces the French *"bien fait"* [well-made]: music about music insists that it is not a microcosm fulfilled within itself, but rather the reflection of shattered depletion. Its calculated errors are related to the open contours of legitimate contemporary painting—such as that of Picasso;[9] such painting dismantles every hermetic aspect of the depicted figure. Parody, the basic form of music about music, implies the imitation of something and its resulting degradation through this imitation. This attitude—which the bourgeois regarded suspiciously as the attitude of the intellectual music-maker—adapts to regression with ease. Infantile music treats its model in a manner much like that of the child who takes apart his toys and puts them

---

9. Pablo Picasso (1881–1973), Spanish painter who lived in France. Adorno is referring to the Cubist style of dismantling a figure into a heap of facets.

together again incorrectly. In this unnaturalness there is an element which is not entirely domesticated, an undisciplined mimetic factor—indeed, something of true nature itself. This might well be the way in which primitives would portray a missionary through dance, before they devour him. The impulse in this direction, however, has proceeded from civilizing forces, which scorn affectionate imitation and tolerate it only as a mutilating force. . . . The evil glance at the model casts a spell of bondage upon music about music. It atrophies through its dependence upon heteronomy. It is as though it could expect of its compositional content nothing more than that which is present in the shabbiness of that music, the reverse reflection which determines fortune. The danger of the musical man of letters with his various reaction patterns, the justification of the music hall against Wagner's *Parsifal*,[10] of the player piano against the intoxication of string instruments, of a romantic dream-America against the childlike horrors of German Romanticism—all of this is not an excess of cognizance, exhaustion, and differentiation, but rather of half-wittedness. It becomes evident as soon as music about music conceals the quotation marks.

DISSOCIATION OF TIME

The remnants of the memory are joined together; direct musical material is not developed out of its own driving force. The composition is realized not through development, but through the faults which permeate its structure. These assume the role which earlier was the province of expression: this recalls the statement which Eisenstein[11] once made about film montage; he explained that the "general concept"—the meaning, that is, or the synthesis of partial elements of the theme—proceeded precisely out of their juxtaposition as separated, isolated elements. This results, however, in the dissociation of the musical time continuum itself. Stravinsky's music remains a peripheral phenomenon in spite of the extension of its style over the entire younger generation, because it avoids the dialectical confrontation with the musical progress of time. This, in turn, is the basis of all great music since Bach. The eradication of time, however, which is accomplished by rhythmic tricks, is no sudden achievement of Stravinsky. Ever since *Sacre*[12] he had been proclaimed as the anti-pope to Impressionism; from Impressionism he learned musical "timelessness." Anyone who has been schooled in German and Austrian music and who has listened to Debussy will be familiar with the experience of frustrated expectation. Throughout any one of his composi-

10. *Parsifal* (1882), a "stage-consecration-festival-play" by Richard Wagner (1813–83). Adorno was suspicious of the highly refined mystical harmonies of late Wagner.

11. Sergei Eisenstein, *The Film Sense* (New York, 1942), 30. [Adorno's note.] Sergei Eisenstein (1898–1948) was a Soviet film director who advocated montage—that is, rapid splicing of not-obviously-related film clips—in order to investigate the aesthetics of juxtaposition in time.

12. *Le sacre du printemps* (*The Rite of Spring*) had a scandalous première in 1913.

tions, the naive ear listens tensely, asking whether "it is coming"; everything appears to be a prelude, the overture to musical fulfillment, to the organic resolution of the *Abgesang* [13]—which, however, never arrives. The ear must be re-educated if it is to understand Debussy correctly, seeking not a process of obstruction and release, but perceiving a juxtaposition of colors and surfaces such as are to be found in a painting. The succession simply expounds what is simultaneous for sensory perception: this is the way the eye wanders over the canvas. Technically, this is accomplished at first by "functionless" harmony. . . . The tensions of step-progression are not executed within the key or by modulations; instead harmonic complexes relieve each other. These complexes can be either static or exchangeable in time. The harmonic play of forces is replaced through the exchange of forces; conceptually, this is not dissimilar to the complementary harmony [14] of twelve-tone technique. Everything else proceeds out of the harmonic thought peculiar to Impressionism: the suspended treatment of form—a treatment which actually excludes "development"; the predominance of a type of character piece, which originated in the salon—it acquires its dominance at the expense of actual symphonic structure even in lengthier compositions; the absence of counterpoint; and finally a superior coloration, allotted to harmonic complexes. There is no "end"; the composition ceases as does the picture, upon which the viewer turns his back. In Debussy this tendency became gradually intensified up to the second volume of the *Preludes* and the ballet *Jeux;* [15] in his works it is characterized by a growing atomization of thematic substance. . . .

MUSIC—A PSEUDOMORPHISM OF PAINTING

The analogy which has been noted repeatedly between the transition from Debussy to Stravinsky in music, and the development from Impressionistic painting to Cubism, demonstrates more than a vague common denominator of cultural history, according to which music limped along behind literature and painting at the customary distance. The development of a spatial perspective in music is much rather a testimony of a pseudomorphism of painting in music. At its innermost core, it is the abdication of music. This might at first be explained with regard to the unique situation in France, where the development of productive forces in painting was so far superior to those in music

13. *Abgesang:* closing section (a term from the *Bar-Abgesang* structure of the songs of the old German *Meistersinger*).

14. "The law of vertical dimension of twelve-tone music might well be called the law of complementary harmony . . . where there is no harmonic progress in terms of the rules of thorough bass, but rather static levels of sound which permit only a selection from the twelve tones and then suddenly change into new levels of sound which provide for the remaining tones." Adorno, *Philosophy of Modern Music,* 81.

15. *Jeux* (1913), Debussy's shadowed and wispy music for a tennis-match ballet (1862–1918).

that musicians involuntarily sought support in great painting. But the victory of genius in painting over genius in music submits to the positivistic trend of the entire age. All painting—even abstract—has its pathos in that which is; all music purports a becoming. This, however, is exactly what, in Stravinsky, music attempts to evade through the fiction of its mere existence.[16] In Debussy the individual color complexes were still related to each other and mediated as in the tradition of Wagner's "art of transition": sound is not devaluated, but soars for the moment beyond its boundaries. A perspective of sensory infinity is attained by means of such confluence. In Impressionistic paintings, whose technique absorbed music, dynamic effects and light impressions are produced according to the same procedures through the juxtaposition of spots of color. That sensory infinity was the poetic-aural nature of Impressionism in its age; the artistic rebellion shortly before the First World War was directed against it. Stravinsky directly adopted the conception of music involving spaciousness and surface expanse from Debussy; and his technique of complexes as well as the make-up of his atomized melodic models also illustrate[s] Debussy's influence. The innovation actually consists only in the severance of the connecting threads and the demolition of remnants of the differential-dynamic procedure. The partial spatial complexes stand in harsh contrast to one another. The polemic negation of the gentle reverberation is fashioned into the proof of force, and the disconnected end-product of dynamics is stratified like blocks of marble. What earlier had sounded congruent unto itself now establishes its independence as an anorganic chord. The spatial dimension becomes absolute: the aspect

16. The bourgeois idea of the pantheon would like to join painting and music in a peaceful relationship. Their relationship, however—in spite of synaesthetic double talents—is contradictory to the point of incompatibility. This became obvious precisely at that point where their union was proclaimed in cultural philosophy, that is, in Wagner's concept of the composite work of art—the *Gesamtkunstwerk* [total art work]. The plastic aspect of this idea was from the outset so rudimentary that it is hardly amazing that Bayreuth performances, representing the absolute height of musical perfections, were presented with hopelessly outmoded stage settings. Thomas Mann has pointed out the "dilettante" aspect involved in the concept of unification of the arts. He defines this dilettantism as an essentially unartistic relationship to painting. From Rome and from Paris, Wagner wrote to Mathilde Wesendonk: ". . . my eyes are not enough for me to use to take in the world," and ". . . Raphael never touches me." He continued: "See everything for me" (Thomas Mann, "The Sufferings and Greatness of Richard Wagner," *Essays of Three Decades*, trans. H. T. Lowe-Porter [New York, 1948], 316–17). For this reason Wagner calls himself a "vandal." He was guided by the presentiment that music contains an element not grasped by the process of civilization—which has not been fully subjugated to objectified reason—while the art of the eye, which holds to the deigned objects—to the objective practical world—reveals itself to be intimately related to the spirit of technological progress. The pseudomorphism of music with the technique of painting capitulates before the superior power of rational technology in that very sphere of art which had its essence in protest against such rational domination and which nevertheless became the victim of progressive rational domination of nature. [Adorno's note.]

of atmosphere, in which all Impressionistic music retains something of the subjective experience of time, is eradicated.

THEORY OF BALLET MUSIC

Stravinsky and his school bring about the end of musical Bergsonianism.[17] They play off *le temps espace*[18] against *le temps durée*. The procedural method originally inspired by irrationalistic philosophy establishes itself as the advocate of rationalization in the sense of that which can be measured and counted without memory.[19] Music,

17. The French philosopher Henri Bergson (1859–1941) emphasized the spontaneous and unpredictable flux of human experience—which takes places not in abstract time but in felt time, *la durée* (duration). Bergson influenced the fiction of Marcel Proust.

18. *le temps espace:* time-space, or spatialized time.

19. The *Histoire du soldat* [*The Soldier's Tale,* 1918] further reveals itself as the true focal point of Stravinsky's work in that, in the composition of the Ramuz [C. F. Ramuz, Swiss author] text, the score leads to the very threshold of consciousness of the state of affairs expressed in the text. The hero—a prototype of that generation after the First World War, out of which fascism recruited the hordes who were ready to march to the battlefields—perishes because he transgresses against the commandment of the unemployed: to live only for the moment. The continuity of experience in his memory is the mortal enemy of self-preservation which can be gained only through self-annihilation. In the English text the narrator warns the soldier:

> One can't add what one had to what one has
> Nor to the thing one is, the thing one was.
> No one has a right to have everything—
> It is forbidden.
> A single happiness is complete happiness
> To add to it is to destroy it. . . .

This is the anxiety-ridden, irrefutable maxim of positivism, the proscription of the recurrence of everything past, which would threaten regression into myth—it would represent deliverance to forces which in the composition are embodied by the devil. The princess complains that she has never heard the soldier speak about his earlier life; thereupon he vaguely mentions the city where his mother lived. His sin—the transgression of the narrow boundaries of the kingdom—can hardly be understood as anything but a visit to that city: as a sacrifice to the past. "La recherche du temps perdu est interdite" ["The search for lost time"—the title of Proust's novel—"is forbidden"]—this is of greater validity for no other art form than that for which the innermost law is regression. The regressive transformation of the subject into its pre-worldly being is made possible by cutting him off from the means by which he might become aware of himself. The soldier remains under the spell of the mere present; this fact unravels the taboo which prevails throughout Stravinsky's music. The jerky, blatantly present repetitions in the music should be understood as the means by which permanence can be given a dimension in memory while remaining static. These repetitions further serve to uproot the protected past from within the music. Traces thereof form the background both of the mother and the taboo. The course "back to the land of childhood"—as prescribed in the song by Brahms [*Heimweh,* op. 63

which has become the victim of its own confusion, fears—in the face of the expansion of technology in the late stage of capitalism—that it might regressively fall victim to the contradiction between itself and technology. Music escapes this momentarily by means of a ballet-like leap, but in so doing it becomes all the more deeply enmeshed in the dilemma. Stravinsky, to be sure, hardly ever concerned himself with machine art in the sense of the ominous "tempos of the time." On the other hand, his music is concerned with types of human attitudes which view the ubiquity of technique as a schema of the entire life process: whoever wishes to avoid being crushed by the wheels of the times must react in the same manner as this music does. Today there is no music showing any trace of the power of the historical hour that has remained totally unaffected by the decline of experience—by the substitution, for "life," of a process of economic adjustment dictated by concentrated economic forces of domination. The dying out of subjective time in music seems totally unavoidable in the midst of a humanity which had made itself into a thing—into an object of its own organization. The result is that similar aspects can be observed at the extreme poles of composition. The Expressionistic miniature of the new Viennese School contracts the time dimension by expressing—in Schoenberg's words—"an entire novel through a single gesture."[20] Furthermore, in the most convincing twelve-tone compositions, time plays a role through an integral procedure seemingly without development, because it tolerates nothing outside itself upon which development could experiment. However, there is a significant difference between such a change in time-consciousness in the inner organization of music and the established pseudomorphism of the spatial dimension within musical time—its inhibition through shock and electric blows which disrupt its continuity. In this inner change, on the one hand, music—in the unconscious depth of its structure—lags far behind the historical destiny of time-consciousness. In the pseudomorphism, on the other hand, it establishes itself as an arbiter of time, causing the listener to forget the subjective and psychological experience of time in music and to abandon himself to its spatialized dimension. It proclaims, as its unique achievement the fact that there is no longer any life—as though it had achieved the objectification of life. For this reason, immanent revenge descends upon it. One trick characterizes all of Stravinsky's formal endeavors: the effort of this music to portray time as in a circus tableau and to present time complexes as though they were spatial. This trick, however, soon exhausts itself. He loses his power over the consciousness of continuousness: continu-

---

no. 8]—becomes the cardinal sin of an art which would like to restore the pre-subjective aspect of childhood. [Adorno's note.]

20. Arnold Schoenberg, foreword to Webern's *Six Bagatelles* (1924)—see *Style and Idea*, ed. Leonard Stein, trans. Leo Black (Berkeley: University of California Press, 1984), 483.

ousness now reveals itself and appears heteronomously. It discloses Stravinsky's musical intentions as a lie, unmasking this intention as nothing but boredom. Instead of working out the tension between music and time in composition, he plays another of his tricks upon this tension. Therefore, all those forces shrivel in his hands, which otherwise thrive in music, whenever it absorbs time into itself. The mannerized impoverishment which asserts itself, as soon as Stravinsky attempts to go beyond his speciality, is encumbered by the spatial expansion. To the extent that he renounced all possible means for the production of time-relationships—transition, intensification, the distinction between the field of tension and the field of release, further of exposition and continuation, and of question and answer—all artistic musical means fall under this edict, with the exception of his one artistic trick.[21] A regression now sets in— justified by the literary-regressive intention—but it becomes his undoing when the absolute musical demand is seriously raised. The weakness of Stravinsky's production during the last twenty-five years—which can be detected even by the most insensitive ear—is not just a matter of the composer having nothing more or new to say. It rather arises out of a chain of events which degrades music to the status of a parasite of painting. That weakness—the non-intrinsic element in the general compositional make-up of Stravinsky—is the price he has had to pay for his restriction to the dance; although this limitation once seemed to him a guarantee of order and objectivity. From the beginning it imposed upon his music an aspect of servitude which required the renunciation of autonomy. True dance—in contrast to mature music—is an art of static time, a turning in a circle, movement without progress. It was in this consciousness that sonata form came to replace dance form: throughout the entire history of modern music—with

21. Stravinsky is in many respects the opposite pole of Gustav Mahler, to whom he is nevertheless related in his thoroughly disjunct compositional procedure. Stravinsky has often opposed the highest ambition of Mahler's symphonic composition: the concluding section, those moments in which music—having come to a standstill—must move on. Essentially he grounds his dictate over the listener (proof of the latter's impotence)—in the withholding of that which he feels entitled to for the sake of the element of tension in the models: this right is denied, and tension in itself—an undefined and irrational effort without a goal—is made the law of the composition and of its adequate perception as well. There is a tendency to become enthusiastic about a wicked man if he once does something respectable; in like manner, such music is praised for its moments of respectability. In rare exceptional cases of cleverness, the music permits conclusion-like sections which, by contrast—precisely by virtue of their rarity—border on ethereal bliss. An example is the intensive final "cantilena" from the "Danse de l'Élue" ["The Dance of the Chosen One," from *The Rite of Spring*] (from number 184 to number 186), before the last entrance of the rondo theme. But even here, where the violins are permitted to "sing themselves out" for a moment, the same, unchanged rigid ostinato remains in the accompaniment. The concluding section is not intrinsic in nature. [Adorno's note.] Presumably Adorno is thinking of the extremely slow endings of Mahler's Ninth Symphony and *Das Lied von der Erde* (both 1908–9).

the exception of Beethoven—minuets and scherzi have always been a matter of convenience and of secondary importance; this is particularly true when they are compared to serious sonata form and to the adagio. Music for the dance lies on this side
of—and not beyond—subjective dynamics; to this extent, it contains an anachronistic
element, which in Stravinsky stands in highly peculiar contrast to the literary-modish
success of his hostility towards expression. The past is foisted upon the future as a
changeling. It is suited to this purpose because of the disciplinary nature of the dance.
Stravinsky has restored it again. His accents are just so many acoustic signals to the
stage. He has, therewith, infused into dance music—from the viewpoint of its useful-
ness—a precision which it had totally forfeited beyond the pantomimic-psychologizing
or illustrative intentions of the Romantic ballet. A glance at Richard Strauss's *Josefslegende*[22] clarifies the drastic effect of the cooperation between Stravinsky and Diaghilev; something of this effect has adhered to the music, which—even as absolute music
—has not forgotten one moment of its danceability. All symbolic intermediate instances, however, have been removed from the relationship between dance and music;
as a result, that fatal principle gains control which everyday speech designates with expressions such as "dancing to one's tune." The effective relationship for which Stravinsky's music strives is, to be sure, not the identification of the public with psychic impulses which are supposedly expressed in the dance. Stravinsky aspired, rather, for an
electrification equal to that of the dancer.

From *Philosophy of Modern Music,* trans. Anne G. Mitchell and Wesley V. Blomster (New York:
Seabury, 1973), 186–97.

Adorno's revulsion against pseudomorphisms of painting in music were echoed by
other critics. For example, the art historian Clement Greenberg (1909–94)—whom
Adorno cited with approval in *Philosophy of Modern Music*—wrote an essay called "Towards a Newer Laocoon" (1940), a deliberate sequel to Lessing's *Laokoon.* Lessing believed that the arts of time and the arts of space should have nothing to do with one another; Greenberg isolates and confines the arts still further by arguing that every art is
confined to its own medium and should have nothing to do with artworks that use other
media—"to restore the identity of an art the opacity of its medium must be emphasized."[23] The puritanical Greenberg resists the slightest erasure of the lines that divide
one art form from another. He provides a simple criterion for success: a work of art is

22. Richard Strauss (1864–1949) wrote *Josephslegende* (*Legend of Joseph,* 1914), commissioned, like
Stravinsky's *Rite of Spring* and Debussy's *Jeux,* for the Ballets Russes by the impresario Serge Diaghilev
(1872–1929).

23. Clement Greenberg, *The Collected Essays and Criticism,* vol. 1, ed. John O'Brien (Chicago: University of Chicago Press, 1986), 32.

good to the extent that it displays the substantiality of its medium, without dissembling or fraud. Painting is a thrusting forth of pigment; sculpture is an extancy of metal, an inertia of stone; music is naked sound. The barrier between music and painting (or any other form of art) should be wholly impermeable. This artistic purism is strongly anti-Romantic, in that it contradicts Wagner's notion of the *Gesamtkunstwerk*, the total artwork in which the component media fuse into a single gigantic experience.

But many composers in the second half of the twentieth century have paid little attention to the warnings of Adorno and Greenberg and have continued to experiment in crossovers from music to painting. One gifted and intelligent worker in this field was the American composer Morton Feldman (1926–87), who felt that the dominant influences in his music came from the painters he knew.

MORTON FELDMAN
[Time-Canvas]

Soon after meeting [Robert] Rauschenberg I met Jackson Pollock, who asked me to write music for a film about him. . . . In thinking back to that time I realize now how much the musical ideas I had in 1951 paralleled his mode of working. Pollock placed his canvas on the ground and painted as he walked around it. I put sheets of graph paper on the wall; each sheet framed the same time duration and was, in effect, a visual rhythmic structure. What resembled Pollock was my "all over" approach to the time-canvas. Rather than the usual left-to-right passage across the page, the horizontal squares of the graph paper represented the tempo—with each box equal to a preestablished ictus; and the vertical squares were the instrumentation of the composition. . . .

Stasis, as it is utilized in painting, is not traditionally part of the apparatus of music. Music can achieve aspects of immobility, or the illusion of it: the Magrittelike world Satie evokes, or the "floating sculptures" of [Edgard] Varèse. The degrees of stasis, found in a [Mark] Rothko or a [Philip] Guston, were perhaps the most significant elements that I brought to my music from painting.

From *Essays*, ed. Walter Zimmermann (Kerpen: Beginner Press, 1985), 136–37.

Some of Feldman's early scores even have the Monopoly-board look of such paintings by the Dutch abstractionist Piet Mondrian as *Broadway Boogie Woogie* (1942–43)—itself an example of the opposite pseudomorphism, of music in painting. Such graphic scores were not Feldman's invention. The remarkable innovator Arthur Lourié (1892–1967), a Russian composer much influenced by Italian Futurism, devised some piano pieces, called *Formes en l'air* (1915), notated as a constellation of musical fragments on a

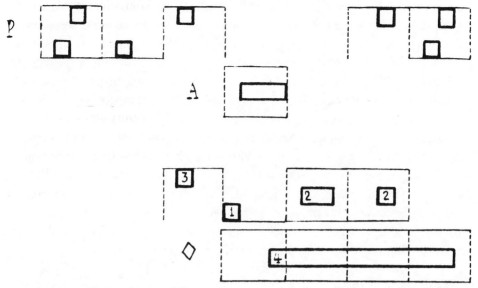

Morton Feldman, *Projection 4* for violin and piano (1951). From Feldman, *Essays,* ed. Walter Zimmerman (Kerpen: Beginner Press, 1985), 27. © 1959 by C. F. Peters Corp. Used by permission. All rights reserved.

white background, so that the pianist has to figure out a strategy for interpreting the spatial configuration as sound and silence.

■

A still more adventurous pseudomorphism can be found in the work of the Greek composer Iannis Xenakis (1922–2001): that of music and architecture. Xenakis was fascinated by the notion that a single idea might develop itself in two different media— might take shape as either a musical composition or a building. He therefore sought equivalents between spatial extension and music, such as line = glissando, or point = string pizzicato. Xenakis had mathematical training and sought to imbue both music and architecture with the rigor of science—but a science of rifts and indeterminacies, of probability distributions, not a science of predictable motions and logical designs.

Xenakis can be formidably technical, but his music draws force from many different Modernist traditions. *Medea* (1967), setting Seneca, and *A Colone* (1977), setting Sophocles, are among a number of his compositions based on classical tragedy; and the stark ritual sonorities of such works as Stravinsky's *Les noces* (*The Wedding,* 1917–23) are sometimes audible. Xenakis's glissandi can be heard as images of the distribution of gas molecules, or they can be heard as shrieks; and in such a work as *Nuits* (1967), the inscription in the score dedicating it to four Greek political prisoners tends to invite the Expressionist interpretation. Xenakis himself was active in the anti-Nazi Greek resistance movement and lost an eye during the battle for Athens; political readings of many of his works are quite possible. It is no accident that he describes stochastic music, in the passage printed below, in terms of the propagation of slogans through crowds at a political rally.

In 1976 Xenakis became interested in ways of using a computer to interpret pictures as sounds; and his *Mycenae-Alpha* (1978) came into being through a computer's interpretation of a drawing of various sorts of steady or wavering lines, free-form ramifying bulges, graphed as frequency over time. Through such models as these, music and the static visual arts can effortlessly trade places, through a cycle of thawings and freezings. Xenakis even insisted that the interpretation of music was exactly like the interpretation of sculpture: "Music is no language. Every piece of music is a sort of complicatedly shaped rock with scratches and patterns cut into it, and people can decipher in a thousand different ways, without any particular way being the best or truest." [24]

IANNIS XENAKIS
from *Formalized Music*

There exists a historical parallel between European music and the successive attempts to explain the world by reason. The music of antiquity, causal and determinate, was already strongly influenced by the schools of Pythagoras and Plato. Plato insisted on the principle of causality, "for it is impossible for anything to come into being with cause." (*Timaeus*). Strict causality lasted until the nineteenth century when it underwent a brutal and fertile transformation as a result of statistical theories in physics. Since antiquity the concepts of chance (*tyche*), disorder (*ataxia*), and disorganization were considered as the opposite and negation of reason (*logos*), order (*taxis*), and organization (*systasis*). It is only recently that knowledge has been able to penetrate chance and to rationalize it progressively. . . .

As a result of the impasse in serial music [which has collapsed from the excessive complexity of linear polyphony], as well as other causes, I originated in 1954 a music constructed from the principle of indeterminism; two years later I named it "Stochastic Music." The laws of the calculus of probabilities entered composition through musical necessity.

But other paths also led to the same stochastic crossroads—first of all, natural events such as the collision of hail or rain with hard surfaces, or the song of cicadas in a summer field. These sonic events are made out of thousands of isolated sounds; this multitude of sounds, seen as a totality, is a new sonic event. This mass event is

---

24. Iannis Xenakis, program note to *La légende d'Eer*, Darmstädter Ferien Kurse für Neue Musik, July 1977.

articulated and forms a plastic mold of time, which itself follows aleatory and stochastic laws. If one then wishes to form a large mass of point-notes, such as string pizzicati, one must know these mathematical laws, which, in any case, are no more than a tight and concise expression of a chain of logical reasoning. Everyone has observed the sonic phenomena of a political crowd of dozens or hundreds of thousands of people. The human river shouts a slogan in a uniform rhythm. Then another slogan springs from the head of the demonstration; it spreads toward the tail, replacing the first. A wave of transition thus passes from the head to the tail. The clamor fills the city, and the inhibiting force of voice and rhythm reaches a climax. It is an event of great power and beauty in its ferocity. Then the impact between the demonstrators and the enemy occurs. The perfect rhythm of the last slogan breaks up in a huge cluster of chaotic shouts, which also spreads to the tail. Imagine, in addition, the reports of dozens of machine guns and the whistle of bullets adding their punctuations to this total disorder. The crowd is then rapidly dispersed, and after sonic and visual hell follows a detonating calm, full of despair, dust, and death. The statistical laws of these events, separated from their political or moral context, are the same as those of the cicadas or the rain. They are the laws of the passage from complete order to total disorder in a continuous or explosive manner. They are stochastic laws.

Here we touch on one of the great problems that have haunted human intelligence since antiquity: continuous or discontinuous transformation. The sophisms of movement (e.g., Achilles and the tortoise) or of definition (e.g., baldness), especially the latter, are solved by statistical definition; that is to say, by stochastics. One may produce continuity with either continuous or discontinuous elements. A multitude of short glissandi on strings can give the impression of continuity, and so can a multitude of pizzicati. Passages from a discontinuous state to a continuous state are controllable with the aid of probability theory. For some time now I have been conducting these fascinating experiments in instrumental works; but the mathematical character of this music has frightened musicians and has made the approach especially difficult.

Here is another direction that converges on indeterminism. The study of the variation of rhythm poses the problem of knowing what the limit of total asymmetry is, and of the consequent complete disruption of causality among durations. The sounds of a Geiger counter in the proximity of a radioactive source give an impressive idea of this. Stochastics provides the necessary laws.

. . . If glissandi are long and sufficiently interlaced, we obtain sonic spaces of continuous evolution. It is possible to produce ruled surfaces by drawing the glissandi as straight lines. I performed this experiment with [the musical composition] *Metastasis* (this work had its premiere in 1955 in Donaueschingen). Several years later, when the architect Le Corbusier, whose collaborator I was, asked me to suggest a design for the architecture of the Philips Pavilion in Brussels [for the World's Fair of 1958], my inspiration was pin-pointed by the experiment with *Metastasis*. Thus I believe that on this occasion music and architecture found an intimate connection.

From *Formalized Music: Thought and Mathematics in Composition*, trans. Christopher Butchers (Bloomington: Indiana University Press, 1971), 1, 4, 9–10.

EMBODYING PHYSICAL MOVEMENT: BALLET AND FILM

Now we turn to the relationship of music to the visual arts that move, such as dance and cinema. Here the problem of pseudomorphism requires less novel solutions, since plastic arts of these kinds have a temporal component. But a good deal of Modernist ingenuity was still required to find satisfactory ways of relating music to visual shape-shiftings.

Adorno's belief that dance is an essentially vain and static art is probably derived in part from the piecemeal construction of many of the older ballet scores, which sometimes seem tacked together, accreted juxtapositively: there is likely to be little musical consequence in a spectacle organized around star turns for solo dancers, who (like opera singers) occasionally inserted favorite numbers from earlier ballets. Despite the existence of such impressive (and to some degree symphonically integrated) scores as Tchaikovsky's *Swan Lake* (1877), the status of ballet at the beginning of the twentieth century was low, and in certain quarters remained low: Adorno's distaste for ballet can be found throughout much of Schoenberg's Second Viennese School—although Schoenberg's teacher Alexander von Zemlinsky wrote a long ballet, *The Triumph of Time* (1901–4), in collaboration with Hugo von Hofmannsthal. It was a daring choice for a composer as ambitious as Stravinsky to stake his career on such a disreputable genre as ballet.

But by the end of the nineteenth century the rehabilitation of ballet had already begun. Edgar Degas had made countless drawings and paintings (and even some sculptures) of ballerinas in tutus; and in 1886 the Symbolist poet Stéphane Mallarmé wrote of ballet in the most transcendentally rhapsodic terms:

The dancing woman . . . *is not a woman who dances* . . . but a metaphor summing up one of the elementary aspects of our form, sword, cup, flower, etc., and . . . suggesting, through the wonder of abridgements and leaps [*élans*], with a corporeal scripture what one would need many paragraphs of dialogue as well as descriptive prose to express . . . a poem disengaged from all the apparatus of writing.[25]

25. Stéphane Mallarmé, *Oeuvres complètes* (Tours: Bibliothèque de la Pléiade, Éditions Gallimard, 1950), 304; translated by the editor.

It is interesting that Mallarmé conceived ballet as a pseudomorphism of written language in dance—as if a ballet were a sequence of hieroglyphs embodied in the visible shapes of the dancers. On the level of language, by means of gestural intensification, music could aspire to meet dance.

One of the most intriguing Modernist writers on the relationship of music to dance came from an area far from classical ballet: calisthenics. Émile Jaques-Dalcroze (1865–1950) was the great exercise guru of Modernism, but, far from being an early version of Richard Simmons or Jane Fonda, he was a widely cultured man who devoted his life to promoting the status of kinesthetics—what he called "living plastic"—as an autonomous art capable of interacting with other arts, especially music. He was a composer and a professor of harmony, but his great contribution was to imagine new ways, far outside the traditional province of dance, to conceive physical movement as art.

Dalcroze's influence was amazingly diverse: in D. H. Lawrence's novel *Women in Love* (1920), two women improvise a little ballet by using Dalcroze movements; and Dalcroze was a crucial factor in the choreography of *The Rite of Spring,* because in 1913 Diaghilev decided that the new choreography of the Ballets Russes should be based on Dalcroze exercise movements. And so the dancers traveled to the Dalcroze institute at Hellerau, near Dresden, to learn the system. In the classes, for example, women would be taught to walk to the 2/4 beat of a piece of music while gesticulating with one arm to a 3/4 beat and with the other to a 4/4 beat—as Bronislava Nijinska, the choreographer of Stravinsky's *Renard* and *Les noces,* explained. Her brother, Vaslav Nijinsky, choreographed *The Rite of Spring* using Dalcroze's method for direct translation of musical rhythm into physical motion—a method that produced such radically antiballetic movement that Debussy complained, after his own ballet *Jeux* was given the same sort of Nijinsky-Dalcroze treatment,

> Nijinsky has given an odd mathematical twist to his perverse genius. This fellow adds up semiquavers with his feet, proves the result with his arms and then as if suddenly struck by paralysis of one side listens for a while to the music, disapprovingly. This it appears is to be called the stylization of gesture. *How awful! It is in fact Dalcrozian and this is to tell you that I hold Monsieur Dalcroze to be one of the worst enemies of music!*[26]

To read this one would think that Dalcroze advocated such a little transposition of music into swaying human bodies that a dance was little more than a sort of oscilloscope—an apparatus for making sound visible.

This, however, was almost exactly the opposite of what Dalcroze wanted. He dreamed of a style of dancing that was essentially autonomous. The translation exercises that so

26. Cited in Bronislava Nijinska, *Early Memoirs,* trans. and ed. Irina Nijinska and Jean Rawlinson (Durham, N.C.: Duke University Press, 1992), 469.

impressed Nijinsky were only rudimentary stuff for beginners, as Dalcroze saw it. Long before Merce Cunningham was devising dances that took place in total silence, Dalcroze wrote that the end point of the evolution of dance would be a dance without music: "The final culmination of studies in moving plastic is certainly the direct expression of aesthetic feelings and emotion without the aid of music or even of speech."[27] It was undignified for dance to be an interpretation of music; instead, the dance should aspire to *be* music. And so Dalcroze hypothesized that dance would some day have its own diatonic scale: "the plastic artist [will] construct for himself a scale of gestures corresponding to that of sounds."[28] If sound music were to occur at the same time as this plastic music, Dalcroze hoped that the two musics would be in counterpoint, not unison.

Dalcroze's most visionary essay is "The Technique of Moving Plastic": there he writes with elation of the future of kinesthetics, imagined as a sort of Olympic Games in which all the sports are organized in the manner of synchronized swimming. Here is something like a symphony translated into pure bodily movement, a large-scale and minutely detailed universe of gesture, which has its sonatas of rising versus falling gymnasts, its fugues of javelin throwers—a totalized art of muscle contraction, in which everything that the human physique can do is done, and done beautifully. Dalcroze insists that each component art in multimedia spectacles must remain autonomous, yet he is fascinated by the ways in which one art can encroach on the domains of other arts—indeed the Dalcrozean Olympics is a game in which kinesthetics has become a whole Wagnerian opera. If Harry Partch called for a corporeal music, Dalcroze takes this idea about as far as it will go, by imagining a silent music incarnate in human bodies.

EMILE JAQUES-DALCROZE
"The Technique of Moving Plastic" (1922)

All the masterpieces of Doric sculpture prove the existence of rhythmic laws which regulate the relations of individuals with one another and the contrasts between various human groupings. All this presupposes on the part of the complete athlete a capacity for adapting himself to every physical rhythm in time and space. Now, in these days, we find many runners who are incapable of performing slow movements; wrestlers who cannot walk lightly; quoit-throwers unable to make any other gesture than that of throwing. Here is the danger of specialization, a danger incurred by many renowned pianists whose hands and fingers are nimble only when employed on the keyboard.

27. Émile Jaques-Dalcroze, *Eurhythmics Art and Education,* trans. Frederick Rothwell (London: Chatto and Windus, 1930), 28–29.
28. Ibid., 33.

Sport, I repeat, requires temperament; art requires in addition the sacrifice of certain individual powers to one collective power. The gymnastic exercises of masses of people frequently have extraordinarily powerful aesthetic effects, but they are all effects in simultaneity, whereas the gymnastic art we wish to create needs effects of opposition and contrast, as do all arts.

At a gymnastic fête in Geneva, some years ago, a few thousand gymnasts went through *ensemble* movements to musical accompaniment. The space of ground covered was so extensive that the musical rhythms were some time in reaching the most distant rows, the result being that movements involving bodily displacement, gestures and kneeling, were performed in "canon" style, i.e. the first rows kept time, those in the center were half a second and those farther away a full second later than the first, etc. The result was admirable, and this naturally-regulated polymotivity impressed the spectators far more powerfully than an exact synchronism would have done. It is effects of this kind that the gymnastic art in mass which we wish to create is called on to produce.

To these must be added the effects of contrast which are produced by opposite directions in bodily movement and displacement. Take, for instance, the simple act of kneeling and rising, and suppose that 100 gymnasts are kneeling whilst another 100 are rising: each of the two actions becomes intensified. Suppose, at the same time, that 100 gymnasts raise their arms, 100 others extend them, and that still other rows act simultaneously, some stepping forward, others backward or sideways, and we obtain an idea of spectacles of combined movements very easy to produce. The same in running: if an entire crowd runs, the impression is grandiose; if half the runners stop whilst the rest continue, the effect is doubled. It will be considerably increased if certain runners run twice as fast as the others, if those in certain rows make periodic leaps, if the runners spread out and draw in according to a previously arranged plan. A game of football (with a real or imaginary ball) arranged so as to obtain decorative groupings and single players crossing one another, will afford the spectators quite a different kind of emotion from that created by a real match. It will not be emotion caused by surprise, but emotion of an aesthetic order, created by the harmonies and counterpoints of movements. Doubtless the runners themselves will have less keen sensations than during a real contest, but the sensations will be quite as satisfying, for the joys procured by subordinating the individual to the whole are certainly equivalent to those procured by affirming one's full individuality. . . .

Think of the contrast between the various athletic activities, the movements of javelin-throwers combined with running and leaping movements, or contrasted with the movements of throwers of balls. Four hundred men hurl balls into the air, at double or quadruple speed, at different degrees of intensity: a veritable symphony of trajectories. All trades, all bodily activities may be distinctly expressed. The gestures of rowers,

of swimmers, of blacksmiths, road-menders, wood-cutters, navvies, mowers and sow-
ers, all supply us with material for distinctive expression. Then, too, the collaboration
of the natural human movements with those which necessitate mechanical intervention: ballets of cyclists, the simultaneous evolutions of motor-cars and riders on horseback! Some of these may seem fantastic, though such is not the case: each of these
suggestions could easily be put in practice.

So far I have said nothing of the humanization of the phenomena of nature, i.e. of
the imitation, by the body, of the motion of the wind upon fields of corn or waves of the
sea, of the placid lines of the horizon, swaying trees, the uneven swirl of a torrent, the
wide meanderings of a river, the gushing of a fountain, the incoming tide, the tumul-
tuous leaping of flames, or the activity of machines. At each Olympic festival, a general
subject might be offered for treatment by human movement, each team being permitted to interpret it after its own fashion. After competitions in strength, suppleness and
endurance, wrestling, running and games, there might be held competitions in imagination, organization and even improvisation.

For there is a new athletic activity to be created: the rapid improvisation of groupings, the arranging and adjusting of this living architecture through the sudden power
shown by some imaginative individual over the crowd, or by the intelligent subordination of groupings to the will of one or more controllers. In teaching *ensemble* gymnastic movements, insufficient scope is given for the development of the faculties of imagination and of the spontaneous creation of movements. This may also be affirmed of
the cinematograph, whose best group effects are most frequently due to chance, and
act on the spectators as picturesque swarmings rather than as aesthetic polyrhythms.
Into this domain also it will be necessary to introduce music, though music of a special
kind, having nothing in common with pure symphony except rhythm and sound, and,
as regards dynamism, obedient to quite new laws. This music will have to be wholly
inspired by a knowledge of corporal impulses and muscular rhythms, as well as of the
relations of space with the moving architecture which must occupy it. All attempt at picturesque harmony or counterpoint, all search for interest of timbre, must be subordinated to the physical action, or at least directly inspired by it. More than this, the music we need should not constantly accompany the physical manifestations. It should
call them forth and sustain them, draw them out without itself attempting to remain in
the foreground. It should also know how to be silent, to oppose its rhythms to those of
the bodily instrument, to counterpoint and unite with them without troubling about any
personal effect. The spectator must forget its very existence, though conscious of its
necessity. This music should originate so directly from corporal rhythms that the
dancers may regard it as the natural expression of their movements. . . .

Still, even though it be admitted that the art of moving plastic seeks further means of affirming its existence, and that, for the time being, it needs the aid of music, it must not be concluded that music needs to be supplemented by gesture. Music, indeed, is self-sufficing. Its aim, clearly defined and attained, is a dual one. On the one hand, thanks to the Apollonian spirit which inspired it, it frees us—as Nietzsche practically tells us in his book on the origin of Greek Tragedy—"from reality by the transfigured representation of appearance." On the other hand, thanks to the Dionysiac spirit with which it is likewise imbued, it initiates us in the most vivid manner into the "generating causes of Being and shows us the most secret bases of things." Simultaneously and successively it gives form to our dreams and opens out a free path to our unchained passions. Whether it manifests itself solely in the Apollonian fashion, as in certain works of Palestrina,[29] or solely in the Dionysiac fashion as in almost the whole of Beethoven's work, it still fully expresses "the essence of dreams and feelings, or that of realities and sensations." When moving plastic is capable, like music, of expressing all emotions without the collaboration of another art whilst giving an impression of order and style, of describing everything by suggestion, of harmoniously combining external forms whilst revealing the wildest rhythms of its subconsciousness—then it will live its own life, vibrate with its own rhythms, assert itself according to its own ordering. Emancipated from the laws of music, it will also be emancipated from those of architecture, it will renounce mimicry—a process accessory to imitation—it will have its own style, its forms and nuances. . . .

When, however, each of the arts becomes autodynamic and autonomous, none of them will be constrained to maintain for ever a splendid isolation. There will still have to be created the laws of a universal harmony, dictating for each specialized art what sacrifices and   eliminations will be necessary for effective collaboration. And then, by means of these eliminations, each of the arts, without losing its own personality, may be called upon to supplement a sister art, which for the time being has voluntarily decided not to be constantly using all its means of expression. And in certain circumstances we shall find all the arts blending in one grand symphony. There will appear works in which moving plastic, for instance, will constitute the element of order; music, the element of emotion; words, the element of dreamland . . . and vice versa. All combinations will become possible, and discussion as to the expediency of a fusion of all aesthetic elements will become futile.

From *Eurhythmics Art and Education,* trans. Frederick Rothwell (London: Chatto and Windus, 1930), 40–46.

29. Giovanni Pierluigi da Palestrina (ca. 1525–94), composer of polyphonic masses and motets, famous for euphony.

■

When the cinema appeared, Jean Cocteau referred to it as the tenth Muse,[30] as if the cinema were a wholly unprecedented novelty in the history of art. It certainly owed something to some of the first nine Muses, including Polyhymnia (mime) and Thalia (comedy); but it is hard to find any Greek Muse that pertains to disrupted images of action spliced together. In any case, the existence of film created for composers both a new market and new challenges. Here was a genre without a history, a technological artifact of Modernism. What role did music have to play in it?

From the beginning, music was considered indispensable, partly because it covered the racket of the projector's sprocket. In provincial movie theaters, a pianist was given a few cues and asked to improvise the rest of the accompaniment: the heroine of D. H. Lawrence's *Lost Girl* (1912–20) is such an accompanist, and the very young Dmitri Shostakovich earned his living in this manner—he once got into trouble with the management because he became so engrossed in a Charlie Chaplin routine that he stopped playing. But in large cities there were a few theaters that spared no expense to provide lavish musical entertainment. The elderly Camille Saint-Saëns was hired in 1908 to write music for a small orchestra for André Calmettes's film *L'assassinat du duc de Guise;* and by the end of the silent film era, in the later 1920s, a certain tendency to musical gargantuanism could be noticed, in Arthur Honegger's lavish score to Abel Gance's *Napoléon* (1926–27), shown at the Paris Opéra-Comique, with a panoramic three-projector system and tinting in the colors of the French flag—or in Shostakovich's huge, rich score to Grigori Kosintsev's and L. Z. Trauberg's *The New Babylon* (1928–29).

To write film music as an immediate reflex of the visual action was no easy matter; as Dalcroze observed, "the extraordinary brevity of visual rhythms—the art of the cinema is one of detail—forces the composer who has undertaken to interpret them to abandon all progressive logic, whether aesthetic or sentimental."[31] If, however, Eisenstein was right in thinking that montage—rapid cuts of discontinuous visual material—was the essence of the art of the cinema, perhaps composers could succeed by abandoning notions of continuity and progressivity, and constructing sound montages to match the sight montages.

In the lower world of movies, where solo pianists supplied all the music, all-purpose books were available to help the pianist to imagine appropriate music for anything occurring on the screen. In 1919 Giuseppe Brecce assembled a *Kinothek,* a library of short standard music-bits correlative to any mood or action, a kind of textbook of musical physiology; and in 1924 Erno Rapée published *Motion Picture Moods for Pianists and*

---

30. See Francis Steegmuller, *Cocteau: A Biography* (Boston: Nonpareil, 1986), 176.

31. Dalcroze, *Eurhythmics Art and Education,* 199.

Organists, which classifies a large number of pieces under fifty-two headings, such as "Aëroplane" (Felix Mendelssohn's *Rondo capriccioso*), "Battle" (the third movement of Beethoven's *Moonlight* Sonata), "Horror" (the bride's abduction from Edvard Grieg's *Peer Gynt*), "Railroad" (the Spinning Song from Wagner's *Flying Dutchman*), "Sadness" (the first movement of the *Moonlight* Sonata)—and, "for use in situations . . . where *there is neither action*, nor atmosphere, nor the elements of human temperament," "Neutral" (Schubert's *Moment musical*, op. 94 no. 3).[32] The customer who closed his or her eyes would hear a collage of abruptly juxtaposed bits of familiar music, a sloppy, free-form version of Neoclassicism. (It is even possible that the early cinothèques influenced the development of the Neoclassical aesthetic in concert music.) Furthermore, the visual component created a sort of conditioned reflex: the audience was slowly being trained, Pavlov-style, to interpret the meaning of the music through the action that it accompanied.

In the artier domain of the high-class cinema, a certain tendency toward musical montage could also be seen. Shostakovich's score to *The New Babylon* (1928–29)—a film glorifying the Paris commune of 1871 as part of the proletariat's movement toward liberation—is sensitive in many ways to the need to create a promiscuous, polystylistic sort of musical discourse to match the directors' abrupt cuts, unlinear narrative, and other sorts of visual flair. The score quotes French revolutionary songs (such as "Ça ira"), a Tchaikovsky children's piece, an Offenbach waltz—at one point Shostakovich counterpoints "The Marseillaise" with the famous can-can from Offenbach's *Orpheus in the Underworld* in order to provide an auditory symbol for the clash between the poor folk and the frivolous bourgeois "ooh-la-la" decadents.

When movies with sound tracks—the "talkies"—took over in the 1930s, some of the zeal for experimental music left the cinema or went underground; a certain routine developed in film scores, even, or especially, in the most expensive Hollywood productions. One of the most thoughtful documents on film music is *Composing for the Films* (1947), by Hanns Eisler (1898–1962), the German communist composer, a veteran of all sorts of film scoring, from Hollywood to propaganda films to experimental documentaries on icebergs. Like most serious composers who worked on film, Eisler stresses the need for music to retain a degree of autonomy, a sense of self-regard despite the undignified conditions under which most film composers work. He begins his book with a section on the prejudices and bad habits of film music: (1) the *Leitmotiv*: Eisler dislikes the rigid slapping-on of tunes to denote the presence of a person or thing; (2) melody and euphony: Eisler resists the tendency to "fetishize" unchallenging and old-fashioned sorts of tunefulness; (3) unobtrusiveness: Eisler is irritated by the belief that music

32. Erno Rapée, *Motion Picture Moods for Pianists and Organists* (New York: Arno Press, 1974).

shouldn't call attention to itself, but should be subordinate to the visual spectacle; (4) visual justification: Eisler lambastes the philistine assumption that the presence of the music should somehow be accounted for in the script, for instance, by having the hero burst into song, or at least turn on his radio; (5) illustration: Eisler notes the "favorite Hollywood gibe: 'Birdie sings, music sings'"[33]—but feels that this demotes the music to a redundancy, since the visual images are so "hyperexplicit" that they scarcely need reinforcement from the orchestra; (6) geography and history: Eisler deplores the fact that a composer is expected to quote a Dutch folk song if the movie takes place in Holland; (7) stock music: Eisler loathes composers who quote the Wedding Chorus from Wagner's *Lohengrin* when someone gets married—or who otherwise follow the procedures laid down by Rapée and his cohort; (8) clichés: all of Eisler's objections reduce to this: composers are hired to provide exactly what the audience expects, as if the film score already existed before the composer began to work.

Eisler's method, by contrast, was to create film music that did not reinforce the meaning of the visual text, but instead provided a counterpoint to the visual text—the music retains its own point of view and offers a critique of what the camera shows. (This notion is derived from Bertolt Brecht, as we will see in chapter 8.) An example is the music that Eisler wrote for *Kuhle Wampe* (1931), a film (in which Brecht had a hand) about mass unemployment—one of the most important attempts to make a proletarian sort of cinema. In one scene showing the wretched condition of the poorest residents of Berlin, Eisler deliberately provided the "wrong" music: where an illustrative composer would have underscored the images in a sentimental, wheedling way, Eisler instead wrote "quick, harsh music," to indicate the theme of rebellion. In other words, Eisler didn't depict what the workers actually were doing—he depicted what the workers *ought* to be doing, namely, resisting their oppressors. The music provides an energizing ethical gloss to the scene, which otherwise might simply evoke a passive state of pity.

The passages from Eisler's book cited here begin with a meditation on a new sort of montage, an intermedia montage in which one element is a picture sequence and the other element is a music sequence. The unrelatedness of picture and music, he stresses, generates a strong degree of aesthetic tension. Throughout the book Eisler notes the foreignness of music in the world of the cinema, its recalcitrance, its refusal to assimilate itself neatly into a prepackaged drama.

---

33. Hanns Eisler, *Composing for the Films* (New York: Oxford University Press, 1947), 12.

HANNS EISLER
from *Composing for the Films* (1947)
"ELEMENTS OF AESTHETICS"

. . . If the concept of montage, so emphatically advocated by Eisenstein,[34] has any justification, it is to be found in the relation between the picture and the music. From the aesthetic point of view, this relation is not one of similarity, but, as a rule, one of question and answer, affirmation and negation, appearance and essence. This is dictated by the divergence of the media in question and the specific nature of each. Music, however well defined in terms of its own structure, is never sharply defined with regard to any object outside itself to which it is related by imitation or expression. Conversely, no picture, not even an abstract painting, is completely emancipated from the world of objects.

The fact that it is the eye, not the ear, that perceives the world of objects affects even the freest artistic process: on the one hand, even the purely geometric figures of abstract painting appear like broken-off fragments of the visible reality; on the other hand, even the most crudely illustrative program music is at most related to this reality as a dream is to awakened consciousness. The facetiousness characteristic of all program music that does not naively attempt something that is impossible to it derives from that very circumstance. It manifests the contradiction between the reflected world of objects and the musical medium, and exploits this contradiction in order to enhance the effect of the music. Roughly speaking, all music, including the most "objective" and nonexpressive, belongs primarily to the sphere of subjective inwardness, whereas even the most spiritualized painting is heavily burdened with unresolved objectivity. Motion-picture music, being at the mercy of this relationship, should attempt to make it productive, rather than to negate it in confused identifications.

Montage
The application of the principle of montage to motion-picture music would help to make it more adequate to the present development phase, to begin with, simply because those media have been evolved independently of each other, and the modern technic by which they are brought together was not generated by them, but by the emergence of new facilities for reproduction. Montage makes the best of the aestheti-

---

34. Sergei Eisenstein (1898–1948) was a Soviet film director who advocated montage—that is, rapid splicing of not-obviously-related film clips—in order to investigate the aesthetics of juxtaposition in time. Eisenstein was concerned with film music, and inspired Sergei Prokofiev to some of his best scores, including *Alexander Nevsky* (1938).

cally accidental form of the sound picture by transforming an entirely extraneous relation into a virtual element of expression.³⁵

The direct merging of two media of such different historical origins would not make
much more sense than the idiotic movie scripts in which a singer loses his voice and
then regains it in order to supply a pretext for exhausting all the possibilities of photographed sound. Such a synthesis would limit motion pictures to those accidental cases
in which both media somehow coincide, that is to say, to the domain of synaesthesia,³⁶
the magic of moods, semi-darkness, and intoxication. In brief, the cinema would be
confined to those expressive contents which, as Walter Benjamin showed, are basically
incompatible with technical reproduction. The effects in which picture and music can
be directly united are inevitably of the type that Benjamin calls "auratic"³⁷—actually
they are degenerated forms of the "aura," in which the spell of the here and now is
technically manipulated.

There can be no greater error than producing pictures of which the aesthetic ideas
are incompatible with their technical premises, and which at the same time camouflage
this incompatibility. In the words of Benjamin,

> It is noteworthy that even today particularly reactionary writers pursue the same
> line of thought, and see as the chief significance of motion pictures their capacity
> for expressing, if not the ritual, at least the supernatural elements of life. Thus, in
> discussing Reinhardt's production, *Midsummer Night's Dream,* Werfel says that it
> is doubtless the sterile imitation of the external world with its streets, interiors, rail-
> way station restaurants, cars and beaches, that has so far stood in the way of the
> rise of the motion picture to the realm of art. "The motion picture," to quote his

35. "Two film pieces of any kind, placed together, inevitably combine into a new concept, a new
quality, arising out of that juxtaposition." (Eisenstein, [*The Film Sense,* New York, 1942,] 4.) This applies not only to the clash of heterogeneous pictorial elements, but also to that of music and picture,
particularly when they are not assimilated to each other. [Eisler's note.]

36. *synaesthesia:* a phenomenon of response through the wrong sense-organ, as when a musical
note is perceived as a color. The poet Charles Baudelaire, in the famous sonnet "Correspondences"
(1857), cited later in this anthology, made synthaesthesia a criterion of advanced artistic consciousness.
For Eisler, as for Brecht, synesthesia is part of an outmoded Wagnerian vision of the mystical fusion
of the arts.

37. "What is stunted in the age of technical reproducibility, is the aura of the work of art." The aura
is "the unrepeatable, single impression of something presented as remote, however close it may be. To
follow with one's eyes a mountain chain on a summer afternoon or a bough that casts its shadow on
one resting under it—is to breathe the aura of those mountains, of that bough." The aura is "bound
with the here and now, there can be no copy of it." (Walter Benjamin, "L'oeuvre d'art à l'époque de
sa reproduction mécanisée," in *Zeitschrift für Sozialforschung,* V., Paris, 1936–37, pp. 40ff.) [Eisler's
note.] Walter Benjamin (1892–1940) was a German aesthetician and literary critic—the essay to
which Eisler refers is one of the seminal documents of Modernism.

words, "has not yet grasped its true significance, its real potentialities. . . . These consist in its unique capacity for expressing the realm of the fairy tale, the miraculous and the supernatural with natural means and incomparable convincing power."[38]

Such magical pictures would be characterized by the tendency to fuse the music and the picture and to avoid montage as an instrument for the cognition of reality. It is hardly necessary to stress the artistic and social implication of Werfel's program—pseudo-individualization achieved by industrial mass production.[39] It would also mark a retrogression from the achievements of modern music, which has freed itself from the *Musikdrama,* the programmatic school, and synaesthesia, and is working with might and main at the dialectical task of becoming unromantic while preserving its character of music. The sound picture without montage would amount to a "selling out" of Richard Wagner's idea—and his work falls to pieces even in its original form.

Aesthetic models of genuine motion-picture music are to be found in the incidental music written for dramas or the topical songs and production numbers in musical comedies. These may be of little musical merit, but they have never served to create the illusion of a unity of the two media or to camouflage the illusionary character of the whole, but functioned as stimulants because they were foreign elements, which interrupted the dramatic context, or tended to raise this context from the realm of literal immediacy into that of meaning. They have never helped the spectator to identify himself with the heroes of the drama, and have been an obstacle to any form of aesthetic empathy.

It has been pointed out above that today's cultural industry unwittingly carries out the verdict that is objectively pronounced by the development of the art forms and materials. Applying this law to the relation between pictures, words, and music in the films, we might say that the insurmountable heterogeneity of these media furthers from the outside the liquidation of romanticism which is an intrinsic historical tendency within each art. The alienation of the media from each other reflects a society alienated

---

38. The quotation is from Franz Werfel, "Ein Sommernachtstraum, Ein Film von Shakespeare und Reinhardt," in *Neues Wiener Journal,* quoted in LU, 15 Nov. 1935. [Eisler's note.] Franz Werfel (1890–1945) was a novelist and critic and the third husband of Alma Mahler; Eisler disliked his nonconfrontational, if not escapist, sort of art. Max Reinhardt (1873–1943) was an Austrian producer; he worked with Werfel and Kurt Weill (among many others), and his productions of *Salome* and *Elektra* inspired Richard Strauss's operas. Strauss left an affectionate caricature of Reinhardt in the role of the theater director La Roche in his last opera, *Capriccio* (1942).

39. Eisenstein is aware of the materialistic potentialities of the principle of montage: the juxtaposition of heterogeneous elements raises them to the level of consciousness and takes over the function of theory. This is probably the meaning of Eisenstein's formulation: "Montage has a realistic significance when the separate pieces produce, in juxtaposition, the generality, the synthesis of one's theme" (op. cit. p. 30). The real achievement of montage is always interpretation. [Eisler's note.]

from itself, men whose functions are severed from each other even within each individual. Therefore the aesthetic divergence of the media is potentially a legitimate means of expression, not merely a regrettable deficiency that has to be concealed as well as possible. And this is perhaps the fundamental reason why many light-entertainment pictures that fall far below the pretentious standards of the usual movie seem to be more substantial than motion pictures that flirt with real art. Movie revues usually come closest to the ideal of montage, hence music fulfils its proper function most adequately in them. Their potentialities are wasted only because of their standardization, their spurious romanticism, and their stupidly super-imposed plots of successful careers. They may be remembered if the motion picture is ever emancipated from the present-day conventions.

However, the principle of montage is suggested not merely by the intrinsic relation between pictures and music and the historical situation of the mechanically reproduced work of art. This principle is probably implied in the need that originally brought pictures and music together and that was of an antithetic character. Since their beginning, motion pictures have been accompanied by music. The pure cinema must have had a ghostly effect like that of the shadow play—shadows and ghosts have always been associated. The magic function of music that has been hinted at above probably consisted in appeasing the evil spirits unconsciously dreaded. Music was introduced as a kind of antidote against the picture. The need was felt to spare the spectator the unpleasantness involved in seeing effigies of living, acting, and even speaking persons, who were at the same time silent. The fact that they are living and nonliving at the same time is what constitutes their ghostly character, and music was introduced not to supply them with the life they lacked—this became its aim only in the era of total ideological planning—but to exorcize fear or help the spectator absorb the shock.[40]

Motion-picture music corresponds to the whistling or singing child in the dark. The

40. Kurt London makes the following illuminating remark: "It [motion-picture music] began not as a result of any artistic urge, but from the dire need of something which would drown the noise made by the projector. For in those times there were as yet no sound-absorbent walls between the projection machine and the auditorium. This painful noise disturbed visual enjoyment to no small extent. Instinctively cinema proprietors had recourse to music, and it was the right way, using an agreeable sound to neutralize one less agreeable." (London, [*Film Music,* Faber and Faber, n.d.] p. 28.) This sounds plausible enough. But there remains the question, why should the sound of the projector have been so unpleasant? Hardly because of its noisiness, but rather because it seemed to belong to that uncanny sphere which anyone who remembers the magic-lantern performances can easily evoke. The grating, whirring sound actually had to be "neutralized," "appeased," not merely muted. If one reconstructed a cinema booth of the type used in 1900 and made the projector work in the audience room, more might be learned about the origin and meaning of motion-picture music than from extensive research. The experience in question is probably a collective one akin to panic, and it involves the flashlike awareness of being a helpless inarticulate mass given over to the power of a mechanism.

real reason for the fear is not even that these people whose silent effigies are moving in front of one seem to be ghosts. The captions do their best to come to the aid of these images. But confronted with gesticulating masks, people experience themselves as creatures of the very same kind, as being threatened by muteness. The origin of motion-picture music is inseparably connected with the decay of spoken language, which has been demonstrated by Karl Kraus.[41] It is hardly accidental that the early motion pictures did not resort to the seemingly most natural device of accompanying the pictures by dialogues of concealed actors, as is done in the Punch and Judy shows, but always resorted to music, although in the old horror or slapstick pictures it had hardly any relation to the plots.

The sound pictures have changed this original function of music less than might be imagined. *For the talking picture, too, is mute.* The characters in it are not speaking people but speaking effigies, endowed with all the features of the pictorial, the photographic two-dimensionality, the lack of spatial depth. Their bodiless mouths utter words in a way that must seem disquieting to anyone uninformed. Although the sound of these words is sufficiently different from the sound of natural words, they are far from providing "images of voices" in the same sense in which photography provides us with images of people.

This technical disparity between picture and word is further accented by something much more deep-lying—the fact that all speech in motion pictures has an artificial, impersonal character. The fundamental principle of the motion picture, its basic invention, is the photographing of motions. This principle is so all-pervading that everything that is not resolved into visual motion has a rigid and heterogeneous effect with regard to the inherent law of the motion-picture form. Every movie director is familiar with the dangers of filmed theater dialogues; and the technical inadequacy of psychological motion pictures partly derives from their inability to free themselves from the dominance of the dialogue. By its material, the cinema is essentially related to the ballet and the pantomime; speech, which presupposes man as a self, rather than the primacy of the gesture, ultimately is only loosely superimposed upon the characters.

Speech in motion pictures is the legitimate heir to the captions; it is a roll retranslated into acoustics, and that is what it sounds like even if the formulation of the words is not bookish but rather feigns the "natural." The fundamental divergencies between words and pictures are unconsciously registered by the spectator, and the obtrusive

---

Such an impulse is easily rationalized, for instance, as fear of fire. It is basically the feeling that something may befall a man even if he be "many." This is precisely the consciousness of one's own mechanization. [Eisler's note.] Kurt London (b. 1900) wrote about politics and films.

41. Karl Kraus (1874–1936), prolific writer and editor of the journal *Die Fackel,* was much concerned with precision in language.

unity of the sound picture that is presented as a complete reduplication of the external world with all its elements is perceived as fraudulent and fragile. Speech in the motion picture is a stop-gap, not unlike wrongly employed music that aims at being identical with the events on the screen. A talking picture without music is not very different from a silent picture, and there is even reason to believe that the more closely pictures and words are coordinated, the more emphatically their intrinsic contradiction and the actual muteness of those who seem to be speaking are felt by the spectators. This may explain—although the requirements of the market supply a more obvious reason— why the sound pictures still need music, while they seem to have all the opportunities of the stage and much greater mobility at their disposal.

Eisenstein's theory regarding movement can be appraised in the light of the foregoing discussion. The concrete factor of unity of music and pictures consists in the gestural element. This does not refer to the movement or "rhythm," of the motion picture as such, but to the photographed motions and their function in the picture as a whole. The function of music, however, is not to "express" this movement—here Eisenstein commits an error under the influence of Wagnerian ideas about the *Gesamtkunstwerk*[42] and the theory of aesthetic empathy—but to release, or more accurately, to justify movement. The photographed picture as such lacks motivation for movement; only indirectly do we realize that the pictures are in motion, that the frozen replica of external reality has suddenly been endowed with the spontaneity that it was deprived of by its fixation, and that something petrified is manifesting a kind of life of its own. At this point music intervenes, supplying momentum, muscular energy, a sense of corporeity, as it were. Its aesthetic effect is that of a stimulus of motion, not a reduplication of motion. In the same way, good ballet music, for instance Stravinsky's,[43] does not express the feelings of the dancers and does not aim at any identity with them, but only summons them to dance. Thus, the relation between music and pictures is antithetic at the very moment when the deepest unity is achieved.

The development of cinema music will be measured by the extent to which it is able to make this antithetic relation fruitful and to dispel the illusion of direct unity. . . .

"SUGGESTIONS AND CONCLUSIONS"

Discretion

A fundamental requirement that taxes all of a composer's sensitiveness is that he should not write a single sequence, not even a single note, that overlooks the social-technological prerequisite of the motion picture, namely, its nature as mass produc-

---

42. *Gesamtkunstwerk*: total artwork—the synthesis of text, music, and stage spectacle into a perfectly amalgamated whole; the artistic goal of Richard Wagner (1813–83). Eisler, unlike Wagner, prefers to keep the component artistic media separate, on individual, cleanly demarcated planes.

43. Igor Stravinsky (1882–1971) indeed believed in the nonexpressivity of his ballet music.

tion. No motion-picture music should have the same character of uniqueness that is desirable in music intended for live performance. In other words, motion-picture music should not become the tool of pseudo-individualization. But therein the greatest, almost insurmountable difficulties are involved. First of all, music, by its nature and origin, seems inseparable from the factor of uniqueness, the *hic et nunc.*[44] The occurrence of the same music in different places at the same time, especially when the intimacy of the moment, its whim, so to speak, is emphasized, implies something that is almost anti-musical, as manifested most clearly in motion pictures of concerts.[45] As a matter of fact, the motion picture itself consists of mass reproductions of unique events, and thus compels the composer to deal with individual situations, whose very nature resists such mass reproduction.

There is no sense in covering up such contradictions, the profoundest that confront motion-picture music, far beyond the bounds of the existing practices; on the contrary they should be made apparent. And since the composer cannot evade them, they should enter as an element into his music. The aim is to write music that abandons itself to its concrete occasion as "unique"—and this is the basic postulate of specific composing—but at the same time takes care not to seek its fulfilment in the triumph of intruding upon something "unique." One might almost say that the profoundest requirement of cinema music is that of "discretion"—namely that it should not behave indiscreetly with regard to its object, that it should not suggest close intimacy, but that on the contrary it should mitigate the inevitable impression of embarrassing closeness to an intimate event, which every motion picture produces. This is the contemporary form of musical "taste" and the picture itself can teach us something in this respect. Thus, the portrayal of the departure of a ship and the crowded pier is rightly considered more appropriate than close-ups of kisses; the reason for this is not prudishness, but the circumstance that in the ship scene the element of the uniqueness, of the *hic et*

44. *hic et nunc:* here and now; the present instant.

45. More generally, the question must at least be raised whether the technification of the work of art does not lead inevitably to the ultimate elimination of art. "Art still has a limitation within itself, and therefore passes into higher forms of conscious activity . . . We no longer hold art to be the highest mode in which truth acquires existence . . . With the progress of culture, every nation reaches a time in which art points beyond itself . . . Such a time is our own." (Hegel, *Vorlesungen ueber die Aesthetik,* vol. 1, 1842, p. 132.) In the second part of his *Aesthetics* Hegel discusses the tendency to self-dissolution historically inherent in art, and connects it with the progress of civilization. The following passage is directly relevant to the problems of the motion picture and aesthetic planning: "For the modern artist to be bound to a particular content and a manner appropriate only to a given material, is a thing of the past. Thereby art has become a free instrument, which he can apply equally with regard to every content of whatever nature, according to the measure of his subjective skill." (Ibid., vol. 2, p. 232). [Eisler's note.] Georg Friedrich Hegel (1770–1831), German dialectical philosopher, argued that history progresses through the resolutions of contradictions into synthesis.

nunc, although present, is not as pronounced and does not affect the picture to the same extent as in the picture of a lover's embrace. The cinema composer who in a sense is constantly driven to behave in the manner of people kissing in public should heed this lesson. From the point of view of advanced composing, music illustrating a noisy crowd seems more appropriate than music illustrating an erotic scene. It is said that a contract with Stravinsky was canceled because he stipulated that he would not illustrate any love scenes.

The paradox inherent in motion-picture music—the fact that it is both technified and obliged to have a character of uniqueness—if it is really as inevitable as it appears to be—leads to a fundamental consequence concerning the general attitude of the music. Being a "multipliable unique" it is always supposed to achieve what it actually cannot achieve. It must give a hint to this situation unless it is blindly to succumb to this contradiction. In other words, motion-picture music must not take itself seriously in the same way as autonomous music does. Analysis of the most fundamental premises of motion-picture music thus confirms what we have inferred from the fact of its subordination to its purpose and the impossibility of its autonomous development. With some exaggeration it may be said that essentially all motion-picture music contains an element of humor, speaks with its tongue in its cheek, as it were, and that it degenerates into a bad kind of naïveté as soon as it forgets this element.

It is hardly an accident that the music for those pictures in which the idea of technification has made the greatest inroads on the function of music, that is, the cartoons, almost always takes on the aspect of a joke through the use of sound effects. The investigations made by the Film Music Project[46] show that almost all new and unconventional solutions are based on ideas that are at least close to humorous elements. This should not be misunderstood. What is advocated here is not that the music as such should have a facetious character; on the contrary, it should make use of the whole gamut of expression. Nor should the music necessarily make mock of the events on the screen. The element of humor is rather to be found in the formal relation of the music to its object and in its function.

For instance (we refer here to an example studied by the Project), the music imitates caution. Actually, this is impossible; caution is a specific human behavior, and music cannot express it and accurately distinguish it from similar impulses without the help of concepts. The music is aware of this, and exaggerates itself in order to enforce the association of caution, which it actually cannot express. Thereby it ceases to take itself literally in its immediacy; it turns into a joke something that it cannot do seriously. By

---

46. The Film Music Project, funded by the Rockefeller Foundation in 1940, employed Eisler for three years as project director; under its aegis he wrote scores for Josef Losey's *The Children's Camp,* Joris Ivens's *Rain,* and other antinarrative films.

doing this, it suspends the claim of the physical immediacy of the *hic et nunc,* which is incompatible with its technological situation. By keeping itself at a distance, it also creates a distance from its place and hour.

Something of this element—the formal self-negation of music that plays with itself—should be present in every composition for motion pictures as an antidote against the danger of pseudo-individualization. The postulate of universal planning leads of itself to such functional jokes, which at the same time are inseparable from technification. The very fact that something is mechanically manufactured and is at the same time music objectively implies a comical element. Music will escape being comical involuntarily only by agreeing to be comical voluntarily. The formal facetious function is nothing but the awareness of music that it is mediated, technically produced, and reproduced. In a certain sense, every productive dramatic musical idea in the motion picture is a paradox. It hardly needs to be shown that such an affinity to jokes reflects the deepest unconscious tensions in the audience's reaction to motion-picture music.[47]

The same problem can be approached from a different angle—in relation to the effect of music, which is today the exclusive consideration, and which, despite its questionableness, is nevertheless always to some extent revealing objectively. Cinema music is not carefully listened to. If this fact is more or less accepted as an inevitable premise, the best of which has to be made, the aim will be to compose music that, even though it is listened to inattentively, can as a whole be perceived correctly and adequately to its function, without having to move along beaten associative tracks that help the listener to grasp the music, but block any adequate fulfilment of its function. The composer is thus faced with a new and strange task—that of producing something sensible, which at the same time can be perceived by way of parenthesis, as it slips by the listener. Such a requirement is closely related to that of music that does not take itself seriously. Good cinema music must achieve everything that it does achieve on the surface, so to speak; it must not become lost in itself. Its whole structure—and it needs structure more than any form of autonomous music—must become visible; and the more it adds the lacking depth dimension to the picture, the less it must itself develop

---

47. The problem of the comical potentialities of music is inseparable from the meaning of the motion picture itself. "This is magnificently shown in the pictures of the Marx Brothers, who demolish an opera set as though to express allegorically the philosophic insight into the disintegration of the opera itself . . . or smash a grand piano and seize the framework and strings as a sample of the harp of the future . . . The main reason for the tendency of music to become comical in the present phase, is that something so completely useless should be practiced with all the visible signs of strenuous serious work. The fact that music is alien to industrious people reveals their alienation with regard to one another, and the awareness of this alienation vents itself in laughter." (T. W. Adorno, "Ueber den Fetisch-charakter in der Musik und die Regression des Hörens," in *Zeitschrift für Sozialforschung,* VII, 1938, p. 353.) [Eisler's note.]

in depth. This is not meant in the sense of musical "superficiality"; on the contrary it is precisely the procedure diametrically opposed to the superficial, fleeting, and comfortable convention. It implies the striving to make everything completely sensuous, in contrast to musical transcendence and inwardness. In technical terms, this means the predominance of movement and color over the musical depth dimension, harmony, which governs just the conventional patterns.

Cinema music should sparkle and glisten. It should attain the quick pace of the casual listening imposed by the picture, and not be left behind. Tonal colors can be perceived faster and with less effort than harmonies, unless the latter follow the tonal pattern and are therefore not registered at all as specific. Sparkling variation and coloristic richness are also most readily compatible with technification. By displaying a tendency to vanish as soon as it appears, motion-picture music renounces its claim that it is *there,* which is today its cardinal sin.

From *Composing for the Films* (New York: Oxford University Press, 1947), 70–78, 128–33.

4 The New Music Theater

In 1982 Virgil Thomson reviewed the history of opera and was struck by the continuity of vocal lines over the centuries:

> From Monteverdi to Nono, from Rameau to Poulenc, from Purcell to Britten, from Schütz to Schönberg, and Glinka to Stravinsky, the voice parts of operas and oratorios in any language are almost interchangeable, though their instrumental accompaniments can vary from Baroque, Rococo, and Romantic to polytonal, non-tonal, even twelve-tone serial. Excellent opera music has indeed been composed in all these styles.[1]

Thomson was also struck by the similarities in operatic story lines. So for Thomson, opera has very little in the way of history, except for the slow mutation of accompaniment styles under fixed procedures for setting text for voices.

Thomson's thesis is debatable, but not negligible: the curriculum for opera that Monteverdi and his colleagues set out between 1598 and 1607 has been pursued with remarkable steadiness up to the present day. Still, it is possible to distinguish certain shifts in emphasis that mark the new styles and themes of music drama of the Modernist period.

1. *Dissonance among the component media.* Wagner thought that the ideal drama was the *Gesamtkunstwerk,* the total artwork in which the component media (text, music, spectacle) fused into a devastating whole, and many composers of the twentieth century, particularly in the domain of Expressionism, have followed his lead. But other composers have laughed at the notion that the mission of the theater is to provoke swoons and jolts by means of total sensory engagement. These composers preferred a dismembered and disengaged sort of theatrical experience, in which the music ignored, criticized, or contradicted the meanings proposed by the text. This tendency is felt most strongly in Surrealist opera (for example, Poulenc's 1944 *Les mamelles de Tirésias,* in which the music deliberately misinterprets the text, in order to induce the spectator to a sort of vertigo) and in the political operas for which Brecht provided librettos (for example, Kurt Weill's 1928 *Threepenny Opera,* in which music and text try to subvert one another, so that the audience will adopted a critical and detached attitude toward the opera, and toward all of culture). This cultivation of dissonance among component media is, for the most part, new to the twentieth century; it is not easy to find precedents in earlier opera.

1. Virgil Thomson, "On Writing Operas and Singing Them," *Parnassus* 10 (1982): 16–17.

2. *Philosophical opera.* Modernist music is sometimes called cerebral, usually as a term of dispraise, though it is hard to see why intelligence is necessarily a bad thing; and this cerebral quality sometimes expresses itself in music drama. Compare Ferruccio Busoni's *Doktor Faustus* (1914–24) with Charles Gounod's *Faust* (1859): Gounod's hero is a crabby old man who wants to be young again and have some fun; Busoni's hero is a metaphysical self-promoter storming the ultimate verges of human experience. (This is not to say that Busoni's opera is better than Gounod's.) Other examples of philosophical opera include Schoenberg's *Moses und Aron* (1930–32), which investigates the artistic ramifications of the commandment against graven images; and Stravinsky's *The Rake's Progress* (1951), which investigates the unnatural extremes of natural human desire. Philosophical opera also lacks many obvious precursors in previous opera: generally, in plot lines where intellectual abstractions were likely to obtrude, the older librettists deflected attention by creating love stories, sometimes quite preposterously, as in Rossini's *Mosè in Egitto* (1818), in which much of the action concerns not Moses, but the love affair between the Pharaoh's son, Osiris, and the Hebrew girl, Elcia.

3. *Meta-opera.* The philosophical opera and the opera that dissociates its media are both the products of a kind of self-consciousness: the composer is asked not to exuberate into passionate melody, but to *think;* not to do the expected thing, but to do something contrived and studied, artificial. This acute attentiveness to the problematic aspects of opera—opera's tendency to the flamboyant and fatuous—sometimes expressed itself as an interest in meta-opera, that is, opera about opera. In the most overt meta-operas, the characters are actually engaged in opera production, as in the prologue to Richard Strauss's *Ariadne auf Naxos* (originally composed 1912, prologue added 1916), in which the Composer is running around backstage, trying frantically to figure out, at the last minute, how to combine a tragedy and a comedy into a single evening's entertainment; or as in Strauss's *Capriccio* (1942), in which the Composer, the Poet, and the Director argue over which of them is preeminent in the world of opera (the Director seems to win).

Ariadne auf Naxos is also an example of another kind of meta-opera, in which the apparatus of an extinct or remote species of music drama is revived in order to provide an abstract, disengaged sort theatrical experience. In *Ariadne,* as in Ferruccio Busoni's *Arlecchino* (inspired by a private performance from another distinguished Modernist clown, the lead character of Schoenberg's *Pierrot Lunaire)* and *Turandot* (both 1917), that species is the old Italian commedia dell'arte, the slapstick buffoonery in which clowns in masks rehearsed stereotyped plots—giddy young couples outwitting the grumpy father, and so forth. Here was a dramaturgy so familiar and routine, so dead, that it can be shocked back to life only by electricity applied from outside; the spectator is conscious of witnessing an artificial resuscitation. These evocations of old stock comedy are the product of an active historical imagination: they do not tend to flatten history, by arranging collages in which the old and the new are squashed together, but rather to respect it, by illustrating how remote the twentieth century is from the world of the madrigal comedy (such as Orazio Vecchi's *L'Amfiparnaso* of 1597) and the Neapolitan *opera buffa* of the early seventeenth century. Giacomo Puccini's *Turandot,* his last opera, unfinished at his death in 1924, also has something of this meta-operatic quality—as if a brawny *verismo* tenor had wandered into a stage set for a Chinese puppet show. The puppet play, for example Paul Hindemith's opera for "Burmese marionettes" *Das Nusch-Nuschi* (1920) and Manuel de Falla's *El retablo de Maese Pedro* (1923), and the Japanese Noh play, for example Weill's *Der Jasager* (1930) and Benjamin Britten's *Curlew River* (1964)—these models provided the composers with clues for an eerie and estranged sort of music drama, an opera for extraterrestrials.

Meta-opera is far from new. Mozart's *Der Schauspieldirektor* (*The Impresario*) and Antonio Salieri's *Prima la musica, poi le parole* (*First Music, Then Words*)—presented together on the same day, 7 February 1786—ridicule the pretensions of poets, composers, and singers; in fact, Giovanni Battista Casti's libretto for Salieri influenced the libretto of Strauss's *Capriccio* centuries later. Felice Romani's hall-of-mirrors libretto for Gioachino Rossini's *Il Turco in Italia* (1814), concerning a Poet who is transcribing the events he's watching, anticipates the meta-dramas of the Modernist playwright Luigi Pirandello. But the older meta-operas tend to be warmer, less brittle than the Modernist ones.

4. *Zeitoper.* This difficult-to-translate German term (literally, "time-opera") refers to a genre of operas set in the present that often strenuously evoke the world of Modernism by concentrating on photography, railroads, cocktail parties, and so forth. The fad was established by Ernst Krenek's wildly popular opera concerning a jazz violinist, *Jonny spielt auf* (1927), which was quickly followed by Weill's *The Tsar Has His Photograph Taken* (1928) and Hindemith's *Neues vom Tage* (*News of the Day,* 1929), among others. An interesting subset of *Zeitoper* consists of stage treatment of the marital spats of composers: Strauss's *Intermezzo* (1924) starred a composer named Storch (German for stork—the word *Strauss* is German for ostrich) made up to look like Strauss himself, and Arnold Schoenberg's *Von Heute auf Morgen* (*From Today to Tomorrow,* 1929) dramatized a taken-for-granted-wife flirting with an operatic tenor—the libretto was indeed written by Schoenberg's second wife. *Zeitoper* seems the exact opposite of meta-opera, since one is self-consciously remote and the other aggressively up to date, but in fact they are oddly similar in effect: the *Zeitoper* often treats modern life in such a parodic manner that it seems to regard the contemporary scene with a skeptical, almost anthropological gaze. A number in *Neues vom Tage* labeled "Duett-Kitsch" gives some sense of the self-mocking tone of this genre: the *Zeitoper* contemplates itself as simply another piece of just-invented dreck. *Zeitoper* is very much a Modernist phenomenon; though there are earlier operas set (more or less) in the present, such as Verdi's *La traviata* (1853), it is not easy to find operas that make thematic use of their contemporaneity.

5. *Greek tragedy revisited.* Most of the operatic modes discussed so far have a certain comic aspect, since they concern a dramaturgy that does not try to enforce empathy between spectator and protagonist. But Modernist music drama is also concerned with tragedy, in the old Aristotelian sense of catharsis—a purging of emotions through overwhelming vicarious excitement. Some of the most compelling experiments of the Modernist theater are settings of Greek texts: Strauss's *Elektra* (1909), Sophocles modified by Hugo von Hofsmannsthal; Igor Stravinsky's *Oedipus Rex* (1927), Sophocles abridged and dehydrated by Jean Cocteau; Arthur Honegger's *Antigone* (1927), Sophocles again as treated by Cocteau; Carl Orff's *Antigonae* (1949), a setting of Friedrich Hölderlin's translation of Sophocles; and Partch's *King Oedipus* (1952), a setting of Yeats's translation of Sophocles. Except for Stravinsky's (in part), these operas are not exercises in irony and parody, but serious attempts at finding some convulsive sort of musical rhetoric, capable of achieving in the twentieth century what the Greek drama achieved so long ago. Some composers, such as Strauss, simply intensified the normal expressive devices of opera (*Leitmotiv* slogans, chromatic torsion, explosions, silence); others, such as Orff and Partch, rethought opera in an archaizing manner by concentrating on percussion in the orchestra and restricting vocal lines to monotone or melismatic chant—procedures that tried to combine Modernist expressivity with Modernist uncanniness and evocation of distance.

Far from being a novelty, the restoration of Greek tragedy was part of the original program of opera; but during the nineteenth century Greek tragedy fell out of favor with composers, with a few great exceptions, such as Felix Mendelssohn's incidental music for *Antigone* (1841). This produced the odd result that the nineteenth century's most prominent opera on a classical Greek theme is Jacques Offenbach's spoof *Orpheus in the Underworld* (1858). The Romantic musical imagination often looked for inspiration to the literature of northern Europe, from Sir Walter Scott's *The Bride of Lammermoor* to the *Nibelungenlied;* Greece could seem a bit stiff-jointed—formal, chaste, clear, reticent, sublime in a somewhat boring way. The rehabilitation of Greece came in 1872 from Friedrich Nietzsche (1844–1900), who helped to generate a reformation of opera through Greek tragedy.

Nietzsche was one of the most precocious scholars of his age—such as master of Greek and Latin that he had been called to a chair and a full professorship in classical philology at the University of Basel by the time he was twenty-five. Two years later he published his first book, *The Birth of Tragedy out of the Spirit of Music,* which had a profound influence on the art and thought of the Modernist movement. Its tenets are:

1. Greek tragedy grew out of choral hymns worshiping Dionysus—the god of drunkenness, riot, pain, ecstatic dismemberment, and the primal oneness of all things.

2. Human beings are too frail to accept the dark truths represented by Dionysus—we have to believe in the illusion that we are private individuals with private wills, and

we have to screen ourselves from the abyss by inventing beautiful images, dreams of glory.

3. We call these beautiful images gods, and identify Apollo in particular—the god of light, music, and clarity—with the principle of the saving illusion.

4. Therefore, instead of simply singing choral hymns to Dionysus, we intersperse these hymns with staged enactments (called tragedies) of the pretty stories that Apollo devises to distract us from the intolerable Dionysiac truth that we spend our lives reeling in a pit and ought never to have been born.

5. The ideal psychic functionality of Greek tragedy was destroyed by Socrates, who substituted abstract rational speculation for the immediate apprehension of the cosmos available only through artistic means, and the first symptoms of this corruption can be found in the decadent tragedies of Sophocles' contemporary, Euripides.

6. When Greek tragedy was resurrected in the form of opera, around 1600, its inventors produced only a bloodless and vain parody of Greek tragedy, suited to the rationalistic temper of the times—instead of the Dionysiac satyr, opera provided only sexless shepherds, so insipid that they could hardly even sing, only speak in recitative.

7. But the spirit of Greek tragedy has at last resurrected itself in the music dramas of Richard Wagner, a composer intimate with both Dionysus and Apollo.

Nietzsche ends his book by prophesying a general rebirth of the Greek spirit in the future composers of Germany.

Nietzsche's book exalted music and provided a good deal of encouragement, even elation, for future composers, and not only in Germany. It was as if Wagner, by means of Nietzsche's superlatively educated mind, had extended himself into the domain of professional philosophy: Nietzsche became a sort of conduit through which music could claim a central position in European culture as a whole. Nietzsche had indeed contemplated a career as a composer, and some of his musical works, such as the Byronic *Manfred-Meditation* (1872, the same year as *The Birth of Tragedy*), show that Nietzsche had listened to Wagner's *Tristan und Isolde* (1865) with almost embarrassingly close attention. But his chief contribution to music was to promote a sense that the composer, not the abstract thinker, was the person closest to the heart of human truth.

After *The Birth of Tragedy*, Nietzsche and Wagner quarreled—partly because Nietzsche was uneasy in the role of acolyte, partly because Wagner was quick to take offense at small criticisms, partly because Nietzsche, a vehement pagan, detested the Christian sentimentalism of Wagner's last music drama, *Parsifal* (1882). Toward the end of the 1880s, Nietzsche's mind started to fail as syphilis invaded his brain, until he broke down completely in 1889—he spent the last eleven years of his life in confinement, almost completely mute. Sometimes he suffered from the delusion that he *was* Richard Wagner: he once broke his silence to explain to his keepers in the asylum that he had been brought there by "his wife," Cosima (Wagner's widow).

At the end of the excerpts printed here—the last pages of *The Birth of Tragedy*—Nietzsche hymns the German soul in a manner that would later embarrass him, for he came to devote much of his energy to showing the defects of the German character. Nietzsche's concluding observation in *The Birth of Tragedy* is that mankind *is* dissonance: a remarkable statement that makes the extraordinary development of musical dissonance during the following century a means of investigating the authentic nature of the human race.

FRIEDRICH NIETZSCHE
from *The Birth of Tragedy* (1872)
§21

The myth protects us against the music, just as on the other side the myth first gives to music the highest freedom. As a return gift music bestows on the tragic myth a penetrating and persuasive metaphysical significance, such as word and image could never attain without music's unique help; and in particular it is through music that the spectator of tragedy is seized by that sure premonition of a highest joy, a joy at the end of the road through ruin and negation, so that he thinks he hears the innermost abyss of things speaking audibly to him.

. . . To true musicians I direct the question, if they can imagine a man capable of perceiving the third act of *Tristan und Isolde*[2] with no help from word and image, purely as a monstrous symphonic movement, without expiring in a convulsion of the soul's wings, loosed from every restraint? A man like this, who has put his ear to the heart chamber of the world-will, who feels the raging hunger for being as a thundering stream or as a brook dispersed to the sweetest mist, gushing from this source through all the world's veins—shouldn't he suddenly break to pieces? Should he endure hearing, in the wretched glass shell of his human individuality, the resounding clamor of numberless summonses to joy and woe out of "wide space of the world-night," without feeling at the shepherd's dance of metaphysics an irresistible need to take shelter in his primal home? If however such a work could be perceived as a whole, without any denial of the individual existence, if such a creation could be created without shattering its creator—where could we find the solution to such a contradiction?

2. *Tristan und Isolde:* music drama (1865) by Wagner in which a love potion compels Tristan to fall violently in love with Isolde, the conquered Irish princess intended as a bride for his uncle, King Marke. Nietzsche understands the convulsive ecstasies of the love duet in act 2 as an authentic shudder of Dionysus—"the heart chamber of the world-will . . . the raging hunger for being"; Nietzsche understands the pathetic cries of Tristan in act 3, as he lies wounded on the shore, waiting for Isolde's ship, as a compensating movement toward Apollo, toward individual personality and attractive spectacle.

Here there is thrust, between this music and our highest music excitement, the tragic myth and the tragic hero, basically only as a simile or image of the most universal facts, of which music alone can speak in a direct way. But as a simile the myth would remain with us completely ineffectual and unnoticed, if we could listen as purely Dionysian beings. . . . Here the *Apollonian* power breaks forth, arising to restore the almost exploded individual with the healing balm of a delightful deception: suddenly we believe we're still seeing only Tristan, as, motionless and muffled, he asks himself: "The old tune; why does it wake me?" And what earlier seemed to us like a hollow sighing from the midpoint of being itself now wants only to say to us, "waste and empty the sea."[3] And where breathless we imagined ourselves snuffed out in convulsive outrackings of every feeling, and we felt only a little bit of a connection to our usual existence, now we see and hear the hero, wounded to death and yet not dying, with his despairing cry: "Yearning! Yearning!" . . .

§24

. . . The first requirement for explaining the tragic myth is just this, to seek its peculiar pleasure in the purely aesthetic sphere, without encroaching onto the region of pity, of terror, of the ethically sublime. How can the ugly and the discordant—the contents of the tragic myth—excite an aesthetic pleasure?

Now here we need to whirl round with a bold advance into a metaphysics of art, while I repeat an earlier sentence [from §5], that being and the world appear justified only as an aesthetic phenomenon: in this sense the tragic myth has to convince us that even the ugly and the discordant are an artistic game that the will, in the eternal fullness of its pleasure, plays with itself. But this difficult-to-grasp primal phenomenon of Dionysiac art will be instantly grasped only in the wonderful meaning of *musical dissonance,* since after all music alone, when set down beside the world, can give an idea of what is meant by the justification of the world as an aesthetic phenomenon. The pleasure that the tragic myth produces has the same country of origin as the pleasurable feeling of dissonance in music. The Dionysiac, with its primal pleasure felt even in pain, is the common womb of music and of the tragic myth.

Meanwhile, with the help of the music-relation of dissonance, shouldn't we essentially have lightened the heavy problem of the tragic effect? We now understand what it is to want to see the tragedy and at the same time to yearn for something above any seeing: for we would have characterized artfully used dissonance as a similar state, in that we want to hear and at the same time we yearn for something above any hearing. This striving into the endless, this wingbeat of yearning at the point of highest pleasure

3. *öd' und leer das Meer:* this is the line that T. S. Eliot quotes in *The Waste Land* (1922), l. 42 — a poem governed by rhythms of Dionysus and Apollo, figureless ecstasy and figured myth.

in clearly perceived reality, reminds us that in both states we have to perceive a Dionysiac phenomenon that reveals to us ever anew the playful building up and smashing apart of the individual world as the outflow of a primal pleasure, as when Heraclitus the Obscure[4] compared the power that shapes worlds to a child at play, who puts stones here and there and builds up and throws down heaps of sand.

So in order to assess the Dionysiac capacity of a people, we have to consider not only the its music, but just as necessarily its tragic myth as a second witness of its capacity. The close relation between music and myth makes us similarly suppose that the degrading and depraving of one will be connected to a shriveling of the other: if indeed in the weakening of the myth there is really manifest a diminishing of Dionysiac potential. But concerning both, a glance at the development of the German identity might leave us in no doubt: in our opera just as in the abstract character of our mythless existence, in our art with its debased amusements just as in our idea-ridden life, we see revealed the inartistic, life-withering nature of Socratic optimism. But to console us there are omens that despite everything the German spirit rests and dreams, undestroyed, in splendid health, depth, and Dionysiac strength, like a slumber-sunk knight in an inaccessible abyss: out of this abyss the Dionysiac song rises up to us, in order to make us understand that this German knight even now is dreaming his primally old Dionysiac myth in blessed solemn visions. Let no one think that the German spirit may have lost forever its mythic home, when it still understands so distinctly the voices of the birds that tell of that home. Some day it will find itself awake in the morning freshness after a monstrous sleep: then it will kill dragons, wipe out the spiteful dwarfs,[5] and awaken Brünnhilde—and Wotan's spear itself won't be able to block its way!

My friends, you who believe in Dionysiac music, you also know what tragedy means for us. In you we have, reborn out of music, the tragic myth—and in it you may hope for everything and forget what is most painful! But most painful for all of us—the long degradation, under which the German genius, estranged from house and home, lived in the service of spiteful dwarfs. You understand the word—as you will also, finally, understand my hopes.

4. Heraclitus of Ephesus was a Greek philosopher who lived before Socrates. Obscure because of the difficulty of his aphorisms and because of his sense of the misery of human life, he was called the weeping philosopher because he stressed the transitoriness of all things—you never put your foot twice into the same river.

5. dwarfs: In *Ecce Homo* (1888), Nietzsche glosses the dwarfs of *The Birth of Tragedy* as "Christian priests"; at the beginning of his career, Nietzsche is circumspect about his opinion that Christianity is a religion fit for slaves. Nietzsche is also thinking here of Wagner's *Siegfried* (1869), in which Siegfried attains glory by forging a sword, killing the evil dwarf Mime, shattering his grandfather Wotan's spear (the source of divine authority), and plunging through flames to embrace the Valkyrie Brünnhilde.

§25

Music and tragic myth are in the same way expressions of the Dionysiac capacity of a people and inseparable from one another. Both stem from a domain of art that lies beyond the Apollonian; both transfigure a region in whose pleasure-chords dissonance as well as the world's terrible image alluringly reverberate and vanish; both play with the thorn of displeasure, trusting their exceedingly powerful arts of magic; both justify through this game the very existence of this "worse world." Here the Dionysiac, measured against the Apollonian, shows itself as the eternal and primordial force of art that really calls into being the whole world of appearance, in whose midst a new halo[6] of transfiguration becomes necessary, in order to keep alive the bustling world of individuation. If we could think ourselves an incarnation of dissonance—and what else is man?[7]—then this dissonance would need, in order to be able to live, a splendid illusion, to cover its own being with a veil of beauty. This is the true art intention of Apollo: in whose name we comprise all these numberless illusions of beautiful appearance, illusions that after all make existence livable at every moment and press us to experience the next moment.

From that foundation of all existence, from the Dionysiac substrate of the world, exactly so much may enter into the human individual's consciousness as can be overcome again by Apollo's transfiguring force, so that these two art urges must necessarily unfold their strengths in strictly reciprocal proportion, according to the law of eternal justice. Where the Dionysiac powers arise so violently as we are experiencing now, there Apollo, wrapped in a cloud, already has descended to us; whose most voluptuous effects of beauty will indeed be seen by the next generation.

But each man will most surely feel for himself how necessary this effect is, through intuition, if he once, even if only in a dream, imagines himself back to an old Hellenic mode of existence: wandering among high Ionic colonnades, looking upward to a horizon cropped by clean and noble lines, beside him reflections of his transfigured shape in shining marble, around him men solemnly striding or delicately moving, with harmonious lutes and a speech of rhythmic gestures—wouldn't he, at this continuous streaming of beauty, have to lift a hand to Apollo and cry out, "Blessed people of Greece! How great must Dionysus be among you, if the Delian God [Apollo] finds such magic necessary to cure your dithyrambic madness!"—but to a man musing in this fashion a gray Athenian, gazing up at him with the sublime eyes of Aeschylus, might

6. The German word is *Schein*. Throughout this passage Nietzsche is punning on various meanings of *Schein*, including "appearance," "illusion," "glory," and "shine."

7. Compare Nietzsche's statement in section 9 of *The Birth of Tragedy:* "In the heroic impulse of the individual toward the universal, in the attempt to stride beyond the curse of individuation and to will himself to be the one world-being, he suffers in himself the primal contradiction hidden in things."

reply: "But you might also say this, you odd stranger: how much did this people have to suffer, in order to be able to become so beautiful! But now follow me to the tragedy and sacrifice with me in the temple of both godheads!"

From *Gesammelte Werke*, Bd. 3 (München: Musarion Verlag, 1920), 142–44, 161–65; translated by the editor.

■

Nietzsche's notion that philosophy and music drama are two forms of the same enterprise—the inquiry into the inner spaces of the human condition—helped to create an intellectual climate in which opera was seen, not as pleasant evening's entertainment, but as something cathartic and edifying. Indeed, a certain tension arose between the model of opera as seizure of reality and the model of opera as fun.

Good examples of this tension can be found in the remarkable series of operas with music by Richard Strauss (1864–1949) and text by Hugo von Hofmannsthal (1874–1929). Their first collaboration, *Elektra* (1909), based on a preexisting play by Hofmannsthal, was a serious exercise in exploring a Nietzschean abyss: as Hofmannsthal remarked, his play is about the "dissolution of the concept of individuality. In *Electra* the individual is dissolved in the empirical way, inasmuch as the very substance of its life blasts it from within, as water about to freeze will crack an earthenware jug. Electra is no longer Electra, just because she has dedicated herself to entirely to being Electra."[8] The opera offers a single trajectory toward catharsis; but even here the grimness is relieved by a few pieces of cruel comedy, such as the scene in which Orestes murders his jaunty, jittery stepfather Aegisthus—a scene that sounds rather like the assassination of Till Eulenspiegel.

But in some of their later operas, such as *Ariadne auf Naxos,* Strauss and Hofmannsthal integrated such profoundly Dionysiac themes into good-humored entertainment. This project first reached the public in 1912 as a divertissement in a production of Molière's *Le bourgeois gentilhomme:* Monsieur Jourdain, the wealthy upstart bourgeois, in his mad attempt to get himself some culture, arranges the performance at his home of a serious opera and a clown comedy; but when time runs short, he commands, to everyone's consternation, that the serious opera and the clown comedy be performed *at the same time.* The serious opera concerns Ariadne: after helping Theseus to slay the minotaur in the labyrinth by showing him the trick with the thread, she and her lover sail away; but the faithless Theseus abandons her on a desert isle; she laments her fate and prays for death; a god appears, and she thinks that it is Death, come to put her out

8. Hugo von Hofmannsthal, *Selected Plays and Libretti,* trans. Michael Hamburger (New York: Pantheon Books, 1963), 88.

of her misery; but the god is not Death but Bacchus (that is, Dionysus), newborn and bewildered—and Ariadne swoons in his arms, is transfigured by his love. All through the opera the clowns regularly butt in, perform little songs and dances to try to cheer the disconsolate heroine, but she ignores them and concentrates on her woe; at last Zerbinetta, the promiscuous lead clown, sings a long virtuosic aria to persuade Ariadne that it's fine for a jilted girl to cry a few tears, but she should soon seek delight in the arms of new gods—though this, too, falls on deaf ears.

Ariadne auf Naxos turned out to be too long to be presented in the midst of Molière's play, so in 1916 Strauss and Hofmannsthal provided a prologue, in which the Composer (male, but played by a mezzo-soprano) runs around backstage, trying to think up tunes for this bizarrely mongrelized spectacle. At first the Composer is contemptuous of the clowns—he's a *serious* creative talent—but eventually he becomes enamored of the coquette Zerbinetta.

The conflict, then, between two models of opera—profundity and amusement—is built into the libretto. But it can also be found in the remarkable correspondence between the two collaborators, in which Hofmannsthal plays the role of the erudite poet-philosopher, and Strauss plays the role of composer-buffoon. This was to some extent a pose on both sides—Hofmannsthal had little knowledge of music and no understanding whatever of Strauss's aesthetics (though he tried to turn his ignorance into a virtue by claiming that, despite the fact that he was a "non-musician and a stranger to musical tastes," he was "almost frighteningly free from ephemeral judgments . . . I am open to all that is creative");[9] and Strauss was sufficiently fascinated by philosophy to have written a tone poem based on Nietzsche, *Also sprach Zarathustra* (1896), and a programmatic symphony *An Alpine Symphony* (1915), to which Strauss thought of attaching the Nietzschean title *The Antichrist.* But Strauss was not an intellectual in Hofmannsthal's class, and liked on occasion to play the simpleton.

On 14 July 1911 Strauss wrote to Hofmannsthal that he had received the libretto to *Ariadne auf Naxos:* "I like it well enough. . . . Only I should have preferred the dialogue between Ariadne and Bacchus to be rather more significant. . . . This bit must soar a little higher . . . harness your Pegasus for a little longer."[10] This fairly mild letter stung Hofmannsthal into a remarkable explication of the libretto's philosophical underpinning, the dualities of steadfastness versus metamorphosis of self; fidelity versus promiscuity; morality versus hedonism; spiritual heroism versus earthly tolerance. Dionysus here escapes from the pages of Nietzsche's book to appear onstage, serving Hofmannsthal's somewhat different philosophical ends.

9. *The Correspondence between Richard Strauss and Hugo von Hofmannsthal,* trans. Hanns Hammelmann and Ewald Osers (New York: Random House, 1961), 494–95.

10. Ibid., 92.

HUGO VON HOFMANNSTHAL
Letter to Richard Strauss (1911)

Aussee, Obertressen (mid July 1911)

My dear Doctor Strauss,

I must confess I was somewhat piqued by your scant and cool reception of the finished manuscript of *Ariadne,* compared with the warm welcome you gave to every single act of *Rosenkavalier*[11]—which stands out in my memory as one of the most significant pleasures connected with that work. I believe that in *Ariadne* I have produced something at least equally good, equally original and novel, and although we certainly agree in wishing to shun anything like the false show of mutual adulation in which mediocre artists indulge, I cannot help asking myself whether any praise in all the world could make up to me for the absence of yours.

You may of course have written your letter or read the manuscript when you were somewhat out of sorts, as happens so easily to creative artists; nor do I overlook the fact that a fairly subtle piece of work like this inevitably suffers seriously by being presented in manuscript rather than clear typescript (unfortunately my typist was ill). And so I am not without hope that closer acquaintance with my libretto will bring home to you its positive qualities. Set pieces like, say, the intermezzo, Zerbinetta's aria and the ensemble will not, I venture to say, be surpassed in their own line by anyone writing in Europe today. The way in which this work—though it adheres to the conventional form (which, properly understood, is full of appeal even to the librettist)—indicates and establishes its central idea quite naturally by making Ariadne and Zerbinetta represent diametrical contrasts in female character, or the manner in which I have led up to the arrival of Bacchus, first by the trio of the three women cutting each other short, next by the little Circe song,[12] and finally by Zerbinetta's announcement which, though important in itself, gives the orchestra predominance in that hymnlike march theme—all this, I must say, seemed to me to deserve some expression of appreciation on the part of the one person for whom my work was visualized, conceived and executed. I doubt, moreover, if one could easily find in any other libretto for a one-act opera three songs of comparable delicacy, and at the same time equally

11. *Der Rosenkavalier* (1911) was the wildly successful second collaboration of Strauss and Hofmannsthal—a comedy set in old Vienna, concerning an aristocratic wife in love with an impetuous boy, a boorish nobleman determined to seduce a serving maid (the impetuous boy in disguise), and the forthcoming marriage of the impetuous boy to an innocent girl. One measure of Hofmannsthal's difficult relationship with Strauss can be found in an anecdote: it is said that Hofmannsthal, after hearing *Der Rosenkavalier,* sighed, "God, how beautiful it would have been, if Lehár [Franz Lehár, composer of operettas] had done *Der Rosenkavalier,* instead of Strauss."

12. Circe was the enchantress of the *Odyssey* who turned men into pigs. Bacchus had just escaped from her clutches before coming upon Naxos.

characteristic in tone, as Harlekin's song, the rondo for Zerbinetta and the Circe song of Bacchus.

Not unnaturally I would rather have heard all this from you than be obliged to write it myself.

No doubt it will be possible to find a way of heightening the intensity of the end along the lines you indicate, but before we proceed to settle the degree and the manner of any such climax-building, let me try and explain in a few sentences the underlying idea or meaning of this little poetic work. What it is about is one of the straightforward and stupendous problems of life: fidelity; whether to hold fast to that which is lost, to cling to it even unto death—or to live, to live on, to get over it, to transform oneself, to sacrifice the integrity of the soul and yet in this transmutation to preserve one's essence, to remain a human being and not to sink to the level of the beast, which is without recollection. It is the fundamental theme of *Elektra,*[13] the voice of Electra opposed to the voice of Chrysothemis, the heroic voice against the human. In the present case we have the group of heroes, demi-gods, gods—Ariadne, Bacchus, (Theseus)—facing the human, the merely human group consisting of the frivolous Zerbinetta and her companions, all of them base figures in life's masquerade. Zerbinetta is in her element drifting out of the arms of one man into the arms of another; Ariadne could be the wife or mistress of *one* man only, just as she can be only *one* man's widow, can be forsaken only by *one* man. One thing, however, is still left even for her: the miracle, the God. To him she gives herself, for she believes him to be Death: he is both Death and Life at once; he it is who reveals to her the immeasurable depths in her own nature, who makes of her an enchantress, the sorceress who herself transforms the poor little Ariadne; he it is who conjures up for her in this world another world beyond, who preserves her for us and at the same time transforms her.

But what to divine souls is a real miracle, is to the earth-bound nature of Zerbinetta just an everyday love-affair. She sees in Ariadne's experience the only thing she *can* see: the exchange of an old lover for a new one. And so these two spiritual worlds are in the end ironically brought together in the only way in which they can be brought together: in non-comprehension.

In this experience of Ariadne's, which is really the monologue of her lonely soul, Bacchus represents no mere *deus ex machina;*[14] for him, too, the experience is vital.

---

13. *Elektra* (1909) was the first operatic collaboration of Strauss and Hofmannsthal. In Hofmannsthal's version (first produced as a play in 1903) of Sophocles' tragedy, Elektra is implacably intent on murdering her mother, Klytämnestra, and her mother's lover, Aegisth (who had conspired to kill Agamemnon, Elektra's father); but Elektra's sister Chrysothemis wants no part of murder and hopes only to have the normal domestic life of a woman.

14. *deus ex machina:* a god hauled down to the stage from a pulley; hence, a dramatist's plot device to impose a happy ending by fiat.

Innocent, young and unaware of his own divinity he travels where the wind takes him, from island to island. His first affair was typical, with a woman of easy virtue, you may say or you may call her Circe. To his youth and innocence with its infinite potentialities the shock has been tremendous: were he Harlekin, this would be merely the beginning of one long round of love affairs. But he is Bacchus; confronted with the enormity of erotic experience all is laid bare to him in a flash—the assimilation with the animal, the transformation, his own divinity. So he escapes from Circe's embraces still but not without a wound, a longing, not without knowledge. The impact on him now of this meeting with a being whom he can love, who is mistaken about him but is enabled by this very mistake to give herself to him wholly and to reveal herself to him in all her loveliness, who entrusts herself to him completely, exactly as one entrusts oneself to Death, this impact I need not expound further to an artist such as you.

It would be a very great joy to me if, by an early reply to this personal, friendly letter, you were to restore to me that sense of fine and intimate contact between us which I so much enjoyed during our earlier collaboration, and which has by now become indispensable to me.

Very sincerely yours,

Hofmannsthal

From *The Correspondence between Richard Strauss and Hugo von Hofmannsthal*, trans. Hanns Hammelmann and Ewald Osers (New York: Random House, 1961), 93–95.

After receiving Hofmannsthal's self-justification, Strauss wrote back on 19 July 1911:

I confess frankly that my first impression [of *Ariadne auf Naxos*] was one of disappointment. . . . The piece did not convince me until after I read your letter, which is so beautiful and explains the meaning of the action so wonderfully that a superficial musician like myself could not, of course, have tumbled into it. But isn't this a little dangerous? [15]

◾

Another approach to the opera problem—seriousness versus frivolity—can be seen in the works of Kurt Weill (1900–1950). Weill hoped that he could use his music for the good of the community; it is difficult to find a single piece from Weill's maturity that does not have a clear ethical intent. He worked to show the untenability of capitalism (*Rise and Fall of the City of Mahagonny*, 1930) and to show the harm of racism (*Lost in*

15. *The Correspondence between Strauss and Hofmannsthal*, 95.

the Stars, 1949) and seems among the most serious of composers. But for Weill this seriousness was completely compatible with the notion of providing pleasure to a wide audience. The terms of the debate have shifted: for a composer such as Schoenberg, seriousness is manifest through the use of advanced musical technology, whereas frivolity is
the consequence of pandering to the audience by providing it with familiar satisfactions;
but for Weill, seriousness is manifest through a sort of expert music that provides good
metaphors for resistance to evil and for human kindness, and frivolity is another name
for irresponsibility. A composer may be irresponsible by writing stupid hit tunes, or by
writing music so full of dissonance that it repels all but the narrowest circle of connoisseurs, and for Weill, these two extremes are equally immoral. But it should be remembered that no composer can be confined to a simple caricature: Schoenberg was no dem-
ocrat and indeed thought that music should be funded by princes, but his chorus
Verbundenheit (*Connectedness,* 1929), op. 35 no. 6, argues in favor of human community—we risk our lives to save the lives of others, you are not alone—in terms very comparable to Weill's.

Nietzsche's dream of a Dionysiac music theater, breaking down all divisions among
human beings, is greatly altered in Weill's music theater. For both Nietzsche and Weill,
community is the ultimate goal of music; but for Weill this community is attained not
through a dissolution into ecstasy, but through the most wide-awake means: a heightening of critical consciousness. For Weill, as for his collaborator Bertolt Brecht, a sharpened Apollo can provide glimpses of the oneness of the human race; Dionysus can provide only a private, complacent-making narcosis, a rapture of the deep.

KURT WEILL
"Shifts in Musical Composition" (1927)

If I am to address the question of the current musical situation from the point of view
of the creative musician, then I must restrict myself to considering that situation as it
relates to the state of development in my own production.

The development of music in recent years has chiefly been an aesthetic one. The
emancipation from the nineteenth century; the opposition to extra-musical influences
(program music, symbolism, realism); the return to absolute music; the hard-won acquisition of new expressive means (the enrichment of harmonic language, the cultivation of a new linearity) or an expansion of the old means—these were the ideas which
claimed musicians' attention. Today we have come a step further. A clear split is becoming apparent between, on the one hand, those musicians who, full of disdain for
their audience, continue as it were by shutting out the public sphere to work on the solution of aesthetic problems and, on the other, those who enter into contact with some
sort of audience, integrating their work into some sort of larger concern, because they

opera problematized — why?
max mahön (symbiotion) TARUSKIN

see that above the artistic there is also a common human attitude that springs from some sense of communal belonging and which has to be the determining factor behind the genesis of a work of art.

It is clear that this withdrawal from the individualistic principle of art, observable everywhere, has nowhere emerged with such eruptive force as in Germany, where the foregoing development (the influence of the nineteenth century and the violent emancipation from it) was much more intense. While the search for a community is, for us, by no means to be confused with any concession to public taste, a large number of musicians from Latin countries are thoroughly attuned to a a very cultivated type of *Gebrauchsmusik*. (Rieti, Poulenc, Auric, etc.)[16] The serious musicians in search of new expressive means are apparently much more isolated and receive much less public attention there than in Germany. Yet precisely in Paris, among a budding generation of musicians, a rejuvenation of Catholicism, which originates from literature, seems to be leading to a new sense of community. Moreover, a ritualistic tendency, untypical for French art and finding expression in the preference for themes from antiquity, is characteristic of the current situation. (Stravinsky's *Oedipus Rex*, Milhaud's minute operas.)[17] As far as they are known to us, however, the Russian musicians seem to have little affinity for communal art, although it is from them that one would most expect it. A conspicuous dependence on Scriabin[18] among many Russian musicians would seem to preclude a "revolutionary" attitude.

In Germany, then, there are the clearest signs that musical production must find a new justification for its existence. Here a restructuring of the public is clearly observable. The arts engendered by established society [*gesellschaftlichen*],[19] originating as

16. *Gebrauchsmusik* (music for use) is a term often associated with the composer Paul Hindemith—the term implies music for the pleasure of the performers, music for everyday, music not to be venerated but to be taken out and played. Vittorio Rieti (1898–1994) was an Italian (later American) composer who wrote brisk, clear, sophisticated music, including ballets for Diaghilev's company; Francis Poulenc (1899–1963) and Georges Auric (1899–1983) were two of the French composers of the group called Les Six, often noted for playful insouciance.

17. Stravinsky's *Oedipus Rex* appeared in 1927. When Hindemith asked Darius Milhaud (1892–1974), one of the group of Les Six, to write a brief opera for a festival in 1927, Milhaud obliged with *L'enlèvement d'Europe*—less than ten minutes long; later Milhaud wrote two other *opéras minutes* to make a trilogy.

18. Alexander Scriabin (1872–1915), Russian composer and synesthete, whose vertiginous aesthetic was far from Weill's—Scriabin dreamed of mystical fusions of hearing, sight, and smell, and even scored his *Prometheus* (1910) for a "light keyboard" as well as orchestra.

19. *gesellschaftlichen*: this refers to music for private societies, such as Schoenberg's Society for Private Performances, where advanced music was played for an audience forbidden to clap or register any other signs of approval or disapproval; Weill tended to deplore any sort of hothouse atmosphere for music reception.

they do from another age and another aesthetic, are increasingly losing ground. The new orchestral and chamber music, for which a genuine demand used to exist on the part of the public, nowadays relies almost exclusively on music societies and organizations devoted to the cultivation of new music whose patrons are themselves mainly musicians. That is why music is seeking a rapprochement with the interests of a wider public since only in this way will it retain its viability. It does so, first of all, by utilizing the lightness and musical facility [*Musizierfreudigkeit*] acquired in recent years, in order to create a worthwhile *Gebrauchsmusik*. The whole area of mechanical music and film music should no longer be the sole preserve of a cheap, everyday commodity. Rather, a young generation of musicians has set about cultivating this area of musical life, for which the public at large also displays an interest. It now depends on the resolve of the appropriate "industry" to lure the most talented young musicians and to provide them with the basis for a new development which by no means needs to involve trivialization of any kind.

In addition, we find attempts to attract an audience specifically for the appreciation and cultivation of New Music. Of decisively symptomatic significance in this connection is the activity of a number of musicians within the Amateur Musicians' Guild [*Musikantengilde*] (Hindemith, Ludwig Weber),[20] though it remains to be seen whether this youth movement is not too restricted to certain circles really to create the basis for the renewal of our musical culture or even for the creation of a people's art. More important than these endeavors is, for me, the fact that a large number of musicians whose merit is beyond doubt are again considering the possibility of speaking directly to a wider public. This much is certain: the clarity of language, the precision of expression and the simplicity of emotion, which new music has regained by pursuing a straight line of development, form together the secure aesthetic foundation for a wider dissemination of this art.

The current situation is most clearly evinced in the field of musical theatre. For opera today no longer represents a discrete musical genre (as in the nineteenth century) but has again taken its rightful place (starting, say, with Busoni's *Doktor Faust*)[21] in the whole area of absolute music. It will also represent a most decisive factor in the development whereby music is no longer accorded the role of an art form engendered by established society [*gesellschaftlichen*], but rather that of a socially regenerative or

20. The German word *Musikant* implies a strolling musician, as in the Middle Ages—a populist kind of musician. Paul Hindemith (1895–1963) was active in every sort of public music-making; Ludwig Weber (1891–1947) organized and wrote music for youth-movement musical groups.

21. Ferruccio Busoni (1866–1924), Weill's principal teacher, left *Doktor Faustus* unfinished at his death. Busoni was striving for an operatic style that would possess the rigor and intensity of purely instrumental music; Weill was perhaps less enamored of Busoni's belief that opera should confine itself to strictly unreal, fairy-tale-like themes.

promoting force [*gemeinschaftsbildenden*].[22] Hence it cannot restrict itself either to a purely aesthetic renaissance, which allows principles of musical style to be the sole determinants, or to representing matters of a merely superficial, topical relevance which are valid only for the briefest period of the work's genesis. I believe, above all, that musicians ought first to overcome their fear of truly equal collaborators. It has proved to be quite possible, working closely with representatives of equal stature in the sister arts, to set about creating the kind of music theatre that can provide an untopical [*unaktuelle*], unique and definitive representation of our age. I am also convinced, thanks to the newly attained inner and outer uncomplicatedness of subject matter and means of expression, that a branch of opera is evolving into a new epic form such as I employed with Brecht in the *Mahagonny* Songspiel.[23] True, this form of music theatre presupposes a basically theatrical type of music. Yet is also makes it possible to give opera a structure that is absolutely musical, even instrumental.

From "Verschiebungen in der musikalischen Produktion," *Berliner Tageblatt*, October 1927. Translated by Stephen Hinton in *Source Readings in Music History*, vol. 7, ed. Robert P. Morgan (New York: W. W. Norton, 1998), 123–25.

KURT WEILL
"Opera—Where To?" (1929)
"GEBRAUCHSMUSIK" AND ITS BOUNDARIES

Today, the idea of *Gebrauchsmusik* has permeated all those camps of modern music for whom it is at all within reach. We have forced back our aesthetic verdicts. We have come to understand that we must again create for our output its natural fertile ground; that music in its significance as the simplest human need can also be offered with heightened artistic means of expression; that the boundaries between "art music" and "music for use" [*Verbrauchsmusik*][24] must be brought closer and gradually eliminated.

For that reason, we have attempted to create music that is capable of satisfying the musical needs of broader levels of the population without giving up artistic substance. Therefore, we have not contented ourselves with simplifying our means of expression a little. We have, in fact, put aside aesthetic appraisal. In our music we want to allow men of our time to speak, and they ought to speak to many. The first question for us: is

22. *gemeinschaftsbildenden:* this refers to music that helps to create a spirit of vibrant community— Weill's explicit goal as a composer.

23. *Mahagonny* Songspiel: a short entertainment (1927) based on songs by Brecht, later expanded into *Rise and Fall of the City of Mahagonny* (1930).

24. *Verbrauchsmusik:* this term implies music that is written to be used and thrown away quickly, music without lasting value.

what we do useful to a general public? It is only a secondary question if what we create is art, for that is determined only by the quality of our work.

This attitude, expressed by a representative of "serious music" would have been inconceivable a few years ago. People would have rejected such a claim on the grounds that such a conversion of "art music" would be tied to the needs of the masses with severe concessions to the so-called public taste. The accuracy of this claim could only be tested through application. Today that has occurred.[25] But in no case is it the purpose of all these efforts to enter into combat with the composer of "hit-tunes," but rather merely to bring our music to the masses. That can be attained only if our music is capable of expressing simple human emotions and actions, only if it reproduces the natural condition of man.

With the attempt to advance this genre and to employ it in different areas, we also naturally recognize the dangers of this overall course. If we attempt gradually to eliminate the boundaries between art music and music for use, under no circumstances should the impression be created that we want to renounce the intellectual bearing of the serious musician in order to be able to compete fully with producers of lighter market wares. The superficial or hostile observer sees (or wants to see) only that simplification of the means of musical expression has been carried out to a high degree here, that the question "tonal or atonal?" is no longer discussed; that the question of originality no longer stands in first place; that fear of banality is finally overcome (which Busoni already had demanded ten years ago); above all, that here, with the use of elements of jazz, simple, easily-comprehensible melodies originate which superficially produce a more or less strong resemblance to the melodies of "light" music. In the process the observer all too often overlooks that the effect of this music is not catchy, but instead rousing; that the intellectual bearing of this music is thoroughly serious, bitter, accusing, and, in the most pleasant cases still ironic; that neither the poetry of this music nor the form of the music itself would be conceivable without the vast background of an ethical or social nature on which it is based. Also, one must not forget that the songs of *Die Dreigroschenoper* discovered or created a totally different attitude on the part of the public, and that this public expects something different from the continuance of this genre than from the older forms of "music for use." Here lie the dangers and at the same time the boundaries of our genre; we must not imitate the

25. To this belongs also the musical *Volksstück* as it is manifested in my *Die Dreigroschenoper* and *Happy End*. [Weill's note.] A *Volksstück* is a popular piece; *Die Dreigroschenoper* (The Threepenny Opera, 1928) was one of the great popular successes of the twentieth century; *Happy End* (1929) was a much less successful attempt at a sequel—almost deliberately sabotaged by strenuous communist rhetoric.

"hit" (and it has been proven often that we are not really able to do that). We may change our music only to the extent that we can carry on our intellectual tasks, the duties of the artist in his time, in an entirely perceptible, entirely understandable language.

THE DEVELOPMENTAL TRENDS OF OPERA

Seen in this way, this musical movement seems especially adapted to influence the development of opera. The situation of opera approximately corresponds to the general situation of music, as I have attempted to sketch it previously. On the one hand, one reckons that today a clearly delimited typical operatic audience still exists. This audience, which is not too large numerically, expects in the opera house quite specific impressions which are not allowed to proceed beyond the traditional concept of opera. Thus, one adjusts for this circle of listeners; in the choice of librettos and in the plan of the music one allows for the demands and the receptive capability of this operatic audience. On the other hand, the attempt is also made not to adjust exclusively for a relatively narrowly defined circle of special-interest groups, but rather to bring opera closer to the theater of the present [*Zeit*]. At the outset this is a daring undertaking, for a genre in which more is supposed to be spoken than sung must always occupy an exceptional position. But the modern theater comes to meet these endeavors forcefully, for its most important representatives have realized that certain stylistic elements of the new drama can only be accomplished musically. Since this new theater is aimed at the representation of man, of what he says and what he does, it approaches our musical endeavors, because we, too, seek new expressive possibilities for simple human events and relationships. If we succeed in finding a musical language which is just as natural as the language of the people in modern theater, it is also possible to deal with the monumental themes of our time with purely musical means in the form of opera. This would have a great advantage in comparison to the spoken drama in that we could determine musically the expression, the *gestus* [26] of the presentation, and in this way could prevent the serious performance errors from which the modern theater has too often suffered. These endeavors toward an approach by opera to spoken drama seem, on the other hand, to be deemed of considerable interest by the leaders of spoken drama. Today it is already possible to mount in a private theater in Berlin an opera with a libretto of literary merit and limited technical demands. . . .

If opera wishes once again to find a connection to "great theater," it must adopt the loose form that probably represents the most valuable achievement of the new theater. The loosest form of operatic theater until now has been the dialogue-opera, in which

26. *gestus:* gesture; a term from the eighteenth-century writer Lessing used by Weill and Brecht to mean the basic vocabulary of music theater, the telling twist of rhythm or melody or bodily movement that embodies a social meaning.

the plot is advanced in the spoken dialogue, while the music enters only at static moments of the plot. The principle of number-opera has been taken up again in many musical stage works of recent years as a reaction to music-drama. But it has been accomplished for purely musical-formal reasons. The music has been arranged in numbers, to be sure, but it has in addition been given the ungrateful duty of supplying the background for the incidents of the stage, of sustaining the plot. In *Die Dreigroschenoper,* which we designated from the beginning as the prototype of opera, the music again assumes its irrational role: it interrupts the plot when the action has arrived at a situation that permits music and song to appear. In the opera, *Aufstieg und Fall der Stadt Mahagonny,*[27] this principle could be pushed still further. Here the plot is nothing more than the history of a city. Every musical number is a complete musical scene and short intervening texts create the possibility for the entry of new music in every case.

From "Die Oper—Wohin?" *Berliner Tageblatt,* 31 October 1929; cited in Kim Kowalke, *Kurt Weill in Europe* (Ann Arbor: UMI Research Press, 1979), 506–9.

■

Weill tried to write music that accomplished two things at once: it served an ethical purpose, community formation; and it succeeded as absolute music, music that would make perfect sense if it had no text at all. Weill perhaps understood these two things as aspects of a single goal: any piece of music that makes perfect internal sense, from a Mozart string quartet to a rousing workers' song, serves the cause of human liberation.

Other operatic composers also insisted that they wrote music that was simultaneously dramatic and absolute. For example, Alban Berg (1885–1935) devised *Wozzeck* according to the recipe of old forms, "all these diverse fugues and inventions, suites and sonatas, variations and passacaglias," as Berg enumerates them below; but these old forms are more visible to the score reader than audible to the spectator, for Berg concealed them in a flexible and arresting dramatic language, sensitive to the most local and intimate motions of the text. The musicologist Theodor Adorno wrote a book about his teacher entitled *Alban Berg: Master of the Smallest Link* (1968); and the combination of attention to tiny textual details and obedience to grand strict formalities of the sort associated with instrumental music, not opera, is perhaps unmatched in the history of music.

Wozzeck (1925) is based on an astonishingly forward-looking play by Georg Büchner (1813–37), *Woyzeck,* not quite finished at Büchner's early death. It concerns a brutal and much-put-upon soldier, the victim of sinister medical experiments ("You've got a

27. *Rise and Fall of the City of Mahagonny* (1930), a parable about the origin of capitalism, concerning the founding of a Florida city in which you can do anything you want—as long as you have money.

splendid *aberratio mentalis partialis* of the second species . . . eat only beans!"), subject to apocalyptic hallucinations, driven mad when his mistress sleeps with a drum major; eventually he stabs her to death and drowns himself. Though Berg doesn't emphasize social commitment in his essays, Büchner wrote pamphlets advocating socialism, and the refrain "Wir arme Leut'"("We poor people") evokes a good deal of sympathy both in the play and the opera. *Wozzeck* may be remarkable for its Neoclassicism, its textures of sonata and fugue and passacaglia; but the listener is less aware of Apollo than of Dionysus, as the music lurches toward the abyss—toward auditory symbols of the earth on fire at the Last Judgment, of a man, lit by moonlight, sinking into a black lake.

ALBAN BERG
"The 'Problem of Opera'" (1928)

"What do you about the further evolution of a timely [*zeitgemäß*] opera?" I think what I think about every evolution in artistic matters: one day there will arise a masterwork, so clearly pointing to the future, that one could, simply by virtue of its existence, speak of the "further evolution of opera." The use of "timely" means, such as cinema,[28] music hall, loudspeaker, or jazz music, only guarantees that these works belong to the present moment. But it can't be called real progress; for this is precisely the point at which we've already arrived, and through those means alone we can go no further.

To be able to speak of the further evolution of the art-form of opera—as happened for example in the operas of Monteverdi, Lully, Gluck, Wagner, and, more recently, Schoenberg—something is needed far beyond the mere pressing into service of recent technical achievements, of procedures that are for a moment in vogue.[29]

But is it always necessary to "evolve further"? Isn't it enough to make beautiful music in the service of good theater, or, better yet, to compose music so beautiful that it might become good theater, in spite of everything?

And now I've arrived at my personal position concerning the "problem of opera," and I need to talk about it, because I must correct an error too often made since my opera *Wozzeck* has become known. . . .

I never even dreamed of wanting to reform the art form of opera by composing *Wozzeck.* I didn't intend this when I began to compose, and just as little did I consider

28. In this paragraph, Berg is trying to distinguish *Wozzeck* from the aggressively contemporary manners of the *Zeitoper;* but Berg himself was to write a musical interlude to accompany a silent film in his second opera, *Lulu,* unfinished at his death in 1935.

29. Most of the renewals that Berg mentions here concern attempts to reorient opera away from show-off singing and toward dramatic verities—a theme especially prominent in Gluck's reform opera *Orfeo* (1762). Jean-Baptiste Lully (1632–1687) was the founder of the musical *tragédie* in France.

the finished opera as a model for my own future work or for the works of other composers, nor did I accept or expect that *Wozzeck* could "found a school."

Apart from the wish to compose good music, to fulfill in music the spiritual content
of Büchner's immortal drama, to transpose its poetical language into musical language,
there was in my mind, at the moment when I decided to write the opera, nothing else
(even with respect to compositional technique nothing else) but the wish to give to the
theater something theatrical, and to fashion music conscious at every moment of its
obligation to serve the drama—and further, to make sure that the music could force out
of itself everything that the drama needed in order to be transformed into the reality of
the stage, a task that demands from the composer all the essential duties of a stage director. To be sure: without prejudice to music's absolute (purely musical) right to exist,
without prejudice to its autonomous life, unhindered by anything nonmusical.

As a result of this, it happened naturally that I brought into play more-or-less ancient
musical forms (one of the most important of my supposed operatic reforms).

For my libretto, I had to make a selection of Büchner's twenty-six scenes, loosely
connected and sometimes fragmentary, while avoiding repetitions that weren't susceptible to musical variation; furthermore, I had to bring the scenes together, juxta-
pose them, and group them into acts. Whether I wished it or not, these problems turned
out to be more musical than literary in nature; they were to be solved only with the laws
of musical architecture, not with the laws of dramaturgy.

The shaping of the fifteen remaining scenes, selected and drawn together in order
to maximize contrast (the only way of assuring clarity and impressiveness), particularly
forbade me from doing what is usual: continuous "through-composition" according to
the contents of the literary text. After a small number of scenes, this sort of absolute
music, so structurally rich, so strikingly illustrative of the dramatic events, would not
have been able to avoid a noticeable feeling of musical monotony, a feeling of aversion
growing through a series of a dozen symphonic interludes, offering nothing but a fulfillment of the consequences of this illustrative style of writing—monotony aggravated to
the point of boredom. And boredom is the last thing you want to feel in the theater!

When I obeyed the commanding requirement, to give each scene, each piece of orchestral music—prelude, postlude, transition, and interlude—its own unmistakable
musical face, rounded off, closed, the result was to bring forward what assures distinct
characterization on one hand and closure on the other: the much-discussed use of
those old or new musical forms, even those previously associated only with absolute
music.

Their introduction into the realm of opera may have been in many respects and to
such a great extent uncustomary, indeed new. What I have just said proves that there is
no merit in the charge! This is why I can and must deny resolutely that I've reformed the
art form of opera through these innovations.

Since I don't make this declaration in order to minimize the value of my work—other people, who know my work less well, can do this much better—I want to reveal what I consider my exclusive success.

No matter how much one knows of the musical forms contained in this opera, of the rigor and logic of their elaboration, of the artistic dexterity lying hidden even in their least detail, from the moment when the curtain rises until it falls for the last time, there can be no member of the audience who notices all these diverse fugues and inventions, suites and sonatas, variations and passacaglias—no one who is full of anything else but this opera's Idea, transcending the individual fate of Wozzeck. In that, I think, I've succeeded!

From "Das 'Opernproblem,'" *Neue Musik-Zeiting*, 49. Jahrgang, Heft 9, Stuttgart 1928; cited in Willi Reich, *Alban Berg: Mit Bergs eigenen Schriften* (Vienna: Herbert Reichner Verlag, 1937); translated by the editor.

■

The Austrian (later American) composer Ernst Krenek (originally Křenek; 1900–1991) was prolific in many different styles and genres. Among the high points of his career are *Reisebuch aus den österreichischen Alpen* (*Travel Book from the Austrian Alps*, 1929)—a sort of sequel to Schubert's *Winterreise*—and *Lamentatio Jeremiae Prophetae* (1940–42), which seeks to combine twelve-tone technique with church modes. But he is best known for writing one of the greatest hits in history of opera, *Jonny spielt auf* (*Jonny Strikes Up the Band*, 1927), in which the drama (concerning a black American fiddler and a sober, sentimental European composer) is mostly generated from the opposition of musical styles, from hot jazz to near atonality. Here the jazz musician—a thief, almost a rapist, a force of misrule—plays the role of Dionysus, as if European art music had become ingrown, conventional, and precious, and needed some external stimulus to goad it to move. It is also a profoundly Nietzschean opera in that the drama (as in operas based on the Orpheus theme) follows from the music, not vice versa: the plot concerns a stolen violin, a symbol of music itself, evidently in danger of expropriation by the New World.

The essay printed here extends the argument of *Jonny spielt auf* into the domain of prose. Here Krenek defends the thesis that, for the first time in history, composers are pursuing operatic reform, not by trying to subordinate music to drama, but by trying to subordinate drama to music. If the tone of this essay is more Apollonian than Dionysian (in that Krenek stresses the artificiality, the contrived, "cold" quality of the operatic experience), this may follow from the devout Roman Catholicism that Krenek adopted in the mid-1930s. This was also the time when he began to write most of his music (beginning with the Christian opera *Karl V*, 1934) in the Schoenbergian twelve-tone style.

Perhaps there is a parallel with Schoenberg's own reconversion to Judaism, as if strict musical discipline accords with strict religious discipline.

ERNST KRENEK
from "Is Opera Still Possible Today?" (1936)

Strictly speaking this question has been asked in every period since the puzzling and contradictory affair which is opera has existed. There is no need even to consult the huge mass of theoretical writings on the problem of opera; the numerous opera-parodies, which are almost as old an institution as opera itself and faithfully attend all its various manifestations, are proof enough. Many of the parodies outgrew the original target they had aimed for, and themselves created new styles, thereby giving new life to the very object of their satire—one need only think of the *Beggar's Opera*[30] in early times, later Offenbach and Nestroy,[31] and in the present era the collaborations of Brecht and Weill and many features of Milhaud, Hindemith and others. One of the essential points about these parodies, I think, is that their darts are not only aimed at the particular contemporary manifestation or style of opera which inspired them; they nearly always attack the essentially operatic features of opera in general. It is not only the values of Handelian opera, by then felt to be stilted, that the *Beggar's Opera* was attempting to reveal as vapid, and not only Meyerbeer's high-flown attitudes that Offenbach attacked in his *Barbe Bleue*,[32] but "opera" as such—and moreover always on the basis of the rational argument that it is absurd for people to "sing" while doing things which are obviously part of normal life. The question of whether opera is "still" possible nearly always implies another question—is it possible at the pitch of rationality then reached to swallow the "nonsensical" essence of opera with equanimity and credulity. Objections of this more aesthetic sort are immediately supplemented by the doubt as to whether it is permissible from an ethical point of view to continue this

30. *The Beggar's Opera* (1728) is a satirical opera by the poet John Gay (1685–1732), who wrote songs designed to fit popular tunes (some by Purcell and Handel)—a musician named Pepusch provided an overture. The plot concerns the thief Macheath, who marries a fence's daughter without her father's consent; the outraged father turns him over to the police. Gay provided many links between the world of thieves and prostitutes and the world of Prime Minister Robert Walpole and high political action. The immense popularity of *The Beggar's Opera* almost drove Handel's company out of England and created a new genre of ballad operas. A new vogue for *The Beggar's Opera* following a 1921 production led to the Brecht-Weill *Threepenny Opera* (1928).

31. The operettas of Jacques Offenbach (1819–80) often contain parodies of serious operas by Gluck, Donizetti, and others. Johann Nestroy (1801–62), Viennese actor-dramatist, wrote satirical plays that often contain musical skits.

32. *Bluebeard* (1866), operetta by Offenbach. The showman-composer Giacomo Meyerbeer (1792–1864) helped to put grandiosity into grand opera.

nonsense, when it obviously contains a fair amount of falsification. Carrying out such an exacting type of nonsense often contrasts with the questionable reality of life itself and this leads to sociological considerations that in the end take the question of opera's possibility out of the purely intellectual, cultural sphere and into a completely practical and material one.

The reason why the nature of opera is called into question again and again in this way doubtless has to do with the fact that opera is an artificial product, in the most literal sense. Whatever crises the theatre may go through nobody directly questions its right to exist, nobody doubts that the theatre is a relatively "constant" activity of the human race—the proof being that its origins are lost in the mists of legend and myth. Opera, on the other hand, at least the form of musical drama we call by that name, is not only a very young form but has clearly visible and even rather suspect origins: it was invented, in a rather cold way, by literary men who were quite remote from any current of musical feeling. Everyone has heard of the papers of the Florentine camerata of enthusiastically humanistic aristocrats who used many of their meetings to create as faithful as possible a reconstruction of Attic tragedy and ended up by finding that their experiment had produced opera.

It is obvious that however one may imagine Greek drama was performed, opera does not bear the slightest resemblance to it, not even the opera that was the result of those early scholarly experiments, let alone opera as it later grew and developed. Yet, although this fact was fairly self-evident and became ever more so as research into antiquity progressed, the questionable link with classical drama remained, for some strange reason, a decisive factor in the development of opera. All the "reformers" of opera, from Monteverdi through Gluck to Wagner, made their ideas revolve round this imagined revival of Greek drama, and often tried to justify the boldness of their innovations by adducing their similarity to the spirit and practice of classical Greek dramaturgy. Wagner, who of course was no longer so ingenuous as to believe that his music-drama resembled Greek tragedy in any technical particular whatever, tried to claim that his "total work of art" [*Gesamtkunstwerk*] at least had the same sociological functions in relation to the wished-for German nation that Hellenic festivals had in relation to the community feeling of the Greek nation. This is a rare phenomenon—a purely paper fiction gaining a very genuine power over the reality of an area of life and culture merely through the force of values and attitudes it had conjured up itself.

The so-called "reforms" which revolutionize the development of opera from time to time are always concerned with giving the intellectual content of the language and drama a new, more crucial position. All the innovators agree in seeing operatic singing as a kind of heightened speech—from Monteverdi who tried to re-create a "Pyrrhic" style[33] he had dreamed of by using the enormously dramatic and bold means of rapid note-repetition, to Richard Wagner, who went to great trouble to demonstrate how the musical conception grew out of the dramatic and linguistic one. These reforms always seem necessary, because opera, when left more to itself, shows a tendency to become an exhibition of vocal qualities and singing achievements. These fulfil a sensual need of the public's, and explain why the "reforms" were and are so passionately fought against at first: they rob opera, for a time at least, of its pleasurable, sensual quality.

This is, in fact, the point from which today's criticism of the opera-phenomenon principally starts. The idea is roughly this: it is a pure fiction that opera can be given a significance higher than sensual pleasure by shifting the accent to the language and drama; this is merely a sort of rationalized superstructure which serves the "reformers" as an excuse for creating new and hitherto unexploited forms of vocal exhibition. The proof of this is supposed to be that the daring and hotly disputed innovations of their day, once they have sufficiently taken root in the consciousness of opera and the public, end by revealing their function as pleasure givers, and hence are then defended against further innovations. Wagner, the argument runs, is not prized and admired for the new quality of his total art-work, as he intended, for the way the music heightens and underlines the significance of his dramatic conceptions; he is valued because, despite all these speculative achievements, the public has learnt to track down the purely operatic side of his work, the side that appeals to the sensual instincts; moreover all his intellectual apparatus only had the result of extending the pleasure-potentialities in the sphere of opera. From this the conclusion is drawn that opera only has life in it in so far as it can satisfy the need for pleasure. And it is not possible for opera to exist in the present day, it is objected, because as regards society in general it cannot compete with the cheaper and more direct pleasure-givers which can satisfy the relevant needs of large social classes much better. What is more, it is not even a desirable thing for these classes to be offered pleasure-givers of this or any other kind, for they distract their attention from much more important general matters.

However much justice there is in this reasoning, it does not entirely get to the heart of the problem, in that it accepts the category "pleasure" undialectically. It may be true that the first impulse to listen to opera is a desire for the pleasant sensual impressions it induces. But as the desire to produce these impressions is not the only motive for

33. In the preface to his eighth book of madrigals (1638), Monteverdi wrote that there were three basic representational styles: the *stile molle* (soft style, associated with pathos and dejection) and the *stile temperato* (calm style) were the normal means of madrigal composers; but Monteverdi claimed to have invented the third style, the *stile concitato* (excited style), suitable for the rhetoric of war. This third style, a stutter of sixteenth notes, was based on the pyrrhic foot (short-short) of classical prosody.

creating opera, the additional—or rather original—values are felt in "consuming" the pleasure and through the pleasure itself, so that it too takes on completely changing virtues. These special modifications of pleasure have been studied by Bert Brecht[34] in particular, and his *Mahagonny* is the significant result of these studies, not only having pleasure as a subject but also presenting what it has to say about it in the form of opera, which is recognized as a particularly "pleasurable" form. Nevertheless it must be admitted that the conclusions Brecht draws from his doctrine are not perhaps entirely unequivocal; they are certainly not the only possible conclusions. For it should be noted that although at first the "pleasure-seekers" reject anything unusual as a bar to pleasure, they really crave it, unwittingly, because in the end they grow tired of the pleasure they cling to so stubbornly. Because novelty is rejected in this way, the innovators always produce polemics against the purely pleasurable function of opera, and to this extent it is true that their theories can be viewed as the framework which supports their innovations. But the really important thing is just the inescapable urge of the truly creative nature to express something new, and viewed from this immanent angle the question of opera's continued feasibility depends purely on whether there are sufficient creative gifts with the need and ability to express something new through the medium of opera. Compared with this, the problem of whether this new element is able to exercise the pleasure-giving functions, or whether and when it will itself become a mere pleasure-giver is entirely unimportant.

To assess correctly the inner justification and feasibility of opera today—and only this can give a worthwhile answer to our question—one needs to examine how the new element manifest in today's opera has altered opera's substance. And here it may be said that this new element eminently justifies its existence in the face of all skeptical opposition, in that it accepts the contradictions with which opera is reproached and tries to make them dialectically productive. First of all, there are all the tendencies towards destroying the illusion[35] of opera as a self-contained form, the tendencies which underline the "non-sense" of sung words. In contrast to Wagner, who aimed to make

---

34. Bertolt Brecht (1898–1956), German poet, playwright, and dramatic theorist, who collaborated with Kurt Weill in the opera *Rise and Fall of the City of Mahagonny* (1930). Krenek is alluding to an essay of Brecht's printed later in this volume.

35. The concept of an anti-illusionistic art is important in Modernist thought. In chapter 21 of Thomas Mann's novel *Dr. Faustus* (1947), the composer-hero opines, "The work of art? It is a fraud. . . . Pretense and play [*Schein und Spiel*] have the conscience of art against them today. Art would like to stop being pretense and play, it would like to become knowledge" (Mann, *Dr. Faustus,* trans. H. T. Lowe-Porter [New York: Modern Library, 1966], 181). Theodor Adorno, however, offers this warning to the anti-illusionist: "Since the work, after all, cannot be reality, the elimination of all illusory features accentuates all the more glaringly the illusory character of its existence" (*Philosophy of Modern Music,* trans. Anne G. Mitchell and Wesley V. Blomster [New York: Seabury, 1973], 70).

the medium of music-drama so tight and self-contained that it could exist autonomously side by side with—or best of all, instead of—spoken drama, without the question of its principles of existence ever arising at all, they accept that there is a wide gulf between sung and spoken drama and that the one is not an organic, gradual heightening of the Other, but an artificial world quite opposite to it.

This destruction of the pretense probably stems from Romantic and Baroque stylistic principles, but in the form in which Cocteau[36] and Claudel[37] have introduced it into the world of opera it means something completely new. Claudel, in particular, has originated the idea of dividing the stage into various levels on which things happening at different times can be played simultaneously, often intertwined with one another. To this trend belongs Brecht's demonstrative-didactic style, in which the action is interrupted by observations, discussions and explanations, so that the pretense of a self-contained formal whole is destroyed. It is interesting that after being in at the birth of opera, literary men have also provided important impulses at various later turning-points of its history.

These impulses would of course remain infertile—indeed they would never occur at all—if new possibilities on the musical side did not tempt creators to approach the dramatic element in a new way. If it had not been for the musical upheaval that made itself felt in the most decisive way at the turn of the century, the writers just mentioned would hardly have thought of applying new ideas to the dramatic aspect of opera. The very fact that in music fundamental changes emerged from the development begun by Schoenberg made the musical element as such take the limelight—a move that had been heralded by Debussy's attitude, which was, of course, considerably removed from that of Wagner. Busoni's attempts at neoclassicism and the reintroduction of old, clearly demarcated forms into opera music are further heralds and symptoms of the new attitude. For the first time in operatic history, perhaps, a movement intent on saving clear musical form from being flooded by the stream of realistic drama is not a reactionary symptom; for once people are trying to safeguard the musical side just because the changes made within music are radical. This neoclassicism only takes on a

---

36. Jean Cocteau (1889–1963), French playwright, poet, novelist, filmmaker, caricaturist, and wit. Krenek might be thinking of a number of anti-illusionistic (or self-consciously illusionistic) stage works in which Cocteau was involved, such as the ballet *Parade* (1917), the technological spoof *Les mariés de la Tour Eiffel* (1921), and *Oedipus Rex* (1927).

37. Paul Claudel (1868–1955), playwright, diplomat, and Roman Catholic apologist, worked closely with Milhaud and Honegger; indeed Milhaud worked as Claudel's secretary when both were attached to the French embassy in Brazil. Krenek is probably thinking of the Milhaud-Claudel exotic ballet *L'homme et son désir* (1918), set in the Brazilian jungle; Claudel divided the stage into four terraces on which Milhaud arrayed his (largely percussion) orchestra.

reactionary character when and where it confines itself to reconstructing archaic forms and tries to take no account of the new musical achievements.

Unlike the reactionaries who, in the name of "pure musicality," have always opposed the "reformers" starting out from the dramatic side, the new, musically orientated current within opera does not aim to increase its sensual pleasure in the customary sense. In fact the new musical language has just the opposite character; its radical quality tends rather to heighten the feeling of alienation. With the further advance of "atonality"—that is, the new, radical musical language—the emphatic use of old forms has disappeared too; at first they had served as clear signs of a resistance to the anarchic arbitrariness of dramatic "truth" (even in *Wozzeck* by Alban Berg these old forms, though camouflaged, play an important if already rather outmoded part). This movement too rests on the ideology of a higher reality, but unlike the ideologies of the early "reforms" of opera, which always thought reality could be attained by laying more emphasis on dramatic realism, on "expression" (actually, of course, this only created more stylizing factors, for opera is a stylized drama by definition)—unlike these, then, the new movement tries to get reality not by perfecting the illusion, but by doing away with it altogether.

Taking the ending of pretenses as the basic intention of a new operatic style makes opera a particularly pregnant expression of the antagonistic outlook of the present age and at the same time makes it the very opposite of present-day political tendencies, which, whether of the right or of the left, go in for concealing antitheses and simulating a united, coherent world—and do not scruple to use force to do so, which in itself is the most blatant symptom of internal paradox.

. . . The essential question is whether opera as such still has an inner life-force, and I think the above considerations lead us to a decided "yes."

From "Is Opera Still Possible Today?," in *Exploring Music: Essays by Ernst Krenek,* trans. Margaret Shenfield and Geoffrey Skelton (New York: October House, 1966), 97–104, 111. First published in *Sonderdruck* (1936).

■

Nietzsche's hope for a future music theater in which Dionysus and Apollo make themselves immanent has been realized in many different aspects of twentieth-century drama. But perhaps the most explicit realization of all can be found in those operas fashioned around Euripides' *Bacchae* (ca. 408 B.C.)—the most Nietzschean plot line of all, in that the play consists of a slow unveiling of the god Dionysus, until he is seen in full loathsomeness and glory. King Pentheus is disturbed that the worship of Dionysus has led to rioting among the women of Thebes, including his own mother, Agave; he tries to arrest the stranger god but fails; then he is tricked into dressing as a woman and climbing a tree to watch the orgy in which the women smear themselves with the blood of animals; the women see him, pull him down from the tree, and tear him limb from limb; finally Agave goes home, thinking she is carrying the head of a lion—but the head is actually her own son's. Nietzsche disliked *The Bacchae,* because he thought that Euripides, a dupe of Socratic rationalism, misrepresented, even depraved, the sacred force of Dionysus; and yet a dramatist inspired by Nietzsche's themes is likely to turn to *The Bacchae,* for nowhere else in Greek literature is the abyss beneath all human knowledge felt so strongly.

Dionysus is an attractive operatic hero—as we see in Karol Szymanowski's *King Roger* (1926), Harry Partch's *Revelation in the Courthouse Park* (1960–61), and Hans Werner Henze's *The Bassarids* (1965–66), all based on *The Bacchae.* Dionysus is popular because he is the most somatic of heroes. He doesn't engage in intellectual speculation, but thinks with his body; he is the god of drunkenness, of blind huggings, of blind rippings, objectless, polymorphous-perverse. It is not far from Dionysus to Don Giovanni. Clearly Partch liked Dionysus because he offered the ideal pretext for the corporeal music he advocated; and W. H. Auden (1907–73), the co-librettist (with Chester Kallman) of *The Bassarids* (and, more famously, Stravinsky's opera *The Rake's Progress*), also thought that music pertained to the physical body:

> Music cannot imitate nature: a musical storm always sounds like the wrath of Zeus. . . .
>
> Man's musical imagination seems to be derived almost exclusively from his primary experiences—his direct experience of his own body, its tensions and rhythms, and his direct experience of desiring . . .
>
> . . . Opera in particular is an imitation of human willfulness; it is rooted in the fact that we not only have feelings but insist upon having them at whatever cost to ourselves. . . .
>
> Every high C accurately struck demolishes the theory that we are the irresponsible puppets of fate and chance.[38]

Auden sees opera as a medium for the assertion of the private bodily will. But perhaps there is another sort of will, not private at all, but communal, destructive, mass-hysterical. This is the sort of will that Auden treats in the libretto to *The Bassarids.* Dionysus is an incarnation of a will that transcends any finite organism—indeed, Nietzsche derived him in part from Schopenhauer's notion of will, the urgency at the heart of creation that sends out its tentacles through every living thing, striving spasmodically, idiotically, onward.

Auden thought that this sort of will was Romantic and immoral. (Auden's attitude toward Romanticism can be seen from the title of a course he taught at Swarthmore:

---

38. W. H. Auden, *The Dyer's Hand* (New York: Random House, 1962), 466–67, 470, 474.

"Romanticism from Rousseau to Hitler.") Auden was a Christian and what he called a Horatian—that is, someone who thought that poetry should be modest, worldly, ironical, self-deprecating, formal, tight, and *civilisé*. These are the least operatic of virtues, and—as the following essay shows—Auden enjoyed the chance to escape from the self-imposed strictures of his poetics by writing opera libretti. But he refused the opportunity to glorify Dionysus: indeed, this essay hints strongly that Dionysus reminded him of the Freudian id (the unconscious locus of repressed desires) and of Hitler. In this sense, Auden was of Socrates' and Euripides' party, not Nietzsche's.

W. H. AUDEN
from "The World of Opera" (1967)

A number of years back Mr. Kallman and I told Mr. Henze [39] that we thought the *Bacchae* of Euripides was excellent potential material for a grand opera libretto, since the myth seemed to us exceptionally relevant to our own day.

The eighteenth century took it for granted that, in a conflict between Reason and Unreason, Reason was bound in the end to be victorious. So, in *Die Zauberflöte*,[40] The Queen of the Night has a daughter, Pamina, Sarastro acquires a princely disciple, Tamino, the two young innocents fall in love, and the curtain falls upon preparations for their wedding. Even a century later, a librettist or a composer, looking for a suitable operatic subject, would probably have rejected the *Bacchae* as too unnatural. Such events, they would have said, may have occurred in a primitive barbaric society, but social and intellectual progress have made it impossible for anything of the kind ever to occur again. For the nineteenth century, the myth was moribund.

Today we know only too well that it is as possible for whole communities to become demonically possessed as it is for individuals to go off their heads. Further, what the psychologists have taught us about repression and its damaging, sometimes fatal effects, makes us look at Sarastro with a more critical eye. Like Pentheus when confronted by the cult of Dionysus, Sarastro's only idea of how to deal with the Queen of the

---

39. Hans Werner Henze (b. 1926), German composer specializing in stage works urging social revolt, such as *El Cimarrón* (1969–70), concerning a Cuban slave rebellion. Henze had previously collaborated with Auden and Kallman on *Elegy for Young Lovers* (1961), an opera about a monstrously selfish poet, based to some extent on Yeats.

40. *The Magic Flute* (1792), by Mozart and Emanuel Schikaneder, is a fairy tale about the daughter of the Queen of the Night, Pamina, who falls in love with Tamino; when she falls into the hands of the agents of Sarastro, Tamino sets out to rescue her; but it turns out that Sarastro intends only good (of an enlightened, Masonic-humanistic sort) and has to defeat the Queen of the Night—which he does, after initiating Tamino and Pamina into the mysteries of Isis and Osiris. Auden and Kallman translated *The Magic Flute* (with many textual alterations) in 1955.

Night is to use force, magical in his case, and banish her to the underworld. "Suppose," we cannot help wondering, "there had been no Tamino and Pamina to provide a tidy and happy ending, would Sarastro have enjoyed his triumph for long? Is it not more likely that, in the end, he would have suffered at the hands of the implacable Queen as horrid a fate as Pentheus?" . . .

Certain scenes in his tragedy, notably the scene in which Pentheus confronts the disguised Dionysus, the scene in which Dionysus hypnotizes Pentheus till he is willing to dress up as a woman and go to Mount Kithairon, and the scene in which Cadmus[41] brings Agave out of her trance to a realization of the appalling thing she has done, seemed to us excellent operatic material as they stood, so that our libretto could in these scenes follow the original text pretty closely. . . .

Agave has lost all faith in the traditional polytheism in which she was brought up, and when the opera opens she believes in nothing. She is lonely and unhappy, feelings she hides behind a mask of cynical bitchiness, though really a passionate nature. The obvious cause of her loneliness is that she has been left a widow when still fairly young, and there is no man of equal rank whom she could take as a second husband. Her dissatisfaction, however, goes much deeper than sexual frustration. Though not consciously aware of it, she is desperately looking for some faith which will give her life meaning and purpose. Such a faith Dionysus seems to offer. . . .

One may suppose, if one likes, that Pentheus has visited Ionia and studies under one of the philosophers there. At any rate, he has discarded polytheism, the gods of which have all the passions and vices of mortals, and come to believe in the One Good, universal, impersonal, apprehensible to human reason. For him, the source of blindness and evil is the flesh with its passions. As King of Thebes, he is willing to tolerate the traditional cults for the time being, but not the new cult of Dionysus, which seems to him the deliberate worship of irrational passion. His attempt to completely repress his own instinctual life instead of trying to integrate it with his rationality puts him into Dionysus' hands. . . .

Lastly, a word about the costumes. To dress all the characters in Greek costume would be risky, since it demands the kind of figure which few opera singers possess. To live, as we do, in an historically conscious age, means that for us, each historical epoch has its typical character and attitude to life, which are reflected in what they wear. It seemed to us, therefore, that we could use clothing as a kind of visual shorthand, so that, when a singer entered, the audience would at once guess the kind of character he or she represented. So Cadmus is dressed as an old king out of a fairy-tale, thousands of years old, Tiresias as an Anglican archdeacon, Pentheus like a portrait of one of

41. Cadmus: Pentheus's grandfather, the founder of Thebes.

those pious mediaeval kings, Dionysus as a Regency dandy, Agave and Autonoe in the fashion of the Second Empire, and when, near the end, the chorus of Bassarids[42] swarm on to the stage, they are dressed as Beats.[43] . . .

Judging by the poetry they have written, all the modern poets whom I admire seem to share my conviction that, in this age, poetry intended to be spoken or read can no longer be written in a High, even in a golden style, only in a Drab one to use these terms as Professor C. S. Lewis[44] has used them. By a Drab style, I mean a quiet tone of voice which deliberately avoids drawing attention to itself as Poetry with a capital P, and a modesty of gesture. Whenever a modern poet raises his voice, he makes me feel embarrassed, like a man wearing a wig or elevator shoes.

I have—I imagine most of my colleagues have too—my theories about why this should be so, but I shall not bore you by inflicting them on you. For non-dramatic poetry, this raises no problem; for verse-drama it does. In writing his verse plays, Mr. Eliot took, I believe, the only possible line. Except at a few unusual moments, he kept the style Drab. I cannot think, however, that he was altogether happy at having to do this, for to perform in public is, as we say, "to put on an act"; this a High style can unashamedly do, but a drab style has to pretend it is not "making a scene." What I have tried to show you is that, as an art-form involving words, Opera is the last refuge of the High style, the only art to which a poet with a nostalgia for those times past when poets could write in the grand manner all by themselves can still contribute, provided he will take the pains to learn the metier, and is lucky enough to find a composer he can believe in.

From W. H. Auden, *Secondary Worlds* (New York: Random House, 1968), 109–10, 112–13, 115–16.

42. Bassarids: followers of Dionysus.

43. Beats: beatniks, 1950s-style existentialists, both hip and cool, often dressed in black. Harry Partch had similar thoughts when he made the Dionysus figure of *Revelation in the Courthouse Park* a charismatic rock musician.

44. Clive Staples Lewis (1898–1963), literary critic and fabulist; his distinction between golden poetry (ornate diction, magniloquent cadences) and drab (close to the texture of common speech) can be found in *English Literature in the Sixteenth Century, Excluding Drama* (Oxford: Clarendon Press, 1954). Auden had strong inclinations to the golden, but forced himself toward the drab.

5 Fuller Universes of Music

Music history is often taught as a story about expansion of resource: from the emancipation of the third (after the earliest medieval music, when only fourths and fifths were considered consonant) to the emancipation of all dissonances. The Modernist age showed such a remarkable acceleration of this outgroping (toward novelties in harmony, toward non-Western instruments and musical procedures) that some musicologists have considered it the chief characteristic of the whole movement. Perhaps this habit of mind tends to ignore the contributions of certain Modernist composers whose talents lay in other fields—but it is certainly true that much of the exhilaration of early Modernism came from a giddy sense that musicians had previously confined themselves to a timid exploration of the seashore, while oceans of musical possibility beckoned over the horizon. The octave, far from being a spectrum with seven distinct shades, concealed worlds of mystery in its interstices.

In *The Brothers Karamazov* (1880), Fyodor Dostoevsky wrote of the strange vertigo that arises from the conviction that "everything is permitted": a sudden entry into a disoriented amoral space, a condition of free fall. In Nietzsche's *The Gay Science* (1882), section 125, a madman seeks God, but finally shouts: "*We have killed him*—you and I. We all are his murderers. But how have we done this? How were we able to drink up the sea? Who gave us this sponge to wipe away the whole horizon? What did we do when we unchained this earth from its sun? . . . Do we yet smell nothing of the divine decomposition?—even Gods decompose! God is dead."[1] For composers, the dissolution of the tonal system, the discovery that every note is permitted and that the tonic is dead, had something of the same sense of elation and terror. Nietzsche's philosophy seemed well suited to the destruction of tonality: for example, at the end of Richard Strauss's tone poem *Also sprach Zarathustra* (1896)—based on the book (1883–85) in which Nietzsche announced that mankind is only a bridge to the Overman—the uncanny juxtaposition of C major and B major triads foreshadows the centerless tone systems that would soon arise in Germany and France.

■ One of the first Modernist composers who devoted great energy to expanding musical resources was Claude Debussy (1862–1918). He was impatient with all the constraints

---

1. Nietzsche, *Werke in drei Bänden,* ed. Karl Schlechta (München: Carl Hanser Verlag, 1966), 2:127.

and legalisms of textbook music, and looked far afield to find new sonorities, new harmonies, new shadings of melody. His pleasure in breaking rules was strong: he took delight in parallel fifths, soft umbras of ninth and eleventh chords—harmony that functioned less as structural undergirding than as chiaroscuro. In his youth he had visited Russia with Madame von Meck (Tchaikovsky's patron) and found in Russian music some of the emancipation he sought: the songs of Musorgsky, in particular, seemed to have no "established, one might say official, form," but consisted of "successive minute touches mysteriously linked together by mean of an instinctive clairvoyance."[2] In 1889 Debussy heard a traveling Javanese gamelan (mostly percussive) orchestra, and later he evoked it on the piano in *Pagodes* (1903).

But his chief new resource was not the exotic East, but nature itself. Unlike, say, Alessandro Poglietti or Olivier Messiaen, Debussy didn't look for truth in the actual sounds of birds and other phenomena of nature; instead, he tried to use nature's constitutive processes to replace the rule book of old texts of harmony. One of Ezra Pound's heroes, the American scholar of Chinese poetry Ernest Fenollosa, wrote that nature has no grammar, no parts of speech:

> A true noun, an isolated thing, does not exist in nature. Things are only the terminal points, or rather the meeting-places, of actions, cross-sections cut through actions. . . . And though we may string ever so many clauses into a single compound sentence, motion leaks everywhere, like electricity from an exposed wire. All processes in nature are interrelated; and thus there could be no complete sentences (according to this definition) save one which it would take all time to pronounce.[3]

The leisurely succession of unrelated chords at the beginning of Debussy's *Nuages* (*Clouds*, 1900)—derived, interestingly, from a Musorgsky song—seems to have no particular sense of beginning or end, as if *Nuages* were a segment of an infinitely long piece of music, as majestically ungrammatical as nature itself. Debussy is sometimes called a composer of musical prose (indeed he wrote in 1895 a song sequence called *Proses lyriques*), and the term is exact: if poetry is an imposed artifice, Debussy's music often aspires to a perfect ease of flow, in which recurrent elements are neither predictable nor startling.

Debussy's most substantial piece of verbal prose is *Monsieur Croche antidilettante,* a series of journal articles written between 1901 and 1905 and assembled later by Debussy

---

2. *Three Classics in the Aesthetic of Music* (New York: Dover, 1962), 19; translated by B. N. Langdon Davies.

3. Fenollosa, *The Chinese Written Character as a Medium for Poetry,* ed. Ezra Pound (San Francisco: City Lights, 1969), 10–11.

(and published posthumously in 1921); the first article of the series is printed below. M. Croche is a persona that Debussy used to express his more crotchety opinions—his name might be translated as Mr. Crooked or Mr. Eighth Note—and it seems that through him music itself speaks. He hates the technical vocabulary of music, however; he speaks mostly through pictorial metaphors, through what Adorno called pseudomorphisms, for to Debussy a painting and a musical composition are two aspects of the same project: the apprehension of the natural world.

CLAUDE DEBUSSY
from *Monsieur Croche antidilettante* (1901)

Monsieur Croche was a spare, wizened man and his gestures were obviously suited to the conduct of metaphysical discussions. . . . He spoke almost in a whisper and never laughed, occasionally enforcing his remarks with a quiet smile which, beginning at his nose, wrinkled his whole face, like a pebble flung into still waters, and lasted for an intolerably long time.

He aroused my curiosity at once by his peculiar views on music. He spoke of an orchestral score as if it were a picture. He seldom used technical words, but the dimmed and slightly worn elegance of his rather unusual vocabulary seemed to ring like old coins. I remember a parallel he drew between Beethoven's orchestration—which he visualized as a black-and-white formula resulting in an exquisite gradation of greys —and that of Wagner, a sort of many-colored "make-up" spread almost uniformly, in which, he said, he could no longer distinguish the tone of a violin from that of a trombone.

Since his intolerable smile was especially evident when he talked of music, I suddenly decided to ask him what his profession might be. He replied in a voice which checked any attempt at comment: "Dilettante Hater." Then he went on monotonously and irritably: "Have you noticed the hostility of a concert-room audience? Have you studied their almost drugged expression of boredom, indifference and even stupidity? They never grasp the noble dramas woven into the symphonic conflict in which one is conscious of the possibility of reaching the summit of the structure of harmony and breathing there an atmosphere of perfect beauty. Such people always seem like guests who are more or less well-bred; they endure the tedium of their position with patience, and they remain only because they wish to be seen taking their leave at the end; otherwise, why come? You must admit that this is a good reason for an eternal hatred of music. . . .

". . . In all compositions I endeavor to fathom the diverse impulses inspiring them and their inner life. Is not this much more interesting than the game of pulling them to pieces, like curious watches?

"People forget that, as children, they were forbidden to pull their jumping-jacks to pieces—even then such behavior was treason against the mysteries—and they continue to want to poke their aesthetic noses where they have no business to be. Though they no longer rip open puppets, yet they explain, pull to pieces and in cold blood slay the mysteries; it is comparatively easy; moreover you can chat about it. Well, well! an obvious lack of understanding excuses some of them; but others, act with greater ferocity and premeditation, for they must of necessity protect their cherished little talents. These last have a loyal following." . . .

. . . There was a long silence, during which there came from him no sign of life save for the smoke ascending in blue spirals from his cigar which he watched curiously as if he were contemplating strange distortions—perhaps bold systems. His silence became disconcerting and rather alarming. At length he resumed:

"Music is a sum total of scattered forces. You make an abstract ballad of them! I prefer the simple notes of an Egyptian shepherd's pipe; for he collaborates with the landscape and hears harmonies unknown to your treatises. Musicians listen only to the music written by cunning hands, never to that which is in nature's script. To see the sun rise is more profitable than to hear the *Pastoral Symphony*.[4] What is the use of your almost incomprehensible art? Ought you not to suppress all the parasitical complexities which make music as ingenious as the lock of a strong-box? You paw the ground because you only know music and submit to strange and barbarous laws. You are hailed with high-sounding praises, but you are merely cunning! Something between a monkey and a lackey."

I ventured to say that some had tried in poetry, others in painting—I added with some trepidation one or two musicians—to shake off the ancient dust of tradition and it had only resulted in their being treated as symbolists or impressionists—convenient terms for pouring scorn on one's fellows. . . .

"Discipline must be sought in freedom, and not within the formulas of an outworn philosophy only fit for the feeble-minded. Give ear to no man's counsel; but listen to the wind which tells in passing the history of the world."

In *Three Classics in the Aesthetic of Music* (New York: Dover, 1962), 3–8; translated by B. N. Langdon Davies.

■

Debussy's program for throwing out the book of musical rules, for composing through instinct aligned with natural process, found strong support from Ferruccio

4. Beethoven's Sixth (1808), which contains musical evocation of a brook, some birdcalls, and a thunderstorm; Beethoven was sufficiently concerned about its pictorialisms to note: "More an expression of feelings than a painting."

Busoni (1866–1924). Busoni—composer, virtuoso pianist, influential teacher—was so perfectly at home in both Italy and Germany that he managed to be that rare thing, a citizen of Europe. He was a man who detested binary categories of every sort: north versus south; good versus evil; absolute versus programmatic music; major versus minor mode. When Busoni was confronted with an either/or, he usually cried out, Both! In his most important treatise, *Sketch of a New Esthetic of Music,* Busoni argues for what he calls a "pan-art," a music that excludes nothing, that is bound by no straitjacket of pre-existing form, no rules about tonic and dominant, no confinement to the measly twelve-part division of the octave, no servitude to representing either external facts or name-able internal feelings. For Busoni, the universe is fundamentally not a collection of hard objects but a vibration, and the vibratory nature of music is best fitted to embrace it, not in part, but as a whole. His aesthetic philosophy was chiefly derived from Goethe and Nietzsche (both of whom he frequently quotes), and from Schopenhauer, whose hatred of nature noises in music Busoni inherited. For Schopenhauer and Busoni alike, music imitates not the sounds of specific natural phenomena, but the mode of operation of nature itself, the growth patterns of plants and animals, the tectonics of things. Much of this sounds like the exultations of late Romanticism, and it would be wrong to minimize the Romantic component of Busoni's thought; but Busoni was altogether devoted to Bach—and indeed Busoni's advocacy of what he called "Young Classicity" became an important stimulus to the Neoclassic movement. Romantic/Classic was yet another binary category that Busoni rejected.

Busoni pleads not only for a large notion of what music is, but also for a larger notion of how music can be interpreted. Musical interpretation is often based on binary categories: for example, the major mode is traditionally considered bright, assertive, cheerful, male, and the minor mode the opposite of these traits—shadowed, oblique, sad, female. (The musicologist Gretchen Wheelock has found an eighteenth-century theorist who argues that the minor mode is female because the inversion of a major triad is a minor triad, and everyone knows that a woman is an upside-down man.) Busoni, by contrast, peremptorily rejects this polarity, just as he rejects most polarities: for him, any meaning ascribed to one mode can easily be generated by the other. In this way Busoni dismantles the normal semantics of music.

The treatise ends with Nietzsche's plea for what we now call world music. The continent of Europe was at last too small for the overarching synthesis that Busoni desired.

FERRUCCIO BUSONI
from *Sketch of a New Esthetic of Music* (1907)
§2

Absolute Music! What the lawgivers mean by this, is perhaps remotest of all from the Absolute in music. "Absolute music" is a form-play without poetic program, in which the form is intended to have the leading part. But Form, in itself, is the opposite pole of absolute music, on which was bestowed the divine prerogative of buoyancy, of freedom from the limitations of matter. In a picture, the illustration of a sunset ends with the frame; the limitless natural phenomenon is enclosed in quadrilateral bounds; the cloud-form chosen for depiction remains unchanging for ever. Music can grow brighter or darker, shift hither or yon, and finally fade away like the sunset glow itself; and instinct leads the creative musician to employ the tones that press the same key within the human breast, and awaken the same response, as the processes in Nature.

Per contra, "absolute music" is something very sober, which reminds one of music-desks in orderly rows, of the relation of Tonic to Dominant, of Developments and Codas.

Methinks I hear the second violin struggling, a fourth below, to emulate the more dexterous first, and contending in needless contest merely to arrive at the starting-point. This sort of music ought rather to be called the "architectonic," or "symmetric," or "sectional," and derives from the circumstance that certain composers poured *their* spirit and *their* emotion into just this mould as lying nearest them or their time. Our lawgivers have identified the spirit and emotion, the individuality of these composers and their time, with "symmetric" music, and finally, being powerless to recreate either the spirit, or the emotion, or the time, have retained the Form as a symbol, and made it into a fetish, a religion. . . .

Is it not singular, to demand of a composer originality in all things, and to forbid it as regards form? No wonder that, once he becomes original, he is accused of "form-lessness." Mozart! the seeker and the finder, the great man with the childlike heart—it is he we marvel at, to whom we are devoted; but not his Tonic and Dominant, his Developments and Codas.

Such lust of liberation filled Beethoven, the romantic revolutionary, that he ascended one short step on the way leading music back to its loftier self—a short step in the great task, a wide step in his own path. He did not quite reach absolute music, but in certain moments he divined it, as in the introduction to the fugue of the Sonata for Hammerclavier.[5] Indeed, all composers have drawn nearest the true nature of music in preparatory and intermediary passages (preludes and transitions), where they felt at liberty to disregard symmetrical proportions, and unconsciously drew free breath. Even a Schumann (of so much lower stature) is seized, in such passages, by some feeling of the boundlessness of this pan-art (recall the transition to the last movement of the D-minor Symphony);[6] and the same may be asserted of Brahms in the introduction to the Finale of his First Symphony.[7]

5. Beethoven's immense Sonata in B♭, op. 106 (1819).
6. Schumann's Fourth Symphony (1841, 1851).
7. Brahm's Symphony in C Minor (1877).

But, the moment they cross the threshold of the Principal Subject, their attitude becomes stiff and conventional, like that of a man entering some bureau of high officialdom.

Next to Beethoven, Bach bears closest affinity to "infinite music" [*Ur-Musik*]. His Organ Fantasias (but not the Fugues) have indubitably a strong dash of what might be overwritten "Man and Nature." In him it appears most ingenuous because he had no reverence for his predecessors (although he esteemed and made use of them), and because the still novel acquisition of equal temperament opened a vista of—for the time being—endless new possibilities.

Therefore, Bach and Beethoven are to be conceived as a beginning, and not as unsurpassable finalities. . . .

§3

[Program-music] has been set up as a contrast to so-called "absolute music," and these concepts have become so petrified that even persons of intelligence hold one or the other dogma, without recognition of a third possibility beyond and above the other two. In reality, program-music is precisely as one-sided and limited as that which is called absolute. In place of architectonic and symmetric formulas, instead of the relation of Tonic to Dominant, it has bound itself in the stays of a connecting poetic—sometimes even philosophic—program.

Every motive—so it seems to me—contains, like a seed, its life-germ within itself. From the different plant-seeds grow different families of plants, dissimilar in form, foliage, blossom, fruit, growth and color.

Even each individual plant belonging to one and the same species assumes, in size, form and strengths growth peculiar to itself. And so, in each motive, there lies the embryo of its fully developed form; each one must unfold itself differently, yet each obediently follows the law of eternal harmony. *This form is imperishable, though each be unlike every other.*

The motive in a composition with program bears within itself the same natural necessity; but it must, even in its earliest phase of development, renounce its own proper mode of growth to mould—or, rather, twist—itself to fit the needs of the program. Thus turned aside, at the outset, from the path traced by nature, it finally arrives at a wholly unexpected climax, whither it has been led, not by its own organization, but by the way laid down in the program, or the action, or the philosophical idea.

And how primitive must this art remain! True, there are unequivocal descriptive effects of tone-painting (from these the entire principle took its rise), but these means of expression are few and trivial, covering but a very small section of musical art. Begin with the most self-evident of all, the debasement of Tone to Noise in imitating the sounds of Nature—the rolling of thunder, the roar of forests, the cries of animals; then those somewhat less evident, symbolic—imitations of visual impressions, like the lightning-flash, springing movement, the flight of birds; again, those intelligible only through the mediation of the reflective brain, such as the trumpet-call as a warlike symbol, the shawm to betoken ruralism, march-rhythm to signify measured strides, the chorale as vehicle for religious feeling. Add to the above the characterization of nationalities—national instruments and airs—and we have a complete inventory of the arsenal of program-music. Movement and repose, minor and major, high and low, in their customary significance, round out the list. These are auxiliaries, of which good use can be made upon a broad canvas, but which, taken by themselves, are no more to be called music than wax figures may pass for monuments.

And, after all, what can the presentation of a little happening upon this earth, the report concerning an annoying neighbor—no matter whether in the next room or in an adjoining quarter of the globe—have in common with that music which pervades the universe?

To music, indeed, it is given to set in vibration our human moods: dread (Leporello),[8] oppression of soul, invigoration, lassitude (Beethoven's last Quartets), decision (Wotan),[9] hesitation, despondency, encouragement, harshness, tenderness, excitement, tranquillization, the feeling of surprise or expectancy, and still others; likewise the inner echo of external occurrences which is bound up in these moods of the soul. But not the moving cause itself of these spiritual affections; not the joy over an avoided danger, not the danger itself, or the kind of danger which caused the dread; an emotional state, yes, but not the psychic species of this emotion, such as envy, or jealousy; and it is equally futile to attempt the expression, through music, of moral characteristics (vanity, cleverness), or abstract ideas like truth and justice. Is it possible to imagine how a poor, but contented man could be represented by music? The contentment, the soul-state, can be interpreted by music; but where does the poverty appear, or the important ethical problem stated in the words "poor, but contented"? This is due to the fact that "poor" connotes a phase of terrestrial and social conditions not to be found in the eternal harmony. And Music is a part of the vibrating universe.

I may be allowed to subjoin a few subsidiary reflections: The greater part of modern theatre music suffers from the mistake of seeking to repeat the scenes passing on the stage, instead of fulfilling its own proper mission of interpreting the soul-states of the persons represented. When the scene presents the illusion of a thunderstorm, this is exhaustively apprehended by the eye. Nevertheless, nearly all composers strive to depict the storm in tones—which is not only a needless and feebler repetition, but likewise a failure to perform their true function. The person on the stage is either psychically influenced by the thunderstorm, or his mood, being absorbed in a train of thought

8. Leporello (Italian for rabbit) is a cowardly servant in Mozart's *Don Giovanni* (1787).
9. Wotan, the authoritative god in Wagner's *Ring of the Nibelung*.

of stronger influence, remains unaffected. The storm is visible and audible without aid from music; it is the invisible and inaudible, the spiritual processes of the personages portrayed, which music should render intelligible. . . .

§6

The creator should take over no traditional law in blind belief, which would make him view his creative endeavor, from the outset, as an exception with that law. For his individual case he should seek out and formulate a fitting individual law, which, after the first complete realization, he should annul, that he himself may not be drawn into repetitions when his next work shall be in the making.

The function of the creative artist consists in making laws, not in following laws ready made. He who follows such laws, ceases to be a creator.

Creative power may be the more readily recognized, the more it shakes itself loose from tradition. But an intentional avoidance of the rules cannot masquerade as creative power, and still less engender it. . . .

What we now call our Tonal System is nothing more than a set of "signs"; an ingenious device to grasp somewhat of that eternal harmony; a meagre pocket-edition of that encyclopedic work; artificial light instead of the sun. Have you ever noticed how people gaze open-mouthed at the brilliant illumination of a hall? They never do so at the millionfold brighter sunshine of noonday.

And so, in music, the signs have assumed greater consequence than that which they ought to stand for, and can only suggest.

How important, indeed, are "Third," "Fifth," and "Octave"! How strictly we divide "consonances" from "dissonances"—*in a sphere where no dissonances can possibly exist!*

We have divided the octave into twelve equidistant degrees, because we had to manage somehow, and have constructed our instruments in such a way that we can never get in above or below or between them. Keyboard instruments, in particular, have so thoroughly schooled our ears that we are no longer capable of hearing anything else—incapable of hearing except through this impure medium. Yet Nature created an *infinite gradation—infinite!* who still knows it nowadays? . . .

. . . We are tyrannized by Major and Minor—by the bifurcated garment.

Strange, that one should feel major and minor as opposites. They both present the same face, now more joyous, now more serious; and a mere touch of the brush suffices to turn the one into the other. The passage from either to the other is easy and imperceptible; when it occurs frequently and swiftly, the two begin to shimmer and coalesce indistinguishably. But when we recognize that major and minor form one Whole with a double meaning, and that the "four-and-twenty keys" are simply an elevenfold transposition of the original twain, we arrive unconstrainedly at a perception of the UNITY *of our system of keys.* The conceptions of "related" and "foreign" keys vanish, and with them the entire intricate theory of degrees and relations. *We possess one single key.* But it is of the most meagre sort. . . .

. . . Let us once again call to mind, that in this latter the gradation of the octave is *infinite,* and let us strive to draw a little nearer to infinitude. The tripartite tone (third of a tone) has for some time been demanding admittance, and we have left the call unheeded. Whoever has experimented, like myself (in a modest way), with this interval . . . will not have failed to discern that tripartite tones are wholly independent intervals with a pronounced character, and not to be confounded with ill-tuned semitones. . . .

. . . Who has not dreamt that he could float on air? and firmly believed his dream to be reality? Let us take thought, how music may be restored to its primitive, natural essence; let us free it from architectonic, acoustic and esthetic dogmas; let it be pure invention and sentiment, in harmonies, in forms, in tone-colors (for invention and sentiment are not the prerogative of melody alone); let it follow the line of the rainbow and vie with the clouds in breaking sunbeams; *let Music be naught else than Nature mirrored by and reflected from the human breast;* for it is sounding air and floats above and beyond the air; within Man himself as universally and absolutely as in Creation entire; for it can gather together and disperse without losing in intensity.

§7

In his book "Beyond the Good and the Bad" (*Jenseits von Gut und Böse* [1886]) Nietzsche says: "With regard to German music I consider precaution necessary in various ways. Assuming that a person loves the South (as I love it) as a great training-school for health of soul and sense in their highest potency, as an uncontrollable flood and glamour of sunshine spreading over a race of independent and self-reliant beings; well, such an one will learn to be more or less on his guard against German music, because while spoiling his taste anew, it undermines his health.

"Such a Southlander (not by descent, but by belief) must, should he dream of the future of music, likewise dream of a redemption of music from the North, while in his ears there rings the prelude to a deeper, mightier, perchance a more evil and more mysterious music, a super-German music, which does not fade, wither and die away in view of the blue, sensuous sea and the splendor of Mediterranean skies, as all German music does; a super-European music, that asserts itself even amid the tawny sunsets of the desert, whose soul is allied with the palm-tree, and can consort and prowl with great, beautiful, lonely beasts of prey.

"I could imagine a music whose rarest charm should consist in its complete divorce from the Good and the Bad; only that its surface might be ruffled, as it were, by a longing as of a sailor for home, by variable golden shadows and tender frailties: an Art which should see fleeing toward it, from afar off, the hues of a perishing moral world become wellnigh incomprehensible, and which should be hospitable and profound enough to harbor such belated fugitives." . . .

Will this music ever be attained?

"Not all reach Nirvana; but he who, gifted from the beginning, learns everything that one ought to learn, experiences all that one should experience, renounces what one should renounce, develops what one should develop, realizes what one should realize—he shall reach Nirvana." (Kern, *Geschichte des Buddhismus in Indien*.)

If Nirvana be the realm "beyond the Good and the Bad," one way leading thither is here pointed out. A way to the very portal. To the bars that divide Man from Eternity— or that open to admit that which was temporal. Beyond that portal sounds music. Not the strains of "musical art." [10] It may be, that we must leave Earth to find that music. But only to the pilgrim who has succeeded on the way in freeing himself from earthly shackles, shall the bars open.

In *Three Classics in the Aesthetic of Music* (New York: Dover, 1962), 78–83, 88–89, 91, 93, 95–97; translated by Th. Baker.

■

Like Ferruccio Busoni, whose musical heroes were Bach and Liszt, the German composer Max Reger (1873–1916) hoped to unite the taut formality of Bach with the sensitive, sometimes extravagant rhetoric of Brahms, Wagner, and Strauss. Whereas a Modernist like Debussy rejected the old forms—if the textures of the music lesson enter his music, it is for the sake of spoof (as in *Dr. Gradus ad Parnassum,* 1908)—Reger sometimes sought a new style through a bizarre excess of textbook procedures: he can pile up counterpoints beyond the limits of intelligibility, especially in the fugues at the end of his favored theme-and-variations form. Reger found it hard to make a career, partly because of his prickly personality (he once, famously, read a review of his music and wrote to the critic, "I am sitting in the smallest room in my house. Your review is in front of me. Soon it will be behind me"), and partly because of the odd swollenness of his music. But it is possible to find his combination of the crabbed and the whimsical quite appealing.

The inflammatory aspects of Reger's personality can be seen in the following essay, a wild polemic in favor of what we now call Modernism. It is also a reply to a music critic (and Reger's former teacher), Hugo Riemann (1849–1919), whose conservative views stung Reger in much the same way as the music critics sting the hero of Strauss's *Ein Heldenleben* (1899). The issue of degeneration was much discussed in these days: Cesare Lombroso studied criminals to observe signs of regression to a more primitive life form, and Max Nordau found in Impressionist paintings the symptoms of eye disease. But

---

10. I think I have read, somewhere, that Liszt confined his Dante Symphony to the two movements, *Inferno* and *Purgatorio,* "because our tone-speech is inadequate to express the felicities of Paradise." [Busoni's note.] Liszt originally planned a third movement, "Paradiso," for his *Dante Symphony* (1857), but Wagner dissuaded him.

Reger may have noticed that the word *Regeneration* (the same in German as in English) was latent in his very surname.

MAX REGER
"Degeneration and Regeneration in Music" (1907)

Under this title Prof. Dr. Hugo Riemann has just published a long article in Max Hesse's *Deutscher Musikerkalender für 1908*. The opinions and "advice" that are developed in this essay compel me to examine them closely from the point of view of a forward-looking musician. . . .

Prof. Dr. Riemann writes that composers perpetually lament that, in spite of the mighty increase in concerts, their "novelties" all-too-seldom get their turn for performance. But Prof. Dr. Riemann's assertion in no way corresponds to the facts. Indeed composers now living have—in comparison to those of the "good old days"—especially little reason to complain over their "not-yet-their-turn-ness." It wasn't too long ago, that even the most important composers had to wait until they were "old men," before they were considered "ripe for performance." Brahms, Wagner were for a long time banned from our concert halls. The concert programs of our time prove undeniably that our concert societies (with a very few exceptions) have realized that living composers also have to be taken into consideration—and even in the most reactionary cities, where twenty or thirty years ago people cried Alas and Woe when a work by Wagner or Brahms was performed "accidentally," nowadays they offer Strauss, Mahler,[11] and †††Reger.

Although the old-inherited musicology, so righteous in its indignation, may keep protesting against these performances, it cannot prevent (even in cities where critical illumination burns as brightly as an oil lamp) the delighted gathering of many supporters under the fresh-fluttering banner of the "lovers of new sounds" [*Neutöner*]—where no old fogies are to be found. The most striking evidence that Riemann is completely wrong is the Fellowship of German Composers (organization for musical performance rights), so undeniably effective for us "living composers."

Prof. Dr. Riemann writes further: "The most prominent distinguishing characteristic of the newer productions, with which the great conductors experiment, is an excessive increase of challenges to the technical performance capacities of the orchestra and its leader. . . . It is again the character of the age, if one wishes the high society of the musical world to pay attention, to leave the path of plain nature and to draw attention to oneself through exaggerations of every kind, difficulties of reading, difficulties of technical execution, increase in the size of the orchestra, the piling up of confusingly intersecting melodic lines and of harmonies bleeding through each other, if possible with

---

11. Gustav Mahler (1860–1911), Austrian symphonist and conductor.

expressive reference to the most newfangled and extravagant productions of poetry or painting."

Above all, concerning the sentence "to leave the path of plain nature and, through exaggerations, etc.," one must confirm it for all ages—in that way Prof. Dr. Riemann is completely right: for fifteen years there have been editions of masterpieces by Bach, Mozart, Beethoven, etc. etc., which were actually created according the principle of "leaving the path of plain nature and, through exaggerations" etc.! Strange to say, these editions are by—Hugo Riemann. Concerning the piling up of technical difficulties, which we †††moderns cultivate only in order to awaken the interest of the musical high society (incidentally, a somewhat noteworthy glimpse of the respectability of our musical aspirations), permit me, as a quite modest non-music-historian, to observe that for example Bach's music was in its time considered unplayable on account of the piling up of technical difficulties—people said that only Bach could play his works. Furthermore: did not Grandfather Haydn, now about 110 years ago, seriously advise the young Beethoven against publishing the three Op. 2 piano sonatas, because—they were too hard to play. Here too are "difficulties of technical execution"! Poor Beethoven! Weren't even Beethoven's greatest creations—the last sonatas and string quartets—considered unperformable for nearly a whole generation? And Brahms! I myself know how, when I was young, people groaned and cursed over the difficult accompaniments of Brahms's songs. Poor Brahms, if you read "Degeneration and Regeneration in Music" (German Music Almanac, 1908), you would become conscious of your gross sins against the Holy Ghost of German musicology!

What Prof. Dr. H. Riemann further charges against us moderns is the old story, that remains always new, even as it has constantly been proved false. (After all, our modern polyphony, for example, should be called "modest," if one considers what monstrous polyphony the old masters of the Netherlands used in their works.) Finally, it is really necessary to establish clearly and emphatically that all the reproaches that Prof. Dr. Riemann directs against us very much "living" shakers-up of the past—reproaches for which he has yet to provide any proof—have always been flung with luscious verbosity and classical insolence etc. etc. against especially those who, several decades later, were considered by reasonable people to have saved music from becoming silted up by dreary epigonism. Have the musicologists really forgotten that Bach in his time appeared so "incomprehensible" that he was known as a virtuoso rather than as a composer? What abuses of all sorts did not the darling of God, Mozart, have to endure? Was it not said that Mozart's music was too "overworked" and orchestrated too "noisily"?

And how did German criticism behave toward Beethoven? Did not the majority of Beethoven's contemporaries consider him totally insane? I cite here a judgment on the great *Leonore* overture: "Rhapsodies of an incurable madman!" (And such judgments on Beethoven from "expert circles" could be adduced by the hundreds.) How many painful struggles it cost, until R. Schumann, for example, "pulled through." (He himself, naturally, didn't live to see it.) Have the unspeakably wretched years of suffering of a R. Wagner already been forgotten? Forgotten even by music historians?

And Brahms: were not the first performances of all his symphonies received with icy coldness? And Bruckner and Hugo Wolf?[12] Could not E. Hanslick[13] write, regarding Bruckner, these lovely words: "This music stinks!" (Note: Hanslick has also composed many books about music!) And when one compares the abundant criticisms against Beethoven, against Schubert, Schumann, Wagner, Brahms, Bruckner, H. Wolf, with what Prof. Dr. Riemann attempts to add with his accusation against the devilish moderns, one finds a notable similarity: it is the struggle of the man who can no longer keep up, against the boisterous progressives! But hail, hail to those who are so "evaluated," in just the way that people used to evaluate the great immortals! That is the incomparable honor for us disciples, that we, unsickened by the consumptive pallor of gray theory, can plant our trees in the ever-blossoming woods of German art with fresh daring and with trust in the germanic spirit.

Prof. Dr. Riemann writes further: "Since the deaths of Wagner and Liszt, the side of the forward-pushing composers has lacked an authoritative personality, someone who could restrain the untamed youth, and through his judgments and through his own example conspicuously mark the borders that must not be transgressed."

No, Professor, that makes us laugh. It would be a sign of true degeneration, deeply to be lamented, if our youth paused in its desire to do great things, to dare to seize the unsuspected, the unheard of, and instead decided to make horse-obedient, innocence-dripping kindergarten music! (By the way, it is really hilarious that Prof. Riemann suddenly declares that Franz Liszt—a composer without any creative gift, according to Prof. Riemann—should be an authority for boisterous youth, and regrets that Liszt is no longer around to restrain untamed youth.) Yes, if the time came when youth lost its forward-pointing ideals, when youth did not shoot forth past the limit—yes, then degeneration would set in, incurable in the worst sense of all! Moreover: who reined in Bach, Beethoven, Schumann, Wagner, Brahms? Did not these great men come forth among their contemporaries frighteningly "unrestrained"?

Further: "mark the borders that must not be transgressed"! What does that mean? Didn't all our great and immortal composers lift their inconsiderate mighty fists and pound back into the illimitable all the borders that their age conceived, the borders that

---

12. Anton Bruckner (1824–96), Austrian composer of symphonies on a grand scale; Hugo Wolf (1860–1903), composer of subtly shaded, expressively potent songs.

13. Eduard Hanslick (1825–1904), formalistic Viennese music critic, opponent of Wagner (who caricatured him as the incompetent Beckmesser in *Die Meistersinger*) and of every sort of program music, champion of Brahms and of absolute music.

the former broken-backed aesthetic had properly glued in place? (Certainly a huge an-noyance to future scholars!) And we who are alive, we who are not Beethoven, Schu-bert, Schumann, Wagner, Brahms, H. Wolf—we don't let anyone restrain us or cudgel us or put us into the custody of musicologists!

Prof. Dr. Riemann then woefully laments, What is left of the successes of E. Grieg, M. Bruch, H. Hofmann, Friedrich Kiel, Joseph Rheinberger? [14] Doesn't he know that these successes have quickly paled for only one reason, because their personalities were too small, because they were obviously too dependent on their elders? Only personality, and the spiritual capacity that a personality radiates, can guarantee immortality.

In Prof. Dr. Riemann's view, we moderns are headed directly to disaster; soon, he writes, we will make the plunge into the abyss, and if one pulls apart the corners of the garment that flutters around the "trembling bones those who ride to the left"—there grins a hollow death's-head!? Oh, how creepy and hideous! It reminds me of a wax mu-seum, where one can pay fifty cents and shudder at the most shocking horrors. Prof. Dr. Riemann: we who ride to the left with our trembling bones are absolutely unafraid of plunging into the abyss! We sit fast in our saddles, we who ride to the left! Much rather do you plunge into the abyss with your attacks—and if there is supporting evidence for those attacks, you are keeping it to yourself!

To speak seriously: does Hugo Riemann really believe that we—Strauss, Mahler, Pfitzner,[15] etc. and finally my insignificant self—dare to ride so "directionlessly" into "fantastic adventures"; that we are so completely unprepared that we allow our muses to drag us into realms accessible only to a few; that like fools we wander ceaselessly from phantom to phantom? Doesn't Prof. Dr. Riemann know that we have artistic con-victions, just as he has, though ours have been matured by practical experience and not by dusty book-learning? If Riemann would acquaint himself with what we have written, he would know that the technical level of our musical equipment lies at least as high as that of Max Bruch or Joseph Rheinberger! Does he live in the error that we are criminals who have thrown overboard all the old masters? Or do we still need to explain to him that every age must naturally have its corresponding manner of artistic expression? Has not Wagner in all his works, Richard Strauss in *Don Juan, Till Eulenspiegel, Death and Transfiguration,* already become classic? (Please throw stones at me!) Have not an incalculable number of the best modern musicians gathered with the most honorable enthusiasm around our soiled, much-spat-on banner? Are all these people so blinded, that they cannot see the daylight of true art???

14. Edvard Grieg (1843–1907), Norwegian composer; Max Bruch (1838–1920), German composer; Heinrich Hofmann (1842–1902), German composer and pianist; Friedrich Kiel (1821–85), German composer; Joseph Rheinberger (1839–1901), prolific German composer, organist, and teacher.

15. Hans Pfitzner (1869–1949), German composer who would outlive his reputation as a pro-gressive.

Prof. Dr. Riemann writes further: "One gnarled oak alone, with deep and mighty roots, has stood fast against the all-destroying whirlwind! (namely J. Brahms). . . . As a living artistic potency he is the complement to the historicizing tendencies of the musicology that has blossomed in the last decades!"

I believe that my wholehearted admiration of Joh. Brahms and my glowing devotion to the great old masters are so well known that I don't need to emphasize them here. But above all I protest here, with all my energy, against the notion that Brahms can be explained as the complement to the historicizing tendencies of the musicology that has blossomed in the last decades. It is a great, great error for Prof. Dr. Riemann to believe that Brahms has therefore become the gnarled oak that outlasts the whirlwind. Brahms as the complement of the musicology of his age!! No, that's divinely beautiful! It is well known that musicology always takes possession of a great man after the cool grass has covered him for a very long time; when one or two hundred years have passed, then an old master is fit for consumption. Or is it ordered otherwise in the collegium musicum? It would be very sad, concerning the immortality of a Brahms, if he were to owe his high rank to the way he leans on the old masters, as Riemann believes. That's the sort of notion that only gray theory can assert, which draws its lonely circles away from the golden stream of life, away from the powerfully pulsing heartbeat of our age! And the most striking evidence against Prof. Dr. Riemann's view is a phenomenon like, for instance, Rheinberger! Whoever studies his development in Munich, the things he did, the things he didn't do, knows that he had at least as strong a feeling for the old masters as Brahms did. And yet, and despite all that, Rheinberger has so quickly faded away. What assures immortality for Brahms is not his "leaning" on the old masters, but the fact that he knew how to generate new and unsuspected psychic moods, by virtue of his own spiritual makeup. In that there rests the root of all immortality—never in leaning on the old masters, for implacable history always sentences to death, in just a few decades, those who merely lean.

Dr. Riemann writes further: "With secret worry, which gradually intensified to open hate, the radical progressives have watched these tendencies (namely the "historicizing" of musicology) sprout and grow strong," etc.

This affair is not so bad as all that. If the tendencies of musicology only aim so far, to bring honor to the old masters, then we radical progressives have every reason to greet these tendencies with complete sympathy! I believe it can be admitted that among the radical progressives there isn't one person who has turned in hate against these meritorious tendencies. If that has nevertheless happened, then the offenders have stricken their names forever from the list of people who can be taken seriously. But one can with "modest" certainty admit that, to a much greater extent, we progressives have been greeted with open or concealed hatred. It may have happened that, when the wild riders felt the "corners of their garments" being tugged all too nicely, the

"trembling bones of those who ride to the left" have occasionally delivered (with sar-
castic gallows humor) not unjustified kicks to those who have never sat in a saddle, or
very badly understand how to ride.

Prof. Dr. Riemann finally writes that our degenerate art can and must regenerate itself. We horrible moderns finally want nothing more, to be sure, than to regenerate, but
in our own way and manner. It is impossible to stand still, and the real degeneration,
degeneration in the truest sense of the word, would be manifest if there weren't to be
found the sorts of "guys" who willfully and boldly accomplish a regeneration, in their
own way! Fresh blood, new life, new goals have never done harm, and have in all ages
proven to be the sole remedy against the real decadence!

Prof. Dr. Riemann is naturally convinced that we find ourselves today in a frankly incurable "confusion in music"! This "confusion" has for several months made a great
stir; people wrote, driveled at random, without changing the "confusion" in any way!
My opinion is that the "confusion" — so suddenly discovered — actually began with *Salome*.[16] The whole musical world — naturally with the exception of some "backwoods-
men" — has quietly consented to the works of Richard Strauss; gradually the conviction
has dawned that Strauss is quite decidedly the most significant representative of
the "symphonic poem" since Franz Liszt. Suddenly came *Salome* and now there is confusion! How remarkable! Has then the Strauss of *Salome* become a different, a completely transformed creative artist? Never! People must not have completely understood Strauss in the first place, if they now "yelp" in pain, after such masterpieces as
Don Juan, Till Eulenspiegel, Death and Transfiguration, even *Ein Heldenleben,* persist
in the repertory with, so to speak, an iron fixity, indeed have become "classics" of their
kind.

Since the pyre has already been set up, on which I'll be soon roasted, to the quiet
delight of all backward-looking people, I'll unburden my conscience concerning a matter that has long bothered me: among our riders there are many who look down, from
their "superior" vantage point, on Schumann and Mendelssohn. It seems to me that
these people will at last be understood by a later generation as underage "Mendels-
sons" or decrepit "Mendels-wives." Their ride goes too little, much too little, to the left,
for we "genuine" riders to the left know only too well that Schumann and even Mendelssohn — each in his own way — rode to the left, and we "genuine" riders to the left dis-
avow none of our own! (They'll also kindle my pyre from the left!)

I regret very much having to find myself, with my artistic convictions, in such a state
of contradiction with the views of my former teacher, whom I revere, whom I regard as

16. *Salome* (1905), Richard Strauss's lurid, chromatically advanced opera, was a great though scandalous success: the Archbishop of Vienna (a man named Piffl) prevented any performance there until 1918.

by far the preeminent theorist, not only of our age, but since Rameau.[17] Only there is a great and extremely precise distinction between theory and the powerfully forward-pressing impulse in our music since Liszt and Wagner! And in spite of my great and generally well known "infinite," unlimited admiration for all the great old masters, without exception, I can only state, with my complete conviction and realization (although I don't know if my physical experience[18] will give any indication of "trembling bones"): "I ride unflinchingly to the left!"

From "Degeneration und Regeneration in der Musik," in *Die Konfusion in der Musik: Felix Draesekes Kampfschrift von 1906 und ihre Folgen,* ed. Susanne Shigihara (Bonn: Gudrun Schröder, 1990), 250–58; translated by the editor.

■

American music has a long history, and much of it consists of colonial obedience to European models. But many American artists have felt that the influence of Europe is shallow, and the immensity of the continent, the absence of a rigidly established culture, invite a certain freedom to experiment. European music, in particularly, could seem to certain composers prissy, four-square, and conventional: according to Roy Harris, Americans have a "unique rhythmic sense" that rebels against the "labored symmetrical rhythms" of European music; "nature abounds in these freer rhythms" to which Americans are sensitive.[19] America, then, seemed a good place to write nature's music, the music that owed nothing to the artifices of textbooks. On the other hand, the tabula rasa quality of American culture had its dangers as well: another adventurous composer, Charles Seeger, exclaimed, "What a great unwieldly corpus this American music is— great talent, great resources, great opportunites; but still a giant without head or feet— no folk-art for us to stand on, no head to direct us."[20] Herman Melville, in *Pierre* (1852), elaborated a nightmare vision of an "American Enceladus," an armless Titan bashing its huge impotent torso in vain; and Seeger perceived that American music might be a sort of Enceladus, growing inane in a vacuum.

The history of American experimental music perhaps began with two nineteenth-century composers who were willing to challenge European musical hegemony, to assert the values of the New World. The first was the New Orleans composer-pianist Louis Moreau Gottschalk (1829–69), who tried in effect to creolize European music by insin-

17. Jean Philippe Rameau (1683–1764), French composer and theorist.

18. This is a joking allusion to Reger's physique: he was about six feet, four inches tall, and very heavy.

19. *American Composers on American Music: A Symposium Edited by Henry Cowell* (Palo Alto: Stanford University Press, 1933), 153.

20. Ibid., 33.

uating into it the rhythms and melodies of Cuba, Uruguay, and other places where he sojourned. Gottschalk was not necessarily an advanced composer, from the standpoint of musical technique; but a second American was willing to contest European music on the fundamental levels of harmony, development, and aesthetic, as well as on the level of thematic content. This was Charles Ives (1874–1954), who, perhaps more than anyone else, laid down the curriculum of American Modernist music.

It is not easy to study Ives's contributions to Modernism, partly because his music was so little known at the time when it was written, partly because in his later years Ives tampered with his scores, by inserting "wrong" notes into conventional passages in order to gain a sort of retrospective prestige for his advanced harmony. Indeed many of Ives's scores are so unsettled that they are less text than hypertext—a locus of possibilities, rather than a determined coordination of notes. But this very incoherence seems to point to the arresting indeterminacies of such later American composers as John Cage; and it is possible to point to several extraordinary forward-looking characteristics of Ives's music:

1. *Music is alive, organic, and can't be arrested or paralyzed by the notation of a score.* As Henry Cowell described Ives's performance goals, "the composition is a germ idea which may develop in any number of different directions. Therefore, if he writes down one certain way, he fears that the form of the piece will become crystallized. [. . . To avoid this] he gives directions in a certain place for a performer to play very loud if his feelings have been worked up sufficiently; if not, he is to continue playing more softly. Very frequently, also, he gives a choice of measures. . . . There are very full chords written, with a footnote stating that, if the player wishes, he may leave out certain notes or, if he wishes, he may add still more! . . . The same fear of hampering the freedom or cramping the feelings of the performer has resulted in his creating very independent parts for each of the men in his orchestral works." [21]

2. *A musical composition is an experience of acoustic theater—an imitation of the ways that sounds impinge on the human mind.* It takes place within a graduated, three-dimensional psychic space, a polyphony not of individual musical lines but of planes. There may be, for example, an underlayer of cricket chirps, on which are superimposed various events, such as brass bands far apart and playing different marches. The polychoral motets of Giovanni Gabrieli, the complex spatial arrangements of Hector Berlioz's Requiem, anticipate certain Ivesian effects; but the *al fresco* effect of ears oriented in a landscape full of agglomerated sounds comes to us new from Ives.

3. *Music has no rule of exclusion.* A melody that sticks in your brain sticks there for a reason—there is no use in questioning whether that melody is good or bad, worthy or unworthy, sentimental or highfalutin, developable or incapable of development. A single

21. Ibid., 133–34.

musical composition, then, may contain childhood hymns, fighting songs from the Civil War, minstrel tunes, political-rally rousers, rags, and quotations from Beethoven. "I think there must be a place in the soul all made of tunes, of tunes of long ago,"[22] Ives wrote; and since the purpose of music is to provide a record of the psychic copresence of tunes, then vulgar songs must coexist equally with European art music.

According to Virgil Thomson, the American artist "selects his materials casually and then with great care arranges them into patterns of hidden symmetry. The difference between such artists and their European counterparts lies . . . in the casual choice of materials. That Europe will have none of. From Bach and Mozart through Debussy and Stravinsky to Boulez and Berio and Xenakis, just as from Chaucer through Byron to Proust and Joyce, or from Giotto through Picasso, forms themselves, the words, the colors, the sounds, the scales, the melodies are ever precious, the psychic themes adventurous and terrible. Their treatment may be comical or tragic, sometimes both; but the matter must be noble no matter how ingenious the design."[23] Thomson was thinking mostly of John Cage and Gertrude Stein; but Ives is the pioneer of Americanness in this sense.

Ives's prose is a long polemic against triviality in music—and Ives understands most European composers of his generation as pursuers of trivial goals. Richard Strauss, especially, is damned for being a sort of musical materialist, playing ingenious games of representing the world of solid objects instead of writing music with more spiritual aspirations: "Can a tune literally represent a stone wall with vines on it or even with nothing on it . . . ? Does the extreme materializing of music appeal strongly to anyone except to those without a sense of humor?"[24] Ives himself, of course, could be called a sort of materialist of music, in that he was fascinated by the re-creation of concrete acoustic facts—exactly how Central Park sounded on a particular evening, for example. But these laborious sound effects are devised not for the sake of the literal representation, but for the sake of catching the reverberations of a psychological moment, the feeling-complex engendered by the sounds.

Ives's accusations against European composers have a strongly masculinist quality. Strauss is a sissy; Debussy could write better music if he learned to handle a hoe. Ives's dislike of effeminacy reached such a pitch that he composed what may be history's first piece of homophobic instrumental music, his Second String Quartet (1907–13), in which the score of the second movement ("Arguments") names the second violinist as a "Rollo," a nice soft-spoken fellow who interjects a few meek comments to try to break

---

22. From Ives's text to his song "The Things Our Fathers Loved" (1917).

23. Virgil Thomson, *A Virgil Thomson Reader* (New York: Dutton, 1981), 481.

24. Ives, *Essays before a Sonata, The Majority, and Other Writings*, ed. Howard Boatwright (New York: W. W. Norton, 1970), 3.

up the violent quarrel that has broken out among the other three string players; Ives's tempo indication here is *Andante emasculata*.

CHARLES IVES
from *Essays before a Sonata* (1920)

We might offer the suggestion that Debussy's content would have been worthier his manner if he had hoed corn or sold newspapers for a living, for in this way he might have gained a deeper vitality and a truer theme to sing at night and of a Sunday. Or we might say that what substance there is, is "too coherent"—it is too clearly expressed in the first thirty seconds. There you have the "whole fragment"—a translucent syllogism; but there the reality, the spirit, the substance stops, and the "form," the "parfume," the "manner" shimmer right along, as the soapsuds glisten after one has finished washing. Or we might say that his substance would have been worthier if his adoration or contemplation of Nature—which is often a part of it, and which rises to great heights, as is felt, for example, in *La Mer*[25]—had been more the quality of Thoreau's.[26] Debussy's attitude toward Nature seems to have a kind of sensual sensuousness underlying it, while Thoreau's is a kind of spiritual sensuousness. It is rare to find a farmer or peasant whose enthusiasm for the beauty in Nature finds outward expression to compare with that of the city man who comes out for a Sunday in the country, but Thoreau is that rare country man and Debussy the city man with his week-end flights into country aesthetics. We would be inclined to say that Thoreau leaned towards substance and Debussy towards manner.

. . . A man may aim as high as Beethoven,[27] or as high as Richard Strauss. . . . Beethoven is always modern and Strauss always mediaeval—try as he may to cover it up in new bottles. He has chosen to capitalize a "talent"—he has chosen the complexity of media, the shining hardness of externals, repose, against the inner, invisible activity of truth. He has chosen the first creed, the easy creed, the philosophy of his fathers, among whom be found a half-idiot-genius (Nietzsche). His choice naturally leads him to glorify and to magnify all kinds of dull things . . . which in turn naturally leads him to windmills and human heads on silver platters.[28] Magnifying the dull into the colossal

25. Debussy's *The Sea: Three Symphonic Sketches* (1905).

26. Henry David Thoreau (1817–62), American writer, who secluded himself at a rural pond to write *Walden;* a pioneer in using civil disobedience to promote public good.

27. Beethoven is important here, not only because he was a model of high musical ideals, but because Ives's Second Piano Sonata (1904–15), subtitled *Concord, Mass., 1840–1860*—the sonata to which *Essays before a Sonata* is prefatory—uses the dot-dot-dot-dash theme from Beethoven's Fifth Symphony as a motto.

28. The windmill is from Strauss's kinesthetically vivid tone poem *Don Quixote* (1898); the head on a platter, from Strauss's opera *Salome* (1905).

produces a kind of "comfort"—the comfort of a woman who takes more pleasure in the fit of fashionable clothes than in a healthy body—the kind of comfort that has brought so many "adventures of baby-carriages at county fairs."[29] . . .

. . . Someone is quoted as saying that "ragtime is the American music." Anyone will admit that it is one of the many true, natural, and, nowadays, conventional means of expression. It is an idiom, perhaps a "set or series of colloquialisms," similar to those that have added through centuries and through natural means some beauty to all languages. Every language is but the evolution of slang, and possibly the broad "A" in Harvard may have come down from the "butcher of Southwark." To examine ragtime rhythms and the syncopations of Schumann or of Brahms seems to the writer to show how much alike they are not. Ragtime, as we hear it, is, of course, more (but not much more) than a natural dogma of shifted accents, or a mixture of shifted and minus accents. It is something like wearing a derby hat on the back of the head, a shuffling lilt of a happy soul just let out of a Baptist church in old Alabama. Ragtime has its possibilities.[30] But it does not "represent the American nation" any more than some fine old senators represent it. Perhaps we know it now as an ore before it has been refined into a product. It may be one of nature's ways of giving art raw material. Time will throw its vices away and weld its virtues into the fabric of our music. It has its uses, as the cruet on the boardinghouse table has, but to make a meat of tomato ketchup and horseradish, to plant a whole farm with sunflowers, even to put a sunflower, into every bouquet, would be calling nature something worse than a politician. Mr. Daniel Gregory Mason,[31] whose wholesome influence, by the way, is doing as much perhaps for music in America as American music is, amusingly says, ". . . if indeed the land of Lincoln and Emerson[32] has degenerated until nothing remains of it but a 'jerk and rattle,' then we at least are free to repudiate the false patriotism of 'My country, right or wrong,' to insist that better than bad music is no music, and to let our beloved art subside finally under the clangor of the subway gongs and automobile horns, dead, but not dishonored."[33] And so may we ask—Is it better to sing inadequately of the "leaf on Walden

29. Ives is alluding to *Adventures in a Perambulator* (1914) by John Alden Carpenter (1876–1951)—a suite of orchestral pieces "told" from a baby's point of view. Ives thought this infantilism ludicrous.

30. Ives should indeed be aware of the possibilities of ragtime, since he wrote *Set of Four Ragtime Dances* (1904) and evoked ragtime in the second and fourth movements of his First Piano Sonata (1902–10).

31. Daniel Gregory Mason (1873–1953), composer and music professor at Columbia University. As we will see later, not everyone would agree that he was a "wholesome influence."

32. Ralph Waldo Emerson (1803–82), American writer and preacher, advocate of transcendentalism and self-reliance—both dear to Ives. Ives devoted movements to both Thoreau and Emerson in his Second Piano Sonata.

33. *Contemporary Composers* (New York, 1918.) [Boatwright's note.]

floating," and die "dead but not dishonored," or to sing adequately of the "cherry on the cocktail," and live forever?

From *Essays before a Sonata, The Majority, and Other Writings,* ed. Howard Boatwright (New York: W. W. Norton, 1970), 82–83, 94–95.

CHARLES IVES
from "Postface to 114 Songs" (1922)

Is not beauty in music too often confused with something which lets the ears lie back in an easy-chair? Many sounds that we are used to do not bother us, and for that reason are we not too easily inclined to call them beautiful? . . . Possibly the fondness for personal expression—the kind in which self-indulgence dresses up and miscalls itself freedom—may throw out a skin-deep arrangement, which is readily accepted at first as beautiful—formulae that weaken rather than toughen the musical-muscles. If a composer's conception of his art, its functions and ideals, even if sincere, coincides to such an extent with these groove-colored permutations of tried-out progressions in expediency so that he can arrange them over and over again to his delight—has he or has he not been drugged with an overdose of habit-forming sounds? And as a result do not the muscles of his clientele become flabbier and flabbier until they give way altogether and find refuge only in exciting platitudes—even the sensual outbursts of an emasculated rubber-stamp, a "Zaza,"[34] a "Salome" or some other money-getting costume of effeminate manhood?

From *Essays before a Sonata, The Majority, and Other Writings,* ed. Howard Boatwright (New York: W. W. Norton, 1970), 125.

CHARLES IVES
"Music and Its Future" (1929)

To give the various instrumental parts of the orchestra in their intended relations is, at times, as conductors and players know, more difficult than it may seem to the casual listener. After a certain point it is a matter which seems to pass beyond the control of any conductor or player into the field of acoustics. In this connection, a distribution of instruments or group of instruments or an arrangement of them at varying distances from the audience is a matter of some interest; as is also the consideration as to the extent it may be advisable and practicable to devise plans in any combination of over two players so that the distance sounds shall travel from the sounding body to the listener's ear may be a favorable element in interpretation. It is difficult to reproduce the sounds and feeling that distance gives to sound wholly by reducing or increasing the number

34. *Zazá* (1900), opera concerning a popular singer by Ruggero Leoncavallo (1857–1919).

of instruments or by varying their intensities. A brass band playing *pianissimo* across the street is a different-sounding thing from the same band, playing the piece *forte,* a block or so away. Experiments, even on a limited scale, as when a conductor separates a chorus from the orchestra or places a choir off the stage or in a remote part of the hall, seem to indicate that there are possibilities in this matter that may benefit the presentation of music, not only from the standpoint of clarifying the harmonic, rhythmic, thematic material, etc., but of bringing the inner content to a deeper realization (assuming, for argument's sake, that there is an inner content). Thoreau found a deeper import even in the symphonies of the Concord church bell when its sounds were rarefied through the distant air. "A melody, as it were, imported into the wilderness . . . at a distance over the woods the sound acquires a certain vibratory hum as if the pine needles in the horizon were the strings of a harp which it swept . . . a vibration of the universal lyre, just as the intervening atmosphere makes a distant ridge of earth interesting to the eye by the azure tint it imparts."

A horn over a lake gives a quality of sound and feeling that it is hard to produce in any other way. It has been asked if the radio might not help in this matter. But it functions in a different way. It has little of the ethereal quality. It is but a photographing process which seems only to hand over the foreground or parts of it in a clump.

The writer remembers hearing, when a boy, the music of a band in which the players were arranged in two or three groups around the town square. The main group in the bandstand at the center usually played the main themes, while the others, from the neighboring roofs and verandas, played the variations, refrains, and so forth. The piece remembered was a kind of paraphrase of "Jerusalem the Golden," a rather elaborate tone-poem for those days. The bandmaster told of a man who, living nearer the variations, insisted that they were the real music and it was more beautiful to hear the hymn come sifting through them than the other way around. Others, walking around the square, were surprised at the different and interesting effects they got as they changed position. It was said also that many thought the music lost in effect when the piece was played by the band all together, though, I think, the town vote was about even. The writer remembers, as a deep impression, the echo parts from the roofs played by a chorus of violins and voices.

Somewhat similar effects may be obtained indoors by partially enclosing the sounding body. For instance, in a piece of music which is based, on its rhythmic side, principally on a primary and wider rhythmic phrase and a secondary one of shorter span, played mostly simultaneously—the first by a grand piano in a larger room which opens into a smaller one in which there is an upright piano playing the secondary part—if the listener stands in the larger room about equidistant from both pianos but not in a direct line between them (the door between the rooms being partially closed), the contrasting rhythms will be more readily felt by the listener than if the pianos are in the same room. The foregoing suggests something in the way of listening that may have a bearing on the interpretation of certain kinds of music.

In the illustration described above, the listener may choose which of these two rhythms he wishes to hold in his mind as primal. If it is the shorter-spaced one and it is played after the longer has had prominence, and the listener stands in the room with the piano playing this, the music may react in a different way, not enough to change its character, but enough to show possibilities in this way of listening. As the eye, in looking at a view, may focus on the sky, clouds, or distant outlines, yet sense the color and form of the foreground, and then, by observing the foreground, may sense the distant outlines and color, so, in some similar way, the listener can choose to arrange in his mind the relation of the rhythmic, harmonic, and other material. In other words, in music the ear may play a role similar to the eye in the foregoing instance.

Some method similar to that of the inclosed parts of a pipe organ played by the choir or swell manuals might be adopted in some way for an orchestra. That similar plans, as suggested, have been tried by conductors and musicians is quite certain, but the writer knows only of the ways mentioned in the instances above.

When one tries to use an analogy between the arts as an illustration, especially of some technical matter, he is liable to get it wrong. But the general aim of the plans under discussion is to bring various parts of the music to the ear in their relation to each other, as the perspective of a picture brings each object to the eye. The distant hills, in a landscape, range upon range, merge at length into the horizon; and there may be something corresponding to this in the presentation of music. Music seems too often all foreground, even if played by a master of dynamics.

Among the physical difficulties to be encountered are those of retarded sounds that may affect the rhythmic plan unfavorably and of sounds that are canceled as far as some of the players are concerned, though the audience in general may better hear the various groups in their intended relationships. Another difficulty, probably less serious, is suggested by the occasional impression, in hearing sounds from a distance, that the pitch is changed to some extent. That pitch is not changed by the distance a sound travels unless the sounding body is moving at a high velocity is an axiom of acoustics; that is, the number of the vibrations of the fundamental is constant; but the effect does not always sound so—at least to the writer—perhaps because, as the overtones become less acute, the pitch seems to sag a little. There are also difficulties transcending those of acoustics. The cost of trial rehearsals, of duplicate players, and of locations or halls suitably arranged and acoustically favorable is very high nowadays. . . .

In closing, and to go still farther afield, it may be suggested that in any music based to some extent on more than one or two rhythmic, melodic, harmonic schemes, the hearer has a rather active part to play. Conductors, players, and composers (as a rule or at least some) do the best they can and for that reason get more out of music and, incidentally, more out of life, though, perhaps, not more in their pockets. Many hearers do the same. But there is a type of auditor who will not meet the performers halfway by projecting himself, as it were, into the premises as best he can, and who will furnish nothing more than a ticket and a receptive inertia which may be induced by predilections or static ear habits, a condition perhaps accounting for the fact that some who consider themselves unmusical will get the "gist of" and sometimes get "all set up" by many modern pieces, which those who call themselves musical (this is not saying they're not) — probably because of long acquaintance solely with certain consonances, single tonalities, monorhythms, formal progressions, and structure — do not like. Some hearers of the latter type seem to require pretty constantly something, desirable at times, which may be called a kind of ear-easing, and under a limited prescription; if they get it, they put the music down as beautiful; if they don't get it, they put it down and out — to them it is bad, ugly, or "awful from beginning to end." It may or may not be all of this; but whatever its shortcomings, they are not those given by the man who does not listen to what he hears.

"Nature cannot be so easily disposed of," says Emerson. "All of the virtues are not final" — neither are the vices.

The hope of all music — of the future, of the past, to say nothing of the present — will not lie with the partialist who raves about an ultra-modern opera (if there is such a thing) but despises Schubert, or with the party man who viciously maintains the opposite assumption. Nor will it lie in any cult or any idiom or in any artist or any composer. "All things in their variety are of one essence and are limited only by themselves."

The future of music may not lie entirely with music itself, but rather in the way it encourages and extends, rather than limits, the aspirations and ideals of the people, in the way it makes itself a part with the finer things that humanity does and dreams of. Or to put it the other way around, what music is and is to be may lie somewhere in the belief of an unknown philosopher of half a century ago who said: "How can there be any bad music? All music is from heaven. If there is anything bad in it, I put it there — by my implications and limitations. Nature builds the mountains and meadows and man puts in the fences and labels." He may have been nearer right than we think.[35]

From "Music and Its Future," in *American Composers on American Music*, ed. Henry Cowell (Palo Alto: Stanford University Press, 1933), 191–98.

■

Another of the wizards of experimentalist music was the Californian Henry Cowell (1897–1965), the closest thing that American Modernist music ever had to an instigator

35. This essay was originally a long footnote in the score of the second movement of the Fourth Symphony — perhaps Ives's furthest reach toward the music of the future.

of Ezra Pound's quality in the field of poetry. Generous and encouraging to many younger American composers, Cowell showed an original mind in a number of musical areas. He was best known for developing the theory and practice of tone clusters (clots of seconds played on the piano with fist or forearm); his patent on this procedure (though Ives had used it earlier in the *Concord* Sonata) seemed so ironclad that Béla Bartók felt it proper to write to Cowell for permission to use tone clusters in his *Out of Doors* piano suite (1926). Cowell felt that his tone clusters constituted an alternative to the entire tonal system of Western music, by providing a harmony based on the interval of the second instead of the third and the fifth—though tone clusters with most other composers have remained a resource for local color instead of a basis for composition.

Cowell worked in electronic music from the very beginning of the discipline: in 1931 he and Léon Thérémin devised a sort of transfigured metronome called the rhythmicon, which could superimpose a number of complex rhythmic patterns. And Cowell was one of the first composers to write music to be strummed on the inside of the piano, as in the eerily resonant *Aeolian Harp* (1923)—a composition in which the motto of Debussy's M. Croche, "Listen to the wind!," seems carried to unusual lengths. (This procedure would be investigated still more remarkably by Cowell's student John Cage.) Cowell also was a pioneer in investigating world music: he worked for many years to find ways of assimilating the sonorities, the scales, the rhythms of non-Western cultures into Western music, and helped to publish, on Folkways Records, *Primitive Music of the World,* including field recordings from Panama, Borneo, and many other places. Cowell's tart definition of primitive music—"we think of music as being primitive if no outside influence can be traced"[36]—remains a useful corrective to the notion that the music of exotic cultures is defective or savage.

Cowell's most significant publication was *American Composers on American Music* (1933), where he is the genial ringleader for the whole circus of American music. But his own ideas are most clearly heard in *New Musical Resources* (1930), an ambitious attempt to develop a general theory of music from the structure of the overtone series. His hope of devising scales of rhythm comparable to scales of pitch strongly recalls a book by another American genius-crank: Ezra Pound's *Treatise on Harmony* (1924). Pound attempts to relate rhythm to harmony through mathematical procedures: "the percussion of the rhythm can enter the harmony exactly as another note would. It enters usually as a Bassus, a still deeper bassus; giving the main form to the sound."[37] For Pound, the fact that the concert A of 440 cycles per second could be subdivided down the octaves—to 220, 110, 55, 27.5, and 13.75 cycles per second (this last one below the threshold of hearing), and finally to something measured in cycles per minute, a tick-tick on a metro-

36. From the note to Folkways Records FE4581 (1962).
37. *Ezra Pound and Music,* ed. R. Murray Schafer (New York: New Directions, 1977), 303.

nome—suggested that a basic rhythm is simply a very slow form of a tonic note. Cowell also tried to identify rhythm and pitch: "a quarter-note is taken as the equivalent of C. The reason for this is evident—a low C in tone is produced by sixteen vibrations per second. If this C be carried down two octaves, the result is a subaudible C of four vibrations per second. If the time-value of a whole note is taken to be one second, four quarter-notes will be produced in one second, just as four vibrations will produce a subaudible C."[38] Karlheinz Stockhausen, in his preparations for *Gruppen* (1958), tried a similar method of relating of rhythm to harmony, thereby producing a sort of unified field theory of the fundamentals of musical composition.

It is possible that Cowell's music and writings still suffer neglect because of his conviction for homosexual conduct with a minor, resulting in his incarceration at San Quentin from 1936 to 1940; in 1942 he was pardoned by the governor of California.

For Ives and Cowell alike, America seemed the proper place for experiments in freeing music from its old shackles of harmony and precut formalities. But Percy Grainger (1882–1961) thought his native land, Australia, a still newer New World, might be even more appropriate. Grainger considered melody the prime factor in music—"Melody seems to me to provide music with an initiative, whereas rhythm appears to me to exert an enslaving influence"[39]—and it might be said that his central project was to discover melodies and to liberate them. He was an indefatigable and much-traveled collector of folksongs (such as Lincolnshire's famous "Brigg Fair," which he took down in 1905), and he enjoyed setting folksongs and sea shanties with arresting harmonies (as in *Shallow Brown*, 1910) in order to recapture the freshness of spirit behind the originals. For Grainger, an aggressively unsnobbish man, there was little distinction between high and low; he profoundly respected Grieg, Stephen Foster, and other of his precursors in the movement to bring art to the domain of the popular and the agreeable. Grainger also wrote original compositions, sometimes folkish in spirit, sometimes playful (for example, the orchestral piece *The Immovable Do*, 1942, inspired by an organ in which a high C was stuck open), sometimes ambitious (such as his ballet *The Warriors*, 1913–16, an evocation of a pagan orgy).

Grainger, like many other Modernists, sought a reconciliation of the archaic and the technologically advanced. He considered that his most valuable contribution was what he called "free music"—music of pure glissandi, disencumbered from the labored stepwise divisions of the scale. Free music could be realized more easily in an electronic medium than with conventional instruments, so in the middle 1930s Grainger began composing pieces for theremin, an electronic instrument named for its inventor, Leon

38. Henry Cowell, *New Musical Resources* (New York: Knopf, 1930), 99.
39. From a letter to Frederick Fennell, 6 August 1959, quoted in the notes to Mercury CD 434 330-2.

Theremin, and played by two hands moving in space: the changing distance of one hand from the antenna creates a continuous variation of pitch, the changing distance of the other hand a continuous variation of volume. In 1938 Grainger wrote the essay reprinted here, explaining that free music had been a dream of his since childhood. Though Grainger here emphasizes the use of expressive machines, he also experimented with free music produced by less novel means, as in "Red Dog" (*Kipling Setting* no. 19, 1941), in which voices imitate the baying of wolves.

The prose of "Free Music" is unusually well behaved by Grainger's standards. A more typical specimen of his literary style can be found in the following sentences: "My *Hill-Songs* arose out of the thought about, and longings for, the wildness, the freshness, the purity of hill-countries. . . . These compositions were part of a back-to-nature urge, and were written as a protest against tame-ness of plain-countries and plain-dwellers and their dullness, samishness and thwartingness of life in towns." [40] Grainger's extraordinary love of blunt Old English words was part of a modernizing movement to rid English of Latinate diction: when Grainger called a string quartet a "fiddle four-some," he was following principles established by William Barnes, who insisted that we replace such a phrase as "terms of comparison" with its Anglo-Saxon equivalent, "pitches of suchness." [41] In language as in music, Grainger sought a slightly contrived version of archaic simplicity.

PERCY GRAINGER
"Free Music" (1938)

Music is an art not yet grown up; its condition is comparable to that stage of Egyptian bas-reliefs when the head and legs were shown in profile while the torso appeared "front face"—the stage of development in which the myriad irregular suggestions of nature can only be taken up in regularized or conventionalized forms. With Free Music we enter the phase of technical maturity such as that enjoyed by the Greek sculptures when all aspects and attitudes of the human body could be shown in arrested movement.

Existing conventional music (whether "classical" or popular) is tied down by set scales, a tyrannical (whether metrical or irregular) rhythmical pulse that holds the whole tonal fabric in a vice-like grasp and a set of harmonic procedures (whether key-bound or atonal) that are merely habits, and certainly do not deserve to be called laws. Many composers have loosened, here and there, the cords that tie music down. Cyril

---

40. Program note to *Hill Songs,* quoted in the notes to Chandos CD 9549, 4–5.
41. Gerard Manley Hopkins, letter to Robert Bridges, 26 November 1882.

Scott[42] and Duke Ellington[43] indulge in sliding tones. . . . Schoenberg has liberated us from the tyranny of conventional harmony. But no non-Australian composer has been willing to combine *all* these innovations into a consistent whole that can be called *Free Music.*

It seems to be absurd to live in an age of flying and yet not be able to execute tonal glides and curves—just as absurd as it would be to have to paint a portrait in little squares (as in the case of mosaics) and not be able to use every type of curved lines. If, in the theatre, several actors (on the stage together) had to continually move in a set metrical relation to one another (to be incapable of individualistic, independent movement) we would think it ridiculous; yet this absurd goose-stepping still persists in music. Out in nature we hear all kinds of lovely and touching "free" (non-harmonic) combinations of tones; yet we are unable to take up these beauties and expressiveness into the art of music because of our archaic notions of harmony.

Personally I have heard free music in my head since I was a boy of eleven or twelve in Auburn, Melbourne. It is my only important contribution to music. My impression is that this world of tonal freedom was suggested to me by wave-movements in the sea that I first observed as a young child at Brighton, Victoria and Albert Park Melbourne.

Yet the matter of Free Music is hardly a personal one. If I do not write it someone else certainly will, for it is the goal that all music is clearly heading for now and has been heading for through the centuries. It seems to me the only music logically suitable to a scientific age.

The first time an example of my Free Music was performed on man-played instruments was when Percy Code conducted it (most skillfully and sympathetically) at one of my Melbourne broadcasting lectures for the Australian Broadcasting Commission, in January, 1935. But Free Music demands a non-human performance. Like most true music, it is an emotional, not a cerebral, product and should pass direct from the imagination of the composer to the ear of the listener by way of delicately controlled musical machines. Too long has music been subject to the limitations of the human hand, and subject to the interfering interpretations of a middle-man: the performer. A composer wants to speak to his public direct. Machines (if properly constructed and properly written for) are capable of niceties of emotional expression impossible to a human performer. That is why I write my Free Music for theremins—the most perfect tonal instruments I know. In the original scores each voice (both on the pitch-staves and on the

42. Cyril Scott (1879–1970), English pianist and Modernist composer, who had studied music in Frankfurt with Grainger in the later 1890s.

43. Edward Kennedy Ellington (1899–1974), jazz composer and bandleader, known for such hits as "Mood Indigo" (1930) and for more ambitious works, e.g. *Black, Brown, and Beige* (1943).

sound-strength staves) is written in its own specially colored ink, so that the voices are easily distinguishable, one from the other.

From *A Musical Genius from Australia: Selected Writings by and about Percy Grainger,* ed. Teresa Balough (Nedlands: University of Western Australia Press, 1983); essay dated 6 December 1938.

PANTONALITY

Cowell, like Grainger and Bartók, sought to refresh Western music by granting equal status to non-Western musical traditions; he thought there was little difference between musical novelties generated from mathematical research and novelties generated through careful attention to the music of exotic cultures. But Arnold Schoenberg (1874–1951) was not particularly charmed by composers who emphasized the folkloristic component of music: "Isolation alone does not guarantee fertility. . . . If songs of the Southern section of West-Parinoxia show Lydian traits in their otherwise Phrygian texture, dances of the neighboring Northern part of Franimonti may display the opposite: Phrygian influence in Lydian melodies. Such differences constitute individuality to the local connoisseur. There exist such differences, for instance, in the Balkans. Their songs and dances are often overwhelmingly deep in expression."[44] As a leading advocate of progressivity, Schoenberg tended to sarcasm when he thought of folklorists: they struck him as spelunkers or troglodytes, not likely to work toward the spiritual advance of music.

Schoenberg himself hoped to improve himself, not from the company of illiterate fiddlers, but from the company of the most sophisticated artists of the age. These included not only musicians but painters, particularly Vassily Kandinsky (1866–1944), a Russian-born artist who settled in Munich. He initiated a correspondence with Schoenberg in the sane year (1911) he published *Concerning the Spiritual in Art,* the momentous book that argues for a nonrepresentational style of painting:

The more abstract the form, the more clear and direct is its appeal. In any composition the material side may be more or less omitted in proportion as the forms used are more or less material, and for them substituted pure abstractions, or largely dematerialized objects. The more an artist uses these abstracted forms, the deeper and more confidently will he advance into the kingdom of the abstract.[45]

---

44. Arnold Schoenberg, *Style and Idea: Selected Writings of Arnold Schoenberg,* ed. Leonard Stein, trans. Leo Black (Berkeley: University of California Press, 1984), 163.

45. Wassily Kandinsky, *Concerning the Spiritual in Art,* trans. M. T. H. Sadler (New York: Dover, 1977), 32.

Schoenberg's *Harmonielehre* (*Theory of Harmony,* also 1911) seemed to Kandinsky the musical equivalent of dematerialization in art: the painter is liberated from enslavement to the shapes of objects in the physical world, just as the composer is liberated from the chains of musical law—"every chord, every progression is permissible," [46] Kandinsky noted with interest after reading the *Harmonielehre.*

As their friendship grew during the following year, Schoenberg and Kandinsky found more and more points of convergence: both desired an emancipated, spiritually intense art, in which all the dead weight of vain tradition was burned away. Schoenberg contributed an article, "The Relationship to the Text," to the almanac *Der blaue Reiter* (*The Blue Rider,* 1912), edited by Kandinsky and Franz Marc; Kandinsky contributed an article on Schoenberg's paintings to a short book on Schoenberg edited by Alban Berg and others. Furthermore, Schoenberg was writing a short opera, *Die glückliche Hand* (*The Lucky Touch*), full of dazzling effects of lighting and scenery, while Kandinsky was writing an abstract play, *Der gelbe Klang* (*The Yellow Sound,* printed in *Der blaue Reiter*), full of instructions about sounding shrill chords of major seconds—as if both artists were trying to prove the thesis that the borders separating one artistic medium from another were effortlessly transgressed. As Kandinsky put it in the introduction to *Der gelbe Klang:*

> The means belonging to the different arts are externally quite different. Sound, color, words!
>
> *In the last essentials,* these means are wholly alike: the final goal extinguished the external dissimilarities and reveals the inner identity.
>
> This *final goal* (knowledge) is attained by the human soul through finer vibrations of the same. These finer vibrations, however, which are identical in their final goal, have in themselves different inner motions and are thereby distinguished from one another. . . .
>
> A certain complex of vibrations—the goal of a work of art.[47]

Kandinsky, like Schoenberg, hoped to abolish all that pertained to externality in the work of art, in order to open space to project a cosmic vibration.

In the following excerpts from their correspondence, Schoenberg approves of Kandinsky's stress on the alogical aspects of art but is a little uneasy about Kandinsky's use of the word "construction," which seems to suggest a too wide-awake and critical sort of art-making. Schoenberg instead emphasizes the intuitive, the unconscious aspect

---

46. *Arnold Schoenberg, Wassily Kandinsky: Letters, Pictures and Documents,* ed. Jelena Hahl-Koch, trans. John C. Crawford (London: Faber and Faber, 1984), 130.

47. Ibid., 111.

of composition, as if unknown psychic forces could find their proper acoustic realization only in a sort of trance state in which all forethought was suspended. Here, perhaps more clearly than anywhere else in his voluminous writings, Schoenberg gives voice to an almost Surrealist hope that spasms of disconnected musical dissonances could imitate the authentic nature of inner reality—an enigma that can never be solved, only recoded in music.

ARNOLD SCHOENBERG AND VASSILY KANDINSKY
Correspondence (1911)
KANDINSKY TO SCHOENBERG, 18 JANUARY 1911
Dear Professor,

Please excuse me for simply writing to you without having the pleasure of knowing you personally. I have just heard your concert here and it has given me real pleasure. You do not know me, of course—that is, my works—since I do not exhibit much in general, and have exhibited in Vienna only briefly once and that was years ago (at the Secession.)[48] However, what we are striving for and our whole manner of thought and feeling have so much in common that I feel completely justified in expressing my empathy.

In your works, you have realized what I, albeit in uncertain form, have so greatly longed for in music. The independent progress through their own destinies, the independent life of the individual voices in your compositions, is exactly what I am trying to find in my paintings. At the moment there is a great tendency in painting to discover the "new" harmony by constructive means, whereby the rhythmic is built on an almost geometric form. My own instinct and striving can support these tendencies only halfway. *Construction* is what has been so woefully lacking in the painting of recent times, and it is good that it is now being sought. But I think differently about the *type* of construction.

I am certain that our own modern harmony is not to be found in the "geometric" way, but rather in the anti-geometric, antilogical way. And this way is that of "dissonances in *art*," in painting, therefore, just much as in music. And "today's" dissonance in painting and music is merely the consonance of "tomorrow." (What I might call the academic-"harmonic" is of course not to be excluded by this: one takes what one needs without worrying from *where* one takes it. And particularly "today," in the time of the coming "Liberalism," there are so many possibilities!) . . .

48. In 1897 Gustav Klimt and other advanced artists founded the Secession, a movement that seceded from traditional academic art to devote itself to *Jugendstil* (or Art Nouveau)—sinuous, decorative, biomorphic.

SCHOENBERG TO KANDINSKY, 24 JANUARY 1911

. . . I am particularly happy when it is an artist creating in another art from mine who finds points of contact with me. Certainly there are such unknown relationships and common grounds among the best artists who are striving today, and I dare say they are not accidental. I am proud that I have most often met with such evidence of solidarity from the best artists.

First of all, my heartfelt thanks for the pictures. I liked the portfolio very much indeed. I understand it completely, and I am sure that our work has much in common—and indeed in the most important respects: In what you call the "unlogical" and I call the "elimination of the conscious will in art." I also agree with what you write about the constructive element. Every formal procedure which aspires to traditional effects is not completely free from conscious motivation. But art belongs to the *unconscious!* One must express *oneself!* Express oneself *directly!* Not one's taste, or one's upbringing, or one's intelligence, knowledge or skill. Not all these *acquired* characteristics, but that which is *inborn, instinctive.* And all form-making, all *conscious* form-making, is connected with some kind of mathematics, or geometry, or with the golden section or suchlike. But only unconscious form-making, which sets up the equation "form = outward shape," really creates forms; that alone brings forth prototypes which are imitated by unoriginal people and become "formulas." . . .

. . . I myself don't believe that painting must necessarily be objective. Indeed, I firmly believe the contrary. Nevertheless, when imagination suggests objective things to us, then, well and good—perhaps this is because our eyes perceive only objective things. The ear has an advantage in this regard! But when the artist reaches the point at which he desires only the expression of inner events and inner scenes in his rhythms and words, then the "object in painting" has ceased to belong to the reproducing eye. . . .

SCHOENBERG TO KANDINSKY, 19 AUGUST 1912

. . . I must also speak to you about your contributions to the *Blaue Reiter*—thus: your stage composition pleases me extremely. Also the preface to it. I am completely in agreement. But how does all this stand in relation to "construction"? It seems to me to be the opposite. It seems to me that he who constructs must weigh and test. Calculate the load capacity, the relationships, etc. *Der gelbe Klang,* however, is not construction, but simply the rendering of an inner vision.

There is the following difference:

An inner vision is a whole which has component parts, but these are linked, already integrated. Something which is constructed consists of parts which try to imitate a whole. But there is no guarantee in this case that the most important parts are not missing and that the binding agent of these missing parts is: the soul.

I am sure that this is only a quarrel over words and that we agree completely about essentials. But "construction," though it is only a word, is nevertheless the word of yours with which I do not agree. Even though it is the only one. But as I said, *Der gelbe Klang* pleases me extraordinarily. It is exactly the same as what I have striven for in my *Glückliche Hand,* only you go still further than I in the renunciation of any conscious thought, any conventional plot.[49] That is naturally a great advantage. We must become conscious that there are puzzles around us. And we must find the courage to look these puzzles in the eye without timidly asking about "the solution." It is important that our creation of such puzzles mirror the puzzles with which we are surrounded, so that our soul may endeavor — not to solve them — but to decipher them. What we gain thereby should not be the solution, but a new method of coding or decoding. The material, worthless in itself, serves in the creation of new puzzles. For the puzzles are an image of the ungraspable. And imperfect, that is, a human image. But if we can only learn from them to consider the ungraspable as possible, we get nearer to God, because we no longer demand to understand him. Because then we no longer measure him with our intelligence, criticize him, deny him, because we cannot reduce him to that human inadequacy which is our clarity. Therefore I rejoice in *Der gelbe Klang,* and imagine that it would make a tremendous impression on me when performed.

I would have been glad to hear what you think of my *Theory of Harmony.* Have you read it? Then also my article in the *B[laue] R[eiter].* There are also many things in it which are very close to what you say in your preface to *Der gelbe Klang. . . .*

KANDINSKY TO SCHOENBERG, 22 AUGUST 1912

. . . This is the sense in which I also understand construction, which does not, in your opinion, combine harmoniously with *Der gelbe Klang.* Surely you understand me already! Up until now the word construction has only been viewed one-sidedly. But everything has at least two sides. . . . In this particular case: by c[onstruction] one understood up until now the obtrusively geometrical (Hodler,[50] the Cubists, and so on). I will show, however, that construction is also to be attained by the "principle" of disso-

---

49. The plotlessness of *Der gelbe Klang* is indeed remarkable: the play consists almost entirely of stage directions. Here is a sample: "*The music is shrill and tempestuous, with oft-repeated a and b and b and a-flat . . . the brilliant white light becomes progressively grayer. On the left side of the hill a big yellow flower suddenly becomes visible. It bears a distant resemblance to a large, bent cucumber, and its color becomes more and more intense. . . . Later, in* complete silence, *the flower begins to sway very slowly from right to left*" (Arnold Schoenberg, Wassily Kandinsky, 119–20). Much later, in 1974, Alfred Schnittke used Kandinsky's *Der gelbe Klang* as the scenario for a mime-ballet.

50. Ferdinand Hodler (1853–1918), allegorical painter fond of rigid bodies.

nance—(or better) that it [construction] now offers many more possibilities which must *unquestionably* be brought to expression in the epoch which is beginning. *Thus* is *Der gelbe Klang* constructed; that is, in the same way as my pictures. This is what people call "anarchy," by which they understand a kind of lawlessness (since they still see only one side of the Ten Commandments) and by which they must come to understand order (in art, construction), but one which has its roots in another sphere. Briefly stated, there is a law which is millions of kilometers distant from us, towards which we strive for thousands of years, of which we have a presentiment, which we guess, apparently see clearly, and therefore give various forms.[51] Thus is the evolution of "God," religion, science, art. And all these forms are "right," since they have all been seen. Except that they are all false, since they are one-sided. And *evolution* consists only of this, that everything appears many-sided, *complicated*. And always more and more so. For example, the history of music is like this: monophony, melody, and so on.

From *Arnold Schoenberg, Wassily Kandinsky: Letters, Pictures and Documents,* ed. Jelena Hahl-Koch, trans. John C. Crawford (London: Faber and Faber, 1984), 21, 23–24, 54–55, 57–58.

NOISE

If the history of music is a story about the continual expansion of the idea of consonance, at first limited to fourths and fifths, then granted to thirds and sixths, and finally to tone clusters of seconds, what is the last chapter? For Schoenberg, there is no last chapter: since the human race is at a far remove both from God and from the unconscious depths of the psyche, music may approach closer and closer through increasingly subtle and recondite combinations of notes; but what is ungraspable can never be grasped. Nor, for Hába and other microtonalists, is there a last chapter, because the number of intervals into which the octave can be cut is infinite; when the musical resources of the forty-three-note octave are fully mapped and exhausted, there is always a forty-four-note octave to be explored.

But for more materialistic composers, there was a simple answer to the question, Where is music going: noise. Listen to a locomotive, a steel mill, a circular saw: these are the highest sorts of musical instruments, if dissonance is the criterion of excellence. If we want to be overwhelmed by sound, sound we can feel through our diaphragms,

51. Schoenberg was attracted to Kandinsky's rhetoric of God's remoteness, as can be seen in a speech by the angel Gabriel in Schoenberg's oratorio *Jacob's Ladder* (1912–22): "Come closer—one who on a middle level is a likeness and possesses radiance, who resembles One far higher, as the distant overtone the fundamental" (trans. Lionel Salter, from Sony CD SMK 48462, p. 25).

sound that so fills the mind that there is no room left for anything else, a boiler room can do more than Bruckner.

This line of speculation may sound more like satire than like an area for serious research. But for certain machine-loving artists, the notion that art and technology might converge had great prestige. Indeed there was a whole school devoted to just this convergence, the first of the major isms of the ism-ridden art of the twentieth century: Futurism, which grandly published its first manifesto in 1909, in the most conspicuous place in Europe, the Paris newspaper *Le Figaro*.

The leader of the movement was Filippo Tommaso Marinetti (1876–1944), the "caffeine of Europe," a histrionic man who hated lethargy and rules of conduct and adored speed and power. He exulted in war, wrote odes in praise of the machine gun, and hoped for destruction—without destruction there would be no room to build new things. His artistic principles are most clearly expressed in "Technical Manifesto of Futurist Literature" (1912):

> One must destroy syntax and scatter one's nouns at random. . . . The noun should be followed, with no conjunction, by the noun to which it is related by analogue. Example: man-torpedo-boat, woman-gulf, crowd-surf, piazza-funnel, door-faucet. . . . Abolish even the punctuation. . . . To accentuate certain movements and indicate their directions, mathematical symbols will be used: $+ - \times : =$ and the musical symbols. . . . Destroy the *I* in literature, that is, all psychology. The man sidetracked by the library and the museum, subjected to a logic and wisdom of fear, is of no interest. . . . To substitute for human psychology, now exhausted, the lyric obsession with matter. . . . The warmth of a piece of iron or wood is in our opinion more impassioned than the smile or tears of a woman.[52]

If a piece of prose were to look like a machine, it would have to be spare, abrupt, efficient, loud.

There was also a "Technical Manifesto of Futurist Painting" (1910), written by some Futurist painters in collaboration with Marinetti:

> All things move, all things run, all things are rapidly changing. A profile is never motionless before our eyes, but it constantly appears and disappears. On account of the persistency of an image on the retina, moving objects constantly multiply themselves: their form changes, like rapid vibrations, in their mad career. Thus a running horse has not four legs but twenty. . . . To paint a human figure you must not paint it: you must render the whole of its surrounding atmosphere. . . . Who can still believe in the

52. Filippo Tommaso Marinetti, *Marinetti: Selected Writings*, trans. R. W. Flint and Arthur A. Coppotelli (New York: Farrar, Straus and Giroux, 1972), 84–85, 87.

opacity of bodies, since our sharpened and multiplied sensitivity has already penetrated the obscure manifestations of the medium? Why should we forget in our creations the doubled power of our sight, capable of giving results analogous to those of X-rays? . . . The motor bus rushes into the house it passes, and in their turn the houses throw themselves upon the motor buses and are blended with it.[53]

The materialism of Futurist art was in no way static, but a manifestation of matter that behaved like energy: objects that superimposed various states of themselves (as in the twenty-legged dachshund in Giacomo Balla's 1912 *Leash in Motion*—the Futurists learned much from the motion-study photographs of Eadweard Muybridge and such Muybridgean paintings as Marcel Duchamp's 1911 *Nude Descending a Staircase*); objects that decompose into fields of force (as in Balla's 1909 *Street Lamp*); and objects generated from the vibration patterns of sound (as in Luigi Russolo's 1912 *Music*, or Balla's 1912 *Rhythms of a Bow*).

What would be Futurist music be like? The Italian Futurists, rich in talented writers and painters, were poor in musicians. So a painter, Luigi Russolo (1885–1947), decided to fill this almost empty ecological niche: he devised a series of noisemakers called *intonarumori*, each enclosed in a black box, so that a concert of them would resemble a Cubist painting. These noisemakers had noisy names—*ululatori, rombatori, crepitatori, gorgogliatori,* and *sibilatori* (howlers, rumblers, cracklers, gurglers, hissers)—and Russolo devised concert-pieces for them, such as the 1913 *Risveglio* [or *Veglio*] *di una città* (*Awakening of a City*), the score to which is a fine piece of Futurist graphic, with its normal bars, clefs, time signatures, and staves, all decorated with thick black lines, holding steadily horizontal, or ascending up and down in slow glides, or proceeding in fast jerks from one flat line to the next.

It is difficult to know what the *intonarumori* sounded like. The instruments themselves seem no longer to exist; in 1977 Mario Abate and Pietro Verardo reconstructed them and recorded *Veglio di una città*—which seems a disappointingly lackadaisical succession of stomach rumbles and distant airplanes. Still more disappointing is the one surviving recording of the original *intonarumori*, unfortunately used as underlay to a conventional *Corale e serenata*, composed by Russolo's brother Antonio and scored for normal instruments: to hear it is to hear ordinary music faintly disrupted by various growls, like a radio broadcast with low-pitched electric interference.

53. Caroline Tisdall and Angelo Bozzolla, *Futurism* (New York: Thames and Hudson, 1989), 33, 35.

Marcel Duchamp, *Nude Descending a Staircase, no. 2* (1912). Philadelphia
Museum of Art: The Louise and Walter Arensberg Collection, 1950. © 2002 Artists
Rights Society (ARS), New York/ADAGP, Paris/Estate of Marcel Duchamp.

Luigi Russolo, *Music* (1911–12). From Caroline Tisdall and Angelo Bozzolla, *Futurism* (London: Thames and Hudson, 1989), 57.

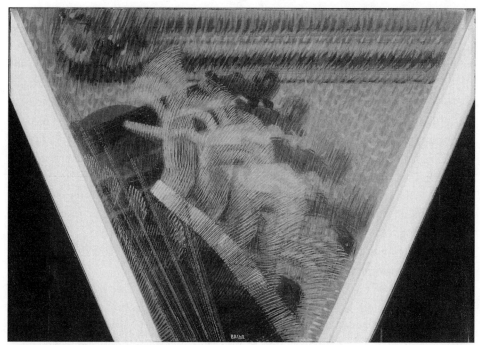

Giacomo Balla, *Rhythms of a Bow* (1912). Private Collection. Alinari/Art Resource, N.Y. © 2002 Artists Rights Society (ARS), New York/SIAE, Rome.

LUIGI RUSSOLO
"The Art of Noises: Futurist Manifesto" (1913)

My Dear Balilla Pratella,[54] great futurist composer:

In the crowded Costanzi Theater, in Rome, while I was listening with my futurist friends Marinetti, Boccioni, and Balla to the orchestral performance of your overwhelming MUSICA FUTURISTA, there came to my mind the idea of a new art: the ART OF NOISES, a logical consequence of your marvelous innovations.

Life in ancient times was silent. In the nineteenth century, with the invention of machines, Noise was born. Today Noise is triumphant, and reigns supreme over the senses of men. For many centuries life evolved in silence, or, at the most, with but a muted sound. The loudest noises that interrupted this silence were neither violent nor prolonged nor varied, since—if we overlook such exceptional phenomena as hurricanes, tempests, avalanches, waterfalls—nature is silent.

54. Francesco Ballila Pratella (1885–1955), composer and mycologist. He was the designated Futurist composer and was to include a few *intonarumori* in his scores, but his music can sound tame.

Noises being so scarce, the first *musical sounds* which man succeeded in drawing from a hollow reed or from a stretched string were a new, astonishing, miraculous discovery. By primitive peoples musical sound was ascribed to the gods, regarded as holy, and entrusted to the sole care of the priests, who made use of it to enrich their rites with mystery. Thus was born the conception of musical sound as a thing having an independent existence, a thing different from life and unconnected with it. From this conception resulted an idea of music as a world of fantasy superimposed upon reality, a world inviolate and sacred. It will be readily understood how this idea of music must inevitably have impeded its progress, as compared with that of the other arts. The Greeks themselves—with their theory of music (systematized mathematically by Pythagoras) [55] which permitted the use of a few consonant intervals only—greatly limited music's scope and excluded all possibility of harmony, of which they knew nothing.

The Middle Ages, with their modifications of the Greek tetrachord system, with their Gregorian chants and their folk songs, enriched the art of music. Yet they continued to regard music from the point of view of *linear development in time*—a narrow view of the art which lasted several centuries and which persists in the more complicated polyphony of the Flemish contrapuntalists. The *chord* did not exist: the flow of the individual parts was never subordinated to the agreeable effect produced at any given moment by the ensemble of those parts. In a word, the medieval conception of music was horizontal, not vertical. An interest in the simultaneous union of different sounds, that is, in the chord as a complex sound, developed gradually, passing from the perfect consonance, with a few incidental dissonances, to the complex and persistent dissonances which characterize the music of today.

The art of music at first sought and achieved purity and sweetness of sound; later, it blended diverse sounds, but always with intent to caress the ear with suave harmonies. Today, growing ever more complicated, it seeks those combinations of sounds that fall most dissonantly, strangely, and harshly upon the ear. We thus approach nearer and nearer to the MUSIC OF NOISE.

This musical evolution parallels the growing multiplicity of machines, which everywhere are assisting mankind. Not only amid the clamor of great cities but even in the countryside, which until yesterday was ordinarily quiet, the machine today has created so many varieties and combinations of noise that pure musical sound—with its poverty and its monotony—no longer awakens any emotion in the hearer.

---

55. Pythagoras: sixth-century B.C. Greek philosopher, reincarnationist, and vegetarian, who noted the arithmetical proportions that determine the pitches of vibrating strings and taught that a similar harmony governs the celestial bodies.

To excite and exalt our senses, music continued to develop toward the most complex polyphony and the greatest variety of orchestral timbres, or colors, devising the most complicated successions of dissonant chords and preparing in a general way for the creation of MUSICAL NOISE. This evolution toward noise was hitherto impossible. An eighteenth-century ear could not have endured the dissonant intensity of certain chords produced by our modern orchestras—triple the size of the orchestras of that day. But our own ears—trained as they are by the modern world, so rich in variegated noises—not only enjoy these dissonances but demand more and more violent acoustic emotions.

Moreover, musical sound is too limited in qualitative variety of timbre. The most complicated of orchestras reduce themselves to four or five classes of instruments differing in timbre: instruments played with the bow, plucked instruments, brass winds, wood winds, and percussion instruments. So that modern music, in its attempts to produce new kinds of timbre, struggles vainly within this little circle.

We must break out of this narrow circle of pure musical sounds, and conquer the infinite variety of noise-sounds.

Everyone will recognize that every musical sound carries with it an incrustation of familiar and stale sense associations, which predispose the hearer to boredom, despite all the efforts of innovating musicians. We futurists have all deeply loved the music of the great composers. Beethoven and Wagner for many years wrung our hearts. But now we are satiated with them and derive much greater pleasure from ideally combining the noises of street-cars, internal-combustion engines, automobiles, and busy crowds than from re-hearing, for example, the "Eroica" or the "Pastorale." [56]

We cannot see the immense apparatus of the modern orchestra without being profoundly disappointed by its feeble acoustic achievements. Is there anything more absurd than to see twenty men breaking their necks to multiply the meowling of a violin? All this will naturally infuriate the musicomaniacs and perhaps disturb the somnolent atmosphere of our concert halls. Let us enter, as futurists, into one of these institutions for musical anemia. The first measure assails your ears with the boredom of the already-heard and causes you to anticipate the boredom of the measure to come. Thus we sip, from measure to measure, two or three different sorts of boredom, while we await an unusual emotion that never arrives. Meanwhile we are revolted by the monotony of the sensations experienced, combined with the idiotic religious excitement of the listeners, Buddhistically intoxicated by the thousandth repetition of their hypocritical and artificial ecstasy. Away! Let us be gone, since we shall not much longer succeed in restraining a desire to create a new musical realism by a generous distribution of

56. Beethoven's Third (1804) and Sixth (1808) Symphonies.

sonorous blows and slaps, leaping nimbly over violins, pianofortes, contrabasses, and groaning organs. Away!

The objection cannot be raised that all noise is loud and disagreeable. I need scarcely enumerate all the small and delicate noises which are pleasing to the ear. To be convinced of their surprising variety one need only think of the rumbling of thunder, the howling of the wind, the roar of a waterfall, the gurgling of a brook, the rustling of leaves, the receding clatter of a horse's hoofs, the bumping of a wagon over cobblestones, and the deep, solemn breathing of a city at night, all the noises made by wild and domesticated animals, and all those that the human mouth can produce, apart from speaking or singing.

Let us wander through a great modern city with our ears more attentive than our eyes, and distinguish the sounds of water, air, or gas in metal pipes, the purring of motors (which breathe and pulsate with an indubitable animalism), the throbbing of valves, the pounding of pistons, the screeching of gears, the clatter of streetcars on their rails, the cracking of whips, the flapping of awnings and flags. We shall amuse ourselves by orchestrating in our minds the noise of the metal shutters of store windows, the slamming of doors, the bustle and shuffle of crowds, the multitudinous uproar of railroad stations, forges, mills, printing presses, power stations, and underground railways.

Nor should the new noises of modern warfare be forgotten. Recently the poet Marinetti, in a letter from the trenches of Adrianopolis, described to me in admirably unfettered language the orchestra of a great battle:

"*every 5 seconds siege guns splitting the belly of space with a* TZANG-TUMB-TUUUMB *chord revolt of 500 echos to tear it to shreds and scatter it to infinity In the center of these* TZANG-TUMB-TUUUMB *spied out breadth 50 square kilometers leap reports knife-thrusts rapid-fire batteries Violence ferocity regularity this deep bass ascending the strange agitated insane high-pitched notes of battle Fury panting breath eyes ears nostrils open! watching! straining! what joy to see hear smell everything everything taratatata of the machine guns frantically screaming amid bites blows traak-traak whipcracks pic-pac pum-tumb strange goings-on leaps height 200 meters of the infantry Down down at the bottom of the orchestra stirring up pools oxen buffaloes goats wagons pluff plaff rearing of horses flic flac tzing tzing shaak hilarious neighing iiiiii stamping clanking 3 Bulgarian battalions on the march croooc-craaac* (lento) Shumi Maritza *or* Karvavena TZANG-TUMB-TUUUMB *toctoctoctoc* (rapidissimo) *crooc-craac* (lento) *officers' yells resounding like sheets of brass bang here crack there* BOOM *ching chak* (Presto) *chachacha-cha-chak up down back forth all around above look out for your head chak good shot! Flames flames flames flames flames collapse of the forts over behind the smoke Shukri Pasha talks to 27 forts over the telephone in*

Turkish in German Hallo! Ibrahim!! Rudolf! Hallo! Hallo, actors playlists echos prompters scenarios of smoke forests applause smell of hay mud dung my feet are frozen numb smell of saltpeter smell of putrefaction Timpani flutes clarinets everywhere low high birds chirping beatitudes shade cheep-cheep-cheep breezes verdure herds dong-dang-dong-ding-baaaa the lunatics are assaulting the musicians of the orchestra the latter soundly thrashed play on Great uproar don't cancel the concert more precision dividing into smaller more minute sounds fragments of echos in the theater area 300 square kilometers Rivers Maritza Tundja stretch out Rudopi Mountains standing up erect boxes balconies 2000 shrapnel spraying exploding snow-white handkerchiefs full of gold srrrrrrrr-TUMB-TUMB *2000 hand-grenades hurled shearing off black-haired heads with their splinters* TZANG-srrrrrr-TUMB-TZANG-TUMB-TUUUMB *the orchestra of the noises of war swells beneath a long-held note of silence in high heaven gilded spherical balloon which surveys the shooting , , ."*

We must fix the pitch and regulate the harmonies and rhythms of these extraordinarily varied sounds. To fix the pitch of noises does not mean to take away from them all the irregularity of tempo and intensity that characterizes their vibrations, but rather to give definite gradation or pitch to the stronger and more predominant of these vibrations. Indeed, noise is differentiated from musical sound merely in that the vibrations that produce it are confused and irregular, both in tempo and in intensity. Every noise has a note—sometimes even a chord—that predominates in the ensemble of its irregular vibrations. Because of this characteristic note it becomes possible to fix the pitch of a given noise, that is, to give it not a single pitch but a variety of pitches, without losing its characteristic quality—its distinguishing timbre. Thus certain noises produced by rotary motion may offer a complete ascending or descending chromatic scale by merely increasing or decreasing the speed of the motion.

Every manifestation of life is accompanied by noise. Noise is therefore familiar to our ears and has the power to remind us immediately of life itself. Musical sound, a thing extraneous to life and independent of it, an occasional and unnecessary adjunct, has become for our ears what a too familiar face is to our eyes. Noise, on the other hand, which comes to us confused and irregular as life itself, never reveals itself wholly but reserves for us innumerable surprises. We are convinced, therefore, that by selecting, coordinating, and controlling noises we shall enrich mankind with a new and unsuspected source of pleasure. Despite the fact that it is characteristic of sound to remind us brutally of life, the ART OF NOISES must not limit itself to reproductive imitation. It will reach its greatest emotional power through the purely acoustic enjoyment which the inspiration of the artist will contrive to evoke from combinations of noises.

These are the futurist orchestra's six families of noises, which we shall soon produce mechanically:

1	2	3	4	5	6
Booms	Whistles	Whispers	Screams	Noises	Voices of animals
Thunderclaps	Hisses	Murmurs	Screeches	obtained by	and men
Explosions	Snorts	Mutterings	Rustlings	percussion	Shouts
Crashes		Bustling	Buzzes	on metals,	Shrieks
Splashes		noises	Cracklings	wood, stone,	Groans
Roars		Gurgles	Sounds	terra-cotta	Howls
			obtained by		Laughs
			friction		Wheezes
					Sobs

In this list we have included the most characteristic fundamental noises; the others are but combinations of these.

The rhythmic movements within a single noise are of infinite variety. There is always, as in a musical note, a predominant rhythm, but around this may be perceived numerous secondary rhythms.

CONCLUSIONS

1. Futurist musicians must constantly broaden and enrich the field of sound. This is a need of our senses. Indeed, we note in present-day composers of genius a tendency toward the most complex dissonances. Moving further and further away from pure musical sound, they have almost reached the *noise-sound*. This need and this tendency can only be satisfied *by the supplementary use of noise and its substitution for musical sounds.*

2. Futurist musicians must substitute for the limited variety of timbres of the orchestral instruments of the day the infinite variety of the timbres of noises, reproduced by suitable mechanisms.

3. The musician's sensibility, liberating itself from facile, traditional rhythm, must find in noises the way to amplify and renew itself, since each offers a union of the most diverse rhythms, in addition to the predominant rhythm.

4. Since every noise has in its irregular vibrations a general, predominating tone, it will be easy to obtain, in constructing the instruments which imitate it, a sufficiently wide variety of tones, semitones, and quarter-tones. This variety of tones will not deprive any single noise of its characteristic timbre but will merely increase its tessitura, or extension.

5. The practical difficulties in the construction of these instruments are not serious. Once the mechanical principle producing a given noise is found, one may vary its pitch by applying the general laws of acoustics. For example, in instruments employing rotary motion the speed of rotation will be increased or diminished; in others, the size or tension of the sounding parts will be varied.

6. Not by means of a succession of noises imitating those of real life, but through a fanciful blending of these varied timbres and rhythms, will the new orchestra obtain the most complex and novel sound effects. Hence every instrument must be capable of varying its pitch and must have a fairly extensive range.

7. There is an infinite variety of noises. If, today, with perhaps a thousand different kinds of machines, we can distinguish a thousand different noises, tomorrow, as the number of new machines is multiplied, we shall be able to distinguish ten, twenty, or thirty thousand different noises, not merely to be imitated but to be combined as our fancy dictates.

8. Let us therefore invite young musicians of genius and audacity to listen attentively to all noises, so that they may understand the varied rhythms of which they are composed, their principal tone, and their secondary tones. Then, comparing the varied timbres of noises with those of musical tones, they will be convinced how much more numerous are the former than the latter. Out of this will come not merely an understanding of noises, but even a taste and an enthusiasm for them. Our increased perceptivity, which has already acquired futurist eyes, will then have futurist ears. Thus the motors and machines of our industrial cities may some day be intelligently pitched, so as to make of every factory an intoxicating orchestra of noises.[57]

I submit these statements, my dear Pratella, to your futuristic genius, and invite you to discuss them with me. I am not a professional musician; I have therefore no acoustic prejudices and no works to defend. I am a futurist painter projecting into an art he loves and has studied his desire to renovate all things. Being therefore more audacious than a professional musician could be, caring nought for my seeming incompetence, and convinced that audacity makes all things lawful and all things possible, I have imagined a great renovation of music through the Art of Noises.

From Nicholas Slonimsky, *Music since 1900,* 4th ed. (New York: Charles Scribner's Sons, 1971), 1298–1302; translated by Stephen Somervell.

■

Italian Futurism was to have many important interactions with later Modernist music. In 1917 Giacomo Balla designed an experimental ballet to the music of Stravinsky's

---

57. As early as 1920 a Concert of Factory Sirens was organized in Soviet Russia to emphasize the aesthetic possibilities of hard labor; and Ezra Pound noted in 1927, "Three years ago Antheil was talking vaguely of 'tuning up' whole cities. . . . With the performance of the Ballet mécanique one can conceive the possibility of organizing the sounds of a factory, let us say of boiler-plate or any other clangorous noisiness, the actual sounds of the labor, the various tones of the grindings; according to the needs of the work, and yet, with such pauses and durées, that at the end of the eight hours, the men go out not with frayed nerves, but elated" (*Ezra Pound and Music,* 315).

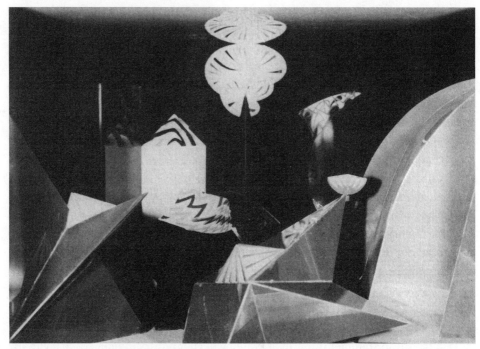

Giacomo Balla, set design for Stravinsky's *Fireworks* (reconstruction). © 2002 Artists Rights Society (ARS), New York/SIAE, Rome.

brief *Fireworks*—a ballet without dancers, in which the action was accomplished by the movement of colored lights across abstract shapes. Futurist adoration of machines can also be heard in a great many musical compositions that simulate mechanical noises, including Honegger's railway fantasy *Pacific 231* (1923), Antheil's *Ballet Mécanique* (1924–25), Vladimir Deshevov's *Rails* and Alexander Mosolov's *Iron Foundry* (both 1926), and Prokofiev's factory ballet *Steel Step* (1927).

A refinement of Futurist musical goals can be heard in the music of the French American Edgard Varèse (1883–1965). Varèse had an orthodox musical education in France, at which he rebelled—he found more inspiration in Busoni's *Sketch of a New Esthetic of Music.* After moving to New York in 1915, Varèse began to write a small canon of pieces in which melody was a property not only of pitch but also of timbre—the shifts of sound-tint (what Schoenberg called *Klangfarbenmelodie*), sometimes among unpitched percussion instruments, determine the musical experience. His music had strong connections to the Futurist school, but Varèse did not like the label: "Futurists believed in reproducing sounds literally; I believe in the metamorphosis of sounds into music."[58] If

58. Cited by Chou Wen-chung in the notes to London CD 460 208-2 (1998), 11.

Futurist composers liked train chuggings and factory bangings, Varèse's titles tend to suggest subtler forms of engagement with technology: *Hyperprism* (1923), *Ionisation* (1930–31), *Poème électronique* (1957–58). This last piece was generated by electronic means (though based on some concrete sounds) and represents a further stage in Varèse's liberation from the vagaries of timbres produced by physical means—scraping, thumping, and blowing. By electronic means Varèse could create timbres more crystalline or opaque, more rarefied or dense. If, as Schoenberg believed, God is in the most remote overtones, then electronics helped Varèse to approach him more closely.

What is striking about Varèse's essays is his continual recourse to visual metaphors. It may seem odd that cultivation of sound-for-sound's-sake leads to a fascination with an analogy between music and painting; but just as Antheil liked to call music a time-canvas, so Varèse conceived music as a balancing of colored masses and planes—a Kandinskian art of abstract sound-forms carefully arranged in space.

EDGARD VARÈSE
"Music and the Times" (1936)

At a time when the very newness of the mechanism of life is forcing our activities and our forms of human association to break with the traditions and the methods of the past in the effort to adapt themselves to circumstances, the urgent choices which we have to make are concerned not with the past but with the future. We cannot, even if we would, live much longer by tradition. The world is changing, and we change with it. The more we allow our minds the romantic luxury of treasuring the past in memory, the less able we become to face the future and to determine the new values which can be created in it.

Art's function is not to prove a formula or an esthetic dogma. Our academic rules were taken out of the living works of former masters. As Debussy has said, *works of art make rules but rules do not make works of art*. Art exists only as a medium of expression. . . .

The emotional impulse that moves a composer to write his scores contains the same element of poetry that incites the scientist to his discoveries. There is solidarity between scientific development and the progress of music. Throwing new light on nature, science permits music to progress—or rather to grow and change with changing times—by revealing to our senses harmonies and sensations before unfelt. On the threshold of beauty science and art collaborate. John Redfield voices the opinion of many when he says: "There should be at least one laboratory in the world where the fundamental facts of music could be investigated under conditions reasonably conducive to success. The interest in music is so widespread and intense, its appeal so intimate and poignant, and its significance for mankind so potent and profound, that it becomes unwise not to devote some portion of the enormous outlay for music to re-search in its fundamental questions."[59]

When new instruments will allow me to write music as I conceive it, the movement of sound-masses, of shifting planes, will be clearly perceived in my work, taking the place of the linear counterpoint. When these sound-masses collide, the phenomena of penetration or repulsion will seem to occur. Certain transmutations taking place on cer-tain planes will seem to be projected onto other planes, moving at different speeds and at different angles. There will no longer be the old conception of melody or interplay of melodies. The entire work will be a melodic totality. The entire work will flow as a river flows.

We have actually [i.e., currently] three dimensions in music: horizontal, vertical, and dynamic swelling or decreasing. I shall add a fourth, sound projection—that feeling that sound is leaving us with no hope of being reflected back, a feeling akin to that aroused by beams of light sent forth by a powerful searchlight—for the ear as for the eye, that sense of projection, of a journey into space.

Today with the technical means that exist and are easily adaptable, the differentia-tion of the various masses and different planes as well as these beams of sound, could be made discernible to the listener by means of certain acoustical arrangements. More-over, such an acoustical arrangement would permit the delimitation of what I call "zones of intensities." These zones would be differentiated by various timbres or col-ors and different loudnesses. Through such a physical process these zones would ap-pear of different colors and of different magnitude, in different perspectives for our per-ception. The role of color or timbre would be completely changed from being incidental, anecdotal, sensual or picturesque; it would become an agent of delineation, like the different colors on a map separating different areas, and an integral part of form. These zones would be felt as isolated, and the hitherto unobtainable non-blending (or at least the sensation of non-blending) would become possible.

In the moving masses you would be conscious of their transmutations when they pass over different layers, when they penetrate certain opacities, or are dilated in cer-tain rarefactions. Moreover, the new musical apparatus I envisage, able to emit sounds of any number of frequencies, will extend the limits of the lowest and highest registers, hence new organizations of the vertical resultants: chords, their arrangements, their spacings—that is, their oxygenation. Not only will the harmonic possibilities of the overtones be revealed in all their splendor, but the use of certain interferences created by the partials will represent an appreciable contribution. The never-before-thought-of use of the inferior resultants and of the differential and additional sounds may also be expected. An entirely new magic of sound! . . .

59. John Redfield, *Music: A Science and an Art* (New York: Knopf, 1928), 304.

I am sure that the time will come when the composer, after he has graphically realized his score, will see this score automatically put on a machine that will faithfully
transmit the musical content to the listener. As frequencies and new rhythms will have
to be indicated on the score, our actual notation will be inadequate. The new notation
will probably be seismographic. And here it is curious to note that at the beginning of
two eras, the Mediaeval primitive and our own primitive era (for we are at a new primitive stage in music today), we are faced with an identical problem: the problem of finding graphic symbols for the transposition of the composer's thought into sound. At a
distance of more than a thousand years we have this analogy: our still primitive electrical instruments find it necessary to abandon staff notation and to use a kind of seismographic writing much like the early ideographic writing originally used for the voice
before the development of staff notation. Formerly the curves of the musical line indicated the melodic fluctuations of the voice; today the machine-instrument requires
precise design indications.[60]

From "New Instruments and New Music," in *Contemporary Composers on Contemporary Music,* ed.
Elliott Schwartz and Barney Childs (New York: Holt, Rinehart and Winston, 1967), 196–97.

■

The art of noise, like visual art, has two basic species: the abstract and the figurative.
In Varèse's work, such as *Ecuatorial* (1932–34), the listener may notice evocations of savage ritual in the manner of Stravinsky's *Rite of Spring;* but Varèse's later compositions
tend to abstraction—some of his titles sound like more like the titles of nonrepresentational paintings than of musical pieces. Varèse said that "I want to encompass all that is
human . . . from the primitive to the farthest reaches of science";[61] and to achieve the
latter goal, he decorated some of his acoustic spaces with swirls and blips that were deliberately meant *not* to remind the hearer of sounds previously heard.

But as Varèse was working in the domain of abstraction, other composers were working in the domain of figuration. Pierre Schaeffer (1910–1995), a radio engineer, and Pierre
Henry (b. 1927), a tape-recorder specialist, collaborated on *Symphonie pour un homme
seul (Symphony for a Solitary Man,* 1949–50), an acoustic collage of knocks, shots, guitar
strums, yelps, garbled speech, shrill laughs, burbles, footsteps, tweets, and (in the *erotica*
section) a woman's delighted breathing; Schaeffer called it "an opera for the blind, an
action without a plot, a poem made of noises and notes, with bursts of text, spoken or

60. This was a lecture given by Varèse in Santa Fe in 1936 under the auspices of the New Mexico
Association on Indian Affairs; it was edited by Chou Wen-chung.

61. From Olivia Mattis, "Varèse's Multimedia Conception of *Déserts*," *Musical Quarterly* 76, no. 4
(Winter 1992): 576.

musical."[62] This sort of music is called *musique concrète,* and is a sort of figure-painting in music—although sometimes the tape-recorded sounds so fully detach themselves from their original context that the composition veers toward that paradoxical thing, an abstract concretion, as (for example) in Henry's *Variations pour une porte et un soupir* (*Variations for a Door and a Sigh,* 1963), in which a long piece is generated mostly through modifications of the sound of a squeaking door.

According to Schaeffer, the tenets of *musique concrète* are as follows:

1. Primacy of the ear. The potential for evolution (and also the limits) of all new music lie in the resources of the ear.

2. In consideration of the first tenet, preference for real acoustic sources to which our ears have long been accustomed (and in particular a refusal to have recourse only to electronic sources).

3. Search for a language. . . . To learn a *new solfège* through systematic listening to sonorous objects of every kind.[63]

Schaeffer invented *musique concrète* after hearing a broken record repeating a groove: "It is a fragment of life caught in a trap";[64] and he saw it as his task to capture these fragments and to let them speak everything that they had to say: "the sound, prisoner of the magnetic tape, repeats itself indefinitely just like itself, isolates itself from contexts, comes to disclose itself in other perspectives of perception, in order to recover this fervor of hearing, this fever of discovery."[65] The language here is almost Proustian, as if Schaeffer hoped to recapture the lost paradise of primal experience through the loopings and splicings of taped sounds.

Musique concrète has had its share of detractors. Stravinsky, for example, said, "It is the transcendent (or 'abstract' or 'self-contained') nature of music that the new so-called concretism—Pop Art, eighteen-hour slices-of-reality films, *musique concrète*—opposes. But instead of bringing art and reality closer together, the new movement merely thins out the distinction."[66] And Schaeffer himself came to agree: in 1989 he told Olivia Mattis that he was convinced that music could only be written using *do-re-mi-fa-sol*—a striking example of Modernist recantation.

Russolo, Varèse, and Schaeffer were concerned with the means of producing sound —sound previously excluded from the domain of music. But John Cage (1912–1992)

62. Pierre Schaeffer, *La musique concrète* (Paris: Presses Universitaires de France, 1967), 22.
63. Ibid., 29; translated by the editor.
64. Cited in *Musique de notre temps,* essay by Claude Samuel (Adès CD 14.122-2, 1988), 89.
65. Pierre Schaeffer, *Traité des objets musicaux* (Paris, Éditions du Seuil, 1966), 33; translated by the editor.
66. Igor Stravinsky and Robert Craft, *Themes and Conclusions* (Berkeley: University of California Press, 1982), 188.

was more concerned with attending to preexisting sounds and with creating stressless environments where sounds could be attended to without too much intervention by the composer. Cage experimented with Russolo's methods (as in *Cartridge Music,* 1960, in which Cage extends the *intonarumori* principle by scraping a phonograph needle over various materials), with Varèse's methods (as in *Fontana Mix,* 1958, an abstract composition for tape), and with Schaeffer's methods (as in *Roaratorio: An Irish Circus on Finnegans Wake,* 1979, a piece of concrete music in which tape-recorded sounds, such as the cries of gulls, illustrate Joyce's text). But Cage rejected the belief, common among Modernist composers, that strenuousness of method and aggressive disposition of sonic resource were signs of excellence; for Cage, the best composer was the person who least tampered with the world's audible events.

Cage strongly distinguished between two methods for achieving a lapse of compositional control, a state of egolessness in music:

1. *Chance procedures,* in which such variables as pitch, rhythm, volume are determined by some generator of randomness, such as casts of dice, imperfections in music paper, star charts, or the *I Ching* (Book of Changes). Others had made some use of these procedures: for example, in 1913 Marcel Duchamp had drawn from a hat pieces of paper with notes written them, and in 1939 Heitor Villa-Lobos had based his piano piece *As três Marias* on the pattern of stars in the constellation Orion. But Duchamp's experiment had few repercussions in the world of music, and Villa-Lobos subjected his stars to more or less orthodox harmonizations. Cage was the first composer to make chance exciting.

2. *Indeterminacy,* in which performers are given latitude, within certain limits, to play such pitches, rhythms, and durations as they wished.

It will be noticed that the first method pertains to composition, the second to performance.

Cage was a pupil of Schoenberg and evidently replaced Schoenberg's rigor with an equally extreme surrender of will; but it might also be argued that he carried out the Schoenbergian revolution through different means, by trading the serialist's chart of retrogrades and inversions for the charts of the *I Ching*.[67] Chance itself can be a stern taskmaster.

Cage's approach to lecturing and writing was as original as his approach to musical composition: for example, when he was asked questions, he sometimes read answers from a prepared list, without any reference to what the questioner had actually asked. He tended to aggregate material, rather to make logical arguments—in the fashion of Marinetti, Cage dispenses with the connective tissues of prose. Therefore it seems best

---

67. Cage makes the comparison between dodecaphony and the *I Ching* in *Silence* (Hanover, N.H.: Wesleyan University Press, 1973), 26.

to print, instead of a single essay, a collection of some of Cage's sayings: speech-bits to be enjoyed as individual sounds, so to speak, without any attempt at harmonization.

JOHN CAGE
Fragments from *Silence* (1961)

Wherever we are, what we hear is mostly noise. When we ignore it, it disturbs us. When we listen to it, we find it fascinating. The sound of a truck at fifty miles per hour. Static between stations. Rain. We want to capture and control these sounds, to use them not as sound effects but as musical instruments. . . . We can compose and perform a quartet for explosive motor, wind, heartbeat, and landslide.

In fact, try as we may to make a silence, we cannot. . . . I entered [an anechoic chamber] at Harvard University several years ago and heard two sounds, one high and one low. When I described them to the engineer in charge, he informed that the high one was my nervous system in operation, the low one my blood in circulation. Until I die there will be sounds. And they will continue following my death. One need not fear about the future of music.

And what is the purpose of writing music? One is, of course, not dealing with purposes but dealing with sounds. Or the answer must take the form of a paradox: a purposeful purposelessness or a purposeless play. This play, however, is an affirmation of life—not an attempt to bring order out of chaos nor to suggest improvements in creation, but simply a way of waking up to the very life we're living, which is so excellent when one gets one's mind and one's desires out of its way and lets it act of its own accord.

Why is it so difficult for so many people to listen?
Why do they start talking when there is something to hear?
Do they have their ears not on the sides of their heads but situated inside their mouths so that when they hear something their first impulse is to start talking?

Hung Mung said, ". . . Cultivate a grand similarity with the chaos of the plastic ether; unloose your mind; set your spirit free; be still as if you had no soul."

The idea of relation . . . being absent, anything . . . may happen. A "mistake" is beside the point, for once anything happens it authentically is.

Is counterpoint good? "The soul itself is so simple that it cannot have more than one idea at a time of anything. . . . A person cannot be more than single in attention." (Eckhart) [68]

. . . Everything is possible. . . . Debussy said quite some time ago, "Any sounds in any combination and in any succession are henceforth free to be used in a musical continuity."

When I said recently in Darmstadt that one could write music by observing the imperfections in the paper upon which one was writing, a student who did not understand because he was full of musical ideas asked, "Would one piece of paper be better than another: one for instance that had more imperfections?"

. . . Cowell remarked at the New School before a concert of works by Christian Wolff, Earle Brown,[69] Morton Feldman, and myself, that here were four composers who were getting rid of glue.

Curiously enough, the twelve-tone system has no zero in it. . . . There is not enough of nothing in it.

I explained that I'd never been interested in symbolism; that I preferred just taking things as themselves, not as standing for other things.

In Zen they say: If something is boring after two minutes, try it for four. If still boring, try it for eight, sixteen, thirty-two, and so on. Eventually one discovers that it's not boring at all but very interesting.

"Art is the imitation of nature in her manner of operation."

Later on I gradually liked all the intervals. As I look back I realize that I began liking the octave; I accepted the major and minor thirds. Perhaps, of all the intervals, I liked these thirds least.

Harmony, so-called, is a forced abstract vertical relation which blots out the spontaneous transmitting nature of each of the sounds forced into it. It is artificial and unrealistic.

68. Johannes Eckhart (?1260–?1327), German mystic.
69. Christian Wolff (b. 1934) and Earle Brown (1926–2002), members, with Feldman and Cage, of the New York School of composers.

A *technique* to be useful (skillful, that is) must be such that it fails to control the elements subjected to it.

The sounds that had accidentally occurred while it was being played were in no sense an interruption. . . . "Why do I write music?" An Indian musician told me the traditional answer in India was "To sober the mind and thus make it susceptible to divine influences."

. . . Chance ought to be very controlled.

Eventually everything will be happening at once.

Well, the grand thing about the human mind is that it can turn its own tables and see meaninglessness as ultimate meaning. . . . Let us say Yes to our presence together in Chaos.

If they say, for instance, "That music hurt my ears," we immediately think it probably didn't, that what were hurt were mental attitudes and feelings.

Nothing needs to be connected to anything else since they are not separated irrevocably to begin with.

From *Silence* (Hanover, N.H.: Wesleyan University Press, 1973), 3, 8, 12, 48–49, 55, 59, 64, 67–68, 70, 71, 79, 85, 93, 100, 115, 152, 154, 157–58, 186, 187, 195, 219, 228–29.

6 New Discipline: The Twelve-Tone Method

By 1922–23, when Schoenberg was announcing his twelve-tone breakthrough—a method for orderly disestablishment of the tonic, by basing composition on a specific array of the twelve notes of the chromatic scale and their transpositions, retrogrades, and inversions—the method was breaking through on several fronts at the same time. By 1915 Nikolay Roslavets (1881–1944) was experimenting with a compositional method based on what he called "synthetic chords"—chords of six or more notes, such as dominant thirteenths—and their transpositions to each of the twelve notes of the chromatic scale; and by 1919 Josef Matthias Hauer (1883–1959) was working on a compositional method (based in part on research into astronomy) in which the "*nomos* lies in the fact that within a certain succession of tones no tone may be repeated and none may be left out."[1] (Schoenberg arranged some performances of Hauer's early work, but started to bristle when it became clear just how closely Hauer's method anticipated the direction of Schoenberg's thought.)[2] The goals and orientations of the three composers were quite different: Roslavets was a Russian Futurist trying to adapt the mystical Symbolist style of Scriabin to a harder-edged, more up-to-date aesthetic; Hauer was a musical absolutist who thought that the perfection of *melos*—abstract melody—could best be accomplished through twelve-note rows; Schoenberg was a dramatic composer, interested in intensifying the meaningfulness of music by making each moment of a composition bear the weight of the whole—by embedding the germ of the music, the row, in each tiny detail, just as a painter might wish to make every square inch of the canvas telling. The twelve-tone method seemed to be the answer to a great many different questions.

But Roslavets, Hauer, and Schoenberg perhaps shared a certain desire for transcendence. An intuitive and unregulated compositional style, such as that of Schoenberg's *Erwartung* (1909) or Scriabin's *Poem of Ecstasy* (1908), refers all questions of form back to the psychology of the composer. This is one reason for its suitability to Freudian themes. But few composers, even the most egotistical, feel capable of supporting the

---

1. From *Vom Wesen des Musikalischen* (1920), quoted by Schoenberg in *Style and Idea,* ed. Leonard Stein, trans. Leo Black (Berkeley: University of California Press, 1984), 211. Schoenberg adds that his *Harmonielehre* (1911) made the same point long before Hauer.

2. "All the laws so apodictically set forth by Hauer . . . are wrong" (ibid., 209).

burden of the whole aesthetic of music; and it was a relief to transfer certain respon-sibilities to a method—especially a method that seemed so unearthly, so replete, as if music itself had devised it, not a human mind. The mathematical symmetry of the magic square (the 144-note table of a row's transpositions, with arrows to indicate retrogrades and inversions) seemed to preexist in an abstract musical space, just as the Pythagorean theorem preexisted before Pythagoras came along to prove it. For Schoenberg, in *Moses und Aron* (1930–32), the tone row would reveal itself as an irresistible metaphor for God.

Schoenberg's twelve-tone music, in its earliest manifestations, showed strong con-nections to Neoclassicism: both sought relief from anarchy. Schoenberg's first twelve-tone works often have the textures, the forms, even the sonorities of eighteenth-century music, especially in the Piano Suite (1923), which contains a gavotte, a musette, and a gigue. Schoenberg could be quite attentive to placements of thirds and fifths in his tone rows and sometimes liked to play games in the margins between twelve-tone and tonal music, as in the third movement of his Suite for Septet (1927), a set of variations on the folksong "Ännchen von Tharau." The notes of the song are picked out on the bass clar-inet, while the piano fills in the other notes of the tone row in order to keep the chastity of the row inviolate. But it would probably be a mistake to consider the twelve-tone method as Schoenberg's retreat to safety from the wilderness of the free atonal music of 1908–13: the new method may have foreclosed some paths of experimentation, but it opened others.

Schoenberg's essays on the twelve-tone method typically have a certain tone of awe. In *Moses und Aron,* the voice from the burning bush tells Moses to take off his shoes—here is holy ground. Schoenberg seems to approach the method with like reverence.

ARNOLD SCHOENBERG
from "Composition with Twelve Tones": [*fiat lux*] (1941)
§1

To understand the very nature of creation one must acknowledge that there was no light before the Lord said: "Let there be Light."[3] And since there was not yet light, the Lord's omniscience embraced a vision of it which only His omnipotence could call forth.

We poor human beings, when we refer to one of the better minds among us as a cre-ator, should never forget what a creator is in reality.

A creator has a vision of something which has not existed before this vision.

And a creator has the power to bring his vision to life, the power to realize it.

In fact, the concept of creator and creation should be formed in harmony with the Di-

---

3. Genesis 1:3. In *Kol Nidre* (1938), Schoenberg set the words "Let there be light" to an amazing sound flash from a flexatone.

vine Model; inspiration and perfection, wish and fulfilment, will and accomplishment coincide spontaneously and simultaneously. In Divine Creation there were no details to be carried out later; "There was Light" at once and in its ultimate perfection.

Alas, human creators, if they be granted a vision, must travel the long path between vision and accomplishment; a hard road where, driven out of Paradise, even geniuses must reap their harvest in the sweat of their brows.

Alas, it is one thing to envision in a creative instant of inspiration and it is another thing to materialize one's vision by painstakingly connecting details until they fuse into a kind of organism.

Alas, suppose it becomes an organism, a homunculus or a robot, and possesses some of the spontaneity of a vision; it remains yet another thing to organize this form so that it becomes a comprehensible message "to whom it may concern."

§II

Form in the arts, and especially in music, aims primarily at comprehensibility. The relaxation which a satisfied listener experiences when he can follow an idea, its development, and the reasons for such development is closely related, psychologically speaking, to a feeling of beauty. Thus, artistic value demands comprehensibility, not only for intellectual, but also for emotional satisfaction. However, the creator's *idea* has to be presented, whatever the mood he is impelled to evoke.

Composition with twelve tones has no other aim than comprehensibility. In view of certain events in recent musical history, this might seem astonishing, for works written in this style have failed to gain understanding in spite of the new medium of organization. Thus, should one forget that contemporaries are not final judges, but are generally overruled by history, one might consider this method doomed. But, though it seems to increase the listener's difficulties, it compensates for this deficiency by penalizing the composer. For composing thus does not become easier, but rather ten times more difficult. Only the better-prepared composer can compose for the better-prepared music lover.

§III

The method of composing with twelve tones grew out of a necessity.

In the last hundred years, the concept of harmony has changed tremendously through the development of chromaticism. The idea that one basic tone, the root, dominated the construction of chords and regulated their succession—the concept of *tonality*—had to develop first into the concept of *extended tonality*. Very soon it became doubtful whether such a root still remained the center to which every harmony and harmonic succession must be referred. Furthermore, it became doubtful whether a tonic appearing at the beginning, at the end, or at any other point really had a constructive meaning. Richard Wagner's harmony had promoted a change in the logic and constructive power of harmony. One of its consequences was the so-called *impressionistic* use of harmonies, especially practiced by Debussy. His harmonies, without constructive meaning, often served the coloristic purpose of expressing moods and pictures. Moods and pictures, though extra-musical, thus became constructive elements, incorporated in the musical functions; they produced a sort of emotional comprehensibility. In this way, tonality was already dethroned in practice, if not in theory. This alone would perhaps not have caused a radical change in compositional technique. However, such a change became necessary when there occurred simultaneously a development which ended in what I call the *emancipation of the dissonance*.

The ear had gradually become acquainted with a great number of dissonances, and so had lost the fear of their "sense-interrupting" effect. One no longer expected preparations of Wagner's dissonances or resolutions of Strauss' discords; one was not disturbed by Debussy's non-functional harmonies, or by the harsh counterpoint of later composers. This state of affairs led to a freer use of dissonances comparable to classic composers' treatment of diminished seventh chords, which could precede and follow any other harmony, consonant or dissonant, as if there were no dissonance at all.

What distinguishes dissonances from consonances is not a greater or lesser degree of beauty, but a greater or lesser degree of *comprehensibility*. In my *Harmonielehre* I presented the theory that dissonant tones appear later among the overtones, for which reason the ear is less intimately acquainted with them. This phenomenon does not justify such sharply contradictory terms as concord and discord. Closer acquaintance with the more remote consonances—the dissonances, that is—gradually eliminated the difficulty of comprehension and finally admitted not only the emancipation of dominant and other seventh chords, diminished sevenths and augmented triads, but also the emancipation of Wagner's, Strauss's, Moussorgsky's, Debussy's, Mahler's, Puccini's, and Reger's more remote dissonances.

The term *emancipation of the dissonance* refers to its comprehensibility, which is considered equivalent to the consonance's comprehensibility. A style based on this premise treats dissonances like consonances and renounces a tonal center. By avoiding the establishment of a key modulation is excluded, since modulation means leaving an established tonality and establishing *another* tonality.

The first compositions in this new style were written by me around 1908 and, soon afterwards, by my pupils, Anton von Webern and Alban Berg. From the very beginning such compositions differed from all preceding music, not only harmonically but also melodically, thematically, and motivally. But the foremost characteristics of these pieces *in statu nascendi* [in the condition of their origin] were their extreme expressiveness and their extraordinary brevity. At that time, neither I nor my pupils were conscious of the reasons for these features. Later I discovered that our sense of form was right when it forced us to counterbalance extreme emotionality with extraordinary shortness. Thus, subconsciously, consequences were drawn from an innovation which, like every innovation, destroys while it produces. New colorful harmony was offered; but much was lost.

Formerly the harmony had served not only as a source of beauty, but, more important, as a means of distinguishing the features of the form. For instance, only a consonance was considered suitable for an ending. Establishing functions demanded different successions of harmonies than roving functions; a bridge, a transition, demanded other successions than a codetta; harmonic variation could be executed intelligently and logically only with due consideration of the fundamental meaning of the harmonies. Fulfilment of all these functions—comparable to the effect of punctuation in the construction of sentences, of subdivision into paragraphs, and of fusion into chapters—could scarcely be assured with chords whose constructive values had not as yet been explored. Hence, it seemed at first impossible to compose pieces of complicated organization or of great length.

A little later I discovered how to construct larger forms by following a text or a poem. The differences in size and shape of its parts and the change in character and mood were mirrored in the shape and size of the composition, in its dynamics and tempo, figuration and accentuation, instrumentation and orchestration. Thus the parts were differentiated as clearly as they had formerly been by the tonal and structural functions of harmony.

§IV

Formerly the use of the fundamental harmony had been theoretically regulated through recognition of the effects of root progressions. This practice had grown into a subconsciously functioning sense of form which gave a real composer an almost somnambulistic sense of security in creating, with utmost precision, the most delicate distinctions of formal elements.

Whether one calls oneself conservative or revolutionary, whether one composes in a conventional or progressive manner, whether one tries to imitate old styles or is destined to express new ideas—whether one is a good composer or not—one must be convinced of the infallibility of one's own fantasy and one must believe in one's own inspiration. Nevertheless, the desire for a conscious control of the new means and forms will arise in every artist's mind; and he will wish to know consciously the laws and rules which govern the forms which he has conceived "as in a dream." Strongly convincing as this dream may have been, the conviction that these new sounds obey the laws of nature and of our manner of thinking—the conviction that order, logic, comprehensibility and form cannot be present without obedience to such laws—forces the composer along the road of exploration. He must find, if not laws or rules, at least ways to justify the dissonant character of these harmonies and their successions.

§V

After many unsuccessful attempts during a period of approximately twelve years, I laid the foundations for a new procedure in musical construction which seemed fitted to replace those structural differentiations provided formerly by tonal harmonies.

I called this procedure *Method of Composing with Twelve Tones Which are Related Only with One Another.*

This method consists primarily of the constant and exclusive use of a set of twelve different tones. This means, of course, that no tone is repeated within the series and that it uses all twelve tones of the chromatic scale, though in a different order. It is in no way identical with the chromatic scale.

[. . . A] basic set (BS) . . . should never be called a scale, although it is invented to substitute for some of the unifying and formative advantages of scale and tonality. The scale is the source of many figurations, parts of melodies and melodies themselves, ascending and descending passages, and even broken chords. In approximately the same manner the tones of the basic set produce similar elements. Of course, cadences produced by the distinction between principal and subsidiary harmonies will scarcely be derived from the basic set. But something different and more important is derived from it with a regularity comparable to the regularity and logic of the earlier harmony; the association of tones into harmonies and their successions is regulated (as will be shown later) by the order of these tones. The basic set functions in the manner of a motive. This explains why such a basic set has to be invented anew for every piece. It has to be the first creative thought. It does not make much difference whether or not the set appears in the composition at once like a theme or a melody, whether or not it is characterized as such by features of rhythm, phrasing, construction, character, etc.

Why such a set should consist of twelve different tones, why none of these tones should be repeated too soon, why, accordingly, only one set should be used in one composition—the answers to all these questions came to me gradually.

Discussing such problems in my *Harmonielehre* (1911), I recommended the avoidance of octave doublings. To double is to emphasize, and an emphasized tone could be interpreted as a root, or even as a tonic; the consequences of such an interpretation must be avoided. Even a slight reminiscence of the former tonal harmony would be disturbing, because it would create false expectations of consequences and continuations. The use of a tonic is deceiving if it is not based on all the relationships of tonality.

The use of more than one set was excluded because in every following set one or more tones would have been repeated too soon. Again there would arise the danger of interpreting the repeated tone as a tonic. Besides, the effect of unity would be lessened.

Justified already by historical development, the method of composing with twelve tones is also not without aesthetic and theoretical support. On the contrary, it is just this support which advances it from a mere technical device to the rank and importance of a scientific theory.

Music is not merely another kind of amusement, but a musical poet's, a musical thinker's representation of musical ideas; these musical ideas must correspond to the laws of human logic; they are a part of what man can apperceive, reason and express. Proceeding from these assumptions, I arrived at the following conclusions:

THE TWO-OR-MORE-DIMENSIONAL SPACE IN WHICH MUSICAL IDEAS ARE PRE-SENTED IS A UNIT. Though the elements of these ideas appear separate and independent to the eye and the ear, they reveal their true meaning only through their co-operation, even as no single word alone can express a thought without relation to other words. All that happens at any point of this musical space has more than a local effect. It functions not only in its own plane, but also in all other directions and planes, and is not without influence even at remote points. For instance, the effect of progressive rhythmical subdivision, through what I call "the tendency of the shortest notes" to multiply themselves, can be observed in every classic composition.

A musical idea, accordingly, though consisting of melody, rhythm, and harmony, is neither the one nor the other alone, but all three together. The elements of a musical idea are partly incorporated in the horizontal plane as successive sounds, and partly in the vertical plane as simultaneous sounds. The mutual relation of tones regulates the succession of intervals as well as their association into harmonies; the rhythm regulates the succession of tones as well as the succession of harmonies and organizes phrasing. And this explains why, as will be shown later, a basic set of twelve tones (BS) can be used in either dimension, as a whole or in parts.

The basic set is used in diverse mirror forms. . . .

. . . The validity of this form of thinking is . . . demonstrated by the previously stated law of the unity of musical space, best formulated as follows: *the unity of musical space demands an absolute and unitary perception.* In this space, as in Swedenborg's[4] heaven (described in Balzac's *Seraphita*),[5] there is no absolute down, no right or left,

---

4. Emanuel Swedenborg (1688–1772), Swedish scientist and mystic, who ideas influenced artists as diverse as William Blake (whose *Marriage of Heaven and Hell* is a riposte to Swedenborg's conception of heaven) and George Bernard Shaw (whose *Man and Superman* owes much to Swedenborg's concept of heaven and hell as affinity states). Yeats was struck by his matter-of-fact approach to the existence of angels—"a mind incredibly dry and arid, tangible and cold, like the minerals he assayed for the Swedish government, studies a new branch of science: the economics, the natural history of Heaven" (*A Vision* [New York: Macmillan, 1961], 161).

5. Honoré de Balzac (1799–1850) wrote an immense series of novels called *La comédie humaine*. *Séraphita* (1834–35) concerns an angel who is at once male and female; it represented to Schoenberg a mystical convergence of opposites. Schoenberg set Ernest Dowson's poem "Seraphita" as the first of

forward or backward. Every musical configuration, every movement of tones has to be comprehended primarily as a mutual relation of sounds, of oscillatory vibrations, appearing at different places and times. To the imaginative and creative faculty, relations in the material sphere are as independent from directions or planes as material objects are, in their sphere, to our perceptive faculties. Just as our mind always recognizes, for instance, a knife, a bottle or a watch, regardless of its position, and can reproduce it in the imagination in every possible position, even so a musical creator's mind can operate subconsciously with a row of tones, regardless of their direction, regardless of the way in which a mirror might show the mutual relations, which remain a given quality.

§VI

The introduction of my method of composing with twelve tones does not facilitate composing; on the contrary, it makes it more difficult. Modernistically-minded beginners often think they should try it before having acquired the necessary technical equipment. This is a great mistake. The restrictions imposed on a composer by the obligation to use only one set in a composition are so severe that they can only be overcome by an imagination which has survived a tremendous number of adventures. Nothing is given by this method; but much is taken away.

It has been mentioned that for every new composition a special set of twelve tones has to be invented. Sometimes a set will not fit every condition an experienced composer can foresee, especially in those ideal cases where the set appears at once in the form, character, and phrasing of a theme. Rectifications in the order of tones may then become necessary.

In the first works in which I employed this method, I was not yet convinced that the exclusive use of one set would not result in monotony. Would it allow the creation of a sufficient number of characteristically differentiated themes, phrases, motives, sentences, and other forms? At this time, I used complicated devices to assure variety. But soon I discovered that my fear was unfounded; I could even base a whole opera, *Moses and Aron,* solely on one set; and I found that, on the contrary, the more familiar I became with this set the more easily I could draw themes from it. Thus, the truth of my first prediction had received splendid proof. One has to follow the basic set; but, nevertheless, one composes as freely as before. . . .

§XII

. . . Prior to Richard Wagner, operas consisted almost exclusively of independent pieces, whose mutual relation did not seem to be a musical one. Personally, I refuse to believe that in the great masterworks pieces are connected only by the superficial coherence of the dramatic proceedings. Even if these pieces were merely "fillers" taken

---

his *Four Orchestral Songs* (1916); and he began a setting of Balzac's work to a libretto by the librettist of *Erwartung,* Marie Pappenheim (now lost).

from earlier works of the same composer, something must have satisfied the master's sense of form and logic. We may not be able to discover it, but certainly it exists. In music there is no form without logic, there is no logic without unity.

I believe that when Richard Wagner introduced his *Leitmotiv* — for the same purpose as that for which I introduced my Basic Set — he may have said: "Let there be unity."

ADDENDUM (1946)

In the course of about the last ten years, some of the strictness of the rules concerning octave doubling and prominent appearances of fundamental chords of harmony have been loosened to some degree.

At first it became clear that such single events could not change the style of nontonality into tonality. There remained still those characteristic melodies, rhythms, phrasings and other formal devices which were born simultaneously with the style of freedom of the dissonances.

Besides, even if the negation of a tonal center's domination would have been temporarily undermined, this need not have destroyed the stylistic merits of a composition.

I have to admit that Alban Berg, who was perhaps the least orthodox of us three — Webern, Berg and I — in his operas mixed pieces or parts of pieces of distinct tonality with those which were distinctly non-tonal. He explained this apologetically, by contending that as an opera composer he could not, for reason of dramatic expression and characterization, renounce the contrast furnished by change from major to minor.

Though he was right as a composer, he was wrong theoretically. I have proved in my operas *Von Heute auf Morgen* [6] and *Moses und Aron* that every expression and characterization can be produced with the style of free dissonance.

From *Style and Idea,* ed. Leonard Stein, trans. Leo Black (Berkeley: University of California Press, 1984), 214–20, 223–24, 224–25.

■

Anton Webern (1883–1945) was one of Schoenberg's oldest and most devoted pupils; he was also one of the best-educated composers of the age, a professional musicologist who wrote a dissertation on the Renaissance polyphonist Heinrich Isaac. Of all the Modernists, Webern was most sensitive to the need for concentration of gesture. Schoenberg himself had written, in 1911, *Six Little Piano Pieces,* op. 19, which range in length from about thirty seconds to a minute and a half; this terseness would be a main characteristic of Webern's career. He tried to achieve authenticity by paring away everything but the essence of the composition — crescendo, scurry, silence. This chastity of expression, this

6. *Von Heute auf Morgen* (1929), Schoenberg's garishly amusing opera (to a text by his second wife) concerning a wife who flirts with an operatic tenor after her husband takes her for granted.

refusal to dilute the significant thing with development or with contrasting material, threatened to lead Webern toward the blank page.

Webern's fury of elimination was more common in the visual arts than in music. In the 1910s, when Webern was writing his first mature works, the Dutch painter Piet Mondrian (1872–1944) was developing an art style, called Neoplasticism, which sought to reduce landscapes to their essentials—to departicularize a tree or a seascape until only its most universal aspects were visible. (Interestingly, a stripped-down tree looked almost exactly like a stripped-down seascape, a pile of flat, slightly bulging or sagging rectangles.) Mondrian sought to look behind the confusions and distractions of normal seeing to discover what was behind ("I am one of those artists who is *most* expressive of the absolute");[7] he was opposed to the traditional goals of painting ("there must be a destruction of the natural and its reconstruction in accordance with the spiritual").[8] Similarly, Webern tended to think that traditional music was fat with superfluities, prevarications, of every sort; he labored to disextend music back to its verities.

Webern saw Schoenberg's twelve-tone method as a sort of salvation, since it enabled a musical composition to stretch out in time without losing its purity of motive, its unity of being. (However, even in Webern's twelve-tone works, it is unusual to find a movement as long as six minutes.) But Webern's approach to row construction differed somewhat from Schoenberg's. As Pierre Boulez has noted, Webern's rows are halls of mirrors: "A series is totally symmetrical when it can be broken down into a greater or lesser number of isomorphic figures. Webern's series, for example, are always of this kind."[9] Boulez's illustration of this property has a strong look of a Mondrian rhomboid:

In 1932 Webern gave some nontechnical lectures on the new music, lectures that reveal his luminous conviction that tonal music is passé, and that the path of twelve-tone music is the only path worth following.

ANTON WEBERN
from "The Path to Twelve-Note Composition" (1932)
§1

I didn't invent the title you've seen. It's Schoenberg's. This year I was to talk in Mondsee on this subject, so I had a brief correspondence with Schoenberg about what such a lecture should be called. He suggested "The path to twelve-note composition."

We must know, above all, what it means: "twelve-note composition." Have you ever

---

7. Yve-Alain Bois, Joop Josten, Angelica Zander Rudenstine, and Hans Janssen, *Piet Mondrian* (Milan: Leonardo Arte, 1994), 150.

8. Ibid., 317.

9. Pierre Boulez, *Boulez on Music Today*, trans. Susan Bradshaw and Richard Rodney Bennett (Cambridge: Harvard University Press, 1971), 71.

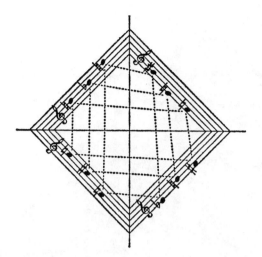

Pierre Boulez, symmetry
diagram of a Webern series.
© 2002 Artists Rights
Society (ARS), New York/
ADAGP, Paris.

looked at a work of that kind? It's my belief that ever since music has been written, all the great composers have instinctively had this before them as a goal. But I don't want to trust you with these secrets straight away—and they really are secrets! Secret keys. Such keys have probably existed in all ages, and people have unconsciously had more or less of an idea of them.

Today I want to deal generally with these things. So what has in fact been achieved by this method of composition? What territory, what doors have been opened with this secret key? To be very general, it's a matter of creating a means to express the greatest possible unity in music. There we have a word we could discuss all day. Perhaps, after all, it's important to talk about these things—I mean things so general that everyone can understand them, even those who only want to sit and listen passively. For I don't know what the future has in store. . . .

Unity is surely the indispensable thing if meaning is to exist. Unity, to be very general, is the establishment of the utmost relatedness between all component parts. So in music, as in all other human utterance, the aim is to make as clear as possible the relationships between the parts of the unity; in short, to show how one thing leads to another.

Turning now to music, it's to some extent historical. What is this "twelve-note composition?" And what preceded it? This music has been given the dreadful name "atonal music." Schoenberg gets a lot of fun out of this,[10] since "atonal" means "without notes";

---

10. "I find above all that the expression, 'atonal music,' is most unfortunate—it is on a par with calling flying 'the art of not falling,' or swimming 'the art of not drowning'" (Schoenberg, *Style and Idea,* 210).

Piet Mondrian, *Composition with Grid 5 (Lozenge)* (1919). © 2002 Mondrian/Holtzman Trust, c/o Beeldrecht/Artists Rights Society (ARS), New York.

but that's meaningless. What's meant is music in no definite key. What has been given up? The key has disappeared!

Let's try to find unity! Until now, tonality has been one of the most important means of establishing unity. It's the only one of the old achievements that has disappeared; everything else is still there. Now we shall try to probe deeper into this story.

So: what is music? Music is language. A human being wants to express ideas in this language, but not ideas that can be translated into concepts—*musical* ideas. Schoenberg went through every dictionary to find a definition of an "idea," but he never found one. What is a musical idea?

(whistled) *"Kommt ein Vogerl geflogen"*

That's a musical idea! Indeed, man only exists insofar as he expresses himself. Music does it in musical ideas. I want to say something, and obviously I try to express it so that others understand it. Schoenberg uses the wonderful word "comprehensibility" (it constantly occurs in Goethe!). Comprehensibility is the highest law of all. Unity must be there. There must be means of ensuring it. All the things familiar to us from primitive life must also be used in works of art. Men have looked for means to give a musical idea the most comprehensible shape possible. Throughout several centuries one of these means was tonality, since the seventeenth century. Since Bach, major has been distinguished from minor. This stage was preceded by the church modes, that's to say seven keys in a way, of which only the two keys, like genders, finally remained. These two have produced something that's above gender, our new system of twelve notes.

Returning to tonality: it was an unprecedented means of shaping form, of producing unity. What did this unity consist of? Of the fact that a piece was written in a certain key. It was the principal key, which was selected, and it was natural for the composer to be anxious to demonstrate this key very explicitly. A piece had a keynote: it was maintained, it was left and returned to. It constantly reappeared, and this made it predominant. There was a main key in the exposition, in the development, in the recapitulation, etc. To crystallize out this main key more definitely, there were codas, in which the main key kept reappearing. I have to keep picking out these things because I'm discussing something that's disappeared. Something had to come and restore order.

There are two paths that led unavoidably to twelve-note composition; it wasn't merely the fact that tonality disappeared and one needed something new to cling to. No! Besides that, there was another very important thing! But for the moment I can't hope to say in one word what it is. Canonic, contrapuntal forms, thematic development can produce many relationships between things, and that's where we must look for the further element in twelve-note composition, by looking back at its predecessors.

The most splendid example of this is Johann Sebastian Bach, who wrote the *Art of Fugue* at the end of his life. This work contains a wealth of relationships of a wholly abstract kind; it's the most abstract music known to us. (Perhaps we are all on the way to writing as abstractly). Although there's still tonality here, there are things that look forward to the most important point about twelve-note composition: a substitute for tonality.

What I'm telling you here is really my life-story. This whole upheaval started just when I began to compose. The matter became really relevant during the time when I was Schoenberg's pupil. Since then a quarter of a century has already gone by, though.

If we want to find historically how tonality suddenly vanished, and what started it, until finally, one day, Schoenberg saw by pure intuition how to restore order, then it was about 1908 when Schoenberg's piano pieces Op. 11 appeared. Those were the first "atonal" pieces; the first of Schoenberg's twelve-note works appeared in 1922. From 1908 to 1922 was the interregnum: 14 years, nearly a decade and half, this stage lasted. But already in the spring of 1917—Schoenberg lived in the Gloriettegasse at the time, and I lived quite near—I went to see him one fine morning, to tell him I had read in some newspaper where a few groceries were to be had. In fact I disturbed him with this, and be explained to me that he was "on the way to something quite new." He didn't tell me more at the time, and I racked my brains—"For goodness' sake, whatever can it be?" (The first beginnings of this music are to be found in the music of *Jacob's Ladder*.) [11]

I'm sure it will be very useful to discuss the last stage of tonal music. We find the first breach in sonata movements, where the main key often has some other key forced into it like a wedge. This means the main key is at times pushed to one side. And then at the cadence. What is a cadence? The attempt to seal off a key against everything that could prejudice it. But composers wanted to give the cadence an ever more individual shape, and this finally led to the break-up of the main key. At first one still landed in the home key at the end, but gradually one went so far that finally there was no longer any feeling that it was necessary really to return to the main key. At first one did think, "Here I am at home—now I'm going out—I look around me—I can wander off as far as I like while I'm about it—until I'm back home at last!" The fact that cadences were shaped ever more richly, that instead of chords of the sub-dominant, dominant and tonic, one increasingly used substitutes for them, and then altered even those—it led to the break-up of tonality. The substitutes got steadily more independent. It was possible to go into another tonality here and there. (When one moved from the white to the black keys, one wondered, "Do I really have to come down again?") The substitutes became so predominant that the need to return to the main key disappeared. All the works that Schoenberg, Berg and I wrote before 1908 belong to this stage of tonality.

"Where has one to go, and does one in fact have to return to the relationships implied by traditional harmony?"—thinking over points like that, we had the feeling, "We don't need these relationships any more, our ear is satisfied without tonality too." The time was simply ripe for the disappearance of tonality. Naturally this was a fierce struggle; inhibitions of the most frightful kind had to be overcome, the panic fear, "Is that possible, then?" So it came about that gradually a piece was written, firmly and consciously, that wasn't in a definite key any more.

You're listening to someone who went through all these things and fought them out. All these experiences tumbled over one another, they happened to us unselfconsciously and intuitively. And never in the history of music has there been such resistance as there was to these things.

11. Schoenberg's unfinished oratorio *Die Jakobsleiter* (1912–22) experiments with tone-row construction, though not as yet embracing all twelve tones of the chromatic scale.

Naturally it's nonsense to advance "social objections." Why don't people understand that? Our push forward had to be made, it was a push forward such as never was before. In fact we have to break new ground with each work: each work is something different, something new. Look at Schoenberg! Max Reger certainly developed, too, as a man develops between his fifteenth year and his fortieth, but stylistically there were no changes; he could reel off fifty works in the same style. We find it downright impossible to repeat anything. Schoenberg said, and this is highly revealing, "Suppose I'd written an opera in the style of the *Gurrelieder?*" [12]

How do people hope to follow this? Obviously it's very difficult. Beethoven and Wagner were also important revolutionaries, they were misunderstood too, because they brought about enormous changes in style.

I've tried to make this stage really clear to you and to convince you that just as a ripe fruit falls from the tree, music has quite simply given up the formal principle of tonality. . . .

§IV

Today we shall examine tonality in its last throes. I want to prove to you that it's really dead. Once that's proves, there's no point in going on dealing with something dead.

Last time we discussed chords built from the whole-tone scale, and arrived at a six-note passing chord (F–A–C♯–G–B–D♯, or E♭–G–B–A–D♭–F). Simply by adding one such chord to another that's analogously constructed, we produce a twelve-note chord.

With all this we approach the catastrophe; 1906, Schoenberg's Chamber Symphony [13] (fourth-chords!); 1908, music by Schoenberg that's no longer in any key. [14] Relationship to a keynote became ever looser. This opened the way to a state where one could finally dispense with the keynote. The possibility of rapid modulation has nothing to do with this development; in fact, just because all this went on in order to safeguard the keynote, to extend tonality—precisely because we took steps to preserve tonality—we broke its neck!

I go out into the hall to knock in a nail. On my way there I decide I'd rather go out. I act on the impulse, get into a tram, come to a railway station, go on traveling and finally end up—in America! That's modulation!

We—Berg and I—went through all that personally. I say this, not so that it will get

---

12. *Gurrelieder* (1901–10), Schoenberg's gargantuan orchestral song cycle, composed in a ripely chromatic idiom, full of extravagant depictions of love, death, madness, phantom horsemen, and pantheistic nature.

13. First Chamber Symphony, op. 9.

14. Though Webern considered that the first experiment in atonal music was the third of the *Three Piano Pieces,* op. 11, others have suggested the fourth movement of Schoenberg's Second String Quartet, op. 10.

into my biography, but because I want to show that it was a development wrested out of feverish struggles and decisively necessary.

§v

. . . In this musical material new laws have come into force that have made it impossible to describe a piece as in one key or another. It was so ambiguous. Things have asserted themselves that made this "key" simply impossible. We sensed that the frequent repetition of a note, either directly or in the course of the piece, in some way "got its own back," that the note "came through." It had to be given its due—that was still possible at this stage; but it proved disturbing, for example, if one note occurred a number of times during some run of all twelve. Individual parts in a polyphonic texture no longer moved in accordance with major and minor, but with chromaticism. (Schoenberg said, "The most important thing in composing is an eraser!") It was a matter of constant testing; "Are these chordal progressions the right ones? Am I putting down what I mean? Is the right form emerging?"

What happened? I can only relate something from my own experience; about 1911 I wrote the *Bagatelles for String Quartet* (Op. 9), all very short pieces, lasting a couple of minutes—perhaps the shortest music so far.[15] Here I had the feeling, "When all twelve notes have gone by, the piece is over." Much later I discovered that all this was a part of the necessary development. In my sketch-book I wrote out the chromatic scale and crossed off the individual notes. Why? Because I had convinced myself, "This note has been there already." It sounds grotesque, incomprehensible, and it was incredibly difficult. The inner ear decided quite rightly that the man who wrote out the chromatic scale and crossed off individual notes *was no fool.* (Josef Matthias Hauer, too, went through and discovered all this in his own way.) In short, a rule of law emerged; until all twelve notes have occurred, none of them may occur again. The most important thing is that each "run" of twelve notes marked a division within the piece, idea or theme.

. . . One day Schoenberg intuitively discovered the law that underlies twelve-note composition. An inevitable development of this law was that one gave the succession of twelve notes a *particular order.* Imagine; twelve parts, sixty parts, and each of them has begun the series of twelve notes! (It isn't note-repetition that's forbidden, but within the order fixed by me for the twelve notes none may be repeated!)

Today we've arrived at the end of this path, i.e. at the goal; the twelve notes have come to power and the practical need for this law is completely clear to us today. We can look back at its development and see no gaps.

---

15. Schoenberg, in his foreword to the Bagatelles, wrote that they conveyed "a novel through a single gesture, or felicity by a single catch of the breath" (*Style and Idea,* 483–84).

§VI

Before we knew about the law we were obeying it. This proves that it really did develop quite naturally. There's no longer a tonic. All twelve notes have equal rights. If one of them is repeated before the other eleven have occurred it would acquire a certain special status. The twelve notes, in a firmly fixed order, form the basis of the entire composition. Twelve-note composition is not a "substitute for tonality" but leads much further.

Great composers have always striven to express unity as clearly as possible. One means of doing it was tonality. Another was provided by polyphony. One of the earliest surviving polyphonic pieces is a canon—an English summer canon from the 13th century.[16] What is a canon? A piece of music in which several voices sing the same thing, only at different times; often what is sung occurs in a different order (crab canon, mirror canon).[17] The crowning glory of polyphonic music was the fugue, based on a fugue theme (answer, stretto, etc.). Why does this crop up again? Indeed, yet again, it was the same thing but different! Thematic unity came with homophonic music, but the fugue, too, is really thematic. Now something very remarkable emerged; soon there was an attempt to create some kind of unifying thematic connection between the principal part and the accompaniment. We see an absolute pull from homophonic music back to polyphony, an urge to deepen and clarify the unity.

An example: Beethoven's *Six easy variations on a Swiss song*. Theme: C–F–G–A–F–C–G–F, then backwards! You won't notice this when the piece is played, and perhaps it isn't at all important, but it is *unity*.

Further development of unity in Brahms, Mahler, Schoenberg. Schoenberg's first string quartet[18] (in D minor)—the accompanying figure is thematic! This urge towards unity, relationships, leads of its own accord to a form the classical composers often turned to, and which in Beethoven became most important—variation form. A theme is given. It is varied. In this sense variation form is a forerunner of twelve-note composition. An example: Beethoven's Ninth Symphony, finale—theme in unison; all that follows is derived from this idea, which is the primeval form. Unheard-of things happen, and yet it's constantly the same thing!

You'll already have seen where I am leading you. Goethe's primeval plant;[19] the root

16. *Sumer is icumen in* (ca. 1240)—the earliest known piece of six-part music.

17. A crab, or cancrizan, is a term for retrograde; mirror here means inversion.

18. First String Quartet, op. 7 (1904–5).

19. *Urpflanze,* the term used by the poet and scientist Johann Wolfgang von Goethe (1749–1832) to describe the single original plant, modified over the ages into the diverse forms of the plants we know today. Charles Darwin thought that Goethe had anticipated, to some degree, the theory of evolution.

is in fact no different from the stalk, the stalk no different from the leaf, and the leaf no different from the flower: variations of the same idea.

§VIII

Last time, starting from Goethe's "primeval plant," we dealt with the "other path." The same law applies to everything living: "variations on a theme"—that's the primeval form, which is at the bottom of everything. Something that seems quite different is really the same. The most comprehensive unity results from this.

This urge to create unity has also been felt by all the masters of the past. Remember the canon form we mentioned last time: everyone sings the same thing. If I repeat several times, "Shut the door," or, as Schoenberg said about a questionable composer, "I am an ass," then unity of that kind is already established. An ash-tray, seen from all sides, is always the same, and yet different. So an idea should be presented in the most multifarious way possible.

One such way is backwards movement—cancrizan; another is mirroring—inversion. The development of tonality meant that these old methods of presentation were pushed into the background, but they still make themselves felt in a way, even in classical times, in "thematic development." This path led to ever-increasing refinement of the thematic network.

How has such an unusual degree of unity come about in twelve-note music? Through the fact that in the course of the row on which the composition is based no note may be repeated before all have occurred. This law developed gradually, on its own, but it would have been impossible without using both the paths we have described. And here the urge toward maximum unity found its fulfilment. For the rest, one composes as before, but on the basis of the row; on the basis of this fixed series one will have to invent. (Here too the result can be rubbish, as in tonal composition: nobody banned major and minor for it!)

If an untutored ear can't always follow the course of the row, there's no harm done—in tonality, too, unity was mostly felt only unconsciously. The course of the row can be repeated several times, even quite identically, as in the Sonnet from Schoenberg's "Serenade."[20] Something will stick in even the naivest soul. So there will be a multiplication of all the things that were aimed at along the second path, bound up with the urge toward thematic development.

All the works created between the disappearance of tonality and the formulation of the new twelve-note law were short, strikingly short. The longer works written at the time were linked with a text which "carried" them (Schoenberg's *Erwartung* and *Die*

---

20. Serenade for Instrumental Septet, op. 24 (1920–23). The fourth movement has a part for baritone singing Petrarch's sonnet no. 256 and is an early example of clear twelve-tone design.

glückliche Hand, Berg's *Wozzeck*),[21] that's to say, with something extra-musical. With the abandoning of tonality the most important means of building up longer pieces was lost. For tonality was supremely important in producing self-contained forms. As if the light had been put out!—that's how it seemed. (At least this is how it strikes us now.) At the time everything was in a state of flux—uncertain, dark, very stimulating and exciting, so that there wasn't time to notice the loss. Only when Schoenberg gave expression to the law were larger forms again possible.

How does the row come to exist? It's not arbitrary, the result of chance; it's arranged with certain points in mind. Here there are certain formal considerations, for example one aims at as many different intervals as possible, or certain correspondences within the row—symmetry, analogy, groupings (thrice four or four times three notes, for instance).

Our—Schoenberg's, Berg's and my—rows mostly came into existence when an idea occurred to us, linked with an intuitive vision of the work as a whole; the idea was then subjected to careful thought, just as one can follow the gradual emergence of themes in Beethoven's sketchbooks. Inspiration, if you like.

Adherence is strict, often burdensome, but it's *salvation!* We couldn't do a thing about the dissolution of tonality, and we didn't create the new law ourselves—it forced itself overwhelmingly on us. This compulsion, adherence, is so powerful that one has to consider very carefully before finally committing oneself to it for a prolonged period, almost as if taking the decision to marry; a difficult moment! Trust your inspiration! There's no alternative!

So the row is there. At once re-casting, development starts. How is the system now built up? Our inventive resourcefulness discovered the following forms: cancrizan, inversion, inversion of the cancrizan. Four forms altogether. There aren't any others. However much the theorists try.

Each of these four forms can be based on each of the twelve degrees of the scale. Bearing these twelve transpositions in mind, each row can manifest itself in 48 different ways.

Considerations of symmetry, regularity are now to the fore, as against the emphasis formerly laid on the principal intervals—dominant, subdominant, mediant, etc. For this reason the middle of the octave—the diminished fifth—is now most important.[22] For the rest, one works as before. The original form and pitch of the row occupy a position

---

21. *Erwartung,* op. 17 (1909); *Die glückliche Hand,* op. 18 (1910–13); Berg's *Wozzeck* (1925).

22. "The initial series of Berg's *Lyric Suite* contains all the possible intervals, the last five being a symmetrical inversion of the first five—pivoting around the diminished fifth, the only non-invertible interval" (Boulez, *Boulez on Music Today,* 71).

akin to that of the "main key" in earlier music; the recapitulation will naturally return to it. We end "in the same key!" This analogy with earlier formal construction is quite consciously fostered; here we find the path that will lead us again to extended forms.

§VIII

... I'll answer a question put to me by one of you: "How is free invention possible when one has to remember to adhere to the order of the series for the work?" ...

The twelve-note row is, as a rule, not a "theme." But I can also work without thematicism, that's to say much more freely, because of the unity that's now been achieved in another way; the row ensures unity. As we gradually gave up tonality an idea occurred to us: "We don't want to repeat, there must constantly be something new!" Obviously this doesn't work, it destroys comprehensibility. At least it's impossible to write long stretches of music in that way. Only after the formulation of the law did it again become possible to write longer pieces.

We want to say "in a quite new way" what has been said before. But now I can invent more freely; everything has a deeper unity. Only now is it possible to compose in free fantasy, adhering to nothing except the row. To put it quite paradoxically, only through these unprecedented fetters has complete freedom become possible!

Here I can only stammer. Everything is still in a state of flux. The old Netherlanders were similarly unclear about the path they were following, and in the end this development led to Schoenberg's *Harmonielehre*! Here there's certainly some underlying rule of law, and it's our faith that a true work of art can come about in this way. It's for a later period to discover the closer unifying laws that are already present in the works themselves. When this true conception of art is achieved, then there will no longer be any possible distinction between science and inspired creation. The further one presses forward, the greater becomes the identity of everything, and finally we have the impression of being faced by a work not of man but of Nature. How does a man keep the 48 forms in his head? How is it that he takes now number seven, then number forty-five, now a cancrizan, now an inversion? Naturally that's a matter for reflection and consideration. I know how I invent a fresh idea, and how it continues, and then I look for the right place to fit it in.

An example: the second movement of my Symphony (Op. 21, written in 1928). The row is F–A♭–G–F♯–B♭–A; E♭–E–C–C♯–D–B. It's peculiar in that the second half is the cancrizan of the first. This is a particularly intimate unity. So here there are only 24 forms, since there are a corresponding number of identical pairs. In the accompaniment to the theme the cancrizan appears at the beginning. The first variation is in the melody a transposition of the row starting on C. The accompaniment is a double canon. Greater unity is impossible. Even the Netherlanders didn't manage it. In the fourth variation there are constant mirrorings. This variation is itself the midpoint of the whole movement, after which everything goes backwards. So the entire movement is itself a double canon by retrograde motion!

Now I must say this: what you see here—cancrizan, canon, etc.—constantly the same thing—isn't to be regarded as a "tour de force"; that would be ludicrous. I was to create as many connections as possible, and you must allow that there are indeed many connections here! Finally I must point out to you that this is so not only in music. We find an analogy in language. I was delighted to find that such connections also often occur in Shakespeare, in alliteration and assonance. He even turns a phrase backwards. Karl Kraus'[23] handling of language is also based on this; unity also has to be created there, since it enhances comprehensibility.

And I leave you with an old Latin saying:[24]

```
S   A   T   O   R
A   R   E   P   O
T   E   N   E   T
O   P   E   R   A
R   O   T   A   S
```

From *The Path to the New Music* (Bryn Mawr: T. Presser, [1963?]), 42–45, 47–48, 51–56.

■

As Webern's lectures suggest, twelve-tone composers had to forestall the objection that their method was so rigid that it left no scope for playfulness—as if the row, once determined, performed the labor of composition without human assistance; for Webern, the row, far from being a cramp, was a great blessing to the composer's imagination. This and other themes from Webern's lectures appear in Thomas Mann's novel *Dr. Faustus* (1947)—not with Webern's serene confidence, but in lurid and agonized doubt. The German writer Thomas Mann (1875–1955) knew a good deal about music, but also had the good fortune, during his exile from Germany during the Second World War, to be the neighbor of the musicologist Theodor Adorno, when both—along with Schoenberg, Stravinsky, and other significant figures in European Modernism—were living in the Los Angeles area. Thus when Mann decided to write the biography of a fictitious composer who happened to invent the twelve-tone system, he could turn to Adorno for intellectual stimulation. Indeed the interaction of Mann and Adorno is one of the most remarkable cases of symbiosis in the Modernist movement.

23. Karl Kraus (1874–1936), prolific writer and editor of the journal *Die Fackel*, was much concerned with precision in language.

24. "Sower Arepo keeps the work in circles"—a magic square that says the same thing backward and forward, up and down; the equivalent in language of the chart of inversions and retrogrades.

The narrator of *Dr. Faustus* is a humane pedant named Serenus Zeitblom, who recounts the story of devoted lifelong friendship with the composer Adrian Leverkühn, a cold but tormented genius. In his youth, Leverkühn was attracted to witchcraft and posted on his wall "a so-called magic square, such as appears also in Dürer's *Melancolia,* along with the hour-glass, the circle, the scale, the polyhedron, and other symbols. Here as there, the figure was divided into sixteen Arabic-numbered fields . . . and the magic, or the oddity, simply consisted in the fact that the sum of these numerals, however you added them, straight down, crosswise, or diagonally, always came to thirty-four."[25] The reference here to Dürer's famous engraving is not random, for in the Renaissance—Dürer's time—it was thought that artistic genius was a refined and intensified form of melancholy; and Leverkühn's genius is intimate with every sort of crazy dejection, self-loathing.

At one point Leverkühn blunders by mistake into a brothel, and when a prostitute kisses him, he recoils and flees. But later he decides to track down the prostitute and decides to sleep with her even though she warns him of venereal disease; for the rest of the novel, Mann carefully coordinates the progress of his syphilis with the evolution of Leverkühn's genius and the frantic degeneration of Nazi Germany. The centerpiece of the novel occurs in chapter 25, in which Zeitblom finds a document written by Leverkühn, a memoir of a dialogue with the devil, in which Leverkühn sells his soul in return for artistic abandon and success. Leverkühn has felt increasingly inhibited by the contraction of his music into shorter and shorter forms, as he disdains the tricks by which previous composers have extended and developed their musical material. But the devil has a method for freeing Leverkühn from this bind—a method not dissimilar to the magic square. Leverkühn goes on to write great music, including an oratorio based on the book of Revelation; but when he calls together all his acquaintances to hear his last work, on the Faust theme, he confesses his bargain with the devil, strikes one hideous dissonance on the piano, and collapses. He remains a mute imbecile for the remaining years of his life.

There are obvious parallels between Leverkühn and Schoenberg, but the descent into syphilic insanity recalls Friedrich Nietzsche, and also the composer Hugo Wolf—who similarly broke down when trying to play his unfinished opera *Manuel Venegas* on the piano in front of his friends. Mann explained to Adorno the novel's method: "The point on which I feel I owe you an explanation concerns the principle of *montage.* . . . I was struck by it again in a recent passage where it occurs in half amusing, half uncanny fashion; I was describing the hero's critical illness, and I included Nietzsche's symptoms word for word as they are set forth in his letters. . . . I pasted them in, so to speak, for

---

25. Thomas Mann, *Doctor Faustus: The Life of the German Composer Adrian Leverkühn, as Told by a Friend,* trans. H. T. Lowe-Porter (New York: Modern Library, 1966), 92.

anyone to recognize." [26] Montage, of course, is a Modernist device; but Mann thought that there were aspects of Modernist art that were profoundly antihuman, that verged on doubtful or forbidden areas, that attempted monstrous convergences of extremes. Mann used twelve-tone music as a metaphor for all that was wrong in Modernism—its strange equivocation between objectivity and subjectivity, between freedom and necessity, between order and chaos. The aged Stravinsky complained, "What I cannot follow are the manic-depressive fluctuations from total control to no control, from the serialization of all elements to chance"; [27] and the peculiar congruity between completely predetermined music and completely random music seemed to Mann a symptom of artistic disease.

One can understand that Schoenberg was not pleased to read *Dr. Faustus.* On 17 February 1948 he sent Mann an extract from the *Encyclopedia Americana* of 1988 (!) stating that the twelve-tone system had been invented by Thomas Mann, who tolerated its appropriation by the thievish composer Arnold Schoenberg. [28] Schoenberg was vexed by Leverkühn's expropriation of dodecaphony and wanted credit, which explains why every copy of Mann's novel ends with a patient, grudging little note explaining Schoenberg's property rights. Perhaps Schoenberg was intrigued by Mann's synthesis of a Nietzsche-Schoenberg hybrid: the last chapter of Schoenberg's *Structural Functions of Harmony* (1948) is called "Apollonian Evaluation of a Dionysian Epoch." There Schoenberg notes:

> Classical music was composed in one of the Apollonian periods, when the application of dissonances and their treatment . . . were governed by rules. . . . But the new chords and dissonances of the next epoch, a Dionysian period (provoked by the romantic composers), had barely been digested and catalogued . . . when a new progressive movement began. . . . Because of the many attempts to connect the past with the future one might be inclined by call this [contemporary period] an Apollonian period. But the fury with which addicts of various schools fight for their theories presents rather a Dionysian aspect. [29]

Schoenberg may have seen himself as a Dionysus who evolved into an Apollo, a lawgiver to dissonance, a tamer of beasts. Leverkühn, by contrast, was a Dionysus whose very self-control was a form of licentiousness, a Dionysus-Faust eventually torn to pieces and dragged into the pit.

26. *The Letters of Thomas Mann,* vol. 2, *1942–1955,* trans. Richard and Clara Winston (London: Secker and Warburg, 1970), 493–94.

27. Igor Stravinsky and Robert Craft, *Themes and Conclusions* (Berkeley: University of California Press, 1982), 33.

28. *The Letters of Thomas Mann,* 2:546.

29. Arnold Schoenberg, *Structural Functions of Harmony* (New York: W. W. Norton, 1969), 192–93.

THOMAS MANN
from *Dr. Faustus* (1947)
CHAPTER 21

. . . Always dominant in [Leverkühn] was a will to go to extremes of expression; together with the intellectual passion for austere order, the *linear* style of the Netherlands composers. In other words, heat and cold prevail alongside each other in his work; sometimes in moments of the greatest genius they play into each other, the *espressivo* takes hold of the strict counterpoint, the objective blushes with feeling. One gets the impression of a glowing mould; this, like nothing else, has brought home to me the idea of the daemonic.

. . . I saw . . . inhibitions hampering the development of his gifts. I have heard him say:

"The work of art? It is a fraud. It is something the burgher wishes there still were. It is contrary to truth, contrary to serious art. Genuine and serious is only the very short, the highly consistent musical moment. . . . Pretense and play [30] have the conscience of art against them today. Art would like to stop being pretense and play, it would like to become knowledge." . . .

CHAPTER 22

". . . One would have to . . . make words out of the twelve letters, as it were, of the tempered semitone alphabet. . . . Every note of the whole composition, both melody and harmony, would have to show its relation to this fixed fundamental series. Not one might recur until the other notes have sounded. Not one might appear which did not fulfil its function in the whole structure. There would no longer be a free note. That is what I would call 'strict composition.'"

"A striking thought," said I. "Rational organization through and through, one might call it. You would gain an extraordinary unity and congruity, a sort of astronomical regularity and legality would be obtained thereby. But when I picture it to myself, it seems to me that the unchanged recurrence of such a succession of intervals, even when used in different parts of the texture, and in rhythmic variations, would result in a probably unavoidable serious musical impoverishment and stagnation."

"Probably," [Leverkühn] answered, with a smile which showed that he had been prepared for this reservation. . . . "And it is not so simple either. One must incorporate into the system all possible techniques of variation, including those decried as artificial; that is, the means which once helped the 'development' to win its hold over the sonata. I ask myself why I practiced so long under Kretschmar [31] the devices of the old counterpoint and covered so much paper with inversion fugues, crabs, and inversions of

---

30. *Schein und Spiel*—a phrase common in Adorno's writings; in fact Mann's next sentence is taken from a passage from Adorno quoted in the next chapter.

31. Kretschmar was the principal music teacher of Leverkühn's youth.

crabs. Well now, all that should come in handy for the ingenious modification of the twelve-note word. In addition to being a fundamental series it could find application in this way, that every one of its intervals is replaced by its inversion. Again, one could begin the figure with its last note and finish it on its first, and then invert this figure as well. . . . The decisive factor is that every note, without exception, has significance and function according to its place in the basic series or its derivatives. That would guarantee what I call the indifference to harmony and melody."

"A magic square," I said. "But do you hope to have people hear all that?"

"Hear?" he countered. "Do you remember a certain lecture given for the Society for the Common Weal from which it followed that in music one certainly need not hear everything? If by 'hearing' you understand the precise realization in detail of the means by which the highest and strictest order is achieved, like the order of the planets, a cosmic order and legality—no, that way one would not hear it. But this order one will or would hear, and the perception of it would afford an unknown aesthetic satisfaction."

"Very remarkable," said I. "The way you describe the thing, it comes to a sort of composing before composition. The whole disposition and organization of the material would have to be ready when the actual work should begin, and all one asks is: which is the actual work? For this preparation of the material is done by variation, and the creative element in variation, which one might call the actual composition, would be transferred back to the material itself—together with the freedom of the composer. When he went to work, he would no longer be free."

"Bound by a self-imposed compulsion to order, hence free."

"Well, of course the dialectic of freedom is unfathomable. But he could scarcely be called a free inventor of his harmony. Would not the making of chords be left to chance and accident?"

"Say, rather, to the context. The polyphonic dignity of every chord-forming note would be guaranteed by the constellation. The historical events—the emancipation of dissonance from its resolution, its becoming 'absolute' as it appears already in some passages of the later Wagner—would warrant any combination of notes which can justify itself before the system."

"And if the constellation produced the banal: consonance, common-chord harmonics, the worn-out, the diminished seventh?"

"That would be a rejuvenation of the worn-out by the constellation."

"I see there a restorative element in your Utopia. It is very radical, but it relaxes the prohibition which after all already hung over consonance. . . ."

CHAPTER 25

I [Leverkühn]: "So you would sell me time?"

He [Devil]: "Time? Simple time? No, my dear fere [companion], that is not devyll's ware.[32] For that we should not earn the reward, namely that the end belongs to us. What manner of time, that is the heart of the matter! Great time, mad time, quite be-divelled time, in which the fun waxes fast and furious, with heaven-high leaping and springing—and again, of course, a bit miserable, very miserable indeed, I not only ad-mit that, I even emphasize it, with pride, for it is sitting and fit, such is artist-way and artist-nature. That, as is well knowen, is given at all times to excess on both sides and is in quite normal way a bit excessive. Alway the pendulum swings very wide to and fro between high spirits and melancholia, that is usual is so to speak still according to moderate bourgeois Nueremberg way, in comparison with that which we purvey. For we purvey the uttermost in this direction; we purvey towering flights and illuminations, ex-periences of upliftings and unfetterings, of freedom, certainty, facility, feeling of power and triumph, that our man does not trust his wits—counting in besides the colossal ad-miration for the made thing, which could soon bring him to renounce every outside, for-eign admiration—the thrills of self-veneration, yes, of exquisite horror of himself, in which he appears to himself like an inspired mouthpiece, as a godlike monster. And correspondingly deep, honorably deep, doth he sink in between-time, not only into void and desolation and unfruitful melancholy but also into pains and sicknesse—familiar incidentally, which had alway been there, which belong to his character, yet which are only most honorably enhanced by the illumination and the well-knowen 'sack of heyre.' Those are pains which a man gladly pays, with pleasure and pride." . . .

I: "Mocker and liar! *Si diabolus non esset mendax et homicida!*[33] If I must listen, at least speak to me not of sane and sound greatness and native gold! I know that gold made with fire instead of by the sun is not genuine."

He: "Who says so? Has the sun better fire then the kitchen? And sane and sound greatness! Whenever I hear of such, I laugh! Do you believe in anything like an *inge-nium* [genius] that has nothing to do with hell? *Non datur!*[34] The artist is the brother of the criminal and the madman. Do you ween that any important work was ever wrought except its maker learned to understand the way of the criminal and madman? Morbid and healthy! Without the morbid would life all its whole life never have survived. . . . We make naught new—that is other people's matter. We only release, only set free. We let the lameness and self-consciousness, the chaste scruples and doubts go to the devil. We physic away fatigue. . . . Who knows today, whoever knew in classical times, what inspiration is, what genuine, old, primeval enthusiasm, insicklied critique, unparalysed by thought or by the mortal domination of reason—who knows the divine raptus? I be-

32. Parts of this chapter are written in archaic German, suitable to an age (such as Faust's or Luther's) when commerce with devils was customary.

33. If the devil were not a liar and a killer of men.

34. It is not given.

lieve, indeed, the devil passes for a man of destructive criticism? Slander and again slander, my friend! Gog's sacrament! If there is anything he cannot abide, if there's one thing in the whole world he cannot stomach, it is destructive criticism. What he wants and gives is triumph over it, is shining, sparkling, vainglorious unreflectiveness!"

I: "Charlatan!"

He: "Yea, of a truth. . . . Let us just for an instance take the 'idea.' . . . The idea, then, a matter of three, four bars, no more, isn't it? All the residue is elaboration, sticking at it. . . . Take Beethoven's notebooks. There is no thematic conception there as God gave it. He remoulds it and adds 'Meilleur' [Better]. Scant confidence in God's prompting, scant respect for it is expressed in that 'Meilleur' — itself not so very enthusiastic either. A genuine inspiration, immediate, absolute, unquestioned, ravishing, where there is no choice, no tinkering, no possible improvement; where all is as a sacred mandate, a visitation received by the possessed one with faltering and stumbling step, with shudders of awe from head to foot, with tears of joy blinding his eyes: no, that is not possible with God, who leaves the understanding too much to do. It comes but from the divel, the true master and giver of such rapture."

Even as he spake, and easily, a change came over the fellow: as I looked straight at him meseemed he was different, sat there no longer a rowdy losel [hoodlum], but changed for the better, I give my word. He now had on a white collar and a bow tie, horn-rimmed spectacles on his hooked nose. Behind them the dark, rather reddened eyes gleamed moistly . . . a member of the intelligentsia, writer on art, on music for the ordinary press, a theoretician and critic. . . .

". . . Look at them, your colleagues. . . . I mean the honest, serious ones, who see the consequences of the situation. I speak not of the folklorists and neoclassic asylists whose modernness consists in their forbidding themselves a musical outbreak and in wearing with more or less dignity the style-garment of a pre-individualistic period. Persuade themselves and others that the tedious has become interesting, because the interesting has begun to grow tedious."

I had to laugh, for although the cold continued to pursue me, I must confess that since his alteration I felt more comfortable in his presence. He smiled as well: that is, the corners of his mouth tensed a little and he slightly narrowed his eyes.

"They are powerless too," he went on, "but I believe we, thou and I, lever [rather] prefer the decent impotence of those who scorn to cloak the general sickness under color of a dignified mummery. But the sickness is general, and the straightforward ones shew the symptoms just as well as the producers of back-formations. Does not production threaten to come to an end? . . . Every composer of the better sort carries within himself a canon of the forbidden, the self-forbidding, which by degrees includes all the possibilities of tonality, in other words all traditional music. What has become false, worn-out cliché, the canon decides. Tonal sounds, chords in a composition with the technical horizon of today, outbid every dissonance. As such they are to be used, but cautiously and only *in extremis,* for the shock is worse than the harshest discord of old. Everything depends on the technical horizon. The diminished seventh is right and full of expression at the beginning of Op. 111.[35] It corresponds to Beethoven's whole technical niveau [level], doesn't it? —the tension between consonance and the harshest dissonance known to him. The principle of tonality and its dynamics lend to the chord its specific weight. It has lost it—by a historical process which nobody reverses. . . . In every bar that one dares to think, the situation as regards technique presents itself to [the modern composer] as a problem. Technique in all its aspects demands of him every moment that he do justice to it, and give the only right answer which it at any moment permits. It comes down to this, that his compositions are nothing more than solutions of that kind; nothing but the solving of technical puzzles. Art becomes critique. . . ."

. . . He seemed no longer to be the spectacled intellectual and amateur of music who had awhile been speaking. And he was no longer just sitting in the comer, he was riding légèrement [lightly], half-sitting, on the curved arm of the sofa, his fingertips crossed in his lap and both thumbs spread out. A little parted beard on his chin wagged up and down as he talked, and above his open lips with the sharp teeth behind them was the little moustache with stiff twisted points. I had to laugh, in all my frozenness, at his metamorphosis into the old familiar.

". . . You have lectured me a good deal about the houre-glasse time you purvey; also about the payment in pains to be made now and again for the higher life; but not about the end, about what comes afterwards, the eternal obliteration. That is what excites curiosity, and you have not, long as you have been squatting there, given space to the question in all your talk. Shall I not know the price . . .? Answer me: what is life like in the Dragon's Den? . . ."

He (laughs a falsetto laugh): "I'll not deny you the information and do not need to palliate, for what can seriously trouble you, that is so far off? Only it is not easy actually to speak thereof—that is, one can really not speak of it at all because the actual is beyond what by word can be declared; many words may be used and fashioned, but all together they are but tokens, standing for names which do not and cannot make claim to describe what is never to be described and denounced in words. That is the secret delight and security of hell, that it is not to be informed on, that it is protected from speech, that it just is, but cannot be public in the newspaper, be brought by any word to critical knowledge, wherefor precisely the words 'subterranean,' 'cellar,' 'thick walls,' 'soundlessness,' 'forgottenness,' 'hopelessness,' are the poor, weak symbols. One must just be satisfied with symbolism, my good man, when one is speaking of hell, for there everything ends—not only the word that describes, but everything

---

35. Beethoven's last piano sonata (1821–22), in C minor.

altogether. This is indeed the chiefest characteristic and what in most general terms is to be uttered about it: both that which the newcomer thither first experiences, and what at first with his as it were sound sense he cannot grasp, and will not understand, because his reason or what limitation soever of his understanding prevents him, in short because it is quite unbelievable enough to make him turn white as a sheet, although it is opened to him in greeting, in the most emphatic and concise words, that *'here everything leaves off.'* Every compassion, every grace, every sparing, every last trace of consideration for the incredulous, imploring objection 'that you verily cannot do so unto a soul': it is done, it happens, and indeed without being called to any reckoning in words; in soundless cellar, far down beneath God's hearing, and happens to all eternity. No, it is bad to speak of it, it lies aside from and outside of speech. . . . True it is that inside these echoless walls it gets right loud, measureless loud, and by much overfilling the ear with screeching and beseeching, gurgling and groaning, with yauling and bauling and caterwauling, with horrid winding and grinding and racking ecstasies of anguish no man can hear his own tune, for that it smothers in the general, in the thick-clotted diapason of trills and chirps lured from this everlasting dispensation of the unbelievable combined with the irresponsible.

From *Doctor Faustus: The Life of the German Composer Adrian Leverkühn, as Told by a Friend,* trans. H. T. Lowe-Porter (New York: Modern Library, 1966), 178, 181; 192–93; 230, 236–39, 244–45.

■

Adorno thought that Schoenberg's music alluded to some state of saturation, in which all twelve tones were sounded at the same time. Webern found himself instinctively selecting notes by crossing off those notes he had already used, as if his music also were moving toward the full spectrum of sound. But Mann's devil imagines hell simply as a huge organ in which all the keys are depressed at once, forever—enriched by glissandi from the screams of the damned. Mann noted that this hellscape was "inconceivable, incidentally, without the psychological experiences of Gestapo cellars."[36] It is going far to identify Nazi torture with an avant-garde revision of the concept of consonance; but Mann found it appropriate.

For a number of twentieth-century musicians, the twelve-tone method, if not a gift straight from the mouth of hell, was certainly unwelcome; and there is an enormous literature of refutations, disparagements, and curses directed at Schoenberg and his system. Much of the anti-twelve-tone discourse makes the point that the system is an artificial contrivance—the tonal system is inevitable because it is given by nature. These

36. Thomas Mann, *The Story of a Novel: The Genesis of Doctor Faustus,* trans. Richard and Clara Winston (New York: Alfred A. Knopf, 1961), 108.

arguments often appeal to the structure of the overtone series, but sometimes to more recondite matters, such as the spiral shape of the cochlea of the inner ear.[37]

One well-informed opponent of Schoenberg was Arthur Honegger (1892–1955).

ARTHUR HONEGGER
[The Twelve-Tone Method] (1951)

What strikes me about [our age] is the haste of reactions, the premature discarding of methods. It took centuries, from Monteverdi to Schoenberg, to arrive at the free use of twelve tones. After this discovery, evolution suddenly became very rapid. We all face a wall; this wall, consisting of all the materials piled up little by little, stands before us today, and everybody is trying to find an opening in it; each one searches for it according to his own intuition.

There are, on the one hand, the champions of Satie's method; they extol the return to simplicity—*sancta simplicitas!*—on the other hand, those who, returning to Schoenberg's researches forty years later, look for an exit by way of atonality, setting up, more arbitrarily still, the twelve-tone system. This system boasts a very narrow codification; the dodecaphonists remind me of convicts who, having broken their chains, voluntarily attach two-hundred-pound balls to their feet in order to run faster. . . .

Music is dying not of anemia but of plethora.

From *Je suis compositeur* (Paris: Conquistador, 1951), 164, 175. Translated by Sam Morgenstern in *Composers on Music: Eight Centuries of Writings,* ed. Josiah Fisk (Boston: Northeastern University Press, 1997), 306–7.

Another example can be found in the rhapsodic conclusion to the Norton lectures of Leonard Bernstein (1918–90).

LEONARD BERNSTEIN
[The Twelve-Tone Method] (1976)

There is a general bubbling and rejoicing and brotherliness among composers. . . . And I believe all this has been made possible by the rediscovery and the reacceptance of tonality, that universal earth out of which such diversity can spring. And I believe that no matter how serial, or stochastic, or otherwise intellectualized music may be, it can always qualify as poetry as long as it is rooted in earth.

I also believe, along with Keats, that the Poetry of Earth is never dead [*Endymion,* l. 1], as long as Spring succeeds Winter, and man is there to perceive it.

37. For an analysis of cochlear logarithms, see Ernest Ansermet, *Écrits sur la musique* (Neuchâtel: Éditions de la Baconnière, 1971), 91.

I believe that from the Earth emerges a musical poetry, which is by the nature of its sources tonal.

From *The Unanswered Question: Six Talks at Harvard* (Cambridge: Harvard University Press, 1976), 423–24.

It is possible to use the twelve-tone method to write in a manner that gratifies ears accustomed to tonal music (Schoenberg's 1942 *Ode to Napoleon* is such a piece, a twelve-tone composition that manages to end in E♭ major); but it's hard to see how a stochastic composition can root itself in the earth of tonality.

Perhaps most modest and compelling of all the resistances to the twelve-tone method comes from Benjamin Britten (1913–76).

BENJAMIN BRITTEN
[The Twelve-Tone Method] (1963)

[Twelve-tone composition] has simply never attracted me as a method, though I respect many composers who have worked in it, and love some of their works. It is beyond me to say why, except that I cannot feel that tonality is outworn, and find many serial "rules" arbitrary. "Socially" I am seriously disturbed by limitations. I can see it taking no part in the music-lover's music-making. Its method makes writing *gratefully* for voices or instruments an impossibility, which inhibits amateurs and young children.

From Humphrey Carpenter, *Benjamin Britten: A Biography* (New York: Charles Scribner's, 1992), 336.

And yet, of those composers who have been skeptical of nontonal music, a surprisingly large number have made some use of serial procedures. Sometimes it has been only for the sake of a joke, as in Britten's *The Prince of the Pagodas* (1956) and *Cantata academica* (1959); but Stravinsky spent the final years of his career making experiments in serial technique—beginning right after Schoenberg's death in 1951, as if Stravinsky wished to extend his empire over every kingdom of music, including that of his principal rival.

Of course, some composers objected to the twelve-tone method from the left instead of the right, so to speak. For Elliott Carter, for example, the twelve-tone system seemed a disappointing attempt to legislate conformity, to stifle the hitherto straightforward process of liberation in twentieth-century music: the pre–World War I works of Schoenberg, Berg, and Webern "give a glimpse of a new universe of emancipated discourse, unfortunately quickly abandoned when Schoenberg returned to the classical musical shapes upon adopting the twelve-tone system."[38]

38. Elliott Carter, *The Writings of Elliott Carter* (Bloomington: Indiana University Press, 1977), 186.

7 Isms

We can no longer subscribe to the notion that music must be imprisoned within the contrived structures of the old counterpoint of Handel and Sebastian Bach, tediously elaborated at the expense of every natural beauty of melodic line. Therefore we propose a new movement, to be called *Classicism,* in which the delight of melody will be supported by discreet and engaging figures of accompaniment, and in which the dominant will ever seek to establish, in the most gracefully flattering manner possible, the tonic.

    (signed) F. J. Haydn   W. A. Mozart

This is a document that was never written, and could never have been written—it is imagined here only to illustrate how distant the eighteenth century is from what Schoenberg called "the fury with which addicts of various [Modernist] schools fight for their theories."[1] In fact Mozart studied the works of Bach and Handel with care and admiration, and even wrote a keyboard overture in the style of Handel, K. 399 (385i). Mozart and Haydn didn't consider themselves Classicists, nor did they have a convenient word, such as Baroque, to characterize the music of preceding generations; they thought in such terms as new and old, or German and Italian, and felt free to avail themselves of all the resources that they knew, depending on the particular purposes of the composition. They regarded the history of music as a continuum, not as something chopped into competing schools or movements.

It would not be quite correct to say that the isms of the music historian are simply imposed from without. Romanticism, for example, was a word in current use in the early nineteenth century. But when, say, E. T. A. Hoffmann discussed the great musical Romantics, he included not only such living composers as Schumann, but also Mozart—the term Romanticism had to mutate considerably before it meant what it has come to mean in contemporary textbooks. As terms such as Romanticism and Classicism grew more restricted and more numerous, they tended to promote a fragmentation in the domain of music, a fragmentation that reached its climax in the Modernist era.

Among the divisions and controversies of pre-twentieth-century music are:

1. The edicts of the Council of Trent in 1562–63 against church music in which the words were inaudible, which led to a paring down of the excesses of polyphony; as early

---

1. Arnold Schoenberg, *Structural Functions of Harmony* (New York: W. W. Norton, 1969), 193.

as 1607 a legend began that Palestrina's *Missa Papae Marcelli* was written to comply with the new requirement.

2. The *seconda prattica,* which developed around 1600: the new expressive monody of Caccini and others, vigorously defended as an alternative to polyphony; in the preface to his fifth book of madrigals (1605), Monteverdi responded to challenges to this new art by the theorist Giovanni Artusi.

3. The amazing brouhaha over the use of an unprepared dissonance (a ninth) in Francisco Valls's *Missa Scala Aretina* (1702); fifty-seven Spanish musicians contributed to the argument.

4. Various operatic reforms (by Gay in 1728 and by Gluck in 1762), designed to discover a music theater based on something other than displays of virtuoso singing.

5. The *querelle des bouffons* (clown fight) of 1752–54 concerning the respective merits of French and Italian music; the philosopher-composer Jean-Jacques Rousseau used Pergolesi's *La serva padrona* to prove that French music was all vanity and artifice, whereas Italian music was direct, unaffected, natural.

6. Schumann's League of David, promoting the value of original genius, such as Beethoven's, against the staid and the philistine—a conflict embedded in Schumann's *Davidsbündlertänze* and especially *Carnaval* (both 1837).

These are only samples of the intellectual discords in music history, but they may suffice to show how the fissures within Modernism differ from earlier controversies.

Most important, the intellectual substance of some of the earlier controversies was weak. Despite Rousseau's best efforts, there was no real argument to be made that French music ought not to exist: all music is artificial, all music is natural. Nor did anyone write a learned pamphlet to prove to Gluck that opera would be much more dramatically incisive and aesthetically satisfying if castrati were paid enormous sums to sing anything they pleased, regardless of any relevance to the plot. Nor did there exist in 1837 an articulate body of philistines prosecuting the case against Beethoven with skill and cogency. The notion that unnaturalness might be deliberately cultivated, or that dramatic inconsequentiality had special charm, or that dissonance could be relished for dissonance's sake, did not appear until around the beginning of the twentieth century. The Modernists may sometimes appear foolhardy, but they were willing to take extreme positions, and to defend them with resourcefulness and wit.

Of the disputes mentioned above, the one that most clearly anticipates the world of Modernist ism controversy is that between *prima* and *seconda prattica.* Here was a well-defined and coherent conflict between two intellectually respectable positions. Furthermore, in the early seventeenth century, monophony and polyphony coexisted, and monophony attained distinction of technique and purpose by contrast with its still-thriving predecessor—just as the New Objectivity was to define itself in contrast to Expressionism.

In studying the welter of isms in the early twentieth century, it is possible to get sick of all the squabbles. As Frank Martin wrote in 1949,

> the work of art, in order to be viable, must everywhere satisfy conditions which at first seem opposed and irreconcilable. . . . The intellect must not defer to the senses, nor vice versa. Surrealism's attempt to render the subconscious all-important is as fatal to art as the systematic refusal to admit any subconscious forces (which characterizes academicism. All the "isms" conceal an impoverishing, in these circumstances a voluntary impoverishing).[2]

To refuse the dialectical structure of isms, to try to supersede it, may indeed be praiseworthy; but it should be remembered that much of the electricity of Modernist art is generated by the high differential between the various isms.

SYMBOLISM

The first great Modernist ism was the Futurism of Marinetti (Russolo's Futurist manifesto concerning music is reprinted in chapter 5). But before Futurism there was Symbolism—a movement that is in some ways belongs to a pre-Modernist cultural climate but it deserves some attention in the context of Modernism as well. Just as the New Objectivity was at once the antidote to Expressionism, and the factor that imparted precision to it, so Symbolism was the antidote / defining-factor to Realism: it is one of history's best coincidences that the culminating novel of Realism, Gustave Flaubert's *Madame Bovary,* and the founding document of Symbolist poetry, Charles Baudelaire's *Les fleurs du mal* (*Flowers of Evil*), were published in the same year, 1857.

"Correspondances"

La Nature est un temple où de vivants piliers
Laissent parfois sortir de confuses paroles;
L'homme y passe à travers des forêts de symboles
Qui l'observent avec des regards familiers.

Comme de longs échos qui de loin se confondent
Dans une ténébreuse et profonde unité,
Vaste comme la nuit et comme la clarté,
Les parfums, les couleurs et les sons se répondent.

2. Frank Martin, *Un compositeur médite sur son art* (Neuchâtel, Éditions de la Baconnière, 1997), 41–42.

Il est des parfums frais comme des chairs d'enfants,
Doux comme les hautbois, verts comme les prairies,
—Et d'autres, corrumpus, riches et triomphants,

Ayant l'expansion des chosen infinies,
Comme l'ambre, le musc, le benjoin et l'encens,
Qui chantent les transports de l'esprit et des sens.

"Correspondences"

The pillars of Nature's temple are alive
and sometimes yield perplexing messages;
forests of symbols between us and the shrine
remark our passage with accustomed eyes.

Like long-held echoes, blending somewhere else
into one deep and shadowy unison
as limitless as darkness and as day,
the sounds, the scents, the colors correspond.

There are odors succulent as young flesh,
sweet as flutes, and green as any grass,
while others—rich, corrupt and masterful—

possess the power of such infinite things
as incense, amber, benjamin and musk,
to praise the senses' raptures and the mind's.[3]

Realism tends to celebrate the world as it is: as George Eliot wrote in book 2, chapter 17, of *Adam Bede* (1864), the novel should take the Dutch genre painting of the seventeenth century as its model, and present the world of stone mugs, flowerpots, all the bric-a-brac of commonplace life, as cherishable, haloed with human feeling. Symbolism, on the other hand, concerns itself with the transcendental, the ideal; it dismisses the physical world as meaningless, except for a few precious objects—symbols—that remain charged with an arcane power to flame into meaning. As Jean Moréas wrote in the Symbolist manifesto (1886):

Symbolic poetry, the enemy of "instruction, declamation, false sensibility, and objective description," seeks to clothe the Idea in a tangible form which will not be that

3. Charles Baudelaire, *Les fleurs du mal*, trans. Richard Howard (Boston: David R. Godine, 1985), 193, 15.

poetry's object but which, while serving to express the Idea, will remain subordinate. Nor must the Idea itself be seen stripped of the sumptuous robes of external analogy; for the essential characteristic of symbolic art is never to go so far as the conception of the Idea in itself. Thus, in this art, neither scenes from nature nor human actions nor any other physical phenomena can be present in themselves: what we have instead are perceptible appearances designed to represent their esoteric affinities with primordial Ideas.

. . . Sometimes mythical phantasms, from ancient Demogorgon to Belial, from the Kabires to the Nigromans, appear elaborately decked out on Caliban's rock or in Titania's forest, to strains of the mixolydian modes of barbitons and eight-stringed lyres.[4]

Symbolism treated not exact appearances, the heft of physical objects, but the far reaches of imagination.

How can art skim above the physical world, enter the azure realm of the ideal? One method is by naming obvious unrealities, such as unicorns; ordinary language isn't well equipped to describe the delicate delirium that Symbolist writers wish to present. A more artful method is the language of synesthesia (that is, the crossing over from one sense to another): in Baudelaire's sonnet, perfumes are like flutes ("oboes" in the original French) or the feel of a child's flesh. Synesthesia is a technique for reconstruing commonplace nature into something fresh, for indicating intuitions of some indwelling transsensuous beauty, a beauty that (since it is beyond the usual range of our sensory apparatus) expresses itself through the "wrong" sense organ. The phenomenon known as *audition colorée*—hearing in color—is not rare; but during the heyday of Symbolism it enjoyed great prestige. A late example can be found in the writings of Katherine Ruth Heyman, concert pianist, composer, friend of Ezra Pound, and enthusiast for Scriabin: she claimed in 1921 that the note E was colored chrome green and had the flavor of chicken liver.[5]

It will be noted that both Baudelaire and Moréas, in describing the power of Symbolism, appeal to music: music was the privileged art of the Symbolist movement, since it is least referential, the least earthbound of the arts. In 1861 Baudelaire saw the revised version of *Tannhäuser,* and immediately understood that the synesthetic elations described in "Correspondences" were immanent in Wagner's music drama. He soon published a long piece in which he described his reactions to many pieces by Wagner, including the prelude to *Lohengrin,* a tone painting of the descent of the Holy Grail—

4. Jean Moréas, cited in Robert L. Delevoy, *Symbolists and Symbolism* (New York: Rizzoli, 1982), 71.

5. See Katherine Ruth Heyman, *The Relation of Ultramodern to Archaic Music* (Boston: Small, Maynard, 1921), 7.

the immanence of pure symbol. First he quoted Liszt's rapturous description, full of synesthetic imagery (Liszt saw in Wagner's music *golden* doors, *iridescent* clouds, a dazzling flash of *color*), and then continued with his own.

CHARLES BAUDELAIRE
from *Richard Wagner and Tannhäuser in Paris* (1861)

May I be allowed to explain and express in words the inevitable translation that my imagination made of the same passage when, with closed eyes, I heard it for the first time, and when I felt as if I were being lifted up above the earth? Certainly I would not dare to speak complacently about my *reveries,* if it were not useful to compare them with the *reveries* just mentioned. The reader knows what we are trying to do: to show that true music suggests analogous ideas to different minds. Besides, it would not be ridiculous in this connection to argue *a priori,* without analysis and without comparisons; for what would be really surprising would be that sound *could not* suggest color, that colors could not convey a melody, and that sound and color were unsuited to translating ideas, things always having been expressed by a reciprocal analogy ever since the day when God created the world as a complex and indivisible whole. [Here Baudelaire quotes the first eight lines of "Correspondences."]

To continue, I remember that, from the first measures, I experienced one of those happy impressions that almost all imaginative men have known in dreams when they were asleep. I felt myself freed from the *bonds of weight,* and in memory I recaptured the extraordinary *pleasure* which floats about *heights.* . . . Next, involuntarily, I imagined to myself the delightful state of a man gripped by a great dream in absolute solitude, but a solitude with *an immense horizon* and filled with a *vast diffused light: an immensity* with no décor except itself. Soon I experience the sensation of a brighter *light, of an intensity of light* increasing so quickly that none of the nuances furnished by the dictionary would suffice to express *this always renascent increase of brilliance and whiteness.* Then I had the full realization of a soul moving in a luminous milieu, of an ecstasy *composed of pleasure and knowledge,* and soaring above and far away from the natural world.

From *Baudelaire as a Literary Critic,* trans. Lois Boe Hyslop and Francis E. Hyslop (University Park: Pennsylvania State University Press, 1964), 197–98.

To Baudelaire, Wagner seemed a nearly perfect Symbolist artist, consuming the insignificant outer world in a signifying blaze.

The composers who read the Symbolist poets sometimes tried to attain the effect that Baudelaire applauded in Wagner, but with more intimate means; when the poet

Mallarmé wrote that Wagner's magnificent temple stood only halfway up the mountain of artistic idealism,[6] he was indicating that one might climb higher using sparer methods, shouldering a less oppressive burden. Henri Duparc's two great settings (1870 and 1884) of Baudelaire poems suggested that insinuating potencies of melody might achieve ecstasy without the clumsy apparatus of the opera house; and Claude Debussy tried to achieve a feeling of transcendence through quiet: the climax of his opera *Pelléas et Mélisande* (1902) occurs in a state of hush, when Pelléas says, "Je t'aime." The libretto was closely based on a play by Maurice Maeterlinck, whose Symbolist dramas often concern helpless, airy characters, so faintly defined that they seem like ghosts in a ghostly world, conjured from wisps of myth; they grope for a path beneath a sun that seems dim even at noon. For Debussy, the preeminent Symbolist composer, the whole-tone scale —a disoriented scale, like any symmetrical division of the octave—provides an effective metaphor for a state of blindness and treacherous footing; and rifted harmonies become metaphors for a condition of disengagement, a concentration on something that can't be grasped. In a number of Symbolist pictures—Odilon Redon's *Closed Eyes* (1890), Jean Delville's *Portrait of Mrs. Stuart Merrill* (1892), Fernand Khnopff's *Blood of the Medusa* (1895)—the eyes are closed, whited out, or turned impossibly up, as if to suggest a mind that has lost touch with the world of visual facts. Debussy sometimes offers the acoustic equivalent of such eyes. Indeed in the 1890s Strauss and Debussy tend to repeat the pairing of the Realist Flaubert and the Symbolist Baudelaire from the 1850s: Strauss's tone poems grip the domain of physical objects with unprecedented precision, whereas Debussy's *Prélude à l'après-midi d'un faune* images a tantalizing state of worldlessness.

One of the most probing literary evocations of the Symbolist quality of music, its capacity to gesture beyond sound itself to some supersensual essence, is the famous description of Vinteuil's sonata in *Swann's Way,* by Marcel Proust (1871–1922). Vinteuil is an imaginary composer of the later nineteenth century, with some resemblances to Saint-Saëns and to César Franck;[7] we first "hear" Vinteuil's music when Charles Swann, a wealthy art connoisseur, the author of a learned monograph on problems of authentication in the paintings of Vermeer, hears a pianist play a reduction of a violin sonata; as he listens he remembers the occasion, the previous year, when he first heard the sonata, then played in the full violin-piano version. For the past year, Swann has been trying to learn the name of the piece that had inspired such a deepening and renewal of his whole (somewhat abstract and barren, routinized) sensibility; and now he finally learns that it is the Andante movement of a sonata by a composer named Vinteuil. In the second

---

6. Delevoy, *Symbolists and Symbolism,* 48.

7. For Proust's musical sources, see George D. Painter, *Marcel Proust: A Biography* (New York: Vintage Books, 1978), 2:245.

excerpt printed here, set long after the first, Swann has come to the end of his long affair with Odette: after Odette has ceased to love him, Swann again has occasion to hear the Vinteuil sonata, and he hears in the "contralto" voice of the violin a personal message to him. Music, the most timebound of the arts, offers an access to the timeless; love vanishes, the human ego liquefies, but the Vinteuil sonata provides a shiver of eternity. Proust's essentializing metaphors are synesthetic in many ways, but are centered around perfume: Vinteuil's sonata unlocks something, hidden, immaterial, exquisite, ideal—as if behind experience lurks a fragrance of pure being, the ultimate object of desire.

MARCEL PROUST
from *Swann's Way* (1913)

At first he had appreciated only the material quality of the sounds which those instruments secreted. And it had been a source of keen pleasure when, below the delicate line of the violin-part, slender but robust, compact and commanding, he had suddenly become aware of the mass of the piano-part beginning to surge upward in plashing waves of sound, multiform but indivisible, smooth yet restless, like the deep blue tumult of the sea, silvered and charmed into a minor key by the moonlight [*que charme et bémolise le clair de lune*]. But then at a certain moment, without being able to distinguish any clear outline, or to give a name to what was pleasing him, suddenly enraptured, he had tried to grasp the phrase or harmony—he did not know which—that had just been played and that had opened and expanded his soul, as the fragrance of certain roses, wafted upon the moist air of evening, has the power of dilating one's nostrils. Perhaps it was owing to his ignorance of music that he had received so confused an impression, one of those that are nonetheless the only purely musical impressions, limited in their extent, entirely original, and irreducible to any other kind. An impression of this order, vanishing in an instant, is, so to speak, *sine materia* [immaterial]. Doubtless the notes which we hear at such moments tend, according to their pitch and volume, to spread out before our eyes over surfaces of varying dimensions, to trace arabesques, to give us the sensation of breadth or tenuity, stability or caprice. But the notes themselves have vanished before these sensations have developed sufficiently to escape submersion under those which the succeeding or even simultaneous notes have already begun to awaken in us. And this impression would continue to envelop in its liquidity, its ceaseless overlapping, the *motifs* which from time to time emerge, barely discernible, to plunge again and disappear and drown, recognized only by the particular kind of pleasure which they instill, impossible to describe, to recollect, to name, ineffable—did not our memory, like a laborer who toils at the laying down of firm foundations beneath the tumult of the waves, by fashioning for us facsimiles of those fugitive phrases, enable us to compare and to contrast them with those that follow. And so, scarcely had the exquisite sensation which Swann had experienced died away, before his memory had furnished him with an immediate transcript, sketchy, it is true, and provisional, which he had been able to glance at while the piece continued, so that, when the same impression suddenly returned, it was no longer impossible to grasp. He could picture to himself its extent, its symmetrical arrangement, its notation, its expressive value; he had before him something that was no longer pure music, but rather design, architecture, thought, and which allowed the actual music to be recalled. This time he had distinguished quite clearly a phrase which emerged for a few moments above the waves of sound. It had at once suggested to him a world of inexpressible delights, of whose existence, before hearing it, he had never dreamed, into which he felt that nothing else could initiate him; and he had been filled with love for it, as with a new and strange desire.

With a slow and rhythmical movement it led him first this way, then that, towards a state of happiness that was noble, unintelligible, and yet precise. . . . But when he returned home he felt the need of it: he was like a man into whose life a woman he has seen for a moment passing by has brought the image of a new beauty which deepens his own sensibility [*qui donne à sa propre sensibilité une valeur plus grande*], although he does not even know her name or whether he will ever see her again.

Indeed this passion for a phrase of music seemed, for a time, to open up before Swann the possibility of a sort of rejuvenation. . . .

. . . One thinks one is listening to a captive genie, struggling in the darkness of the sapient, quivering and enchanted box [the violin], like a devil immersed in a stoup of holy water; sometimes, again, it is in the air, at large, like a pure and supernatural being that unfolds its invisible message as it goes by.

As though the musicians were not nearly so much playing the little phrase as performing the rites on which it insisted before it would consent to appear, and proceeding to utter the incantations necessary to procure, and to prolong for a few moments, the miracle of its apparition, Swann, who was no more able to see it than if it had belonged to a world of ultraviolet light, who experienced something like the refreshing sense of a metamorphosis in the momentary blindness with which he was struck as he approached it, Swann felt its presence like that of a protective goddess, a confidante of his love, who, in order to be able to come to him, had disguised herself in this sweeping cloak of sound [*apparence sonore*]. And as she passed, light, soothing, murmurous as the perfume of a flower, telling him what she had to say . . . he made involuntarily with his lips the motion of kissing, as it went by him, the harmonious, fleeting form. He felt that he was no longer in exile and alone since she, who addressed herself to him, was whispering to him of Odette. For he had no longer, as of old, the impression that Odette and he were unknown to the little phrase. Had it not often been the witness of their joys? True that, as often, it had warned them of their frailty. And indeed, whereas in the earlier time he had divined an element of suffering in its smile, in its limpid, disenchanted tones, tonight he found there rather the grace of a resignation that was almost gay. Of those sorrows which the little phrase foreshadowed to him then, which, without being affected by them himself, he had seen it carry past him, smiling, on its sinuous and rapid course, of those sorrows which had now become his own, without his having any hope of being ever delivered from them, it seemed to say to him, as once it had said of his happiness: "What does it all matter? It means nothing." And Swann's thoughts were borne towards Vinteuil, towards that unknown, exalted brother who must also have suffered so greatly. . . .

When it was the little phrase that spoke to him of the vanity of his sufferings, Swann found a solace in that very wisdom. . . . But ever since, more than a year before, discovering to him many of the riches of his own soul, the love of music had . . . been born in him, Swann had regarded musical *motifs* as actual ideas, of another world, of another order, ideas veiled in shadow, unknown, impenetrable.

From *Remembrance of Things Past,* trans. C. K. Scott Moncrieff and Terence Kilmartin, 3 vols. (New York: Random House, 1981), 1:227–29, 378–79.

Symbolist music of the quieter sort—intensity that verges on silence—continued through the twentieth century, in such works such Luigi Nono's string quartet *Fragmente—Stille, an Diotima* (1980) and Toru Takemitsu's two piano pieces entitled *Yeux clos (Closed Eyes,* 1979 and 1988), based on Redon's picture. But the too loud as well as the too soft could also be used as an auditory symbol of potencies beyond our life. In 1907 there appeared two French Symbolist works of music, both of which were inclined to sensory overload: Dukas's opera *Ariane et Barbe-bleue,* based on a Maeterlinck play, the opening scenes of which depict a torrent of jewels—amethysts, emerald, rubies, pearls, diamonds—pouring down on the overwhelmed heroine as she opens one of Bluebeard's doors after another; and Florent Schmitt's ballet *La tragédie de Salomé,* a work admired by Stravinsky and an important precursor to *The Rite of Spring.* Both of these compositions have famous relatives elsewhere among Symbolist music dramas: Strauss's *Salome* (1905), based on Oscar Wilde's 1893 play, and Bartók's *Duke Bluebeard's Castle* (1911, 1918), to a haunting text by Béla Balázs. In all four works, huge swells of sound, sometimes containing too many notes of the chromatic scale, attempt to induce a state of rapture, the peak of feeling that Freud called the oceanic experience; a spasm of some more authentic mode of being. From this point of view, Expressionism itself can be understood as a derivative of Symbolism.

The culmination of Symbolist pan-sensual fury came in the work of the Russian composer and mystic Alexander Scriabin (1872–1915); his last completed orchestral work, *Prometheus* (1908–10), was designed to dazzle the eye as well as the ear—the orchestra is to be accompanied by a "light keyboard." Indeed Scriabin came to regard *Prometheus* as, so to speak, an anticipation of World War I, and a continuation of it by other means. He wrote on the educational significance of war:

> . . . At certain times the masses urgently need to be shaken up, in order to purify the human organization and fit it for the reception of more delicate vibrations than those to which it has hitherto responded. . . .
>
> The history of races is the expression at the periphery of the development of a central idea, which comes to the mediating prophet and is felt by the creative artist, but is completely hidden from the masses.
>
> The development of this idea is dependent upon the rhythm of the individual attainments, and the periodic accumulation of creative energy, acting at the periphery, produces the upheavals whereby the evolutionary movement of races is accomplished. These upheavals (cataclysms, catastrophes, wars, revolutions, etc.), in shaking the souls of men, open them to the reception of the idea hidden behind the outward happenings.
>
> . . . The time has come to summon [artists and scientists] to the construction of new forms, and the solution of new synthetic problems. These problems are not yet fully recognized, but are dimly perceptible in the quest of complex experiences, in tendencies such as those manifested by artists to reunite arts which have hitherto been differentiated, to federate provinces heretofore entirely foreign to one another. The public is particularly aroused by the performance of productions which have philosophic ideas as a basis, and combine the elements of various arts. Personally I was distinctly conscious of this at the fine rendering of Prometheus at the Queen's Hall, London. As I now reflect on the meaning of war, I am inclined to attribute the public enthusiasm, which touched me greatly at the time, not so much to the musical side of the work as to its combination of music and mysticism.[8]

At the time of his death in 1915, Scriabin was working on *Mysterium,* a colossal piece of sound and light intended, through an intensity of synesthetic delirium, to hasten the end of the world.

PRIMITIVISM AND EXOTICISM

In D. H. Lawrence's novel *Women in Love* (1920), the hero remembers an African statuette that he saw in the living room of a London painter with advanced taste:

---

8. Letter from Scriabin to Brianchaninov, cited in Heyman, *The Relation of Ultramodern to Archaic Music,* 128–29, citing A. Eaglefield Hull, *Scriabin,* 70.

It was a woman, with hair dressed high, a tall, slim, elegant figure from West Africa, in dark wood, glossy and suave. It was a woman, with hair dressed high, like a melon-shaped dome. He remembered her vividly: she was one of his soul's intimates. Her body was long and elegant, her faced was crushed tiny like a beetle's, she had rows of round heavy collars, like a column of quoits, on her neck. He remembered her: her astonishing cultured elegance, her diminished, beetle face, the astounding long elegant body, on short, ugly legs, with such protuberant buttocks, so weighty and unexpected below her slim long loins. She knew what he himself did not know. She had thousands of years of purely sensual, purely unspiritual knowledge behind her . . . knowledge such as the beetles have, which live purely within the world of corruption and cold dissolution. This was why her face looked like a beetle's: this was why the Egyptians worship the ball-rolling scarab.[9]

Modernist Primitivism tends to be just such a mixture of fascination, disgust, and something like terror: the statuette is, for Lawrence, an image of a knowing body, a body that Western civilization has lost through the bleaching, attenuating effect of cerebral thought—a body that is the source of wonder, and yet is intimate with dung and pus. The vogue for African art was instigated in part by Picasso, whose Cubism owed much to his Primitivist studies: indeed his famous *Les demoiselles d'Avignon* (1907), one of the seminal paintings of the Cubist revolution, shows a woman whose face is simply an African mask. Picasso approached African art very much as Lawrence did: the title is a reference to a brothel on Avignon street in Barcelona, and the first design for the painting showed a medical student holding a skull. Recent scholarship has connected Picasso's painting both with images of harem girls and with photographs of faces ravaged by venereal disease;[10] and it is entirely possible to read *Les demoiselles d'Avignon* as an allegory of syphilis. The copresence of sexual desire and sexual anxiety, the eerie intimacy of love and death, are the motivating forces of Primitivism, from Gauguin's Tahiti onward.

Primitivism in music tends to differ from Primitivism in literature and painting, in that the darker side is sometimes minimized. When folksong researchers carried their recording equipment to out-of-the-way places, they reported their experiences in an almost completely positive manner: here, in Transylvania, or Lincolnshire, was something unspoiled and precious. One such researcher was the Australian-born Percy Grainger, who spoke of the primitive in the most ebullient manner conceivable: Grainger considered "the root emotion of my life [to be] the love of savagery, the belief that savages are sweeter and more peaceable and artistic than civilized people, the belief that primitive-

9. D. H. Lawrence, *Women in Love* (New York: Modern Library, 1950), 288–89.
10. Charles Harrison, Francis Frascina, and Gill Perry, *Primitivism, Cubism, Abstractionism: The Early Twentieth Century* (New Haven: Yale University Press, 1993), 109, 129.

ness is purity and civilization filthy corruption, the agony of seeing civilization advance and pass its blighting hand over the world." [11]

But musical Primitivism wasn't a matter of pure research; it also involved the application of the fruits of research into sophisticated new contexts. The works of another folksong researcher, Bartók (especially the *Cantata Profana* of 1930), often explicitly celebrate the rural over the urban; but his stage pieces, such as *Duke Bluebeard's Castle* and *The Miraculous Mandarin* (1918–26), depict not cheerful peasants clapping their hands in a round dance, but Symbolist spectacles full of sadism and angst—such as a murdered Mandarin, dripping blood, who refuses to die until he embraces a prostitute. Even in Bartók's music, the ritualistic aspect of Primitivism is sometimes transposed into expressions of terror, terror before archaic sexual intensities that are beyond our power to comprehend.

Similarly, in the most famous of all Primitivist experiments, *The Rite of Spring*, the whole urgent complex of attraction and revulsion is clearly on display, for the chief rite of spring is the collective execution of a virgin. The defining moment of Modernism—not just in music, but in all the arts—took place on 29 May 1913, at the première of Stravinsky's ballet *The Rite of Spring*. This established the gold standard for twentieth-century artistic scandals: from that day on, young composers such as George Antheil clung to the hope that they, too, could achieve a comparable riot. At *The Rite of Spring*, a rite of spring occurred in the auditorium as well as on stage.

The ballet had a rich cast of characters. The organizer of the Ballets Russes was Serge Diaghilev (Sergei Dyagilev, 1872–1929), a man of sensitive taste in the field of the astonishing. His lead dancer at the time was Vaslav Nijinsky (1890–1950), a short, somewhat stocky man capable of inhumanly high leaps—one critic called him a "celestial insect." The scenarist and set designer of *The Rite of Spring* was Nicholas Roerich (Nikolay Ryorikh, 1874–1947), a painter, archeologist, and folklorist specializing in pagan Russia. Similarly, Stravinsky's music was built up, as Richard Taruskin has shown, out of fragments of folk tunes.

The music, with its rapid shifts of meter and displaced accents, presented insuperable challenges to conventional choreography. So Diaghilev had Nijinsky, the choreographer of *The Rite of Spring*, attend Dalcroze's exercise classes, to learn a calisthenic method for translating musical rhythm into bodily gesture. Using this system, Nijinsky was able to move in a manner amazingly crammed with musical detail. His sister Bronislava, who would have danced the role of the Chosen One at the première if pregnancy had not interfered, left this account:

Nijinsky demonstrated a *pas mouvement* in the choreography to the musical count of 5/4. During his huge leap he counted 5 (3 + 2). On count 1, high in the air, he bent one

11. Cited by Barry Peter Ould in the notes to *Grainger's Jungle Book*, Hyperion CDA 66863 (1996), 8.

leg at the knee and stretched his right arm above his head, on count 2 he bent his body towards the left, on count 3 he bent his body towards the right, then on count 1, still high in the air, he stretched his body upwards again and then finally came down lowering his arm on count 2, graphically rendering each note of the uneven measure.[12]

In *The Rite of Spring,* Nijinsky found a way of letting the strange meters generate strange gestural icons. Instead of the traditional turned-out style of classical ballet, he devised a turned-in, huddled style: if classical ballet pretended that dancers could fly, the dancers in *The Rite of Spring* seemed to dwell in a domain of too-intense gravity, as if they could hardly straighten their legs. The heaviness of the gestures was designed to evoke the sheer weight of ancient ritual, burdened by an excess of meaning; and yet interweavings of the dancers' lines had a strongly abstract character. The ballet represented a remarkable intersection of the plausibly primitive and the obviously studied—no one spontaneously moves by counting threes and twos with different body parts.

Almost every spectator had some reservations about Nijinsky's choreography, which seemed more appropriate to the American Indian wild-west shows that Nijinsky had seen in his childhood than to a Parisian ballet. Stravinsky's reservations will be only too clear in the following passages. But Stravinsky owed much to the scandal that Nijinsky, not his music, created: no one at the première could hear the music, which was drowned out by the hisses and the boos.

It should be remembered that Stravinsky cavalierly rewrote his past in any way that suited him. It may be true, as he says in his autobiography, that the article in *Montjoie!,* published on the day of the première under the name Stravinsky, was a complete misrepresentation of his opinions; on the other hand, the authority of the autobiography is itself somewhat shaky, since it was ghostwritten by Walter Nouvel. But the falsehoods that surround the origin of *The Rite of Spring,* as well as the truths, play a significant role in the mythology of Modernism.

IGOR STRAVINSKY
"What I Wished to Express in *The Consecration of Spring*" (1913)

Some years ago the Parisian public was kind enough to receive favorably my Firebird and Petrushka. My friends have noted the evolution of the underlying idea, which passes from the fantastic fable of one of these works to the purely human generalization of the other. I fear that *The Consecration of Spring,* in which I appeal neither to the spirit of fairy tales nor to human joy and grief, but in which I strive toward a somewhat

12. Bronislava Nijinska, *Early Memoirs,* trans. and ed. Irina Nijinska and Jean Rawlinson (Durham, N.C.: Duke University Press, 1992), 460.

vaster abstraction, may confuse those who have until now manifested a precious sympathy towards me.

In *The Consecration of Spring* I wished to express the sublime uprising of Nature renewing herself—the whole pantheistic uprising of the universal harvest.

In the Prelude, before the curtain rises, I have confided to my orchestra the great fear which weighs on every sensitive soul confronted with potentialities, the "thing in one's self," which may increase and develop infinitely. A feeble flute tone may contain potentiality, spreading throughout the orchestra. It is the obscure and immense sensation of which all things are conscious when Nature renews its forms; it is the vague and profound uneasiness of a universal puberty. Even in my orchestration and my melodic development I have sought to define it.

The whole Prelude is based upon a continuous "mezzo forte." The melody develops in a horizontal line that only masses of instruments (the intense dynamic power of the orchestra and not the melodic line itself) increase or diminish. In consequence, I have not given this melody to the strings, which are too symbolic and representative of the human voice; with the crescendi and diminuendi, I have brought forward the wind instruments which have a drier tone, which are more precise, less endowed with facile expression, and on this account more suitable for my purpose.

In short, I have tried to express in this Prelude the fear of nature before the arising of beauty, a sacred terror at the midday sun, a sort of pagan cry. The musical material itself swells, enlarges, expands. Each instrument is like a bud which grows on the bark of an aged tree; it becomes part of an imposing whole. And the whole orchestra, all this massing of instruments, should have the significance of the Birth of Spring.

In the first scene, some adolescent boys appear with a very old woman, whose age and even whose century is unknown, who knows the secrets of nature, and teaches her sons Prediction. She runs, bent over the earth, half-woman, half-beast. The adolescents at her side are Augurs of Spring, who mark in their steps the rhythm of spring, the pulse-beat of spring.

During this time the adolescent girls come from the river. They form a circle which mingles with the boys' circle. They are not entirely formed beings; their sex is single and double like that of the tree. The groups mingle, but in their rhythms one feels the cataclysm of groups about to form. In fact they divide right and left. It is the realization of form, the synthesis of rhythms, and the thing formed produces a new rhythm.

The groups separate and compete, messengers come from one to the other and they quarrel. It is the defining of forces through struggle, that is to say through games. But a Procession arrives. It is the Saint, the Sage, the Pontifex, the oldest of the clan. All are seized with terror. The Sage gives a benediction to the Earth, stretched flat, his arms and legs stretched out, becoming one with the soil. His benediction is as a signal for an eruption of rhythm. Each, covering his head, runs in spirals, pouring forth in numbers, like the new energies of nature. It is the Dance of the Earth.

The second scene begins with an obscure game of the adolescent girls. At the beginning, a musical picture is based upon a song which accompanies the young girls' dances. The latter mark in their dance the place where the Elect will be confined, and whence she cannot move. The Elect is she whom the Spring is to consecrate, and who will give back to Spring the force that youth has taken from it.

The young girls dance about the Elect, a sort of glorification. Then comes the purification of the soil and the Evocation of the Ancestors. The Ancestors gather around the Elect, who begins the "Dance of Consecration." When she is on the point of falling exhausted, the Ancestors recognize it and glide toward her like rapacious monsters in order that she may not touch the ground; they pick her up and raise her toward heaven. The annual cycle of forces which are born again, and which fall again into the bosom of nature, is accomplished in its essential rhythms.

I am happy to have found in M. Nijinsky the ideal [choreographic] collaborator, and in M. Roerich, the creator of the decorative atmosphere for this work of faith.

From *Stravinsky in Pictures and Documents,* by Vera Stravinsky and Robert Craft (New York: Simon and Schuster, 1978), 524–26. First published in *Montjoie!* This is a reprint of a translation published in the *Boston Evening Transcript* on 12 February 1916 by Edward B. Hill.

IGOR STRAVINSKY
from *An Autobiography* (1934)

One day, when I was finishing the last pages of *L'Oiseau de Feu* in St. Petersburg, I had a fleeting vision which came to me as a complete surprise, my mind at the moment being full of other things. I saw in imagination a solemn pagan rite: sage elders, seated in a circle, watched a young girl dance herself to death. They were sacrificing her to propitiate the god of spring. Such was the theme of the *Sacre du Printemps*. I must confess that this vision made a deep impression on me, and I at once described it to my friend, Nicholas Roerich, he being a painter who had specialized in pagan subjects. He welcomed my inspiration with enthusiasm, and became my collaborator in this creation. In Paris I told Diaghileff about it, and he was at once carried away by the idea. . . .

Although I had conceived the subject of the *Sacre du Printemps* without any plot, some plan had to be designed for the sacrificial action. For this it was necessary that I should see Roerich. He was staying at the moment at Talachkino, the estate of Princess Tenicheva, a great patron of Russian art. I joined him, and it was there that we settled the visual embodiment of the Sacre and the definite sequence of its different episodes. . . .

Diaghileff made up his mind that year that he would spare no effort to make a choreographer of Nijinsky. I do not know whether he really believed in his choreographic gifts, or whether he thought that his talented dancing, about which he raved, indicated that he would show equal talent as a ballet master. However that may be, his idea was to make Nijinsky compose, under his own strict supervision, a sort of antique tableau conjuring up the erotic gambols of a faun importuning nymphs. At the suggestion of Bakst,[13] who was obsessed by ancient Greece, this tableau was to be presented as an animated bas-relief, with the figures in profile. Bakst dominated this production. Besides creating the decorative setting and the beautiful costumes, he inspired the choreography even to the slightest movements. Nothing better could be found for this ballet than the impressionist music of Debussy,[14] who, however, evinced little enthusiasm for the project. Diaghileff nevertheless, by dint of his persistence, wrung a half-hearted consent from him, and, after repeated and laborious rehearsals, the ballet was set afoot and was produced in Paris in the spring. The scandal which it produced is a matter of history, but that scandal was in nowise due to the so-called novelty of the performance, but to a gesture, too audacious and too intimate, which Nijiusky made, doubtless thinking that anything was permissible with an erotic subject and perhaps wishing thereby to enhance the effect of the production.[15] I mention this only because it was so much discussed at the time. . . .

But to return to the *Sacre*. To be perfectly frank, I must say here and now that the idea of working with Nijinsky filled me with misgiving, notwithstanding our friendliness and my great admiration for his talent as dancer and mime. His ignorance of the most elementary notions of music was flagrant. The poor boy knew nothing of music. He could neither read it nor play any instrument, and his reactions to music were expressed in banal phrases or the repetition of what he had heard others say. As one was unable to discover any individual impressions, one began to doubt whether he had any. These lacunae were so serious that his plastic vision, often of great beauty, could not compensate for them. My apprehensions can be readily understood, but I had no choice in the matter. . . .

Nijinsky began by demanding such a fantastic number of rehearsals that it was physically impossible to give them to him. It will not be difficult to understand why he wanted so many, when I say that in trying to explain to him the construction of my work in general outline and in detail I discovered that I should achieve nothing until I had taught him the very rudiments of music: values—semibreve, minim, crotchet, quaver, etc.—bars, rhythm, tempo, and so on. He had the greatest difficulty in remembering

13. Léon Bakst (1866–1924), painter of sumptuous fantasies, stage designer for the Ballets Russes.
14. *Prélude à l'après-midi d'un faune* (1892–94). Nijinsky's ballet appeared in 1912.
15. Nijinsky, dancing the faun, masturbated with the nymph's scarf.

any of this. Nor was that all. When, in listening to music, he contemplated movements, it was always necessary to remind him that he must make them accord with the tempo, its divisions and values. It was exasperating and we advanced at a snail's pace. It was all the more trying because Nijinsky complicated and encumbered his dances beyond all reason, thus creating difficulties for the dancers that were sometimes impossible to overcome. This was due as much to his lack of experience as to the complexity of a task with which he was unfamiliar.

Under these conditions I did not want to leave him to his own devices, partly because of my kindly feeling for him. . . . It was evident that the poor boy had been saddled with a task beyond his capacity. . . .

I have now come to the spring season of 1913 in Paris, when the Russian Ballet inaugurated the opening of the Théâtre des Champs-Elysées. It began with a revival of *L'Oiseau de Feu,* and the *Sacre du Printemps* was given on May 28 at the evening performance. The complexity of my score had demanded a great number of rehearsals, which Monteux had conducted with his usual skill and attention. As for the actual performance, I am not in a position to as I left the auditorium at the first bars of the prelude, which had at once evoked derisive laughter. I was disgusted. These demonstrations, at first isolated, soon became general, provoking counter-demonstrations and very quickly developing into a terrific uproar. During the whole performance I was at Nijinsky's side in the wings. He was standing on a chair, screaming "sixteen, seventeen, eighteen"—they had their own method of counting to keep time. Naturally the poor dancers could hear nothing by reason of the row in the auditorium and the sound of their own dance steps. I had to hold Nijinsky by his clothes, for he was furious, and ready to dash on to the stage at any moment and create a scandal. Diaghileff kept ordering the electricians to turn the lights on or off, hoping in that way to put a stop to the noise. That is all I can remember about that first performance. Oddly enough, at the dress rehearsal, to which we had, as usual, invited a number of actors, painters, musicians, writers, and the most cultured representatives of society, everything had gone off peacefully, and I was very far from expecting such an outburst.

Now, after the lapse of more than twenty years, it is naturally difficult for me to recall in any detail the choreography of the *Sacre* without being influenced by the admiration with which it met in the set known as the avant-garde—ready, as always, to welcome as a new discovery anything that differs, be it ever so little, from the *déjà vu.* But what struck me then, and still strikes me most, about the choreography, was and is Nijinsky's lack of consciousness of what he was doing in creating it. He showed therein his complete inability to accept and assimilate those revolutionary ideas which Diaghileff had made his creed, and obstinately and industriously strove to inculcate. What the choreography expressed was a very labored and barren effort rather than a plastic realization flowing simply and naturally from what the music demanded.

. . . Among the most assiduous onlookers the rehearsals had been a certain Ricciotto Canuedo,[16] a charming man, devoted to everything advanced and up to date. He
was at that time publishing a review called *Montjoie*. When he asked me for an interview, I very willingly granted it. Unfortunately, it appeared in the form of a pronouncement on the *Sacre,* at once grandiloquent and naïve and, to my great astonishment,
signed with my name. I could not recognize myself, and was much disturbed by this distortion of my language and even of my ideas, especially as the pronouncement was
generally regarded as authentic, and the scandal over the *Sacre* had noticeably increased the sale of the review. But I was too ill at the time to be able to set things right.

From *An Autobiography* (New York: W. W. Norton, 1962), 31, 35–37, 41–42, 46–49.

■

Primitivism could be used to defend the most extraordinary sorts of musical practices. During the Modernist period, critics often denounced the extensions of musical
resources (polyrhythms, quarter-tones, clots of nontriadic chords, and so forth) as vain
contrivances, unfeeling cerebrations; but composers often defended them as recourses
to the authentic roots of music. This convergence of the artificial and the natural is one
of the great paradoxes of Modernism. A composer such as Harry Partch or Henry Cowell, for example, will haul out the most formidable charts of frequency ratios to defend
his procedures, but will also argue that non-Western (that is, unspoiled) music makes
constant use of those matters (scales with too few or too many notes, rhythms with a
too-unintelligible beat) that seem, to the skeptical critic, derived from a sort of arithmetical phantasmagoria.

Modernist approaches to the quarter-tone can be profitably compared. Busoni
argued that music should avail itself of intervals narrower than the semitone because
they're there: nature provides a continuum within the octave, and it is a useless artifice
to try to chop the octave into twelve equal divisions. N. Kulbin made a similar case in
Der blaue Reiter Almanach (1912): "Like the nightingale, the artist of free music is not
restricted by tone and half tones. He also uses quarter tones and eighth tones."[17] According to Ives, the sheer plenitude of acoustic phenomena, the whole world's out-of-
tuneness, compels us to hear very small intervals all the time—though we usually try to
ignore them; when he devised his *Three Quarter-Tone Pieces* (?1903–14), Ives simulated
uncoordinated sound-sources by taking two pianos and carefully tuning them a quarter-
tone apart. The Czech composer Alois Hába (1893–1973) argued, still less theoretically,
that he should write quarter-tone music because he listened to quarter-tone music all

16. Properly Ricciotto Canudo, the interviewer for *Montjoie!*
17. N. Kulbin, "Free Music," in *The Blaue Reiter Almanac,* ed. Wassily Kandinsky and Franz Marc;
new ed. edited by Klaus Lankheit (New York: Da Capo Press, 1974), 141.

the time—the folk singers of his native land never sang in such gross and unmelodic intervals as semitones:

> The folksong collectors Bartók (Hungary) and Plicka (Czechoslovakia) notated the
> perceived interval deviations with a plus or minus sign (+, −). Older folksong col-
> lectors had notated all the intervals in the system of semitones, not observing the
> finer modifications of intervals. This first gained currency from the phonograph and
> tape recordings of folk music from various lands. . . . From folksong I learned to per-
> ceive melodic intervals a little smaller or greater than those of the semitone-system.
> . . . In my youth it often happened that the folk singers, who during the intermissions
> of dance festivals sang songs of "their kind," deviating from the semitone system, de-
> manded that the first violinist of the Wisowitzer Kapelle play "their" melody just as
> they sang it. Once a temperamental singer threatened to strike the double-bass player
> with a beer mug if he didn't "play along" with the song, exactly as he sang it.[18]

Of course the string players had a good deal of trouble following the subtle contours of
the folksong—they hadn't been trained in this style. Hába sought to provide training by
writing books on the theory of quarter-tones and still finer intervals and by writing such
music, and not only for stringed instruments: he commissioned the building of quarter-
tone clarinets, trumpets, pianos, and so forth.

Hába even wrote a full quarter-tone opera, *Mother* (1930), a remarkable work: slightly
in awe of its own daring, in that Hába seemed more fascinated by the quarter-tone scale
themselves than by any melody that might be constructed from them, and yet resolute
in refusing to employ the small intervals in the expected way, as a resource for denoting
pain or disorientation. An Expressionist would use an exotic musical language to mean
extreme states of feeling; but Hába—not an Expressionist, but a searcher for authenticity—intended *Mother* to be a peasant comedy in the tradition of Smetana's *Bartered
Bride* (1866).

Hába's younger contemporary, Béla Bartók (1881–1945), made only occasional use
of microtonal intervals, as in the first version of his solo violin sonata (1944); but he
strongly believed that eastern European folk music offered a potent challenge to the harmonic system of Western music, by inviting harmonies based not on dominants but on
such intervals as fourths and sevenths. For Richard Strauss and for Schoenberg, the desire to use such intervals sprang from a mythology of historical progress in Western music; but for Bartók, it sprang from a mythology of some archaic vigor of which traces survived in remote corners of Europe—a vigor capable of renewing the West. As Bartók
says in the following essay, he considered that he was turning his back on the evolution

---

18. From Alois Hába, *Mein Weg zur Viertel- und Sechsteltonmusik* (Düsseldorf: Verlag der Ge-
sellschaft zur Förderung der systematische Musikwissenschaft, 1971), 12, 14; translated by the editor.

of nineteenth-century music—not extending it. (But this perhaps wasn't quite the whole truth: in such Strauss-influenced works as *Duke Bluebeard's Castle,* Bartók used dissonance for purposes of post-Romantic expression, not simply as an appeal to the primal art of sound.)

Just as Bartók lugged a phonograph recorder around Hungary, Romania, and Turkey, so Milman Perry studied bardic epics in the Balkans in the hope that he could find vestiges of the oral Homeric tradition responsible for the *Iliad.* Orpheus himself, the primal musician of Greek legend, lived in Thrace, where modern Bulgaria, Turkey, and Greece meet; and if the voice of Orpheus could be heard anywhere today, Perry and Bartók were determined to hear it.

BÉLA BARTÓK
"The Influence of Peasant Music on Modern Music" (1931)

There have always been folk music influences on the higher types of art music. In order not to go back too far into hardly known ages, let us begin by referring to the pastorals and musettes of the seventeenth and eighteenth centuries, which are nothing but copies of the folk music of that time performed on the bagpipe or the hurdy-gurdy.

It is a well-known fact the Viennese classical composers were influenced to a considerable extent by folk music. In Beethoven's Pastoral Symphony, for instance, the main motive of the first movement is a Yugoslav dance melody. Beethoven obviously heard this theme from bagpipers, perhaps even in Western Hungary; the ostinato-like repetition of one of the measures, at the beginning of the movement, points to such an association.

But it was only a number of so-called "national" composers who yielded deliberately and methodically to folk music influences, such as Liszt (Hungarian Rhapsodies) and Chopin (Polonaises and other works with Polish characteristics). Grieg, Smetana, Dvořák, and the late nineteenth-century composers continued in that vein, stressing even more distinctly the racial character in their works. In fact, Moussorgsky is the only composer among the latter to yield completely and exclusively to the influence of peasant music, thereby forestalling his age—as it is said. For it seems that the popular art music of the eastern and northern countries provided enough impulse to the other "blatantly nationalistic" composers of the nineteenth century, with very few exceptions. There is no doubt that such music also contained quite a number of peculiarities missing till then in the higher types of Western art music, but it was mixed . . . with Western hackneyed patterns and Romantic sentimentality. . . .

At the beginning of the twentieth century there was a turning point in the history of modern music.

The excesses of the Romanticists began to be unbearable for many. There were composers who felt: "this road does not lead us anywhere; there is no other solution but a complete break with the nineteenth century."

Invaluable help was given to this change (or let us rather call it rejuvenation) by a kind of peasant music unknown till then.

The right type of peasant music is most varied and perfect in its forms. Its expressive power is amazing, and at the same time it is devoid of all sentimentality and superfluous ornaments. It is simple, sometimes primitive, but never silly. It is the ideal starting point for a musical renaissance, and a composer in search of new ways cannot be led by a better master. What is the best way for a composer to reap the full benefits of his studies in peasant music? It is to assimilate the idiom of peasant music so completely that he is able to forget all about it and use it as his musical mother tongue.

In order to achieve this, Hungarian composers went into the country and made their collections there. It may be that the Russian Stravinsky and the Spaniard Falla did not go on journeys of collection, and mainly drew their material from the collections of others, but they too, I feel sure, must have studied not only books and museums but the living music of their countries.

In my opinion, the effects of peasant music cannot be deep and permanent unless this music is studied in the country as part of a life shared with the peasants. It is not enough to study it as it is stored up in museums. It is the character of peasant music, indescribable in words, that must find its way into our music. It must be pervaded by the very atmosphere of peasant culture. Peasant motives (or imitations of such motives) will only lend our music some new ornaments; nothing more.

Some twenty to twenty-five years ago well-disposed people often marveled at our enthusiasm. How was it possible, they asked, that trained musicians, fit to give concerts, took upon themselves the "subaltern" task of going into the country and studying the music of the people on the spot. What a pity, they said, that this task was not carried out by people unsuitable for a higher type of musical work. Many thought our perseverance in our work was due to some crazy idea that had got hold of us.

Little did they know how much this work meant to us. We went into the country and obtained first-hand knowledge of a music that opened up new ways to us.

The question is, what are the ways in which peasant music is taken over and becomes transmuted into modern music?

We may, for instance, take over a peasant melody unchanged or only slightly varied, write an accompaniment to it and possibly some opening and concluding phrases. This kind of work would show a certain analogy with Bach's treatment of chorales.

Two main types can be distinguished among works of this character.

In the one case accompaniment, introductory and concluding phrases are of secondary importance, and they only serve as an ornamental setting for the precious stone: the peasant melody.

It is the other way round in the second case: the melody only serves as a "motto" while that which is built round it is of real importance.

All shades of transition are possible between these two extremes and sometimes it is not even possible to decide which of the elements is predominant in any given case. But in every case it is of the greatest importance that the musical qualities of the setting should be derived from the musical qualities of the melody, from such characteristics as are contained in it openly or covertly, so that melody and all additions create the impression of complete unity.

At this point I have to mention a strange notion widespread some thirty or forty years ago. Most trained and good musicians then believed that only simple harmonizations were well suited to folk melodies. And even worse, by simple harmonies they meant a succession of triads of tonic, dominant and possibly subdominant.

How can we account for this strange belief? What kind of folk songs did these musicians know? Mostly new German and Western European songs and so-called folk songs made up by popular composers. The melody of such songs usually moves along the triad of tonic and dominant; the main melody consists of a breaking up of these chords into single notes, for example, the opening measures of "O du lieber Augustin" and "Kutya, kutya tarka." It is obvious that melodies of this description do not go well with a more complex harmonization.

But our musicians wanted to apply the theory derived from this type of song to an entirely different type of Hungarian song built up on pentatonic scales.

It may sound odd, but I do not hesitate to say: the simpler the melody the more complex and strange may be the harmonization and accompaniment that go well with it. Let us for instance take a melody that moves on two successive notes only (there are many such melodies in Arab peasant music). It is obvious that we are much freer in the invention of an accompaniment than in the case of a melody of a more complex character. These primitive melodies moreover, show no trace of the stereotyped joining of triads. That again means greater freedom for us in the treatment of the melody. It allows us to bring out the melody most clearly by building round it harmonies of the widest range varying along different keynotes. I might almost say that the traces of polytonality in modern Hungarian music and in Stravinsky's music are to be explained by this possibility.

Similarly, the strange turnings of melodies in our Eastern European peasant music showed us new ways of harmonization. For instance the new chord of the seventh which we use as a concord may be traced back to the fact that in our folk melodies of a pentatonic character the seventh appears as an interval of equal importance with the third and the fifth. We so often heard these intervals as of equal value in the succession, that nothing was more natural than that we should try to make them sound of equal importance when used simultaneously. We sounded the four notes together in a setting which made us feel it not necessary to break them up. In other words: the four notes were made to form a concord.

The frequent use of fourth-intervals in our old melodies suggested to us the use of fourth chords. Here again what we heard in succession we tried to build up in a simultaneous chord.

Another method by which peasant music becomes transmuted into modern music is the following: the composer does not make use of a real peasant melody but invents his own imitation of such melodies. There is no true difference between this method and the one described above.

Stravinsky never mentions the sources of his themes. Neither in his titles nor in footnotes does he ever allude to whether a theme of his is his own invention or whether it is taken over from folk music. In the same way the old composers never gave any data: let me simply mention the beginning of the Pastoral Symphony. Stravinsky apparently takes this course deliberately. He wants to demonstrate that it does not matter a jot whether a composer invents his own themes or uses themes from elsewhere. He has a right to use musical material taken from all sources. What he has judged suitable for his purpose has become through this very use his mental property. In the same manner Molière is reported to have replied to a charge of plagiarism: "je prends mon bien où je le trouve." [19] In maintaining that the question of the origin of a theme is completely unimportant from the artist's point of view, Stravinsky is right. The question of origins can only be interesting from the point of view of musical documentation.

Lacking any data I am unable to tell which themes of Stravinsky's in his so-called, "Russian" period are his own inventions and which are borrowed from folk music. This much is certain, that if among the thematic material of Stravinsky's there are some of his own invention (and who can doubt that there are) these are the most faithful and clever imitations of folk songs. It is also notable that during his "Russian" period, from Le Sacre du Printemps [20] onward, he seldom uses melodies of a closed form consisting of three or four lines, but short motives of two or three measures, and repeats them "à la ostinato." These short recurring primitive motives are very characteristic of Russian music of a certain category. This type of construction occurs in some of our old music for wind instruments and also in Arab peasant dances.

This primitive construction of the thematic material may partly account for the strange mosaic-like character of Stravinsky's work during his early period.

19. "I take what I need where I find it." Molière (Jean Baptiste Poquelin, 1622–73) was a French playwright.

20. *The Rite of Spring* indeed contains far more folk material than Stravinsky confessed.

The steady repetition of primitive motives creates an air of strange feverish excitement even in the sort of folk music where it occurs. The effect is increased a hundredfold if a master of Stravinsky's supreme skill and his precise knowledge of dynamic effects employs these rapidly chasing sets of motives.

There is yet a third way in which the influence of peasant music can be traced in a composer's work. Neither peasant melodies nor imitations of peasant melodies can be found in his music, but it is pervaded by the atmosphere of peasant music. In this case we may say, he has completely absorbed the idiom of peasant music which has become his musical mother tongue. He masters it as completely as a poet masters his mother tongue.

In Hungarian music the best example of this kind can be found in Kodály's[21] work. It is enough to mention *Psalmus Hungaricus,* which would not have been written without Hungarian peasant music. (Neither, of course, would it have been written without Kodály.)

From *Béla Bartók Essays,* ed. Benjamin Suchoff (London: Faber and Faber, 1976), trans. Richard Tószeghy et al., 340–44. First published in *Új Idők* 37, no. 23 (May 1931): 718–19.

■

Exoticism is to space what Primitivism is to time: a search for meaning at great distances. This is not to say that a firm line can be drawn between the two: since so little actual music has survived from the remote past, we reconstruct the Primitive from the evidence of the Exotic, under the sometimes dubious assumption that in hard-to-reach places exist vestiges of extremely old practices. In the late twentieth century, Primitivism and Exoticism both came under attack. To speak of Primitivism requires a strong sense of history; and as Postmodernism tends to flatten time consciousness, the prestige of the Bronze Age has diminished: it is understood that archaic societies went about their business as ineptly, as ingeniously, as we go about ours; they were no closer to the sacred. Postmodernism is even more skeptical about the exotic, since, as Edward Said and others have argued, Orientalism tends to be a blind for the predations of colonialism. Still, it is not hard to see why, in the early twentieth century, the sheer diversity, the overwhelming unfamiliarity, of non-Western cultures provided a certain excitement of strangeness. The exotic may have seemed to offer even more than the primitive. In the eighteenth century, Telemann had listened carefully to Polish folk fiddlers and bagpipe ensembles, and had made use (for example, in the *Concerto polonois*) of what he heard, and Bartók considered that Western art music had always been rejuvenated by the

21. Zoltán Kodály (1882–1967), Bartók's fellow explorer in Hungarian folk music. His *Psalmus Hungaricus* (1923) commemorates the fiftieth anniversary of the uniting of three cities to form Budapest.

primitive. But neither Telemann nor any other of the older European composers knew the music of Amazon rain forests or New Guinea highlands.

The not-too-distantly exotic entered gingerly into Western art music, through (for example) the gypsies that provided material for Liszt and Brahms, and through the American Indian melodies that provided barbaric yawps (but genteelly harmonized) for a whole school of composers, including Edward MacDowell and Arthur Farwell, from about 1890 to 1910. This school partly came into being through Dvořák's urging American composers to look to Negro and Indian material for inspiration. But just as Bartók tried to re-create his whole compositional style through thorough assimilation of folk technique, so some of the Modernists tried to use exotic material not just superficially, on the level of borrowed tunes, but profoundly, on the level of structure and harmony. In the United States, for example, Charles Tomlinson Griffes composed *Sketches for String Quartet on Indian Themes* (published 1921), and *Three Japanese Melodies* (1917), in which he deliberately omitted all thirds and sixths from the harmony in order to produce an effect "as Japanese as possible: thin and delicate, and the muted string points d'orgue serve as a neutral-tinted background like the empty spaces in a Japanese print."[22] By the 1930s there existed all over the world composers trained in Western music who strove to rework, with varying success, indigenous material and forms as contributions to the Modernist movement: in Mexico, Silvestre Revueltas (*Sensemayá*, 1938); in Argentina, Alberto Ginastera (*Panambí*, 1937); and in Australia, John Antill (*Corroboree*, 1936), to mention only a few. Their distinguished forerunner was the Brazilian Heitor Villa-Lobos, long engaged in this project (*Uirapurú*, 1917).

In Asia, Western composers found a trove of music that was exotic but in no way primitive—indeed, music with a history older than that of Western art music. In the nineteenth century, Asiatic music typically seemed intolerable even to the most sophisticated Western ears: when Berlioz heard a Chinese musician, he wrote:

> What a violin! it's a bamboo tube. . . . Between its two strings, lightly twisted around each other, pass the hairs of a fantastic bow. . . . These two strings are discordant. . . . The Chinese Paganini . . . holding his instrument supported on his knee, uses the fingers of his left hand on the top of the double string in order to vary its intonation, as we do in playing a cello, but without heeding any division concerning whole-tones, half-tones, or any interval whatsoever. He thus produces a continuous series of gratings, weak meowings, which give the impression of the wailings of the new-born child of a ghoul and a vampire.[23]

22. From notes by Donna K. Anderson, Newport Classic CD NPD 85634 (1998), 7.

23. Hector Berlioz, *Les soirées de l'orchestre* (Paris: Michel Levy, 1854), 317–18; translated by the editor.

But the child of the ghoul and the vampire would soon start to sound much more attractive.

Before the Modernist age, the effect of the East on Western music had been limited to a few tropes (drones, jangly percussion) used in the "Turkish" music of Gluck, Mozart, Beethoven, and others; and to a few special stunts, such as Weber's incorporation of an actual Chinese tune (discovered in Rousseau's *Dictionary of Music*) in his *Turandot* incidental music (1809). But Western creative adaption of Eastern music may be said to begin in 1903, when Debussy evoked the percussive sound of the Javanese gamelan orchestra in his *Pagodes* (from *Estampes*)—a gamelan orchestra had come to Paris in 1889.

The notion of a music founded on intricacies of rhythm, on the contrasts of timbre of various sorts of beaten metal, seemed so starkly different from the usual melodic-harmonic notion of music that composers felt that, in Indonesia, Western music had discovered its Other. The attraction was described by the Canadian composer Colin McPhee, so ravished that he devoted himself to writing gamelan music for Western orchestra such as *Tabuh-Tabuhan* (1936) and eventually set up residence in Bali during 1938–39:

> Most enchanting . . . to a young composer in search of new sounds were the recordings of the gamelan, the Indonesian orchestra composed primarily of tuned bronze gongs of many shapes and sizes, various forms of metallophones, little cymbals, and hand-beaten drums. The Balinese recordings in particular had a polyrhythmic complexity, an animation and metallic shimmer, like nothing I had ever heard.[24]

The gamelan seemed to prove that the Western orchestra had been incomplete, and to offer possibilities for a richer understanding of music itself. Its influence has been incalculable: Poulenc's Concerto for Two Pianos (1932) and Hindemith's Sonata for Two Pianos (1942) were written under its spell; Lou Harrison's *La Koro Sutra* (1972) and many other works were composed for what he called an "American gamelan"; and Britten's gamelan evocations in both *The Prince of the Pagodas* (1957) and *Death in Venice* (1973) represent an erotic domain of transcendental eeriness.

The gamelan is only one of a number of Eastern exotic traditions that Modernist music was to find compelling. India left many traces, starting perhaps with Maurice Delage's *Quatre poèmes hindous* (1913) and continuing through Messiaen's work with *deçî-tâlas,* classes of Indian rhythms.[25] Minimalism evolved partly out of Philip Glass's study of Indian music:

24. Colin McPhee, *Music in Bali: A Study in Form and Instrumental Organization in Balinese Orchestral Music* (New Haven: Yale University Press, 1966), xiii.

25. Olivier Messiaen, *Music and Color: Conversations with Claude Samuel,* trans. E. Thomas Glasow (Portland, Ore.: Amadeus Press, 1994), 75.

What came to me as a revelation was the use of rhythm in developing an overall structure in music. I would explain the difference between the use of rhythm in Western and Indian music in the following way: In Western music we divide time—as if you were to take a length of time and slice it the way you slice a loaf of bread. In Indian music (and all the non-Western music with which I'm familiar), you take small units, or "beats," and string them together to make up larger time values.[26]

The elementary harmonic schemes of early Minimalism allow for the greatest possible concentration on the moiré effects of rhythmic overlay—for Exoticism usually requires that some element must be kept as familiar as possible, precisely so that the exotic element can fully register its deviance from the expected.

EXPRESSIONISM

Expression has for centuries been considered a normal aspect of composition and performance, not necessarily something to which special attention had to be called. But Expressionist music is different from expressive music per se in that aggressive technical developments were considered embodiments of new and intense feeling states. Modulation, for example, shifts from a purely musical procedure involving local change of key, to an institutionalized metaphor for a change of feeling; nonfunctional harmony is made to represent dysfunctional emotion; bizarre chromaticism becomes a sign of a discolored psyche. The older composers often used tonal shadings to convey emotional shadings: but in the second half of the nineteenth century, the shadings tended to overwhelm the thing being shaded—a chiaroscuro in which the object is difficult to make out.

In Handelian opera, the nobility of the character is a reflex of the steadfastness of his or her emotion. A hero, when he rages, rages in an even, equable, wholehearted manner; when he loves, he is thoroughly tender, unable to think of anything except tenderness. The B section of an ABA aria may offer a significant contrast of feeling, especially if the singer is caught in an emotional bind. But musical feeling is still terraced, divided into distinct psychic planes. The affect conventions of opera provide a list of clear captions, as if the singer had adopted a statuesque pose and the music underscored this pose with a name: Rage, or Joy, or Dejection.

But in Handel's world are characters who don't follow the rules: the ignoble and the insane. In *Orlando* (1733), for example, the mad Orlando hallucinates that he has found his great enemy and starts to shadow-box, to fight empty air; he bawls out his fury—to the tune of a gavotte, as if he's lost his place in the opera's table of captions. This extreme

26. Philip Glass, *Music by Philip Glass,* ed. Robert T. Jones (New York: Harper and Row, 1987), 17.

instability of musical cues for feeling seems old-fashioned, in that it resembles the seventeenth-century conventions for madness, as in Henry Purcell's *Bess of Bedlam,* or Barbara Strozzi's *L'astratto,* pieces in which the music switches wildly between contradictory feeling states, a perfect embodiment of manic-depressiveness. But all such pieces strongly anticipate the instantaneous responsiveness of Expressionist music, where emotion is continually darting in and out of focus, mutating into some new emotion, in such continuous transition that it is hard to isolate any finite feeling. Expressionist music is captionless, either because the expression is at such a peak of violence that it is useless to ask whether it is hate, or love, or simply a dentist's drill hitting a raw nerve, or because the expression is shifting, iridescing so rapidly among various states that it can't be pinned down, except through a sort of differential calculus of music criticism. The gradual loss of a tonic was felt as a loss of a dominating affect, a key emotion from which other emotions deviate; instead there is only an endless psychic flux.

The great master of transition in nineteenth-century music was Richard Wagner (1813–83), and Wagner perhaps deserves the title of the first Expressionist composer, both as practitioner and theoretician. Wagner's music dramas tend to be long and earnest, but Nietzsche (the anti-Wagnerian Nietzsche of 1888) claimed that Wagner was chiefly a psychopathologist and miniaturist:

> Wagner's art is sick. The problems he brings to the stage—purely problems of hysterics—the convulsiveness of his affect, his overexcited sensibility, his taste that required ever stronger spices . . . : all this taken together represents without any doubt a picture of sickness. *Wagner est une névrose* [Wagner is a neurosis]. . . . Wagner is . . . our greatest *miniaturist* of music: he crowds into the smallest space an infinity of sense and sweetness. His richness in colors, in half-shadows, in the secrecies of dying light spoils you to such an extent that after him almost all other composers seem too robust.[27]

Wagner understood his art somewhat similarly: he considered his music a set of momentary seizures of nameless emotions or "indefinite presentiments"—a "pure organ of feeling [that] speaks out the very thing which word speech in itself can not speak out . . . *the unspeakable.*"[28] Perhaps it was inevitable that a composer who relied on the old conventions of musical insanity (fast evolutions of vehement feeling) should be denounced as a hysteric. But it may be relevant that Nietzsche, not Wagner, was the one carried off to an asylum.

27. Friedrich Nietzsche, *Werke in drei Bänden,* ed. Karl Schlechta (München: Carl Hanser Verlag, 1966), 2:918.

28. *Wagner on Music and Drama,* ed. Albert Goldman and Evert Sprinchorn, trans. H. Ashton Ellis (New York: E. P. Dutton, 1964), 225, 217.

A predominant influence on the thought of both Nietzsche and Wagner was the philosopher Arthur Schopenhauer (1788–1860), whose crucial book, *The World as Will and Representation,* appeared in 1819. There Schopenhauer understands the universe as the blind, spastic groping of the will (all human or subhuman desire) toward further entanglements of itself; in Thomas Mann's summary, the will "forgets its original unity and, although in all its divisions it remains essentially one, it becomes a will a million times divided against itself. Thus it strives against itself . . . and so constantly sets its teeth in its own flesh, like that dweller in Tartarus who avidly devoured his own members."[29] Only through chaste intellection, through choosing a dispassionate life of ideas, can we hope to save ourselves from will. As Wagner told Liszt, Schopenhauer's "chief idea, the final negation of the desire of life, is terribly serious, but it shows the only salvation possible."[30] Schopenhauer thought that music was the only art that did not merely copy ideas, but actually embodied the will itself.

The following passages, from Wagner's centennial essay on Beethoven, show how strongly Wagner's theory of musical expression is based on his reading of Schopenhauer. Here Wagner claims that every finite expression of emotion is a weakening or dilution of some primal pan-expressive, "will"-ful act. A scream, a lullaby, an expression of pious devotion, a tender cooing of lovers—all are simply shadings-down of a shriek, its refractions into an infinite variety of colors. Wagner's doctrine of the primal scream seems to anticipate Nietzsche's *The Birth of Tragedy* (1872—only two years after Wagner's essay), in which Dionysian ecstatic dismemberment underlies all the calm beauties of art; and also to anticipate the Expressionism of Edvard Munch's famous painting *The Scream* (1895), in which a screamer who seems at once a fetus and a corpse stands on a bridge under a lurid sky: as Munch wrote, "I felt a loud, unending scream piercing nature."[31]

The Beethoven essay anticipates Expressionism also in its fascination with the unconscious. For Wagner, music addresses itself to some hidden place beneath the critical, vigilant, analytic and alert conscious mind—music constitutes itself in a shadowy and amorphous, insinuating sound world that has nothing to do with the hard facts of the outer world as revealed to the eye. In this sense, the essay is a prose version of *Tristan und Isolde* (1865), in which the codes and precisions of the daytime world vanish into a tremulous night violence, where orgasm and death shudder are one—as Tristan tells his Uncle King Marke, Isolde's husband, near the end of act 2:

29. Thomas Mann, *Essays of Three Decades,* trans. H. T. Lowe-Porter (New York: Alfred A. Knopf, 1948), 381.

30. *Wagner on Music and Drama,* 271.

31. Elizabeth Prelinger and Michael Parke-Taylor, *The Symbolist Prints of Edward Munch* (New Haven: Yale University Press, 1996), 98.

Edvard Munch, *The Scream* (1895). The Museum of Modern Art, New York, Matthew T. Mellon Fund (19. 1960). © 2002 The Munch Museum/The Munch-Ellingsen Group/Artists Rights Society (ARS), New York. Digital Image © The Museum of Modern Art/Licensed by SCALA/Art Resource, N.Y.

> In the land that Tristan means
> the sun's light never shines;
> the dark land of always-night
> from which my mother sent me out.

The final words of Isolde, collapsing over Tristan's corpse during the transfiguration scene, are also a paean to the unconscious: "unbewußt—höchste Lust!" (unconsciousness—highest bliss!).

Wagner's essay started to influence the history of music almost from the moment of its first publication. Alma Mahler recalled: "Mahler often said that apart from Wagner's *Beethoven* the only writer who had said anything of value about the nature of music was Schopenhauer."[32]

32. *Selected Letters of Gustav Mahler: The Original Edition Selected by Alma Mahler,* ed. Knud Martner, trans. Eithne Wilkins et al. (New York: Farrar, Straus, Giroux, 1979), 412.

RICHARD WAGNER
"Beethoven" (1870)

It was Schopenhauer who first defined the position of music among the fine arts with philosophic clearness, ascribing to it a totally different nature from that of either plastic or poetic art. He starts from wonder at music's speaking a language immediately intelligible by everyone, since it needs no whit of intermediation through abstract concepts; which completely distinguishes it from poetry, in the first place, whose sole material consists of concepts, employed by it to visualize the idea. For according to this philosopher's so luminous definition, it is the ideas of the world and of its essential phenomena, in the sense of Plato,[33] that constitute the "object" of the fine arts; whereas, however, the poet interprets these ideas to the visual consciousness through an employment of strictly rationalistic concepts in a manner quite peculiar to his art, Schopenhauer believes he must recognize *in music itself an idea of the world,* since he who could entirely translate it into abstract concepts would have found withal a philosophy to explain the world itself.

... If we [consider] what Schopenhauer postulates as the condition for entry of an idea into our consciousness, namely, "a temporary preponderance of intellect over will, or to put it physiologically, a strong excitation of the sensory faculty of the brain without the smallest excitation of the passions or desires," we have only further to pay close heed to the elucidation which directly follows it, namely, that our consciousness has two sides: in part it is a consciousness of *one's own self,* which is the will; in part a consciousness of *other things,* and chiefly then a *visual* knowledge of the outer world, the apprehension of objects. "The more the one side of the aggregate consciousness comes to the front, the more does the other retreat."

After well weighing these extracts from Schopenhauer's principal work, it must be obvious to us that musical conception, as it has nothing in common with the seizure of an idea (for the latter is absolutely bound to physical perception of the world), can have its origin nowhere but upon that side of consciousness which Schopenhauer defines as facing inward. Though this side may temporarily retire completely, to make way for entry of the purely apprehending "subject" on its function (that is, the seizure of ideas), on the other hand it transpires that only from this inward-facing side of consciousness can the intellect derive its ability to seize the character of things. If this consciousness, however, is the consciousness of one's own self, that is, of the will, we must take it that its repression is indispensable indeed for purity of the outward-facing consciousness, but that the nature of the thing-in-itself—inconceivable by that physical [or "visual"]

33. Plato (c. 427–348 B.C.) taught that human ideas are copies of transcendental ideas, beyond the range of the human senses—as if we only saw, in front of us, the shadows cast by objects that were always behind our backs. So the artist makes copies of copies.

mode of knowledge—would be revealed to this inward-facing consciousness only when it had attained the faculty of seeing within as clearly as that other side of consciousness is able in its seizure of ideas to see without.

For a further pursuit of this path, Schopenhauer has also given us the best of guides, through his profound hypothesis concerning the physiologic phenomenon of clairvoyance, and the dream theory he has based thereon. For as in that phenomenon the inward-facing consciousness attains the actual power of sight where our waking daylight consciousness feels nothing but a vague impression of the midnight background of our will's emotions, so from out this night *tone* bursts upon the world of waking, a direct utterance of the will. As dreams must have brought to everyone's experience, beside the world envisaged by the functions of the waking brain there dwells a second, distinct as is itself, no less a world displayed to vision; since this second world can in no case be an object lying outside us, it therefore must be brought to our cognizance by an *inward* function of the brain; and this form of the brain's perception Schopenhauer here calls the dream organ.

Now, a no less positive experience is this: besides the world that presents itself to sight, in waking as in dreams, we are conscious of the existence of a second world, perceptible only through the ear, manifesting itself through sound; literally a *sound world* beside the *light world,* a world of which we may say that it bears the same relation to the visible world as dreaming to waking: for it is quite as plain to us as is the other, though we must recognize it as being entirely different. As the world of dreams can come to vision only through a special operation of the brain, so music enters our consciousness through a kindred operation; only, the latter differs exactly as much from the operation consequent on sight, as that dream organ from the function of the waking brain under the stimulus of outer impressions.

As the dream organ cannot be roused into action by outer impressions, against which the brain is now fast locked, this must take place through happenings in the inner organism that our waking consciousness merely feels as vague sensations. But it is this inner life through which we are directly allied with the whole of nature, and thus are brought into a relation with the essence of things that eludes the forms of outer knowledge, time and space; whereby Schopenhauer so convincingly explains the genesis of prophetic or telepathic, fatidical dreams, ay, in rare and extreme cases the occurrence of somnambulistic clairvoyance. From the most terrifying of such dreams we wake with a scream, the immediate expression of the anguished will, which thus makes definite entrance into the sound world first of all, to manifest itself without. Now, if we take the scream in all the diminutions of its vehemence, down to the gentler cry of longing, as the root element of every human message to the ear; and if we cannot but find in it the most immediate utterance of the will, through which the latter turns the swiftest and the surest toward without, then we have less cause to wonder at its immediate intelligibility than at an art arising from this element: for it is evident, upon the other hand, that neither artistic beholding nor artistic fashioning can result from aught but a diversion of the consciousness from the agitations of the will.

... Here [in music] the world outside us speaks to us in terms intelligible beyond compare, since its sounding message to our ear is of the selfsame nature as the cry sent forth to it from the depths of our own inner heart. The object of the tone perceived is brought into immediate rapport with the subject of the tone emitted: without any reasoning go-between we understand the cry for help, the wail, the shout of joy, and straightway answer it in its own tongue. If the scream, the moan, the murmured happiness in our own mouth is the most direct utterance of the will's emotion, so when brought us by our ear we understand it past denial as utterance of the same emotion; no illusion is possible here, as in the daylight show, to make us deem the essence of the world outside us not wholly identical with our own; and thus that gulf which seems to sight is closed forthwith.

Now, if we see an art arise from this immediate consciousness of the oneness of our inner essence with that of the outer world, our most obvious inference is that this art must be subject to aesthetic laws quite distinct from those of every other. All aesthetes hitherto have rebelled against the notion of deducing a veritable art from what appears to them a purely pathologic element, and have consequently refused to music any recognition until its products show themselves in a light as cold as that peculiar to the fashionings of plastic art. Yet that its very rudiment is felt, not seen, by our deepest consciousness as a world's idea, we have learned to recognize forthwith through Schopenhauer's eventful aid, and we understand that idea as a direct revelation of the oneness of the will; starting with the oneness of all human beings, our consciousness is thereby shown beyond dispute our unity with nature, whom equally we recognize through sound.

[. . .] We can but take it that the *individual will*, silenced in the plastic artist through pure beholding, awakes in the musician as the *universal will*, and—above and beyond all power of vision—now recognizes itself as such in full self-consciousness. Hence the great difference in the mental state of the concipient musician and the designing artist; hence the radically diverse effects of music and of painting: here profoundest stilling, there utmost excitation of the will. In other words we here have the will in the individual as such, the will imprisoned by the fancy of its difference from the essence of things outside, and unable to lift itself above its barriers save in the purely disinterested beholding of objects; whilst there, in the musician's case, the will feels *one* forthwith, above all bounds of individuality: for hearing has opened it the gate through which the world thrusts home to it, it to the world.

This prodigious breaking down the floodgates of appearance must necessarily call forth in the inspired musician a state of ecstasy wherewith no other can compare: in it the will perceives itself the almighty will of all things: it has not mutely to yield place to contemplation, but proclaims itself aloud as conscious world idea. One state surpasses his, and one alone—the saint's, and chiefly through its permanence and imperturbability; whereas the clairvoyant ecstasy of the musician has to alternate with a perpetually recurrent state of individual consciousness, which we must account the more distressful, the higher has his inspiration carried him above all bounds of individuality. And this suffering again, allotted him as penalty for the state of inspiration in which he so unutterably entrances us, might make us hold the musician in higher reverence than other artists, ay, well-nigh give him claim to rank as holy. For his art, in truth, compares with the communion of all the other arts as *religion* with the *Church*. . . .

Sleepless one night in Venice, I stepped upon the balcony of my window overlooking the Grand Canal: like a deep dream the fairy city of lagoons lay stretched in shade before me. From out of the breathless silence rose the strident cry of a gondolier just woken on his bark; again and again his voice went forth into the night, till from the remotest distance its fellow cry came answering down the midnight length of the Canal: I recognized the drear melodic phrase to which the well-known lines of Tasso[34] were also wedded in his day, but which in itself is certainly as old as Venice's canals and people. After many a solemn pause the ringing dialogue took quicker life, and seemed at last to melt in unison; till finally the sounds from far and near died softly back to new-won slumber. Whate'er could sun-steeped, color-swarming Venice of the daylight tell me of itself, that that sounding dream of night had not brought infinitely deeper, closer, to my consciousness?

Another time I wandered through the lofty solitude of an upland vale in Uri. In broad daylight from a hanging pasture-land came shouting the shrill yodel of a cowherd, sent forth across the broadening valley; from the other side anon there answered it, athwart the monstrous silence, a like exultant herd call: the echo of the towering mountain walls here mingled in; the brooding valley leaped into the merry lists of sound. So wakes the child from the night of the mother womb, and answer it the mother's crooning kisses; so understands the yearning youth the woodbird's mate call, so speaks to the musing man the moan of beasts, the whistling wind, the howling hurricane, till over him there comes that dreamlike state in which the ear reveals to him the inmost essence of all his eye had held suspended in the cheat of scattered show, and tells him

---

34. Torquato Tasso (1544–1595), best known for his epic *Gerusalemma liberata (Jerusalem Delivered)*. Venetian gondoliers chanted stanzas from Tasso to a tune that appears in Liszt's tone poem *Tasso: lamento e trionfo* (1849).

that his inmost being is one therewith, that only in *this* wise can the essence of things without be learned in truth.

The dreamlike nature of the state into which we thus are plunged through sympathetic hearing—and wherein there dawns on us that other world, that world from whence the musician speaks to us—we recognize at once from an experience at the door of every man: namely, that our eyesight is paralyzed to such a degree by the effect of music upon us, that with eyes wide open we no longer intensively see.

Wagner on Music and Drama, ed. Albert Goldman and Evert Sprinchorn, trans. H. Ashton Ellis (New York: E. P. Dutton, 1964), 179–86.

■

Expressionism was a term coined in 1910 by a Czech art historian, Antonin Matějček, who saw the movement as the opposite of Impressionism:

> An Expressionist wishes, above all, to express himself. . . . [He rejects] immediate perception and builds on more complex psychic structures. . . . Impressions and mental images pass through his soul as through a filter which rids them of all substantial accretions to produce their clear essence [. . . and] are assimilated and condense into more general forms, into types, which he transcribes through simple short-hand formulae and symbols.[35]

Expressionism, then, is distilled and internalized Impressionism: raw sensory data concentrated into hieroglyphs, terse equivalents of psychic states. Many Expressionist painters agreed with this definition. One of the early Expressionist schools, called *Die Brücke* (*The Bridge*—the name is derived from Nietzsche's Zarathustra, who considered mankind a bridge passing to the *Übermensch,* the Overman), arose in 1905 at a Jugendstil art school in Dresden led by Hermann Obrist. Obrist taught that the purpose of art was to give "a deepened expression and intensification of the essence, instead of a hasty impression";[36] and Ernest Ludwig Kirchner (1880–1938), one of the leading painters of *Die Brücke,* spoke of his drawings as "hieroglyphs in that sense that they represent natural forms in simplified, two-dimensional forms and suggest their meaning to the onlooker."[37] Instead of providing news of the look of the outer world, Expressionist pictures provide glimpses of the inner workings of the mind.

35. Cited in Donald E. Gordon, *Expressionism: Art and Idea* (New Haven: Yale University Press, 1987), 175.

36. Cited in Wolf–Dieter Dube, *The Expressionists,* trans. Mary Whittall (New York: Thames and Hudson, 1990), 37.

37. Ibid., 40.

But Expressionism is more than a discipline of essences; it is also a discipline of violence. How is it possible for pictorial forms to acquire psychic potency? The chief answer is, through distortion, since by distortion the mind's processes of assimilating nature are reflected in the assimilated shape. From this need to illustrate the interiority of the image—the status of the image as something registered by the mind, not by the eye—there arises the calculated hideousness of Expressionist art, its intimacy with psychosis and other states of breakdown between the mind and the outer world. Robert Wiene's film *The Cabinet of Dr. Caligari* (1919), in which the camera tries to imitate schizophrenic visual cognition, is one of many Expressionist experiments with insanity; in 1915 Kirchner, on the edge of nervous breakdown, made a series of woodcuts to illustrate *Peter Schlemihl*—"really the life story of a paranoid," as Kirchner said.[38] The woodcut is a typical Expressionist technique, because the evidence of deep knife gashes is a visible reminder of the sort of wound that the artwork seeks to inflict on the mind of the spectator. Expressionist art tries to cut deep; it is intimate with mutilation, since such terrors best promote the intensity of response that artist seeks. The artists of *Die Brücke* not only used knives in the their work, but devised pictorial shapes consisting of knife forms: the personages in Kirchner's *Women at Potsdamer Platz* (1914) move like blades, slice the city into sharp chunks; and the nude in Erich Heckel's *Glassy Day* (1913) seems precariously posed in a bright but edgy landscape consisting entirely of shards of glass.

This surgical quality of Expressionism is especially prominent in its crime stories. One of the great heroes of the Expressionist movement is the London serial killer Jack the Ripper: Frank Wedekind's play *Lulu* (1913, but assembled from two earlier plays of 1895 and 1902) tells the story of an irresistible seductress who descends from wealth into street prostitution and is finally murdered by Jack; and a Berlin revival led the master caricaturist Georg Grosz to paint *Jack the Ripper* (1918), in which a ripe nude sprawls before the viewer's gaze, as sexually confrontational as a nearly decapitated woman can be. Jack the Ripper, scuttling away in Grosz's picture, was finally to find a lasting home in Alban Berg's opera *Lulu* (1935).

Another grisly tale of seduction and murder can found in Oskar Kokoschka's *Mörder, Hoffnung der Frauen* (*Murderer, Hope of Women*, 1907), by some accounts the first Expressionist play. Oskar Kokoschka (1886–1980) was best known as a painter, specializing in spindly human figures—he said that he liked extremely thin models, such as circus children, "because you can see their joints, sinews, and muscles so clearly, and because the effect of each movement is modeled more emphatically with them."[39] Starvation, like other forms of violence, imparts a certain psychic stress to the image; and Kokoschka's preference for skinless, flayed figures, in which the nerves and muscles are

38. Ibid, 46–47.
39. Ibid., 181.

Ernest Ludwig Kirchner, *The Women at Potsdamer Platz* (1914). From Wolf-Dieter Dube, *The Expressionists* (London: Thames and Hudson, 1990), 45.

Erich Heckel, *Glassy Day* (1913). © 2002 Artists Rights Society (ARS), New York/VG Bild-Kunst, Bonn.

Georg Grosz, *Jack the Ripper* (1918). © Estate of George Grosz/Licensed by VAGA, New York, N.Y.

stripped open, suggests that the inside of the body could serve as a potent metaphor for the inside of the mind.

Kokoschka helped to involve Expressionist art with the world of music, as well. In 1911, the year of Mahler's death, he began an affair with Mahler's widow, Alma; on the very evening when she first met Kokoschka she "took me to the piano in the next room, where she played and sang—for me alone, she said—Isolde's *Liebestod.*"[40] Kokoschka

40. Gordon, *Expressionism,* 48. *Liebestod (Love-Death)* is the name that Liszt gave to the final scene of Wagner's *Tristan und Isolde* when he arranged it for piano in 1867.

returned the favor by painting Alma having sexual intercourse with him (*The Tempest*, 1914) in a billowy Wagnerian way.

But *Mörder, Hoffnung der Frauen* is Expressionistic in a bleak and hard-edged manner, far from the Wagnerian. It is a play designed to be challenging and offensive: it combines love and death in an ecstasy of revulsion. Kokoschka derived his black fable of human sexuality from Otto Weininger's *Geschlecht und Charakter* (*Sex and Character*, 1903). Weininger was perhaps the most precocious scholar since Nietzsche, widely read in biology, philosophy, and the literature of several languages, an anti-Semitic Jew who in 1903, at the age of twenty-three, staged his suicide at the house where Beethoven died. Weininger's book is a mythology of misogyny, presented along the following lines: maleness is essentially spiritual, antimaterialistic, pure; but maleness suffered a Fall when it was tempted by sensuality. This fallen manhood created woman, to embody and express its evil, to revel in it. Femaleness is therefore a contingency and an inauthenticity; a virtuous man will have nothing to do with women, and will certainly never stoop to procreation. Women are fundamentally filthy creatures, who have no interest in anything except phallus worship and sexual intercourse. Weininger concludes his book with a recommendation of universal chastity, in the hope that the biological extinction of the human race will lead to its reunion with the spiritual One, lost so long ago when we descended to coarse material existence. The whole book, garish and overtechnical, suggests what Expressionist nausea would look like, translated into the world of intellectual debate.

There are two points in *Geschlecht und Charakter* that touch closely on Kokoschka's play. The first lies in Weininger's sense of the deep ferocity of sex:

> all sexual urge is related to cruelty. The "association" has a deep foundation. Everything born of a woman must die. Birth and death stand in an indissoluble relation. In the presence of untimely death the sex drive awakens most violently in every being, as the need to propagate itself. And so coitus, not only psychologically as an act, but also from an ethical and scientific viewpoint, is related to murder: . . . love is murder.[41]

The second lies in Weininger's conclusion concerning the ultimate formlessness and nonentity of women. For Weininger, women aren't even evil, since they lack any sort of decisive interior lives:

---

41. Otto Weininger, *Geschlecht und Charakter: eine prinzipielle Untersuchung* (Vienna: W. Braunmüller, 1903), 333–34; translated by the editor. For more on the theme of Expressionist sexual violence, see Maria Tatar, *Lustmord: Sexual Murder in Weimar Germany* (Princeton: Princeton University Press, 1995).

Women have no existence and no essence, they *are* not, they are *nothing*. . . . Woman has no relation to idea, she neither affirms it nor denies it: she is neither moral nor anti-moral, . . . neither good nor evil, neither angel nor devil. [. . .] Woman is a lie.[42]

Kokoschka's play is an allegory of coition, from a Weininger-like point of view. Sex is an act in which a man tries to brand a woman, establish ownership; and an act in which a woman tries to kill a man, drink his blood, incorporate his force. Sex is also a game of mutual imprisonment, torture, and general cramp of being. In sexual intercourse a man confronts the formless horror of biological existence; the murderer is the only hope of women, and the only hope of men too, for the woman must be destroyed if the man is to achieve freedom and purity of being. A man can hope to escape; a woman, being nothing to begin with, can only hope to be annihilated. Kokoschka regarded human sexual relations as a raw wound; his play attempts not to heal it, but to tear it open further, by using every resource of various arts—painting, speech, and bodily movement—in order to maximize sensation.

In 1917 Kokoschka published the revised text of *Mörder, Hoffnung der Frauen;* and in October of that year the magazine *Kunstblatt* devoted a special issue to Kokoschka. When Hindemith read this issue he wrote to a friend that he took a strong interest in this "ultra-overstressed"[43] artistic direction, though he found it difficult to grasp. In 1919 he set almost the whole text of Kokoschka's play, and proved resourceful in finding musical figures equivalent to flaying and branding. The opera begins with a chord made of a semitone, the musical equivalent of a fingernail scraping a blackboard; and Hindemith characterizes the Woman with a quotation from the prelude to *Tristan und Isolde,* as if to show what Wagnerian love-intensity sounds like in the harsh and convulsive world of Modernism.

OSKAR KOKOSCHKA
Murderer, Hope of Women (1907, 1917)
Characters:
The Man
The Woman
Warriors
Maidens

The action takes place in antiquity.
Night sky. Tower with great latticed iron door.
Torchlight. Floor rising to the tower.

42. Ibid., 388–89.
43. *ultra-überspannte: Hindemith-Jahrbuch* 1972, no. 2, 191; cited in Giselher Schubert's notes to Wergo CD WER 60132–50.

Oskar Kokoschka, drawing for *Mörder, Hoffnung der Frauen* (1908). © 2002 Artists Rights Society (ARS), New York/ProLitteris, Zurich.

The Man. *(White face, armored in blue, around his forehead a cloth that covers a wound; with the host of warriors, wild heads, gray and red headcloths, white, black, and brown clothes, emblems on the clothes, naked legs, torches on long poles, ringing, uproar. They crawl up with outstretched poles and lights, try tiredly and unwillingly to hold back the impetuous adventurer, to pull down his horse. He keeps going. They draw back to form a looser circle around him while they cry out, slowly getting louder.)*

Warriors: We were the flaming wheel around him. We were the flaming wheel around you, you assaulter of locked fortresses! *(Hesitantly they make a chain behind him; he goes forward, with the torchbearer in front.)*

Warriors: Lead us, pale man! *(While they want to pull down his horse, maidens, along with the chief woman, descend the right-hand stairs, which lead out of the fortress wall.)*

Woman *(Red dress, yellow hair unbound, tall.) (loud):* At my breath the yellow disk of the sun flares. My eye gathers the rejoicings of men. Their stammering pleasure crawls like a beast around me.

Maidens *(disperse from her, see now the stranger for the first time).*

First Maiden *(curious):* Our lady! His breath hangs on her.

First Warrior *(afterward, to the others):* Our lord comes like the day, rising in the east.

Second Maiden *(naively):* When will she be embraced with delight!

Woman *(looks fixedly at the Man):* Who is the strange man who looks at me?

First Maiden *(points at him, cries):* Scared away by the mother of sorrow, the boy with snakes on his brow escaped. Do you recognize him?

Second Maiden *(smiling):* The abyss totters. If she drives the dear guest away?

The Man *(astonished, his procession halts):* What did the shadow say? *(Lifting his face to the Woman)* Did you look at me, did I see you?

Woman *(fearing and longing):* Who is the pale man? Hold him back!

First Maiden *(shrilly crying, runs back):* Are you letting him in? He suspects that we're defenseless? The fortress stands open!

First Warrior: Whatever parts air and water, whatever wears skin, feathers, and scales, is subject to him—even ghosts, hairy and naked.

Second Maiden: There the golden-haired woman laughs and weeps, with one eye. Hunter, catch us already . . . *(Laughter.)*

First Warrior *(to the Man):* Embrace her! The neighing drives the mare mad. Offer your thigh to the beast.

First Maiden *(craftily):* Our lady has been entangled in a web, she hasn't yet attained shape.

Second Maiden *(boasting):* Our lady rises and sinks, yet never comes to the earth.

Third Maiden: Our lady is naked and smooth, and she never closes her eyes.

Third Warrior *(to the Third Maiden, mocking):* The little fish gets caught on the hook. The lady fish is hooked by the fisherman.

Second Warrior *(to the Second Maiden; he has understood):* Curls fly about! Her face out in the open . . . The spider has climbed out of the nest.

The Man *(has exposed the Woman's veil; angry):* Who is she?

First Warrior *(urging him on):* She seems to you afraid, catch her! It is only fear that paralyzes. Be afraid of what you grasp for yourself!

First Maiden *(fearful):* Lady, let us flee! Quench the leader's lights!

Second Maiden *(stubborn):* Lady, let me wait for daylight here . . . Don't tell me to go to sleep, with unrest in all my limbs!

Third Maiden *(imploring):* He should not be our guest, should not breathe our air! Don't let him spend the night here. He terrifies away our sleep!

First Maiden: He has no luck!

First Warrior: She has no shame!

Woman: Why do you charm me, Man, with your glance? All-devouring light, you confuse my flame! All-consuming life comes over me. O take away from me this horrible hope—

The Man *(goes up, raging):* You men! Take a hot iron, and burn my sign into her red flesh! *(Warriors carry out the command. First the crowd with the torches scuffling with her, then the Old Man with the iron rips off her dress and brands her.)*

Woman *(crying out in terrible pain):* Beat it back, the evil plague. *(She leaps onto the Man with a knife and makes a wound in his side. The Man falls.)*

Warriors: Flee the possessed man, kill the devil! Woe to us innocent ones, bury the conqueror quickly.

The Man *(cramped by wounds, singing with visibly bleeding wounds):* Senseless craving from horror to horror, ceaseless circling in the void. Childbearing without birth, plunge of suns, reeling space. End of those who praised me. Oh, Oh, your merciless word!

Warriors *(to the Man):* We don't know him. Spare us! Come, you Greek maidens, let us hold a wedding on his sickbed.

All Maidens: He terrifies us, we loved you when you came.

(The Maidens lie down seductively in front of the Warriors, stage right.)

(Three Warriors make a bier out of sticks and branches, and put it, with the weakly moving Man, into the tower. Women throw open the latticed door and draw back to the men.)

The Old Man. *(Stands up and barricades. Everything dark, little light in the cage.)*

Woman *(alone, weeping, stubborn):* He cannot live, cannot die, he is all pale. *(She prowls around the cage; forcibly grabs the bars, threatens with her fist.)*

Woman *(defiantly):* Open the door, I must go to him! *(Shakes the door despairingly.)*

Warriors and Women *(enjoying themselves, in the shadows, disordered):* We've lost the key—we find it—do you have it?—did you see it—we're not guilty. We don't know you—what do we know about you! The struggle is incomprehensible and lasts an eternity. *(They go back again. Cock crow, the background lights up.)*

Woman *(reaches through the lattice with her arm, malevolently gasping):* Pale man! Are you terrified? Do you know fear? Are you sleeping? Are you awake? Do you hear me?

The Man *(inside, breathing with difficulty, lifts his head tiredly, later moves one hand, then both hands, gets up slowly, singing, enraptured):* Wind that pulls, time after time. Loneliness, calm, and hunger confuse me. Worlds circling past, no air, it will be evening-long.

Woman *(beginning to be afraid):* So much life flows out of the gap, so much strength out of the gate, he is pale as a corpse. *(Slips again up the stairs, with her body trembling, again laughing out loud.)*

The Man *(having slowly stood up, leans on the lattice).*

Woman *(becoming weaker, fiercely):* I tame a wild beast in a cage here, does your song of hunger bark out?

The Man *(opens his mouth to speak):* . . . . *(Cock crow.)*

Woman *(trembling):* You, you don't die?

The Man *(powerful):* Stars and moon! Woman! Brightly shining, in dreams or in waking, I saw a singing being . . . dark things breathing reveal themselves to me. Mother . . . You lost me here.

Woman *(lies completely on him; separated from him through the lattice, she opens the gate) (softly):* Don't forget me . . .

The Man *(wipes over his eyes):* A blighted thought clings to my head . . .

Woman *(tenderly):* It is your wife!

The Man *(gently):* A short stretch of timid light!—

Woman *(beggingly):* Man!! Sleep . . . me . . .

The Man *(louder):* Peace, peace, deceitful thought, leave me . . .

Woman *(opens her mouth to speak):* . . . .

The Man *(lonely):* I'm afraid—

Woman *(ever more violent, crying out):* I will not let you live. You! You weaken me— I kill you—you chain me! I captured you—and you hold me! Let loose from me— you clasp me—as with iron chains—strangled—loose—help! I lost the key—that holds you fast. *(Leaves the lattice, collapses on the stairs.)*

The Man. *(Stands fully up, tears the gate open, touches with the finger of his outstretched hand the rigidly towering Woman, who is completely white. She feels*

*her end near, stretches her limbs, relaxes them in a scream that slowly falls away.
The Woman falls down, and during her fall snatches the torch from the Old Man.
It goes out and envelops everything in a shower of sparks.)*

The Man. *(Stands on the highest stair; Warriors and Maidens, wishing to flee from
him, run from him screaming.)*

Warriors and Maidens: The devil! Subdue him, save yourselves! Save yourself if you
can—all lost!

The Man. *(Goes up to them immediately. He kills them like flies. The flame spreads to
the tower and rips it from top to bottom. Through the fiery street the Man hurries
away. Cock crow in the far distance.)*

END

From *Schriften 1907–1955,* ed. Hans Maria Wingler (Munich: Albert Langen–Georg Müller, 1956),
140–51; translated by the editor.

■

Expressionist art justifies itself on the grounds of psychic authenticity: the artwork
may not resemble any familiar thing—in fact it has been so contorted that it cannot resemble any familiar thing—but its validity is guaranteed by our recognition of the mind
stresses that bent the image out of shape. This sort of argument is carried as far as it will
go in the defense of Expressionist music by Theodor Adorno (1903–69), who claims that
all previous composers present only representations of passion, flimsy symbolic equivalents to passion; but Schoenberg has managed to write music that embodies the brain's
physiological responses to shock and trauma. It is as if the score of Schoenberg's *Erwartung* were a sound generator hooked up to an electroencephalograph: Schoenberg
descended beneath all codes and conventions to discover what the nervous system actually sounds like. Adorno goes on to distinguish Schoenberg's organically intense Expressionism from other artistic movements which fail because of their falsity: Surrealism, considered a movement for zombies or automata, not for human beings; and the
New Objectivity, considered a spiffy fake of streamlined functionality.

These arguments are venturesome, as are all arguments that claim a superior natu-
ralness for one sort of music rather than another. But Adorno may be on safer ground
when he contemplates the inadequacy of what appears to be, by the standards of Expressionist music, the ultimate expressive act: the sounding of all twelve notes of the
scale at the same time. Music had been attempting for many years, from the *Schreckens-
fanfare* (terror fanfare) at the beginning of the finale of Beethoven's Ninth Symphony
(1824), to the nine-note chord at the climax of the Adagio of Mahler's Tenth Symphony
(1911), to approach this pan-expressive agglomeration of sound. Here, if anywhere, was

the scream that Wagner mentioned in his essay on Beethoven. But, as Adorno notes, when it finally happened—for example, in Berg's *Lulu*—it did not manage to terminate the art of music, or to leave all hair on all heads permanently raised.

Expressionist art is always haunted by the hope that it can have an effect something like an epileptic seizure, what Freud calls the oceanic experience, a condition of complete sensory overload. Schoenberg was profoundly attracted to such peaks of sensation.

ARNOLD SCHOENBERG
from *Die glückliche Hand* (1910–13): [brain-storm]

[The MAN] goes to the anvil . . . picks up a piece of gold lying on the ground, lays it on the anvil and grasps the hammer with his right hand. . . . Radiant, swelled with a sense of power—he grasps the hammer with both hands and brings it down in a powerful swing. . . . The anvil splits down the middle and the gold sinks into the cleft.

The MAN bends down and pulls it out with his left hand. Raises it slowly on high. It is a diadem set with precious stones. . . .

The WORKERS' gestures grow threatening again; then disdainful; they take counsel together and seem to be planning to make some move against the MAN. The MAN throws his handiwork to them, laughing. They prepare to rush upon him. He has turned away and does not see them. He stoops to pick up his sword.

As he touches it with his left hand, the grotto grows dark.

Every trace of the workshop disappears behind the dark curtain.

As it darkens, a wind springs up. At first it murmurs softly, then steadily louder (along with the music).

Conjoined with this wind-crescendo is a light-crescendo. It begins with dull red light (from above) that turns to brown and then a dirty green. Next it changes to a dark blue-gray, followed by violet. This grows, in turn, into an intense dark red which becomes ever brighter and more glaring until, after reaching a blood-red, it is mixed more and more with orange and then bright yellow; finally a glaring yellow light alone remains and inundates the second grotto from all sides. This grotto was already visible at the beginning of the light-crescendo and underwent the same gamut of color changes from within (although less brightly than the rest of the stage). Now it too streams with yellow light.

During this crescendo of light and storm, the MAN reacts as though both emanated from him. He looks first at his hand (the reddish light); it sinks, completely exhausted; slowly, his eyes grow excited (dirty green). His excitement increases; his limbs stiffen convulsively, trembling, he stretches both arms out (blood-red); his eyes start from his head and he opens his mouth in horror. When the yellow light appears, his head seems as though it is about to burst.

He does not turn toward the grotto, but looks straight ahead.

When it is completely bright, the storm breaks off and the yellow light changes swiftly to a mild, bluish light. For a moment the grotto remains empty, bathed in this light. Then the WOMAN enters from the left, quickly and lightly. She is dressed as in the second scene, but the upper left section of her clothing is missing, so that this part of her upper body is completely naked to her hip.

From *Arnold Schoenberg, Wassily Kandinsky: Letters, Pictures, and Documents,* ed. Jelena Hahl-Koch, trans. John C. Crawford (London: Faber and Faber, 1984), 96.

These are stage directions from Schoenberg's *The Lucky Touch,* a short opera about a genius's difficulties with sexuality and with an uncomprehending public; here the genius is seized with inspiration, an inspiration that takes the form of a brain explosion. Schoenberg represented the hammer blow with a chord that contains all twelve notes of the chromatic scale, But it is doubtful that any technical procedure, even a twelve-note chord, can constitute once and for all an appropriate image of this electrocuted state of mind. Indeed the twelve-tone chord fairly quickly became normalized: Ruth Crawford Seeger used it in her *Three Chants* (1930), in the context of monks chanting a (made-up) Asiatic language—a gesture of rapture, but not suggestive of total convulsion.

THEODOR ADORNO
from *Philosophy of Modern Music* (1948)

Today [historical] process has turned against the self-sufficient work of art and everything determined thereby. The illness which has befallen the idea of the work might well have its roots in a social condition which reflects nothing binding and affirmative enough to guarantee the internal harmony of the work sufficient unto itself. The prohibitive difficulties of the work are, however, evident not only in the reflection upon it, but in the dark interior of the work itself. If one thinks of the most conspicuous symptom—namely, the shrinking of the expansion in time—which in music is only an external factor of the work, then it must be stated that only individual impotence, incapacity for structural formulation—not sparseness—is to be made responsible for the lack of success of a given work. No works could exhibit greater concentration and consistency of formal structure than Schoenberg's and Webern's shortest movements. Their brevity is a direct result of the demand for the greatest consistency. This demand precludes the superfluous. In so doing this consistency opposes expansion in time, which has been the basis for the conception of the musical work since the eighteenth century, certainly since Beethoven. The work, the age, and illusion are all struck by a single blow. Criticism of the extensive scheme is interlocked with criticism of the content, in terms of phrase and ideology. Music, compressed into a moment, is

valid as an eruptive revelation of negative experience. It is closely related to actual suffering. In this spirit of compression modern music destroys all decorative elements
and, therewith, symmetrically extended works. Among the arguments which would attempt to relegate the disquieting phenomenon of Schoenberg into the past of Romanticism and individualism (in order to be able to serve the operations of modern collec-
tives with a better conscience), the most widely spread is the one which brands him as
an "*espressivo* composer" and his music as an "exaggeration" of a decayed mode of
expression. It is neither necessary to deny his origin in the Wagnerian *espressivo* style
nor to overlook the traditional *espressivo* elements in his earlier works. These compositions, nonetheless, prove their ability to come to terms with this barren emptiness. At
the same time, Schoenberg's *espressivo* style since the break—if not from the very beginning, at least since the *Piano Pieces* and the [Stefan] George songs, *Das Buch der
hängenden Gärten* [*The Book of the Hanging Gardens,* 1908–9]—differs in quality from
Romantic expression precisely by means of that intensification which thinks this
espressivo thought to its logical conclusion. The expressive music of the West, since
the beginning of the seventeenth century, assumed an expressiveness which the composer allotted to his musical structures in much the same way as the dramatist did
to his theatrical figures, without the expressed emotions claiming to have immediate
presence and reality within the work. Dramatic music, just as true *musica ficta,*[44] from
Monteverdi to Verdi presented expression as stylized communication—as the representation of passions. Whenever this music extended beyond this, laying claim to a
substantiality beyond the appearance of expressed feelings, this claim hardly restricted
itself to specific musical emotions, reflecting in turn such emotions of the soul. This
claim was validated only by the totality of the form, which exercises control over the
musical characters and their correlation. The process is totally different in the case of
Schoenberg. The actual revolutionary moment for him is the change in function of musical expression. Passions are no longer simulated, but rather genuine emotions of the
unconscious—of shock, of trauma—are registered without disguise through the medium of music. These emotions attack the taboos of form because these taboos subject such emotions to their own censure, rationalizing them and transforming them into
images. Schoenberg's formal innovations were closely related to the change in the content of expression. These innovations serve the breakthrough of the reality of this content. The first atonal works are case studies in the sense of psychoanalytical dream
case studies. In the very first publication on Schoenberg,[45] Vassily Kandinsky called the

44. *musica ficta:* a term from early music, in which the line is colored with unnotated sharps and flats.
45. *Arnold Schönberg,* ed. Berg et al. Kandinsky's essay is reproduced in *Arnold Schoenberg, Wassily
Kandinsky: Letters, Pictures, and Documents,* ed. Jelena Hahl-Koch, trans. John C. Crawford (London:

composer's paintings "acts of the mind" [*Gehirnakte,* or brain acts]. The scars of this revolution of expression, however, are the blotches which have become fixed in his music as well as in his pictures, as the heralds of the id against the compositional will.[46] They destroy the surface and are as little to be removed by subsequent correction as are the traces of blood in a fairy tale. Authentic suffering has implanted these in the work of art as a sign that the autonomy of the work is no longer recognized by this suffering. The heteronomy of the scars—and the blotches—challenges music's façade of self-sufficiency. . . . Schoenberg's attitude towards play is just as polemic as is his attitude towards illusion. He turns just as sharply against the New Objectivity music-makers and their collective retinue as he does against the decorative elements of Romanticism. He has formulated both attitudes in his theoretical writings: "Music is not to be decorative; it is to be true," and "Art does not arise out of ability but rather out of necessity."[47] With the negation of illusion and play music tends towards the direction of knowledge.[48] . . .

. . . Expressionistic music did remain "organic"; it was a language; it was subjective and psychological. . . . In its attitude towards the organic, Expressionism distinguishes itself from Surrealism. The "inner strife" of Expressionism is a result of its organic irrationality. This strife is definable in terms of opposites: sudden gesture and motionlessness of the body. Its rhythm is patterned after that of waking and sleeping. Surrealistic irrationality, on the other hand, assumes that the physiological unity of the body has collapsed—Paul Bekker[49] once called Schoenberg's Expressionism "physiological music." Surrealism is anti-organic and rooted in lifelessness. It destroys the boundary between the body and the world of objects. . . .

. . . All New Objectivity secretly threatens to fall into the hands of that which it most bitterly opposes: the ornament. The interior-design charlatans, sitting in full view in their streamlined club chairs, publicly confess what the loneliness of constructivist painting and twelve-tone music grasped as a matter of necessity. Illusion vanishes from the work of art as soon as the work begins to define itself in its battle against the ornament; in the process the position of the work of art in general gradually becomes

---

Faber and Faber, 1984), 125–28. Kandinsky there remarks that Schoenberg paints "in order to give expressions to those motions of the spirit [*Gehirnakte*] that are not couched in musical form."

46. The tremolo passage in the first piano piece from opus 19 or measures 10, 269, and 382 of *Erwartung* are examples of such blotches. [Adorno's note.]

47. Arnold Schoenberg, *Probleme des Kunstunterrichts* [*Problems of Art Instruction*], Musikalisches Taschenbuch, Vienna, 1911. [Adorno's note.]

48. A sentence appropriated by Thomas Mann in *Dr. Faustus.* See chapter 6 of this anthology.

49. Paul Bekker (1882–1937), German music critic, enthusiastic about Schoenberg and other avant-garde composers.

untenable. Everything having no function in the work of art—and therefore everything transcending the law of mere existence—is withdrawn. The function of the work of art lies precisely in its transcendence beyond mere existence. Thus the height of justice becomes the height of injustice: the consummately functional work of art becomes consummately functionless. Since the work, after all, cannot be reality, the elimination of all illusory features accentuates all the more glaringly the illusory character of its existence. This process is inescapable. The dissolution of the illusory features in the work of art is demanded by its very consistency. . . .

. . . The law of vertical dimension of twelve-tone music might well be called the law of complementary harmony.[50] Precursory forms of complementary harmony are found less in Schoenberg's middle period than in Debussy and Stravinsky. They are to be found above all where there is no harmonic progress in terms of the rules of thorough bass, but rather static levels of sound which permit only a selection from the twelve tones and then suddenly change into new levels of sound which provide for the remaining tones. In complementary harmony every sound is complexly constructed: it contains its individual pitches as independent and differing moments of the whole, without causing their differences to disappear, as would be the case in triadic harmony. Within the range of the twelve tones the experimenting ear cannot withdraw from the chroma of experience, whereby each complex sound fundamentally demands for completion those pitches of the chromatic scale which are not present in the sound itself. This demand can be fulfilled simultaneously or successively. Tension and release in twelve-tone music are always to be understood in the perspective of the individual sounds of the twelve tones viewed comprehensively. The single complex chord becomes capable of attracting musical forces unto itself which formerly had meaning only within entire melodic lines or harmonic structures. At the same time, complementary harmony, through sudden transformation, is able to cause these chords to radiate in such a manner that all their latent power is revealed. The change from one harmonic stratum, defined by chord, to the next complementary stratum, produces harmonic effects of depth—a type of perspective that traditional music has often sought, and attempted, for example, in Bruckner; but hardly ever achieved. If one is to take Lulu's twelve-tone death chord[51] as the integral totality of complementary harmony, then Berg's allegorical genius proves itself within a historical perspective which makes the

50. Adorno took the notion of complementary harmony from Schoenberg: "The chord progression seems to be regulated by the tendency to include in the second chord tones that were missing in the first"—Arnold Schoenberg, *Theory of Harmony,* trans. Roy E. Carter (Berkeley: University of California Press, 1983), 420.

51. In his last opera, *Lulu* (1935), Alban Berg uses a chord sounding all the notes of the chromatic scale at certain climactic moments.

brain reel: just as Lulu in the world of total illusion longs for nothing but her murderer and finally finds him in that sound, so does all harmony of unrequited happiness long for its fatal chord as the cipher of fulfillment—twelve-tone music is not to be separated from dissonance. Fatal: because all dynamics come to a standstill within it without finding release. The law of complementary harmony already implies the end of the musical experience of time, as this was heralded in the dissociation of time according to Expressionistic extremes.

From *Philosophy of Modern Music,* trans. Anne G. Mitchell and Wesley V. Blomster (New York: Seabury, 1973), 37–39, 40, 51, 70, 81–82.

NEOCLASSICISM AND THE NEW OBJECTIVITY

Technical extremism in one direction often breeds technical extremism in contrary directions; so it is not surprising that Expressionism's cultivation of musical electroshock therapy would lead to various advocacies of milder, more familiar music. But in these countermovements there is often something confrontational, even aggressive; Modernist preoccupation with technique prevails even where nothing grates on the ear or challenges common notions of continuity. Anti-Expressionism took the following forms (among others):

1. *Neoclassicism.* Stravinsky gave himself credit for originating the movement (in *Pulcinella,* written in 1919), but fascination with Baroque and Classical forms had in fact never gone far enough way to require much reviving. Liszt's *À la Chapelle Sixtine* (1862), Grieg's *Holberg Suite* (1884), Tchaikovsky's pastiche-Mozart divertissement in *The Queen of Spades* (1890), Reger's *Concerto in the Old Style* (1912)—all these and many more testify to the ongoing vigor of the eighteenth century, as composers dressed up their music in old clothes in order to create a smiling or pensive evocation of the past. Still, Modernist Neoclassicism is different: rarely easygoing, often tense, the Neoclassicists self-consciously advertise their contemporaneity through slight or gross deviations from the old-fashioned. (Stravinsky's particular game is to see how little he can change in an old text and still Stravinskyize the musical experience.) In *Pulcinella* Stravinsky worked to translate eighteenth-century music published under the name of Pergolesi into a Modernist idiom, just as Ezra Pound (in *Homage to Sextus Propertius,* 1917) translated Latin poetry into an English so contemporary it referred to Frigidaire patents. But to translate is to assume that the material translated has become illegible. It is as if the eighteenth century had at last died during World War I and suddenly needed artificial resuscitation in order to live—or at least to attain a parody of life. Neoclassicism renders the classics up-to-date, jaunty, but also calls attention to the distance between the eighteenth

century and the twentieth, and thus demonstrates the pastness of the past. The border between Neoclassicism and Expressionism seemed distinct in the early 1920s but soon grew blurry: for example, Schoenberg's Concerto for String Quartet and Orchestra (1933) is simultaneously Expressionist and Neoclassicist, a vivacious hallucination of Handel's Concerto Grosso, op. 6 no. 7.

2. *The New Objectivity (neue Sachlichkeit).* In German, *Sache* means "thing," and *sachlich* means "matter-of-fact"; and there arose during the 1920s an artistic movement that understood the artwork not as an expression, not as an attempt to capture some fleeting mental state, but as a self-standing uncontingent object, equal in dignity to other phenomena in the world. In literature, this entailed a desire to understand a poem as a verbal icon, a well-wrought urn, not connected to the poet's biography or to the political culture around it—a doctrine that followed from T. S. Eliot's "Tradition and the Individual Talent" (1919). In painting, this entailed a rejection of what Wilhelm Hausenstein called the "objectlessness of expressionism"—its preoccupation with "intestinal convolutions, nerves, and blood vessels," all that is "horribly deformed, cross-eyed, loutish, mangled"[52]—in favor of cool colors, unstrenuous facture, and clear outlines. In 1925 Franz Roh compiled a useful table of the differences between Expressionism and its successor movement:

Expressionism	Post-Expressionism
ecstatic objects	plain objects
many religious themes	few religious themes
the stifled object	the explanatory object
rhythmic	representative
arousing	engrossing
dynamic	static
loud	quiet
summary	sustained
obvious	obvious and enigmatic . . .
monumental	miniature
warm	cool to cold
thick coloration	thin layer of color
roughened	smooth, dislodged
like uncut stone	like polished metal
work process preserved	work process effaced
leaving traces	pure objectification
expressive deformation of objects	harmonic cleansing of objects

52. Cited in *The Weimar Republic Sourcebook,* ed. Anton Kaes et al. (Berkeley: University of California Press, 1994), 481.

Expressionism	*Post-Expressionism*
rich in diagonals	rectangular to the frame
often acute-angled	parallel
working against the edges of image	fixed within edges of image
primitive	civilized [53]

The musical equivalent can be found in Paul Hindemith's wind quintet *Kleine Kammermusik,* op. 24 no. 2 (1922), in which the inner workings of the music are completely and cheerfully exposed, like the ductwork of a building without interior walls. Hindemith designed it as *Gebrauchsmusik* — music for everyday use, not a special experience to be approached reverentially or nervously, for music should a part of the normal rhythm of human life: you brush your teeth, you go to work, you get together with friends for some fun with your bassoon. A wind quintet can be crafted with Bauhaus simplicity, elegance, and delight in firmness of line, as opposed to the haunted, broody gothicism of an earlier style.

This sort of object music is not necessarily Neoclassical, in that it may not employ devices typical of the eighteenth century; but it tends to have the same spruce clarity as the music of Bach or Haydn. It is remarkable how equably the Expressionist and the New Objectivist could coexist in Hindemith in the 1920s: at one moment he could write an opera about a mad nun who presses her naked body against a statue of Jesus (*Sancta Susanna,* 1921); at another, an opera about the casual affairs of normal businessmen and the wives, caught in the bathtub or strolling in a museum (*Neues vom Tage,* 1928–29). But this ease of passage between seemingly opposite artistic movements perhaps shows the easy commerce between all forms of technical extremism in art.

3. *Neoromanticism.* This was an art movement associated with Virgil Thomson, the painter Francis Rose, and others — a sort of reaction to Neoclassicism that retained much of the Neoclassicist aesthetic. As Thomson described it, "Neo-Romanticism involves rounded melodic material (the neo-Classicists affected angular themes) and the frank expression of personal sentiments. The neo-Romantic position is an esthetic one purely, because technically we are eclectic. Our contribution to contemporary esthetics has been to pose the problem of sincerity in a new way. We are not out to impress, and we dislike inflated emotions. The feelings we really have are the only ones we think worthy of expression. . . . Sentiment is our subject and sometimes landscape, but preferably a landscape with figures." [54] In the late twentieth century, the term Neoromanticism came to suggest a music that imitated the high emotional saturation of the music of (for

---

53. Ibid., 493.

54. Virgil Thomson, *Possibilities,* 1:1, cited in Kathleen Hoover and John Cage, *Virgil Thomson: His Life and Music* (New York: Thomas Yoseloff, 1959), 250.

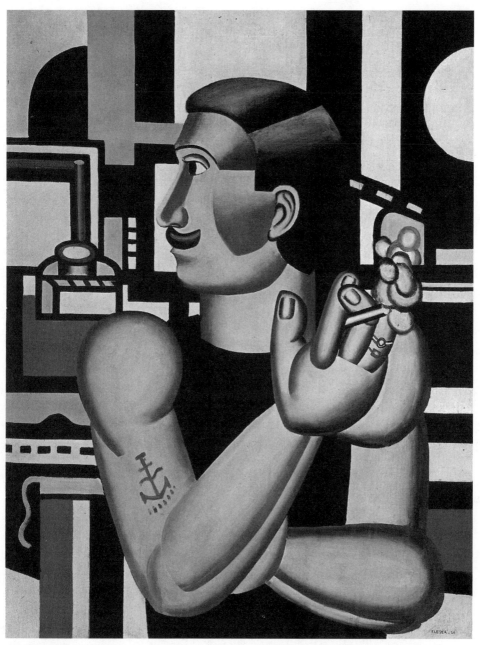

Fernand Léger, *The Mechanic* (1920). © 2002 Artists Rights Society (ARS), New York/ADAGP, Paris.

example) Schumann, but in the 1920s it meant a subdued and modest sort of emotion-alism, in which the excessive gestures of the Expressionists were boiled down into some solid residue of stable feeling.

■ Neoclassicism and the New Objectivity would seem quite remote from Symbolism; and yet they derived part of their force from it. The poet Rainer Maria Rilke (1875–1926), much influenced by the Symbolist movement, worked for a time as the secretary to the sculptor Auguste Rodin, and was much attracted to sculptural precision in verse—in-deed his poetry is governed by rhythms of objectifying and liquidating of intense emo-tion. In "Archaic Torso of Apollo," a fragmentary statue of the god tells the poet, "You must change your life": and Rilke believed that we must discipline ourselves according to the moral imperative of great art—shape our lives, shape our deaths, to strict for-mality. During a period of two weeks in February 1922, Rilke suddenly wrote a long se-ries of *Sonnets to Orpheus;* and in the third sonnet Rilke imagines the god Apollo telling mankind that song is not desire but *being*—a passage that can be taken as a motto of that post-Expressionist music that seeks genuineness not in its conformity to human feelings but in its remoteness from them.

RAINER MARIA RILKE
Sonnets to Orpheus 1.3 (1922)

Ein Gott vermags. Wie aber, sag mir, soll
ein Mann ihm folgend durch die schmale Leier?
Sein Sinn ist Zwiespalt. An der Kreuzung zweier
Herzwege steht kein Tempel für Apoll.

Gesang, wie du ihn lehrst, ist nicht Begehr,
nicht Werbung um ein endlich noch Erreichtes;
Gesang ist Dasein. Für den Gott ein Leichtes.
Wann aber *sind* wir? Und wann wendet *er*

an unser Sein die Erde und die Sterne?
Dies *ists* nicht, Jüngling, daß du liebst, wenn auch
die Stimme dann den Mund dir aufstößt,—lerne

vergessen, daß du aufsangst. Das verrinnt.
In Wahrheit singen, ist ein andrer Hauch.
Ein Hauch um nichts. Ein Wehn im Gott. Ein Wind.

A god can. But say, what shall a man do,
since through the narrow lyre no man can pass?

No temple for Apollo stands at the cross
of two heartways. Man is split in two.

You make him know that song is not burning
desire, nor wooing what at last he'll reach;
Song is being. Easy for a god to teach.
But when will we *be?* When is *he* turning

earth and the stars into our existence?
This *is* not, youth, that you love, even if
your voice shoves your mouth wide open—listen,

singer, forget that you sang out. All's going.
To sing the truth, you need another breath.
Breath about nothing. Wind in the god. Blowing.

From *Sämtliche Werke,* ed. Ruth Sieber-Rilke and Ernst Zinn (Insel-Verlag, 1955), 1:732; translated by the editor.

■

The instigator of Neoclassicism was Igor Stravinsky (1882–1971)—at least according to Stravinsky, for musicologists have made prior claims for Busoni (who wrote an essay, "Junge Klassizität," or "New Classicity," 1920), Prokofiev, Ravel, and others. After Stravinsky's opulent and spectacular ballets just before World War I—*The Firebird* (1910), *Petrushka* (1911), and *The Rite of Spring* (1913)—he experimented with various sorts of reduction of scale, partly because, during and after the war, no one had much money for lavish productions, and partly because he wanted new aesthetic challenges. In 1915 Debussy wrote a suite for two pianos, *En blanc et noir,* one movement of which was dedicated to Stravinsky; and Stravinsky also sought more a linear, black-and-white style, in which the virtues were those of the engraver, not those of the *fauve* colorist.

As early as 1913 Stravinsky was writing pieces (*Three Japanese Lyrics*) almost as abrupt and terse as Webern's. But Webern was led to brevity by the search for concentration in expression; Stravinsky, on the other hand, was moving toward a music that sought to express nothing, music that had something of the flatness and all-overness of modern painting, but had no illustrative content whatsoever. Stravinsky had several strategies for objectifying music: one was a preference for the cool sonorities of wind instruments; another was the method of eliminating the human performer (so likely to add expressive phrasing and emphasis) by composing for the pianola—a player piano operated by compressed air and governed by holes punched on paper rolls. Stravinsky's *Étude for pianola* was first performed in 1921; other composers with a predilection for the objective also experimented with similar devices—Paul Hindemith, for example, composed his *Triadic Ballet* for mechanical organ in 1926.

When Stravinsky published his autobiography in 1936, he made the famous claim that music—not just his music, but all music—lacks any power to express. This desemanticizing of music is, as Stravinsky himself later admitted, a polemical exaggeration— more useful for distinguishing himself from the Expressionism of Schoenberg and his followers than for eliminating the doctrine of expression from the history of music. In his later life Stravinsky stressed the unity of twentieth-century music, the ways in which he and Schoenberg (the twin popes of Modernist music, in Robert Craft's phrase) were engaged in a common enterprise. But the younger Stravinsky needed to carve out space in which his exuberant musical imagination could operate.

Stravinsky's prose reveals many of the same virtues as his music: impudence, learning, wit, high intellectual tension. But it should be remembered that Stravinsky, like Socrates, is an elusive presence, since he wrote almost nothing and depended on a battery of ghostwriters and interviewers to make his opinions known. Still, there is a sense of a distinct personality in Stravinsky's writing, whether the actual writer was Walter Nouvel (author of Stravinsky's autobiography), Alexis Roland-Manuel (author of Stravinsky's *Poetics of Music*), or Robert Craft.

IGOR STRAVINSKY
from *An Autobiography* (1936)

What fascinated me in this [Russian folk] verse was not so much the stories, which were often crude, or the pictures and metaphors, always so deliciously unexpected, as the sequence of words and syllables, and the cadence they create, which produces an effect on one's sensibility very closely akin to that of music. For I consider that music is, by its very nature, essentially powerless to *express* anything at all, whether a feeling, an attitude of mind, a psychological mood, a phenomenon of nature, etc. . . . *Expression* has never been an inherent property of music. That is by no means the purpose of its existence. If, as is nearly always the case, music appears to express something, this is only an illusion and not a reality. It is simply an additional attribute which, by tacit and inveterate agreement, we have lent it, thrust upon it, as a label, a convention—in short, an aspect unconsciously or by force of habit, we have come to confuse with its essential being.

Music is the sole domain in which man realizes the present. By the imperfection of his nature, man is doomed to submit to the passage of time—to its categories of past and future—without ever being able to give substance, and therefore stability, to the category of the present.

The phenomenon of music is given to us with the sole purpose of establishing an order in things, including, and particularly, the coordination between man and time. To be put into practice, its indispensable and single requirement is construction. Construction once completed, this order has been attained, and there is nothing more to be said. It would be futile to look for, or expect anything else from it. It is precisely this construction, this achieved order, which produces in us a unique emotion having nothing in common with our ordinary sensations and our responses to the impressions of daily life. One could not better define the sensation produced by music than by saying that it is identical with that evoked by contemplation of the interplay of architectural forms. Goethe thoroughly understood that when he called architecture petrified music.

From *An Autobiography* (New York: W. W. Norton, 1962), 53–54.

IGOR STRAVINSKY AND ROBERT CRAFT
from *Expositions and Developments* [Expressivity] (1962)

The over-publicized bit about expression (or non-expression) was simply a way of saying that music is supra-personal and super-real and as such beyond verbal meanings and verbal descriptions. It was aimed against the notion that a piece of music is in reality a transcendental idea "expressed in terms of" music, with the *reductio ad absurdum* implication that exact sets of correlatives must exist between a composer's feelings and his notation. It was offhand and annoyingly incomplete, but even the stupider critics could have seen that it did not deny musical expressivity, but only the validity of a type of verbal statement about musical expressivity. I stand by the remark, incidentally, though today I would put it the other way around: music expresses itself.[55]

A composer's work *is* the embodiment of his feelings and, of course, it may be considered as expressing or symbolizing them—though consciousness of this step does not concern the composer. More important is the fact that the composition is something entirely new *beyond* what can be called the composer's feelings. . . . A new piece of music *is* a new reality.

On another level, of course, a piece of music may be "beautiful," "religious," "poetic," "sweet," or as many other expletives as listeners can be found to utter them. All right. But when someone asserts that a composer "seeks to express" an emotion for which the someone then provides a verbal description, that is to debase words *and* music.

From *Expositions and Developments* (Berkeley: University of California Press, 1981), 101–2.

55. Compare Oscar Wilde in "The Decay of Lying" (1891): "Art never expresses anything but itself. . . . It is not necessarily realistic in an age of realism, nor spiritual in an age of faith. So far from being the creation of its time, it is usually in direct opposition to it . . . Sometimes it returns upon its footsteps, and revives some antique form" (*Complete Works of Oscar Wilde* [London: Collins, 1973], 991).

IGOR STRAVINSKY AND ROBERT CRAFT
from *Expositions and Developments* [*Pulcinella*] (1962)

The suggestion that was to lead to *Pulcinella* came from Diaghilev[56] one spring afternoon while we were walking together in the Place de la Concorde: "Don't protest at what I am about to say. . . . I want you to look at some delightful eighteenth-century music with the idea of orchestrating it for a ballet." When he said that the composer was Pergolesi,[57] I thought he must be deranged. I knew Pergolesi only by the *Stabat Mater* and *La Serva Padrona,* and though I had just seen a production of the latter in Barcelona, Diaghilev knew I wasn't in the least excited by it. I did promise to look, however, and to give him my opinion.

I looked, and I fell in love. My ultimate selection of pieces derived only partly from Diaghilev's examples, however, and partly from published editions, but I did play through the whole of the available Pergolesi before making my choices. My first step was to fix a plan of action and an accompanying sequence of pieces. Diaghilev had found a book of Pulcinella stories in Rome. We studied this book together and selected certain episodes.[58] The final construction of the plot and ordering of the dance numbers was the work of Diaghilev, Leonid Massine, and myself, all three of us working together. But the libretto—or argument, for *Pulcinella* is more an *action dansante* than a ballet—does not come from the same source as the texts of the songs; the latter were borrowed from two operas and a cantata. As in *Les Noces,*[59] the singers are not identified with stage characters. They sing "in character" songs—serenades, duets, trios—as interpolated numbers.

Pulcinella was the swan song of my Swiss years. It was composed in a small attic room of the Maison Bornand in Morges, a room crowded by a cimbalom, a piano, a harmonium, and a whole *cuisine* of percussion instruments. I began by composing on the Pergolesi manuscripts themselves, as though I were correcting an old work of my own.

---

56. Serge Diaghilev (1872–1929), impresario of the Ballets Russes, whose taste helped shape the whole Modernist movement.

57. Giovanni Battista Pergolesi (1710–36), whose best-known works are the comic intermezzo *La serva padrona* (1733) and the Stabat Mater (1736). Because of his popularity and his early death, publishers forged his name to many works he didn't write, including a number that found their way into *Pulcinella.*

58. This account of the composition of the ballet is not altogether true. See Richard Taruskin, *Stravinsky and the Russian Traditions: A Biography of the Works through "Mavra,"* 2 vols. (Berkeley: University of California Press, 1996), 2:1463–65. There Taruskin also provides an up-to-date list of the sources of the borrowings or thefts in *Pulcinella.*

59. *Les noces* (or *Svadebka* [*Little Wedding*], 1915–23) is a ballet for chorus and an orchestra of four pianos and percussion, in which a peasant wedding in enacted in a manner at once hieratic and Dionysian. The solo singers are not identified with particular characters, but keep switching roles.

I began without preconceptions or aesthetic attitudes, and I could not have predicted anything about the result. I knew that I could not produce a "forgery" of Pergolesi because my motor habits are so different; at best, I could repeat him in my own accent. That the result was to some extent a satire was probably inevitable—who could have treated that material in 1919 without satire?—but even this observation is hindsight; I did not set out to compose a satire and, of course, Diaghilev hadn't even considered the possibility of such a thing. A stylish orchestration was what Diaghilev wanted, and nothing more, and my music so shocked him that he went about for a long time with a look that suggested The Offended Eighteenth Century. In fact, however, the remarkable thing about *Pulcinella* is not how much but how little has been added or changed.

If I had an *a priori* conception of the problems involved in re-composing an eighteenth-century work it was that I should somehow have to convert operatic and concert pieces into dance pieces. I therefore began to look through Pergolesi for "rhythmic" rather than "melodic" numbers. I did not go far, of course, before discovering that this distinction does not exist. Whether instrumental or vocal, whether sacred or secular, eighteenth-century music is, in one sense, all dance music. Performance tradition ignores this. For example, in the famous recording of an eminent conductor rehearsing the *Linz* Symphony,[60] he is continually heard inviting the orchestra to "sing," while he never reminds it to "dance." The result of this is that the music's simple melodic content is burdened with a thick-throated late-nineteenth-century sentiment that it cannot bear, while the rhythmic movement remains turgid.

Pulcinella was my discovery of the past, the epiphany through which the whole of my late work became possible. It was a backward look, of course—the first of many love affairs in that direction—but it was a look in the mirror, too. No critic understood this at the time, and I was therefore attacked for being a *pasticheur,* chided for composing "simple" music, blamed for deserting "modernism," accused of renouncing my "true Russian heritage." People who had never heard of, or cared about, the originals cried "sacrilege": "The classics are ours. Leave the classics alone." To them all my answer was and is the same: You "respect," but I love.

Picasso accepted the commission to design the décor for the same reason that I agreed to arrange the music—for the fun of it—and Diaghilev was as shocked with his set as he was with my sounds. Picasso's stage was a volumetric view of balconied, Spanish-style houses. It filled only a part of the huge stage of the Paris Opéra and it was described by its own frame, rather than by that of the Opéra. The costumes were simple. Six Pulcinellas appear in the course of the ballet.[61] They were all dressed in

---

60. *Linz* Symphony: by Mozart, in C, K. 425 (1784).

61. The plot of the ballet concerns four young men who, jealous of Pulcinella's success with women, dress up in Pulcinella costumes; they intend to give a beating to the original Pulcinella to remove him

baggy, white costumes, with red stockings. The women wore black corselets and red, candy-stripe shirts with black fringes and red pompoms.

When musicians talk among themselves about the masterpieces of their art, a moment always comes when someone will demonstrate what he means by singing it; i.e., instead of saying, "three quavers of G followed by a minim E flat," he will sing the opening of Beethoven's Fifth. The limits of criticism could hardly be better defined. I, too, would rather "sing" *Pulcinella* than try to talk about it.

From *Expositions and Developments* (Berkeley: University of California Press, 1981),, 111–14.

IGOR STRAVINSKY AND ROBERT CRAFT
from *Dialogues* (1968)

STRAVINSKY	SCHOENBERG
1. Reaction against "German music" or "German romanticism." No "*Sehnsucht,*" no "*ausdrucksvoll.*"[62]	"Today I have discovered something which will assure the supremacy of German music for the hundred years." Schoenberg, July 1921.
2. Fox[63] (eclectic and abundant variety). (Aron)	Hedgehog. (Moses)
3. "Music is powerless to express anything at all."	"Music expresses all that dwells in us . . ."
4. Chief production is of ballets.	"Ballet is not a musical form."
5. Learns from others, a lifelong need for outside nourishment and a constant confluence with new influences. Never a teacher. No writing about musical theory.	An autodidact. After the early works, no influence from other composers. Also a teacher. Large amount of writing on musical theory. His philosophy of teaching is "Genius learns only from itself; talent from others. Genius learns from its own nature; talent learns from art."

from competition, but in fact beat a fifth double, who seems to die; then the original Pulcinella, disguised as a magician, pretends to revive the fifth double from the dead; all ends happily, with multiple marriages.

62. *Sehnsucht:* yearning; *ausdrucksvoll:* expressive.

63. Fox and hedgehog refer to categories popularized by Isaiah Berlin, based on a Greek proverb: "The fox knows many small things, the hedgehog knows one big thing." Aron and Moses are characters in Schoenberg's opera *Moses und Aron* (1930–32): Aron is slippery and compromising, Moses stern and unbending.

6. Composes only at the piano.	Never composes at the piano.
7. Composes every day, regularly, like a man with banking hours. Hardly a scrap unfinished or unused.	Composed fitfully, at lightning speed, and in the heat of inspiration. Therefore, many unfinished works.
8. Remote-in-time subjects: *The Rake's Progress*.[64]	Contemporary subjects (protest music): *Survivor from Warsaw*.[65]
9. Metronomic strictness, no *rubato*.[66] Ideal is of mechanical regularity (Octuor, Piano Concerto,[67] etc.).	Much use of *rubato*.
10. Diatonicism.	Chromaticism.
11. *Secco*. Scores contain minimum of expression marks.	*Espressivo*. Scores full of expression marks.
12. Prefers spare, two-part counterpoint.	Preferred dense eight-part counterpoint (the choruses, op. 35; the *Genesis Prelude* canon).[68]
13. "What the Chinese philosopher says cannot be separated from the fact that he says it in Chinese." (Preoccupation with manner and style.)	"A Chinese philosopher speaks Chinese, but what does he say?" ("What is *style?*")

A parlour game, no more, and in any case the parallelisms are more interesting. For example:

1. The common belief in Divine Authority, the Hebrew God and Biblical mythology, Catholic culture.

---

64. Stravinsky's opera *The Rake's Progress* (1951), with text by W. H. Auden and Chester Kallman, is a moral fable drawn from eighteenth-century pictures by William Hogarth.

65. *A Survivor from Warsaw* (1947), Schoenberg's harrowing six-minute melodrama concerning Nazi brutality to Jews.

66. *tempo rubato*: stolen time, that is, a lilting prolongation of one note at the expense of another.

67. These are Neoclassical works: the Octet for Winds (1922–23) and the Concerto for Piano and Winds (1923–24).

68. Schoenberg's Six Pieces for Male Chorus (1929–30); and prelude to the *Genesis Suite* (1945)— this suite to illustrate the Bible was commissioned by Nat Schilkret, who also obtained a piece from Stravinsky (*Babel*).

2. The success obstacle of the first pieces, *Verklärte Nacht* and *The Firebird*,[69] which remained the most popular of all our works, all our lives and after.

3. The common exile to the same alien culture, in which we wrote some of our best works (his Fourth Quartet, my *Abraham and Isaac*)[70] and in which we are still played far less than in the Europe that exiled us.

4. Both family men and fathers of several children, both hypochondriac, both deeply superstitious.

5. For both of us, numbers are things.

6. Both of us were devoted to The Word, and each wrote some of his own librettos (*Moses und Aron, Die glückliche Hand, Jacobsleiter, Les Noces, Renard*).[71]

7. Each of us composed for concrete sounds, unlike the later Webern, in which choice of sound is a final stage.

8. For both of us, the row is thematic and we are ultimately less interested in the construction of the row, *per se,* than is Webern.

From *Dialogues* (Berkeley: University of California Press, 1982), 105–7.

IGOR STRAVINSKY AND ROBERT CRAFT
from *Themes and Conclusions* (1969)

Mr. Auden's recent thoughts on opera, *Words and Notes* (Festungsverlag Salzburg, 1968), include a number of distinctions between the requirements of libretti and those of spoken drama, all well worth [considering], at any rate by aspirants to the librettist's art. Even more valuable, however, is a distinction, expressed in terms of grammatical function, concerning the nature of music itself. Thus he says that in contrast to the actors in a naturalistic stage drama, "the singers in an opera address themselves primarily to the audience." Whether they *do* anymore, on the *surface* level, is of course debatable, but "address" is meant in the largest sense, the sense in which "All musical statements are intransitive, in the First Person, singular or plural, and in the Present

---

69. Schoenberg's string sextet (later arranged for string orchestra) *Verklärte Nacht* (*Transfigured Night,* 1899); Stravinsky's ballet for Diaghilev *The Firebird* (1910).

70. Schoenberg's Fourth String Quartet (1937) and Stravinsky's sacred ballad *Abraham and Isaac* (1962–63) were both written in southern California.

71. Schoenberg based the text of his opera *Moses und Aron* (1930–32) on Exodus; his opera *Die glückliche Hand* (*The Lucky Touch,* 1910–13) is an original fable about the terror and ecstasy of artistic inspiration; his oratorio *Die Jakobsleiter* (1917–22) concerns the levels of enlightenment available in heaven to the dead. Stravinsky's choral ballet *Les noces* (1915–23), and his burlesque in song and dance *Renard* (*Bayka,* 1915–16), have texts assembled by Stravinsky from folk sources.

Indicative."[72] Music, in other words, is for everyone and no one, and it is always in the Present Tense. And Mr. Auden establishes his grammatical classification by comparing music to poetry, which does not have these limits, and should not, in his opinion, seek them. The attempt of the *Symbolistes* "to make poetry as intransitive as music," could get no farther, he says, than a "narcissistic reflexive."

But music's intransitiveness is also proven by the circumstance that "We may sing a tune without words, or a song where the notes are associated with words, but when we *feel* like singing, the notes will always seem the more important element." (My italics.) And does the qualification, "when we *feel* like singing," not say, as I would say, that the words even of the Ninth Symphony can be reduced to nonsense without affecting the meaning of the music?

From *Themes and Conclusions* (Berkeley: University of California Press, 1982), 289–90.

■

If Stravinsky was somewhat uneasy about Schoenberg, Schoenberg was also uneasy about Stravinsky—especially the Neoclassical Stravinsky. In the foreword to his *Three Satires* (1925), Schoenberg notes that the targets of his gibes include those composers who refuse to challenge the listener; academic composers; and those backward-pointing people who try to renew the tonic and the dominant. But it is not hard to see that his particular target is the "little Modernsky," Igor Stravinsky.

ARNOLD SCHOENBERG
from *Three Satires* (1925)
> "Versatility"
> Well, who's drumming over there?
> That's the little Modernsky!
> He's got a cute haircut;
> Looks good!

72. "In verbal speech one can say *I love you*. Music can, I believe, express the equivalent of *I love*, but it is incapable of saying whom or what I love, you, God, or the decimal system. In this respect it is at the opposite pole of the language of painting. A painting can portray someone as beautiful, lovable, etc. but it cannot say who, if anybody, loves this person. Music, one might say, is always intransitive and in the first person; painting has only one voice, the passive, and only the third person singular or plural. Both of them, also have only the present indicative tense, and no negative. For this reason, it makes no sense to ask of a piece of music or a painting: Does the composer or the painter mean what he says, or is he just pretending?" (W. H. Auden, *Secondary Worlds* [New York: Random House, 1968], 91). Stravinsky wishes to remove still more of the semantic component of music, to leave music still more incapable of expression.

Like genuine false hair!
Like a wig!
Just like (as the little Modernsky conceives him),
Just like Papa Bach!

"The New Classicism"
I won't be Romantic any more,
I hate Romantic;
Starting tomorrow I write
Only purest Classic!
The might of the ages
Has no effect on the composer
—See Riemann!—[73]
Who obeys the laws of art
To the letter.
Letters, for those who can learn them!
I'm astonished, how quickly the transformation:
between today and tomorrow
it's possible to possess perfection of form!

From Arnold Schönberg, *Sämtliche Werke*, Abteilung V: *Chorwerke*, Reihe B, Bd. 18, 2: *Chorwerke I*, ed. Tadeusz Okuljar and Dorothee Schubel (Mainz: Schott Musik International, 1996), 117–18; translated by the editor.

■

After having set the fashion for using modish technology with his *Jonny spielt auf* (1927)—an aggressively modern opera full of railroad trains, loudspeakers, and jazz— Ernst Krenek (1900–91) wrote a thoughtful essay in which he distinguished his opera (in which technological appliances are, he claims, only stage props, secondary to the human interest of the drama) from a genuinely dehumanized, thing-glorifying sort of art for which the term New Objectivity might be more appropriate. (Perhaps the economically depressed world of the 1930s made Krenek less optimistic about the future that technology promised.) The essay begins with some speculations about a crisis in art: Krenek believes that the artists of the early twentieth century are handicapped by the incoherence of European culture (the fact that artists are geographically and intellectually scattered) and by the absence of a live tradition, such as that of Renaissance artists, who could paint

73. Hugo Riemann (1849–1919), the same conservative critic who so vexed Reger in an extract printed in chapter 5 of this anthology. The 1916 edition of his encyclopedia of music spoke ill of Schoenberg's *Harmonielehre*.

and repaint images of the Madonna. The Modernist period, then, is no Golden Age. In the passage cited here, Krenek meditates on the role of technology in art, at a time when commercial success seems the main criterion of excellence.

Appended at the end is an excerpt from Krenek's "Music and Mathematics" (1937), in which Krenek toys with the notion of an axiomatics of music, as if a musical composition could be constructed on scientifically irrefutable foundations—a profoundly New Objectivist dream, which would seem to leave little room for the humanity Krenek espoused in 1931.

ERNST KRENEK
from "New Humanity and Old Objectivity" (1931)

The telegraph and telephone make it possible to hear an enormous amount enormously quickly about an enormous number of things, and this fact undoubtedly creates a situation where people do so, and the damage is already done. Once the idea of quantity, as a virtue, becomes rooted in culture (and applied science undoubtedly brings this in its train), it spreads like dry-rot and increases by feeding on itself incessantly. If people know they can know everything, they immediately want to know more. The press puts itself at the service of this news-apparatus, and floods the defenseless public with information. Intellectual inventions, wrung from the imagination with great effort, naturally have very little news value. Probably the best-known fact about the theory of relativity, the fact that has made the most impact, is that Einstein[74] plays the violin; this after all, is hard news.

Nowadays the radio fills in the gap between the morning and evening newspaper so that there is not a moment of silence in which anyone might become conscious of a void. . . .

The truth of the matter is that every society has its art, and the aristocrats of pre-revolutionary Germany had Beethoven because they valued intellect and perhaps even had some themselves. I am not saying that as a class they understood Beethoven, even approximately, or could have met him on an equal footing intellectually, but they valued what he did enough to spend time and money on it. Today this social class no longer exists; instead we have the general public and that procures what it wants to spend its time and money on. But since its aim is to be economical with both, the goods it gets are correspondingly low in value.

Now the really essential question arises: is it possible for art to go along with this

74. The physicist Albert Einstein (1879–1955) was an amateur violinist, and even premièred Martinů's (not difficult) *Five Madrigal Stanzas* (1943). His enjoyment of the violin was to provide a motive in the Philip Glass opera *Einstein on the Beach* (1976), shortly after Einstein appeared as a tool of capitalist tyranny in Paul Dessau's opera *Einstein* (1974).

social change? The answer is bound to be no. . . . It is well known that in a majority, the standard is always set by the lowest and never by the highest, for the level is a line common to all and that is always the bottom line, not the top one.

Despite this state of affairs, attempts have recently been made, and more will be made in the future, to create an art, particularly an art of the musical theatre, which will fit the enlarged society as earlier art fitted the limited society—in other words to find a basis for an art that the general public could enter into and assimilate. In this connection I must mention my own efforts. They consisted mainly of including some parts of the rhythmic and harmonic elements of jazz in my works. The motives that led me to this now strike me as twofold. Firstly I thought that by using the jazz elements I might hit on an atmosphere which would fit the collective feeling of the age. As jazz music in practice enjoyed undisputed mastery and general validity, it seemed conceivable that from it one might derive an artistic means that after all belonged to the sphere of music, and so was capable of the most serious and intellectual development, while at the same time having a natural place in the life of modern man. This, I felt, might give me the possibility of saying something generally valid.

The second consideration was an internal musical one. As must be fairly well known, there has been a complete disruption of musical systems of organization along with the democratic opening-up of the conventions of life. At first, atonality, which tried to replace these systems, extended the range of musical means to infinity, theoretically at least, so that today there is really nothing that is musically "impossible." Every conceivable harmonic combination can be produced at any time, without special preparation, and a new organization from this quarter is not to be hoped for. So far, atonality has not proved particularly suitable for versatile dramatic presentation and in the circumstances jazz, with its stereotyped harmonic and rhythmic elements, seemed an effective protection against the ineffectual ubiquity of all musical possibilities, because it offered a sort of new convention. But there was never any idea, least of all in my mind, of its being a complete substitute for every other kind of expressive world; only if that were successfully achieved would the product really deserve the name of "jazz opera." In my attempt, as in all the others I know of, jazz was only alluded to at the points demanded by the action; apart from this the harmony was colored by its elements, thus guaranteeing the homogeneity of the whole and justifying the way I had deliberately limited the means—a protection against atonality.

Looking back on the results, one is bound to be aware that works of this kind were only connected with the general public "atmospherically"—that is, by being reminiscent of the familiar pop-style—while their real artistic value remained irrelevant and obscure. Nevertheless it must be admitted that in this sphere the good is still usually more successful than the inferior, while just the reverse seems to be true of operetta, for example. The amazement and agitation I caused by showing a station and having somebody telephone on the stage have since died down, and there is not much point now in going into the programmatic interpretations people read into these things. There have always been naturalistic operas, and the props, if they are no more than that, are probably the least important symptoms of an attitude of mind. From any moderately reasonable point of view, my *Jonny spielt auf* is one of the unhappiest examples to quote in connection with Neue Sachlichkeit, "new objectivity," for although new objects occur in it they do so only as objects surrounding present-day people, without proclaiming any positive attitude concerning them. Nobody prays to the engine or lauds the virtues of the telephone; these things merely play a subordinate, functional role as props needed by the action, and there is no more reason why a present-day work should do without them than why a drama taking place in the past should do without the modern props of that age.

But there are other efforts along these lines which must be taken much more seriously; in them the essential thing is not just using daily objects for personal reasons, as in *Jonny spielt auf,* but assenting to everyday aims as such. Of course it is true that anything can be made into artistic material, but it is essential that the object should stand in a dynamic relationship to man. The object must release a feeling;[75] to apply this to the complicated conditions of a theatrical process, the object must be an obvious vehicle of dramatic movement within the course of an emotional pattern translated into action. For example, the fact that there is a telephone means absolutely nothing artistically; however intensely the instrument is accepted, as it may be by many people, this cannot give any occasion for artistic creation. For even if you wanted to address a poem to the telephone you would have no choice but to gear it to man's use of the machine, its position in man's life; and to get the emotional content needed for the poem you would have to examine whether and how the fact of telephoning plays a part in the expression of man's inner life. Description alone is not enough, and even a list of all the component parts of an aeroplane would not add up to a Homeric epic.

On the stage the telephone can only be used as a prop, a characteristic feature of a milieu, as stage-coaches, distaffs, shepherds' crooks, spears and swords were features of other milieus, and no one milieu is *a priori* better than another. Nothing further can be derived from this—no theory, no aesthetic position, no dogma, nothing to gladden the heart of the philistine thirsting for knowledge. But the Neue Sachlichkeit I have criticized puts the prop in the center of the picture and so reflects the situation described

---

75. Compare T. S. Eliot in 1919: "The only way of expressing emotion in the form of art is by finding an "objective correlative"; in other words, a set of objects, a situation, a chain of events which shall be the formula of that *particular* emotion; such that when the external facts, which must terminate in sensory experience, are given, the emotion is immediately evoked" (*Selected Essays* [New York: Harcourt, Brace and World, 1960], 124–25).

above—the fact that the technical devices created by man have long since become ends in themselves and reduced their erstwhile masters to servitude. Instead of machines serving us silently and exactly, and setting us free to find ourselves more quickly and easily, they get in our way and themselves become the monuments they have destroyed, for which we have such an ineradicable taste. The divine in man has been replaced by the fact that he can travel faster than a bird flies; and in the advertisements, the inventor of a new kind of engine rivals the creator of the world.

We now have the "rhythm of the age" and so know all the less about the rhythms of music; we are bored to death with the "tempo of the age," but nobody is allowed to fall behind. Now I conceive of a work of art as the intellectual form of an emotional content, and so can see little point in an art which rejects emotion as too human and not mechanical enough, and intellect as too exhausting. However, the "easiness" of an object is one of the first conditions of its intrinsic value in this age. As I indicated, we are dealing with a race of overworked and distrait consumers. . . .

This "new objectivity" has led to another, equally doubtful venture in the specific field of music. I mean the musical guilds and societies with their amateur music and Gebrauchsmusik. This is a predominantly German movement which sees, quite correctly, that today there is no society as a culture-medium for music, and so is trying to use the "general public," as I call it, as a culture-medium instead. Its promoters are rightly trying to build up a new amateur-structure, but unfortunately they are doing it by trying to get down to the sunken level of present-day people. In other words, this is another attempt to combat the "de-animation" of life on the ground of that very de-animation, and to compete with the "convenience" of present-day objects. The error is that in the cultural field one does not have to compete in convenience—only in love, talent and effort. Imagine trying to write music so easy to play that even a distrait, overworked and unimaginative consumer feels inclined to buy! . . .

Nothing has really been done about meeting the spirit of the age, in any of these ways. If earlier art epochs fitted the spirit of their ages, it was because age and spirit were not such opposites as they now are. I am not trying to advocate any one trend, or condemn any other, because really there are no trends. We know that the truly great works of every age are essentially alike, whatever historical "movement" we neatly fit them into on the grounds of their equipment or some unimportant individual traits. Just as Expressionism, as a movement, perished because of the daubers who thought every ill-splashed canvas was an example of abstract painting, so Neue Sachlichkeit is dying of the support given by those who believe that every postcard is a work of art, that writing a drama consists merely of setting four out of five scenes in a brothel and filling them with the coarser swear-words. Fortunately a new movement will soon emerge and then we shall see that the good works of this period are still good even if nobody knows that they were once supposed to be Neue Sachlichkeit, or why.

It is humanity, directness, uniqueness, the originality of the experience that make a work of art, not the subject-matter, or the intention behind it, or the artist's attitude to an ephemeral public. "Objectivity" is a process but not something to express, and to this extent every art, however Romantic, is "objective" if it is good. For if so, it aims at expressing itself clearly, and this is the essential thing about every usable artistic method, whatever intellectual purpose it may be devoted to; in so far as any art attains this clarity it may be called "objective." Consequently I would like to mention the old Sachlichkeit, the good old Sachlichkeit of Sophocles and Goethe, Shakespeare and Novalis,[76] Monteverdi and Schubert. And humanity, in the work of art the fact that it centers on man and the things that always affect him—love, faith, hope, passion, intellect, grace—this humanity should only be new because we of today have to recapture it anew. The battle of the spirit cannot be settled on the level of the inanimate object.

From *Exploring Music: Essays by Ernst Krenek,* trans. Margaret Shenfield and Geoffrey Skelton (New York: October House, 1966), 49–50, 53–60.

ERNST KRENEK
from "Music and Mathematics" (1937)

In this general form [i.e., sound as a symbol of spiritual reality] our engagement of music with mathematics touches on the domain of the so-called *axiomatics*. By that term we understand that sort of mathematical science which proves that no absolute validity is attained from the systems of arithmetic and geometry, but that validity depends on determinate presuppositions which are set down in axioms. An axiom is usually defined as a proposition that is true and whose truth is immediately evident, but that cannot be proved—moreover on account of its certainty it does not need to be proved. To my mind the shedding of new light in this area is one of the most magnificent results of modern mathematics, and I can never reread the crucial sentences of the first section of David Hilbert's *Foundations of Geometry* (Leipzig 1922)[77] without the characteristic trembling, aroused by encountering fundamental knowledge. Hilbert says: "We think of three different systems of things: the things of the first system we call points and denominate with A, B, C . . . ; the things of the second system we call lines and denominate with a, b, c . . . ; the things of the third system we call planes and denominate with α, β, γ. . . . We think of points, lines, and planes in certain reciprocal relations and denominate these relations through words such as 'lie,' 'between,' 'paral-

76. Novalis, pseudonym of the German Romantic poet Friedrich von Hardenberg (1772–1801), whose "Hymns of Night" influenced the rhetoric of Wagner's *Tristan und Isolde.*

77. The mathematician David Hilbert (1862–1943) hoped to devise a set of axioms sufficient to generate the whole of mathematics, but Kurt Gödel proved that this was impossible.

lel,' 'congruent,' 'constant'; the exact and for mathematical purposes complete description of these relations results through the axioms of geometry."

... For long enough, music has been considered an impenetrable terra incognita, whose border zones stand at the disposal of the advances of physics and psychology, as desired. Yet it is necessary to fetch music back into the zone of pure thought which is appropriate to its worth, and which alone grounds its worth. Only we must make no mistake and not lose ourselves in fantastic fabulations, in vague similes and metaphors, if we are to make the category of musical thought precise. At first glance one thinks that there could be no common ground between the seemingly thin, sober, insubstantial, and prickly object of mathematical thinking and the elemental exuberance from which music's being streams forth. But the common ground rests just in that category of thought. When Hilbert says, "We *think* of three different systems of things: the things of the first system we call points," etc., he very clearly differentiates the two acts of thinking and of name-giving. . . . According to this presupposition we now say, very approximately: "We think of three systems of things, the things of the first system we call notes, the things of the second we call chords, the things of the third we call melodies. We think of these systems in different relations, which we denominate with words such as 'interval,' 'consonance,' 'dissonance,' 'motion,' 'inversion' and others. In this way the autonomy of music is usefully pronounced."

From *Über neue Musik: Sechs Vorlesungen zu Einführung in die Theoretischen Grundlagen* (Darmstadt: Wissenschaftliche Buchgesellschaft, 1977), 82–83; translated by the editor.

■

Perhaps the most stinging of all rebukes to Neoclassicism came from Constant Lambert (1905–51). Lambert was a man of paradoxes: he detested Gershwin for attempting to add jazz elements to classical forms, but Lambert's most popular composition, *The Rio Grande* (1927), is a wild cantata in which a jazz pianist makes frequent interjections. Lambert often railed against the morbid, even gangrenous quality of twentieth-century music, and yet his own music was fascinated with disease: perhaps his most sustained effort is *Summer's Last Will and Testament* (1935), an evocation of plague.

His book *Music Ho! A Study of Music in Decline* (1936), from which the following excerpts are taken, is a brilliant polemic against the fetishizing of style that he found in the work of Stravinsky; and yet Lambert's diagnosis of the "disease" is so acutely rendered that, with a few changes of minus signs to plus signs, the book could be a panegyric to what we now call Postmodernism. It is instructive, for example, to compare Lambert's curses against pastiche with the recent comments of the literary critic Fredric Jameson, himself uneasy about the late-capitalist aspects of Postmodernism:

Pastiche is, like parody, the imitation of a peculiar or unique, idiosyncratic style, the wearing of a linguistic mask, speech in a dead language. But it is a neutral practice of such mimicry, without any of parody's ulterior motives, amputated of the satiric impulse, devoid of laughter and of any conviction that alongside the abnormal tongue you have momentarily borrowed, some healthy linguistic normality still exists. Pastiche is thus blank parody, a statue with blind eyeballs: it is to parody what that other interesting and historically original modern thing, the practice of a kind of blank irony, is to what Wayne Booth calls the "stable ironies" of the eighteenth century.[78]

This paragraph constitutes, in effect, Stravinsky's rejoinder against Lambert: if all music is based on arbitrary convention, then an overstressing of the conventional aspects of musical composition is a form of deference to music's true nature.

CONSTANT LAMBERT
"The Age of Pastiche" (1934)

To describe the present age in music as one of pastiche may seem a sweeping generalization but, like the description of the Impressionist period as one of disruption, it is a generalization with a strong basis in fact. There are many contemporary composers of note who stand to some extent outside this classification . . . but the dominant characteristic of post-war music is either pastiche or an attempted consolidation that achieves only pastiche.

Pastiche has existed in music for many years, but it is only since the war that it has taken the place of development and experiment. In the nineteenth century a number of minor composers turned out suites in the olden style, but these mild pièces d'occasion no more affected the main course of music than an Olde Worlde Bunne Shoppe affects the architectural experiments of Corbusier and Mallet-Stevens.[79] Apart from these studio pieces, pastiche has always existed in the form of stage decoration as, for example, the Mozartean divertissement in Tchaikovsky's *Queen of Spades*,[80] or the music offstage in the second act of Puccini's *Tosca*. It need hardly be pointed out, though, that these touches of dramatic color indicated no change of heart on the part of the composer. Tchaikovsky did not write symphonies modeled on Haydn any more than Puccini set out to imitate Rossini or Mercadante.[81]

78. Fredric Jameson, *Postmodernism; or The Cultural Logic of Late Capitalism* (Durham, N.C.: Duke University Press, 1991), 17.

79. Le Corbusier (Charles Jeanneret-Gris, 1887–1965) and Robert Mallet-Stevens (1886–1945), French Modernist architects.

80. The main theme of Tchaikovsky's divertissement seems to be the Papageno-ish theme from Mozart's Piano Concerto in C, K. 503 (1786).

81. Saverio Mercadante (1795–1870), Italian composer of operas and chamber music.

The deliberate and serious use of pastiche, not as a curiosity or as a pièce d'occasion but as a chosen medium for self-expression, is the property of the post-war period alone. The idea that music of an earlier age can be better than the music of one's own is an essentially modern attitude. The Elizabethans did not tire of their conceits and go back to the sweet simplicity of Hucbald,[82] any more than the late Caroline composers deserted the new and airy Italian style for the grave fantasias of Dowland.[83] Burney's *History of Music*[84] is an astonishing example of the complete satisfaction with its own period so typical of the eighteenth century. To him the earlier composers were only of interest as stepping stones to the glorious and unassailable music of his own day. Passages in the earlier music which do not display the smoothness of texture that the eighteenth century looked on as technical perfection were dismissed as crudities due to lack of taste and skill. The nineteenth century was to carry this smug attitude one stage further. The eighteenth-century masters were admired not so much for their own sake as for being precursors of the romantic school which through its sheer position in time was naturally an improvement. Once Beethoven's Symphonies were accepted they were considered as being superior to Mozart's in the way that a six-cylinder car is preferred to a four-cylinder car, or a talking to a silent film. Schumann, it is true, admired Scarlatti,[85] but with a touch of the patronage displayed by a Lady Bountiful visiting the village, and Clara Schumann[86] simply could not understand how Brahms could take any interest in composers earlier than Bach. Wagner's followers did not look upon *The Ring* as a way of writing operas that was different from Bellini's,[87] but as a way that clearly was a much better one.

Even in the early twentieth century, when the attitude towards music of a past age was broader and more cultured, showing at times a certain humility, the direction taken, not only by composers but by the public and the critics, was progressive in the mechanical sense of the word. Those who were swept off their feet by Strauss and, later, by Scriabin—and they included some of our most levelheaded critics—thought nothing of referring to Mozart as a snuffbox composer in comparison with these cosmic masters; and it is clear that the more fervent admirers of Debussy and Stravinsky regarded their music as not only a reaction against Wagner, but as the death of Wagner.

That is not to say that music until the present has proceeded in a mechanical series

---

82. Hucbald (ca. 840–930), French monk who wrote a treatise on music.

83. John Dowland (1563–1626), English lutenist and composer, famously melancholic.

84. Dr. Charles Burney (1726–1814) wrote a four-volume *History of Music* (1776–89), for which he did extensive research in Europe.

85. Domenico Scarlatti (1685–1757), Italo-Spanish composer of harpsichord sonatas.

86. Clara Wieck Schumann (1819–96), virtuoso pianist and composer, wife of Robert.

87. Vincenzo Bellini (1801–35), who composed operas in the sinuously melodic *bel canto* style.

of reactions. It is not until Stravinsky that a new movement in music is held to have automatically wiped out all traces of the preceding one (of which the wretched followers,
like Babylonian courtiers, are forcibly immolated on the tomb of their master). . . .

Revolutionary, in fact, is an unsuitable word with which to describe the experimental periods of past ages. The revolutionaries of the seventeenth century were hardy pioneers who struck out boldly across undiscovered plains and cultivated the virgin soil.
The revolutionaries of today are no more hardy than the man who takes a ticket on the
Inner Circle, and is at liberty to travel in either direction, knowing that eventually he will
arrive at the station which the fashion of the day has decreed to be the center of the
town. The modern musical revolutions are revolutions in the meanest sense of the
word—the mere turning of a stationary wheel. A great deal of pre-war music, may have
sounded, to use a dear old phrase, "like nothing on earth," but that at least is a negative merit from the revolutionaries' point of view. Most music of today sounds only too
reminiscent of something that has previously been in existence.

Comparison to an earlier composer, at one time a well-known form of musician-
baiting, is now come to be a delicate compliment. If you had told Wagner that you admired his operas because they were "like" Cimarosa[88] he would probably have kicked
you out of the house. . . .

But today every composer's overcoat has its corresponding hook in the cloakroom
of the past. Stravinsky's concertos (we have it on his own authority) are "like" Bach and
Mozart. . . . The composer can no longer pride himself on being true to himself—he can
only received the pale reflected glory of being true to whichever past composer is cred-
ited at the moment with having possessed the Elixir of Life. . . .

Unlike the experimental period of the seventeenth century the pre-war period has
led to a psychological cul-de-sac. There are many explanations of this, of which the
most convincing is a simple and practical one. By 1913 music had already reached the
absolute limit of complication allowed by the capacity of composers, players, listeners
and instrument makers. With very few exceptions in detail—such as the piano writing
of Sorabji,[89] the polytonal choral writing of Milhaud and the quarter-tone writing of
Aloys Haba—there is nothing in present-day music more complicated from any point of
view than what we find in the music of twenty years ago. The composer is now faced,
not with further experiment but with the more difficult task of consolidating the experiments of this vertiginous period. He is like a man in a high-powered motor car that has
got out of control. He must either steer it back to the road, or leap out of it altogether.

---

88. Domenico Cimarosa (1749–1801), best known for comic operas in a somewhat Mozartean style.

89. Kaikhosru Shapurji Sorabji (1892–1988), composer of sonorous and intricate piano music on
a grand scale.

Most modern composers have chosen the latter plan, remarking as they dexterously save their precious lives, "I think motor cars are a little *vieux jeu* [old hat]—don't you?"

There is an obvious end to the amount of purely physical experiment in music, just as there is an obvious end to geographic exploration. Wyndham Lewis[90] has pointed out that when speed and familiarity have reduced traveling in space to the level of the humdrum, those in search of the exotic will have to travel in time; and this is what has already happened in music.

From *Music Ho! A Study of Music in Decline* (New York: Charles Scribner's Sons, 1936), 63–68.

CONSTANT LAMBERT
[Stravinsky as Pasticheur] (1934)

In *Renard*[91] the obsession with rhythmic jigsaw puzzles is still tinged with the old national color, though the Russian folk dance is by now no long a live and kicking peasant but a dead kulak whose corpse is material for a lecture by the dissecting surgeon. . . . By the time we reach *L'Histoire du Soldat,*[92] written in 1918, the remnant of vitality provided by the Russian folk song is gone, and the material used is less picturesque and more international. The Russian folk dance gives way to the pasodoblé of the street band, the polka of the musical box, and the valse of the mechanical piano. The constant rhythmic changes, which had some logic when applied to the asymmetrical line of the Russian folk song, acquire a new perversity when attached to the left-right-left and the one-two-three-hop of the wooden soldiers' march and the baby's polka. The valse, ragtime and tango which the soldier plays on his violin are not parodies like the polkas of Walton and Berners,[93] nor are they meant to have the René Clair[94]-like evocative significance, the bal-musette sentimentality of the valses of Auric.[95] They are like the familiar objects, the bottle of wine, the guitar, and the pack of cards used by the Cubist painters because their very familiarity would draw added attention to their geometrical

90. Wyndham Lewis (1882–1957), English novelist, painter, and essayist, whose *Time and Western Man* (1927) claims that Modernist literature, such as Joyce's *Ulysses,* has been depraved through too much concern with the fluidity of time and too little concern with the solidity of space.

91. *Renard* (*Bayka,* 1915–16), a burlesque in song and dance, concerns a fox who schemes to eat a rooster.

92. *The Soldier's Tale* (1918), a spare drama concerning a soldier who sells his violin to the devil.

93. William Walton (1902–83) evoked many popular styles in his recitation *Façade* (1923), dedicated to Lambert (who composed four bars of it). Lord Berners (Gerald Tyrwhitt, 1883–1950) wrote music in a Satie-like style; Lambert is probably thinking of his ballet *The Triumph of Neptune,* which includes a polka.

94. René Clair (1898–1981), French film director.

95. Georges Auric (1899–1983), one of the group of French composers called Les Six, wrote music evocative of popular styles.

distortion. To dance to these movements is absurd as it would be to read the news in the sections of *Le journal* incorporated by Picasso or Juan Gris[96] in one of their "abstracts." Stravinsky was quite right to protest against Massine using the *Ragtime*[97]—a work of much the same type, and of roughly the same period—for dancing purposes. The *Ragtime,* like the piano *Rag Music,* is an abstract pattern created out of the raw material of certain syncopated devices. It has no connection whatsoever with either the technique or the emotional world of jazz.

L'Histoire du Soldat is chiefly of interest as the most elaborate and convincing work of Stravinsky's abstract period, that is to say, the period in which he uses popular and humorous material for the purposes of abstract rhythmical dissection. The abstraction of these nursery- rhyme works is more significant than their buffoonery, for there is singularly little geniality or gusto about their self-conscious clowning.

The paraphernalia of the harlequinade are not of necessity humorous in themselves. One man may laugh like a child when he sees the red-hot poker applied to the butcher's inviting rump, another man may use the occasion for a lecture on the origins of laughter, with some notes on the connection between sadistic impulses and the risible faculties in the mentality of the infant. In the hands of Stravinsky the red-hot poker becomes the ruler of the maths master. We should not allow the outré orchestration of this work—always, with Stravinsky, the most accomplished side of it—to blind us to its essentially coldblooded abstraction.

Apart from the two short chorales, which point forward to his neoclassical period, *L'Histoire du Soldat* consists almost entirely of an objective juggling with rhythm, or rather meter, for there can be no true rhythm where there is no melodic life. Like Gertrude Stein, Stravinsky chooses the drabbest and least significant phrases for material of his experiments, because if the melodic line had life dissection would be impossible. "Everyday they were gay there, they were regularly gay there everyday" etc., from Gertrude Stein's *Helen Furr and Georgine Skeene,*[98] has no particular value as content, least of all is it meant to be gay. It is merely material for a fantasia in rhythmic values whose effect would be equally appreciated by someone with no knowledge of English whatsoever. Similarly, the melodic fragments in *L'Histoire du Soldat* are completely meaningless themselves. They are merely successions of notes that can conveniently be divided up into groups of three, five and seven and set against other mathematical groupings.

96. Pablo Picasso (1881–1973) and Juan Gris (1887–1927). The Cubist painters sometimes incorporated actual fragments of newspapers in their collages.

97. Stravinsky's *Rag-Time* for small orchestra and *Piano-Rag-Music* (both 1919) are stylizations of American popular music.

98. "Miss Furr and Miss Skeene" (1922), a piece of repetitious experimental prose by Gertrude Stein (1874–1946).

The melodic poverty, or even nullity, of such a movement as the *Petit Concert* reaches its logical development in the final section, a cadenza for drums alone that is actually the most consistently satisfying feature of the whole work. It represents the goal towards which the earlier compositions of this period had been tending. Harmony, melody, all that could give the least emotional significance to his music, has been banished in the interests of abstraction, and musical purity has been achieved by a species of musical castration. The formula of sound for sound's sake is here reduced to its ludicrous essentials, and there is no further progress possible on these lines. The percussion solo which ends *L'Histoire du Soldat* has much the same satisfaction of finality as the map of that pioneer of abstraction The Bellman,[99] which was, we are told, "a perfect and absolute blank."

Unlike Debussy, who was strong enough to conquer his early mannerisms and put his revolutionary technique to a flexibly expressive use, Stravinsky was caught in the mechanics of his technical mannerisms, and the deliberate exploitation of certain facets of musical thought for their own sake led him to a definite blind alley from which there was no escape except by a deliberate reaction. He is like a motorist who spends all his time with his head inside the bonnet [hood]. *Chi ha vissuto per amore, per amore si morì* ("Those who live for love are killed by love") sings the street musician in Puccini's *Il Tabarro* [1918]—and he might have added: "Those who live by technique are killed by technique." . . .

. . . The time traveling of the *Pulcinella* ballet probably provided the impetus for Stravinsky's neoclassical period, which, apart from the adoption of eighteenth-century forms and titles, is chiefly noticeable for its attempt to create melody by synthetic manufacture. One cannot create a creature of flesh and blood out of fossil fragments.

It need hardly be pointed out that the sequences, cadences, and other stylistic features of the best classical tunes are not their most important element. They take their place in the scheme of things, they have a formal and even an emotional logic, but they are the façade, not the whole building. It is the easiest possible thing to take four bars out of one of the best-constructed and most moving of Mozart's arias and find that in themselves they have remarkably little value. This, in fact, is what Stravinsky often does without, however, realizing that he is confusing the periwig with the face beneath it. The turns of phrase that occur at the end of a melody with much the same conventional beauty and constructional logic as a Corinthian capital occurring at the top of a column are taken by Stravinsky, isolated from their surroundings and plastered over the façade with a complete disregard of their true function and a complete inability to add anything to them except a little incongruous color. Lest I should be thought to

---

99. Bellman: a character in Lewis Carroll's poem "The Hunting of the Snark" (1876), whose not very helpful map is a blank page.

be exaggerating the confusion between eighteenth-century thought and eighteenth-century mannerism exhibited by Stravinsky and his followers, I should like to recall the occasion when Diaghileff[100] included as a symphonic interlude at the Russian ballet Mozart's *Musical Joke* [K. 522, 1787], a brilliant parody of the stupid and mechanical application of eighteenth-century formulas to insignificant and ludicrous material. No one saw the joke except Diaghileff himself. His entourage took the piece with perfect gravity as an example of classicism to be admired and imitated.

To create even a synthetic melody — such as the one in the slow movement of Ravel's concerto [in G, 1930–31] — to any degree of satisfaction requires a power of sustained linear construction which it is only too clear Stravinsky does not possess. His melodic style has always been marked by extreme shortwindedness and a curious inability to get away from the principal note of the tune. . . .

That Stravinsky's shortwinded methods are incapable of producing even a satisfactory synthesis of this type of melody we can see by taking a concrete example, the theme which opens the slow movement of his Piano Concerto [1923–24] — a movement which may be said to set the type of Stravinsky's adagios for the next few years. It opens with a two-bar phrase in the eighteenth-century manner — commonplace enough, but still, capable of yielding results of a certain distinction in the hands of a composer such as Vivaldi. Stravinsky, however, is unable to continue this phrase or even find a contrasting two bars. He repeats it with a slight rhythmic variation — the only type of treatment that comes easily to him — twists its tail for a moment and then lets it fall gradually back on itself, the process of extinction being artificially held up by the mechanical application of sequential figures, which derive not from eighteenth-century lyricism, but from eighteenth-century passage work. . . .

A phrase like "Ladies and gentlemen, unaccustomed as I am to public speaking" is flat enough in all conscience, but if it occurs at the beginning of a speech as a prelude to a remark of some weight we can accept it readily enough as an unavoidable and inoffensive formula; but we can hardly be expected to keep patience with a speaker whose whole oration consists of a portentously solemn Mene Mene Tekel Upharsin[101] delivery of a Stein-like fantasia such as "Ladies and gentle ladies and gentlemenu-manumissionaries unaccustomed as I am to a Siamese customary una-menu-mina-mo ('alf a mo' ladies) to a ladies' public bar and gentlemen's speak-easy I mean to easy public speak I-N-G spells ING."

From *Music Ho! A Study of Music in Decline* (New York: Charles Scribner's Sons, 1936), *Music Ho!*, 94–97, 101–5.

---

100. Serge Diaghilev (1872–1929), impresario of the Ballets Russes; Lambert's *Romeo and Juliet* (1926) was the first ballet for Diaghilev's company composed by an Englishman.

101. These are the mysterious words on the wall that terrify King Belshazzar (Daniel 5:25).

Lambert thought that Stravinsky's music had the deliberate inconsequentiality of Stein's prose. Gertrude Stein (1874–1946) also believed that her prose could lend itself to musical treatment: in 1927 she and the composer Virgil Thomson (1896–1989) decided to write an opera together, *Four Saints in Three Acts* (first performed in 1934). If Stravinskyan Neoclassicism, in Lambert's and Adorno's opinion, is essentially static, secondhand, and vitiated, Stein and Thomson tried to make stasis and a sort of twisted banality into virtues—and in the opinion of some critics, they succeeded. Stein considered that drama is the exact opposite of narrative: narratives concern events, whereas plays concern the absence of events: "Everyone knows so many stories and what is the use of telling another story. . . . I concluded that anything that was not a story could be a play and I even made plays in letters and advertisements";[102] all successful plays were plays in which "nothing was happening . . . after all Hamlet Shakespeare's most interesting play has really nothing happening except that they live and die . . . an interesting thing is when there is nothing happening. I said that the moon excited dogs because it did nothing, lights coming and going do not excite them."[103] An opera in which a number of saints sit around or stand and discuss at great length just how to go about sitting and standing ("Saint Therese seated and not surrounded. There are a great many persons and places near together")[104] had a low enough density of event to please her. But it should be remembered that the mad success of the first performances—special trains were hired to take society folk from New York to the Hartford theater where it played— owed much to the extravagant décor by Florine Stettheimer (full of feathers, shells, and yards of cellophane) and the novel feature of an all–African American cast; the stage itself had a far from minimalist look.

Thomson considered himself not a Neoclassicist but a Neoromanticist—unobtrusively expressive, never straining for effect. But his Neoromanticism has many Neoclassical elements. The music of *Four Saints in Three Acts* only rarely indulges in quotation (though "My Country 'Tis of Thee" appears briefly). But it resembles Lambert's description of Stravinsky in that it pieces together in a jumbled order the elementary preparations and cadences of a "boob-simple" diatonicism. As Thomson explained:

> My skill was to be employed not for protecting such composers as had invested in the dissonant manner but for avoiding all those interval frictions and contrapuntal viscosities which are built into the dissonant style and which if indulged unduly might trip up my verbal speeds. Not to have skirted standard modernism would have been to fall into a booby trap. On the contrary, I built up my accompaniments by select-

102. Gertrude Stein, *Lectures in America* (New York: Vintage, 1975), 118–19.
103. Gertrude Stein, *Everybody's Autobiography* (Cambridge: Exact Change, 1993), 292.
104. Gertrude Stein, *Selected Writings,* ed. Carl van Vechten (New York: Vintage Books, 1990), 587.

ing chords for their tensile strength and by employing in a vast majority of cases only those melodic elements from the liturgical vernacular of Christendom, both Catholic and Protestant, that had for centuries borne the weight of long prayers.[105]

Just as Stein created a plotless drama, so Thomson created a purely non-progressive music, falling easily on the ears but going nowhere—an acoustic labyrinth.

In the following passage, Stein describes how she created *Four Saints in Three Acts* as a pseudomorphism (Adorno's term) between landscape and drama by adapting the unchanging flatness of the Spanish desert into the text for an opera. And indeed the opera remains one of the most weightless and evacuated theatrical contrivances in the history of art—almost an exact opposite of Schoenberg's *Erwartung*.

GERTRUDE STEIN
from *Lectures in America* (1935)

In Four Saints I made the Saints the landscape. All the saints that I made and I made a number of them because after all a great many pieces of things are in a landscape all these saints together made my landscape. These attendant saints were the landscape and it the play really is a landscape.

A landscape does not move nothing really moves in a landscape but things are there, and I put into the play the things that were there.

Magpies are in the landscape that is they are in the sky of a landscape, they are black and white and they are in the sky of the landscape in Bilignin [106] and in Spain, especially in Avila. When they are in the sky they do something that I have never seen any other bird do they hold themselves up and down and look flat against the sky.

A very famous French inventor of things that have to do with stabilization in aviation told me that what I told him magpies did could not be done by any bird but anyway whether the magpies at Avila do do it or do not at least they look as if they do it. They look exactly like the birds in the Annunciation pictures the bird which is the Holy Ghost and rests flat against the side sky very high.

There were magpies in my landscape and there were scarecrows.

The scarecrows on the ground are the same thing as the magpies in the sky, they are a part of the landscape.

They the magpies may tell their story if they and you like or even if I like but stories are only stories but that they stay in the air is not a story but a landscape. That scarecrows stay on the ground is the same thing it could be a story but it is a piece of the landscape.

While I was writing the Four Saints I wanted one always does want the saints to be

105. Virgil Thomson, *Virgil Thomson* (New York: Alfred A. Knopf, 1966), 106.
106. Bilignin: in Southern France, where Stein lived.

actually saints before them as well as inside them, I had to see them as well as feel them. As it happened there is on the Boulevard Raspail a place where they make photographs that have always held my attention. They take a photograph of a young girl dressed in the costume of her ordinary life and little by little in successive photographs they change it into a nun. These photographs are small and the thing takes four or five changes but at the end it is a nun and this is done for the family when the nun is dead and in memoriam. For years I had stood and looked at these when I was walking and finally when I was writing Saint Therese [107] in looking at these photographs I saw how Saint Therese existed from the life of an ordinary young lady to that of the nun. And so everything was actual and I went on writing.

All these things might have been a story but as a landscape they were just there and a play is just there.

Then in another window this time on the rue de Rennes there was a rather large porcelain group and it was of a young soldier giving alms to a beggar and taking off his helmet and his armour and leaving them in the charge of another.

It was somehow just what the young Ignatius [108] did and anyway it looked like him as I had known about him and so he became actual not as actual as Saint Therese in the photographs but still actual and so the Four Saints got written.

All these things might have been a story but as a landscape they were just there and a play is just there. That is at least the way I feel about it.

Anyway I did write Four Saints an Opera to be Sung and I think it did almost what I wanted, it made a landscape and the movement in it was like a movement in and out with which anybody looking on can keep in time. I also wanted it to have the movement of nuns very busy and in continuous movement but placid as a landscape has to be because after all the life in a convent is the life of a landscape, it may look excited but its quality is that of a landscape if it ever did go away would have to go away to stay.

Anyway the play as I see it is exciting and it moves but it also stays and that is as I said in the beginning might be what a play should do.

Anyway I am pleased. People write me that they are having a good time while the opera is going on a thing which they say does not very often happen to them at the theatre.

So you do see what I have after all meant.

And so this is just at present all I know about the theatre.

From *Lectures in America* (New York: Vintage, 1975), 128–31.

107. Teresa of Ávila (1515–1582), Spanish mystic and saint, who once had a vision of an angel pointing a flaming dart at her. Stein imagined a calm and aimless version of her as the female lead in the opera.

108. Ignatius Loyola (1491–1556), Spanish missionary and saint; Stein's male lead, his militancy much toned down.

■

The French composer Maurice Ravel (1875–1937) adopted an aesthetic not far from Neoclassicism. He was, from his youth, attracted to classical forms—*Menuet antique* (1895), *Sonatine* (1903–5)—not, perhaps, out of particular love for the academic, but out of an extraordinary affection for the contrived. Ravel impressed his contemporaries as a man who fashioned music with a jeweler's loupe. Though Ravel worked in many styles, the sound of the music box is often conspicuous, as in the "Laideronnette, impératrice des pagodes" movement of the ballet *Ma mère l'oye* (1908–11), or the song "Noël des jouets" (1905). Also remarkable is Ravel's tendency to associate clockwork precision of rhythm with sexuality, as in his opera *L'heure espagnole* (1911), in which the ticking of clocks seems to arouse adulterous passion. For Ravel, the dry sound of machines seems not an escape from human feelings but an excitement of them—as if the goals of Expressionism were best pursued by the means of Neoclassicism. As the following interviews show, Ravel managed, one might say, to live inside a music box; and he was inspired by the pounding noises of factories—though in his music all Futurist heavy metal was refined to delicacy.

MAURICE RAVEL
Interview: [Ravel's Toys] (1933)

A padded landing. A silent door. Here is the study, cell or dream-room, a box of dark grey ply wood, with a high border of precious Japanese prints.

—"A new type of stained-glass window will replace this window, which will hide this odious landscape of the industrial suburbs to the point of making one forget it."

Another silent door. . . . A large library rises above a spacious couch.

"It won't be big enough to contain my collection of memorialists," the maître says. He then shows me his treasures: Viennese crystal, bibelots brought back from Arizona ("Doesn't it look like a Picasso?"), a delightful miniature village from a toy box for a fairy godchild. . . .

"As for this, done by [Bolette] Natanson, it may well be the most beautiful surrealist tableau of all . . ."

How can one describe it? Under a globe, overlapping strips of glass are lit by a small tinted bulb of glaucous blue or emerald green, revealing the bottom of the sea, in which the volute of a shell and the lacework of an alga are spun out.

"This finally? . . ."

But it's only a mechanical toy. Ravel winds it up: a puppet seizes a marble, throws it with a gesture toward a "numbered box," as in Satie's song[109]—and does it again. But

---

109. In Satie's song "La statue de bronze," a frog tries to catch coins but misses, and the coins clank against a *piédestal numéroté*.

it suddenly strikes me that the mechanical toy and the surrealist tableau thus placed side by side illuminate all of Ravel's oeuvre. Ariel and Vaucanson:[110] isn't this how Roland-Manuel[111]—his most penetrating biographer—explained it?

—"I am stopping my little pelota player," Ravel says. . . .

His mother was Basque. His father was from Versoix, the small port which Voltaire had established on blue Lake Geneva. Ravel has also been called "the most perfect of Swiss clockmakers"—or the most enchanting of Iberian magicians: think of *L'Heure espagnole.*[112]

From José Bruyr, "An Interview with Maurice Ravel" (1931), in *A Ravel Reader: Correpondence, Articles, Interviews,* ed. Arbie Orenstein (New York: Columbia University Press, 1990) 479–80.

MAURICE RAVEL
Interview: "Finding Tunes in Factories" (1933)

M. Maurice Ravel, the French composer, who has come to England to conduct the first performance in this country of his new pianoforte concerto tomorrow, confessed today that he admired jazz. He said:

"Each movement of my new symphony[113] has some jazz in it. I frankly admit that I am an admirer of jazz, and I think it is bound to influence modern music. It is not just a passing phase, but has come to stay. It is thrilling and inspiring, and I spend many hours listening to it in night clubs and over the wireless."

M. Ravel said he thought that the mechanics and machinery of the age would also leave their imprint on music of the present day. He added: "I gained much of my inspiration from machinery.

"I love going over factories and seeing vast machinery at work. It is awe-inspiring and great. It was a factory which inspired my *Boléro.*[114] I would like it always to be played with a vast factory in the background.

"Do I think that at some future date we shall see on a concert platform rows of typewriters, lathes and saws in place of the usual instruments? It is not improbable; it has

110. Ariel is the spirit of imagination in Shakespeare's *Tempest* (1611); Jacques de Vaucanson (1709–82) constructed automata.

111. Alexis Roland-Manuel (1891–1966), composer and writer on music, who published *Maurice Ravel et son oeuvre* in 1914.

112. Ravel's opera *L'heure espagnole* (1911) takes place in a clockmaker's shop and concerns an unfaithful wife whose lover hides in a grandfather's clock.

113. new symphony: that is, the new piano concerto, in G (1930–31).

114. *Boléro* (1927), Ravel's hypnotic exercise in monothematicism.

already been tried in one of the Russian ballets,[115] where a typewriter being tapped was a legitimate instrument of the orchestra.

"But, if it does come about, I do not think it can truly be called art. I do think it is art to make violins, horns, trombones, and all the other instruments of the orchestra sound like machinery. If machinery were put on the concert platform instead of musical instruments, however, it would conversely only be art if that machinery were made to sound like music. At present I do not see how this could be done."

Then M. Ravel discussed another idea. That was that in these days of cacophony it might be quite an original idea for the orchestra to start, say, in C major, and then, through a series of discords the instruments should divide, some going up a semitone at every three or four bars, while others went down in the same way, eventually ending in perfect harmony in C major two octaves apart. He said:

"It is just an idea but it might be rather fun working it out and certainly a novel way of resolving harmony from discord."

From an unattributed interview in the *Evening Standard,* London, 24 February 1932, in *A Ravel Reader: Correpondence, Articles, Interviews,* ed. Arbie Orenstein (New York: Columbia University Press, 1990), 490 – 91.

DADAISM AND SURREALISM

José Bruyr thought that Ravel was a combination of a Surrealist and a designer of mechanical toys. To speak of Ravel as a Surrealist is not hard: his opera *L'enfant et les sortilèges* (1920 – 25), to a fine libretto by Colette, concerns furniture that comes to life in order to chide a wicked child. Surrealism is a movement that transgresses boundaries; and the instability of such categories as animate and inanimate, or human and animal, is the modality of Ravel's opera.

Expressionism, Neoclassicism, and the New Objectivity are important Modernist movements in which music took an obvious leading role. But the role of music in Dadaism and Surrealism is perhaps undervalued—partly because the Dadaist and Surrealist writers and painters tended to know little about music. Francis Poulenc, a composer strongly attracted to Surrealism, complained that except for Paul Éluard the Surrealists were musically illiterate; and the leading Surrealist of the 1930s and 1940s, André Breton, publicly confessed his dislike of music in an essay entitled "Silence Is Golden"

---

115. Satie's *Parade* (1917), performed at the Ballets Russes, has parts for a typewriter, a pistol, and other odd sound effects.

(1946). Surrealism was an organized, almost regimented artistic movement, despite its anarchic attitude toward art, which is why Breton was able to excommunicate the art of music if he chose. Expressionism and Neoclassicism were powerful but loosely defined tendencies; Surrealism, on the other hand, had not only elaborate manifestoes but a whole dictionary of its own.[116] But as Surrealism becomes emancipated from Breton's heavy hand, it becomes possible to understand its influences on, and contributions from, the art of music.

In 1924 Breton defined Surrealism as follows:

> SURREALISM, n. Pure psychic automatism, by which one proposes to express, either verbally, or in writing, or by any other manner, the real functioning of thought. Dictation of thought in the absence of all control exercised by reason, outside of all aesthetic and moral preoccupation.[117]

This is a radical doctrine for writer or a painter: the writer must learn to surrender logic and temporal sequence of event; the painter must learn to work in an incoherent pictorial space where perspective is established only to be outraged. But how might a composer interpret the command of Surrealism? It could easily be argued that Bach's *Art of Fugue* displays "the real functioning of thought"; and if the older music seemed too reasonable, too rule driven, there were already plenty of voices in the early twentieth century—such as Debussy's and Busoni's—telling the composer to forget all the rules. In Virgil Thomson's opinion, all composers are Surrealists: "I got myself into a lovely little—shall we say controversy—with André Breton, by pointing out that the discipline of spontaneity, which he was asking his surrealist neophytes to adopt, was new for language but something that composers had been practicing for centuries."[118]

Still, it is possible to speak of Surrealist music in a narrower sense. A short catalog might include settings by Poulenc, Honegger, Jean Wiéner, and Joseph Kosma of poems by Surrealist writers; Milhaud's *Le boeuf sur le toit* (1920), a ballet to a scenario by Cocteau; the collaboration by five of the composers known as Les Six on Cocteau's *Les mariés de la Tour Eiffel* (1921); operas by Bohuslav Martinů based on plays by Georges Neveux (*Julietta, Ariane*), along with Martinů's ballet *The Revolt* (1925), in which dancers costumed as musical notes rebel against their abuse by musicians—eventually Igor Stravinsky (a character in the ballet) is forced to seek refuge on a Pacific island;

116. The *Abridged Dictionary of Surrealism* is reprinted in the second volume of Breton, *Oeuvres complètes,* ed. Marguerite Bonnet, 2 vols. (Paris: Éditions Gallimard, 1988), vol. 2.

117. Ibid., 1:328; translated by the editor.

118. Virgil Thomson, *A Virgil Thomson Reader* (New York: E. P. Dutton, Inc., 1981), 548.

René Magritte, *The Discovery of Fire* (ca. 1934–35). © 2003 C. Herscovici, Brussels/Artists Rights Society (ARS), New York. Photo: Bridgeman Art Library.

Stravinsky's own *Oedipus Rex* (1927), also to a scenario by Cocteau; George Antheil's set of piano preludes (1933) for Max Ernst's collage-novel *La femme 100 têtes;* and Poulenc's opera *Les mamelles de Tirésias* (1944) to a text by Apollinaire.

A common feature of a number of these pieces is wrongness. Just as the Surrealist painter René Magritte might show a flaming tuba or a crowd of little men in bowler hats raining from the sky, so the Surrealist composer dislocates and miscontextualizes. The music is frequently expressive, but expressive of something that the text didn't call for. Poulenc has the discourse of the general in *Les mariés de la Tour Eiffel* voiced by two cornets playing a little polka; the peppy, frivolous tune discords strongly with the pompous militarism the situation might call for. The music of *Oedipus Rex* is, by Stravinsky's own account, slapped together from the most untragic and ignoble stuff imaginable: "Much of the music is a *Merzbild,* put together from whatever came to hand. I mean, for example . . . the Alberti-bass horn solo accompanying the Messenger. I also mean the fusion of such widely divergent types of music as the *Folies Bergères* tune at No. 40 ('The girls enter, kicking') and the Wagnerian 7th-chords at Nos. 58 and 74." [119]

A *Merzbild* is one of Kurt Schwitters's Dada collages—Schwitters was fascinated by the nonsense syllable *Merz* and often included it in assemblages of junk. The reasonable, Apollonian Stravinsky is such a powerful construct of Modernist mythology that it is perhaps hard to remember that there is a Dada irrationalist in Stravinsky also, dismantling Greek temples and putting them back together with the pediment on the bottom, the columns plastered into shattered diagonals, and a movie-house marquee smacked on top.

The explicitly Dadaist music of the 1910s tends to be composed by chance procedures and disruptive to the point of complete unintelligibility; Surrealistic music, on the other hand, is often rather conservative in harmony and melody. There is a simple explanation for this: Dada music aspired to mean nothing, Surrealist music to mean wrong; and in to order to mean wrong, music must mean something. Thus Surrealist music depended on semantic cues interpretable by traditional means—just as Salvador Dalí had to paint a watch that looked like watch before he could mollify it into a limp dishrag hanging over a tree branch in *The Persistence of Memory* (1931).

Surrealist music, though chiefly French, was not exclusively so. A fine example can be found in Paul Hindemith's *Cardillac* (1926). At the end of the first act, there is a long pantomime during which a man quietly opens a woman's bedroom door, awakens her (with a hushing finger on his lips), and presents her with a magnificent belt of gold; delighted, she tries it on, then takes it off and starts to kiss and fondle the man; at the end, a masked figure dressed in black climbs in through the bedroom window, crawls toward the bed like an animal, and suddenly interrupts the lovers: he stabs the man in the neck, steals the gold belt, and flees. It is easy to imagine the sort of music that a film composer (Bernard Hermann, say) would supply for this scene; but Hindemith, radically contravening expectations, supplied a neo-Baroque duet for two flutes. Nothing in the music expresses the slumber or the passionate kiss, and certainly not the stealthy murderer, just outside the window, about to crawl in at the instant the duet ends—the flutes remain tranquil, self-possessed, rhythmically even, oblivious to sex and death alike. The only aspect of the text that Hindemith wished to notice was the idea of pairing: two entwined lovers equal two entwined flutes. But by allowing the concept of *duet* to dominate the musical proceedings, Hindemith flouted normal notions of what's important and what's trivial in the domain of musical expression.

119. Stravinsky and Craft, *Dialogues*, 27.

■ Dada preceded Surrealism: it was born in a Zurich cabaret in 1915–16. By the early 1920s, after a period of flamboyant research into methods of negating almost everything suggested by the word *art*, its force was almost spent. Some sense of the anti-Expressionist, anti-logical, anti-everything flavor of early Dada can be seen in Hugo Ball's description of a 1915 reading he gave at the Cabaret Voltaire, in a special costume:

> I invented a new species of verse, "verse without words," or sound poems. . . . I looked liked an obelisk [. . . and] wore a high top hat striped with white and blue. I recited the following:
>
> gadji beri bimba
glandridi lauli lonni cadori . . .
>
> The accents became heavier, the expression increased an intensification of the consonants. I soon noticed that my means of expression (if I wanted to remain serious, which I did at any cost), was not adequate to the pomp of my stage setting.[120]

A more famous Dada poem, by Kurt Schwitters, consisted entirely of the letter W. If Dada was suspicious of Expressionism, it also took care to ridicule all other isms (ultimately including Dadaism itself). As a poster of December 1918 put it:

> Let us destroy let us be good let us create a new force of gravity NO = YES Dada means nothing life Who? catalogue of insects / Arp's woodcuts / each page a resurrection each eye a daredevil-leaping down with cubism and futurism every sentence a blast of an automobile horn.[121]

Despite this extreme negativism, the Romanian poet Tristan Tzara (who claimed that he invented the term Dada, a French word meaning "hobby-horse" found "by accident in the Larousse dictionary")[122] defended Dada as a direct imitation of nature and human cognition:

> We [Dadaists] are often told that we are incoherent, but into this word people try to put an insult that it is rather hard for me to fathom. Everything is incoherent. . . . There is no logic. . . . The acts of life have no beginning and no end. Everything happens in a completely idiotic way. That is why everything is alike. Simplicity is called

---

120. Robert Motherwell, ed., *The Dada Painters and Poets: An Anthology* (Cambridge: Belknap Press, 1981), xxv.

121. Richard Huelsenbeck, ed., *The Dada Almanac: Berlin 1920*, trans. Malcolm Green et al. (London: Atlas, 1983), 28.

122. William S. Rubin, *Dada, Surrealism, and Their Heritage* (New York: Museum of Modern Art, 1968), 189.

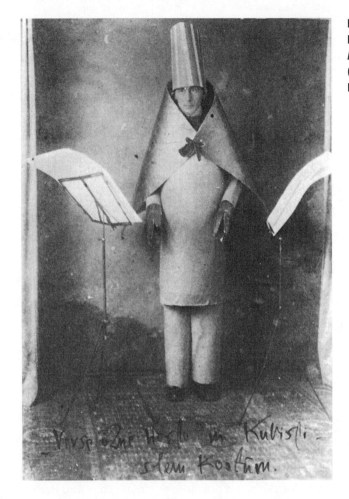

Hugo Ball in costume.
From Donald E. Gordon,
Expressionism: Art and Idea
(New Haven: Yale University
Press, 1987), 163.

Dada. Any attempt to conciliate an inexplicable momentary state with logic strikes me as a boring kind of game. . . . Like everything in life, Dada is useless. . . . Perhaps you will understand me better when I tell you that Dada is a virgin microbe that penetrates with the insistence of art into all the spaces that reason has not been able to fill with words or conventions.[123]

If I shout:

> *Ideal, Ideal, Ideal*
> *Knowledge, Knowledge, Knowledge,*
> *Boomboom, Boomboom, Boomboom*

123. Motherwell, *The Dada Painters and Poets,* 250–51.

I have recorded fairly accurately Progress, Law, Morals, and all the other magnificent qualities that various very intelligent people have discussed in so many books.[124]

Dada, then (from the Dadaists' point of view), is Realism, as the twentieth century understands reality.

Dada recognized a number of forerunners, such as Gertrude Stein[125] and most of all Marcel Duchamp (1887–1968). Duchamp appealed to the Dadaists through his "readymades," such as an ordinary shovel taken out of the context of a tool shed, placed in an art exhibition, and given the title *In Advance of a Broken Arm* (1915); later came a urinal entitled *Fountain,* which made a splash at the 1917 Exhibition of Independent Painters in New York. This tweaking of the boundary between high art and non-art prefigured the more sustained aggressions of the Dadaists against the concept of art itself. Duchamp was not a violent man, but he showed his skepticism toward the grand tradition of art history in many forms, as in his 1919 *L.H.O.O.Q,* in which he drew an elegant little mustache on a print of the *Mona Lisa* (the title is an obscene pun: *Elle a chaud au cul,* her bottom is hot).

Years before Tzara began to generate poems by cutting up newsprint into separate words and mixing them in a hat, Duchamp was generating music by an almost identical procedure: in 1913 (or at least he claimed in 1934 that it was 1913) he wrote a composition for three voices (his own and those of his sisters Yvonne and Magdeleine) by taking as his text the dictionary definition of "imprint," a sentence with twenty-five syllables—the number of notes in the chromatic scale of two octaves; then writing the name of each of these twenty-five notes on a card, so that he eventually compiled three sets of twenty-five cards; then scrambling each set in a hat; and finally conducting drawings to determine the pitches to which the definition should be sung by each of the three performers. He notated the score without any indication of rhythm or instruction as to whether the parts were to be performed consecutively or simultaneously. Performed simultaneously, and with even note values, the effect tends to be less strident than calm; as with all (not too dense) randomly generated music, the occasional consonances suggest an inhuman stresslessness of being. Random music quickly became a Dada institution: Tzara liked to have a pianist playing notes determined by chance, punctuated by blasts from a klaxon, at his performance-lectures.[126]

124. Huelsenbeck, *The Dada Almanac,* 127.
125. Moholy-Nagy thought that Schwitters, by using the technique of verbal collage, "like Gertrude Stein . . . uncovers all the symptom of social decay" (Motherwell, *The Dada Painters and Poets,* xxviii).
126. Huelsenbeck, *The Dada Almanac,* 88.

Kurt Schwitters, *The Hitler Gang* (1944). © 2002 Artists Rights Society (ARS), New York/VG Bild-Kunst, Bonn.

Faire une empreinte, marquer des traits, une figure sur une surface, imprimer un sceau sur cire. [To make an imprint, to mark with lines, a figure on a surface, to impress a seal on wax.] [127]

■ Perhaps the most ambitious of Dada music projects was the *Ursonate* (*Primal Sonata,* 1921–32) of the collagist and poet Kurt Schwitters (1887–1948). Of all the Dadaists, Schwitters understood most clearly that if Dada removed the halo from the work of art, canceled its every privilege, then art diffused into a whole environment instead of con-

127. From Edition Block CD EB 202 (1991), 3.

centrating itself in a finite object. In other words, if nothing is art, then everything is art. Following this reasoning, Schwitters converted his home into what he called a *Merzbau,* a *Merz* construct:

> I could not, in fact, see the reason why old tickets, driftwood, cloakroom tabs, wires and parts of wheels, buttons and old rubbish found in attics and refuse dumps should not be as suitable for painting as the paints made in factories. This was, as it were, a social attitude. . . . I called my new works utilizing such materials *Merz.* This is the second syllable of *Kommerz* [commerce]. It originated in the *Merzbild* [*Merz Picture*], a work in which the word *Merz,* cut out from an advertisement of the *Kommerz und Privatbank* and pasted on, could be read among the abstract elements. . . . Later I extended the word *Merz,* first to my poetry, which I have written since 1917, and finally to all my related activities. Now I call myself *Merz.*[128]

Schwitters's house in Hanover resembled the lunatic sets of Wiene's film *The Cabinet of Dr. Caligari:* it seemed to defy human habitation, since the interior spaces were crammed with beams and parallelepipeds set at challenging angles.

The *Ursonate,* however, bears little relation to *Merzbau.* It is speech-music, based on a single word in a 1918 poem by Raoul Hausmann: *fmsbwtözäu.* Schwitters began by devising a way of pronouncing this word (*Fümms bö wö tää zää Uu*) and then declared this line the first theme of a rondo. He then invented some other themes for the rondo, adjoined three other movements (Largo; Scherzo-Trio-Scherzo; Presto-Kadenz-Schluss), and prepared a score for a reciter. Though the word themes lack all meaning, Schwitters's obedience to the strictly regulated recurrence patterns of his musical form is absolute: he seems to delight in the contrast between disorderly phonemes and the symmetrical rigidity, the dry logic, of the rondo. At the end of the fourth movement, the recitation turns into letters from the German alphabet, as if a basis for sense is at last crystallizing out of madly insistent nonsense. Whereas Duchamp accepted musical notes and abolished any principle of order, Schwitters accepted the traditional ordering of musical events and abolished the notes.

128. Rubin, *Dada, Surrealism, and Their Heritage,* 53.

KURT SCHWITTERS
Ursonate: **Rondo** (1921–32)

1922–1932   **Ur Sonata**

---

prelude:

Fümms bö wö tää zää Uu,   1
          pögiff,
                    kwii Ee.

Ooooooooooooooooooooooooooooooooo,   6

     dll rrrrrr beeeee bö,   (A)   5
     dll rrrrrr beeeee bö fümms bö,
          rrrrrr beeeee bö fümms bö wö,
               beeeee bö fümms bö wö tää,
                    bö fümms bö wö tää zää,
                         fümms bö wö tää zää Uu:

---

first movement:

theme 1:
Fümms bö wö tää zää Uu,   1
          pögiff,
                    kwii Ee.

theme 2:
Dedesnn nn rrrrrr,   2
               Ii Ee,
                    mpiff tillff too,
                         tillll,
                              Jüü Kaa? (*sung*)

theme 3:
Rinnzekete bee bee nnz krr müü?   3
                    ziiuu ennze, ziiuu rinnzkrrmüü,

     rakete bee bee.   3 a

theme 4:
Rrummpff tillff toooo?   4

From *Das literarische Werk,* vol. 1: *Lyrik,* ed. Friedhelm Lach (Cologne: Verlag M. Dumont Schauberg, 1973), 214. © 2002 Artists Rights Society (ARS), New York / VG Bild-Kunst, Bonn.

■

Not surprisingly, Dada music provoked some fury; for example, Frederick Delius wrote in 1920 of the "musically imbecile productions" of the "devotees of Dada." [129] Of course, this was exactly the reaction for which the revolutionaries hoped: Dadaism can be understood as a hammer designed to shatter our notions of music (and the other arts). The term Surrealism, however, originated in a program note praising a musical composition. The coiner of the word was the French poet and art critic Guillaume Apollinaire (Wilhelm Apollinaris Kostrowitzky, 1880–1918); and the piece of music was the Satie-Picasso ballet *Parade* (1917).

"Surreal" has two meanings: more-real, and more-than-real. Apollinaire thought that *Parade* gave a stronger impression of the heft, the texture of felt experience than commonplace "realistic" art could achieve; but *Parade* also delaminates the coherent world of the senses into jagged planes, where what is seen has little relation to what is heard—a Cubist deconstruction and reconstruction of reality, an "analysis-synthesis." The circus performers on stage are full of crowd-pleasing routines: the Chinese Conjurer pulls an egg out of his toe, the American Girl does exciting stunts stolen from the *Perils of Pauline* movie serial, the Acrobats perform their death-defying tricks; but the music goes about its business in a cool, anti-expressive manner, as if it were unconcerned with the affairs on the stage. The music is punctuated by pistol shots, typewriting, lottery wheels, Morse code apparatus, and other sounds of modern life, but in the blanched domain of Satie's score these effects seem neutralized, reduced to pure abstract percussion. This dissonance between layers of reality imparts a strong sense of the eeriness that Surrealism would always prize. The concept of wrongness in art is promoted into an entire theatrical event.

Soon after *Parade*, Apollinaire would stage a revised reversion of his 1903 skit *Les mamelles de Tirésias* (*The Breasts of Tiresias*), the prologue of which describes a new kind of theater: "Marrying often without apparent bond as in life / The sounds the gestures the colors the cries the noises." [130] This line is in effect the motto of the Surrealist theater: disconnection of sound from gesture, of gesture from cry.

Apollinaire's program note for *Parade* keeps returning to the notion of surprise, and he imagined that Surrealism had a future in which continual novelty would play a strong role. But Apollinaire was to die the next year, in the great influenza pandemic of 1918, and the future of Surrealism would be left to others.

---

129. Frederick Delius, "At the Cross-Roads," *Sackbut* 1, no. 5 (September 1920): 205.

130. Guillaume Apollinaire, *Les mamelles de Tirésias, avec six portraits inédits par Picasso* (Paris: Éditions du Bélier, 1946), 30.

GUILLAUME APOLLINAIRE
Program Note for *Parade* (1917)

The cubist painter Picasso and the boldest of choreographers, Léonide Massine,[131] have effected it, consummating for the first time the alliance of painting and dance, of plastic and mime, which is the sign of the advent of a more complete art.

Let no one cry paradox! The Ancients, in whose life music held such a great place, knew absolutely nothing of harmony, which is almost everything in modern music.

From this new alliance, for until now stage sets and costumes on one side and choreography on the other had only a sham bond between them, there has come about, in *Parade,* a kind of super-realism [*sur-réalisme*], in which I see the starting point of a series of manifestations of this new spirit [*esprit nouveau*], which, finding today the opportunity to reveal itself, will not fail to seduce the elite, and which promises to modify arts and manners from top to bottom for the world's delight, since it is only common sense to wish that arts and manners reach at least to the same height as scientific and industrial progress.

Breaking with the tradition dear to those who were so bizarrely called (not long ago in Russia) "balletomanes," Massine has kept himself from falling into pantomime. He has effected this thing entirely new, marvelously seductive, with a truth so lyrical, so human, so joyous, that it might well be capable of illuminating, if it were worth the trouble, the frightening black sun of Dürer's *Melancolia*[132]—what Jean Cocteau calls a realistic ballet. Picasso's cubist stage sets and costumes bear witness to the realism of his art.

This realism, or this cubism, if you like, is what has most deeply stirred the arts during the last ten years.

The stage sets and costumes of *Parade* clearly demonstrate his preoccupation with extracting from an object all the aesthetic emotion that it can give. Quite often, they have sought to bring painting back to its strictly necessary elements [*stricts éléments*]. . . .

Picasso[133] goes much further than all of them. You see it in *Parade,* with an astonishment that quickly becomes admiration. Above all it's a question of translating reality. However, the motif is no longer reproduced but only represented and rather than

---

131. Léonide Massine (1896–1979) was a principal choreographer for Diaghilev's Ballets Russes, continuing Fokine's sinuous liquidations of classical ballet. Massine choreographed *Parade* (with the assistance of Cocteau) and danced the Chinese Conjurer.

132. *Melancolia* (1514), by Albrecht Dürer (1471–1528), shows a pensive winged figure, with an hourglass and a magic number-square. Leverkühn, in Mann's *Dr. Faustus,* often alludes to it.

133. Pablo Picasso (1881–1973) designed the backdrop and the costumes for *Parade,* his first work for the theater.

being represented it would like to be suggested by a kind of analysis-synthesis embracing all its visible elements and something more, if possible, an integral schematization that would seek to reconcile contradictions while sometimes deliberately renouncing any rendering of the immediate outward aspect of the object. Massine has complied with the Picassian discipline in a surprising fashion. He has identified himself with it and his art is enriched with such cherishable inventions as the realistic steps of the horse in *Parade*—one dancer makes the front feet and another the rear.

The fantastic constructions that represent these gigantic and unexpected personages: The Managers,[134] far from being an obstacle to Massine's fantasy, have given him, one might say, more unconstraint [*désinvolture*].

In sum, *Parade* will overturn the ideas of not a few of the spectators. They will certainly be surprised, but in the most agreeable fashion; charmed, they will learn to recognize all the undoubted grace of modern movement.

A magnificent music-hall Chinaman will give flight to their free fantasy, and, turning the crank of an imaginary auto, the American Girl will express the magic of their everyday life, whose mute rites are celebrated by an Acrobat in blue tights, with an exquisite and surprising agility.

From *Oeuvres en prose complètes*, ed. Pierre Caizergues and Michel Décaudin (Paris: Éditions Gallimard, 1991), 2:865–66; translated by the editor.

■

The collaborators of *Parade* contributed to the literature of Surrealism as well as to the theater of it. The composer Erik Satie (1866–1925) was a Dadaist or Surrealist *avant la lettre*—if Schwitters could announce "I call myself *Merz*" and live in a *Merzbau*, the dandyesque Satie, many years before, managed (he claimed) to regulate his life according to equally absurdist principles: "I eat only white foods: eggs, sugar, grated bones, the fat of dead animals; veal, salt, coconut, chicken cooked in white water; fruit mold, rice, turnips; camphorated sausage, dough, cheese (white), cotton salad, and certain fish (skinless)."[135] But Schwitters was trying to express something about the nature of human life through *Merzbau;* Satie, on the other hand, seemed, through various fictitious or real abstractions of conduct, to be insulating himself from human life.

134. Picasso designed cardboard costumes for Managers (who introduce the three circus acts) as walking Cubist sculpture: the French Manager (who looked like Diaghilev) had a row of trees on his back; the American Manager was a reconstructed skyscraper; the third Manager was supposed to be a Negro on horseback, but the costume proved so troublesome that the Manager was eventually reduced to a mere pantomime horse.

135. Rollo H. Myers, *Erik Satie* (New York: Dover, 1968), 135.

Surrealist dissonance—as opposed to the harmonic dissonance of the Schoenberg school—can be found everywhere in Satie's work. The titles generally discord with the music, either by being incomprehensible or by arousing expectations that the actual sounds will violate: a title such as *Disagreeable Glimpses* or *Pickled Embryos* or *Flabby Preludes for a Dog* seems to register the composer's faint disgust with the music, instead of providing some cue for interpretation of these cheerful autisms for piano. Satie was perhaps the first composer since the Renaissance completely to reject the notion of expression. He prided himself on inventing what he called furniture music—unobtrusive commonplace figures, taken from such familiar sources as Saint-Saëns's *Danse macabre* and Thomas's *Mignon,* repeated over and over (more information on furniture music can be found in the "Painting and Architecture" section of chapter 3).

But all of Satie's music, whether intended as furniture or otherwise, has a certain thinglikeness—self-enclosed, polished, demure. The following extract from *Memoirs of an Amnesiac* anticipates Surrealism in its systematic wrenching away from the plane of the audible to the plane of the tangible. It also reads like a parody of the New Objectivity—though it was written some years before New Objective music came into existence; and Satie's false claim that he generates his music by means of machines anticipates the genuinely machine-assisted music that would soon come into being.

ERIK SATIE
Memoirs of an Amnesiac (1912)

Everyone will tell you that I am not a musician. It's true.

Since the beginning of my career, I have classified myself among the phonometrographers. My labors are pure phonometrics. Take the *Fils des étoiles* or the *Morceaux en forme de poire, En habit de cheval* or the *Sarabandes:* [136] one sees that no musical idea presided in the creation of these works. It is scientific thought that dominates.

Besides, I have more pleasure in measuring a sound than in hearing it. Phonometer in hand, I labor joyously and confidently.

What have I not weighed or measured? All Beethoven, all Verdi, etc. Very curious.

The first time I provided myself with a phonoscope, I examined a B♭ of middle size. I assure you, I have never seen anything more repugnant. I called my servant to make him see it.

With the phono-weigher [*phono-peseur*], a very common, ordinary F♯ attained 93 kilograms. It emanated from a fat tenor whose weight I took.

---

136. *Son of the Stars,* "Chaldean pastoral" for a Rosicrucian ceremony (1891); *Three Pieces in the Form of a Pear,* for piano four hands (1890–1903); *In Riding Costume,* for piano four hands (1911); *Sarabandes,* for piano (1887).

Do you know sound-cleaning? It's rather dirty. Spinning is more proper; to know how to classify them is very exacting and requires a good view. Here we are into phono-technique.

As to explosions of sound, often so disagreeable, cotton stuffed in the ears attenuates them suitably. Here we are into pyrophony.

In order to write my *Pièces froides,*[137] I availed myself of a kaleidophone-recorder. That took seven minutes. I called my servant to make him hear them.

I can well say that phonology is superior to music. It's more varied. The pecuniary reward is greater. I owe my fortune to it.

In any case, with a motodynamophone, a phonometrician with mediocre training can easily notate more sounds than the most skilled musician can, in the same amount of time, with the same effort. It is thanks to that machine that I've written so much.

The future lies with philophony.

From Rollo H. Myers, *Erik Satie* (New York: Dover, 1968), 135.

■

The scenarist of *Parade* was Jean Cocteau (1889–1963), the instigator of much of the Surrealist music theater, including Milhaud's *Le boeuf sur le toit* (1920), *Les mariés de la Tour Eiffel,* composed by five of Les Six (1921), and Stravinsky's *Oedipus Rex* (1927). The official Surrealists considered Cocteau a flighty, fatuous, effeminate man—Breton considered that the whole art of music was rendered distasteful because its main champion was the "notorious *false poet* [Cocteau], a versifier who happens to *debase* rather than to *elevate* everything he touches."[138] But Cocteau's versatility—he was a gifted poet, playwright, critic, filmmaker, caricaturist, even choreographer—allowed him to contemplate artistic transgressions on a field larger than Breton could easily understand. It might even be said that Apollinaire devised the term Surrealism to describe what Cocteau was trying to accomplish.

The year after *Parade,* Cocteau published *Cock and Harlequin* (1918), a series of reflections about music and the other arts, arguing for an art at once hard and fanciful, down-to-earth and astonishing. If Henri Matisse thought that a painting should be like an armchair, Cocteau thought that any piece of art should be as useful and securely constructed as a chair; it is possible to find in these aphorisms many pre-echoes of the rhetoric of the New Objectivity as well that of Surrealism. Of particular interest to the student of comparative arts is Cocteau's presentation of *Parade* as an exercise in "synthetic" Cubism—

137. *Cold Cuts,* for piano (1897).
138. André Breton, *La clé des champs* (Paris: Éditions du Sagittaire, 1953), 77.

putting together a ballet out of scraps of real machine noises and real gestures of people observed in the street, just as Picasso glued swatches of real cloth and strips of real newsprint onto his paintings.

JEAN COCTEAU
from *Cock and Harlequin* (1918)

Simplicity progresses in the same way as refinement. . . .

Art is science in the flesh.

The musician opens the cage-door to arithmetic; the draughtsman gives geometry its freedom.

A work of art must satisfy all the muses—that is what I call "proof by nine." . . .

TACT IN AUDACITY CONSISTS IN KNOWING HOW FAR WE MAY GO TOO FAR.

We must get rid of a Baudelairean prejudice;[139] Baudelaire is bourgeois. The "Bourgeoisie" is the bed-rock of France from which all our artists emerge. They may possibly get clear of it, but it allows them to build dangerously on substantial foundations.

With us there is a house, a lamp, a plate of soup, a fire, wine and pipes at the back of every important of art. . . .

The nightingale sings badly. . . .

Truth is too naked; she does not inflame men.

A sentimental scruple, which prevents us from speaking the whole truth, makes us represent Venus hiding her sex with her hand. But truth points to her sex with her hand.

Satie said: "I want to write a play for dogs, and I have got my scenery. The curtain goes up on a bone." Poor dogs! it is their first play. Afterwards they will be shown more difficult ones, but it will always come back to the bone in the end.

Musicians ought to cure music of its convolutions, its dodges and its tricks, and force it as far as possible to keep *in front of the hearer.*

A POET ALWAYS HAS TOO MANY WORDS IN HIS VOCABULARY, A PAINTER TOO MANY COLORS ON HIS PALETTE, AND A MUSICIAN TOO MANY NOTES ON HIS KEYBOARD. . . .

Let us read again Nietzsche's *The Case of Wagner.*[140]

Never have shallower or profounder things been said. When Nietzsche praises *Carmen,* he praises the crudity that our generation seek in the music-hall. . . .

Satie . . . warned Debussy against Wagner. "Be on your guard," he said. "A scenery

---

139. The poet Charles Baudelaire (1821–67) detested the French bourgeois and hoped to write a poetry of "artificial paradises," sheltered from public complacency and indifferent to questions of good and evil.

140. Nietzsche's *Der Fall Wagner* (1888) contrasts Wagnerian neurotic fog with the Mediterranean clarity and human scale of Georges Bizet's *Carmen* (1873–74).

tree is not upset [*ne se convulse pas*] because somebody comes on to the stage." That is the whole aesthetic of *Pelléas*. . . .

SMALL WORKS. There are certain small works of art whose whole importance lies in their depth; the size of their orifice is of small account.

In music, line is melody. The return to design will necessarily involve a return to melody. . . . Wagner, Stravinsky, and even Debussy are first-rate octopuses. Whoever goes near them is sore put to it to escape from their tentacles; Satie leaves a clear road open. . . .

Satie is the opposite of an improviser. His works might be said to have been completed beforehand, while he meticulously unpicks them, note by note.

Satie teaches what, in our age, is the greatest audacity, simplicity. Has he not proved that he could refine better than anyone? But he clears, simplifies, and strips rhythm naked. Is this once more the music on which, as Nietzsche said, "the spirit dances," as compared with the music "in which the spirit swims"?

Not music one swims in, nor music one dances on; MUSIC ON WHICH ONE WALKS. . . .

Enough of clouds, waves, aquariums, water-sprites, and nocturnal scents;[141] what we need is a music of the earth, everyday music.

Enough of hammocks, garlands, and gondolas; I want someone to build me music I can live in, like a house. . . .

Music is not all the time a gondola, or a racehouse, or a tightrope. It is sometimes a chair as well.

A Holy Family is not necessarily a holy family; it may also consist of a pipe, a pint of beer, a pack of cards and a pouch of tobacco. . . .

THE CAFE-CONCERT IS OFTEN PURE; THE THEATRE IS ALWAYS CORRUPT. . . .

The music-hall, the circus, and the American Negro bands, all these things fertilize an artist just as life does. . . . These entertainments are not art. They stimulate in the same way as machinery, animals, natural scenery, or danger. . . .

A LIGHT STEP PRODUCED BY HEAVY FEEDING. Much fun has been made of an aphorism of mine . . . : "an artist must swallow a locomotive and bring up a pipe." I meant by this that neither painter nor musician should make use of the spectacle afforded by machinery to render their art mechanical, but should make use of the measured exaltation aroused in them by that spectacle in order to express other things of a more intimate kind.

141. Each item in this catalog seems derived from an Impressionist composition: the clouds from Debussy's *Nuages* (from *Nocturnes,* 1899), the waves from his *La mer* (1905), the aquarium from his *Poissons d'or* (*Images 2,* no. 3, 1907), the water sprite from Ravel's "Ondine" (from *Gaspard de la nuit,* 1908), the nocturnal scent from Debussy's *Ibéria* (1909).

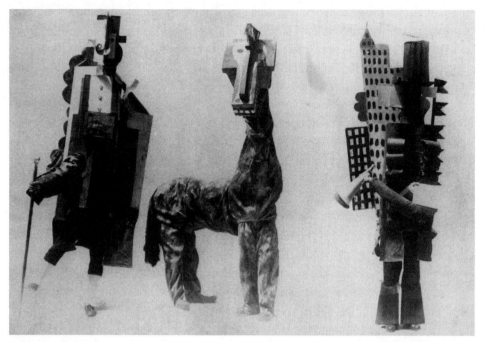

Pablo Picasso, costumes for the Managers in *Parade* (1917). © 2002 Estate of Pablo Picasso/ Artists Rights Society (ARS), New York.

Machinery and American buildings resemble Greek art in so far as their utility endows them with an aridity and a grandeur devoid of any superfluity.

But they are not art. . . .

The score of *Parade* was meant to supply a musical background to suggestive noises, e.g. of sirens, typewriters, aeroplanes and dynamos, placed there like what Georges Braque so aptly calls "facts." . . .

[In *Parade* there was] no humbug, no repetition, no underhand caresses, no feverishness or miasma. Satie never "stirs up the bog." His is the poetical imagination of childhood moulded by a master technician.

In *Parade* the public thought that the transposition of the music-hall was a bad kind of music-hall. . . .

Contrary to the belief of the public, these characters [the Chinese Conjuror, the American Girl, and the two Acrobats in *Parade*] are more Cubist than our "managers." The managers are a sort of human scenery [*hommes-décor*], animated pictures by Picasso, and their very structure necessitates a certain choreographic formula. In the case of these four characters, the problem was to take a series of natural gestures [*gestes réels*] and to metamorphose them into a dance without depriving them of their realistic force, as a modern painter seeks his inspiration in natural objects in order to metamorphose them into pure painting, but without losing sight of the force of their volume, substance, color and shade.

FOR REALITY ALONE, EVEN WHEN WELL CONCEALED, HAS THE POWER TO AROUSE EMOTION.

From *Cocteau's World: An Anthology of Writings by Jean Cocteau,* ed. Margaret Crosland (New York: Dodd, Mead, 1972), 304–14, 328.

■

France was not the only country in which Surrealism thrived; there was an important Czech tradition, for example, represented by such painters as Jindřich Štyrský and such composers as Erwin Schulhoff. Schulhoff (1894–1942) was a versatile composer, who wrote such diverse pieces as the satire against German militarism *Symphonia Germanica* (1919), the American Indian ballet *Ogelala* (1925), the fox-trot *Orinoco* (1934), and a long cantata to the text of the Communist Manifesto (1936). His leftist politics led to his death in German detention in 1942.

He was involved with the Dadaists and the Surrealists almost from the beginning. In 1919 he composed *Sonata Erotica for Solo Mother-Trumpet,* in which a soprano spends several minutes faking a carefully notated orgasm; in 1922 he wrote his jazz-influenced work *The Cloud-Pump,* a set of "serious songs" to "words from the holy ghost Hans Arp." One of Schulhoff's most inventive works in this style is *Bassnightingale* (1922), in which a solo contrabassoon does its best to make soulful liquid birdcalls; Schulhoff also supplied this preface denouncing putrefied Expressionists and nervous aesthetes.

ERWIN SCHULHOFF
"For General Intelligibility as a Confession" (1919)

> The divine spark may be present
> in a liver sausage or in a contrabassoon.
> Hence a dedication to lyrical friends and aesthetes, in short,
> to all you high-strung folks as an "experience."
> If all the others sob in sweet tones on violins,
> then, mark you, I always do just the opposite
> to stir you up, you little marionettes, soulish fops,
> horn-rimmed salon intellectuals, you pathological tea-plants
> and putrefied expressionists.
> I confess without shame to be made from muck
> and to love muck!

But you were born with immaculately ironed pleats
and with a tiptop tailcoat, Your Existencies!
If distance is what I want to keep between me and you,
then I clamp in my monocle, and you show me respect!!!

From MDG CD 304 0617-2 (1995), trans. Susan Marie Praeder.

■

At about the same time that Schulhoff was setting Arp's text, the young William Walton (1902–83) was a houseguest at the Sitwells', composing madcap music for the Surrealistic *Façade* poems of Edith Sitwell (1887–1964). Sitwell intended her poems as pseudomorphisms (in Adorno's term) of music into words: "The poems in *Façade* are *abstract* poems—that is, they are patterns in sound. They are . . . virtuoso exercises in technique of extreme difficulty, in the same sense as that in which certain studies by Liszt are studies in transcendental technique in music." [142] Sitwell mentions Liszt, but she also might have mentioned Stravinsky: she considered Diaghilev's Ballets Russes a liberating influence in art, and she wrote of *Petrushka* in terms that might apply both to her own poetry and to Walton's music: "this ballet, alone among them all, shatters our glass house about our ears. . . . The music, harsh, crackling rags of laughter, shrieks at us like some brightly painted Punch and Judy show." [143]

In *Façade* the phonetic elements of language are overwhelmingly prominent and the semantic elements fairly unimportant—although the continual presence of Queen Victoria and Lord Tennyson, transposed into an orgiastic domain in which Hottentots, Venus, Bacchus, and Hell figure conspicuously, suggests that anti-Victorian satire is part of the poems' project. In Sitwell's *Études transcendentales* of language, the displacement of complicated rhymes to the middle of lines becomes a sort of syncopation; the rhythms never settle into a routine but continually startle. These poems may recall the nonsense verse of Lewis Carroll—but in any case Breton considered Lewis Carroll a great precursor of Surrealism

Walton's music is sensitive to the poems' suggestions of hornpipe, fox-trot, and tango; he may quote traditional tunes, or the *William Tell* overture, but always with some disguise or eccentricity, as if the crank that ground out the music were being turned by an unsteady hand. At the first public performance, in 1923 in London, the curtain rose to reveal another curtain, on which was painted a large face, half pink, half white; the face's mouth was the opening of a megaphone, through which Sitwell recited her poems, to

142. Edith Sitwell, *The Canticle of the Rose Poems: 1917–1949* (New York: Vanguard Press, 1949), xii.
143. Edith Sitwell, *Fire of the Mind,* ed. Elizabeth Salter and Allanah Harper (New York: Vanguard, 1976), 119.

the accompaniment of the tootles and slinks of Walton's little orchestra. The audience was scandalized, enraged; but by 1926 *Façade* was a hit.

In the poem printed here, Sitwell seems to be pondering the old metaphor of waves as horses of the sea—though the horses keep metamorphosing into a whole zoo of odd quadrupeds. The most prominent phoneme theme in the poem is *-or-* or *-ori-* (horse, gloria, boreal, Victoria, memorial, etc.); but the coda is a fantasy on *-inx*.

EDITH SITWELL
"Hornpipe" (1922)

> Sailors come
> To the drum
> Out of Babylon;
> Hobby-horses
> Foam, the dumb
> Sky rhinoceros-glum
>
> Watched the courses of the breakers' rocking horses and with Glaucis,
> Lady Venus [144] on the settee of the horsehair sea!
> Where Lord Tennyson [145] in laurels wrote a gloria free,
> In a borealic iceberg came Victoria; [146] she
> Knew Prince Albert's tall memorial [147] took the colors of the floreal
> And the borealic iceberg; floating on they see
> New-arisen Madam Venus for whose sake from far
> Came the fat and zebra'd emperor from Zanzibar
> Where the golden bouquets lay far Asia, Africa, Cathay,
> All laid before that shady lady by the fibroid Shah.
> Captain Fracasse [148] stout as any water-butt came, stood
> With Sir Bacchus both a-drinking the black tarr'd grapes' blood [149]
> Plucked among the tartan leafage
> By the furry wind whose grief age

144. Venus was born from sea foam, according to myth. Sitwell probably considered Glaucis an escorting sea nymph.

145. Alfred Lord Tennyson (1809–92), British poet laureate and defender of imperialism.

146. Queen Victoria (1819–1901), right-minded British monarch and watchword for prudery.

147. When Victoria's consort, Prince Albert, died in 1861, a monument in his memory was erected in Hyde Park—a cluttered monstrosity, to Modernist eyes.

148. Compare *fracasser,* French for "to shatter."

149. The emblems of Bacchus, the god of wine and orgy, include the grape and the lynx.

Could not wither[150]—like a squirrel with a gold star-nut.
Queen Victoria sitting shocked upon the rocking horse
Of a wave said to the Laureate, "This minx[151] of course
Is as sharp as any lynx and blacker-deeper than the drinks and quite as
Hot as any hottentot, without remorse!
   "For the minx,"
     Said she,
   "And the drinks,
     You can see
Are hot as any hottentot and not the goods for me!"

From *The Canticle of the Rose Poems: 1917–1949* (New York: Vanguard Press, 1949), 60.

■

This section on isms will end with an essay of Krenek's offering some shrewd comments on the relations between Surrealism and Neoclassicism, as well as a brilliant, if somewhat fatigued, overview of musical Modernism—written within the Modernist movement itself.

ERNST KRENEK
"What Is Called the New Music, and Why?" (1937)

We must first pose the question in a quite practical, empirical manner: What does the "New Music" consist of? Schoenberg—his name always appears first, when the New Music is discussed. Berg, Webern, the Schoenberg school. Other striking, generally visible names: Hindemith, Bartók, Stravinsky. Perhaps we should also mention Kurt Weill, certain works of his in any case. Milhaud, Honegger, Alois Hába and many others. . . . One could naturally extend the sequence in many directions, but the essential thing is already clear: in the matter of the acoustic phenomenon, in the matter of the music *qua* music, we can at first glance establish no common ground whatsoever among these different composers. Between a piano piece of Schoenberg's and a song of Kurt Weill's there seem to lie abysses scarcely to be bridged. Nevertheless some common ground must be sought, since our instinct tells us of a certain close connection among these phenomena. Viewed again, empirically, their common ground is an outward-streaming *shock effect* upon the unprejudiced listener who is knowledge-

---

150. Compare Enobarbus on Cleopatra: "Age cannot wither her, nor custom stale / Her infinite variety" (Shakespeare, *Antony and Cleopatra*, act 2, scene 2, ll. 234–35).

151. The minx is presumably Venus, who represents everything that Queen Victoria detests.

able about the musical tradition. Moreover we must not think of our small circle, in which the effect of hearing music is highly graduated and differentiated through a great deal of experience. As we step into a larger, heterogeneous circle of listeners, we can distinctly observe the shock. The best proof that the shock is present lies in the panicky need to ward it off; the aversion against this experience and the fear of it have caused the New Music to be banned from every performance organization in which such a heterogeneous circle, accustomed to traditional sounds, is preponderant. The fact that this shock was and still is felt also demonstrates the well-known phrase *épater le bourgeois*—an intention that is always attributed accusingly to the new music. It would not be very original to react apologetically to such a reproach, seeing that lying is always the weakest sort of defense. We must calmly accept that the reproach is justified. . . .

The shock, this characteristic, uneasy-making shattering of equilibrium, this nervous reaction, which a piece by Schoenberg calls forth, is very different from that of Stravinsky or Weill. No wonder, since their music is obviously very different. What exactly are the factors that make these differences? In a piece by Schoenberg, it is clear that a strange effect emanates from it; its musical habitus is decidedly deviant from the customary; its harmony consists exclusively of dissonances, no known key is to be found, the melodies indulge themselves in extreme intervals. In Bartók similar principles govern, in which the characteristic national coloring of the material is conspicuous. From Hindemith to Weill, however, the habitus of the music is displaced so far that it again becomes, so to speak, "normal"—flagrantly, provocatively normal. And that is plainly it: here the shock effectively proceeds from the provocative character of the normality. In the *Threepenny Opera*[152] song no sort of "modern" effect comes forth from the musical elements, and yet, in a definite sense, the result is modern.

To begin with, it is well known that Schoenberg's special stylistic properties result from a consistent intensification of the expressive means of earlier times. Many melodies of the *Gurrelieder*[153]—in which the connection with Brahms and Wagner is evident—already show in their wide-stretched intervals the germ of later developments, and Schoenberg himself says that he attained the new tonal language by way of intensified need for expressive means. Thus in the domain of expression there is a straight line, which has led to a radical transformation of the means of expression. The expressive will, i.e., the intention with which the means are seized, remains until late atonal music is aligned in all essentials with that of the romantics; indeed this similarity of will compels a transformation of means, if something new, something personal,

152. *Die Dreigroschenoper* (1928), Kurt Weill's very popular setting of Brecht.
153. *Gurrelieder* (1900–11), Schoenberg's richly chromatic song sequence for a gigantic orchestra.

is to be said. It is therefore possible to explain why *Expressionism*—the realm where the middle-period Schoenberg certainly belongs—seems to be so totally overcome. While the immediate reaction to art proceeds mainly from the sensuous impression and while this adheres above all to the material, Expressionism, having brought up a sheerly anarchic transmogrification of material, seemed to indicate a progress so unheard of, so rapid, so dizzy-making, that one feels oneself unable to grasp the Primitivism that came after it, so powerful does the regression seem. Meanwhile this is how matters stand: the expressionistic contents entailed less of a new intention than the boldness of the transformation of material first allowed one to suppose; and the new later-appearing artistic intentions (with regard to the contents) left Expressionism the more in the background, the more pointedly those intentions were coupled with a restitution of the old-accustomed materials, so that one hoped to be able to send home the disagreeable guest, the more satisfied that one no longer ran the danger to be considered reactionary—when one was in reality altogether reactionary. So it comes out: our first task is to retrieve Expressionism's honor.

The new intentions of these others, certainly also the style forms belonging to the New Music, consist above all in their wish to bring into question the validity of the expressive means that they themselves used, which, often unexpected, sometimes intended, brings about a total reversal of plus and minus, and from the intended destruction there arises a real restoration. Even if the catchwords of the visual arts do not allow themselves to be transferred exactly to musical conditions, they still have their value, as distinguishing marks of general attitudes more than as descriptions of concrete facts. Therefore one can use, with respect to the New Music of this kind, the terms "New Objectivity" "Surrealism," and "Neoclassicism," three attitudes with a common tendency to retain or recover the old material. . . .

Taking this restorative tendency furthest is *Neoclassicism,* a term that must have first come into use in Busoni's circle. Behind the habitus of a lucid spiritual reaction against the chaotic darkness of late Romanticism there is concealed, naturally, a genuinely romantic attitude, crystallized in the idea that one could again attain the treasured grace and worthiness, the noble symmetry and the eternal *serenità* of the classics, if one could first divest the wildly fabricated means of Expressionism, and then, as far as possible, tame them and smooth them. That is not a completely naive procedure, especially when it is practiced by ingenious men, as later by Stravinsky. The classicism [*Klassizität*] of antiquity in *Oedipus Rex* is just as problematic as de Chirico's[154] landscape of ruins and Picasso's academy. What is brought to light here looks more like

---

154. Giorgio de Chirico (1888–1978) was an important precursor to the Surrealists—his enigmatic paintings often contain elements of classical architecture.

excavations after an earthquake than like something freshly copied out of the atelier. Everything questionable in the age is engraved on the smooth façades erected here; and the ground, which bears the weight of the whole splendor, is furrowed by many uncanny rifts and fissures. The classicism of antiquity lives here anew and in the same shape in which it genuinely came to us: in the form of fragments. The torso, mutilated by invisible forces, has a more mysteriously intense and charged life than the whole that it perhaps once was; in Neoclassicism (distinguished from the Renaissance in that it falls short of perfection because it lacks any intention for wholeness and illusion), the scars and fractures that a work carries, with or without the intention of the maker, are not only its charm, but also represent its sole truth. . . . In the domain of the fragmentary the development of Neoclassicism is connected with *Surrealism*, which, more energetically destructive, lives in the montage of the ruins that it comes across.[155] If, in the case of Neoclassicism, the intention is primarily directed toward the production of an appearance of closedness [*Geschlossenheit*], and the discovery of its seeming captivity [*Scheinhaftigkeit*] is often a secondary effect compelled from without, so the intention of Surrealism is directed from the first toward the unmasking of illusion. The pieces are mounted in an ensemble so that one can see that they do not fit together. Here rules the seriousness of the clown, and the melancholy of his humor. From the beginning on, it is established that nothing here is established, that everything has fallen out of joint, and the attempt to make any order proves that a desperate disorder prevails. The material cannot be used up enough, for the isolated model specimen of normality shows most ostentatiously that there exists no norm into which it fits, and that out of such stuff one can only patch together a cabinet of abnormalities. An eminently polemical trait is characteristic of Surrealism, in contrast to Neoclassicism, which confronts its distrust concerning the normality of the material in a rather calming manner, in that it tries to transfigure that normality. Neoclassicism has a significant tendency to be ahistorical, in that it would like to recover the lost *primal meaning* [*Ursinn*]. In this matter Surrealism is its exact opposite, in that Surrealism dissects [*herauspräpariert*] the *nonsense* [*Unsinn*] that arises when a consciousness that has not kept up with history treats a world falling into ruin as if it were still whole.

. . . In the end, Neoclassicism thrives all too easily in the suspicion that it owes its existence merely to the masking of the fact that one would not like to be separated

155. Compare Adorno (1956): "Surrealism forms the complement to the . . . New Objectivity, which came into being at the same time. The *Neue Sachlichkeit*'s horror at the crime of ornamentation, as Adolf Loos called it, is mobilized by Surrealist shocks. . . . Surrealism gathers up the things the *Neue Sachlichkeit* denies to human beings; the distortions attest to the violence that the prohibition has done to the objects of desire" (Adorno, *Notes to Literature*, vol. 1, trans. Shierry Weber Nicholsen [New York: Columbia University Press, 1991], 89–90).

from the old material; one sees how Neoclassicism passes, more or less worthily, into a solemn conformity, for show alone. A similar danger threatens Surrealism. Of the macabre operetta, in which the twisted limbs of withered strength had been mounted, there gradually remains left only the operetta—the skeletons become, if desired, slim bodies, and the disagreeable stench of corpses becomes, through the simple removal of some corrosive ingredients, transformed into the more popular odor of hit-tune merchandise. Moreover, in the case of surrealistic music there predominated from the beginning the character of the text to which it was joined. The process of "transfunctioning" [*Umfunktionierens*], however, which is an essential means of montage technique and consists of splitting the customary unity of text and music and forcing on each of the halves a new meaning opposed to its earlier one, is unfortunately reversible, and all too quickly it happens that music, freed from its compromising text, finds its home, its primal ground: only a pair of false basses are needed to rectify it, and in the panopticon of horror it becomes completely cozy.

The direction that could be called the "New Objectivity," embodied in many works by Hindemith and above all his multifarious imitators, threatens to go down the same path toward conformism. It has in common with Neoclassicism the Anti-Espressivo-Tendency, and it originated in the same way: by neutralizing the material newly formed by Expressionism under the compulsion of its will to express; by freeing it of the burden of affect; and by regarding it as self-given, indifferent. The affectlessness, the absence of emotion, of which composers were inordinately proud, is conditioned by a certain frenzy in the handiwork, and the essential characteristic of this music became a motorlikeness [*Motorik*]—the less talented examples of which were often reminiscent of water pipes and sewing machines. Here the shock proceeded from the spectacle of inhuman thinness of feeling and emptiness of thought, never so baldly produced before; but it was soon paralyzed and weakened through the fact that such music, while it did not engage the mind of the interpreter, was all the more enjoyable for his fingers. The concept of "enjoyment in playing" [*Spielfreudigkeit*] soon excused everything else, while the emotional side, greatly neglected for so long, found itself satisfied through the renaissance of the strolling musician [*Musikanten*]. Concerning the newly discovered virtue of strolling musicians, even the better heads temporarily let themselves become stupid, and thought of them as excellent musicians whenever reminded of the topic. For the present we do not wish to criticize the spirit of the strolling musician sociologically, where it is most vulnerable, but only to establish that under this rubric, which seems to express something touchingly harmless and, beyond all the rubbish, forgivable, there creeps everything lazy, muggy, boring, moldy—which otherwise would have long been recognizable and obvious. Not in vain have the pitiless motor composers discovered their elective affinity with those birds of passage, the strolling musicians—even as their motor urges began to contrast all too sharply with the revived estimation of the value of feelings. From there the culture of recorder-tootling took its point of departure, and its spread permitted every fool to march in the vanguard of the age, while he played a bad composition by a recognized master still more badly. Even here the shock is at length muffled; the prevailing coarseness of heart does not get excited at its mirror image in motoric New Objective music and is comforted through the vital enjoyment in it, as it is so gaily, fervently, piped and fiddled.

Folkloristic music, developing primarily in the east, also demonstrates a certain kinship with this motoric music; here also there is an attempt to take up the transformed material of Expressionism, without renouncing basic givens, in this cause of a national sort. The folk music of the eastern peoples is especially well suited to such amalgamating, for its melodies are based on scales that deviate from our major-minor system. Therefore the application of modern achievements to this substrate does not seem as violent as would be the case if our folk melodies were so employed. On the other side, the rhythmic structure of this eastern folk music, with its long monotonous sections in a uniform tempo, establishes from the beginning an elective affinity with the development of the "New Objective" music discussed above. Here too we see a gradual increase of nationalistic substance, over the contents of transformed sound material, which, in the case of Bartók, is still very strongly present, rendering his music a truly lasting achievement. All the Tartar, Uzbek, Turkmenic, and other suites that are today produced in eastern Europe in great numbers have scarcely anything to do with the New Music, and offer at best a fitting-out of national raw material for an unpretentious civic use.

Since this long decontaminated and completely conformist music is now played everywhere—in fact not especially much of it, since it is in general rather insignificant—it looks as if the New Music has the success that it deserves, or even more success, and lamenting would not be warranted. But such objections can only be raised by someone who has noticed nothing of the great fissure that goes through what is called the New Music. . . .

When we comprehensively ask what is called the New Music, we can fix our eyes on the whole formal complex of contemporary music: a very great anti-espressivo sector, and a quantitatively very small espressivo sector. The essential distinguishing mark of the New Music is the posing of the form-question, i.e., the problem of how the relationship of the musical composition to the age is realized in the arrangements that regulate the discharging [Ablauf] of the work's component elements. The anti-espressivo music can only interest us as far as it also broaches the form problem, which it does only indirectly. While the old form shapes are made questionable through certain distortions and ruptures, the whole composition does not categorically pose the form question, because the conserving of the old material does not demand or admit raising such a question. In the espressivo music, on the contrary, the form-problem is central, because the transformation of the material has dissolved the old forms.

From *Über neue Musik: Sechs Vorlesungen zu Einführung in die Theoretischen Grundlagen* (Darmstadt: Wissenschaftliche Buchgesellschaft, 1977), 5–13, 17; translated by the editor.

8 Music, Social Responsibility, and Politics

Many of the Modernist composers intended their music as an instrument of ethical or political reform. But the relation between politics and aesthetic technique is vexing.

A number of composers would have liked to identify the forward march toward a more egalitarian society with the avant-garde harmony promoted by Schoenberg—and some, especially Hanns Eisler, skillfully combined the progressive in both areas. But Eisler, like all the rest, knew that factory laborers don't bustle into taverns at the end of the day to sing twelve-tone canons, no matter how cheering. This led to a certain tension between the two different notions of progress.

In the Soviet Union, this tension became institutionalized. Receptive in its early days to the experimental music of Nicolay Roslavets and others, the Soviet Union under Stalin attempted to denounce (under such names as Formalism and Obscurantism) and exterminate every sort of music that would trouble an ignorant ear. Therefore the composers who felt frustrated by restrictions were forced to cultivate irony as a technique for obeying the letter but subverting the spirit of state control: the triumphalist gestures in certain works of Shostakovich, for example, seem puffed up, calculated to sneer (hand hiding mouth) at the authorities that command them. In Germany of the 1920s, on the other hand, such left-wing composers as Kurt Weill cultivated similar forms of irony to mock the bourgeois, leading to the odd result that anti-bourgeois and anti-Soviet music have the same sort of in-quotation-marks, somebody-else-is-saying-this-not-me flavor—though Weill's irony is more conspicuous, since his game (until Hitler took power) was less dangerous.

In the Germany of the 1930s, there were few composers well known today who were committed Nazis, though Hans Pfitzner did what he could to court the favor of Joseph Goebbels, Hitler's minister of propaganda. Most of the Jewish composers either fled (like Weill and Schoenberg) or were executed (like Viktor Ullmann); the non-Jewish composers either fled (like Hindemith—rather reluctantly) or found some form of accommodation with the government. A senior composer like Richard Strauss, who knew that his cultural prestige was immense, could probe the limits of his freedom in various ways: Strauss tried to have a clear public acknowledgment of the role of his Jewish librettist Stefan Zweig, a loud opponent of Hitler, at the première of *Die schweigsame Frau* in 1935; on the other hand, in 1933 Strauss had dedicated to Goebbels his song *Das Bächlein,* op. 88, no. 1 (the otherwise harmless text contains a reference to "mein Führer"), to celebrate Strauss's appointment as president of the Reichsmusikkammer. Less monumental composers tended to acquiescence to the regime, either grudgingly or not: Carl Orff worked in Germany, and Anton Webern in Nazi-occupied Austria, without much difficulty.

But it is venturesome to say that there is a Nazi or an anti-Nazi musical style, or a Soviet or an anti-Soviet style. The Nazi exhibitions of *entartete Kunst* (degenerate art) pretended to have some stylistic basis for the category; but in fact any sort of music composed by a degenerate composer (that is, Jewish or otherwise unsatisfactory from the Nazi point of view) would be discovered, on careful examination, to be degenerate. Music officially approved by totalitarian governments certainly tended to be simple, or simplistic, on the level of harmony and structure. But it is rarely easy to say whether the accessible style of Carl Orff or the later (Soviet) Prokofiev is the result of conformity to political demands or of engagement with one of many aesthetic movements that exalt the ritualistic and the communal over individual expression. Furthermore, it is impossible to make clear stylistic distinctions between the political rightists and leftists. The rightist Webern (who was enthusiastic for the Nazi Party) and the leftist Eisler were both pupils of Schoenberg (a monarchist Jew) and continually stressed their admiration of him. Both Webern and Eisler were active in the workers' choral movement—in 1929 Webern wrote to Eisler congratulating him for the "uncommon beauty" of his op. 35 male choruses, which urged solidarity among laborers. Furthermore, Orff began by composing choral cantatas on texts by the leftist Brecht, such as *Vom Frühjahr, Öltank und vom Fliegen* (1930), in which seven hundred intellectuals worship an oil tank. It is odd to hear a pounding triadic style that anticipates *Carmina Burana* (1937) used as a vehicle for socialist satire; but it teaches the indifference of technique to the politics it serves—which is not to say that politics is indifferent to the technique that serves it.

The elderly Schoenberg pondered the issue of the politics of the twelve-tone method with some acuity:

It has become a habit of late to qualify aesthetic and artistic subjects in terms borrowed from the jargon of politics. . . . There are people who call the method of composing with twelve tones "bolshevik." They pretend that in a "set of twelve tones," upon which such compositions are founded, since there is no tonic nor dominant, every tone is considered independent, and consequently exerts equal functions.

This is wrong in every respect; yet it is curious to note that even the exact contrary has been contended. The German composer, Paul von Klenau, during Hitler's time, composed a whole opera in the twelve-tone style.[1] After a successful performance, he published an essay in which he "demonstrated" that this method is a true image of national-socialist principles! . . .

1. The opera *Elisabeth von England*, first performed at Kassel in 1939, by Paul von Klenau (1883–1946).

In a "fascist" interpretation, the basic set accordingly would represent the leader, the Duce, the Fuehrer, on whom all depends, who distributes power and function to every tone.[2]

Schoenberg, however, was perhaps too dismissive of the power of music as political metaphor. Even if the relation between the musical signifier and the political signified is wholly arbitrary, music insinuates itself into politics and every other aspect of life. Even highly technical aspects of music can attain great metaphorical power.

■ In 1925 the young Hanns Eisler (1898–1962) wrote the following lively essay claiming that the new music isn't new at all—that composers have always responded to their contemporary world, and in a world in which love letters are delivered by railway train, not a postal coach, it is necessary to write music that takes this factor into account. This argument, of course, has the corollary that the most sensitive sort of music is that which takes into account the greatest number of factors in the present world—the whole apparatus of economic production, distribution, and consumption. In his collaborations with Bertolt Brecht, such as *Die Mutter* (1931) and *Die Rundköpfe und die Spitzköpfe* (1934–36), Eisler would attempt just this sort of pan-cultural sensitivity.

HANNS EISLER
"On Old and New Music" (1925)

What isn't new music accused of! (By new music I mean music after Richard Strauss.) They say it has no tradition, is all bluff or is construed; it does away—so they say—with the musical idea, melody and especially with form. All these accusations, were they true, would show the differences between old and new music. But one thing is forgotten, namely, that the same accusations were leveled against old music when it was new. Today Mozart is counted among the easily understandable composers, yet in his time he was considered complicated, florid and recklessly discordant. And what about Beethoven's Symphony No. 9, or even more, his last quartets? It has always been the same when together with new sound effects a new style appears.

The fact that we wear different clothes today [from those] we wore five hundred years ago is not questioned, for people adapt themselves to new ways of living. For a worker standing at a machine eight hours a day wearing clothes of the Renaissance would be absurd; as well as an office worker sitting at his desk in a toga; or a woman wearing a crinoline. How would she climb into a streetcar got up like that for example, or get through the bustling crowds thronging the streets today? None of Schubert's

2. Arnold Schoenberg, *Style and Idea: Selected Writings of Arnold Schoenberg*, ed. Leonard Stein, trans. Leo Black (Berkeley: University of California, 1984), 249–50.

contemporaries made fun of the subject of his song *Die Post* (Mailcoach).[3] Yet people make fun of the piece *Pacific 231*[4] by Honegger (a young Swiss-born French composer) before they have heard it, because it is about an express train. (Here it is not a question of comparing the composers or the compositions but the subject of the compositions.) Schubert wrote his song about the mailcoach, not as a "vehicle," but as a "messenger of love." Today mailcoaches no longer exist. You will agree that with the best will in the world the modern musician cannot regard an "express train" as a "messenger of love," although it may well be so, just as Schubert's mailcoach was. But he is fascinated perhaps by the speed of it, the power, or perhaps something else typical of the time. Why, one might ask, shouldn't an express train mean something to a child of his time?

Take another example: the mill was a popular lyrical subject. Countless poems were composed about the mill, the millstream, the miller and the miller's daughter, drawing various conclusions. For the composer today it is more difficult. There are few romantic mills left and who wants to lie down by a stream under a signboard. Today's mill is usually a factory filled with the noise of rushing, pounding and hissing. The composer of earlier days saw his mill as an ornament to nature. Together with the mill he loved its inhabitants and their patriarchal way of life. Today's artist, if he is emotionally honest and thinks clearly, would have to draw quite different conclusions were he confronted with a Mill Company Limited. Possibly he would see hundreds of people working, he would see poverty and distress. Even declarations of love sound different in a factory yard [from those] in nature. And he will be wary of asking today's millstream—the factory waste—whither it is flowing so fast, as Schubert asks his millstream.

The modern artist is impressed by quite different things, accordingly he must feel quite differently. If these different sensations are given a form of expression, then the way of expressing them, the musical configuration will also be different. And the material with which the artist fashions his new ideas will consequently have to change with his changed intentions. This process and the results of it are called "new" by some people and "modern" by others. In reality it is neither new nor modern, only different. Now it would be wrong to believe that the modern artist regards his musical predecessors without respect or with contempt. No one admires the masters of old music more and needs to understand them better than does the modern artist. But this admiration and understanding must never become philistine, rejecting all that differs from the old school.

No one needs to understand them better?

3. "Die Post": song in Schubert's *Winterreise* cycle (1828).
4. Honegger's *Pacific 231* (1923) is an orchestral evocation of a railway train.

No branch of art in the world has ever broken completely with the work of its predecessors. Elements common to the past can always be found even in works decried as "radical." Not only are the older forms frequently used (concerto grosso, fugue, suite; in opera the aria and recitative), but also in details the continuity from classical or preclassical music can be seen. You may judge from this that today's artist must have had a very comprehensive schooling with a profound comprehension of the work of his predecessors. To be able to play an instrument and have a superficial knowledge of music of the past, are not enough. He himself must have experienced the whole development of music in order to move freely in his art. No matter how much the presentation of an art may change, the criteria for the work of art itself will always remain the same. Whether about a mill or a Mill Company Limited is immaterial when all is said and done. In the end the listener will only ask himself, did the composer have a musical idea and was he able to give shape to it? The question of a triad in C major or a new chord is equally immaterial. The main thing will always be—whether the artist can express with the highest degree of perfection what he wishes to express emotionally. . . .

Let me say this to all music lovers and music listeners: don't come to a concert only as guardians of cherished traditions. Don't cling to a standard of beauty by which you assess a work, for it may not be what you really feel. Don't look up reference books to see "whether it is right" or whether this chord was "allowed" a hundred years ago. And if you hear a complicated sound, then try to understand it, don't scold the creator. You must not believe that all modern composers are revolutionaries or are poking fun. They simply want to make music, that is all, as our great masters wanted to, young or old. Everyone in his own time and within the framework of that time. That is the whole secret!

From *A Rebel in Music,* ed. Manfred Grabs, trans. Marjorie Meyer (Berlin: Seven Seas, 1978), 19–23.

■

If Karl Marx considered that religion was the opiate of the masses, Brecht found music to be a still more sinister drug. The German poet, playwright, and drama theoretician Bertolt Brecht (1898–1956) fought to reform the music theater: he was the successor of Calzabigi (the librettist of Gluck's 1762 *Orfeo,* the great reform opera of the mid-eighteenth century) and John Gay (the poet of *The Beggar's Opera,* 1728)—indeed Brecht's affinity to Gay is clear from his adaptation of *The Beggar's Opera* as *The Threepenny Opera,* first performed in 1928.

Brecht's most significant essay on music theater is a critique, signed by both Brecht and Peter Suhrkamp (1891–1959), of the Brecht and Kurt Weill opera *Aufstieg und Fall der Stadt Mahagonny* (*Rise and Fall of the City of Mahagonny,* 1930)—an expansion of a short theater piece called *Mahagonny-Songspiel* (1927). Brecht's analysis falls along these lines: (1) the public chiefly desires to be put into a stupor, to forget the miseries of life, and opera, especially the swoony Wagnerian opera, arose to provide this anesthesia; (2) the public needs to be forced to wake up, to confront exploitation and inequality; (3) but, since the public doesn't want to wake up, the amphetamine, the antidote to opera, must be smuggled into an opera that provides many of the old narcotic satisfactions. This is why Brecht keeps insisting that his opera is "culinary," dishing up the familiar fun—the sentimental duet, the hit tune; *but* it is also critical, and calls into question its own pleasurability. Brecht was a realist, according to his personal definition: "*Realist* means: laying bare society's causal network / showing up the dominant viewpoint as the viewpoint of the dominators";[5] and in *Rise and Fall of the City of Mahagonny* Brecht hoped to attain realism in an indirect matter by erecting a self-consciously flimsy structure of illusion and then making sure that the soufflé fizzles, deflates—thereby providing the shock of facing fact that would be impossible for an opera to provide directly. At the end of the opera, the city of Mahagonny meets the fate of Sodom, as a mock God descends to blast it into nonentity; just as capitalism is shown to be an untenable system of economics, so opera is shown to be an untenable mode of art.

The opera's plot is a parable about the origin of capitalism: a little band of gangsters founds a city in Florida (or somewhere) called Mahagonny, under the motto, Here you can do anything you want. To illustrate this motto Brecht and Weill devised a snappy chorale for the jazz age:

> First thing, remember, stuff your maw;
> Second, don't forget to fuck;
> Third, a fist right to the jaw;
> Fourth, drink till you fall in the muck.
> Most of all, the rule is: you
> Do everything you want to do.

The naive hero falls in love with a prostitute, and all is mostly well until he runs out of money and fails to pay his bill—a capital offense in the realm of capitalism. Everyone, including the prostitute, forsakes the hero, and he is put to death. In the death scene, and indeed throughout the work, there is a tension between operatic sentimentality and some harsher and larger point of view, an anger in which all pathos vanishes, a recoil against the whole mechanism of opera and its bourgeois patrons. This dissonance among the components of the theater itself is akin to the dissonances of Surrealism; and indeed the last important collaboration between Weill and Brecht was *The Seven Deadly Sins* (1933), a spectacle organized by the Surrealist poet Edward James.

---

5. *Brecht on Theatre*, trans. John Willett (New York: Hill and Wang, 1991), 109.

BERTOLT BRECHT AND PETER SUHRKAMP
"The Modern Theatre Is the Epic Theatre" (1930)

Our existing opera is a culinary opera. It was a means of pleasure long before it turned into merchandise. It furthers pleasure even where it requires, or promotes, a certain degree of education, for the education in question is an education of taste. To every object it adopts a hedonistic approach. It "experiences," and it ranks as an "experience." Why is *Mahagonny* an opera? Because its basic attitude is that of an opera: that is to say, culinary. Does *Mahagonny* adopt a hedonistic approach? It does. Is *Mahagonny* an experience? It is an experience. For . . . *Mahagonny* is a piece of fun.

The opera *Mahagonny* pays conscious tribute to the senselessness of the operatic form. The irrationality of opera lies in the fact that rational elements are employed, solid reality is aimed at, but at the same time it is all washed out by the music. A dying man is real. If at the same time he sings we are translated to the sphere of the irrational. (If the audience sang at the sight of him the case would be different.) The more unreal and unclear the music can make the reality—though there is of course a third, highly complex and in itself quite real element which can have quite real effects but is utterly remote from the reality of which it treats—the more pleasurable the whole process becomes: the pleasure grows in proportion to the degree of unreality.

The term "opera"—far be it from us to profane it—leads, in *Mahagonny*'s case, to all the rest. The intention was that a certain unreality, irrationality and lack of seriousness should be introduced at the right moment, and so strike with a double meaning.

The irrationality which makes its appearance in this way only fits the occasion on which it appears.

It is a purely hedonistic approach.

As for the content of this opera, *its content is pleasure*. Fun, in other words, not only as form but as subject-matter. At least, enjoyment was meant to be the object of the inquiry even if the inquiry was intended to be an object of enjoyment. Enjoyment here appears in its current historical role: as merchandise.

It is undeniable that at present this content must have a provocative effect. In the thirteenth section, for example, where the glutton stuffs himself to death; because hunger is the rule. We never even hinted that others were going hungry while he stuffed, but the effect was provocative all the same. It is not everyone who is in a position to stuff himself full that dies of it, yet many are dying of hunger because this man stuffs himself to death. His pleasure provokes, because it implies so much.

In contexts like these the use of opera as a means of pleasure must have provocative effects today. Though not of course on the handful of opera-goers. Its power to provoke introduces reality once more. *Mahagonny* may not taste particularly agreeable; it may even (thanks to guilty conscience) make a point of not doing so. But it is culinary through and through.

Mahagonny is nothing more or less than an opera. . . .

Opera had to be brought up to the technical level of the modern theatre. The modern theatre is the epic theatre. The following table shows certain changes of emphasis as between the dramatic and the epic theatre:[6]

Dramatic Theatre	Epic Theatre
plot	narrative
implicates the spectator in a stage situation	turns the spectator into an observer, but
wears down his capacity for action	arouses his capacity for action
provides him with sensations	forces him to take decisions
experience	picture of the world
the spectator is involved in something	he is made to face something
suggestion	argument
instinctive feelings are preserved	brought to the point of recognition
the spectator is in the thick of it, shares the experience	the spectator stands outside, studies
the human being is taken for granted	the human being is the object of the inquiry
he is unalterable	he is alterable and able to alter
eyes on the finish	eyes on the course
one scene makes another	each scene for itself
growth	montage
linear development	in curves
evolutionary determinism	jumps
man as a fixed point	man as a process
thought determines being	social being determines thought
feeling	reason

When the epic theatre's methods begin to penetrate the opera the first result is a radical *separation of the elements*. The great struggle for supremacy between words, music and production—which always brings up the question "which is the pretext for what?": is the music the pretext for the events on the stage, or are these the pretext for the music? etc.—can simply be by-passed by radically separating the elements. So long as the expression "Gesamtkunstwerk" (or "integrated work of art") means that

---

6. This table does not show absolute antitheses but mere shifts of accent. In a communication of fact, for instance, we may choose whether to stress the element of emotional suggestion or that of plain rational argument. [Brecht's note.]

the integration is a muddle, so long as the arts are supposed to be "fused" together, the various elements will all be equally degraded, and each will act as a mere "feed" to the rest. The process of fusion extends to the spectator, who gets thrown into the melting pot too and becomes a passive (suffering) part of the total work of art. Witch-craft of this sort must of course be fought against. Whatever is intended to produce hypnosis, is likely to induce sordid intoxication, or creates fog, has got to be given up.

Words, music and setting must become more independent of one another.

MUSIC

For the music, the change of emphasis proved to be as follows:

Dramatic Opera	Epic Opera
The music dishes up [*serviert*]	the music communicates
music which heightens the text	music which sets forth the text
music which proclaims the text	music which takes the text for granted
music which illustrates	which takes a position
music which paints the psychological situation	which gives the attitude

Music plays the chief part in our thesis.

TEXT

We had to make something straightforward and instructive of our fun, if it was not to be irrational and nothing more. The form employed was that of the moral tableau. The tableau is performed by the characters in the play. The text had to be neither mor-alizing nor sentimental, but to put morals and sentimentality on view. Equally impor-tant was the spoken word and the written word (of the titles). Reading seems to en-courage the audience to adopt the most natural attitude towards the work.

SETTING

Showing independent works of art as part of a theatrical performance is a new de-parture. Neher's[7] projections adopt an attitude towards the events on the stage; as when the real glutton sits in front of the glutton whom Neher has drawn. In the same way the stage unreels the events that are fixed on the screen. These projections of Ne-her's are quite as much an independent component of the opera as are Weill's music and the text. They provide its visual aids.

Of course such innovations also demand a new attitude on the part of the audiences who frequent opera houses. . . .

7. Brecht's old friend the painter (and sometime librettist) Caspar Neher designed the stage sets and devised a series of projections for *Rise and Fall of the City of Mahagonny*.

It is true that the audience had certain desires which were easily satisfied by the old opera but are no longer taken into account by the new. What is the audience's attitude during an opera; and is there any chance that it will change?

Bursting out of the underground stations, eager to become as wax in the magicians' hands, grown-up men, their resolution proved in the struggle for existence, rush to the box office. They hand in their hat at the cloakroom, and with it they hand in their normal behavior: the attitudes of "everyday life." Once out of the cloakroom they take their seats with the bearing of kings. How can we blame them? You may think a grocer's bearing better than a king's and still find this ridiculous. For the attitude that these people adopt in the opera is unworthy of them. Is there any possibility that they may change it? Can we persuade them to get out their cigars?

Once the content becomes, technically speaking, an independent component, to which text, music and setting "adopt attitudes"; once illusion is sacrificed to free discussion, and once the spectator, instead of being enabled to have an experience, is forced as it were to cast his vote; then a change has been launched which goes far beyond formal matters and begins for the first time to affect the theatre's social function.

In the old operas all discussion of the content is rigidly excluded. If a member of the audience had happened to see a particular set of circumstances portrayed and had taken up a position *vis-à-vis* them, then the old opera would have lost its battle: the "spell would have been broken." Of course there were elements in the old opera which were not purely culinary; one has to distinguish between the period of its development and that of its decline. *The Magic Flute, Fidelio, Figaro*[8] all included elements that were philosophical, dynamic. And yet the element of philosophy, almost of daring, in these operas was so subordinated to the culinary principle that their sense was in effect tottering and was soon absorbed in sensual satisfaction. Once its original "sense" had died away the opera was by no means left bereft of sense, but had simply acquired another one—a sense *qua* opera. The content had been smothered in the opera. Our Wagnerites are now pleased to remember that the original Wagnerites posited a sense of which they were presumably aware. Those composers who stem from Wagner still insist on posing as philosophers. A philosophy which is of no use to man or beast, and can only be disposed of as a means of sensual satisfaction (*Elektra, Jonny spielt auf*).[9] We still maintain the whole highly-developed technique which made this pose possible: the vulgarian strikes a philosophical attitude from which to conduct his hackneyed ruminations. It is only from this point, from the death of the sense (and it is understood that this sense could die), that we can start to understand the further innovations which are now plaguing opera: to see them as desperate attempts to supply this art

8. Mozart's *Die Zauberflöte* (1791); Beethoven's *Fidelio* (1804–14); Mozart's *Le nozze di Figaro* (1786).
9. Strauss's *Elektra* (1909); Krenek's *Jonny spielt auf* (1927).

with a posthumous sense, a "new" sense, by which the sense comes ultimately to lie in the music itself, so that the sequence of musical forms acquires a sense simply *qua* sequence, and certain proportions, changes, etc. from being a means are promoted to become an end. Progress which has neither roots nor result; which does not spring from new requirements but satisfies the old ones with new titillations, thus furthering a purely conservative aim. New material is absorbed which is unfamiliar "in this context," because at the time when "this context" was evolved it was not known in any context at all. (Railway engines, factories, aeroplanes, bathrooms, etc. act as a diversion. Better composers choose instead to deny all content by performing—or rather smothering—it in the Latin tongue.) [10] This sort of progress only indicates that something has been left behind. It is achieved without the overall function being changed; or rather, with a view to stopping any such change from taking place. And what about *Gebrauchsmusik?* [11]

At the very moment when neoclassicism, in other words stark Art for Art's sake, took the field (it came as a reaction against the emotional element in musical impressionism) the idea of utilitarian music, or *Gebrauchsmusik,* emerged like Venus from the waves: music was to make use of the amateur. The amateur was used as a woman is "used." Innovation upon innovation. The punch-drunk listener suddenly wants to play. The struggle against idle listening turned into a struggle for keen listening, then for keen playing. The cellist in the orchestra, father of a numerous family, now began to play not from philosophical conviction but for pleasure. The culinary principle was saved. What is the point, we wonder, of chasing one's own tail like this? Why this obstinate clinging to the pleasure element? This addiction to drugs? Why so little concern with one's own interests as soon as one steps outside one's own home? Why this refusal to discuss? Answer: nothing can come of discussion. To discuss the present form of our society, or even of one of its least important parts, would lead inevitably and at once to an outright threat to our society's form as such.

We have seen that opera is sold as evening entertainment, and that this puts definite bounds to all attempts to transform it. We see that this entertainment has to be devoted to illusion, and must be of a ceremonial kind. Why?

In our present society the old opera cannot be just "wished away." Its illusions have an important social function. The drug is irreplaceable; it cannot be done without. [12]

---

10. This is a swipe at Stravinsky, whose *Oedipus Rex* (1927) is composed to a Latin translation of Cocteau's adaptation of Sophocles.

11. *Gebrauchsmusik:* music for daily use, instead of music reserved for concert performance—a term often associated with Paul Hindemith.

12. The life imposed on us is too hard; it brings us too many agonies, disappointments, impossible tasks. In order to stand it we have to have some kind of palliative. There seem to be three classes of these: overpowering distractions, which allow us to find our sufferings unimportant, pseudo-satisfactions

Only in the opera does the human being have a chance to be human. His entire mental capacities have long since been ground down to a timid mistrustfulness, an envy of others, a selfish calculation. The old opera survives not just because it is old, but chiefly because the situation which it is able to meet is still the old one. This is not wholly so. And here lies the hope for the new opera. Today we can begin to ask whether opera hasn't come to such a pass that further innovations, instead of leading to the renovation of this whole form, will bring about its destruction.

Perhaps *Mahagonny* is as culinary as ever—just as culinary as an opera ought to be—but one of its functions is to change society; it brings the culinary principle under discussion, it attacks the society that needs operas of such a sort; it still perches happily on the old bough, perhaps, but at least it has started (out of absentmindedness or bad conscience) to saw it through. . . . And here you have the effect of the innovations and the song they sing.

Real innovations attack the roots.

The opera *Mahagonny* was written three years ago, in 1927.[13] In subsequent works attempts were made to emphasize the didactic more and more at the expense of the culinary element. And so to develop the means of pleasure into an object of instruction, and to convert certain institutions from places of entertainment into organs of mass communication.

From *Brecht on Theatre*, trans. John Willett (New York: Hill and Wang, 1991), 33–42.

■

In the days of the Weimar Republic—the democratic, increasingly inflation-riddled government that existed in Germany between the end of World War I and Hitler's regime—the main form of politically engaged music theater was the cabaret. There had been a cabaret before the war, the *Überbrettl* of Ernst von Wolzogen; in 1901, the little-known Arnold Schoenberg earned some money by writing *ooh-la-la* songs for it (in one, for example, a bald man has a girl friend who likes to stroke her pussycat; and so, when he wants attention, he puts the cat on his pate). Wolzogen's cabaret was noticeably tamer, though, than the postwar cabarets, which crossed the threshold of many taboo areas of

---

which reduce them and drugs which make us insensitive to them, The pseudo-satisfactions offered by art are illusions if compared with reality, but are none the less psychologically effective for that, thanks to the part played by the imagination in our inner life. (Freud: *Das Unbehagen in der Kultur* [*Civilization and its Discontents*], page 72.) Such drugs are sometimes responsible for the wastage of great stores of energy which might have been applied to bettering the human lot. (Ibid., page 28.) [Brecht's note.]

13. This date is valid only for the terse *Songspiel* version.

European life. Now, two women, disgusted with their boyfriends, might decide to hug one another; or a vamp might say that she had stolen Hitler's mustache.

The potential for artistic experimentation found its clearest expression in the Cabaret Voltaire in Zurich, where Dada was born; but the popular cabaret of Germany was also capable of serious artistic and social critique. Indeed the influence of cabaret (and cabaret-like informal performance) on opera was strong: Frank Wedekind, whose plays provided the basis for Alban Berg's *Lulu* (1935), strummed the guitar and sang erotic (and homoerotic) songs for money; in the third act of *Lulu* Berg builds a set of orchestral variations out of a raunchy song that Wedekind composed. Wedekind was the mentor of the young Bertolt Brecht, who developed a similar performance style; and it was in the cabarets of Berlin that Brecht and Kurt Weill found one of the stars of *The Threepenny Opera,* the famous Rosa Valetti, who played Mrs. Peachum—though she, who spent her life singing obscene songs, thought that Brecht's lyrics were far too raw for her tender soul. The whole milieu of Brecht and Weill was saturated with cabaret; though Weill claimed, with some justice, that his carefully crafted melodies bore only a superficial resemblance to cabaret style, that superficial resemblance is sometimes striking—as in the Weillian song "Baby" (1931, text by Walter Mehring, music by Friedrich Hollaender).

Friedrich Hollaender (1896–1976) was one of the most articulate and politically engaged of the cabaret composers. *Münchhausen* (1931)—Hollaender wrote both words and music—is an amazingly direct challenge to the Nazis; and the next year he wrote an essay on cabaret, completely frank about the "poison cookie" that lurks inside cabaret songs—a Brechtian sort of admission. The year after that, 1933, Hitler came to power and put an end to all these hijinks.

FRIEDRICH HOLLAENDER
Münchhausen (1931)

> I came across a wond'rous tree
> as prickly as a porcupine
> This cactus tree bore luscious fruit
> and giant roses red as wine
> It rose so high into the sky
> its top was far, far out of sight
> Its leaves recoiled from the day
> and then they turned to gold at night
> And if you bored into its bark
> hot coffee poured out rich and dark
> Liar liar liar liar liar liar

I'm sick and tired of lies from you
but how I wish your lies were true
Liar liar liar liar liar liar
truth is hard and tough as nails
that's why we need fairy tales
I'm all through with logical conclusions
why should I deny myself illusions

I saw a film the other day
that really varied from the norm
There were no soldiers on parade
and no one marched in uniform
Its heroes were not supermen
and no one even shot a gun
The audience still loved the film
though not a single war was won
But I was really shocked to see
this film was made in Germany
Liar liar liar liar liar liar, *etc.*

I saw a court of law where all
the justices were just again
Where all the lawyers worked for free
and all of them were honest men
You could be rich you could be poor
you could be Christian or a Jew
Your politics did not have sway
on how a judge would rule on you
Their hearts were young, their minds were free
they judged all men equally

I saw a woman trying hard
to feed her family of ten
She was poor and destitute
and worse was pregnant once again
She knew what they would say in church
she sought a doctor out instead
who told her if she had the child
that she herself might well end dead
Then in a calm and gentle voice

he said the law says it's your choice
Liar liar liar liar liar liar, *etc.*

I saw a brave republic where
one banner flew for all to see
Its stripes of black and red and gold
proclaim a new democracy
All banners from the past were banned
the empire's black and white and red
Yes now the black and red and gold
is flying everywhere instead
And nowhere will you see those flags
which sport that thing that zigs and zags [14]
Liar liar liar liar liar liar, *etc.*

I saw a land that hated war
and melted all its weapons down
to build a boat of love for kids
who planned to sail from town to town
declaring peace for all the world
Let killing now come to an end
embrace your enemies instead
your former foe is now your friend
Ev'ry conflict now will cease
and all of us will live in peace
Liar liar liar liar liar liar, *etc.* [15]

From *Ute Lemper: Berlin Cabaret Songs,* London CD 452 601-2, 38–40; translated by Alan Lareau and Jeremy Lawrence.

FRIEDRICH HOLLAENDER
"Cabaret" (1932)
The cabaret—which those terribly serious, bearded sorts are fond of dismissing as the undernourished half-sister of the verbal arts—is more like the happy child of an eleventh muse, conceived in an easy-going love affair with theater, variety shows, and political tribunals. Though no less serious than its three fathers whose sharpest

14. zigs and zags: the Swastika.
15. The title of the piece refers to Baron Münchhausen, said to have lived from 1720 to 1797 and to have served in the Russian army against the Turks; a collection of his tall tales (1785) by Rudolph Erich Raspe made his name proverbial for fantastic lies.

criticism constantly reaffirms its mission, cabaret would nevertheless like to appear more lucid and less weighty but also more unruly. This might be explained by the fact that it often falls into the hands of unqualified pedagogues who from time to time, darken its path with their own frivolous behavior. Thus it happens that the cabaret is always being dragged down from its conquered heights, from its jovial perspective, and sometimes even descends to a level beneath that of the coasters under the beer glasses on the bar.

But we are speaking of restrained cabaret, which, true to its ironic mission, floats like a soap bubble above the things in our difficult-to-live life, reflecting them wickedly or tenderly, now using the distorting effects of color and light to render their value overwhelming, now screwing them back down to the diminutive status that is in truth their due. In Copenhagen "cabarets" mean the colorful bowls in the restaurants offering the hurried palate manifold stimuli in concentrated form. Where do connoisseurs begin? How can they secure for themselves a taste of all of them? And before they get to the enchanting taste of all these sophisticated little morsels, the bowls are empty, leaving behind, aside from a symphony of appetizing aromas, that splendid, not quite satisfied desire without which we would not be able to live.

That is the secret of the cabaret: the aphoristic novel, the burst of a short-lived drama, the two-minute song of our times, the sweetness of love, the heartbeat of unemployment, the bewilderment of politics, the standard-issue uniform of cheap amusement. All without the drain of five acts, three volumes, a thousand kilos of psychology—in the form of a pill, which might be bitter into the bargain. Who has ever seen enough of a fireworks display?

The laws inherent to this compressed form demand not only the rapid effect of the arresting word and the quickly understood gesture, they call imperiously for music that is provocative, short, revealing, essential; in its rhythm and coloring, in its melody and drama, the music must explode in a lightning flash and can permit itself no time to develop and build; the course of its burning away must be the moment of its birth. Its mood has to be present in the first beats. In the serious *chanson* the potential lies in the tightly arched bow of an instantaneous, dramatic flash; in the cheerful *chanson,* in the lethal precision of its pause (which must be one with the verbal joke), the way an arrow fired at the nearest target hits its mark. In taste it obediently follows the fashion of its time; the bourgeois romanticism proper to Wolzogen's variety show[16] would be too cheap for the modern political cabaret. The fashionable horror music played by the eleven hangmen in Wolzogen's time was enough to tighten the throats of the listeners, who were the delinquents of the piece, but now that music causes nothing but a tickle.

---

16. The turn-of-the-century cabaret of Ernst von Wolzogen (1855–1934)—a versatile man of the theatre and librettist for Strauss's second opera, *Feuersnot* (1901).

Only one person from that time wrote music that would still be adequate for today's cabaret: [Jean] Bruyant in Paris, whose stomping, revolutionary rhythms excited the crowd to forsake song for action. For—and this should be a further law of the cabaret—within it there lies an aggressiveness that will forever distinguish it from all operatic, choral, and symphonic music. Cabaret that fails to take pleasure in the attack, that lacks the taste for battle, is not fit to live. It is the traditional battlefield on which the only proper weapons—sharp words and loaded music—are capable of beating into retreat those cast of iron. They are stronger and more successful than anything in the much-praised contemporary theater, that usually sober forum of dry theory that nearly always lacks the seductive magic of the ironic or forceful music needed to achieve a gratifying effect. The effect achieved by the contrasting moods in cabaret is truly not to be outdone; if one considers that eight-hundred people out of a thousand regard cabaret as an innocent amusement and attend it in this spirit, then it becomes possible to assess the healthy jolt to the psyche that a socially minded *chanson* fired off between two amusing parodies can occasion. Under the cover of an evening's relaxing entertainment, cabaret, like nothing else, suddenly dispenses a poison cookie. Suggestively administered and hastily swallowed, its effect reaches far beyond the harmless evening to make otherwise placid blood boil and inspire a sluggish brain to think. Music as seductress—it always succeeds whenever it has magic in its gut: as a hymn in church, as a military march before the campaign, as an indictment from the podium.

That is a profile of music in the cabaret. The joke is different, and a few words should be said about that. I do not mean the cheap shot as an end in itself, the musical chestnut that wrings a laugh from the listener who later recalls it in shame. I mean rather the regal joke, which, in affectionate derision of all-too-human frailties, returns the listener to a consciousness of his strength. That will make him happy on the journey home. Everyone who, in this age of fashions and the record book, has occasionally found himself being more snobbish than a snob, more knowing than an ignorant know-it-all, more beloved than Goethe's Werther,[17] will see his hobby-horse put mercilessly through its paces—with himself in the saddle.

Now the music—if its caricatures of people, things, habits, and the commonplaces of daily life are to hit their mark with split-second timing—has to be superlative; that is, it has to bear within itself and bring to expression the sickest of the sick, the emptiest babble of the babbler, the most perverse of the perverse, the stingiest of the stingy. If it chooses, for example, the stingy Scot of popular anecdotes for its focus, it would best invent a model one-note melody. For a modish gigolo the musician ought to

---

17. Goethe's first great success was his epistolary novel *The Sorrows of Young Werther* (1774), concerning a sensitive young man in love with another man's fiancée. His sad end led to a vogue for suicides throughout Europe.

create an exaggerated tango, the supreme stylization of mock slow-motion. If a farcical Gandhi [18] appears on the stage, the music must immediately become more Indian than real Indian music; once again, the most emancipated of the emancipated. To take the Gandhi example to its conclusion, one might conceive a contrapuntal battle between this "guaranteed genuine Indian hermit music" and the English national anthem. Those in the know will grin, and the others relish it just the same. But I am not talking here about unintelligent onomatopoeia. A satire of the automobile craze does not gain a musical dimension from a couple of cheap honking effects; the music must contain within it eighty miles per hour and high-test gasoline.

From *The Weimar Republic Sourcebook,* ed. Anton Kaes, Martin Jay, and Edward Dimendberg (Berkeley: University of California Press, 1994), 566–67; reprinted from "Cabaret," *Die Weltbühne* 28, no. 5 (2 February 1932): 169–71.

■

At the very moment the Nazi government was taking power, Paul Hindemith (1895–1963) was working on an opera about the torments of an artist's role in a botched civilization: *Mathis der Maler* (1932–34; first performed in Zurich in 1938). The time is 1525; the protagonist is Matthias Grünewald, struggling to keep on painting in a Germany torn apart by the Peasants' War, as Luther's Protestants rebel against the Roman Catholic authorities. Mathis is a friend to the poor and eventually stops painting to join their fight; but neither action nor withdrawal from action satisfies him, and the opera ends with the elderly painter, too worn out to paint, musing over his tool kit, lingeringly lovingly over paints, brushes, rulers, and compasses. Shakespeare's Prospero, the magician-hero of *The Tempest,* drowned his book and broke his staff, but Hindemith's Mathis seems incapable of deciding either to renounce art or to employ it. Just as his patron, the enlightened Cardinal Albrecht, withdraws from public life to meditate in solitude, so Mathis seems attracted to a hermit's life; but the same discipline that makes Mathis a great painter reinforces his ethical obligations to help others.

Hindemith's libretto for the opera shows his extraordinary uncertainty about his own role in a world where politics was hard to ignore. In his Norton lectures at Harvard (1949–50), Hindemith—far from worn out, but far from young—lingers lovingly over the tool kit of *his* art: the books of musical rules, the tonal system itself. He quotes with approval Augustine's thought that "music has to be converted into moral power"; also Boethius's aphorism "Music is a part of our human nature; it has the power either to im-

18. Mohandas K. Gandhi (1869–1948), ascetic who advocated nonviolent protest to gain India's political independence from England. His emaciated frame, clothed only in a homespun loincloth, made him an easily recognized figure.

prove or to debase our character."[19] And the lectures explain over and over again that our only hope for cultural salvation is obedience to law, an obedience that manifests itself in music as conformity to the principles of tonality—principles that, to Hindemith, have the utterly inviolable status of physical laws, such as the law of gravity. Hindemith even reconceives totalitarianism from political to musical terms: he applies the word Nazi to those false theorists who invent such inhumane systems as dode*cacophony*. (Like Thomas Mann, Hindemith seems to find an unnatural order to be equivalent to total disorder.) He goes so far as to argue that madrigal singing might promote enough brotherhood to save us from the atomic bombs of World War III—though here we may see the anguish of a supremely cultured, somewhat introverted sensibility that has trouble looking beyond madrigal singing to contemplate other remedies for human ills.

PAUL HINDEMITH
from *A Composer's World* (1949–50)
[THE GRAVITATION OF TONALITY]
    . . . In painting the impression of visual depth is created by so drawing all receding lines of the picture's object that their prolongations meet in one single point—the vanishing point; and in musical perspective, all harmonies [. . . will] be understood as in close relationship to . . . tonics.
    . . . In painting it is up to the painter to decide whether he wants to have perspective as a part of the pictorial effect or not. In music we cannot escape the analogous effect of tonal unification, of tonality. The intervals which constitute the building material of melodies and harmonies fall into tonal groupments, necessitated by their own physical structure and without our consent.
    Have we not heard many times of tendencies in modern music to avoid these tonal effects? It seems to me that attempts at avoiding them are as promising as attempts at avoiding the effects of gravitation. Of course, we can use airplanes to fly away from the center of gravitation, but is not an airplane the best evidence for our incapacity to escape gravitation? Tonality doubtless is a very subtle form of gravitation, and in order to feel it in action we do not even need to take our usual musical detour from actual experience via the image of it, released by music. It suffices to sing in a chorus or a madrigal group to experience the strength of tonal gravitation: to sense how a synoptic tonal order has a healthy, refreshing effect on our moods and how structures that in their obscurity reach the point of impracticability lead to real physical pain.
    Certainly, there is a way to escape the effects of earthly gravitation, by using a

19. Paul Hindemith, *A Composer's World: Horizons and Limitations* (Gloucester: Peter Smith, 1969), 6, 8.

powerful rocket that overshoots the critical point of terrestrial attraction, but I cannot see how music's less harmful projectiles could ever reach this point of its imaginary equivalent. And yet, some composers who have the ambition to eliminate tonality, succeed to a certain degree in depriving the listener of the benefits of gravitation. To be sure they do not, contrary to their conviction, eliminate tonality: they rather avail themselves of the same trick as those sickeningly wonderful merry-go-rounds on fair grounds and in amusement parks, in which the pleasure-seeking visitor is tossed around simultaneously in circles, and up and down, and sideways, in such fashion that even the innocent onlooker feels his inside turned into a pretzel-shaped distortion. The idea is, of course, to disturb the customer's feeling of gravitational attraction by combining at any given moment so many different forms of attraction that his sense of location cannot adjust itself fast enough. So-called atonal music, music which pretends to work without acknowledging the relationships of harmonies to tonics, acts just the same as those devilish gadgets; harmonies both in vertical and in horizontal form are arranged so that the tonics to which they refer change too rapidly. Thus we cannot adjust ourselves, cannot satisfy our desire for gravitational orientation. Again spatial dizziness is the result, this time in the sublimated realm of spatial images in our mind.

I personally do not see why we should use music to produce the effect of seasickness, which can be provided more convincingly by our amusement industry. Future ages will probably never understand why music ever went into competition with so powerful an adversary. . . .

[A NEW *MUSICA MUNDANA*]

. . . There is some sound foundation in the ancient idea of a universe regulated by musical laws—or, to be more modest, a universe whose laws of construction and operation are complemented by a spiritual reflection in musical organisms.

The time may perhaps return, when musical rules will be, as they were in olden times, an essential part of the code of the physical sciences. It is an alluring idea to think of a reorganization of scientific concepts on a musical basis. Instead of a plan for the world's destruction by superbombs, a blueprint of music theory would be drawn up to serve as a plan for a tremendous reformation of the universe. Harmonic, melodic, and rhythmic laws, as worked out in a most beautiful and exalted composition, would transform the world's woes and falsehood into the ideal habitat for human beings, who by the same process of musical ennoblement would have grown into creatures worthy of such a paradise.

[TOTALITARIAN MUSICAL SYSTEMS]

Let us investigate briefly some of those allegedly "modern" achievements. The best known and most frequently mentioned is the so-called twelve-tone technique, or composition in preëstablished tone series. The idea is to take the twelve tones of our chromatic scale, select one of its some four hundred million permutations, and use it as the basis for the harmonic (and possibly melodic) structure of a piece. This rule of construction is established arbitrarily and without any reference to basic musical facts. . . .

Twelve-tone operations are not the only nightmares that haunt the composing zealot who wants to be up-to-date. Are there not city sky lines whose ragged contours demand to be reproduced in melodic lines?[20] . . . We could go on counting such methods of tonal equations, but only to enter a sphere in which there is almost nothing that could not be brought into direct equational relationship with harmony and melody: fever cures, cooking recipes, railroad timetables (the music resulting from them may be rather monotonous, though), catalogues of country fairs, the depth of the ocean between Halifax and Ireland, and so on.

If the inventors of such systems had looked into music history, they would have found that their methods are by no means as modern as they think. . . .

The method which in my opinion showed the greatest subtlety is one suggested in a little book published in 1751 by the English musician William Hayes. Its title is *The Art of Composing Music by a Method Entirely New, Suited to the Meanest Capacity.* It is a satire on the wave of Italian music, with its composers of frequently inferior quality, which at that time swept over London. His advice is, to take a brush with stiff bristles (like a toothbrush), dip it into an inkwell, and, by scraping the bristles with the finger, spatter with one sweep a whole composition onto the staff paper. You have only to add stems, bar lines, slurs, et cetera, to make the opus ready for immediate performance. Whole and half notes are entirely absent, but who cares for sustained tones anyway! (What a striking forecast of one of the ugliest modern musical diseases!)

Despite the intentional humor of these directions, the similarity with our twelve-tone technique cannot be overlooked. The characteristic difference seems to be that Hayes's method gives the composer . . . a greater freedom in artistic enterprises than does the rather rigorous twelve-tone technique. Moreover, it prevents the once accepted technique from degenerating into stylistic irrelevancies.

Movements of this kind spring up like epidemics of measles, and they disappear just as enigmatically. We have already once seen a twelve-tone movement die, due to lack of interest on the part of musicians who liked music more than operations on music. That was shortly after World War I. At that time the germ was introduced to this country and caused minor disturbances, which by now have all but disappeared, with a few scars remaining. After World War II, Europe was again infected, but already the patients are feeling better and there is hope that after some minor relapses only a few diehards will survive to be the prophets who, in quiet solitude, will prepare the next big outburst.

20. Hindemith is mocking Villa-Lobos's piano piece *New York Sky Line Melody* (1939).

This, if we can trust past experience, will probably occur after World War III, provided any people are left over to be interested in tone combinations. One little sign of reconvalescence may perhaps be seen in the following fact, which could not remain hidden even to the most stalwart dodecaphonists (or is it dodecacophonists, as many people have it?): with this method no pieces can be produced which could fill big spaces with broad symphonic colors, or which could satisfy many people's demands for simplicity, directness, and personal sympathy.[21]

A strange feature of all these movements is their sectarian character. It is almost as in the Nazi state or in a Red dictatorship: the supreme condition for your participation is that you have no disbelief whatsoever in the perfection of the system. You will have to fight against the adherents of other "systems," against the writers of program music, and against those who use sky lines and numerical equivalents other than the permutations of the numbers one to twelve, although your "meanest capacity" would tell you, that their activities are of the same kind as those you adore. The parallelism to religious sects goes so far, that an idol is felt to be necessary, to whom everything of importance ever created or uttered in music is ascribed, although for his glory some real instigators and inventors may have to be obscured and rendered innocuous. It is all so reminiscent of some kind of voodoo cult. . . .

[POSTWAR MADRIGALS]

. . . If there is any form of musical reproduction that is able to touch the collective feelings of large groups of people, it can only be choral singing. I am convinced that such singing, on a scale completely unknown thus far, will be one of the important forms of musical life in the future. Although it will make use of all possible achievements that an advanced knowledge of conditions of performance can provide (new instruments for accompaniment, effective means of amplifying and transmitting, adequate localities for performance), the heaviness of such tremendous musical apparatus will force the composer into stylistic considerations foreign to our present writers.

An art of this kind can never be a replacement for the cultured musical communication of ensemble singing. Nevertheless, subtlety may not entirely disappear from the musical world. Musical development may progress on lines parallel with general social advancement. After further wars, political and economic upheavals, after destruction, grief, and desolation, after the final detrition of generalissimos, führers, and dictators, a human society may emerge that in addition to its grand collective deeds strongly emphasizes the small-scale gregariousness of the individual. The reason for such gregariousness is the eternal longing for human warmth and sympathy, which can never be

---

21. This paragraph does not represent Hindemith's last word on the subject: during the 1950s he himself experimented with twelve-tone rows, as in his Tuba Sonata (1955).

provided by a government-organized mass movement, and without which such mass movements would in the long run lose their driving power. If in some political theories the mass movement is proclaimed as the fulfillment of the human being's desire for mutual understanding, one should note that this is true only in times of low culture. The genuine satisfaction of such a desire is achieved in the voluntary union of individuals who may then project it onto the background of the general human community.

If the fear of earthly loneliness is the reason for all this, we may see in music the sublime way of dispelling it. Since there is no nobler way of making music than ensemble singing, we may nourish the conviction that with a clear recognition of man's collective desires a new epoch of madrigalesque musical art will spring up as an encouraging model for other collective enterprises.

From *A Composer's World: Horizons and Limitations* (Gloucester: Peter Smith, 1969), 62–65, 117, 141–43, 200–201.

■

Five years before Hindemith elaborated his vision of a peaceful future in which the steelworker joins the shepherd in his madrigals, a number of people were making music in more difficult conditions. Sixty kilometers north of Prague, at the Nazi concentration camp of Terezín (in German, Theresienstadt), some of Europe's most skilled musicians were gathered. Originally they made music in secret—they even managed to smuggle a cut-apart cello into the camp in a rucksack, together with the glue to reassemble it—but eventually the guards decided to permit the music openly. In abandoned stables they performed Bedřich Smetana's *The Bartered Bride* and other demanding works—the audience of fellow prisoners paid for admission with pieces of bread. It occurred to the Nazis that Terezín could be useful in demonstrating the happy conditions that prevailed within their concentration camps; so, after the camp was freshly painted, and outfitted with rose bushes and a children's playground, the International Red Cross came, on 23 June 1944, to behold the delight of being a Jew in Fortress Europe. The musicians were given evening dress and told to perform; a little barrier of flowers was erected in front of the stage to disguise the fact that the orchestra members had no real shoes. A few months later, on 16 October, most of the players were transported to Auschwitz, a concentration camp that did not resemble a health resort.

Some remarkable composers were housed at Terezín; those who contributed new compositions for Karel Ančerl's prisoners' orchestra included Gideon Klein (1919–44), Pavel Haas (1899–1944), and Viktor Ullmann (1898–1944). Ullmann, a pupil of Schoenberg's, was astonishingly productive during his Terezín years: he wrote at least twenty-five works, including an opera, *Der Kaiser von Atlantis* (*The Emperor of Atlantis*, 1943–44), to a text by a fellow prisoner, the writer and artist Peter Kien. Ullmann's music is oddly peppy, even cheeky, with pert distortions of Haydn's tune for "Deutschland über

Alles" (originally a hymn for Emperor Franz Joseph) and Mahler's *Das Lied von der Erde;* even the motto of Josef Suk's death-haunted *Asrael Symphony* (1904–6) is turned into chipper tritonal fanfare. But a grisly gaiety is one response to terror.

Kien's starkly amusing fable concerns Emperor Overall, who makes a declaration of total war; but Death himself is offended by this upstart competitor and decides to punish him by refusing to let anyone die—even the mortally wounded. The Emperor realizes that this is an intolerable state of affairs; but Death will relent only if the Emperor will allow himself to be the first victim. The Emperor agrees—in an aria of surprising gentleness—and the opera ends, like Berg's Violin Concerto (1935), with a valedictory Protestant chorale, in this case *Ein' feste Burg.* The Emperor's aria dwells on the beauty of the physical world, persisting after his death; and it will serve as well as for the victims as for the torturer, in that it represents a fantasy of the relief from brutality offered by sheer absence of being. Here Kien and Ullmann offer delicacy, learning, parody, grace: the authors try to constitute a cultural space by conspicuous espousal of the values that the Nazis have tried to destroy.

PETER KIEN

Der Kaiser von Atlantis: **Final Scene** (1943–44)

Kaiser Overall *(Death gradually takes on the features of Hermes):* [22] I will follow this strange young man—where to, I cannot tell, but I still hope that one day I may return.

Rivers will flow and mountains will surround me. Flowers will bloom in the alpine meadows, warmed by the sun and buffeted by pitiless winds. Snow falls, though you are not there. The summer rains pour down, though you are not there. Many things are there, but you are elsewhere.

And when you think: now a child goes to the well, a horse stands in front of a blacksmith to be shod, then think of me without lamenting.

For that which is far away should not be mourned, but rather that which is near, and lies in everlasting shadow.

(Death takes the Emperor gently by the hand and leads him through the mirror, while the chorale is sung off-stage.)

Bubikopf, Drummer-Girl, Harlequin, Loudspeaker: [23]

> Come, Death, our honored guest,
> enter the chamber of our hearts.

22. The Greek god Hermes conducted the souls of the dead to the afterlife.

23. Bubikopf is a young soldier woman who falls in love with her enemy; the Drummer-Girl summons people to war; Harlequin is a clown representing the pleasures of life; the Loudspeaker is the opera's mechanical narrator.

Take from us life's pain and woe,
lead us to rest after grief and sorrow.

Teach us to honor in our brothers
the joys and sorrows of life.
Teach us the most holy commandment:
Thou shalt not take
Death's great name in vain.

(The curtain falls.)

From the notes to *Der Kaiser von Atlantis*, trans. Paula Kennedy, London CD 440 854-2 (1994), 33.

■

Ullmann died at Auschwitz, probably in 1944; and soon the reports of the mass extermination of Jews would start to have wide influence on art. Thomas Mann was writing *Doktor Faustus*, in which the description of hell is based, as Mann himself noted, on the gas chambers. In 1947 Schoenberg (living, like Mann, in California) heard accounts of Nazi atrocities in the Warsaw Ghetto, and in a period of twelve days (11–23 August) wrote the text (in English) and music for *A Survivor from Warsaw*, for narrator, chorus, and orchestra. In this brief and harrowing piece, in which twelve-tone means are used for Expressionistic ends, the ability of the Jews to form a chorus, to sing the *Šəma' Yiśro'ēl* becomes a musical symbol of human solidarity, resistance to tyranny.

ARNOLD SCHOENBERG
A Survivor from Warsaw (1947)

Narrator. I cannot remember ev'rything. I must have been unconscious most of the time. I remember only the grandiose moment when they all start to sing, as if prearranged, the old prayer they had neglected for so many years—the forgotten creed! But I have no recollection how I got underground to live in the sewers of Warsaw for so long a time.

The day began as usual: Reveille when it still was dark. Get out! Whether you slept or whether worries kept you awake the whole night. You had been separated from your children, from your wife, from your parents; you don't know what happened to them—how could you sleep?

The trumpets again—Get out! The sergeant will be furious! They came out; some very slow: the old ones, the sick ones; some with nervous agility. They fear the sergeant. They hurry as much as they can. In vain! Much too much noise; much too much commotion—and not fast enough! The Feldwebel[24] shouts: "Achtung!

---

24. *Feldwebel:* sergeant.

Stilljestanden! Na wirds mal? Oder soll ich mit dem Jewehrkolben nachhelfen? Na jutt; wenn ihrs durchaus haben wollt!"[25] The sergeant and his subordinates hit everybody: young or old, quiet or nervous, guilty or innocent. It was painful to hear them groaning and moaning. I heard it though I had been hit very hard, so hard that I could not help falling down. We all on the ground who could not stand up were then beaten over the head.

I must have been unconscious. The next thing I knew was a soldier saying: "They are all dead," whereupon the sergeant ordered to do away with us. There I lay aside—half-conscious. It had become very still—fear and pain. Then I heard the sergeant shouting: "Abzählen!"[26] They started slowly and irregularly: one, two, three, four—"Achtung!" the sergeant shouted again, "Rascher! Nochmal von vorn anfangen! In einer Minute will ich wissen, wie viele ich zur Gaskammer abliefere! Abzählen!"[27] They began again, first slowly: one, two, three, four, became faster and faster, so fast that it finally sounded like a stampede of wild horses, and all of a sudden, in the middle of it, they began singing the Šəma' Yiśro'ēl.

Male Choir:[28]

Hear, O Israel: the Lord our God *is* one Lord:
And thou shalt love the Lord thy God with all thine heart, and with all thy soul, and with all thy might.
And these words, which I command thee this day, shall be in thine heart.
And thou shalt teach them diligently unto thy children, and shalt talk of them when thou sittest in thine house, and when thou walkest by the way, and when thou liest down, and when thou risest up.

From *Sämtliche Werke*, Abt. V: *Chorwerke, Reihe B*, Bd. 19, *Chorwerke II*, ed. Christian Martin Schmidt (Mainz: B. Schott's Söhne, 1977), 72–73.

German and Czech artists were not alone in their persecution. Olivier Messiaen spent time in Stalag 8-A in Silesia, where he wrote *Quartet for the End of Time* (1941)—opposing fascism with an urgent preaudition of Christian apocalypse. In the Soviet Union

---

25. "Attention! Stop! Looking for trouble? Or should I help you along with my rifle butt! All right, if that's how you want it!" (The Nazi sergeant barks his commands in a Prussian accent.)

26. "Count off!"

27. "Faster! Start over! In a minute I'll know how many of you to send to the gas chamber! Count off!"

28. The chorus sings Deuteronomy 6:4–7 in Hebrew; the King James translation is given here.

arose a music of anti-Communist protest, which took various forms. One form consisted of hidden meanings in publicly performed works—if Solomon Volkov's *Testimony: The Memoirs of Dmitri Shostakovich* is correct, much of Shostakovich's later music contains subtextual undercuttings of its ostensible celebrations of Communist purposes. The degree of irony in Shostakovich's music is likely to continue to be disputed; but in any case Shostakovich also wrote secret music, in which his disgust with the artistic manipulations of the Communist state is quite clear.

Dmitri Shostakovich (1906–75) first ran afoul of the authorities in 1936, when the official newspaper *Pravda* printed "Chaos Instead of Music," an article denouncing Shostakovich's opera *Lady Macbeth of Mtsenk* as dissonant, cheap, vulgar, effete, formalistic, neurotic, bourgeois, spasmodic, insignificant, and full of quacks and grunts. This led Shostakovich, if not to sincere repentance, at least to a pose of conformity: his Fifth Symphony (1937) was delivered with the subtitle "A Soviet Artist's Reply to Just Criticism," and for the rest of his life he was fairly compliant—as in, for example, *Song of the Forests* (1949), an oratorio concerning the reforestation of the Volga by Communist youth; or *March for the Soviet Police,* composed soon after Nikolai Shcholokov, the Minister of Police in Brezhnev's time, asked for such a march at a dinner party both attended.

But in private Shostakovich expressed other feelings. In 1957 he composed a satirical cantata, *Rayok* (*Gallery* or *Peepshow*), to a text by the musicologist L. N. Lebedinski. Mstislav Rostropovich, who revealed the work's existence in 1989, recorded it under the title as *The Music Lesson: The Struggle of the School of Realism with the School of Formalism in Music;* and the text presents that great aesthetic debate in the silliest way possible. To understand it, it is necessary to recall that many Soviet composers were injured by the consequences of a seemingly small event: on 7 November 1947 Stalin attended a performance of *The Great Friendship,* a harmless opera by the Georgian Vano Muradeli. To supply local color the composer wrote a *lezghinka* (a Caucasian dance)—but to an original melody, not the familiar folk dance. Stalin, himself from Georgia, was outraged to hear a *lezghinka* that failed to supply his favorite tune; and this led the Party secretary, Andrey Zhdanov, to make life miserable for Prokofiev, Shostakovich, and other composers by insisting on a strict criterion of "realism" to be applied to every musical composition.

Rayok was written for four basses, chorus, and piano. One bass is the presiding officer of the session; the other three, whose names could be translated Onesy, Twosy, and Threesy, are caricatures of Stalin, Zhdanov, and Shepilov (a Party functionary whose role was similar to Zhdanov's). Stalin keeps reverting to a Georgian song he liked, "Suliko"; Zhdanov begins his section with voice warm-up exercises, because he had some training as a singer, and liked to remind people that he had technical knowledge of music; Shepilov's brain is filled with the folksong "Kamarinskaya," which Mikhail Glinka had used in 1848 as the basis of an influential set of orchestral variations. Shepilov is lost in admiration for the great old Russian composers Glinka, Tchaikovsky, and Rimsky-Korsakov—but he is so ignorant that he keeps accenting the name Rimsky-Korsakov on the wrong syllable. In 1870 Musorgsky had written a *Rayok* to satirize foolish music critics who rhapsodized over the soprano Adelina Patti or who forbade the use of the minor mode; but in the 1950s Shostakovich had to contend with even stupider and infinitely more powerful music critics.

In the prologue to the work, evidently written by Shostakovich himself, a Comrade Detestable (Opostýlov—a pun on Shostakovich's enemy Pavel Apostolov) notes that he has discovered the manuscript of this valuable work in a box of excrement and goes on to praise the erudition, indeed the genius, of all three speakers.

L. N. LEBEDINSKI
Rayok: **The Music Lesson** (1957)

The President: Comrades, it is time to begin. It is a pity there are so few of us today. It is true that we have not attained the goal set by our cultural and ideological propaganda services. But since we have planned for today a series of lectures on the theme "Realism and formalism in music," it is about this, comrades, this subject that we shall talk during this meeting. Adopted?

Adopted.

The introductory speech on this question will be given by the learned, the great musicologist and music critic, the comrade and great master, Onesy. So let us welcome, comrades, our very dear comrade who is the master of us all: Onesy. *(Everyone stands up. Prolonged applause.)*

Onesy: Comrades, popular composers always write realistic music, while anti-popular composers always write formalist music. And we can ask ourselves the question, why do popular composers write realistic music, while anti-popular composers always write formalist music? Popular composers write realistic music because, comrades, being realists by nature, they cannot write anything but realistic music, while formalist composers, being anti-popular by nature, cannot write anything but formalist music. Our task therefore consists in encouraging popular composers to stick to the path of realism, while we must once and for all forbid anti-popular composers all their dubious experiments in the field of formalist music. *(Everyone stands up. Prolonged applause.)*

The President: What a fine speech ! My dear comrades, let us, therefore, all together thank our dear, our beloved comrade Onesy for his contribution to this cardinal question of musical aesthetics, which he has clarified for us so well in his speech.

Chorus: Thanks, thanks to our dear comrade!

The President: According to the regulations of the agenda of the day, I now give the platform to comrade number two, a musicologist and, what is more, a singer capable of executing vocalises. I leave the stand to comrade Twosy.
(No one rises. The applause is energetic but soon breaks off.)

Twosy *(affecting humor):* Comrades! I should not like to introduce any dissonance in my speech. And particularly no atonality in the ideas I shall express. We wish, comrades, that music should always be agreeable! That surprises you? Yes? I can see that it surprises you! La, la-la-la-la-la . . . And yet, that's exactly it! That's exactly what I wanted to say. We want music that charms our ear! Because music without harmony, music without melody, unaesthetic music, antipathetic music, can be compared to a dentist's drill! It is utter musical balderdash! So let us love what is graceful, pretty, pleasant, harmonious, and everything that is logical, polyphonic, true to the classical, rhythmic rules of our great popular art. And moreover, comrades, I should like to remind you that in Caucasian operas there must always be an authentic lezghinka, a truly authentic one!

> A real Causasian lezghinka
> Is so lovely to see on the stage,
> Really rousing, really popular,
> Everything about it must be pleasing.
> It must be authentic,
> Always genuine folklore,
> Exclusively authentic,
> Yes, Yes, Yes, Yes, folklore.

(Applause, but no one rises.)

The President *(applauding):* That is what I call a scientific discourse, sparkling with so many profound ideas. Now let us hear comrade Threesy.
(One person applauds, but quickly stops.)

Threesy: Comrades! We must take the classics as models. We must all do what the classics did. Yes! Glinka, Tchaikovsky, Rimsky-Korsákov,

> You are marvelously melodic!
> Glinka, Tchaikovsky, Rimsky-Korsákov,
> The very fibers of our being tremble on listening to you.
> That's normal, because we are sensitive.
> The human organism is so complex!
> That is why, comrades, we need symphonies, poems, quartets,
> cantatas, sonatas, sonatas, sonatas . . .

> Sonatas, sonatas, sonatas, always,
> Quartets and cantatas, love cantatas,
> Kalinka, kalinka, kalinka moya,
> Sonatas, poems, quartets, et cetera . . .

The President, the Chorus: And do not forget: vigilance, vigilance, always and everywhere. Keep your eyes open, but hold your tongue.

> The great leader teaches us that, constantly repeating it:
> Look here, look there, and always inspire terror in our enemies.
> Look here, look there, and eradicate all our enemies!
> Vigilance, vigilance, always and everywhere.
> Let no attempt at subversion reach our ears.

Keep watch over our youth, that is the only way to protect our ideas. And if anyone ever allows himself to be swayed by this influence, we shall put him for a good length of time into a hard-labor camp. The great leader teaches us this, constantly repeating it: look here, look there, and inspire terror in our enemies!

From an anonymous, slightly condensed translation in container insert in Saison Russe/Chant Du Monde CD LDC 2888 075 (1994), 26–29.

9 Testing the Boundaries between Popular and High Art

Some of the movements within Modernism were strongly highbrow in character. Expressionism in particular tended to cherish its exclusivity, its concentration on subtle psychic intensities. Schoenberg, for example, hated any intrusions of low art into high: as he wrote in 1949, "Why not play a boogie-woogie when Wotan walks across a rainbow to Valhalla?"[1] But even Schoenberg quoted the popular song "Ach, du lieber Augustin" in his Second String Quartet (1907–13) and used a folksong as the basis of a movement in his Suite, op. 29 (1925–26); and many of the Modernists regarded destabilization of the boundary between high and low art as one of the great freedoms of twentieth century. T. S. Eliot (in *Sweeney Agonistes*, 1926–27) and Jean Cocteau both found material for advanced art in the music hall. And low art returned the favor by quoting high art as well: Wolfram's hymn to the evening star in Wagner's *Tannhäuser* became the musical basis for a cabaret song by Willy Rosen: "Frau Abendstern, Frau Abendstern, ist heute wieder ganz modern" (Mrs. Evening Star, today she's modern once again). Another cabaret song notices that the commodification of music into phonograph records provides for an easy interchange between the highfalutin and the down-and-dirty: "You can exchange three Jolsons for one Rienzi. . . . Who wants two Chaliapins?—much too blaring for me! I prefer the Revellers for their sexuality!"[2]

Most of the Modernist composers (but with such exceptions as Varèse and Webern) participated, at least to an extent, in the assimilation of low art into high. Indeed the prolific Darius Milhaud was a one-man conversion industry, from Brazil (*Scaramouche,* 1937) to bluegrass (*Kentuckiana,* 1948). But one especially intense area for Modernist research was African American music. Some composers heard in jazz a music that had already attained Modernist goals (sophistication, sinuosity, planar textures) without any particular fuss. Indeed Duke Ellington (1899–1974) argued in 1947 that jazz was the logical successor of Romanticism—a thesis that tends to promote a strict identity between jazz and Modernism:

1. Arnold Schoenberg, *Style and Idea: Selected Writings of Arnold Schoenberg,* ed. Leonard Stein, trans. Leo Black (Berkeley: University of California Press, 1984), 146.
2. *Das spricht Bände* (*That Speaks Volumes,* 1929), a revue with text by Friedrich Hollaender and music by Rudolf Nelson. Al Jolson was an American popular singer specializing in blackface roles; *Rienzi* is Wagner's third opera; Fyodor Shalyapin was a Russian bass best known for singing Modest Musorgsky's Boris Godunov.

What, exactly, is jazz? A matter of trick rhythms, blues-notes, and unorthodox harmonies? I think not. Those matters may enter into it, but only in the nature of the result and not of a cause. To my mind, jazz is simply the expression of an age, in music. . . . Just as the classic form represents strict adherence to a structural standard, just as romantic music represents a rebellion against fixed forms in favor of more personal utterance, so jazz continues the pattern of barrier-breaking and emerges as the freest musical expression we have yet seen. To me, then, jazz means simply freedom of musical speech! [3]

Some European and European American composers found this argument persuasive. Others heard in jazz something primeval and tantalizing, sexy, the musical equivalent of the African masks that Picasso quoted in his *Demoiselles d'Avignon* (1907); still others regarded jazz as loathsome and contagious. For example, by 1926 the president of the Société de Musicologie, Lionel de la Laurencie, called jazz "a collection of melodic dust, a puzzle of little imitations, of audacious anticipations, of farcical *glissandos,* of deafening timbres or of pinching sonorities." [4] But in many ways jazz helped to define Modernism, both by attraction and by repulsion. It is characteristic of Modernism that the *Ebony Concerto* (1945) for Woody Herman's swing band was written by Stravinsky, while incidental music for Shakespeare's recondite play *Timon of Athens* (1963) was written by Duke Ellington.

Perhaps the first significant European essay on American jazz was written by Ernest Ansermet (1883–1969), an important force in Modernist music: he conducted the premières of Satie's *Parade* and Stravinsky's *Soldier's Tale* and *Pulcinella.* Many things about African American music seemed strange to Ansermet—the banjoes, the swaying of the performers' bodies, the altered scales—yet he recognized familiar European elements as well, intriguingly infused with the alien. Despite his (in places) obvious condescension, Ansermet listened with extraordinary attention, and admired much that he heard.

ERNEST ANSERMET
"On a Negro Orchestra" (1919)
This is not about African Negroes but about those of the Southern states of the U.S.A., who have created the musical style commonly known as the rag. Rag music is founded essentially on rhythm and in particular on the qualities of syncopation in rhythm. Rag music first came to Europe in the form of the cake-walk, as I recall, and then with the one-step, two-step, fox-trot, and all the American dances and songs to

3. *The Duke Ellington Reader,* ed. Mark Tucker (New York: Oxford University Press, 1993), 256.

4. André Coeuroy and André Schaeffner, *Le jazz* (Paris: Éditions Claude Aveline, 1926), 118; cited in Jeffrey H. Jackson, "Making Jazz French: Music and Cosmopolitanism in Interwar Paris" (Ph.D. diss., University of Rochester, 1999), 33.

which the subtitle of rag-time is applied. America is full of small instrumental ensembles devoted to rag-time, and if the national music of a people is none other than its popular music, one can say that rag-time has become the true national popular music of America. I remember having traveled by railroad between Berne and Lausanne with a group of young Americans. One of them began to hum a piece of rag-music, whereupon they all joined in, marking the rhythm, by beating their hands on the wooden benches, just as the Swiss in a foreign land, yodel in remembrance of the homeland. Today, rag-time has conquered Europe; we dance to rag-time under the name of jazz in all our cities, and the hundreds of musicians who contribute to our popular music are all applying themselves at this very moment, to adapt this new art to the taste for the insipid and the sentimental, to the coarse and mediocre sensuality of their clientele.[5] Rag-time is even passing into what I will call for lack of another name, the field of learned music: Stravinsky has used it as material for several works, Debussy has already written a cake-walk, and I well believe Ravel will lose no time in giving us a fox-trot.[6] But, under the name of Southern Syncopated Orchestra, there is an ensemble of authentic musicians of Negro race to be heard in London. Instrumentalists and singers, they present us pell-mell with all sorts of manifestations of their art, the old with the new, the best with the worst. It's a mysterious new world which we were acquainted with only through its more or less distant repercussions, and which finally reaches us in its living reality. One can hardly imagine a more opportune manifestation, and it is to be hoped, for our common edification, that the British metropolis will not alone reap its benefits.

The first thing that strikes one about the Southern Syncopated Orchestra is the astonishing perfection, the superb taste, and the fervor of its playing. I couldn't say if these artists make it their duty to be sincere, if they are penetrated by the idea that they have a "mission" to fulfill, if they are convinced of the "nobility" of their task, if they have the holy "audacity" and that sacred "valor" which our code of musical morals requires of our European musicians, nor indeed if they are animated by any "idea" whatsoever. But I can see they have a very keen sense of the music they love, and a pleasure in making it which they communicate to the hearer with irresistible force, a pleasure

5. Permit me another anecdote on this point. One clay, while seeking some examples of rag-time at an American publishers I found one which I rejected because of its dullness and lack of character. Slightly hesitant, the publisher offered me another which he designated as the model of the first; it was a remarkable thing whose accent and force of character seized me at once, but which his clientele would not have, declaring it too trying. The publisher had then made the sugary replica which he had shown me at first, and had withdrawn the original from circulation. [Ansermet's note.]

6. Debussy's *Golliwog's Cake-Walk* (1908); Stravinsky's *Rag-Time* and *Piano-Rag-Music* (both 1919). As for Ravel, Ansermet may have been thinking of *L'enfant et les sortilèges* (1924), on which Ravel was working in 1919—Ravel called it his "opérette américaine."

which pushes them to outdo themselves all the time, to constantly enrich and refine their medium. They play generally without notes, and even when they have some, it only serves to indicate the general line, for there are very few numbers I have heard them execute twice with exactly the same effects. I imagine that, knowing the voice attributed to them in the harmonic ensemble, and conscious of the role their instrument is to play, they can let themselves go, in a certain direction and within certain limits, as their heart desires. They are so entirely possessed by the music they play that they can't stop themselves from dancing inwardly to it in such a way that their playing is a real show, and when they indulge in one of their favorite effects which is to take up the refrain of a dance in a tempo suddenly twice as slow and with redoubled intensity and figuration, a truly gripping thing takes place, it seems as if a great wind is passing over a forest or as if a door is suddenly opened on a wild orgy.

The musician who directs them and to whom the constitution of the ensemble is due, Mr. Will Marion Cook,[7] is moreover a master in every respect, and there is no orchestra leader I delight as much in seeing conduct. As for the music which makes up their repertory, it is purely vocal, or for one voice, a vocal quartet, or a choir accompanied by instruments, or again purely instrumental; it bears the names of the composers (all unknown by our world) or is simply marked "Traditional." This traditional music is religious in inspiration. It is the index of a whole mode of religion and of a veritable religious art which, by themselves, merit a study. The whole Old Testament is related with a very touching realism and familiarity. There is much about Moses, Gideon, the Jordan, and Pharaoh. In an immense unison, the voices intone: "Go down, Moses, way down in Egypt land, Tell old Pharaoh: Let my people go." And suddenly, there they are clapping their hands and beating their feet with the joy of a schoolboy told that the teacher is sick: "Good news! Good news! Sweet Chariot's coming."

Or else a singer gets up, "I got a shoes (pronouncing the s to make it sound nice), you got a shoes, all God's children got a shoes. When I get to heaven, gonna put on my shoes, gonna walk all over God's heaven." And the word *heaven* they pronounce in one syllable as *he'm,* which makes a long resonance in their closed mouths, like a gong. Another time, a deep bass points out the empty platform to one of his companions and invites him to come and relate the battle of Jericho, and it's a terrible story which begins with the mighty deeds of King Joshua and all sorts of menacing fists and martial treads; their hands are raised and then lowered, and the walls come tumbling down. . . .

In the non-anonymous works, some are related to a greater or lesser extent to these religiously inspired works, others sing the sweetness of Georgia peaches, the perfume of flowers, country, mammy, or sweetheart; the instrumental works are rags or even Eu-

7. Will Marion Cook (1869–1944), African American composer and bandleader.

ropean dances. Among the authors, some are Negroes, but these are the exceptions. The others are of European origin, and even when this is not true of the author, it is of the music; most rag-time is founded on well-known motifs or on formuli peculiar to our art, there is one on the "Wedding March" from *Midsummer Night's Dream,* another on Rachmaninoff's celebrated *Prelude* [in C♯ minor], another on typical Debussy chords, another simply on the major scale.[8] The aforementioned traditional music itself has its source, as could doubtless be easily rediscovered, in the songs the Negroes learned from the English missionaries. Thus, all, or nearly all, the music of the Southern Syncopated Orchestra is, in origin, foreign to these Negroes. How is this possible? Because it is not the material that makes Negro music, it is the spirit.

The Negro population of North America is African in origin. I am acquainted with the music of the African Negroes. They say it consists in work-songs and ritual dances, that it is based on melodic modes differing from ours, and that it is particularly rich in its rhythm which already practices syncopation. In losing their land, have the Negroes carried off to America lost their songs as well? (One shudders in conjuring up such an image.) At least, they didn't lose the taste for them. In their new villages by the cotton fields, the first music they find is the songs which the missionaries teach them. And immediately, they make it over to suit themselves.

The desire to give certain syllables a particular emphasis or a prolonged resonance, that is to say preoccupations of an expressive order, seem to have determined in Negro singing their anticipation or delay of a fraction of rhythmic unity. This is the birth of syncopation. All the traditional Negro songs are strewn with syncopes which issue from the voice while the movement of the body marks the regular rhythm. Then, when the Anglo-Saxon ballad or the banal dance forms reach the Dixieland land of the plantations, the Negroes appropriate them in the same fashion, and the rag is born. But it is not enough to say that Negro music consists in the habit of syncopating any musical material whatsoever. We have shown that syncopation itself is but the effect of an expressive need, the manifestation in the field of rhythm of a particular taste, in a word, the genius of the race. This genius demonstrates itself in all the musical elements, it transfigures everything in the music it appropriates. The Negro takes a trombone, and

8. Some time ago, I met in New York, one of the most celebrated rag-time composers, Irving Berlin. A Russian Jew by origin, he had . . . been a jack-of-all trades, and known all kinds of fortune before becoming rich in writing Negro music. Devoid of any musical culture, incapable of writing his notes, hardly knowing how to play the piano, he told me himself how be used to pick out the notes on the piano with one finger, or whistle to a professional who noted down the melodies which entered his spirit, and how then, he'd have the professional seek out the harmonies until he was satisfied. Having assimilated the Negro style perfectly, it is to this style that he applies his gift of musical invention, which is indeed remarkable. [Ansermet's note.]

he has a knack of vibrating each note by a continual quivering of the slide, and a sense of glissando, and a taste for muted notes which make it a new instrument; he takes a clarinet or saxophone and he has a way of hitting the notes with a slight *inferior appoggiatura,* he discovers a whole series of effects produced by the lips alone, which make it a new instrument. There is a Negro way of playing the violin, a Negro way of singing. As for our orchestra tympani, needless to say with what alacrity the Negro runs out to greet them, he grasps all the paraphernalia instantaneously including the most excessive refinements, to set up an inexhaustible jugglery.

The banjo itself (string instrument strummed with a pick) is perhaps not the invention of the Negro, but the modification for his use of a type of instrument represented elsewhere by the mandolin.

By the grouping of these chosen instruments, following the most diversified combinations, a more or less definite type of Negro orchestra constituted itself, of which the Southern Syncopated Orchestra is as the first milestone, an attempt at a synthesis of great style. . . . And the ensemble displays a terrific dynamic range, going from a subtle sonority reminiscent of Ravel's orchestra to a terrifying tumult in which shouts and hand-clapping are mixed.

In the field of melody, although his habituation to our scales has effaced the memory of the African modes, an old instinct pushes the Negro to pursue his pleasure outside the orthodox intervals: he performs thirds which are neither major nor minor and false seconds, and falls often by instinct on the natural harmonic sounds of a given note—it is here especially that no written music can give the idea of his playing. I have often noticed, for example, that in their melodies the A♯ and the B♭, the E and the E♭ are not the sounds of our scale. It is only in the field of harmony that the Negro hasn't yet created his own distinct means of expression. But even here, he uses a succession of seventh chords, and ambiguous major-minors with a deftness which many European musicians should envy. But, in general, harmony is perhaps a musical element which appears in the scheme of musical evolution only at a stage which the Negro art has not yet attained.

All the characteristics of this art, in fact, show it to be a perfect example of what is called popular art—an art which is still in its period of oral tradition. It doesn't matter a whit, after all, whether Negro music be written by Russian Jews, German Jews, or some corrupted Anglo-Saxon. It is a fact that the best numbers are those written by the Negroes themselves. But with these as with the others, the importance of the writer in the creation of the work is counterbalanced by the action of tradition, represented by the performer. The work may be written, but it is not fixed and it finds complete expression only in actual performance.

Nevertheless, some works in the repertory of the Southern Syncopated Orchestra mark the passage from oral tradition to written tradition, or if you choose, from popular art to learned art. First we have a number for choir, soprano, and orchestra, inspired by the traditional works, and signed Dett.[9] On a Biblical text, "Listen to the Lambs," which Handel too has treated in the *Messiah,* this musician has written a very simple yet very pure and beautifully enraptured work. Or we have some works of Mr. Will Marion Cook including a very fine vocal scene entitled "Rainsong." Perhaps one of these days we shall see the Glinka[10] of Negro music. But I am inclined to think that the strongest manifestation of the racial genius lies in the blues.

The blues occurs when the Negro is sad, when he is far from his mammy, or his sweetheart. Then, he thinks of a motif or a preferred rhythm, and takes his trombone, or his violin, or his banjo, or his clarinet, or his drum, or else he sings, or simply dances. And on the chosen motif, he plumbs the depths of his imagination. This makes his sadness pass away—it is the blues.

"These great blue holes which the naughty birds make."

But, for the bitterness of this line, the most refined poet and the Negro coincide here in their expression.

There is in the Southern Syncopated Orchestra an extraordinary clarinet virtuoso who is, so it seems, the first of his race to have composed perfectly formed blues on the clarinet. I've heard two of them which he had elaborated at great length, then played to his companions so that they are equally admirable for their richness of invention, force of accent, and daring in novelty and the unexpected. Already, they gave the idea of a style, and their form was gripping, abrupt, harsh, with a brusque and pitiless ending like that of Bach's second *Brandenburg* Concerto. I wish to set down the name of this artist of genius; as for myself, I shall never forget it—it is Sidney Bechet.[11] When one has tried so often to rediscover in the past one of those figures to whom we owe the advent of our art—those men of the seventeenth and eighteenth centuries, for example, who made expressive works of dance airs, clearing the way for Haydn and Mozart who mark, not the starting point, but the first milestone—what a moving thing it is to meet this very black, fat boy with white teeth and that narrow forehead, who is very glad one likes what he does, but who can say nothing of his art, save that he follows his "own way" and when one thinks that his "own way" is perhaps the highway the whole world will swing along tomorrow.

From *Reading Jazz: A Gathering of Autobiography, Reportage, and Criticism from 1919 to Now,* ed. Robert Gottlieb (New York: Pantheon, 1996), 741–46; translated by Walter Schaap from "Sur un orchèstre nègre" in *Revue romande* (1919).

9. R. Nathaniel Dett (1882–1943), African American composer, not limited to the jazz style.

10. Mikhail Glinka (1804–57) established the Russian national style by infusing folk elements in European forms.

11. Sidney Bechet (1897–1959), jazz clarinetist and saxophonist.

■

Ansermet's essays shows how an erudite European saw the African American entertainers in Paris. A complementary point of view can be found in the autobiography of the African American poet Langston Hughes (1902–67), who spent part of 1924 working in the kitchen of a Paris nightclub specializing in African American music. Ansermet—sitting in the audience—traced the complex of permeations between jazz and European art music. But Hughes—backstage—saw his nightclub as a as a sealed enclave of America's South, a domain of corn fritters and blues music, established in the center of a foreign land: the singer Florence Embry, a warm, hospitable presence to her fellow Americans, adopts a pose of aloofness to gratify the Parisian taste for the exotic. It is possible that much of the European vogue for the American demotic came from the performers' deliberate cultivation of strangeness.

Part of Hughes's mission was the translation of bebop and earlier jazz styles into the language of poetry—as in his poem "Likewise":

> What's the use
> In Harlem?
> What's the Harlem
> use in Harlem
> what's the lick?
>
> *Hey!*
> *Baba-re-bop!*
> *Mop!*
> *On a be-bop kick!*[12]

Hughes noted that his poetry "is marked by conflicting changes, sudden nuances, sharp and impudent interjections, broken rhythms, and passages sometimes in the manner of the jam session, sometimes the popular song, punctuated by riffs, runs, breaks."[13] Hughes's prose, as well as his poetry, skillfully evokes the languor and the hectic of jazz. He assisted music in other ways as well, such as by providing lyrics for Kurt Weill's *Street Scene* (1946–47), and by writing a libretto for James P. Johnson's opera on labor relations, *De Organizer* (ca. 1940).

12. Langston Hughes, *The Collected Poems of Langston Hughes,* ed. Arnold Rampersad (New York: Alfred A. Knopf, 1994), 424.

13. Ibid., 387.

LANGSTON HUGHES
from *The Big Sea* (1940)

The cook at the Grand Duc's name was Bruce, an enormous brownskin fellow, with one eye, and nearing fifty. He wore a white apron, a white cap, and a very fierce frown. He could look at you so fiercely out of his one eye that you would quake in your shoes. His other eye was closed tight. But the one he had looked like three.

Bruce was boss in his own domain, the kitchen. During his hours there, from 11 P.M. to 7 A.M., he would let no one else come in the kitchen, not even the boss or the manager. Only his helper, myself, was permitted. The others called for what they wished at the service window, and woe to the impatient waiter who set foot inside door. Bruce had once hung a pan of pancake batter over such a waiter's head, and several others had often seen the threat of a raised knife. Bruce was highly respected by the employees of the Grand Duc, and addressed with great gentility.

Because he could fry the best chicken à la Maryland in Paris, with corn fritters and gravy, because he could bake beans the way Boston bakes them, and make a golden brown Virginia corn bread that would melt in your mouth, Bruce had a public all his own, was a distinct asset to the place, and his little vagaries were permitted.

They had to be permitted or he would quit.

It was good, working with Bruce, because he would let no one else give you any orders of any kind, neither the French owners nor the Negro manager. And if any waiter said to me: "Hurry up, boy, and hand me some butter," Bruce would bellow: "If you're in such a rush, why don't you tell *me* to hurry up? I'm in charge of this kitchen."

Not another peep out of the waiter, for Bruce's one big eye would petrify him. . . .

A great many celebrities and millionaires came to the Grand Duc in those days, drawn by the fame of Florence Embry—known simply as Florence—the beautiful brownskin girl from Harlem who sang there. Anita Loos[14] and John Emerson, young William Leeds, the Dolly Sisters, Lady Nancy Cunard,[15] various of the McCormicks, the writer, Robert McAlmon, and Belle Livingston with her son and daughter, Fannie Ward, looking not so very young, Prince Tuvalou of Dahomey, Sparrow Robertson of the *Paris Herald*'s sport page, Joe Alix, who became Josephine Baker's[16] dancing partner, the surrealist poet, Louis Aragon,[17] all came—and Florence would notice none of them unless they were very celebrated or very rich.

14. Anita Loos, American novelist and screenwriter, best known for *Gentlemen Prefer Blondes* (1925).

15. Nancy Cunard (1896–1965), patron, collector of African art, and editor of *Negro: An Anthology*.

16. Josephine Baker (1906–75), African American dancer and singer at the Folies Bergères.

17. The French poet Louis Aragon (1897–1982), one of the founders of Surrealism, later abandoned the movement in favor of Communism.

Part of Florence's reputation was based on snobbishness, no doubt, a professional snobbishness which she deliberately cultivated, because outside the club she was as kind and sociable a person as you would ever wish to find. And those who worked with her, from musicians to waiters, loved her. But to the patrons, she adopted an air of unattainable aloofness. She would sing a requested song with only the most casual glance at the table she was singing for—unless a duke, or a steel magnate, or a world celebrity sat there.

Rich, but lowly, patrons could tip Florence ever so heavily, and she would not even condescend to a glass of champagne with them. But the amazing thing was that they would come back and tip her even better for her songs the next time. In the snob world of *de luxe boîte de nuit* society it was considered a mark of distinction for Florence to sit for a moment at your table. Most of the time when Florence was not singing she would remain at her own table by the orchestra saying: "Tell them, 'No, thank you!'" to the waiters who came with offers of champagne from guests who admired her looks or her singing. These frequent "No, thank you's" greatly infuriated the management, who were too short-sighted to see that that was, no doubt, a part of her spell over her following—because she was by no means a great singer of popular songs. She was no Raquel Mellers or Yvette Guilbert.[18] But she was very pretty and brown and could wear the gowns of the great Paris couturières as few other women could. At that time she went home every morning and got plenty of sleep, and would come to work every night looking as fresh and lovely as a black-eyed Susan from some unheard-of Alabama *jardin de luxe,* where sophisticated darkies grow.

In the early part of the evening Florence would often laugh and talk with the waiters and the musicians, or with Bruce and me—but an hour later be as remote as you please to a party of well-to-do tourists from Wisconsin, spending a thousand francs at the front table. It was the first time I had ever seen a colored person deliberately and openly snubbing white people, so it always amused me no end to watch Florence move away from a table of money-spending Americans, who wanted nothing in the world so much as to have her sit down with them.

Her full name was Florence Embry Jones and her husband's name was Palmer Jones. Palmer was a fine piano player, and they frequently sang together. But Palmer at that time was working at the Ambassadeurs, and didn't arrive at the Grand Duc until about three in the morning so, until he came, Florence sang with the orchestra—perhaps a couple of songs an hour between dances, the popular American tunes of the day. Then when Palmer arrived, she would do a group of special numbers with him at the piano, if they felt like it. Palmer himself knew a great many old blues and folksongs—

18. Yvette Guilbert (1867–1944), French actress, singer of Parisian low life. Toulouse-Lautrec painted a famous poster of her.

like "Frankie and Johnnie" and "Henrico." He would occasionally sing one or two of those songs for the guests, inserting off-color lyrics if the crowd was that kind of crowd.

Then when all the other clubs were closed, the best of musicians and entertainers from various other smart places would often drop into the Grand Duc, and there'd be a jam session until seven or eight in the morning—only in 1924 they had no such name for it. They'd just get together and the music would be on. The cream of the Negro musicians then in France . . . would weave out music that would almost make your heart stand still at dawn in a Paris night club in the rue Pigalle, when most of the guests were gone and you were washing the last pots and pans in a two-by-four kitchen, with the fire in the range dying and the one high window letting the soft dawn in.

Blues in the rue Pigalle. Black and laughing, heart-breaking blues in the Paris dawn, pounding like a pulse-beat, moving like the Mississippi!

> *Lawd, I looked and saw a spider*
> *Goin' up de wall.*
> *I say, I looked and saw a spider*
> *Going' up de wall.*
> *I said where you goin', Mister Spider?*
> *I'm goin' to get my ashes hauled!*

Through the mist of smoke and champagne, you laughed at the loneliness of a tiny little spider, going up a great big wall to get his ashes hauled. . . .

Play it, Mister Palmer Jones! Lawd! Lawd! Lawd! Play it, Buddy Gilmore! What you doin' to them drums? Man, you gonna bust your diamond studs in a minute!

From *The Big Sea: An Autobiography by Langston Hughes* (New York: Alfred A. Knopf, 1940), 158–63.

LANGSTON HUGHES
"Moon-Faced, Starry-Eyed" (1946–47)

Moon-faced, starry-eyed,
Peaches and cream with nuts on the side.
I never knew there was anyone living like you.
Moon-faced, starry-eyed,
I'm gonne bust my vest with pride.
I never lived, Baby, not at all 'til I met you.

At six o'clock I expect your call,
At seven o'clock I am in the hall,
At eight o'clock if you don't come by,
By nine o'clock, Baby, I die!

Moon-faced, starry-eyed,
Cooking with gas when I'm by your side.
I swear my heart's nowhere without you.

From the vocal score of *Street Scene: An American Opera,* music by Kurt Weill, book by Elmer Rice, lyrics by Langston Hughes (New York: Chappell Music Company, 1948), 139–41.

■

The Germans as well as the French were beguiled by African American performers. In 1926 the poet Ivan Goll (1891–1950) hailed their arrival—he was elated that an influx of African energy was about to overwhelm anemic, withered, cerebral Europe. The exaltation of the corporeal (seen earlier in this anthology in connection with Harry Partch and D. H. Lawrence) could easily take the form of a fascination with the archaic and the savage. In 1927 appeared Kurt Weill's cantata to a text by Goll, *Der neue Orpheus,* in which Orpheus does everything he can to awaken a culture in full rigor mortis: in clown costume he plays a big drum, at subscription concerts he conducts Mahler symphonies, from the Eiffel Tower he broadcasts his music. In the cantata, Orpheus fails; but Goll may have hoped that the African American entertainers could more successfully galvanize a paralyzed culture. Here Goll employed a caricature that would become familiar in the twentieth century: the black Orpheus, the black Dionysus.

Other observers of the Berlin cultural scene in the later 1920s were also impressed by its exhaustion, thinness, and decadence, but proposed a different solution: "There is the snobby flaneur in a fur coat and patent leather; the worldly lady, *garçon* from head to toe with a monocle and smoking cigarette, taps on high heels across its walkways and disappears into one of thousands of abodes of delirium and drugs. . . . The German people is alien and superfluous here. To speak in the national language is to be nearly conspicuous. Pan-Europe, the *Internationale,* jazz, France . . . —those are the watchwords." [19] The essayist was Joseph Goebbels, soon to be Hitler's minister of propaganda.

IVAN GOLL
"The Negroes Are Conquering Europe" (1926)

The Negroes are conquering Paris. They are conquering Berlin. They have already filled the whole continent with their howls, with their laughter. And we are not shocked, we are not amazed: on the contrary, the old world calls on its failing strength to applaud them.

Yesterday some of us were still saying, art is dead!—the terrible confession of a life-

19. *The Weimar Republic Sourcebook,* ed. Anton Kaes et al. (Berkeley: University of California Press, 1994), 561.

less, enervated, hopeless age. Art dead? Then original art, superior art, lives again! The last art was: disintegration of the ego; disintegration of the world; despair over the world in the ego; the constant, mad revolution of the ego about itself. We experience that in all the twenty-year-old novelists finding fame in Paris just now—and there are dozens of them. . . . And what otherwise is not the product of such pain remains precious and fin-de-siècle, thin and frivolous.

And yet, why complain? The Negroes are here. All of Europe is dancing to their banjo. It cannot help itself. Some say it is the rhythm of Sodom and Gomorrah. . . . Why should it not be from paradise? In this case, rise and fall are one.

The Revue Nègre, which is rousing the tired public in the Théâtre des Champs-Elysées to thrills and madness as otherwise only a boxing match can do, is symbolic. Negroes dance with their senses. (While Europeans can only dance with their minds.) They dance with their legs, breasts, and bellies. This was the dance of the Egyptians, the whole of antiquity, the Orient. This is the dance of the Negroes. One can only envy them, for this is life, sun, primeval forests, the singing of birds and the roar of a leopard, earth. They never dance naked: and yet, how naked is the dance! They have put on clothes only to show that clothes do not exist for them.

Their revue is an unmitigated challenge to moral Europe. There are eight beautiful girls whose figures conjure up a stylized purity, reminiscent of deer and Greek youths. And at their head, the star, Josephine Baker.[20] They have all oiled their curly hair smooth with a process just invented in New York. And on these rounded heads they don hats of manifold fashions, from 1830, 1900, or by the designer Lewis. This mix exudes a glowing irony. A belly dance is performed in a brocade dress by Poiret.[21] In front of a church that could have been painted by Chagall, dressed in bourgeois skirts like women going to market, they dance around a white, bespectacled pastor strumming a banjo (American Negroes are pious and faithful Christians—you only have to listen to their modern songs to know that!). They dance a dance one might expect in a lunatic asylum.

It confronts us all, it confronts everything with the strange impression of a snarling parody. And it is a parody. They make fun of themselves when they perform the "Dance of the Savages" with the same mockery, wearing only the usual loin cloth—and a silk brassiere. And here we see original art becoming one with the latest. These Negroes come out of the darkest parts of New York. There they were disdained, outlawed; these beautiful women might have been rescued from a miserable ghetto. These magnificent

20. Josephine Baker (1906–75), African American dancer and singer, notorious for a dance at the Folies Bergères in Paris in which she wore a costume consisting only of bananas.

21. Paul Poiret (1879–1944), French couturier famous for flamboyant evening dresses, in vogue during the 1910s.

limbs bathed in rinse water. They do not come from the primeval forests at all. We do not want to fool ourselves. But they are a new, unspoiled race. They dance with their blood, with their life, with all the memories in their short history: memories of transport in stinking ships, of early slave labor in America, of much misfortune. Sentimentality breaks through. They become sentimental when they sing, "Swanee River" and "Give Me Just a Little Bit"—these universal hits in provincial jazz apply the rouge on civilization. Alas, these primeval people will be used up fast! Will they have the time to express what is in them in an art of their own making? It is doubtful.

The leader, director, and principal dancer of the troupe is Louis Douglas, the equal of the perfect Baker. He is the only one who wears a dark black mask, while all the others are nearly light brown. He has a gigantic white mouth. But his feet! They are what inspires the music. The orchestra takes its lead from them, not the other way around. He walks, he drags, he slips—and the beat rises from the floor, not from the flutes, which merely offer their accompaniment in secret. One number is called "My Feet Are Talking." And with his feet he tells us of his voyage from New York to Europe: the first day on the boat, the third in the storm, then the trip by railroad and a race at Longchamp.

The musicians play with, they do not merely play along! They are located left of the stage, then soon enough they are following after a dancer or tossing off their remarks in a song. They are genuine actors. They also help to emphasize the parody. They laugh continuously. Whom are they making fun of? No—they aren't making fun of anyone: they are just enjoying, the playing, the dancing, the beat. They enjoy themselves with their faces, with their legs, with their shoulders; everything shakes and plays its part. It often seems as if they had the leading roles.

But the leading role belongs to Negro blood. Its drops are slowly falling over Europe, a long-since dried-up land that can scarcely breathe. Is that perhaps the cloud that looks so black on the horizon but whose fearsome downpours are capable of so white a shine? . . . The Negro question is pressing for our entire civilization. It runs like this: Do the Negroes need us? Or are we not sooner in need of them?

From *The Weimar Republic Sourcebook,* ed. Anton Kaes et al. (Berkeley: University of California Press, 1994), 559–60; originally published as "Die Neger erobern Europa," *Die literarische Welt* 2 (15 January 1926): 3–4.

The controversies concerning jazz were most intense in America. One of the loudest voices raised against it was that of Daniel Gregory Mason (1873–1953), an establishmentarian of the first rank: professor at Columbia University, composer in a conservative Brahmsian idiom, descendent of the distinguished hymn writer Lowell Mason. He was a pioneer in the American music appreciation movement, and he tried his best to make sure that American ears appreciated American music, uncontaminated by the insidious music of Jews or the pathologies of jazz (as he considered them). Yet even Mason, despite his hopes for racial purity in music, tried his hand at assimilating African American elements into European forms: his *String Quartet on Negro Themes* (1920) is based on "Deep River" and other spirituals—treated with all the antiseptics at Mason's disposal.

DANIEL GREGORY MASON
from *Tune In, America* (1931)

Vital nationalism . . . depends less on distinctive idioms, even for those nations that possess them, than on distinctive temperamental attitudes toward life, and on loyalty to local experience, displacing servility to foreign points of view, and prompting in its place a simple sincerity of expression. . . .

Such a characteristic American attitude . . . is the reserve, the dislike of ostentation, the repressed but strong emotion masked by dry humor, that belong to our New England type, as we have seen it in Elgar to belong to the prevailing type in the older England. This Anglo-Saxon element in our heterogeneous national character, however quantitatively in the minority nowadays, is qualitatively of crucial significance in determining what we call the American temper. The name popularly symbolizing it—the word "Yankee"—is often extended from New England to cover the whole country; and that other and most far-reaching of all our popular symbols—Uncle Sam—is only a universalized and glorified Yankee. In our literature the type is immortally enshrined in the work of Emerson and Thoreau and, in our own day, of Robinson and Frost.[22] We hear it often in the music of Chadwick, sometimes in MacDowell.[23] . . . The essence of it is a kind of moderation—not negative, as those who do not understand it imagine, but strongly positive; the moderation that, as Chesterton[24] says, is "not a compromise, but a passion, the passion of great judges"; a moderation, in Tennyson's fine phrase:

> Turning to scorn with lips divine
> The falsehood of extremes.[25]

Why an attitude thus based on moderation should have received so far such slight and sporadic expression in our music, instead of infusing it with a pervasive and dominating individuality, is not hard to understand when we reflect that the particular type

22. Ralph Waldo Emerson (1803–82) and Henry David Thoreau (1817–62), Transcendentalist writers; Edwin Arlington Robinson (1869–1935) and Robert Frost (1874–1963), poets.
23. George Whitefield Chadwick (1854–1931) and Edward MacDowell (1860–1908), composers.
24. Gilbert Keith Chesterton (1874–1936), conservative British writer.
25. From "Of Old Sat Freedom on the Heights" (1842), by Alfred Lord Tennyson (1809–92).

of foreign prestige to which we have most completely capitulated is precisely that Jewish type which, if not exactly based on the "falsehood of extremes," at least tolerates,
perhaps even enjoys, extremes, as a soberer music cannot. The Jew and the Yankee
stand, in human temperament, at polar points; where one thrives, the other is bound
to languish. And our whole contemporary aesthetic attitude toward instrumental music, especially in New York, is dominated by Jewish tastes and standards, with their Oriental extravagance, their sensuous brilliancy and intellectual facility and superficiality,
their general tendency to exaggeration and disproportion. "The insidiousness of the
Jewish menace to our artistic integrity," wrote the present writer more than ten years
ago,[26] when the domination was far less complete than it has since become, "is due to
the speciousness, the superficial charm and persuasiveness of Hebrew art, its violently
juxtaposed extremes of passion, its poignant eroticism and pessimism. . . . For how
shall a public accustomed by prevailing fashion to the exaggeration, the constant running to extremes, of eastern expression, divine the poignant beauty of Anglo-Saxon so-
briety and restraint? How shall it pierce the Anglo-Saxon reticence, the fine reserve so
polar to the garrulous self-confession, the almost indecent stripping of the soul, it wit-
nesses in every concert hall and opera house? How shall it value as it deserves the
balance, the sense of proportion, which is the finest of Anglo-Saxon qualities, and to
which, like the sense of humor to which it is akin (since both depend upon the sense of
congruity or incongruity), nothing is more alien than the Oriental abandonment to excess? Our public taste is in danger of being permanently debauched, made lastingly insensitive to qualities most subtly and quintessentially our own, by the intoxication of
what is, after all, an alien art."

It was several years after these warnings had been written that Ernest Bloch,[27] long
the chief minister of that intoxication to our public, capped his dealings with us by the
grim jest of presenting to us a long, brilliant, megalomaniac, and thoroughly Jewish
symphony—entitled *America*. (In calling attention to this irony, it is hardly necessary to
state that no "anti-Jewish propaganda" is intended. All propaganda is apt to be either
indifferent or positively injurious to art. Besides, no judgment on the intrinsic value of
the Jewish element in American art in general, or of Mr. Bloch's music in particular, is
here undertaken. All that is being pointed out is that our own subservience to fashion
allows one type of art to make us deaf to the possibilities of another that is more pe-
culiarly our own.)

26. "Is American Music Growing Up? Our Emancipation from Alien Influences," in *Arts and Decoration*, November 1920. [Mason's note.]

27. Ernest Bloch (1880–1959), American immigrant from Switzerland, wrote an "epic rhapsody"
America (1926), for chorus and orchestra, celebrating the history of his adopted home. Some of his
other works have conspicuously Jewish themes.

If we look for idiosyncrasies more widespread among us than the ancestral Anglo-Saxon seriousness, our attention may fall on what has been called "American hustle"—a group of qualities induced or encouraged by our present business and industrial life, such as haste, practical "efficiency," good humor of a superficial sort, inventiveness, an extravert preference of action to thought—in short, all that is suggested by such popular slogans as "Step lively" and "Keep smiling." Its natural musical expression is found, of course, in jazz; and for a long time now certain critics have been persistently telling us that jazz is in fact the one distinctive American music, and that by cultivating it sedulously we shall find our musical "place in the sun" among the nations. In jazz, moreover, suppression of native qualities by imported standards seems not to be in operation. On the contrary, jazz has been distinctly "taken up" by some of the more advanced European groups, for whom America has thus become a source of musical importations as well as the ever profitable market for exports. If jazz, as one of its panegyrists claims, expresses "the jerk and rattle" of the American city, "its restless bustle and motion, its multitude of unrelated details, and its underlying progress toward a vague somewhere"[28] and if this expression of the more trivial side of American life meets with no such opposition from fashion as confronts that of more serious aspects, the question inevitably arises whether we should not find here a hopeful lead for American music. In spite of these apparently promising features, however, the answer given by the more discerning critics from the first, and recently with increasing inescapability by experience itself, has turned out to be a negative one, for reasons that throw some light on our whole problem. First of all, jazz is not, like the varied types of European folk-song to which it is often misleadingly compared, a spontaneous artistic activity of our people; it is a commercial product, like so many others "put over" upon the people. It does not grow up in simple minds, voicing their feelings; it is manufactured by calculating ones, seeking profit. In a word, it is not an expression at all; it is an exploitation. Consequently, instinctively felt by all sensitive minds to be artificial, it leaves them cold; it has no persuasiveness, no magic, no psychological truth.

In the second place, even if jazz were true, its truth would be to a pathological state in us, not to the mental health on which alone a valid art can be reared. For it reflects, not our health, vitality, and hope, but our restlessness, our fatigue, and our despair. It is a symptom of a sick moment in the progress of the human soul: the moment of industrial turmoil, fever, and distress that we can but hope to survive, not to perpetuate. To its tense, false gayety the hearing ear responds never with the joy that comes only in relaxation but with a sense of depression that may be tinged with tragedy. Even its most distinguished exploiters seem to recognize its hysterical character. Ernest

28. Hiram K. Moderwell, in the *New Republic,* October 16, 1915. [Mason's note.]

Schelling's *A Victory Ball*[29] is built on a program of post-war disillusion. Mr. Carpenter's *Skyscrapers*[30] is said to represent "the hurry and din of American life . . . its violent alternations of work and play." Despite its kinship with an undeniable if superficial side of our character, and in spite of its acceptability to Europeans in search rather of new sensations than of living art, the bankruptcy of jazz as a source of serious music is becoming daily more evident.

Yet surely there is something in this liveliness of ours, this brisk good cheer, this kindly if superficial cordiality, that gives significance and distinctiveness to our national character. Perhaps, if we could but detach it from the morbid excitement of jazz, product of industrial cities poisoned with nervous fatigue, it might afford a valid ingredient in our art. One hears such a quality, tranquilized and balanced, as it were, by open air and wide spaces, without losing any of its energy, in much of Grainger and Powell[31] and in such a real American folk-song as David Guion's *Turkey in the Straw*. Such animation is native to us, as that in the finales of Haydn's symphonies was native to his Croatian people. It is like the liveliness of children, innocent and gay. Genuinely American is this childlike innocence, since we are in our fundamental mentality childlike or even childish, not to say infantile.

And this brings us to a final trait of ours, perhaps potentially the most American of all, though for the present suffering the severest repression: our sentiment. There can be no doubt that sentiment, often of the naïvest, most unself-conscious kind, existing in a separate compartment from our humor and untouched by it, is a deep ingredient of our character. Not only the American of nineteenth-century fiction, but the American of twentieth-century fact, is naïve in a way and to a degree often surprising to Europeans; his emotions, wonders, vanities, ideals, hopes, are those of a child, not yet made realist by bitter experience. Our most characteristic men of letters both depict these traits and illustrate them in their own persons; think of the trusting optimism of Emerson, the boyish swagger of Bret Harte and Mark Twain.[32] . . .

29. Ernest Schelling (1876–1939), American pianist, composer, and lecturer, wrote the symphonic poem *A Victory Ball* (1925).

30. The ballet *Skyscrapers* (1926), by John Alden Carpenter (1876–1951), celebrates construction and industry with hammer rhythms and fox-trots, using an orchestra that includes saxophones, banjo, and compressed air whistle.

31. Percy Grainger (1882–1961), Australian-born composer whose timbral and harmonic imagination was often stimulated by folksongs, and John Powell (1882–1963), American composer, perhaps best known for *Rhapsodie Nègre* (1918); in the previous year Powell had founded the Society for the Preservation of Racial Integrity at the University of Virginia.

32. Bret Harte (1836–1902) and Mark Twain (Samuel Langhorne Clemens, 1835–1910) both wrote stories about the American West.

Now it is an undeniable fact, of the most far-reaching import to our future growth, that precisely this childlike sentiment, perhaps our deepest quality, surely one of our most characteristic, is the one most irreconcilably antipathetic of all to the qualities of European music that at present set the vogue all over the world, and consequently the one most relentlessly repressed by them. A childlike people, in both the good and the bad senses of the word, musically undeveloped but promising, we find ourselves paralyzed on the very threshold of musical experience by the disillusionment, the cynicism, the blasé striving after novelty, of a Europe old and in some ways effete. The ruling fashion among the sophisticates today is neo-classicism, a dry, hard aesthetic which derides sentiment, repudiates romance, and almost measures the success of a piece of music by the absence of all expression from it. And the pity is that in a complete capitulation to these foreign models our young composers have almost to a man abjured their youth, personal and national. They are like conscientious and aspiring school drunkards and college roués, as pathetic as they are absurd. One hardly knows whether to laugh or cry when one hears young Bostonians striving to outdo Schönberg in sterile, ugly counterpoint, young New Yorkers vying with Stravinsky in brittle pseudo classicism, young Californians trying to be more starkly primitive than Prokofieff!

. . . One dares to hope that at last we are getting ready to outgrow our unmanly awe of Europe, preparing to look hopefully about us at our own life, and, interpreting it as it strikes our naïve, unspoiled sentiment, make some music of our own.

From Daniel Gregory Mason, *Tune In, America: A Study of Our Coming Musical Independence* (Freeport, N.Y.: Books for Libraries Press, 1969), 158–69.

■

George Gershwin (1898–1937)—one of those Jews whom Mason found so insidious—began his career plugging hit tunes at the piano for Tin Pan Alley (as the popular music industry in New York City was called); by the end of his career he was a tennis partner of Arnold Schoenberg's and a respected composer of a concerto and an opera. Of all the Modernist composers, Gershwin had perhaps the most remarkable faculty for assimilating and fusing diverse styles: whereas Stravinsky *uses* many styles—Russian folk, ragtime, Baroque, twelve-tone—holding them all gingerly at arm's length, Gershwin synthesizes so enthusiastically it is difficult (in his concert pieces) to tell where the world of Ravel stops and where the blues begin. Of course, this discrimination is sometimes troublesome in Ravel's own work, such as the Violin Sonata (1923–27), with its "Blues" second movement; but Gershwin may have done more than anyone else to show just how flimsy the division between high and low music can be.

While researching his opera *Porgy and Bess* (1935), Gershwin visited Folly Island off the South Carolina coast, to hear the music of the Gullahs, perhaps the closest thing to a pure African culture surviving in North America; he quickly became so expert in the patterns of hand-and-foot stompings that the locals applauded his skill. Gershwin was also applauded by Schoenberg as an "innovator. . . . Melody, harmony, and rhythm are not welded together, but cast." [33] It is not easy to think of another composer who could receive tributes from such divergent sources.

Gershwin's prose, as well as his music, exemplifies the values of the Melting Pot.

GEORGE GERSHWIN
"The Composer and the Machine Age" (1933)

Unquestionably modern musical America has been influenced by modern musical Europe. But it seems to me that modern European composers, in turn, have very largely received their stimulus, their rhythms and impulses from Machine Age America. They have a much older tradition of musical technique which has helped them put into musical terms a little more clearly the thoughts that originated here. They can express themselves more glibly.

The Machine Age has influenced practically everything. I do not mean only music but everything from the arts to finance. The machine has not affected our age in form as much as in tempo, speed and sound. It has affected us in sound whenever composers utilize new instruments to imitate its aspects. In my *American in Paris* [34] I used four taxi horns for musical effect. George Antheil has used everything, including aeroplane propellers, door bells, typewriter keys, and so forth. [35] By the use of the old instruments, too, we are able to obtain modern effects. Take a composition like Honegger's *Pacific No. 231,* [36] written and dedicated to a steam engine. It reproduces the whole effect of a train stopping and starting and it is all done with familiar instruments.

There is only one important thing in music and that is ideas and feeling. The various tonalities and sounds mean nothing unless they grow out of ideas. Not many composers have ideas. Far more of them know how to use strange instruments which do not require ideas. Whoever has inspired ideas will write the great music of our period. We are plowing the ground for that genius who may be alive or may be born today or tomorrow. If he is alive, he is recognized to a certain degree, although it is impossible for the public at large to assimilate real greatness quickly. Take a composer like Bach. In his lifetime, he was recognized as one of the greatest organists in the world, but he was

---

33. Schoenberg, *Style and Idea,* 476.

34. *An American in Paris* (1928), an orchestral composition that synthesizes raucousness and elegance.

35. Gershwin means the *Ballet Mécanique* (1926) by George Antheil (1900–59).

36. *Pacific 231* (1923), an orchestral evocation of a train, by Arthur Honegger (1892–1955).

not acclaimed as one of the greatest composers of his time or of all time until genera-tions after his death.

I do not think there is any such thing as mechanized musical composition without feeling, without emotion. Music is one of the arts which appeals directly through the emotions. Mechanism and feeling will have to go hand in hand, in the same way that a skyscraper is at the same time a triumph of the machine and a tremendous emotional experience, almost breath-taking. Not merely its height but its mass and proportions are the result of an emotion, as well as of calculation.

Any discussion of the distinction between presentation and representation in music resolves itself into an attempt to determine the relative values of abstract music and program music. It is very difficult for anyone to tell where abstract music starts and pro-gram music finishes. There must have been a picture of something in the composer's mind. What it was nobody knows, often not even the composer. But music has a mar-velous faculty of recording a picture in someone else's mind. In my own case, every-body who has ever listened to *Rhapsody in Blue*[37] — and that embraces thousands of people — has a story for it but myself. *An American in Paris* is obviously a program piece, although I would say half of it or more is abstract music tied together by a few representative themes. Imitation never gets anyone anywhere. Originality is the only thing that counts. But the originator uses material and ideas that occur around him and pass through him. And out of his experience comes this original creation or work of art, unquestionably influenced by his surroundings which include largely what we call the Machine Age.

It is difficult to determine what enduring values, esthetically, jazz has contributed, because jazz is a word which has been used for at least five or six different types of mu-sic. It is really a conglomeration of many things. It has a little bit of ragtime, the blues, classicism and spirituals. Basically, it is a matter of rhythm. After rhythm in importance come intervals, music intervals which are peculiar to the rhythm. After all, there is noth-ing new in music. I maintained years ago that there is very little difference in the music of different nations. There is just that little individual touch. One country may prefer a peculiar rhythm or a note like the seventh. This it stresses, and it becomes identified with that nation. In America this preferred rhythm is called jazz. Jazz is music; it used the same notes that Bach used. When jazz is played in another nation, it is called Amer-ican. When it is played in another country, it sounds false. Jazz is the result of the en-ergy stored up in America. It is a very energetic kind of music, noisy, boisterous and even vulgar. One thing is certain. Jazz has contributed an enduring value to America in the sense that it has expressed ourselves. It is an original American achievement which

---

37. *Rhapsody in Blue* (1924), Gershwin's wildly popular composition for piano and orchestra.

will endure, not as jazz, perhaps, but which will leave its mark on future music in one form or another. The only kinds of music which endure are those which possess form in the universal sense and folk music. All else dies. But unquestionably folk songs are being written and have been written which contain enduring elements of jazz. To be sure, that is only an element; it is not the whole. An entire composition written in jazz could not live.

As for further esthetic developments in musical composition, American composers may in time use quarter notes, but then so will Europe use quarter notes. Eventually our ears will become sensitive to a much finer degree than they were a hundred, fifty or twenty-five years ago. Music deemed ugly then is accepted without question today. It stands to reason, therefore, that composers will continue to alter their language. That might lead to anything. They have been writing already in two keys. There is no reason why they will not go further and ask us to recognize quarter or sixteenth notes. Such notes, whether written or not, are used all the time, only we are not conscious of them. In India they use quarter tones and, I believe, consciously. Music is a phenomenon that to me has a very marked effect on the emotions. It can have various effects. It has the power of moving people to all of the various moods. Through the emotions, it can have a cleansing effect on the mind, a disturbing effect, a drowsy effect, an exciting effect. I do not know to what extent it can finally become a part of the people. I do not think music as we know it now is indispensable although we have music all around us in some form or other. There is music in the wind. People can live more or less satisfactorily without orchestral music, for instance. And who can tell that we would not be better off if we weren't as civilized as we are, if we lacked many of our emotions? But we have them and we are more or less egotistic about them. We think that they are important and that they make us what we are. We think that we are an improvement over people of other ages who didn't have them. Music has become a very important part of civilization, and one of the main reasons is that one does not need a formal education to appreciate it. Music can be appreciated by a person who can neither read nor write and it can also be appreciated by people who have the highest form of intelligence. For example, Einstein plays the violin and listens to music. People in the underworld, dope-fiends and gun men, invariably are music lovers and, if not, they are affected by it. Music is entering into medicine. Music sets up a certain vibration which unquestionably results in a physical reaction. Eventually the proper vibration for every person will be found and utilized. I like to think of music as an emotional science.

Almost every great composer profoundly influences the age in which he lives. Bach, Beethoven, Wagner, Brahms, Debussy, Strawinsky. They have all recreated something of their time so that millions of people could feel it more forcefully and better understand their time.

The composer, in my estimation, has been helped a great deal by the mechanical reproduction of music. Music is written to be heard, and any instrument that tends to help it to be heard more frequently and by greater numbers is advantageous to the person who writes it. Aside from royalties or anything like that, I should think that the theory that music is written to be heard is a good one. To enable millions of people to listen to music by radio or phonograph is helpful to the composer. The composer who writes music for himself and doesn't want it to be heard is generally a bad composer. The first incursion of mechanized reproduction was a stimulus to the composer and the second wave has merely intensified that stimulus. In the past, composers have starved because of lack of performance, lack of being heard. That is impossible today. Schubert could not make any money because he did not have an opportunity through the means of distribution of his day to reach the public. He died at the age of thirty-one and had a certain reputation. If he had lived to be fifty or sixty, unquestionably he would have obtained recognition in his own day. If he were living today, he would be well-off and comfortable.

The radio and the phonograph are harmful to the extent that they bastardize music and give currency to a lot of cheap things. They are not harmful to the composer. The more people listen to music, the more they will be able to criticize it and know when it is good. When we speak of machine-made music, however, we are not speaking of music in the highest sense, because, no matter how much the world becomes a Machine Age, music will have to be created in the same old way. The Machine Age can affect music only in its distribution. Composers must compose in the same way the old composers did. No one has found a new method in which to write music. We still use the old signatures, the old symbols. The composer has to do every bit of his work himself. Hand work can never be replaced in the composition of music. If music ever became machine-made in that sense, it would cease to be an art.

From *1938 Gershwin*, ed. Merle Armitage (London: Longmans, Green, 1938), 225–30.

■

When Gershwin thought of modern music, he thought of machines and jazz; and the affiliations between the mechanical and the African are often strong in the Modernist imagination. Violently emphasized beats might mean a steel factory, or might mean tom-toms in a jungle. This convergence between the Futuristic and the prehistoric is especially noticeable in the work of the American composer George Antheil (1900–59), whose piano sonatas *The Airplane* (1921) and *Sonata sauvage* (1923; its movements are "Niggers," "Snakes," and the "xylophonic" "Ivory") are strikingly similar in sonority and technique. In 1934 Antheil contributed to Nancy Cunard's anthology *Negro* a feverish and elated essay in praise of the African strain in contemporary music. Here Antheil takes Ivan Goll's argument that all cultural rejuvenation must originate in the black races about as far as it will go—Antheil even constructs a whole history of music from this mythic perspective. Ultimately Antheil sees Modernism as a movement that will Africanize the whole continent of Europe—much to Europe's advantage. Of course, other composers had labored to do the exact opposite: to Europeanize African music. For example, the African British composer Samuel Coleridge-Taylor (1875–1912), son of a physician from Sierra Leone, wrote in his preface to *Twenty-Four Negro Melodies* that he hoped to do for the melodies of Africa and the American South "what Brahms has done for the Hungarian folk music, Dvořák for the Bohemian, and Grieg for the Norwegian . . . primitive as it is, it nevertheless has all the elements of the European folk song." But where Coleridge-Taylor imagined an Africa on the brink of evolving into Europe, Antheil saw a Europe that desperately needed Africa's energy.

Cunard's anthology remains a trove of material highly useful to the student of Modernism. She prints, for example, a poem by Ernst Moerman, "Louis Armstrong," translated from the French by Samuel Beckett:

> suddenly in the midst of a game of lotto with his sisters
> Armstrong let a roar out of him that he had the raw meat
> red wet flesh for Louis
> and he up and he sliced him two rumplips
> since when his trumpet bubbles
> their fust buss [38]

To Moerman, the young trumpet virtuoso seems close to a cannibal. In Antheil's essay also, as we will see, there can be felt the Primitivist combination of fascination and terror in the presence of the "savage"—in Antheil's own words, love and panic.

GEORGE ANTHEIL
"The Negro on the Spiral, or A Method of Negro Music" (1934)

Since Wagner, music has had two gigantic blood infusions—first the Slavic, and, in recent times, the Negroid. The Russian Five, leading gradually into young Debussy, and eventually into young Strawinsky, seemed to pass naturally into the present Negroidian epoch, especially after the great and world-shaking events of the *Sacre du Printemps* and *Noces*. It is not difficult to understand the transition when one examines these two last-named works and realizes how completely they exhausted Slavic music, and how the Negroidian music, already used to existence under the most terrible heat

---

38. From *Negro: An Anthology,* ed. Nancy Cunard and Hugh Ford (New York: Frederick Ungar, 1970), 185.

when all other life and musics must perish, was the predestined influence to carry music through the difficult after-war period until the present time. The Negro music, like the Negro, has been living for a number of million years under terrible heat; Negro music has, in consequence, been baked as hard and as beautiful as a diamond; it was the only thinkable influence after the *Sacre* and *Noces* had exhausted once and for all every last drop of blood that the primitive Slavic music had in it. The first Negro jazz band arriving in Paris during the last year of the great war was as prophetic of the after-war period immediately to come as the *Sacre* was prophetic of this selfsame war, declared only a year after the stormy scenes at the Champs Elysées Theatre in 1913. And this was the war which exhausted the world and left it without a grain of its former "spirituality." Likewise the *Sacre* left music sunbaked, parched, without a drop of water, and without a blade of green grass; the famine was here; there was no hope; a cataclysm; a great work marking a finality. Nothing could survive underneath this dense heat and smoke except Negro music. It absorbed this period so naturally that in 1919 we find the greatest Slavic composer living writing "Piano-rag-music" and "Ragtime" almost without knowing it, and a whole school of young composers springing up in Paris deeply influenced by American Negro music. By 1920 the gigantic Slavic influence of the past 40 years ended; not even the long-delayed performance of *Noces* [*The Wedding*] could call it back; in 1923, with this premiere of *Noces* we realized that *Noces* was written in 1914, and that *something* had happened in between time, and that *we were no longer the same*. Strawinsky himself began to forsake Slavic music. Then, frightened at the gigantic black apparition, each European people scurried hurriedly towards their own racial music; the Latins became more Latin, and the Germans more German (and the Britons and white Americans of that time, having mixed French impressionism with Russian and German avant-gardism, became absolutely incomprehensible). From 1920 to 1925 we see one definite trend . . . no matter how absolutely Latin the Latins might become . . . or how Germanic the Germanics might become . . . deep down (or perhaps not even concealed at all) . . . is *ever* present the new *note* of the Congo. This *note* has erroneously been called "American," but this note belongs no more specifically to the North American Negro than to those of the West Indies or South America. It is *black* . . . not white, nor yellow. It is strongly marked and recognizable, never to be mistaken, even by the musical illiterate. Rhythmically it comes from the groins, the hips, and the sexual organs, and not from the belly, the interior organs, the arms and legs, as in the Hindu, Javanese, and Chinese musics, or from the breast, the brain, the ears and eyes of the white races. It is angular and elliptical like the lines of a Brancusi[39] sculpture . . . or better . . . like the sculptures of the African Negroes themselves. In its original state in Africa, this music first impresses us as hard, wooden, incredibly complicated rhyth-

39. Constantin Brancusi (1876–1957), Romanian sculptor of polished abstractions.

mically, so that even the most involved Arabic music must seem tame in comparison. To a white European musician, hearing for the first time choruses from the Congo (even though it be upon gramophone records) . . . he is invariably stunned by the machine-precision of the black choirs in rhythms and counter-rhythms even more difficult than the last cataclysm of the *Sacre,* which demands for its performance musicians of the highest order and many painstaking rehearsals. The idea of correctly presenting these choruses with such vital and direct rhythmic accuracy *is unthinkable with even the best-disciplined white chorus in the world.* One thing is certain, the Negro has a rhythmic sense second to none in the world; one can scarcely believe that one has not to do with a highly civilized race, masters of steel, mathematics, and engineering, in hearing these choruses from the Congo . . . so intricate in rhythmic pattern, so delicately balanced in contra-rhythms and proportions, and so breathtaking in unisons and choral *impact* are these extraordinary performances. One is reminded of a colossal *Noces* fabricated by a *single* people for ages . . . broader . . . wider . . . infinitely more intricate and at the same time more epic; not accompanied by four pianos in a Parisian ballet, but by the gigantic xylophones of a thousand wooden drums fashioned from the hollow trunks of trees; the sound of the tragxylophone, iron bells, the rattle of baskets of stone, primitive but sonorous harps fashioned from a memory of thousands of years back which long ago came down the Nile, one-stringed zithers on long narrow poles, harps with gourds attached to their middles, violins with zebra-hair strings played by a zebra-hair bow with several gourds attached and sounding like clarinets of the richest quality, palm flutes, *wooden* trumpets, great horns made of elephant tusk, the twisted horns of antelopes, each one with a stranger sound (a sound which no European orchestra could possibly duplicate). Imagine added to this the great Negro choirs themselves, and the strange high vibrant treble of the Negro women, and the special Negro throats of the men, and . . . incredible co-ordination.

It is inevitable that this tremendous musical impetus originating in the heat of central Africa was carried over through the slave deportations to North and South America and the West Indies, and that each one of these black populations overflowed with its own separate music in an infinite number of new designs and phenomena, due to the new musical absorptions and influences the original African impetus underwent. But it is important to notice that these influences, whether they be of Yankee hymn tunes, or the Habaneras of the Portuguese or Spanish, or other points further southward in the New World, were always completely absorbed, and did not conceal or hinder the original pure Africanism underlying every measure of this music. This exact quality is hard to define technically, as it has an infinite amount of variants, but in general one might say that the African "sound" in music is usually a tightening-up of the musical force, an intensive concentration and compactness, and thinning-out of line, and brilliant and sudden rhythmical decisions more daring than those of any other people or race, a marked tendency towards the "black" on the pianoforte, and the inevitable eighth-note on the strong beats throwing into an immediate quarter-note following, the latter with an accent (almost the Negro signature, for go where one will in Negro music, these two notes occur like the signature of Alexander the Great in the ancient world). The least common denominator of the Negro music has not changed; one still finds it in an almost pure state upon the islands off the coast of the American southern states where the fire-ritual dances are still played and sung after two hundred years and three thousand miles distant from the Congo. In the interior of the United States the work-songs and the children's songs and occasionally the well-known and often overestimated "spirituals" attest to this. . . . Who can deny that the popular music of the United States has become definitely mulatto, even if only partially so; the union between a Negro and a white invariably produces a Negro and not a white. The Negro music, like the Negro, absorbs, but does not become. It is a definite compactness, and an invulnerable, indestructible quality. It has existed under the broiling sun for thousands of years . . . the sun which blinded in the day and left the night full of jungle steam, terrors, and sounds. Being in the midst of Nature at her cruellest, it is not pastoral. It has survived and built up an incredible musical machinery.

And in 1919 it made its official appearance in Europe.

The fact that Europe was ready for it can only be accredited to the Russian Five, Tschaikowsky, Strawinsky, and the great Frenchman, Debussy, who had spent his early life in Russia as a tutor, and came back to Paris filled full of *Boris Godounov.* Debussy came back to a French Capital that was somewhat surfeited with Wagner, at least in intellectual circles. It is France that we have to thank for the western European support of the revolution against the ponderous scores from Germany, growing ever more bulky and pseudo-Olympian. Borodin, Moussorgsky, Tschaikowsky (and eventually, when everything was ready for his entrance, Strawinsky) turned the desert cyclones of the Gobi and Mongolia loose upon this German music and swept it away for the time being, to the new adventures and progress of music. . . . Then came the war, one single terrible flattening blast; indeed what could survive after this whirlpool of ideas and events? The American Negroes advanced upon musical Paris, took command, reigned for a time, and then disappeared, leaving everywhere gigantic mulatto patches; musicians particularly seemed to have turned at least to octoroons. Like wildfire the *Negro patch* spread everywhere in Europe. . . . Thereupon came the reaction. Every time a white composer was caught consorting with Negro music he was promptly run off and musically lynched; after a vigorous year of campaigning Europe sat back and told itself that Negro music was no more.

Still, papal decrees continued to be issued against jazz; dancing approximated more and more to the St. Vitus sickness; people went back to the old music and found out they could not even listen to it. . . .

. . . For look where we may today beneath this classical music of Strawinsky, or beneath the cheap but infinitely touching "Berlinese" of Weill, or beneath the beery but interesting and strong (in a Breughel-like way) [40] fabrications of Krenek, or for that matter the last creations of Schönberg, Milhaud, Auric . . . we find the note . . . the technic . . . the *aesthetic* of the Congo . . . all the more important and insidious in its influence because now it is more deeply hidden but now *everywhere* present. . . . The violin concerto of Strawinsky is full of recognizable jazz (the first outright jazz Strawinsky has allowed himself in some time); the last opera of Schönberg concerns itself with the present day [41] and contains some of the very worst jazz that white man has ever written; I could go on easily filling up this page. The Negro is *not* absorbed, but absorbs. Even though a white might lay with an octoroon of the whitest color, still after one or two white children a child absolutely black might be born. Europe has been impregnated, and impregnated deeply. We need no longer be surprised by our dark children. Music will no longer be all the white keys of the piano, but will have keys of ebony as well.

The tremendous détour that Negro music has taken to reach the European continent at its most torrid, barren, smoking, and psychological moment has been via the Americas, because this music could never have adequately pierced the Arabian veil thrown over the top of the African continent like magic, or as an iron lid to keep this boiling and seething musical ferment in the jug of Africa. . . . We scarcely realize today exactly how near to the soil was the whole Russian movement. Strawinsky has a partially Asiatic cast of countenance; he comes naturally to the barbaric heritage he has so adequately expressed. But we cannot try to part Russian music and Mongolian and Arabic music. The three have a blood kinship, even though today the Arab might be far removed from the north Russian; the Arabic music in a far-flung western and African branch was sufficiently strange and strong to keep any Negroid inflections from crossing the Mediterranean to the new music cultures of 16th to 19th century Europe. This European music culture drifted in one way or another from the earliest church composers, through Mozart and Beethoven (both of whom wrote "Turkish" music) [42] to Wagner, who (as might suit your own taste) was either Viking or pseudo-Viking . . . from the viewpoint

40. Pieter Bruegel the Younger painted visions of hell and other proto-Surrealist scenes in the seventeenth century.

41. *Von Heute auf Morgen* (1929), Schoenberg's *Zeitoper* concerning a wife who flirts with an operatic tenor; at one point husband and wife dance to what Schoenberg pretended was a popular tune.

42. "Turkish" music used to mean drones and jangling percussion—as in Mozart's *Abduction from the Seraglio* (1782) and Beethoven's *Ruins of Athens* (1811).

of tendency it does not much matter which. It is interesting to note that this culture passes to culture, and influence to influence, like a gigantic spiral starting from a central point and throwing out its long spiral line like those peculiar revolving optical illusions which we spun upon a pinwheel as children. It is like a gigantic radio station. For if we start with Bach we go immediately afterwards to Vienna (still remaining purists and classicists) with Mozart and Beethoven; and then clockwise (in ever larger circles) to Paris (and southern Germany) with Schumann, Chopin, Berlioz, and early Wagner; then in still larger expanding spiral to northern Germany and Scandinavia, with later Wagner and Grieg; then to Petrograd with Tschaikowsky in ever larger spiral (still clockwise) to Moussorgsky, Borodin, Rimsky-Korsakow and Strawinsky through eastern Russia, western Asia, and downward to Arabia; then the line passes invisibly through the very center of Africa (although no one knew it at that exact moment!). I called the Americas an enormous détour, but perhaps indeed they were no détour at all, but absolutely upon the path of this gigantic spiral now throwing out its enormous circle over the South Atlantic, taking in South America, the West Indies, and North America in one gigantic swing. Then in 1919, the line, still swinging clockwise, comes back over the North Atlantic and hits Europe. Wagner at the very height of his northern music culture succeeds to Strawinsky who, at the very height of his eastern Tartar culture, succeeds to the Congo. Clockwise the Viking passes onto the Slav, and again the Slav passes on to the African. It is twelve o'clock with Wagner; three o'clock with Strawinsky; and when the height of African influence and culture is reached, it will be six o'clock. But the point I wish to make clear by the example of this gigantic spiral going clockwise throughout the centuries is this: music progresses logically; even geographically it is possible to trace its course; can one with some optimism be clairvoyant? Certainly it is not impossible to see immediately the kinship between Slav and African, and how one must inevitably pass to the other; and how the utmost end of one development is not unsympathetic to the other. . . . Negro music appeared suddenly (after a gigantic preparation) after the greatest war of all time. It came upon a bankrupt spirituality; to have continued within Slavic mysticism would have induced us all, in 1918, to commit suicide; Negro music made us to remember at least that we still had bodies which had not been exploded by shrapnel and that the cool 4 o'clock morning sunshine still coming over the hot veldt of yesterday was this morning very, very sweet. We needed at this time the licorice smell of Africa and of camel dung . . . the roar of the lion to remind us that life had been going on a long while and would probably go on a while longer. Weak, miserable, and anaemic, we needed the stalwart shoulders of a younger race to hold the cart awhile till we had gotten the wheel back on. But first acquaintance with this charming and beautiful creature, the Negro, made us love him at first sight; we could not resist him.

Then the panic seized us . . . a usual first reaction of love!

Perhaps it was also self-preservation. In 1919 nothing else could have borne the strain, the terrible strain. Nothing else was strong enough, hard enough, new enough. This music came with absolute sympathy and a complete collateral aesthetic in the other arts. Modigliani[43] had already devoted his life to painting marvelous elliptical heads; Gaudier-Breszka and Brancusi had sculpted them; Chirico painted rooms full of Roman ruins with egg-heads; the Dadaists collected every bit of Negro sculpture they could lay their hands upon; the Surrealists in 1924 exhibited the best of it with their own painters. Without knowing it we were learning to live again in the bright torrid sunshine of reasonable animals without mystical northern lights, without any spiritual food except that which we lay in wait for or *trapped* by ourselves. Everywhere the traps were laid; everywhere the lions roared menacingly; at every moment we remembered the years of famine which were directly behind us. The Germans sat down in their methodical way and tried to build up another world-supremacy in music, as they once had done, but they built with counterpoint and scholastic "durchkomponierte Musik"[44] . . . these were the only principles they knew, and these principles had worked for a long time before and they thought they would work again now. But in Paris everyone was like a hunter of wild beasts; we found ourselves suddenly in a dangerous epoch like a wilderness without end, without food, and without life. The Negro taught us to throw away our useless folding baths, our hot-water bottles, our traveling frigidaires . . . to put our noses to the ground, to follow the scent, to come back to the most elementary principles of self-preservation. We found ourselves in the Parisian veldt; Chirico, Picasso, Strawinsky, Cocteau, and many others were hunters who roamed the wild jungles and trapped every day, every month, without fail, our existence. No longer could we arrive at the water-well with an automatic graph or synthetic compass. The Viennese meanwhile, full of automatic-synthesis, invented a system whereby they could reproduce genius upon purely mechanical principles; they thought their science would outdo itself in reproducing life; but so far it his produced nothing but a breath-taking and awesome system. The twelve-tone system is such that each and every melody to attain pure atonal balance must sound at some point within itself, *the whole chromatic scale . . . no more, no less. In consequence, the soul of music has passed out of the hands of the old Germans* (Schönberg and followers) into the hands of the young Germans. And the young Germans embraced mulattoism after their fashion. It is true that they are often as much Negroid as a German performance of *Green*

43. Amedeo Modigliani (1884–1920), Italian painter; Henri Gaudier-Brzeska (1891–1915), French sculptor, friend (like Antheil) of Ezra Pound; Giorgio de Chirico (1888–1978), Italian painter, precursor to the Surrealists.

44. Through-composed music—i.e., not sectionalized, but conceived as a single continuous span.

Pastures[45] with native Berliners in blackface might be, but at least they black their faces unabashedly; *Jonny Spielt Auf*[46] did a considerable lot of good in opening up the new operatic movement in Germany. And their new operatic movement in Germany is the first step they have made towards the recovery of any of their lost musical supremacy. The hero of this last-named opera is a Negro called "Jonny" (!), albeit a beery and Viennese Negro who achieves his highest moment by breaking into "Swanee River." But in Paris it was different. The water-holes were watched and set with traps; Bunuel[47] caught enormous alligators in grand pianos with their life-blood dripping down upon the white keys. Houses were no longer made in Wotan-like architecture, or pseudo-baroc, or what-not; men began building houses, white, like tents, and filled them with campstools made of nickel stretched with canvas. Everywhere we looked we saw the long straight lines of the whitewashed houses of North Africa; we began to realize that home is but a camping ground which we can make simple and beautiful with modern engineering and glass and steel. Still all of these houses carry the feeling of clean straw thatch and mud, as if built for torrid climates. Europe became dotted with white simple architecture as if we hourly expected the gulf-stream to change its course and the temperature of Europe to reach again the torrid temperatures of the pre-ice ages and the saber-toothed tiger. One came to many streets where by looking at the houses in brilliant white, steel, and glass, one felt as if one should approach and enter them only in a sun helmet and white duck pants. Europe began in the early twenties to assume the aesthetic of the desert camp; subconsciously it came within the plan of things to live upon the veldt. The great war had come and gone, we had been robbed and ransacked of everything; *and we were on the march again.* Therefore we welcomed this sunburnt and primitive feeling, we laid our blankets in the sun and it killed all of our civilized microbes. The Negro came naturally into this blazing light, and has remained there. The black man (the exact opposite color of ourselves!) has appeared to us suddenly like a true phenomenon. Like a photograph of ourselves he is the sole negative from which a positive may be drawn! Holding this negative up to the sun we see in essence that which so many eyes and cars have been trying to demonstrate on canvas, paper, and stone . . . the other side of that which we cannot see, but which we can put our arms around; the hard indestructible object with air around it, a world transferred over into the opposite world, a new start, the black man. . . .

A [great] duty would be to trace, scientifically and carefully, the development of the

45. *Green Pastures* (1930), by Marc Connelly (1890–1980), retold Old Testament stories with African American actors.

46. Ernst Krenek's hit *Jonny spielt auf* (1927) stars a jazz violinist; it was the first European opera in which American popular music played a significant role.

47. Luis Buñuel (1900–83), Spanish film director, collaborator with Salvador Dalí on the Surrealist film *Un chien andalou* (1928).

Great Spiral, the victory of the Slav over the German, and the victory of the Negro over the Slav.

From *Negro: An Anthology,* ed. Nancy Cunard and Hugh Ford (New York: Frederick Ungar, 1970), 214–19.

■

In 1947 the jazz drummer Gene Krupa (1909–73), famous for flashy solos, and the then little-known conductor Leonard Bernstein (1918–90) debated in the *Esquire Jazz Book* the thesis, "Has Jazz Influenced the Symphony?" Bernstein argued the positive, along now-familiar Modernist lines, though the influences he noted were much more local than those Antheil found. Krupa, on the other hand, wished to isolate and defend his craft from any encroachment from the highbrow—though he was intrigued by the possibility of some fruitful dialogue between the longhairs and the cool cats, and was even writing, in that very year, a "concerto for swing band and philharmonic orchestra." It should be noted that Krupa's riff concerning the lack of creativity among the African American founders of jazz was venturesome in 1947, as it is today.

GENE KRUPA AND LEONARD BERNSTEIN
"Has Jazz Influenced the Symphony?" (1947)
EMPHATICALLY NO! SAYS GENE KRUPA

My good friend Leonard Bernstein says that symphonic music, "serious" music written for performance by the full orchestra, has been influenced by jazz. The jazz influence is said by some critics to be especially apparent in Leonard Bernstein's own compositions.

I disagree. I have never heard anything genuinely and honestly derivative of jazz in any such music, even, maybe especially, in such works as Igor Stravinsky's Ebony Suite, which Woody Herman, with his usual swing instrumentation, brilliantly performed last season in Carnegie Hall and several other places. I've never heard it in a single one of the "serious" pieces of George Gershwin, who, anybody will tell you, was preeminently "the American jazz composer."

But, then, I've never heard it, as has John Hammond, in the works of Darius Milhaud, for all that during his American visit in the early thirties, Milhaud listened, entranced, to the unsurpassable jazz virtuosity at the hot piano of such great artists as Fats Waller, Earl Hines, and Jimmy Johnson. I watched Maurice Ravel, at the old Sunset in Chicago, marvel at Jimmy Noone's[48] transcendent clarinet—an instrument which seems

---

48. Jimmie Noone (1895–1949), African American jazz clarinetist from New Orleans.

to have a special meaning for the French. Jimmy could fly over a clarinet like no one before him or since—ask Benny Goodman—and it was undoubtedly Noone's technical virtuosity, not the music itself, which obsessed Maurice Ravel. For all his preoccupation with rhythm, I've never heard the least echo of that music, or any music like it, in his compositions.

Leonard Bernstein and others profess to hear traces, echoes, derivations of jazz in Frederick Delius, John Alden Carpenter, Manuel De Falla, Honegger, Prokofiev, even Shostakovitch.

The influence of jazz has been found by someone or other, unnecessarily eager to make out a case for jazz that it doesn't need, anxious perhaps to endow it with reflected "respectability" so that he won't need to make excuses to himself and others for liking it, in the works of every one of these composers. But, in my opinion, it isn't there.

Let's pay a little more attention to two of the composers mentioned earlier, Stravinsky and Gershwin. They are reputed to show the most jazz influence. The contention might well stand or fall with them. Stravinsky did evince preoccupation with jazz music. He talked about it. He wrote a series of compositions with titles referring to "ragtime," but no evidence of that preoccupation appears in the actual music, honestly examined, honestly listened to. That preoccupation was purely verbal. Although apparently able to sense, to feel, the jazz tempo, he has been unable to express it. For all his tremendous musical vitality, that vitality did not encompass the peculiar rhythmic, driving, let us say American quality which is the essence of jazz. Nor is that essence to be found in the more pretentious work of George Gershwin. It exists in the blues feeling of some of his popular songs, particularly when played in the authentic jazz spirit by authentic jazz instrumentalists. But it does not exist in his Concerto in F—even if in some passages he did use derbies to mute the trumpets.

His "Rhapsody in Blue," which too often has been labeled "The Jazz Symphony," is much more—as is Gershwin's serious work as a whole—in the tradition of Claude Debussy. And I don't believe the opening of *L'Après-midi d'un faune* is reminiscent of Jimmy Noone's clarinet work.

Does this mean that I believe that jazz can never and will never form part of the mainstream of America's and of the world's music? To say it can't is to say that America, out of itself, has nothing to contribute musically to the world. Jazz is the United States' own native, original musical idiom. Jazz can be the basis of great music to be written by an American composer just as much as, say, Czech folk tunes were the basis of the music of Smetana and Dvořák.

But jazz can only make its proper contribution to the whole of music, will only make that contribution when both its composition and performance of the music which is developing out of it, are executed by musicians who are completely at home in the idiom. Music must be both conceived and performed. It must be both composed and played.

And jazz cannot be approached from outside. It cannot be approached synthetically and artificially. Above all, it cannot be approached unsympathetically.

Too many "good," "pure," and "serious" musicians, and let's admit that, composing and playing in the idiom to which they are accustomed, are *good* musicians—approach the native American idiom, the jazz idiom, with intolerance, even with condescension. They stoop, but not to conquer. And so, they almost invariably make an unholy mess of their attempts. Then, of course, they sneer at jazz. They tell anyone who will listen that the stuff wasn't music in the first place, but naturally. However, the failure was with them, and all the name calling in the world cannot disguise that fact.

Are there in existence musicians who can compose and, equally important, play this music? A generation ago my answer would have had to be no. The traditional "great men" of jazz . . . came up the hard way. They played for dough. . . . They never had the chance to get highly technical classical training. And, essentially, they were performers, virtuosos, not creators. At most, they were improvisers. They attained a certain measure of greatness in performance because they'd never been told that this or that was "impossible." They achieved, through very lack of classical training, effects which transcended themselves and their instruments. Don't misunderstand me. I'm not questioning their inherent musicianship. Louis Armstrong,[49] "Satchmo," one of the very greatest of jazz trumpeters, could stand up in front of the New York Philharmonic and improvise a brilliant contrapuntal concerto flawless in color and tone against anything they might play. . . .

Let me pass along a word, with great respect, to Mr. Stokowski and Mr. Koussevitzky[50] and their august brethren:

> Gentlemen, if you should sometime in the future schedule for performance a work based on jazz, containing jazz passages, when such music is written, don't entrust its execution entirely to the regular members of your organizations. They are highly competent musicians—but this is not for them.
>
> The most skilled Cordon Bleu would look silly beside a Rhode Island cook at a shore dinner, or a Texas ranch hand at a barbecue.
>
> American music, jazz music, must be played by men who were brought up to drink rye and Coke in juke joints. A lifetime of blond beer in Munch or Torino Vermouth isn't quite the same thing. . . .

49. Louis "Satchmo" Armstrong (1900–71), African American jazz trumpeter and scat singer from New Orleans.

50. Leopold Stokowski (1882–1977) and Serge Koussevitzky (1874–1951) were European conductors who held prominent positions in American orchestras.

POSITIVELY YES! SAYS LEONARD BERNSTEIN

. . . Actually, if I am supposed to be the voice of serious music against that of jazz, I must confess an unfair advantage. Having started out with a Beethoven sonata in one hand and an Archie Bleyer arrangement in the other, I have kept a rather ambidextrous grip on both. So if I appear to live on the other side of the tracks, I do keep a little shack handy on this side too. I therefore take the liberty of being somewhat historical.

To begin with, American music in the nineteenth century was anything but American. Our country was a brand-new one, comparatively speaking, but a full-grown baby, like Minerva springing adult from Jupiter's brain. As such, America was faced with the great and delicate problem of being a pioneer society, dedicated to revolutionary and daring propositions, but with no traditions except European ones. Anyone who was really anyone in music had first to prove it by studying in Europe, and then coming home with a big Lisztian piano concerto or a Wagnerian tone-epic under his arm. Yet the nineteenth century was the greatest nationalistic cauldron of all A.D. history. To use only musical examples, it was the century when Russian music was being glorified by Moussorgsky, Norwegian music by Grieg, Spanish music by Albeniz, Hungarian music by Liszt, Bohemian music by Dvořák.

It was this same Dvořák[51] who arrived on these shores and pointed out to the bewildered and unnationalistic American composers that they, too, could be nationalist glorifiers. He saw a wealth of indigenous folk material latent in America, unused, and ever so usable. Indian and Negro melodies in particular seemed to him to be crying for symphonic transfiguration. And to prove it, he wrote a New World Symphony, based on some of these self-same tunes, and a more beautifully Bohemian symphony was never written.

Immediately the American composers got the point; and there ensued such an outpouring of Indian and Negro operas, suites, cantatas, and tone-poems as I can give an idea of only by refraining from listing them. They are mostly forgotten now, or to be dug for in the dustiest back rooms of the dustiest used-book shops. Out of every movement, however it is based, does emerge some positive asset; and in this case it is the music of MacDowell (Indian school) and of Henry Gilbert (Negro school)[52] which remains with us today; genial, sometimes inspired, European music trying its best to be American.

51. Antonín Dvořák (1841–1904) was director of the National Conservatory in New York from 1892 to 1895 and encouraged American composers to use American folk materials. In 1893 he wrote his Symphony no. 9, *From the New World*, a work influenced by spirituals sung by Harry T. Burleigh.

52. Edward MacDowell (1860–1908) composed several pieces on American Indian themes, including an *Indian Suite;* Henry F. Gilbert (1868–1928) was perhaps best known for *The Dance in Place Congo.*

Why did this movement fail? For fail it did, in the sense of a healthy, historical construction. After all, it was large, it was active, it was earnest, it was sincere. But it was unnatural. It was trying, however sincerely, to be something it was not. A national music is national in direct proportion to how close to its home audiences feel. And when such an audience was presented with an Indian lament, they could think it all very pretty and even touching, but it wasn't *their* music. The fact remained that they were not Indians, any more than we are today. Or, to make the case complete, any more than they were all Poles or all Irish. They were, and we are today, a tough audience. For to what indigenous folk-material could they all respond in common?

Our swift survey has carried us approximately to the point of World War I. . . . There was a necessity to be original at all costs, to be chic, and to be American. But now no Dvořák was needed to promulgate a movement. Something new had been added. Jazz had come to stay.

The really remarkable thing about jazz for the serious composer was that it solved simultaneously the two problems of being original and of being American. For here at last was a musical material which was everybody's bread and butter. No real American could fail to understand a symphonic work which sounded like jazz. . . .

Something new had been added: but something old had been omitted — the element of the unconscious. If we accept the principle that what we call "inspiration" in music is an impulse that springs from the unconscious and attains fruition through the medium of conscious manipulation, then it simply won't do for a composer to seat himself at his table and decide that he is going to be American or anything else. His output should be the natural expression of his psyche, or his soul, or his collected experiences, or his frustrations, or his adjustment, or whatever you choose to call it. If he is American, the music will be American in terms of his place in the development of American history. Thus the composers of the twenties were American in a different sense from, but on about the some plane as, the Indian school of earlier decades. Both groups were trying too hard.

I think I have already said that some positive asset emerges out of every movement, however it is based. The man who gave this postwar movement life, controversy, and real genius was George Gershwin. His aim, in contradistinction to that of the "serious" composers, was to make of the material of jazz, with which he was so intimate, a sort of symphonization in the tradition of the European masters, rather than to paste jazz onto already crystallized personal styles and forms, as did Stravinsky and Ravel. Gershwin approached this great merger from the left, so to speak, from the realm of wah-wah mutes and ga-ga chorus girls. Stravinsky approached it from the bulwark of European musical strength, backed up with orchestras with woodwinds in fives, and the guardian spirits of Debussy and Rimsky-Korsakov. Neither really reached the middle: Stravinsky's jazz was really Stravinsky *plus* jazz; Gershwin's concert music was Gershwin plus everyone else under the sun. In neither case was a real integration attained.

Came the crash. Again, many things stopped happening, and many new things began to happen. Again, a new decade ran itself out, this time at a far slower and wearier pace. Musically, it meant a new reflectiveness, a reconsideration of traditional values. It was just at this point, that, for the very first time, the moment arrived for the sober absorption of all that had happened, and the consequent opportunity for the development of a real, unconsciously derived, American style. And it is the music of this decade which I feel owes the greatest debt to jazz.

We must first take a strong stand on what we mean by "jazz." Avoiding all the lengthy discussion that usually accompanies attempts to define the word, let us make the simple distinction between the commercial song, as we understand the term on Broadway, and the freely improvised jazz of Negro origin, which we know usually in the few formal variants of the Blues. The "popular song" has had, and can have, no influence whatsoever on music. It is created for money, sung for money, and dies when the money stops rolling in. It is imitative, conventional, emotionless. This has nothing to do with the fact that there are many such songs of which I am very fond. I wish I had written "I Get a Kick Out of You"; but I must insist that Mr. Porter[53] has no influence on serious music. I love a Gershwin or a [Richard] Rodgers tune; but the same truth still holds. There are those who show, for example, the influence of a song like "Fascinatin' Rhythm" on symphonic music. Well and good, but the influence is not original with "Fascinatin' Rhythm." Those charming, truncated phrases of Gershwin's go back to the improvised jazz, the real source. It is this jazz, then, that we have to take into account.

. . . In the twenties, when [the serious composer] borrowed overtly from jazz, he used [rhythms in irregular groups of twos and threes] as jazz used them, over a steady and momentous bass which kept the old reliable quarter-note constantly beating. But now that he does consciously borrow from jazz, these rhythms crop in a non-jazzy context, without a meter-bass necessarily holding them up, but with a life of their own. They have acquired personal qualities not always hard and percussive, but sometimes graceful, sometimes singing, sometimes even nostalgic. The whole procedure has unconsciously become common usage among American composers. And the startling thing is that very rarely does this music ever sound like jazz! The scherzo movement of my symphony *Jeremiah* would certainly not bring any connotation of jazz to mind; and yet it could never have been written if jazz were not an integral part of my life.

53. Cole Porter (1891–1964) wrote "I Get a Kick out of You" for the Broadway show *Anything Goes* (1934). In his youth Porter aspired to compose serious music, and his ballet *Within the Quota* was produced by the Ballets Suédois in 1923—a rival company to Diaghilev's.

... Just listen to the best in jazz and the best in serious American music, and enjoy it. For analyses and diagnoses notwithstanding, the great synthesis goes irrevocably on.

From *Reading Jazz: A Gathering of Autobiography, Reportage, and Criticism from 1919 to Now,* ed. Robert Gottlieb (New York: Pantheon, 1996), 774–84.

Unlike Ellington, Gershwin, Antheil, and Bernstein, certain American composers were anxious to establish a firm barrier between art music and popular music. Elliott Carter (b. 1908) devoted much of his effort as a composer to the principle of independence of line—to the careful coordination of wildly divergent polyphonic strands. Similarly, he tended to stress the independence of line between jazz style and the European musical tradition. For Carter, jazz depends on unnotatable deformities of rhythm—and if European composers in the 1920s took an interest in jazz's use of small rhythmic bits, it was because of an accidental convergence of evolution. American composers, he says, find jazz somewhat tiresome; European composers already knew most of jazz's tricks before any jazz came their way.

Carter's tendency to keep the low and the high on separate planes of musical discourse can be understood as part of Modernist purism: just as Clement Greenberg and Theodor Adorno insisted that one artistic medium had nothing to do with any other, so Carter tries to discriminate bounded regions within music itself.

ELLIOTT CARTER
"Once Again Swing" (1939)

Swing. Most everything has already been said about swing. A good many people get more thrills out of swing than out of "classical music," though some say it is a kind of dope—lots of kick that puts your mind to sleep. Some call it non-indigenous and African, though it was really invented by whites. Others call it entertainment music having no emotional or intellectual appeal, with the same relation to "art music" that *Saturday Evening Post* illustrations or comic strips have to the works by [Pavel] Tchelitchev or [Salvador] Dali. Some say the future of American music lies here. Still others, hating its illiteracy and routine formulas, predict it will shortly die of emotional and intellectual starvation. Foreigners recall that gypsy orchestras used to play with the same kind of abandoned improvisation, and historians report that the "polka mania" was just the same sort of craze in the last century. All our lives we have been hearing this astonishing and vigorous music develop. It makes the money, it gets the performances, its popularity exceeds the wildest dreams of serious composers. It has set the feet of the whole world stamping in four-four time.

At Carnegie Hall, during the holidays, the intellectuals of swing organized a fascinating historical concert. Starting with African records, they traced its development through the spiritual, jazz, boogie-woogie on up to Count Basie.[54] Performers from little churches in the deep South who had never traveled before were brought out on Carnegie Hall stage, and in this spacious and, perhaps, specious atmosphere attempted to project the charm they exhibited back home. Negroes, probably because of their social history, have always been a race of entertainers like the gypsies in Europe. Theatrically their tradition is outside that of serious music. But this concert, since it was given in Carnegie Hall, challenged comparisons. Certainly the main factor is the hall itself. A concert hall performance of the usual kind takes place as a ritual in which public and performer are ultimately subservient to the ideas of a composer who has put his notes on paper. Swing, on the other hand, is the glorification of the performer. All the adulatory swing slang: "a killerdiller beating his chops," "gut-bucket licks," "in the groove," "boogie-woogie," "jitterbug," "a solid sender doin' some tall rug cuttin'" refer to the performer, to the type of performance, to the audience, but never to the actual, composed "paper" or music. It is, as we well know, a performance that stresses the intensity of nervous excitement "sent out" by the performer rather than the stuffed-shirt feeling of the concert hall. In order to make serious music palatable to the swing audience, composers like Bach and Debussy have to be arranged, to eliminate everything but the tune; rhythms, developments, and harmonies which might confound the jitterbug must be straightened out. When played in the appropriate jam style (for the "paper men," or men that can read music, do not play the notes in the classical time values but have a tradition which, from the point of view of the serious musician, distorts or "swings" eighths and quarters into rhythms impossible to notate) this becomes the genuine article and loses its original flavor. Just so, swing tends to lose its character and take on another when appropriated by serious composers for the concert hall. In that setting the music will never interest audiences until a serious composer with artistic ambition has been able to stylize and make it express his personal, creative attitude toward American life. Up to now swing still remains, except for a few isolated instances, in the stage of Russian folk song or gypsy music before Glinka, Mussorgsky, Liszt, or Brahms.

From *The Writings of Elliott Carter: An American Composer Looks at Modern Music,* ed. Else Stone and Kurt Stone (Bloomington: Indiana University Press, 1977), 43–45.

ELLIOTT CARTER
"The Rhythmic Basis of American Music" (1955)

It would be convenient if one could say—as so many have done—that the distinguishing mark of serious American music is its employment (or re-working) of the

54. William "Count" Basie (1904–84), big-band jazz leader.

rhythms of our native folk or popular music, particularly jazz. Yet the attempt to reduce national characteristics to a few simple traits is a game that quickly wears thin in the artistic world, as in life itself. In earlier years when American music was just beginning to take shape, such an attempt may have been useful; but now that a substantial number of works has accumulated, neither critics nor composers feel it any longer necessary to emphasize national characteristics. On the contrary, instead of insisting that American music stands apart from that of Europe, it becomes interesting to consider the many foreign influences by which it has been nourished.

During the nineteen-twenties, jazz had a great influence on European music as well as on ours. Its impact in Europe was strong precisely because its techniques had already been anticipated by various composers. Bartók, Stravinsky, and even Schoenberg (in the first of his *Five Pieces for Orchestra,* written in 1909) had all been using irregular rhythmic patterns, and the appearance of jazz stimulated further interest in this rhythmic procedure. Indeed, European composers adopted only those aspects of jazz that had already been tried to some extent before its arrival. These very same aspects influenced the young American modernists of the time; but through greater familiarity with the source they had a different feeling for rhythm. As a result, jazz had far more effect abroad than in many quarters at home.

The American composer's relationship to jazz is in fact quite different from what one might expect. Heard constantly from every corner, this music has lost its original freshness; the techniques have become shopworn, the performances routine and dull. It is perhaps for these reasons that most composers have avoided using the jazz idiom in their concert music; and also because orchestral musicians often do not play jazz well, and cannot under the conditions of concert life be afforded the rehearsals needed for good jazz. Today in out-of-the-way places one can still find fresh lively jazz performances, and the improvisatory character of what is played is impossible to imitate with concert musicians. There are Marc Blitzstein, Leonard Bernstein, and Morton Gould,[55] who, writing in the jazz idiom for popular consumption, have tried to place it (as Kurt Weill did) on a more meaningful and artistic level. But the majority of composers interested in this trend have drawn only on certain characteristics of popular music, combining them with other folk sources or neoclassic ones to produce works of larger scope, more interesting formal possibilities, and more variety.

There were four composers who helped to establish these techniques in the early stages of the contemporary movement in America. Roy Harris, Aaron Copland, and

---

55. Marc Blitzstein (1905–64), composer of politically engaged stage works; Morton Gould (1913–96), composer of snappy American music.

Roger Sessions[56] followed the lead given them by contemporary European music and jazz and embodied a new feeling for rhythm in their music. The fourth, Charles Ives, living in seclusion, followed a different and more curious path, and his achievements are not yet well enough known to be properly judged.

Early in his career, Harris made a remark that has often been quoted: "Our rhythmic sense is less symmetrical than the European rhythmic sense. European musicians are trained to think of rhythm in its largest common denominator, while we are born with a feeling for its smallest units." Although this appeared after a number of outstanding works by Stravinsky, and Bartók had revealed the possibilities of irregular groupings of small units—which is what Harris is talking about—there is no doubt that he had a point in mind which becomes clear in the context of his own music and of jazz practice. For in spite of their irregular rhythmic patterns, written with constantly changing meters, Stravinsky and Bartók do often treat their irregular accents as displacements of regular ones by marking them with the same kind of vigor that was reserved in older music for syncopations. The quality of these accents is quite different from those used in jazz and in much new American music. . . .

Aaron Copland has been outspoken about his relationship with popular music both in his writings and in his composition. He drew from the jazz of the nineteen-twenties a principle of polyrhythm. . . . But although he mentions the fact that jazz performers often play their improvisations with great rhythmic freedom, sounding their notes a bit before or after the beat, Copland has never incorporated this into his own music. . . .

It must be said, however, that only a few American composers are seriously concerned with rhythmic problems. Owing to the influence of Copland, Harris, and Sessions, many seem to have an innate rhythmic sense that is different from that of European composers. But there has been little temptation to explore the field, since each of these three has lately become much more conservative in this respect, and performances of their rhythmically difficult works are rare.

From *The Writings of Elliott Carter: An American Composer Looks at Modern Music*, ed. Else Stone and Kurt Stone (Bloomington: Indiana University Press, 1977), 160–62, 166.

56. Roy Harris (1898–1979), composer who sought a distinctively American style; Aaron Copland (1900–90), composer who did much to define Americanness as a musical trait; Roger Sessions (1896–1985), learned American composer.

Bibliographical Note

For those who wish to continue the pleasures of studying Modernism as an artistic movement on a large scale, the following books (not mentioned elsewhere in this anthology) might be a good start.

Butler, Christopher. *Early Modernism: Literature, Music, and Painting in Europe, 1900–1916.* Oxford: Clarendon Press, 1994.

Ellmann, Richard, and Charles Feidelson Jr., eds. *The Modern Tradition: Backgrounds of Modern Literature.* New York: Oxford University Press, 1965.

Everdell, William R. *The First Moderns: Profiles in the Origin of Twentieth-Century Thought.* Chicago: University of Chicago Press, 1997.

Kolocotroni, Vassiliki, et al., eds. *Modernism: An Anthology of Sources and Documents.* Chicago: University of Chicago Press, 1998.

Levenson, Michael. *A Genealogy of Modernism: A Study of English Literary Doctrine, 1908–22.* Cambridge: Cambridge University Press, 1984.

Watkins, Glenn. *Soundings: Music in the Twentieth Century.* New York: Schirmer, 1995.

Credits

Theodor Adorno, from *Philosophy of Modern Music* (1948): Copyright © 1973 by The Seabury
    Press. Reprinted with the permision of the publisher, The Continuum International Publishing
    Group
Morton Feldman, [Time-canvas] (1983): Reprinted by permission of the Morton Feldman Estate
Iannis Xenakis, from *Formalized Music* (1971): Reprinted with the kind permission of François
    Xenakis
Émile Jaques-Dalcroze, "The Technique of Moving Plastic" (1922): Reprinted by permission of the
    Dalcroze Society, UK (Incorporated)
Hanns Eisler, from *Composing for the Films* (1947): Reprinted by permission of The Continuum
    International Publishing Group

CHAPTER FOUR

Hugo von Hofmannsthal, Letter to Richard Strauss (1911): From *A Working Friendship* by Richard
    Strauss and Hugo von Hofmannsthal, translated by Hanns Himmelmann and Ewald Osers, copy-
    right © 1961 by William Collins Sons & Co. Ltd. Used by permission of Random House, Inc.
Kurt Weill, "Shifts in Musical Composition" (1927) and "Opera—Where To?" (1929): Reprinted
    with permission from the Kurt Weill Foundation for Music, New York. All rights reserved
Alban Berg, "The 'Problem of Opera'" (1928): © 1928 Universal Edition, © renewed, all rights re-
    served; reprinted by permission of European American Music Distributors LLC, sole U.S. and
    Canadian agent for Universal Edition A.G., Vienna
Ernst Krenek, from "Is Opera Still Possible Today?" (1936): Reprinted with the kind permission of
    Gladys Krenek
W. H. Auden, "The World of Opera" (1967): From *Secondary Worlds,* by W. H. Auden, copyright
    © 1968 by W. H. Auden. Used by permission of Random House, Inc. and of Faber and Faber Ltd.,
    London, UK

CHAPTER FIVE

Charles Ives, excerpts from *Essays before a Sonata, The Majority and Other Writings by Charles Ives,*
    ed. Howard Boatwright, copyright © 1961, 1962 by W. W. Norton & Company, Inc., renewed 1990.
    Used by permission of W. W. Norton & Company, Inc.
Charles Ives, "Music and Its Future," in *American Composers on American Music,* ed. Henry Cowell,
    copyright © 1933 by the Board of Trustees of the Leland Stanford Junior University. Copyright
    renewed 1961 by Henry Cowell. Reprinted with the permission of Stanford University Press,
    www.sup.org
Percy Grainger, "Free Music" (1938): Reprinted by permission of the publisher
Arnold Schoenberg and Vassily Kandinsky, from Correspondence (1911): Reprinted by permission of
    Belmont Music Publishers, Pacific Palisades, CA 90272 and of Faber and Faber Ltd., London, UK
Luigi Russolo, "The Art of Noises: Futurist Manifesto" (1913): From *Music since 1900,* 4th edition, by
    Nicholas Slonimsky, copyright © 1971, Charles Scribner's Sons. Reprinted by permission of The
    Gale Group
John Cage, fragments from *Silence,* copyright © 1961 by John Cage and reprinted by permission of
    Wesleyan University Press

CHAPTER SIX

Arnold Schoenberg, from "Composition with Twelve Tones": [*fiat lux*] (1941), trans. and ed. Leo
Black, in *Style and Idea: Selected Writings,* ed. Leonard Stein: © 1975 by Belmont Music Publishers;
reprinted by permission of The University of California Press, Berkeley, CA and of Faber and
Faber Ltd, London, UK

Anton Webern, from "The Path to Twelve-Note Composition" (1932): © 1961 by Universal Edition
A.G., Vienna. With kind permission of the publisher

Extract from *Dr. Faustus,* by Thomas Mann, trans. H. T. Lowe-Porter, published by Secker & Warburg. Used by permission of The Random House Group Limited. Copyright © 1948 and renewed
1976 by Alfred A. Knopf, a division of Random House, Inc. Used by permission of Alfred A.
Knopf, a division of Random House, Inc.

Leonard Bernstein, [The Twelve-Tone Method] (1976): Reprinted by permission of the publisher
from *The Unanswered Question: Six Talks at Harvard,* by Leonard Bernstein, Cambridge, Mass.:
Harvard University Press, copyright © 1976 by Leonard Bernstein

CHAPTER SEVEN

Charles Baudelaire, extract from *Baudelaire as a Literary Critic,* trans. Lois Boe Hyslop and Francis E. Hyslop, copyright © 1964 by The Pennsylvania State University. Reproduced by permission
of the publisher

Marcel Proust, excerpt from *Swann's Way* (1913): From *Remembrance of Things Past,* vol. 1, by
Marcel Proust, trans. C. K. Scott Moncrieff and Terence Kilmartin, copyright © 1981 by Random
House, Inc. and Chatto & Windus. Used by permission of The Random House Group, Ltd.

Excerpts from Igor Stravinsky, *An Autobiography.* Copyright 1962 by W. W. Norton & Company
and Marion Boyars Publishers (UK). Reprinted with permission.

Extract from "The Influence of Peasant Music on Modern Music" (1931): Reprinted from *Béla
Bartók Essays,* selected and edited by Benjamin Suchoff by permission of the University of
Nebraska Press and of Faber and Faber Ltd., London, UK. Copyright © 1976 by Dr. Benjamin
Suchoff, Successor-Trustee, The Estate of Béla Bartók

Richard Wagner, "Beethoven" (1870): from *Wagner on Music and Drama,* by Albert Goldman and
Evert Sprinchorn. Copyright © 1964 by Albert Goldman and Evert Sprinchorn. Used by permission of Dutton, a division of Penguin Putnam Inc.

Extract from Oskar Kokoschka, *Schriften 1907–1955,* ed. Hans maria Wingler, reprinted with the
permission of Artists Rights Society

Arnold Schoenberg, *Die glückliche Hand* (1910–13), [brain-storm]: Reprinted by permission of
Belmont Music Publishers, Pacific Palisades, CA 90272

Theodor Adorno, from *Philosophy of Modern Music* (1948): Copyright © 1973 by The Seabury Press.
Reprinted with the permision of the publisher, The Continuum International Publishing Group

Rainer Maria Rilke, *Sonnets to Orpheus* 1.3 (1922): Reprinted with the permission of the publisher

Excerpts from Igor Stravinsky and Robert Craft, *Expositions and Developments* (1981), *Dialogues*
(1982), and *Themes and Conclusions* (1982), copyright © 1959, 1960, 1961, 1962 by Igor Stravinsky,
are reprinted by permission of The University of California Press

Arnold Schoenberg, "Versatility," from *Three Satires* (1925): Reprinted by permission of Belmont
Music Publishers, Pacific Palisades, CA 90272

Ernst Krenek, "New Humanity and Old Objectivity" (1931), "Music and Mathematics" (1937), and "What Is Called the New Music, and Why?" (1937): Reprinted with the kind permission of Gladys Krenek

Constant Lambert, "The Age of Pastiche" (1934) and [Stravinsky as Pasticheur] (1934), from *Music Ho! A Study of Music in Decline*: Reprinted by permission of Faber and Faber Ltd., London, UK

Gertrude Stein, from *Lectures in America* (1935): Copyright © 1935 and renewed 1963 by Alice B. Toklas. Used by permission of Random House, Inc.

Extracts from *A Ravel Reader: Correspondence, Articles, Interviews,* ed. Arbie Orenstein, © 1990 by Columbia University Press. Reprinted with the permission of the publisher

Extract from Jean Cocteau, *Cock and Harlequin* (1918), reprinted by permission of Artists Rights Society (ARS), New York

CHAPTER EIGHT

Hanns Eisler, "On Old and New Music" (1925): Reprinted from *A Rebel in Music,* ed. Manfred Grabs, with the permission of the publisher, Kahn and Averill, London, UK

Bertolt Brecht and Peter Suhrkamp, from "The Modern Theatre Is the Epic Theatre" (1930): Copyright © 1957, 1963 & 1964 Suhrkamp Verlag. Translation copyright © 1964, renewed 1992 by John Willett. Reprinted by permission of Hill and Wang, a division of Farrar, Straus and Giroux, LLC. and Methuen Publishing Limited, London, UK

Friedrich Hollaender, "Cabaret" (1932), excerpt from *The Weimer Republic Sourcebook,* ed. Anton Kaes, Martin Jay, and Edward Dimendberg: Copyright © 1994 The Regents of the University of California. Used by permission of The University of California Press

Paul Hindemith, from *A Composer's World* (1949–50): Reprinted by permission of the publisher

Arnold Schoenberg, *A Survivor from Warsaw* (1947): Reprinted by permission of Belmont Music Publishers, Pacific Palisades, CA 90272

CHAPTER NINE

"Le Grand Duc" from *The Big Sea,* by Langston Hughes: Copyright © 1940 by Langston Hughes. Copyright renewed 1968 by Arna Bontemps and George Houston Bass. Reprinted by permission of Hill and Wang, a division of Farrar, Straus, and Giroux, LLC.

Langston Hughes, "Moon-Faced, Starry-Eyed" (1946–47): from the vocal score of *Street Scenes: An American Opera,* Music by Kurt Weill, Lyrics by Langston Hughes, TRO—© Copyright 1947 (renewed 1975), Hampshire House Publishing Corp. and Chappell & Co. All rights reserved. Used by permission

George Gershwin, "The Composer and the Machine Age" (1933): Reprinted courtesy of Todd Gershwin

Excerpt from George Antheil, "The Negro on the Spiral, or A Method of Negro Music" (1934) in *Negro: An Anthology,* edited by Nancy Cunard and Hugh Ford. Copyright © 1970 by the Frederick Ungar Publishing Company. Reprinted by permission of the Continuum International Publishing Group

Gene Krupa and Leonard Bernstein, "Has Jazz Influenced the Symphony?" (1947): © 1947 by Leonard Bernstein. Used by permission of The Leonard Bernstein Office, Inc.

Elliott Carter, "Once Again Swing" (1939) and "The Rhythmic Basis of American Music" (1955): Reprinted by permission of the publisher

Index

Abate, Mario, 174
Abgesang, 74
absolute music, 141–42, 143
Abstractionism, 11, 31, 187, 193
"Ach, du lieber Augustin," 367
acoustical arrangement, 186
acoustics, 159
Adorno, Theodor Wiesengrund, 71–72, 130, 213, 270, 271, 333; *Alban Berg: Master of the Smallest Link,* 123; belief that dance is an essentially vain and static art, 84; *Philosophy of Modern Music,* **72–79,** 79, **272–76;** revulsion against pseudomorphisms of painting in music, 79; on Schoenberg's music, 221; *The Treasure of Indian Joe,* 72
African American music, 367–407
African art, 235
Allegri, Gregorio, *Miserere,* 1
Amateur Musicians' Guild, 119
American Modernist music, 162
American music, 154
"America's Musical Tendencies" (Partch), **34–36**
Ansermet, Ernest, "On a Negro Orchestra," **368–73**
Antheil, George, 28, 236, 311, 389–90; *Bad Boys of Music,* 69; *Ballet Mécanique,* 69–70, **71,** 184, 386; "Composer's Notes on 1952–53 Re-Editing" [of *Ballet Mécanique*], **71;** letter to Nicolas Slonimsky, **71;** *Sonata sauvage,* 389; *The Airplane,* 389; "The Negro on the Spiral, or A Method of Negro Music," **390–98**
Anti-Expressionism, 276
anti-illusionistic art, 130–31
anti-twelve-tone discourse, 221–23
Apollinaire, Guillaume, 19, 319; *Les mamelles de Tirésias* (*The Breasts of Tiresias*), 319; Program Note for *Parade,* **320–21**
Apollo, 107, 111

Aragon, Louis, 375
archicembalo, 9
Arlen, Harold, 20
Armstrong, Louis "Satchmo," 400
ars subtilior movement, 10
art music, 16
arts, unification of, 75
Artusi, Giovanni, 225
atonality, 65, 132, 203, 292
Auber, Daniel François, 4
Auden, W. H., 2, 133–34, 287, 289; "The World of Opera," **134–36;** *Words and Notes,* 288
audition colorée, 228
aura, 94
Auric, Georges, 118, 300
Auschwitz, 361
axiomatics, 295

Bach, Johann Sebastian, 141, 143, 386–87; *Art of Fugue,* 205, 310; *Passion According to St. Matthew,* 56–57; *Well-Tempered Clavier,* 4
background, concept of, 70
Baker, Josephine, 375, 379
Bakst, Léon, 240
Balázs, Béla, 233
Ball, Hugo, 313; in costume, 314
Balla, Giacomo, 183–84; *Leash in Motion,* 174; *Rhythms of a Bow,* 174, **177;** *Street Lamp,* 174
ballet, 84–86
ballet music, 76–80
Ballets Russes, 236
Balzac, Honoré de, 199
banjo, 372
Barber, Samuel, 47
Barnes, William, 165
Baroque opera, 19
Barthes, Roland: "The Death of the Author," 13; "Rasch," 30
Bartók, Béla, 18, 243–44, 335; *Cantata Profana,*

Bartók, Béla (*continued*) 236; *Duke Bluebeard's Castle,* 233, 236, 244; *Out of Doors* piano suite, 163; "The Influence of Peasant Music on Modern Music," **244–48**; *The Miraculous Mandarin,* 236

Basie, William "Count," 405

Baudelaire, Charles, 2, 94, **229**, 324; *Les fleurs du mal (Flowers of Evil),* 226–27

beats, 136

Bechet, Sidney, 373

Beckett, Samuel, 13, 47

Beethoven, Ludwig van, 142, 143; *Egmont,* 38; *Fidelio,* 38, 346; Fifth Symphony, 157; German criticism of, 149; Ninth Symphony, 8, 270; Pastoral Symphony, 140, 244; *Ruins of Athens,* 394; *Six easy variations on a Swiss song,* 209

Bekker, Paul, 274

bel canto, 43

Bell, Clive, 48

Bell, Vanessa Stephen, 48

Bellini, Vincenzo, 2, 298

bel parlare, 44

Benjamin, Walter, 94–95

Berberian, Cathy, 47

Berg, Alban, 11, 42, 72, 168, 196, 201; *Lulu,* 260, 271, 275–76, 349; *Lyric Suite,* 211; "The Problem of Opera," **124–26**; "Voice in Opera," **43–44**; *Wozzeck,* 43, 123–26, 132, 211

Bergson, Henri, 76

Berio, Luciano: *Sinfonia,* 13; *Thema (Omaggio a Joyce),* 47–48

Berlin, Irving, 13, 371, 378

Berlin, Isaiah, 286

Berlioz, Hector, 2, 155

Bernstein, Leonard, 398, 406; "Has Jazz Influenced the Symphony?" [positively yes! says Bernstein], **401–4**; *Jeremiah,* 403; [The Twelve-Tone Method], **222–23**

Biber, Heinrich, *Battalia a 10,* 9

binary poles, 16–17

Blake, William, 199

Blitzstein, Marc, 406

Bloch, Ernest, *America,* 382

Bloomsbury, 48

blues, 373, 403

Boethius, 354–55

Boulanger, Lili, 18

Boulanger, Nadia, 19

Boulez, Pierre, 1–2, 12, 202; symmetry diagram of a Webern series, **203**

Brahms, Johannes, 4, 11, 142, 152

Brancusi, Constantin, 391

Brecce, Giuseppe, 90

Brecht, Bertolt, 92, 103, 117; *Aufstieg und Fall der Stadt Mahagonny (Rise and Fall of the City of Mahagonny),* 130, 341–42, 343–48; *Die Mutter,* 339; *Die Rundköpfe und die Spitzköpfe,* 339; fight to reform music theater, 341–42; "The Modern Theatre Is the Epic Theatre," **343–48**; *The Seven Deadly Sins,* 342; *Threepenny Opera,* 127, 341, 349

Breton, André, 26, 310; on Cocteau, 323; "Silence Is Golden," 309

bricolage, 12, 13, 14

British Modernism, 25

Britten, Benjamin: *Cantata academica,* 223; *Curlew River,* 105; *The Prince of the Pagodas,* 223; [The Twelve-Tone Method], **223**

Brown, Earle, 191

Bruch, Max, 151

Bruckner, Anton, 150

Bruegel, Pieter, 394

Bruyant, Jean, 353

Bruyr, José, 309

Büchner, Georg, *Woyzeck,* 123, 125

Buñuel, Luis, 397

Burleigh, Harry T., 401

Burney, Charles, *History of Music,* 298

Busnoys, Antoine, *In hydraulis,* 1

Busoni, Ferruccio, 131, 140–41, 242, 281, 332; *Arlecchino,* 104; *Doktor Faustus,* 104, 119; *Sketch of a New Esthetic of Music,* **141–47**, 184

cabaret, 348–54

Cabinet of Dr. Caligari, The, 260

Caccini, Giulio, 28, 33, 37, 225

cadence, 206

Cage, John, 155, 156, 163, 188–90; *Cartridge Music,* 189; *Fontana Mix,* 189; *Music of*

Changes, 13; *Roaratorio: An Irish Circus on Finnegans Wake*, 189; *Silence*, **190–92**
cake-walk, 368, 369
calisthenics, 85
Calmettes, André, *L'assassinat du duc de Guise*, 90
Calzabigi, Raniero de, 341
cancrizan, 210, 211, 212, 213
canon, 209, 213
Carpenter, John Alden: *Adventures in a Perambulator*, 158; *Skyscrapers*, 384
Carroll, Lewis, 328
Carter, Elliott, 11, 223; "Once Again Swing," **404–5;** "The Rhythmic Basis of American Music," **405–7**
Casti, Giovanni Battista, 105
catharsis, 106
causality, 82
Chadwick, George Whitefield, 381
change procedures, 189
Charpentier, Marc-Antoine, *Les plaisirs de Versailles*, 64
Chesterton, Gilbert Keith, 381
chien andalou, 397
choral singing, 358–59
chromaticism, 8, 9, 195, 208
chromatic scale, 198
Cimarosa, Domenico, 299
cinema, 16
cinothèques, 91
Clair, René, 300
clairvoyance, 256
Clarke, Rebecca, 18
classical ballet, 237
Classicism, 224, 332, 333
Claudel, Paul, *L'homme et son désir*, 131
Cocteau, Jean, 19, 90, 106, 131, 367; *Cock and Harlequin*, 323, **324–27**; *Les mariés de la Tour Eiffel*, 310; *Parade*, 323–24; realistic ballet, 320
Code, Percy, 166
Coleridge-Taylor, Samuel, 390
Colette, 18, 309
commedia dell'arte, 104
complementary harmony, 275

component media, dissonance among, 103
comprehensiveness, 6–7
Concert of Factory Sirens, 183
Confucius, 8
Conrad, Joseph, 5
consonance, 196, 197, 221
Cook, Will Marion, 370, 373
Copeland, Aaron, 19, 406, 407
Cordier, Baude, *Tout par compas*, 10
corporeal music, 30–31, 33–34, 44, 60
Council of Trent, 224
Cowell, Henry, 15, 155, 162–64, 167, 242; *Aeolian Harp*, 163; *American Composers on American Music*, 163; *New Musical Resources*, 163
Craft, Robert, 282; *Dialogues*, **286–88**; *Expositions and Developments* [Expressivity], **283**; *Themes and Conclusions*, **288–89**
Cubism, 74, 235, 319
Cunard, Nancy, 375, 389, 390
Cunningham, Merce, 86
Czech Surrealism, 327

Dada, 309–18, 349
Dahlhaus, Carl, 5–6, 10–11
Dalcroze. *See* Jaques-Dalcroze
Dalí, Salvador, 397; *The Persistence of Memory*, 312
dance form, 78
dance music, 79
Dante Alighieri, *Purgatorio*, 33
Dargomizhky, Alexander, *The Stone Guest*, 33
Darwin, Charles, 209
Davray, Henry D., 10
Debussy, Claude, 7, 11, 67, 75, 131, 137–38, 185, 393; *Dr. Gradus ad Parnassum*, 147; *En blanc et noir*, 281; *Et la lune descend sur le temple qui fut (And the Moon Descends above the Ruins of the Temple)*, 10; *Golliwog's Cake-Walk*, 369; harmonies, 196; *Jeux*, 74, 85; *Monsieur Croche antidilettante*, 138–39, **139–40**; *Nuages*, 138; *Pagodes*, 138; *Pelléas et Mélisande*, 25, 230; *Prélude à l'après-midi d'un faune*, 3, 13, 230, 399; *Preludes*, 74; *The Sea: Three Symphonic Sketches*, 157
de Chirico, Giorgio, 332, 396

Degas, Edgar, 84
degenerate art, 338
Delius, Frederick, 319; *A Mass of Life,* 7
Delville, Jean, *Portrait of Mrs. Stuart Merrill,* 230
Der blaue Reiter, 41
Derrida, Jacques, 12, 14, 17
Deshevov, Vladimir, *Rails,* 184
Dessau, Paul, *Einstein,* 291
Dett, R. Nathaniel, 373
deus ex machina, 115
Diaghilev, Serge, 19, 85, 236, 240, 241, 284, 303
dialogue-opera, 122–23
Die Brücke, 259, 260
diminished fifth, 211
diminished seventh, 196
Dionysiac music, 110, 112
Dionysus, 106, 132, 133
dissonance, 8, 103, 109, 196
dodecaphonists, 222, 358
Dolmetsch, Arnold, 27
Dostoevsky, Fyodor, *The Brothers Karamazov,* 137
Douglas, Louis, 380
Dowland, John, 298
Dowson, Ernest, 199
Drab style, 136
dramatic opera, compared to epic opera, 345
dramatic theatre, compared to epic theatre, 344
dream theory, 256
Duchamp, Marcel, 189; *In Advance of a Broken Arm,* 315; *Fountain,* 315; *L.H.O.O.Q.,* 315; *Musical Erratum,* 14; *Nude Descending a Staircase,* 174, **175**
Dufay, Guillaume, 2
Dukas, Paul, *Ariane et Barbe-bleue,* 233
Duparc, Henri, 230
Dürer, Albrecht, *Melancolia,* 214, 320
Dvořák, Antonín, 12; Symphony no. 9, *From the New World,* 401

Eckhart, Johannes, 191
Einstein, Albert, 291
Eisenstein, Sergei, 73, 90, 93, 95, 98

Eisler, Hanns, 337, 338; *Composing for the Films,* 91–92, **93–102;** *Die Mutter,* 339; "On Old and New Music," **339–41;** *Die Rundköpfe und die Spitzköpfe,* 339
electronic music, 163, 185
Elgar, Edward, 28
Eliot, George, *Adam Bede,* 227
Eliot, T. S., 2, 10, 17, 68; *Four Quartets,* 50; "The Metaphysical Poets," 5; "The Music of Poetry," 51–52, **52–54;** *Sweeney Agonistes,* 367; "Tradition and the Individual Talent," 50, 277; *The Waste Land,* 12, 50
elitism, 16
Ellington, Duke, 166, 367, 368
Éluard, Paul, 309
Embry, Florence, 374, 375–77
Emerson, Ralph Waldo, 158, 162, 381
Emmet, Robert, 47
epic chant, 30
epic opera, 345
Ernst, Max, *La femme 100 têtes,* 311
espressivo, 273
Euripides, *Bacchae,* 30, 132–33
European Modernism, 213
Exoticism, 18, **248–51**
Expressionism, 7–8, 50, 253, 259–76, 332; as a derivative of Symbolism, 233; exclusivity, 367; and *Gesamtkunstwerk,* 103; New Objectivity as antidote to, 225, 226; vs. Post-Expressionism, 277–78; and volatility of emotion, 11
extended tonality, 195
eye music, 68

Falla, Manuel de, *El retablo de Maese Pedro,* 105
Farr, Florence, 26–28
Feldman, Morton, 191; *Projection 4,* **81;** [Time-Canvas], **80**
Fenollosa, Ernest, 138
figure, concept of, 70, 187
film montage, 73
Film Music Project, 100
Flaubert, Gustave, *Madame Bovary,* 226
folkloristic music, 335

folksongs, 164, 246
forty-three-tone scale, 28
Foster, Stephen, 164
fox-trot, 369
Franz, Robert, 58
free music, 164, 165
French Symbolists, 233
Freud, Sigmund, 4, 8, 233
"From Emperor Chun to the Vacant Lot"
    (Partch), 30–34
Frost, Robert, 381
Fry, Roger, 48
fugue, 68, 209
furniture music, 322
Futurism, 11, 18, 173, 174, 182, 226

Gabrieli, Giovanni, 155
Gade, Niels W., 58
Galilei, Vicenzo, 33
Gance, Abel, *Napoléon*, 90
Gandhi, Mohandas K., 354
Gaudier-Brzeska, Henri, 396
gavotte, 194
Gay, John, 225; *The Beggar's Opera*, 127, 341
Gebrauchsmusik, 118, 119, 120–22, 278, 294, 347
gemeinschaftsbildenden, 120
gender, and Poststructuralist theory, 18
George, Stefan, 41
Gershwin, George, 385–86, 398; *An American in
    Paris*, 386, 387; jazz influence on, 399, 402–3;
    Porgy and Bess, 385; *Rhapsody in Blue*, 387,
    399; "The Composer and the Machine Age,"
    386–89
Gesamtkunstwerk, 103, 344–45
gesellschaftlichen, 118–19
gestus, 122
Gesualdo, Carlo: *Tres Sacrae Cantiones di
    Gesualdo*, 9; *Tristis est anima mea*, 9
Gibbons, Orlando, *The Cries of London*, 8
gigue, 194
Gilbert, W. S., 61
Gilbert, Henry F., *The Dance in Place Congo*, 401
Gilbert, Stuart, 47
Giraud, Albert, *Pierrot Lunaire*, 38

Glass, Philip, 19, 68–69; *Einstein on the Beach*,
    291
Glinka, Mikhail, 373
glissandi, 83
Gluck, Christoph Willibald, 225; *Iphigenia in
    Aulis*, 4; *Orfeo ed Euridice*, 56, 124, 341
Gödel, Kurt, 295
Goebbels, Joseph, 378
Goethe, Johann Wolfgang von, 209; *The Sorrows
    of Young Werther*, 353
golden poetry, 136
Goll, Ivan, 390; "The Negroes Are Conquering
    Europe," **378–80**
Gombert, Nicholas, *Diversi diversa orant*, 9
Goodman, Benny, 399
Gottschalk, Louis Moreau, 154–55
Gould, Morton, 406
Gounod, Charles, *Faust*, 104
Grainger, Percy, 164–65, 384; "Free Music,"
    165–67; *Hill-Songs*, 165; on primitivism,
    235–36; "Red Dog," 165; *Shallow Brown*,
    164; *The Immovable Do*, 164; *The Warriors*,
    164
Greek tragedy, 106–8, 107, 128
Greenberg, Clement, "Towards a Newer
    Laocoon," 79–80
Gregory, Daniel, 158
Grieg, Edvard, 58, 151, 164; *Holberg Suite*, 276
Grimace, 10
Gris, Juan, 301
Grosz, Georg, *Jack the Ripper*, 260, **263**
Guilbert, Yvette, 376
Guion, David, *Turkey in the Straw*, 384
Guston, Philip, 80

Haas, Pavel, 359
Hába, Alois, 9, 37, 172, 242–43, 299
Hammond, John, 398
Handel, George Frideric, 4
Hanslick, Eduard, 54, 150
Hardenberg, Friedrich von. *See* Novalis
harmony, 195–96, 197, 198, 199, 246;
    complementary, 275
Harris, Roy, 154, 406, 407

Harte, Bret, 384

Hartmann, Dane, 59

Hartmann, J. P. E., 58

Hauer, Josef Matthias, 193, 208

Hausenstein, Wilhelm, 277

Hausmann, Raoul, 317

Haydn, Joseph, 224; *The Creation,* 8; *The Seasons,* 9

Hayes, William, *The Art of Composing Music by a Method Entirely New, Suited to the Meanest Capacity,* 357

Heckel, Erich, *Glassy Day,* 260, **262**

Hegel, Georg Friedrich, 99

Henry, Pierre, *Symphonie pour un homme seul* (Symphony for a Solitary Man), 187–88; *Variations pour une porte et un soupir* (Variations for a Door and a Sigh), 188

Hensel, Fanny Mendelssohn, 18

Henze, Hans Werner: *El Cimarrón,* 134; *The Bassarids,* 133

Heraclitus, 110

Herman, Woody, 368, 398

Hesse, Max, 148

Heyman, Katherine Ruth, 228

hieroglyphs, 259

high vs. low art, 367–407

Hilbert, David, 295–96

Hildegard von Bingen, *Ordo Virtutum,* 8

Hindemith, Paul, 5, 118, 119; *A Composer's World,* **60–63, 355–59**; *Cardillac,* 312; *Das Nusch-Nuschi,* 105; *Gebrauchsmusik,* 347; *Kleine Kammermusik,* 278; *Mathis der Maler,* 354; *Neues vom Tage,* 105, 278; *Sancta Susanna,* 278; *Triadic Ballet,* 282

Hines, Earl, 398

Hitler, Adolph, 337, 348, 349

Hodler, Ferdinand, 171

Hoffmann, E. T. A., 224

Hofmann, Heinrich, 151

Hofmannsthal, Hugo von, 84, 106, 112, 113; letter to Richard Strauss, **114–16**

Hogarth, William, 287

Hölderlin, Friedrich, 106

Hollaender, Friedrich: "Cabaret," **351–54;** *Münchhausen,* **349–51**

homophonic music, 209

homosexuality, 19

Honegger, Arthur, 90; *Antigone,* 106; *Pacific 231,* 184, 340, 386; [The Twelve-Tone Method], **222**

Hucbald, 298

Hughes, Langston, 374; "Likewise," 374; "Moon-Faced, Starry-Eyed," **377–78;** *The Big Sea,* **375–77**

Hyperrealism, 11

I Ching, 189

Impressionistic painting, 74

indeterminacy, 189

intonarumori, 174, 177, 189

inversion, 210, 211

inward-facing consciousness, 255–56

Isaac, Heinrich, 201

Italian Futurism, 80, 174, 183–87

Iven, Joris, 100

Ives, Charles, 3, 9, 18, 407; *Central Park in the Dark,* 7; characteristics of music, 155–56; *Concord* Sonata, 163; *Essays before a Sonata,* **157–59;** First Piano Sonata, 158; "Music and Its Future," **159–62;** "Postface to 114 Songs," **159;** Second Piano Sonata, 157; Second String Quartet, 156–57; *Set of Four Ragtime Dances,* 158; *Three Quarter-Tone Pieces,* 242

James, Edward, 342

Jameson, Fredric, 296–97

Janáček, Leoš, *Her Stepmother Jenůfa,* 33, 37

Janequin, Clément, *Le chant des oyseaulx,* 9

Jaques-Dalcroze, Émile, 85–86, 236; "The Technique of Moving Plastic," **86–89**

jazz, 121, 292, 393; Elliott Carter on, 404, 405–7; Gershwin, 387–88; Krupa and Bernstein on, 398–404; Mason on, 383; and Modernism, 367–68

Johnson, James P., *De Organizer,* 374

Johnson, Jimmy, 398

Jolson, Al, 367

Jones, Palmer, 376–77

Joyce, James: *Chamber Music,* 47; *Finnegans Wake,* 47; "Sirens," **44–47;** *Ulysses,* 44–47

Jugendstil, 7, 259

Kallman, Chester, 133, 134, 287

Kandinsky, Vassily: *Concerning the Spiritual in Art*, 41, 167; correspondence with Arnold Schoenberg, **169–72**; *Der gelbe Klang*, 65, 168, 171–72; and Schoenberg, 167–69; on Schoenberg, 273–74

Keynes, John Maynard, 48

keynote, 205

Khnopff, Fernand, *Blood of the Medusa*, 230

Kiel, Friedrich, 151

Kien, Peter, 359; *Der Kaiser von Atlantis*, final scene, **360–61**

kinesthetics, 85, 86

King Roger (Szymanowski), 133

Kinothek, 90

Kirchner, Ernest Ludwig, 259; *Women at Potsdamer Platz*, 260, **261**

Klangfarbenmelodie, 184

klaxon, 315

Klein, Gideon, 359

Klimt, Gustav, 169

Knight, G. Wilson, 52

Kodály, Zoltán, 248

Kokoschka, Oskar, 41, 260, 263–64; *Mörder, Hoffnung der Frauen* (Murderer, Hope of Women), 260, 264, **265–70**

Kosintsev, Grigori, 90

Koussevitzky, Serge, 400

Kraus, Karl, 41, 97, 213

Krenek, Ernst: "Is Opera Still Possible Today?", **127–32;** *Jonny spielt auf*, 105, 126, 290, 293, 346, 397; *Karl V*, 126; *Lamentatio Jeremiae Prophetae*, 126; "Music and Mathematics," **295–96;** "New Humanity and Old Objectivity," **291–95;** *Reisebuch aus den österreichischen Alpen*, 126; "What Is Called the New Music, and Why?" **330–36**

Krupa, Gene, "Has Jazz Influenced the Symphony?" [emphatically no! says Gene Krupa], **398–400**

Kuhle Wampe, 92

Kulbin, N., *Der blaue Reiter Almanach*, 242

Laloy, Louis, 10

Lamarr, Hedy, 69

Lambert, Constant: "The Age of Pastiche," **297–300;** *Music Ho! A Study of Music in Decline*, 296; *The Rio Grande*, 296; [Stravinsky as Pasticheur], **300–304;** *Summer's Last Will and Testament*, 296

Laurencie, Lionel de la, 368

Lawrence, D. H., 378; *Lady Chatterley's Lover*, 32; *Lost Girl*, 90; *Phoenix*, 36; *Women in Love*, 85, 234–35

League of David, 225

Lebedinski, L. N., 363; *Rayok*, The Music Lesson, **364–66**

Le Corbusier, 83

Léger, Fernand, *The Mechanic*, **279**

Léhar, Franz, 114

Leitmotiv, 65

Leoncavallo, Ruggero, *Zazá*, 159

Lessing, Gotthold Ephraim, 72; *Laokoon*, 64–65, 79

Les Six, 118, 300, 310, 323

Lévi-Strauss, Claude, 17

Lewis, C. S., 136

Lewis, Wyndham, 300

libretti, 288

Liszt, Franz, 18, 21, 150; *A la Chapelle Sixtine*, 276; *Dante Symphony*, 147; *Tasso: lamento e trionfo*, 258

Lloyd, Marie, 50

London, Kurt, 96–97

Loos, Adolf, 333

Loos, Anita, 375

Lopokova, Lydia, 48

Losey, Josef, 100

Lourié, Arthur, *Formes en l'air*, 80–81

Lully, Jean-Baptiste, 1, 124

Lyotard, Jean-François, 14, 15

MacDowell, Edward, 381; *Indian Suite*, 401

Machine Age, 386–89, 387, 389

Maeterlinck, Maurice, 230, 233

Magritte, René, 311; *The Discovery of Fire*, **311**

Mahler, Alma, 18, 95, 254, 263, 264

Mahler, Gustav, 6, 8, 78; *Das Lied von der Erde*, 360; Second Symphony, 13; Tenth Symphony, 270

Mallarmé, Stéphane, 25, 230; on ballet, 84–85; "L'après-midi d'un faune," 2–3

Mann, Thomas, 75, 253; *Dr. Faustus,* 130, 213–15, **216–21,** 361

Marc, Franz, 168

Marinetti, Filippo Tommaso, 189, 226; "Technical Manifesto of Futurist Literature," 173

Marschner, Heinrich, 58

Martin, Frank, 226

Martinů, Bohuslav, *The Revolt,* 310

Marx, Karl, 341

Mason, Daniel Gregory, 158, 380–81; *String Quartet on Negro Themes,* 381; *Tune In, America,* **381–85**

Massine, Léonide, 284, 320–21

Matějček, Antonin, 259

Matisse, Henri, 323

Mattis, Olivia, 188

Meck, Madame von, 138

Mehring, Walter, 349

melodrama, 38

melody, 164, 199

melos, 193

Melville, Herman, *Pierre,* 154

Mendelssohn, Felix, 4, 106

Merzbau, 317

Merzbild, 311, 312

Messiaen, Olivier, 68, 138; *Quartet for the End of Time,* 362

metanarrative, 14–15

meta-opera, 104–5

Meyerbeer, Giacomo, 58, 127

microtonalism, 9, 172

Milhaud, Darius, 131, 299, 367, 398; *Le boeuf sur le toit,* 19, 310, 323; *L'enlèvement d'Europe,* 118; *Les mariés de la Tour Eiffel,* 323

Minimalist music, 68

Modernism, 1–2, 54; in American music, 162; assumption that technical liberation can lead to artistic liberation, 10; awe of genius, 14; British, 25; composers, 3, 4–5, 10; Dahlhaus's definition, 6–9; establishes and subverts claims of male privilege, 18–20; and jazz, 367–68; main features, 6; motto of, 8; multilingualism, 21; and music theater, 103–36; search for authenticity, 17–18; termination, 12; as a testing of the limits of aesthetic construction, 11–12; uneasy relationship between a given artistic medium and all others, 23

Modernist Primitivism, 235

Modigliani, Amedeo, 396

Moerman, Ernst, 390

Molière, *Le bourgeois gentilhomme,* 112

Mondrian, Piet, 202; *Broadway Boogie Woogie,* 80; *Composition with Grid 5 (Lozenge),* **204**

monophony, 225

monothematicism, 308

montage, 90, 91, 93, 215, 334

Monteverdi, Claudio, 29, 38, 128–29, 225; *Orfeo,* 28

mood cues, 16

Moréas, Jean, Symbolist manifesto, 227–28

Mosolov, Alexander, *Iron Foundry,* 184

Mozart, Leopold, 4

Mozart, Wolfgang Amadeus, 4, 142, 224; *Abduction from the Seraglio,* 394; *Der Schauspieldirektor,* 105; *Die Zauberflöte (The Magic Flute),* 134–35, 346; *Don Giovanni,* 57; *Le nozze di Figaro,* 346; *Linz* Symphony, 285; *Musical Joke,* 303; *Zaide,* 38

Munch, Edvard, 5; *The Scream,* 253, **254**

Muradeli, Vano, 363

musette, 194

music: absolute, 141–42, 143; American, 154; and architecture, 81–84; art, 16; ballet, 76–80; capacity for language, 23–26; and cinema, 90–102; corporeal, 30–31, 33–34, 44, 60; dance, 79; Dionysiac, 110, 112; electronic, 163, 185; eye, 68; folkloristic, 335; free, 164, 165; furniture, 322; homophonic, 209; mechanical reproduction of, 389; Minimalist, 68; and politics, 337–66; progressive, 9; as a pseudomorphism of painting, 74–76; random, 315; relationship to dance, 84–89; and speech, 37–44; stochastic, 82–83, 223; through-composed, 396; and tragic myth, 108–12; world, 163

musica ficta, 273

musical laws, 356

musical noise, 179

musical onomatopoeia, 7

musical prose, 138

musical sound, 178, 179

musical tragédie, 124

music history, intellectual discords in, 224–25

music theater, in modernist period, 103–36

musique concrète, 188

Musorgsky, Modest Petrovich, 37, 138, 244, 364, 367; *Khovanshchina*, 33–34

Muybridge, Eadweard, 174

My Fair Lady, 64

Mythic Method, 11

Nabokov, Vladimir, 69

nature, 17

Nazi concentration camps, 359

Nazis, 337–38, 354

Neher, Caspar, 345

Nelson, Rudolf, 367

Nelson, Willie, 20

Neobarbarism, 11

Neoclassicism, 11, 50, 91, 276–90; Busoni and, 131, 141, 332; Krenek on, 131–32, 332–34; and twelve-tone music, 194

Neoplasticism, 202

Neoromanticism, 278, 280, 304

Nestroy, Johann, 127

Neveux, Georges, 310

New Music, 330–36, 332, 339–41

New Objectivity, 11, 277–78, 290–96; Adorno on, 270; defined in contrast to Expressionism, 225, 226; Krenek on, 334, 335; Schoenberg and, 274

Nibelungenlied, 106

Nielsen, Carl, 54, 65; "Words, Music, and Program Music," **55–60**

Nietzsche, Friedrich, 24; *Also sprach Zarathustra*, 6, 7; *Beyond the Good and the Bad* (*Jenseits von Gut und Böse*), 146; descent into insanity, 214; dislike of *The Bacchae*, 133; *Ecce Homo*, 110; *Der Fall Wagner*, 324; hope for a future music theater, 117, 132; *Manfred-Meditation*, 107; *The Birth of Tragedy out of the Spirit of Music*, 2, 106–8, **108–12**, 253; *The Gay Science*, 137

Nijinska, Bronislava, 85

Nijinsky, Vaslav, 19, 85, 236–37, 240–41

Noh, 105

noise, 172–83, 179

Nono, Luigi, *Fragmente–Stille, an Diotima*, 233

nontriadic formations, 7

non-Western musical traditions, 167

Noone, Jimmy, 398–99

Nordau, Max, 147

Nouvel, Walter, 237, 282

Novalis, "Hymns of Night," 295

Obrist, Hermann, 259

oceanic experience, 233

Ockeghem, Johannes, 1

octave doubling, 198, 201

Offenbach, Jacques, 91, 127; *Bluebeard*, 127; *Orpheus in the Underworld*, 106

onomatopoeia, 8

opera: Baroque, 19; developmental trends of, 122–23; dialogue, 122–23; dramatic and epic, 345; meta, 104–5; philosophical, 104; reforms, 124, 128–29, 225; of speech, 29

opera buffa, 105

opera-parodies, 127

opéras minutes, 118

Orff, Carl, 338; *Antigonae*, 29, 106; *Klage der Ariadne*, 29; *Orpheus*, 29; *Vom Frühjahr, Öltank und vom Fliegen*, 338

Orpheus, 244

overlay, 9

Palestrina, Giovanni Pierluigi da, 4, 89; *Missa Papae Marcelli*, 225

Palmer, Geoffrey Molyneux, 47

"pan-art," 141

pantonality, 167–69

Pappenheim, Bertha, 8

Pappenheim, Marie, 8, 18–19, 200

parody, 72

Partch, Harry, 9, 11, 28–36, 242, 378; "America's Musical Tendencies," **34–36**; *And on the Seventh Day Petals Fell in Petaluma*, 30; "From Emperor Chun to the Vacant Lot," 30–34; *Genesis of a Music*, **29**, 30–36; *King*

Partch, Harry (*continued*)
  Oedipus, 29, 106; *Revelation in the Courthouse Park,* 30, 133, 136; *Revelation in the Courthouse Square,* 30; *Water! Water!,* 30
pastiche, 296
Pater, Walter, 25; *The Renaissance,* 2
Pergolesi, Giovanni Battista, 13; *La serva padrona,* 225, 284
Peri, Jacopo, 29
Perry, Milman, 244
Pfitzner, Hans, 11, 151, 337
philosophical opera, 104
phonology, 323
pianola, 281
Picasso, Pablo, 72, 285, 301; costumes for the Managers in *Parade,* **326;** *Les demoiselles d'Avignon,* 235, 368; *Parade,* 226, 320–21
Pictorialisms, 140
Pirandello, Luigi, 105
pitch, 67, 181
pizzicati, 83
plainchant, 1, 8
Plato, 32, 82; *The Republic,* 32
Poglietti, Alessandro, 138; *Rossignolo,* 9
Poiret, Paul, 379
politics: and music, 337–66; of the twelve-tone method, 338
Pollock, Jackson, 80
polyphony, 209, 224, 225
polyrhythm, 407
polystylism, 12–13, 14
polytonality, 246
popular art, assimilation into high art, 367–407
Porter, Cole, 403
Postimpressionism, 48
Postmodernism, 12–13, 14–17, 296
Poststructuralism, 17, 18
Poulenc, Francis, 11, 118, 309; *Les mamelles de Tirésias,* 19–20, 103, 311; *Les mariés de la Tour Eiffel,* 311
Pound, Ezra, 8, 10, 138, 183, 228; on Antheil, 70; on Dolmetsch, 27; *Ezra Pound and Music,* 67–68; *Homage to Sextus Propertius,* 276; on painting with sound, 69; *Le testament,* 25–26, 29; *Treatise on Harmony,* 163; on Yeats, 26

Powell, John, *Rhapsodie Nègre,* 384
Pratella, Francesco Ballila, 177
primal scream, 253
Primitivism, 18, 234–48, 235
Prince, artist known as, 20
program-music, 143–44
progressive music, 9
Prokofiev, Sergei, 5, 338, 363; *Alexander Nevsky,* 93; *From My Life,* **20–21;** *Steel Step,* 184
Proust, Marcel, 76; *Swann's Way,* 230–31, **231–33**
psaltery chanting, 27–28
pseudomorphism, 72, 77, 81, 84, 305, 328
Puccini, Giacomo, 11; *Tosca,* 297; *Turandot,* 104, 105
Pulcinella ballet, 302
puppet play, 105
purism, 80
pyrrhic foot, 129
Pythagoras, 1, 82, 178

Quantz, Johann Joachim, 4
quarter-tone, 242–43
quarter-tone piano, 9

Rachmaninov, Sergei, 11, 13
ragtime, 158, 368–69
Rameau, Jean-Philippe, 4, 154
random music, 315
randomness, 13, 14
Rapée, Erno, *Motion Picture Moods for Pianists and Organists,* 90–91
Rauschenberg, Robert, 80
Ravel, Maurice, 19, 307, 399; *Boléro,* 308; Interview: "Finding Tunes in Factories," **308–9;** Interview: [Ravel's Toys], **307–8;** *L'enfant et les sortilèges,* 309, 369; *L'heure espagnole,* 307, 308; Violin Sonata, 385
Realism, 226, 227, 315, 342
Redfield, John, 185
Redon, Odilon, *Closed Eyes,* 230
reform opera, 124
Reger, Max, 147–48, 207; *Concerto in the Old Style,* 276; "Degeneration and Regeneration in Music," **148–54**
Reich, Steve, *Come Out,* 48

Reinhardt, Max, 95
Rheinberger, Joseph, 151
rhythm, 164, 199, 368, 387
rhythmicon, 163
Riemann, Hugo, 147, 148–54, 290
Rieti, Vittorio, 118
Rilke, Rainer Maria, 280; *Sonnets to Orpheus* 1.3, **280–81**
Robinson, Edwin Arlington, 381
Rodgers, Richard, 403
Rodin, Auguste, 280
Roerich, Nicholas, 236, 239
Roh, Franz, 277
Roland-Manuel, Alexis, 282
Romani, Felice, 105
Romanticism, 2, 14, 224
rondo, 68, 317
Rose, Francis, 278
Rosen, Willy, 367
Roslavets, Nikolay, 193, 337
Rossini, Gioachino: *Mosè in Egitto,* 104; *Il Turco in Italia,* 105
Rostropovich, Mstislav, 363
Rothko, Mark, 80
Rousseau, Jean-Jacques, 225; *Essay on the Origin of Languages,* 23–24
rows, 202, 211, 212, 213
Russian Five, 390, 393
Russolo, Luigi, 189, 226; "The Art of Noises: Futurist Manifesto," **177–83**; *Music,* 174, **176**; *Risveglio* [or *Veglio*] *di una città* (*Awakening of a City*), 174

Saint-Saëns, Camille, 90; *Danse macabre,* 69
Salieri, Antonio, *Prima la musica, poi le parole,* 105
Sartre, Jean-Paul, 4
Satie, Erik, 11, 68, 321–22; *Furniture Music,* 68–69; *Memoirs of an Amnesiac,* **322–23**; *Parade,* 13–14, 19, 309, 319
Saussure, Ferdinand de, 24–25
Scarlatti, Domenico, 298
Schaeffer, Pierre, 189; *Symphonie pour un homme seul* (Symphony for a Solitary Man), 187–88; tenets of *musique concrète,* 188

Schelling, Ernest, *A Victory Ball,* 383–84
Schikaneder, Emanuel, 134
Schilkret, Nat, 287
Schmitt, Florent, *La tragédie de Salomé,* 233
Schnittke, Alfred, 13, 171; *Peer Gynt,* 13
Schoenberg, Arnold, 4–5, 11, 19, 77, 131, 282, 338; *A Survivor from Warsaw,* 287, **361–62**; *Bagatelles for String Quartet,* 208; *Das Buch der hängenden Gärten,* 41; cabaret songs, 348; "Composition with Twelve Tones," *fiat lux,* **194–201**; Concerto for String Quartet and Orchestra, 277; correspondence with Vassily Kandinsky, **169–72**; *Der rote Blick* (The Red Gaze), 65; *Die Jakobsleiter,* 172, 288; *Erwartung,* 8, 43, 193, 210, 270; Expressionism, 273–75; First Chamber Symphony, 207; Five Orchestral Pieces, 65; *Five Pieces for Orchestra,* 406; on folklorists, 167; forward to *Pierrot Lunaire,* **38–39**; *Four Orchestral Songs,* 199–200; Fourth String Quartet, 288; "The Future of the Opera," **15–16**; *Genesis Suite,* 287; *Die glückliche Hand* (The Lucky Touch), 16, 43–44, 168, 210–11, **271–72**, 288; *Gurrelieder,* 207, 331; *Harmonielehre* (Theory of Harmony), **65–67**, 168, 196, 198, 212; and Kandinsky, 167–69; *Kol Nidre,* 194; on low art, 367; *Moses und Aron,* 42, 104, 194, 200, 201, 286, 288; *Music to Accompany a Film Scene,* 16; notion of complementary harmony, 275; *Ode to Napoleon,* 223; on reaction to *Dr. Faustus,* 215; *Pelleas und Melisande,* 7; Piano Suite, 194; *Pierrot Lunaire,* 104; *Six Little Piano Pieces,* 201; *Six Pieces for Male Chorus,* 287; and Stravinsky, 289; *Structural Functions of Harmony,* 215; style of vocal recitation, 37–38; Suite for Septet, 194; *The Biblical Way,* 3; "The Relationship to the Text," **39–42**; *Three Satires,* **289–90**; training as a painter, 65; twelve-tone method, 21, 193, 194, 202, 206, 338–39; *Verklärte Nacht* (Transfigured Night), 7, 288; *Von Heute auf Morgen,* 105, 201, 394; *Zwei Lieder,* 41
Schopenhauer, Arthur, 133, 141, 255–56; *The World as Will and Representation,* 39, 253
Schubert, Franz, 2, 11; *Die Post* (Mailcoach), 340

Schulhoff, Erwin: *Bassnightingale*, 327; *The Cloud-Pump*, 327; "For General Intelligibility as a Confession," **327–28;** *Sonata Erotica for Solo Mother-Trumpet*, 327

Schumann, Clara Wieck, 18, 298

Schumann, Robert: *Carnaval*, 225; *Davidsbündlertänze*, 225; Fourth Symphony, 142; *Kreisleriana*, 30

Schütz, Heinrich, *Psalmen Davids*, 8

Schwitters, Kurt, 312, 313; *The Hitler Gang,* **316;** *Ursonate*, 316–17, **318**

Scott, Cyril, 165–66

Scott, Sir Walter, *The Bride of Lammermoor*, 106

Scriabin, Alexander: *Mysterium*, 234; *Poem of Ecstasy*, 193; *Prometheus*, 118, 233–34

sea shanties, 164

seconda prattica, 225

Second Viennese School, 84

Seeger, Ruth Crawford, 18; *Three Chants*, 272

semantic specificity, 7, 9

semitone, 265

Serialism, 18, 82, 223

Sessions, Roger, 407

Seventeen Lyrics by Li Po, 29

Shalyapin, Fyodor, 367

Shaw, George Bernard, 199

Shostakovich, Dmitri, 90, 337; Fifth Symphony, 363; *Lady Macbeth of Mtsenk*, 363; *March for the Soviet Police*, 363; *Rayok* (*Gallery* or *Peepshow*), 363; score to *The New Babylon*, 91; *Song of the Forests*, 363

Sibelius, Jean, 11

signs, 25

Sitwell, Edith, *Façade*, 328–29; "Hornpipe," **329–30**

Smetana, Bedřich, *The Bartered Bride*, 243

Smyth, Ethel, 48

Society for Private Performances, 118

Socrates, 107

Solage, 10

somathemes, 30

sonata form, 78–79

Sophocles, 106

Sorabji, Kaikhosru Shapurji, 299

sound projection, 186

sound-tint, 184

sound tracks, 91

Southern Syncopated Orchestra, 369–73

Soviet Union, 337, 362–63

speech: in motion pictures, 97–98; and music, 37–44

speech melody, 37

Spencer, Herbert, 56

Spohr, Louis, *Historical Symphony*, 4

Stabat Mater, 284

Stalag 8-A, 362

Stalin, Josef, 363

stasis, 80

Stein, Gertrude, 18, 156, 315; *Four Saints in Three Acts*, 304–5; *Lectures in America*, 305–6; "Miss Furr and Miss Skeene," 301; *A Sonatina Followed by Another*, 48

Stephen, Sir Leslie, 48

stochastic music, 82–83, 223

Stockhausen, Karlheinz, *Gruppen*, 164

Stokowski, Leopold, 400

Strauss, Richard, 11, 156; *Also sprach Zarathustra*, 6, 113, 137; *An Alpine Symphony*, 113; *Ariadne auf Naxos*, 104, 112–16; *Capriccio*, 95, 104, 105; *Das Bächlein*, 337; *Der Rosenkavalier*, 114; *Die schweigsame Frau*, 337; *Don Quixote*, 7, 157; *Ein Heldenleben*, 147; *Elektra*, 106, 112, 115, 346; *Feuersnot*, 352; *Intermezzo*, 105; *Josefslegende* (Legend of Joseph), 79; *Salome*, 11, 153, 157, 233; *Till Eulenspiegels lustige Streiche*, 13; tone poems, 230

Stravinsky, Igor, 5, 11, 21, 68, 75, 77–78; *Abraham and Isaac*, 288; *An Autobiography*, **239–42, 282–83;** borrowing from folk music, 247–48; "Danse de l'Élue," 78; and Diaghilev, 79; *Dialogues*, **286–88;** *Ebony Concerto*, 368, 398; *Étude for pianola*, 281; experiments in serial technique, 223; *Expositions and Developments* [Expressivity], **283;** *Expositions and Developments* [Pulcinella], 13, 50, 72, 276, 284–86, **284–86;** *Fireworks*, 183–84; *Le sacre du printemps* (The Rite of Spring), 12, 70, 73, 85, 187, 233, 236–37, 247, 281, 390–91; *Les noces* (The Wedding), 81, 85, 288, 391; *L'Histoire du Soldat*, 76, 300–302; influence of jazz on, 399,

402–3; *Monumentum pro Gesualdo,* 9; on *musique concrète,* 188; neoclassical period, 276, 281, 302–3; *Oedipus Rex,* 13, 19, 28, 106, 118, 311–12, 323, 347; *Petrushka,* 2, 281; *Piano-Rag-Music,* 369, 391; *Rag-Time,* 369, 391; *Renard,* 69, 85, 288, 300; *The Firebird,* 281, 288; *Themes and Conclusions,* **288–89;** *The Rake's Progress,* 104, 133, 287; *Three Japanese Lyrics,* 281; "What I Wished to Express in *The Consecration of Spring,*" **237–39;** on Yeats, 26

Structuralist models, 18

Štyrský, Jindřich, 327

Suhrkamp, Peter, 341; "The Modern Theatre Is the Epic Theatre," **343–48**

Suk, Josef, *Asrael Symphony,* 360

Sullivan, Arthur, 61

Surrealism, 26, 270, 274, 309–12, 319, 333–34, 342

Surrealist opera, 103

Swedenborg, Emanuel, 199

swing, 404–5

Symbolism, 226–34, 280

syncopation, 368, 371

synesthesia, 94, 228

synthetic chords, 193

Szymanowski, Karol, 133

Taft, William Howard, 3

Tailleferre, Germaine, 18

Takemitsu, Toru, *Yeux clos (Closed Eyes),* 233

Taruskin, Richard, 236

Tasso, Torquato, *Gerusalemma liberata,* 258

Tchaikovsky, Pyotr Illich, 138; *Swan Lake,* 84; *The Queen of Spades,* 276, 297

"Technical Manifesto of Futurist Painting," 173–74

Telemann, Georg Philipp, *Gulliver Suite,* 9

tempo rubato, 287

Terpander, 30

theremin, 164–65, 166

Theremin, Leon, 163, 164–65

Theresienstadt, 359

Thomas, Ambroise, *Mignon,* 69

Thomson, Virgil, 19, 22, 103, 156, 278, 310; *Four Saints in Three Acts,* 304–5

Thoreau, Henry David, 160, 381; *Walden,* 157

through-composed music, 396

timbre, 179, 181, 184, 186

Tinctoris, Johannes, 4

Tin Pan Alley, 385

tonality, 7–8, 195, 196, 198, 205, 206, 210, 355–56

tonal system, 137, 145

tone clusters, 163

tone color (*Klangfarbe*), 66, 67

tone-painting, 143

tone poem, 7

tone-row construction, 206

totalitarian musical systems, 356–58

transvestism, 19

Trauberg, L. Z., *The New Babylon,* 90

tripartite tone, 146

trombone glissando, 7

Twain, Mark, 72, 384

twelve-tone method, 21, 77, 193–223, 338, 356–57, 396

Tzara, Tristan, 313–15

Ullmann, Viktor, 337, 359–60, 361

Urpflanze, 209

Valetti, Rosa, 349

Valls, Francisco, *Missa Scala Aretina,* 225

Varèse, Edgard, 11, 184–85, 189; *Ecuatorial,* 187; *Hyperprism,* 185; *Ionisation,* 185; "Music and the Times," **185–87**

Vecchi, Orazio, *L'Amfiparnaso,* 105

Verardo, Pietro, 174

Verbrauchsmusik, 120

Verdi, Giuseppe: *La traviata,* 105; *Rigoletto,* 43

Verlaine, Paul, 25; "Art poétique," 2

Vicentino, Nicola, 9

Viennese School, 77

Villa-Lobos, Heitor: *As três Marias,* 189; *New York Sky Line Melody,* 357

Villon, François, 25

viola, adapted, 29

visual metaphors, 185

Vivaldi, Antonio, *Four Seasons,* 9

Volkov, Solomon, *Testimony: The Memoirs of Dmitri Shostakovich,* 363

Wagner, Richard, 200–201; "art of transition," 75; "Beethoven," **255–59;** concept of the *Gesamtkunstwerk* (total art work), 24, 75, 80, 98, 128; *Der Ring des Nibelungen,* 24; *Die Walküre,* 59; *Götterdämmerung,* 50; harmony, 195–96; *Lohengrin,* 228; and *Nietzsche,* 107; *Parsifal,* 73, 107; prefiguration of the Modernist composer-intellectual, 3–4; and Schopenhauer, 253; *Siegfried,* 110; *Tannhäuser,* 2, 228, 367; *Tristan und Isolde,* 2, 50, 107, 108, 253–54, 295

Waller, Fats, 398

Walton, William, 300, 328

Warlock, Peter (Philip Heseltine), *The Curlew,* 28

Warsaw Ghetto, 361

Weber, Carl Maria von, 58

Weber, Ludwig, 119

Webern, Anton, 5, 11, 196, 201–2, 221, 281, 338; "The Path to Twelve-Note Composition," **202–13**

Wedekind, Frank, 349; *Lulu,* 260

Weill, Kurt, 130; anti-bourgeois music, 337; *Aufstieg und Fall der Stadt Mahagonny (Rise and Fall of the City of Mahagonny),* 116, 120, 123, 341–42, 343–48; *Der Jasager,* 105; *Der neue Orpheus,* 378; *Die Dreigroschenoper,* 121, 123; *Happy End,* 121; *Lost in the Stars,* 116–17; "Opera—Where To?", **120–23;** "Shifts in Musical Composition," **117–20;** *Street Scene,* 374; *The Seven Deadly Sins,* 342; *The Threepenny Opera,* 103, 349; *The Tsar Has His Photograph Taken,* 105

Weimar Republic, 348

Weininger, Otto, *Geschlecht und Charakter,* 264–65

Werfel, Franz, 95

Wheelock, Gretchen, 141

whole-tone scale, 230

Wiene, Robert, 260; *The Cabinet of Dr. Caligari,* 317

Wilde, Oscar, 233; "The Decay of Lying," 283

Wittgenstein, Ludwig, 25

Wolf, Hugo, 150; *Manuel Venegas,* 214

Wolff, Christian, 191

Wolzogen, Ernst von, 348, 352

Woolf, Virginia, 48, 49, 54; "A Sketch of the Past," 48; *The Waves,* **49–50**

world music, 163

world theater, 8

Xenakis, Iannis, 81–82; *A Colone,* 81; *Formalized Music,* **82–84;** *Medea,* 81; *Metastasis,* 83–84; *Mycenae-Alpha,* 82; *Nuits,* 81

Yeats, William Butler, 26–28, 106; *A Vision,* 26; *Diarmuid and Grania,* 28; *Fighting the Waves,* 28; "Sailing to Byzantium," 26; "The Lake Isle of Innisfree," 26–28; translation of Sophocles' *King Oedipus,* 29

Zeitoper, 105, 124, 394

Zemlinsky, Alexander von, *The Triumph of Time,* 84

Zweig, Stefan, 337